Sports and Recreation Facilities

for school and community

CONTRIBUTORS

The Asphalt Institute
UNIVERSITY OF MARYLAND, COLLEGE PARK, MARYLAND

N. L. Engelhardt, Sr.
CONSULTING EDITOR, *The School Executive;* PRESIDENT, ENGELHARDT, ENGELHARDT, LEGGETT AND CORNELL, EDUCATIONAL CONSULTANTS, NEW YORK CITY

The Charles M. Graves Organization
PARK AND RECREATION ENGINEERS, ATLANTA, GEORGIA

Gerald J. Hase, Ed.D.
SUPERVISOR OF PHYSICAL EDUCATION AND RECREATION, NEW YORK STATE DEPARTMENT OF EDUCATION, ALBANY, NEW YORK

George Hjelte
MANAGER, DEPARTMENT OF RECREATION AND PARKS, CITY OF LOS ANGELES, CALIFORNIA

Lloyd Hollingsworth, Ed.D.
PROFESSOR OF EDUCATION AND DIRECTOR OF ATHLETICS, GUSTAVUS ADOLPHUS COLLEGE, ST. PETER, MINNESOTA

The Illuminating Engineering Society
COMMITTEE ON SPORTS AND RECREATIONAL AREA LIGHTING, NEW YORK CITY

H. Frederick Kilander, Ph.D.
PROFESSOR OF EDUCATION AND COORDINATOR OF HEALTH EDUCATION, SCHOOL OF EDUCATION, NEW YORK UNIVERSITY

National Golf Foundation, Rex McMorris
EXECUTIVE DIRECTOR, CHICAGO, ILLINOIS

C. A. Meadows and Associates, Limited
CONSULTING ENGINEERS, TORONTO, CANADA

John H. Melady
TURF EXPERT AND AUTHOR OF THE MELADY GARDEN BOOKS, HACKENSACK, NEW JERSEY

Walter L. Pate
FORMER CAPTAIN, UNITED STATES DAVIS CUP TEAM; CHAIRMAN OF COURT CONSTRUCTION COMMITTEE, U. S. LAWN TENNIS ASSOCIATION, NEW YORK CITY

Portland Cement Association, Richard G. Knox
MANAGER OF PUBLIC RELATIONS BUREAU, CHICAGO, ILLINOIS

Charles Pound
ENGINEER AND SUPERINTENDENT OF PARKS, WESTCHESTER COUNTY PARK COMMISSION, WHITE PLAINS, NEW YORK

William R. Shirley
ARCHITECT, NEW YORK CITY

R. Jackson Smith
ARCHITECT WITH EGGERS & HIGGINS, NEW YORK CITY

Lee L. Starr
PARK SUPERVISOR, BOROUGH OF RICHMOND, STATEN ISLAND, NEW YORK

A. Carl Stelling Associates
NEW YORK CITY AND WEST HARTFORD, CONNECTICUT

E. Parker Yutzler, B.PE.
RECREATION PLANNING CONSULTANT AND MANUFACTURER'S REPRESENTATIVE; FORMERLY RECREATION DIRECTOR, LONG ISLAND STATE PARK COMMISSION

Sports and Recreation Facilities

FOR SCHOOL AND COMMUNITY

EDITORS

M. Alexander Gabrielsen, Ph.D.
PROFESSOR OF EDUCATION
NEW YORK UNIVERSITY

Caswell M. Miles
CHIEF, BUREAU OF PHYSICAL EDUCATION AND RECREATION
NEW YORK STATE DEPARTMENT OF EDUCATION,
ALBANY, NEW YORK

Englewood Cliffs, N. J.

PRENTICE-HALL, INC. 1958

PRENTICE-HALL PHYSICAL EDUCATION SERIES

Elmer D. Mitchell, Editor

LIBRARY OF CONGRESS CATALOG CARD NUMBER: 58-13133

PRINTED IN THE UNITED STATES OF AMERICA

83578

Title-page illustration: **Ohio State University fieldhouse**

Courtesy of Department of Photography, Ohio State University

FOREWORD

Editors Gabrielsen and Miles have planned and developed an important and interesting book that should be extremely helpful to all those concerned with the sports facilities and the recreation facilities of both schools and communities.

This book fills a real need. For too long the recreational facilities of schools and communities have grown largely unplanned and unrelated. The Editors and their colleagues have brought order out of chaos. They prove to the community how important it is that all its facilities be included in a comprehensive plan. They present advice and know-how in the development and construction of grounds, buildings, equipment, and the other facilities necessary to a well-rounded program.

The essential thesis of the book is the interrelationship of school and community facilities. The authors' position is that many, if not all, the facilities should be used not only by the schools but also by the other agencies found in the community. They emphasize further that, once it has decided to carry on a given sport or form of recreation, the community must realize that proper facilities properly developed will be required.

This book brings together the best that is known about proper and justifiable programs of sports and other types of recreation and gives explicit directions for carrying out those programs. All who are interested in wholesome recreation will find this book absorbing, and will find in it an authentic handbook of what to do and how to do it. It will be particularly helpful to school administrators, community planners, architects, and health, physical education, and recreation personnel. It fills a real place in the literature in an area that was heretofore a void.

Walter D. Cocking, Editor

The School Executive

PREFACE

Sports and recreation facilities represent substantial financial investments on the part of any community. These facilities serve both public and voluntary agencies and are made available to people of all ages. In the last decade requirements for new facilities, and for new types of facilities, have gone up unceasingly. During that time one advance has been the standardization of space requirements.

The widely varying designs and methods of construction employed in modern sports and recreation facilities have created a need for specialization on the part of engineers and architects. Few architects are completely familiar with the designs and standards involved in the multiplicity of facilities found in recreation today—ranging from the artificial ice-skating rink to swimming pools. To cope with that problem organizations have been developed to promote and improve the design and construction of sports facilities in specific areas. Individual architects have specialized as planners of certain types of facilities, such as golf courses, swimming pools, and skating rinks.

Recognizing the highly specialized nature of many sports facilities, the Editors concluded that a comprehensive treatment of the field could only be accomplished with the help of the many technical organizations and individual experts associated with the planning and construction of sports and recreation facilities. Consequently, the authors of the individual chapters of this book are outstanding authorities in their respective fields.

Although the viewpoints expressed by the contributors are primarily their own, the Editors attempted to guide their analyses by expressing the problems confronting professional personnel in recreation, physical education, health, and camping. Similarly, the modern philosophy underlying community and school programs in physical education and recreation served as a basis for the preparation of each chapter.

The book provides limited detail specifications for the planning and construction of many facilities and suggestions of sources from which additional information may be obtained. It is designed neither to minimize the role of the architect nor to cut down on opportunities for creativity, but is intended to stimulate better planning of facilities for sports and recreation.

It is hoped that this book will prove to be a helpful guide and reference book for community planners, school administrators, architects, and professional sports and recreation personnel.

The Editors wish to acknowledge with sincere appreciation the excellent cooperation given by the chapter authors in the preparation of this book. Without their help this book could never have been written.

M. Alexander Gabrielsen

Caswell M. Miles

CONTENTS

CHAPTER 1

COMMUNITY PLANNING FOR FACILITIES

George Hjelte

THE EARLY AMERICAN INDUSTRIAL CITIES GREW up as compact communities in which most community business was conducted in a nucleus called the downtown area at the center of the city. Major and minor streets, surface transportation lines, subway systems, elevated railways, and telephonic communications radiated from the center.

In some instances growth of a city according to this pattern was hemmed in by barriers such as rivers, estuaries, or hills, which confined the city's nucleus to a given area and cramped its growth, resulting in more congestion of structures and people than would otherwise have occurred. Growth was not to be contained—it surmounted the barriers and settlements sprang up and became glorified communities, each with autonomous governmental status as municipal corporations. As available area between the separate settlements or independent cities filled up with homes and industry, the whole became an integral unit having identity as a metropolis but with several independent local government systems.

Cities that grew up in the main after the appearance of the automobile as a common method of transportation—midwestern and western cities, for example—and that were not hemmed in by barriers were able to extend their boundaries by progressive annexation of newly developed areas. Each newborn community prior to annexation tended to cultivate autonomy and identity as a community. Dependence of the satellites upon the central nucleus was much less extensive than it was in the pre-automobile era. One large metropolis was described as a collection of communities looking for the city. This description was offered as a witticism but upon analysis it was found not to be as facetious as it was realistic. Eventually the several communities yielded their government prerogatives to the whole city while continuing to foster local enterprises and

Illustration: Use of space for recreation along highways—Henry Hudson Parkway, New York

certain independent community activities.[1] Many modern industrial cities followed this pattern in their growth from collections of communities to genuine municipalities. They began as a group of communities and were eventually incorporated into a single metropolitan unit.

Offhand, it would seem that each of the communities comprising an industrial metropolis would have so much individuality and pride in autonomy as to desire to continue as an independent city or as a borough within the city. The high cost of local municipal services and an insufficient industrial tax base discourages retention of local government in satellite cities, and the borough plan does not in practice commend itself. The idea of the borough was that "local affairs" could be administered by a borough government with only a few over-all functions, such as collection of taxes and administration of justice remaining to be administered by a central municipal government. In practice, however, this theory proved not to be efficacious or practicable, except perhaps in the city of New York. Early commitments and limitations of the environment had apparently suited this city to the borough type of government, while other metropolises found it unadaptable to their needs. The difficulty is to distinguish which are local affairs and which functions can be more economically administered by a borough rather than by a central government.

The recently developed industrial city is and will continue to be a collection of communities with a common central government, with uniform government controls and standardized municipal services. Such is the pattern dictated by considerations of convenience and economy, and by recognition of a commonality of problems and uniform solutions of them for all related communities, though not, however, without some local adaptations.

[1] This remark is attributed to Peter B. Kyne in an address before a Chamber of Commerce in which San Francisco, a highly centralized metropolis concentrated at the top of a peninsula, was compared to Los Angeles, to which many formerly independent cities were annexed and which contains 456 square miles, the largest area of any American city.

THE COMMUNITY AND THE NEIGHBORHOOD

The "community" in industrial cities is an area populated by people who have acquired a sense of community identity deriving from its location, history, traditions, and participation of its citizens in the many activities suited to their needs. The uniqueness of communities is also a reflection of the character of leadership that has been available to them. In the development of various community services, community-mindedness is stressed and unique community qualities are pointed up. Facilities for services and for controls are planned and located in relation to the variable community phenomena.

A community, however, is itself subject to subdivision into neighborhoods. The community may be likened to a living organism, which is a collection of cells, each cell being a neighborhood, and all together being more or less in a state of flux. The neighborhood, somewhat like the community, is an area where a consciousness of interdependence exists among the people who live there, a consciousness possibly derived from the common use of facilities and the acquaintance of neighbor with neighbor. Propinquity of people promotes neighborly feelings. With improvement in communication and refinement of home conveniences tending to increase the self-sufficiency of each home, the sense of neighborhood has perhaps suffered some decline. It is notable, however, that when disaster strikes or threatens, people find elements of security in their neighborhood.

One city that has studied its community and neighborhood conformation has identified its neighborhoods within such natural and artificial barriers as highways, rivers, storm channels, and, industrial or commercial plants, which confine a given number of residences to a locality that is the neighborhood. The communities were easily identified, most of them having acquired distinctive names. The average population of each neighborhood was about 2,000. The communities into which these neighborhoods grouped themselves were populated by 25,000 to 50,000 persons. The communities together, each having more or less exact boundaries, constitute a city whose population is measured in seven figures. Growth of this city proceeds by a process of expansion by addition of communities, each with a variable number of neighborhoods. This process has gone on decade after decade and even though the population of older communities has sometimes declined, the gross population increase of the whole city has been phenomenal.

COMMUNITY AND NEIGHBORHOOD BASIS FOR PLANNING

Community planning for sports and recreation facilities must necessarily be based upon the structural organization of the city, and is to be considered from the standpoint of planning within the single community as well as within the collection of communities that constitute the city. Facilities for sports and other recreation activities must be located in reference to the convenience of the people who will use them. If not conveniently located their potentiality will be greatly diminished and their benefit to the community lessened. It is necessary, therefore, to study the variable needs of different age groups on the one hand, and the requirements for different activities on the other.

PLANNING ADAPTED TO AGE GROUPS

The requirements for recreation facilities vary for people of different ages. Facilities for the accommodation of children may be conveniently planned for children in elementary school, kindergarten, and secondary school. Planning facilities for preschool children continues to be a private parental responsibility. The problem of distribution of facilities for recreation has important resemblance to the problem of distribution of school facilities. The mobility of the elementary school child, who is generally less than 12 years of age, scarcely extends beyond the neighborhood in which he resides. School planners have recognized this fact and have located elementary schools in reference to the neighborhood. Secondary school children have greater mobility afforded them by their freedom from close parental supervision, their greater endurance and capacity to walk, and their ability to use mechanical transportation—once only the bicycle, but now including for the older youth the automobile—and also commercial transportation.

The same planning principles apply to recreation facilities; hence, we speak of the neighborhood playground and recreation center, occupying comparatively limited space on a block in the neighborhood but not necessarily over a single block in size, where outdoor and indoor play facilities are maintained and play activities organized and supervised. Likewise there is the community park-playground and recreation center in which are located the facilities that youth beyond the elementary school age require for day-to-day activities. These activities are highly organized, requiring specialized equipment as well as large space. The community park-playground may also contain a neighborhood playground.

There are some municipal recreation installations that are serviceable to nearly all the population and need not necessarily be planned in relation to other installations. They should be located with reference to the convenience of all potential users. The city hall, the central library, the municipal art gallery, are examples. This is true also of regional parks and recreation areas that may possess attractions or facilities to be enjoyed for a sufficient block of time to justify a trip across the city. Regional parks are usually large areas of land affording extraordinary features of terrain and flora or other natural resources useful for recreation purposes. Their location has no relation to neighborhood or community areas. Such parks are most frequently located on marginal lands on the outskirts of cities. Occasionally they are large tracts that are closer to the center of the city, which were set aside at a period of early growth of the city and have since become surrounded by metropolitan urban development. Griffith Park in Los Angeles, 4,250 acres in size, the largest municipal park in America; Golden Gate Park in San Francisco with its 1,013 acres; Fairmont Park in Philadelphia with its 3,882 acres; and Lincoln Park in Chicago, are examples of close-in regional parks. All regional recreation areas, however, are not necessarily parks in the strict sense, for lakes and lake fronts and public beaches of seacoast cities may be included in this category.

Until recently recreational planning for children and youth was necessary on only the neighborhood and community level. It is now becoming increasingly necessary to plan and provide areas and facilities for adults, including senior citizens, many of whom are retired from gainful occupations at 60 to 70 years of age, with limited income from annuities and pensions. The adult population of today is the product of a universal public education system that forty years ago dedicated itself to "preparation for the worthy use of leisure time" as one of the cardinal principles of education.[2] For decades schools have been indoctrinating the population with the traditional American leisure time culture, and they have been aided and abetted by an alert industry which sells commodities and services consumed in leisure. The blandishments and enticements of advertising are apparently irresistible in a time of good economy.

The responsibility for adult recreation to date is largely a regional problem. Facilities for the exercise of many kinds of hobbies—motoring, boating in its many forms, fishing, hunting, horseback riding, hiking, nature contacting, golfing, bowling on the green, and a host of other sports—are best provided in regional parks. This summary does not take in the whole picture. There are also gatherings of small groups, mostly comprised of senior citizens, in parks in congested urban areas. These citizens find pleasure in curb discussion, checkers, chess, shuffleboard, horseshoe pitching, bowling on the green, and the like. Card playing, square and social dancing, group singing, and other indoor pastimes take place in community recreation centers. In some neighborhoods the park-playground will have to be adapted to the needs of adults, senior citizens included, in a manner that will not result in age group conflicts. These adult needs should be primarily accommodated in the community park-playground.

Public policy as determined by elective bodies is always influenced by the pressure of public opinion. Park and recreation administrators long in service remember when the public pressure to establish neighborhood and community parks and to institute recreation activity programs arose out of compassion for children, especially for children living in underprivileged areas of the city. There was also some pressure for the preservation of scenic spots and historical locations. Now the force of public opinion is pre-eminently in behalf of all children and youth and all adults, wherever they reside. Most notable are the sentiments in behalf of senior citizens. It requires no prophetic vision to foresee a strong public pressure emerging in the interest of providing recreation centers for senior citizens when employment tapers off and the older ones are the first recipients of enforced leisure. A universal park and recreation service is desired.

DEPENDENCE UPON PUBLIC PARK SYSTEMS

The importance of a comprehensive system of parks and other recreation areas becomes more apparent with each decade of social progress. Dependence of urban population upon a public system of parks and recreation facilities has increased decade by decade until now it is almost universal. When the population of an area was relatively small and land in private ownership in large blocks was plenteous, there was comparatively little need for a well distributed system of parks and recreation areas. Privately owned land and facilities were sufficient for the needs of a population that had little leisure. As population increased, the number of close-in landed estates situated near urban centers diminished, and the willingness of private owners to permit the use of their lands for many public recreation activities likewise decreased. The increasing burden of taxes upon land has also resulted in decreased private land ownership, especially in the vicinity of urban development.

[2] National Education Association, Committee Report, *Cardinal Principles of Secondary Education* (Washington, D.C.: Bureau of Education, Dept. of the Interior, U.S. Govt.), 1917.

A marginal park in congested Lower Manhattan (Battery Park).

It has now come to pass that in large cities the public has become almost entirely dependent upon publicly owned land for outdoor recreation. To take a single example: golf courses, once provided only by clubs with memberships of a few persons of means are now disappearing. Contributing to this result are the high taxes on land, the cost of water, the increasing labor cost for maintenance, and the capital gains that can be made by subdivision of club grounds for residential, commercial, and industrial purposes. Private golf courses in metropolitan centers will inevitably become exceptional facilities maintained by a limited number of golf enthusiasts who can afford high monthly dues and extraordinary initiation fees. Meanwhile, the number of golfers increases as the leisure time available to play golf also increases; hence, plans for expansion of municipal golf facilities become more and more necessary.

Other facilities required for sports and other recreations are experiencing the same difficulty. Those who find their recreation in fishing today cast their line from a public beach or put out to sea from a public harbor or whip a stream in a state or national park or forest preserve. Those who find pleasure in horseback riding no longer ride through great landed estates but follow the bridle trails in the regional and state and national parks. Those who play baseball or soccer, whether children or youth or young adults —and the number who seek recreation outlets in these sports is increasing year by year —do so upon public fields which are all too limited to care for the demand. Cities suddenly find that "sand lots," once the cradle of the American national pastime, have disappeared. Hundreds of cities, or parts of cities, populated by 50,000 and more persons have not a single baseball lot big enough to allow baseball to be played according to the official rules.

THE PLACE OF SCHOOLS IN THE RECREATION PLAN

It is evident from examination of the facilities required for neighborhood park-playgrounds and community park-playgrounds that the separate facilities to some extent are not unlike those found in the modern elementary and secondary school. The practical suggestion presents itself that planning of neighborhood and community facilities for any city should include the play areas and facilities that are inevitably provided in the schools. Considerations of economy dictate that the elementary school, wherever it is located, shall become the neighborhood playground. This development is not the total answer to the neighborhood need, however. Useful as the large city school playground areas and facilities may be, they are deficient: first, the ground surface is usually hard pavement; second, their equipment is limited; and third, the great number of elementary school areas in a given city frequently demands that an elementary school must serve more than one neighborhood. If all elementary schools were administered as neighborhood park-playgrounds there would still be a need for supplementary areas to provide for neighborhoods not served by schools. Supplementary areas would also be needed for activities that cannot be conveniently and pleasantly accommodated on the limited school ground.

The same rationale may be applied to the planning of community park-playgrounds, the need for which may be only partially relieved by making the areas and facilities of secondary schools available for community play. Supplementation of the secondary school facilities usually requires greater open area, more fields for outdoor sports with grass or well conditioned earth surfaces, and with picnic grounds, batteries of tennis and other play courts, illumination for night play, and other playground essentials.

School planners envision the school in the future as the all-sufficient local institution to provide the areas, facilities, and programs of recreation required in the neighborhood and community. The Educational Policies Commission, appointed by the National Education Association and the American Association of School Administrators, in a report published in 1939 under the title, "Social Services and the Schools," made the following observations:

> The schools are educational institutions which offer some leisure-time activities to a portion of the general population; as institutions for public education, the schools are slowly but steadily increasing the scope of their activities, in accordance with modern philosophies of education, to the point of offering an integrated program of education and recreation for children, youth and adults. Playgrounds and recreation centers are likewise educational institutions offering a balanced leisure-time program to much the same population. To a large degree both institutions use the same facilities in conducting their programs.
>
> School authorities are now administering programs of public recreation in a number of communities. One reason for this is that the school is to be found everywhere, even in the most sparsely settled regions. Legislatures of several states have coupled this fact with the universal need for recreation and have empowered boards of education to establish and provide personnel and equipment for community leisure-time programs. Even without legislative authority, people in some rural areas are utilizing school facilities and personnel for recreation purposes because to them the public school is an acceptable channel for the disbursement of tax-monies devoted to activities associated with their education and well-being.
>
> To say the least, the status of public recreation today is dynamic and subject continuously to change under new laws and judicial interpretations. However, the fact that certain states have made express provision for the establishment of public recreation services and facilities by local boards of education clearly indicates that unification of these educational services is not outside the realm of possibility.

The Commission recognized, however, that merging city local recreation and park activities is not practicable in many cities, and that separate agencies must necessarily continue, but that cooperation between school and other public agencies must be fostered and often committed to formal agreement encompassing, among other things, full use of school facilities for public recreation.

In the regional picture schools hardly enter into the problem of planning at all, for the schools do not possess facilities usually found in regional parks. It is apparent that regional areas and facilities are a special charge of the municipality itself (if it is big enough), or of a county, or state, planned for the use of people of the whole region.

In this discussion of the urban park and recreation problem the metropolitan city has been the urbanized area to which the problem has been oriented. What of the thousands of smaller cities which have no pretensions to metropolitan status? What of the villages and crossroads settlements, which are hardly cities at all? Whenever people are living close enough together to recognize a need for a community recreation program, intelligent planning must precede any action. The very small isolated village can be likened to the neighborhood in the big city. Basically it needs a "neighborhood" park and recreation center, perhaps a "community center." For regional and larger community services in this field it necessarily must look to the county and the state. "In such places emphasis can well be placed upon the gradual assumption of greater recreation responsibilities by the schools," says the Educational Policies Commission.[3] In many states, counties are beginning to provide the means for service to unincorporated areas. They are also entering into the field of providing regional recreation parks, a prerogative also exercised in most states through state park commissions.

In a paper entitled "Future Suburban Parks," prepared for the International Recreation Congress at Philadelphia, 1956, Robert Moses, head of the New York City and State Park Systems, pointed out:

Our State Parks fall into three general categories:

1. Areas near large centers of population where people can go for a day's outing.
2. Areas within driving, walking or boating distance of cities and towns where people can go for a day's recreation and perhaps stay overnight if they wish.
3. Areas where individuals, families and groups can go to spend several days, a week or an entire vacation.

The relationship between national, state, regional, county and municipal parks requires careful planning and cooperation, because no logical balance of recreation needs is possible without a clear understanding of the territory each unit of government should attempt to cover.[4]

With population growing as it is, with increasing congestion in urban and suburban areas, and with the ever-greater mobility of people that automotive transportation has brought about, it is apparent that counties and states in the future must undertake an increasingly larger role in this field of public service.

THE "MASTER PLAN" OF AREAS

A master plan to guide the acquisition and development of areas for sports and general recreation activities is essential if orderly development of a thorough system of parks and recreation facilities is to be accomplished. The master plan is predicated upon an acceptance of principles that have evolved from good practice and are adapted to the local situation. It anticipates the probable changes in total population, in population of the separate neighborhoods and communities, and in population of age groups. It predicts the direction in which urban development will probably take place, and where areas and facilities for new and expanding neighborhoods and communities will be required. It also sets forth the areas of land best suited for acquisition for regional types of facilities and activities.

The growth of a park and recreation system, though conforming more or less to plan, often occurs to some extent through

---

[3] *Social Services and the Schools,* Educational Policies Commission, 1939.

[4] Robert Moses, *Future Suburban Parks* (New York: *Recreation,* December, 1956).

fortuitous or accidental means, which are seldom predictable. Thus cities have come into possession of marginal lands that were unsuited to profitable residential or commercial development and were subsequently made available for municipal purposes. An example of such unpredictable possession would be the transfer of land to the city with cancellation of delinquent taxes or the gift of part of an estate with purchase of the remainder. Development of a park system under these conditions can be orderly and more rapid if a master plan exists.

STANDARDS FOR PLANNING

Planning of neighborhood and community areas for sports and other recreation activities can be reduced more or less to a formula, whereas planning of regional areas is more fortuitous. Various estimates have been made by professional and promotional bodies, such as the American Institute of Park Executives and the National Recreation Association, as to total space required for park and recreation needs. Their estimate is one acre for every 100 residents, or not less than one-tenth of the total area of the city. Such estimates are of little help as a guide to planning, although they do give a limited basis for comparisons between cities. The difficulty with such estimates is that they do not recognize the principle of distribution of land in usable units to meet the requirements of neighborhoods and communities. A more realistic approach to this problem has recently been developed by the California Committee on Planning for Recreation, Park Areas and Facilities. The Committee's report, published in 1956, goes further in setting up a basic standard than has any other agency.[5]

This report recommends for metropolitan cities neighborhood playgrounds of 6 acres if adjoining a school, and of 16 acres if separately established in metropolitan centers. A neighborhood is defined as an area with a population of 2,000 to 3,000 people. It further recommends one community park-playground of approximately 20 acres for each community if adjoining a secondary school, and 32 acres if separately established. The community is considered to be an area of about 25,000 population. The definition of size of area for regional needs is understandably not so specific because opportunities to develop regional areas are less subject to exact planning. They are more dependent upon accidental circumstances of location of natural recreation resources, such as beach, lake, forested area, desert, mountain, or other features about which a park might be developed. The municipal regional parks have usually been marginal lands insofar as their potentiality for economic utilization is concerned. Nevertheless, the California report recommends "city-wide" sports and recreation centers of one to 100,000 population, and other regional reservations, without reference to space standards.

The whole scheme of planning park and recreation areas can now be seen to fall into a pattern of planning for neighborhood playgrounds or parks, community park-playgrounds, regional parks, and sports centers, each with its own function, each serving its own clientele, with some overlapping of clientele between them. All together they constitute the network of park and recreation facilities designed to serve the whole population.

The separate facilities that may be located in each of the areas included within the total plan are adapted to suit the recreation interests and requirements of a clientele related to each type. The kinds of facilities to be developed within the types are somewhat as shown in Table 1-1.

PLANNING OF FACILITIES

Nearly all the master planning of parks and recreation facilities has been done in terms of areas and their distribution and not of facilities of various kinds. Given areas well located, would it not be well to know how many play courts, diamonds, fields, and other facilities should be necessary to meet the expected demand? School planners can compute the numbers of classrooms required for a stated population. This task is comparatively easy because the curriculum is fixed

[5] *Guide for Planning Recreation Parks in California*, California Committee on Planning for Recreation, Park Areas and Facilities, 1956.

TABLE 1-1

Desirable Standards for Public Park and Recreation Areas and Facilities

Nature of Area	*Age Group Primarily Served*	*Approximate Minimum Size*	*Units in re Population*	*Service Area*	*Desirable facilities and Characteristics*
Neighborhood park & playground. Need may be satisfied partially by school play areas.	5 to 14 inc.	10 acres	One per 3,000	½ mile radius	Grassed area for informal games, play apparatus, shelter building (or access to school bldg.), paved courts area, border landscaping, fencing.
Community Park-playground	All groups; but youth essentially	15 acres	One per 25,000	Related to characteristic community; Radius: one mile (more or less)	Grassed area for field sports, moderate spectator accommodations, paved area for court games (basketball, volleyball, etc.), tennis courts (4 or more), picnic facilities, moderate lighting, swimming pool, all-purpose building, landscape features and border planting, area and equipment for adult passive recreation, sanitary conveniences available to outdoors, moderate on site parking lot. (May also include neighborhood playground.)
Unique and specialized park, recreation and historical sites.	Any or all	Variable	Fortuitous as determined by public interest	Unlimited	As indicated by public demand and need.
Regional park	Any or all	Unlimited	Determined by opportunity and public demand	The Metropolitan Region	Natural geographic and geological features; lake, stream, native flora and fauna, camp and picnic areas, hiking and riding trails, roads and parking areas, sports fields, zoo, golf courses, etc.

and attendance of pupils is required by law. Recreation attendance is variable and is dependent upon many things—for example, available facilities, quality of promotion and leadership, local and national fads, competition for attention and time of people, weather, economic conditions, and so forth. A sport may spring up with unpredicted popularity and a community may find itself woefully behind in space and equipment for its accommodation. Through a combination of unpredictable circumstances "kid" baseball for boys suddenly became exceedingly popular. New play fields had to be improvised in private and public land.

Although enough statistics are not available to permit accurate computation of existing conditions, it is unlikely that any city of considerable size can claim to be adequately supplied with facilities for public recreation. The National Recreation Association has gathered statistics for nearly a half century and its reports are now published each five years in *Recreation*, the monthly magazine of the Association.[6] No complete analysis of the statistical reports has been attempted, so far as is known, but central tendencies have been computed for selected cities, grouped according to population. One study conducted for the city of Tulsa deduced statistics for the 23 cities in the population group 200,000 to 400,000 (1957). The median provision of certain public recreation facilities among these cities was computed and this revealed some interesting facts, even though the basic information cannot be considered strictly accurate. The following are some of the statistical media:

Regulation baseball diamonds—one per 35,000 people

[6] *Recreation and Park Yearbook* (New York: National Recreation Association), 1956.

A state park beach, New Sebago Beach, Palisades Interstate Park, Bear Mountain, New York.
Photo by Stockmeyer

Junior baseball diamonds—one per 20,000 people
Softball diamonds—one per 15,000 people
Diamonds of any kind—one per 7,000 people
Tennis courts—one per 5,700 people
Swimming pools (outdoors)—one per 53,000 people
Golf courses (units of 9 holes)—one per 70,000 people

It is obvious from these fragmentary statistics that large cities are undersupplied with public recreation facilities considered apart from areas. Small cities would no doubt show a better record than larger ones. Consider baseball alone, which is often referred to as our "national game." With one diamond for 7,000 people it is apparent that not many could play at one time. Seven thousand people of all ages would include only about 600 male youth from 10 to 20 years of age. Organized in 60 teams of 10 they would need 60 diamonds to play simultaneously. If only one third were to play and if two teams used each diamond, 10 diamonds would be needed. The median is but one. Should it be inferred that the cities in this population group have only $1/10$ as many diamonds as they should have, or that only $1/10$ of the male youth, disregarding girls, are to be expected to play baseball? The former is the more realistic conclusion.

The quantities of facilities required for general participation must be considered in the refining of recreation planning. Agreement should be sought on what constitutes adequate recreation programs and what facilities under given conditions of organization and leadership will be required. More adequate reporting and compilation of statistics is an immediate need if facilities standards are to be developed.

GOVERNMENT STRUCTURE AND POLICY

The traditional hierarchy of governmental structure and organization, *i.e.*, village, city, county, and state, is not always well adapted to the creation of a universal system of recreation areas, facilities, and programs. It has been pointed out that the school district, which is a municipal corporation independent of the city, is a logical agency to make some provisions for public recreation. Counties in some states are only beginning to undertake responsibility for recreation areas and programs. Since the functions of county government are customarily very limited, and usually less inclusive than cities under home rule, special legislation is required to authorize counties to enter this field of service. If all the people of a state are to be served with recreation facilities, counties must be expected to undertake this role with assistance from the school system.

In most states a new form of administration of local functions in a locality has been developed, the *Special District*. Special districts are authorized to acquire and improve property and to administer recreational services. The districts are financed by ad valorem taxes assessed against real property in the district and are governed by administrative boards created by election or by appointment. Such districts sometimes include two or more cities, as well as populated areas in unincorporated parts of a county.

Whatever the government organization for administration of parks and recreation areas, administrative boundaries do not fence in the people. People flow from one area to another in their quest for recreation. It is impractical to limit use of facilities to local residents. Almost everywhere reciprocity is observed in the use of recreation facilities in much the same way as it is in the use of public roads and streets.

The administration of public recreation areas is often carried out by government agencies as a public service, but not without cost to the public. Utility services provided by government agencies are furnished for a fee calculated on the basis of measured service. Some recreation services are financed in this manner. Services for children are usually provided free but adult services that are more costly to maintain are sometimes charged for. Some of the services thus financed include golf-playing privileges, use of swimming pools, special instruction, admittance to entertainment events, and automobile parking privileges. Charging for parking has become a convenient means of collecting revenue in amounts related to use. In the larger systems of public recreation

Photo by Stockmeyer

Well-planned layout for a recreation area. Anthony Wayne Recreation Area, Palisades Interstate Park, New York.

about one-fifth of the revenue required to operate is derived from fees and charges of various kinds.

PRINCIPLES FOR PLANNING

Although provision of public recreation is a comparatively new function of government, practice in America has developed common tendencies among cities. Experience has been shared and from this experience a body of principles has taken form. The following list is suggested as a tentative set of principles upon which there is common agreement among administrators of public recreation:

1. *Properties* should be acquired in the path of urban development, according to a master plan and in advance of the ability and the need of the city to improve them.
2. *Properties for recreation and park* use in areas already fully developed should be acquired as opportunities afford, and as part of a plan of urban redevelopment.
3. *Park lands* should be dedicated for public park and recreation use and should not be permitted to be used for other purposes nor diverted to private use or to uses under control of private parties or corporations.
4. *Public parks and recreation facilities* should be located with the convenience of the whole public in mind, and should be distributed to give all equal opportunity, so far as practicable, for their enjoyment.
5. *Public park and recreation areas* should be improved in a manner creditable to the neighborhood or community in which they are located, and maintained in an attractive, clean, and safe condition.
6. *Facilities* should be arranged according to the most efficient use of the land, convenience of the age group or groups for which they are planned, safety of users, spectators and others, economy, effectiveness of supervision, and pleasing appearance.
7. *Buildings within parks* should provide the essential public conveniences of quality equal to those provided in other public buildings, facilities for effective maintenance and supervision, and indoor rooms suitable to the requirements of the public recreation program.
8. *Public schools,* including buildings and grounds, should be designed and

planned for and be available for use by community groups when such use does not interfere with the established education program, when the use is for a public purpose and activity open to all citizens, and under necessary regulations, including reasonable and not prohibitive charges.

9. *The facilities* of the public park and recreation system should be made readily available to organized school uses under reciprocal arrangements incorporated in official agreements.

10. *Parks* may, with advantages to the total situation, be acquired and developed adjacent to public schools but not as a fixed rule, nor as a reason for the acquirement by the school district of less space than would otherwise be needed for school purposes. Since the complete school is in itself a potential local park and recreation facility to serve the neighborhood of which it is a center, it is often expedient for a park to be located in a neighborhood that cannot be effectively served by an existing school.

11. *In a large city* it may be impossible to plan for as many parks as there may be schools. If appropriate inter-agency agreement can be reached between municipal government and school government wherein schools may be incorporated in the total plan of providing neighborhood recreation service, duplication of areas and facilities is avoided.

12. *Sharing of responsibility* for year-round recreation service to all parts of the city between municipal and school governments is a practical matter subject to negotiation. It is also conditioned by legal authority granted by the legislature, adaptability of the facilities controlled by each public agency to the public needs, financial ability to meet the needs, and other factors.

13. *Constant administrative coordination* between the public agencies having recreation responsibilities and between them and the various voluntary youth serving agencies conducting recreation for the public welfare should be established. Formal agreements should exist among the several agencies. Cooperation should be further implemented by a committee or council composed of top level lay representatives with responsible chief executives serving in technical and advisory capacity.

14. *Enlightened administration* of public parks and schools for wide community recreation use lightens the financial burden upon the voluntary youth-serving agencies, especially in respect to provision of capital funds for land and structures. A goodly part, but not all, of the recreation programs of the private agencies may be accommodated in schools and parks. The public investment in recreation areas and facilities yields far greater return to the taxpayers in terms of volume of effective use when public agencies pursue liberal policies in extending privileges to the youth-serving agencies in the use of facilities without preference over the public agency's own program.

15. *The public park and recreation areas and facilities* require competent management on the site, efficient maintenance and skilled supervision. Management and supervision extend also to the activities that take place daily, seasonally, and annually, and are termed the "program." The program consists of participation by individuals and groups with many complex arrangements within them. For the most part the activities are self-directed by the participants under their recognized leaders with such assistance as the professional public recreation staff may give. The role of publicly financed recreation leadership in parks, playgrounds, and schools (insofar as schools accept a place in the recreation program) is a multiple role that includes the following: (1) management of the physical plant; (2) supervision of the public in use of the plant; (3) promotion of activities with a view to larger and more beneficial use; (4) organization of groups; (5) scheduling uses of the facilities; and (6) incidental instruction.

16. *The role of leadership* in a park and recreation system is a professional role requiring personal and technical preparation parallel to but not identical to that of teaching. Competence in performance of this role cannot be achieved without the benefits of year-round employment at a professional salary. Part-time or seasonal volunteer leadership is effective only when undertaken under the general guidance of professionals.

17. *The public parks of a city* should provide the floor upon which the superstructure of recreation activities of the community may rise. This structure consists of the multiform hobbies and group activities that constitute leisure time culture. They are becoming more and more numerous and increasingly complex. Cities generally provide for the accommodation of sports hobbies, especially competitive games in the park system; now they are urged to provide the locale for a wide range of water activities—sailing, speedboating, water skiing, fly casting, fishing; for mechanical hobbies—motor-driven airplane flying, model motorcar racing, sportscar racing, motorcycling, model railroading; for nature hobbies—bird watching, collecting of natural specimens, prospecting for minerals; for social hobbies—social dancing, square dancing, folk dancing; for dramatics—stage plays and pageants. All of these and other hobbies are subject to voluntary organization and to some extent they can be pursued at home or in private establishments of various kinds; but for the most part they find their greatest development in modern parks and other public recreation centers planned and improved for their accommodation.

18. *The executive personnel* in a park system should consist of professional persons trained in their respective technical fields and imbued with the philosophy that a park department plans constantly with people to facilitate the adaptation of the park areas and structures to the variable recreation needs of the people, and to expedite the widespread use of the facilities by the public. Only through these means are parks used to the extent that the taxpayers may obtain full return from the investment they make in the parks.

19. *The use of public parks and schools* should generally be free of charge. The right to enjoy a park should not be denied anyone because he may lack the price of admission. Special services, however, which are enjoyed by relatively few or which are extraordinarily costly to provide in comparison with ordinary uses may properly be subject to a moderate fee. The assessment of fees for adult activities is more justifiable than for children's activities. Inexpensive supplies should be furnished for group activi-

Courtesy E. I. du Pont de Nemours & Co.

Vinyl all-weather playground of tomorrow.

ties of children; adult groups should provide their own. Failure to provide free a moderate supply of expendable play implements, such as baseballs, softballs, bats, basketballs, volleyballs, table games, and the like, serves to deprive many children and youth the right to enjoy a satisfactory play experience with their peers in the park system.

20. *The use of public parks and special outdoor facilities* within them should not be limited to the daylight hours. Recreation is practiced in the early evening hours possibly more generally than in daytime. Efficient illumination, becoming more and more effective and economical, permits parks to yield much greater returns to the public than formerly. Lighting of areas attracts youth from other places of recreation which are often negative and destructive in influence. Lighting should be discreetly planned and installed to encourage participation in recreation activities and not merely the observation of others at play.

21. *The program of public recreation* should consist essentially of the activities that the people themselves bring to the public place, such as are planned, organized, and led by them. These activities should be facilitated by improvements to grounds and by structures, by equipment which is essential for their enjoyment, and by the leadership of a professional staff assigned to the center. For children and youth, however, the program requires leadership of professional and voluntary staff without which little program ensues, and for the lack of which the salutary outcomes in skill, interest, and good citizenship are not achieved.

22. A *municipal park and recreation system* is not effectively administered unless it is atune to public interest, demand, and constructive opinion. In this respect it may be considered as akin to the system of public schools and education. Regardless of opinion as to how other municipal functions may best be administered, it is a highly prevalent opinion among recreation and park experts and their professional associations that a city does well to have a recreation and park board or commission of lay citizens (or perhaps a park board and a recreation board as in many cities), and that such board or boards should have definitive responsibility for the planning, establishment, and operation of the system with authority to direct the chief executive of the department.

23. *The function of a park and recreation board* should be to organize the city for wholesome recreation insofar as the municipal facilities will permit, and as authorized by law. A board should not become essentially a land acquisition or land development agency, for the resources at its command include also people, activities, interests, and traditions, the utilization of which in democratic ways eventuates in a program of public recreation that has an important place in the urban culture.

CHAPTER 2

THE SCHOOL AS A COMMUNITY CENTER

N. L. Engelhardt, Sr.

SINCE WORLD WAR II GREAT FORCES HAVE been set in motion affecting the fundamental nature of American communities, the character of our homes, the daily use of man's time, the ease of transportation, and the number and nature of agencies for communicating ideas, knowledge, and understanding. Man is creating for himself a new environment and seeks to establish a more significant and universally more satisfying way of life. In the process old types of communities are giving way to more livable centers; the modern thruway, freeway, or parkway is replacing the railroad; dense population centers are unloading many families into modern communities taking root in the open country; and emerging problems of community administration and financing, as well as providing facilities for common use, cry for solution. The communities rising out of the open lands of the country will find the answers. The solutions need not follow the timeworn patterns of the older cities but will, without doubt, be molded to the new needs and the new ways of life.

Illustration: Edgemont High School, Westchester County, New York
Architect: Warren H. Ashley

THE COMMUNITY SCHOOL HAS LONG EXISTED

The new schools serving the emerging social, economic, and cultural changes have in the two decades 1940 and 1950 given an inkling of what communities want in the way of educational facilities. They are on large sites, the buildings are functionally conceived, (the probability of expansion to serve new needs has been acknowledged in the planning), and the adaptation of facilities for general community use has had official approval. In other words, the community school is coming into its own. To be sure, the concept has always had wide

acceptance in this country; unfortunately, however, there has not always been the provision of facilities that would permit the purpose to bear real fruit.

The early colonial schools were community schools in spite of their limitations of space and equipment. Basically the school was built to educate the young. In a democracy this is certainly a delimiting purpose of education. More and more our present 170,000,000 population is veering to a recognition of the need for a "cradle-to-grave" educational program. The growing youth must constantly adjust his educational bearings to new situations and the adult citizen must be constantly alert to the educational implications of a new earning situation, of a more significant use of increased leisure time, or of an alluring opportunity for creative achievement. The narrowly conceived community school of the past century must be supplanted by an honest-to-goodness comprehensive community school where youth as well as adult, man as well as woman, the individual as well as the family, will find opportunity for economic, social, intellectual, physical, creative, and moral growth on their way to the heights of American citizenship.

COMMUNITIES CHANGE OVER THE YEARS

The conquest of time, space, and distance has not only changed the community, but has also de-emphasized or sidetracked the motives behind community building and brought confusion to the main urges that gave rise to many cities and towns.

If America could today start anew in city building, how many of our large and medium-sized cities would be built on their present locations? How many would tend to seek more advantageous placement? How many would wish to better regulate their size? What dominant characteristics would they prefer? The relative proximity of the airfield; the protective nature of the hinterland; high lands instead of bottom marsh or spring-flooded terrain and the sections where lake and mountain contribute to comfortable, happy living are probable choices for location. Satisfactory housing for all, reasonable travel distance to work centers, population in less than astronomical figures, freedom from slums, retention of nature's advantages, superior school and recreational centers, would be powerful guides in the creation of the new city. The American people have changed their outlook. They have come to appreciate what a good modern community can be like. The examples of what the combination of architects, city planners, school planners, builders, writers, and visionaries have accomplished, have stimulated us to be content with none but the best. The making of better communities to fit American ideals holds great promise.

THE FUTURE COMMUNITY IS IN THE MAKING

The future community is in the making. To have the old city indulge in perimeter building will not suffice. To replan the core of the old city pulls at the purse strings and takes interminable time. Starting anew with approved standards of size and character may be a partial answer. At least, many efforts point in that direction.

The old city cannot long continue to thrive with its most competent leadership moving out to the peripheral areas and its old housing turning into congested slums for low-income groups. The congestion of narrow streets, the extensive loss of time to motor vehicle occupants, the illogical long-distance movement of workers to their wage-earning stations and the fears and dangers of this atomic age are mounting obstacles to continued prosperity and growth of the old large city.

Man has discovered easier means of providing food, shelter, and clothing than he had in the days of early community formation. Time and distance, that once loomed as barriers to progress, today take on new and less frightening meaning. Power for production need no longer be used at its source but may be delivered hundreds of miles away. Long lanes of concrete clearly surpass parallel steel rails as a means of transportation in many services to our people. The jet age promises to make neighbors of all mankind.

Today man can easily transport raw materials to any point of production; the nec-

FACILITIES IN A GENERAL EDUCATION LABORATORY

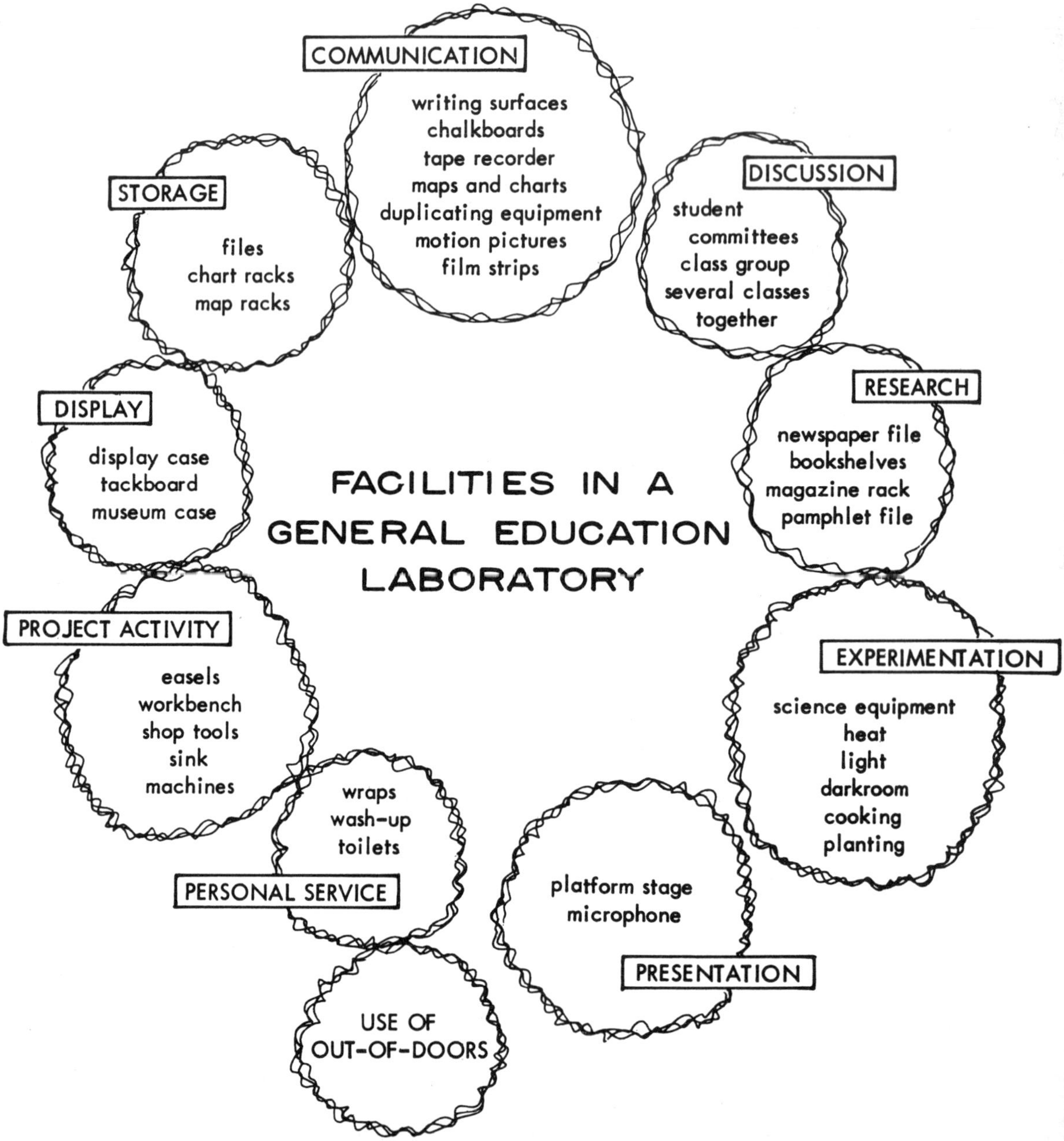

ENGELHARDT, ENGELHARDT AND LEGGETT
Educational Consultants

essary motive power for his machinery is available from a network of seemingly endless wires and pipelines. Millions of cars, trucks, and buses carry man and his goods with ease to any point of vantage. The important elements basic to early community planning have less significance today. Man can produce with ease and in abundance the material necessities and luxuries to satisfy his wants. To accomplish this, he can build his production centers where safety, climatic desirability, and living advantages dictate. Nature's controls over the determination of man's abode have slowly but definitely been losing their potency.

The intangible instruments of community creation and promotion have, however, not lost their power. Happy home living, meaningful objectives, the drive of successful achievement, and assured continuity of life service in the work of the world underlie man's interest in community building. Future community gains are more and more dependent upon more and more education, more and more strengthening of the intangibles. School and community interests are intertwined. Greater understanding of human nature, fundamental appreciation of man's past achievements, and belief in man's limitless potentials can come from the vast resources of the community school and make for a fundamental contribution to community growth.

LAND NEEDS OF THE COMMUNITY SCHOOL

Adequate amounts of land set aside to serve the common needs of the people provide the best safeguards for keeping a community as a desirable place for bringing up children and satisfying family needs during the maturing years. Many old communities duplicated their facilities as their administrative patterns evolved under political, social, and economic pressures. Certain recreational and cultural needs were served by parks, public recreation departments as well as by Boards of Education. Tomorrow's communities will desire to conserve their financial resources by encouraging a single organization to serve where in the past two or more have been providing facilities, staff, and programs. One well-conceived budget provides more efficacious service than two diluted ones. Agencies and municipal departments have tended slowly but definitely to assume functions that properly belong to the school. In the better administered communities mergers are encouraged to eliminate overlapping in community services. The schools tend to render the best service in recreation and physical education, as well as in the social and cultural programs of the various community groups. A single but ample pattern of play areas, indoor and out-of-doors, properly belongs under the school-board's administration.

Thus the best is assured that the community can provide for its available funds. The musical and dramatic arts should have its school facilities planned so that all interested community groups may also utilize them to the full. The industrial arts facilities of the school may serve the many men and women who crave the chance for further work in this field but cannot provide the facilities in their own homes. Duplication of shops and stages, outdoor playfields and indoor play floors, and the like, does not bring the community advantages that would be gained through a well-rounded, single plan developed to serve all community sections and types of neighborhoods.

The fact that land safeguards the future as well as the present community program has become clear to many school boards, as the following list will testify. In early colonial times when land was plentiful, only a fraction of an acre was frequently set aside for school purposes. In the mid-twentieth century, when open land prices rose to new highs, many communities from coast to coast acquired 40 to 100 acres and more for their secondary schools with the prospect that they would serve community purposes in many fields of human desires and achievement.

FACILITIES FOUND ON COMMUNITY SCHOOL SITES

The following checklist gives a comprehensive idea of what needs might be served on a community school site. To be sure, the community school must be the creation of the people it is to serve. There is nothing

TABLE 2-1

Some Senior High School Planning Throughout the Nation with Sites of 40 to 100 and More Acres, 1947-1956*

	Size of Site in Acres
CONNECTICUT	
Groton Senior High	65
Somers High	100
Wallingford High	92
ILLINOIS	
Piasa Community High	40
New West High, Rockford	100
KANSAS	
Manhattan High (including extensive park acreage which adjoins site)	27+
MARYLAND	
Boonsboro High	90
Hancock High	51
Mace's Lane High, Dorchester County	92
North County High, Dorchester County	68
North Hagerstown High	57
Salisbury High	50
Wicomico Senior High, Salisbury	56
MASSACHUSETTS	
Agawam High	40
Ludlow High (1st unit)	89
Mount Everett Regional School	85
Silver Lake Regional Jr.-Sr. High, Kingston	80
Tantasqua-Sturbridge Jr.-Sr. High	116
Wayland High	93.5
West Springfield High	64
MISSISSIPPI	
Greenwood High	50
MISSOURI	
Kirkwood High	41
Riverview Gardens High	47
NEW JERSEY	
Bridgewater Township High, Raritan	81
NEW YORK	
Ballston Spa Jr.-Sr. High	46.5
Clarkstown High, New City	40
Edgemont Jr.-Sr. High, Greenburgh	72
Great Neck Jr.-Sr. High	115
Herricks High	75
Hudson Falls Jr.-Sr. High	97
Massena High	65
North Colonie High	50
Syosset Senior High	73
Wheatley School, East Williston	60
NORTH CAROLINA	
Myers Park High, Charlotte	76
North East High, Charlotte	40+
South West High, Charlotte	60
West Charlotte High, Charlotte (40 park acres adjoining)	50+
West Mecklenburg County High, Charlotte	46
PENNSYLVANIA	
Lower Merion Township High, Ardmore	50
RHODE ISLAND	
New Rogers High, Newport	40
North Kingstown High, Wickford	43+
SOUTH CAROLINA	
Aiken Senior High	46
Blue Ridge High—6 yrs., Greenville County	45
Bryson—6 yr. School, Greenville County	89
Langley-Bath-Clearwater High, Aiken County, Aiken	69
Ridge Spring-Monetta-6 yr. High, Aiken County, Aiken	92
St. Marks—12 yr. School, Greenville County	40
Wagener—12 yr. School, Aiken County	62
VIRGINIA	
Danville High	55+
E. C. Glass High, Lynchburg	54

* Checked for accuracy by the school officials in each community.
Source: **Engelhardt, Engelhardt, Leggett and Cornell, Educational Consultants, New York, N.Y.**

so abhorrent to the American concept of education as the standardization of its schools. The school must fit the community of whose flesh and blood it is part. It must capitalize on the community's resources, both human and material. It must not be a closed proposition but should provide growth opportunities arising out of a thrilling, inspirational community life. The school and the land will be joined. The least expensive laboratory may be the land. The brook, the wooded area, the meadow, and the swamp have all been used fruitfully for learning.

Each community may be comprised of many neighborhoods, all of which will gain from their own type of school. The home-school, the neighborhood school, the regional school may define the type of school but certainly not the content. These should vary according to service needs. The building, as well as the site, should be tailored to fit community needs.

LIMITED PHYSICAL EDUCATION AND HEALTH FACILITIES

All too frequently in the past, the facilities for physical education and health in many schools have spelled a denial of opportunity to all boys and girls attending. Some of the disadvantages of limited physical education facilities are:

1. One hour of physical education per week per student instead of one hour per day.
2. The training of a small high-powered group of specialized athletes instead of training and game competition for all the students.
3. Extended opportunities for boys as contrasted with limited provisions for girls.
4. Emphasis on spectator games and less on recognition of games and exercise for pleasure, individual growth, and full recognition of individual needs.

ELEMENTARY SCHOOLS AND JUNIOR HIGH SCHOOLS

What has been written above about high schools applies equally to other types of public educational facilities, such as elementary schools, junior high schools, and junior colleges. The score card reproduced below reviews the factors that must be considered in site selection for the several types of schools. It must always be kept in mind that:

1. The community school must provide long service for its people.
2. It should be recognized as one of the most significant assets of the community.
3. The community plan should be built around the school.
4. Highways should be planned in such a way that no detriment to the school will result.
5. The school grounds and other facilities should contribute to the welfare, advancement, and happiness of all the people.

TABLE 2-2

Checklist of Items Affecting Size of Senior High School Sites*

Items	*Wanted* Now	*Wanted* Later	*Wanted* Not at All
A. *Required Building Area*			
1. School building or buildings			
2. Transportation garage			
3. Field house			
4. Caretaker's cottage			
5. Agricultural sheds or barns			
6. Greenhouse			
7. Storage sheds			
8. Stadium			
9. Outdoor swimming pool			
10. Heating plant			
11. Housing for animals			
12. Bicycle shed			
13. Amphitheater			
14. Boy Scout or other clubhouse for boys			

TABLE 2-2 (*continued*)

Items	Wanted: Now	Wanted: Later	Wanted: Not at All
15. Girl Scout or other clubhouse for girls			
16. Shelter house for outdoor group protection against storms			
17. Flagstaff and base			
18. Community memorials			
B. *Areas Required to Service or Protect Buildings and Occupants*			
1. Areas provided for building expansion			
2. Necessary set-back from streets			
3. Sidewalks and pedestrian approaches to buildings			
4. Automobile driveways			
5. Fuel, garbage, and supply service drives			
6. Bus loading and unloading areas			
7. Service loading aprons			
8. Parking areas for auditorium, gymnasiums, and outdoor events			
9. Bicycle approaches			
10. Landscaping adjacent to building			
11. Building court areas fully safeguarding sunlight and air in adjoining building units			
C. *Out-of-Doors Educational Areas*			
1. Terraces directly adjoining first floor classrooms			
2. Out-of-doors shop areas adjacent to shop unit			
3. Area for student construction of model cottage			
4. Storage, dressing, orchestra, and audience areas for amphitheater			
5. Pageantry areas			
6. Outdoor classroom areas for biology, plant life, and agriculture			
7. Protective spacing of educational areas from interference			

Items	Wanted: Now	Wanted: Later	Wanted: Not at All
8. Vocational practice in gardening and horticulture			
D. *Playgrounds and Play Fields*			
1. American football field running north and south, surrounded by a ¼ mile track with a 220-yard straightaway and jumping pits			
2. Doubles badminton court			
3. Singles badminton court			
4. Baseball field for boys			
5. Playground baseball field			
6. Basketball court for boys			
7. Basketball court for girls			
8. Clock golf course			
9. Four-wall handball courts			
10. Single-wall handball courts			
11. Field hockey courts			
12. Ice hockey rink			
13. Soccer football field for boys			
14. Soccer football field for girls			
15. Doubles tennis court			
16. Singles tennis court			
17. Volleyball court			
18. Speedball field			
19. Softball field for boys			
20. Softball field for girls			
21. Roller skating area			
22. Archery range			
23. Outdoor baseball diamonds			
24. Horseshoe courts			
25. Croquet courts			
26. Six-man football field			
E. *Other Recreational and Educational Areas*			
1. Hard-surface play area			
2. Areas assigned to scoutcraft			
3. Picnicking grounds including wooded area			
4. Swimming			
5. Hiking trails			
6. Automobile driving instruction area			

TABLE 2-2 (*continued*)

Items	Wanted: *Now*	*Later*	*Not at All*
F. *Protective Areas for Play and Recreational Spaces*			
1. Adequate set-back from streets to prevent conflict with traffic			
2. Essential spacing between play areas			
3. Playground areas adjacent to building for rest and lunch periods			
4. Area required for spectators and their seating			
5. Areas needed for duplicate adult activities			
6. Areas for expansion			

Items	Wanted: *Now*	*Later*	*Not at All*
G. *Other Land Uses*			
1. Formal school lawns, flower beds, trees, and shrubs			
2. Individual student gardens			
3. Experimental planting areas			
4. Play areas for young children of the nursery group used in the home-training department			
H. *Unassigned Areas Held in Reservation for Future Needs*			
1. Vocational extension 2. Junior college			

* From School Planning and Building Handbook, p. 255, by Engelhardt, Engelhardt and Leggett. New York: F. W. Dodge Corporation, 1956.

THE COMMUNITY SCHOOL OF TOMORROW

Tomorrow's community schools, in their various forms, will serve the young, the old, and those in between. The physical education and recreational facilities will be geared to the broadest possible community needs. All the facilities will serve many groups—the producers, the distributors, the human and material service fields, and the professional areas. They will stress the opportunity for broad as well as intensive learnings. The school's environment will add joy and inspiration to the learning tasks. The laboratories of learning will recognize that citizens grow as individuals as well as members of groups, and that opportunity for exercising initiative, participating in planning and action, and the privilege of accepting responsibility are essential elements in the growth processes. This school values the inheritances from past human achievements and furnishes the background for their thorough understanding. The school also welcomes and makes provision for the new media of enlightenment and stresses their values for individual as well as mass use.

The school is planned around all phases of human growth and achievement. The social development of youth to take his constructive place in a well-rounded community is planned for. Participation in the drama, the fine arts, and the home arts comes from programs planned for the earliest learning levels through the later reaches of life. Health and physical education are not just given lip service, but wholesome and comprehensive guidance and participation are made realities.

THE COMMUNITY SCHOOL MIRRORS THE FUTURE

The community school, in its corridors, its library and museum spaces, and its citizens' and parents' conference rooms, pictures the community's growth and its future plans. Here the story is told of individual achievement and of group accomplishments, and the inspiration is found for the creation of the best kinds of homes, the building of constructive and productive lives, and the molding of community and national loyalties that will meet every future test and challenge.

SPACE RELATIONSHIPS IN A JUNIOR HIGH SCHOOL

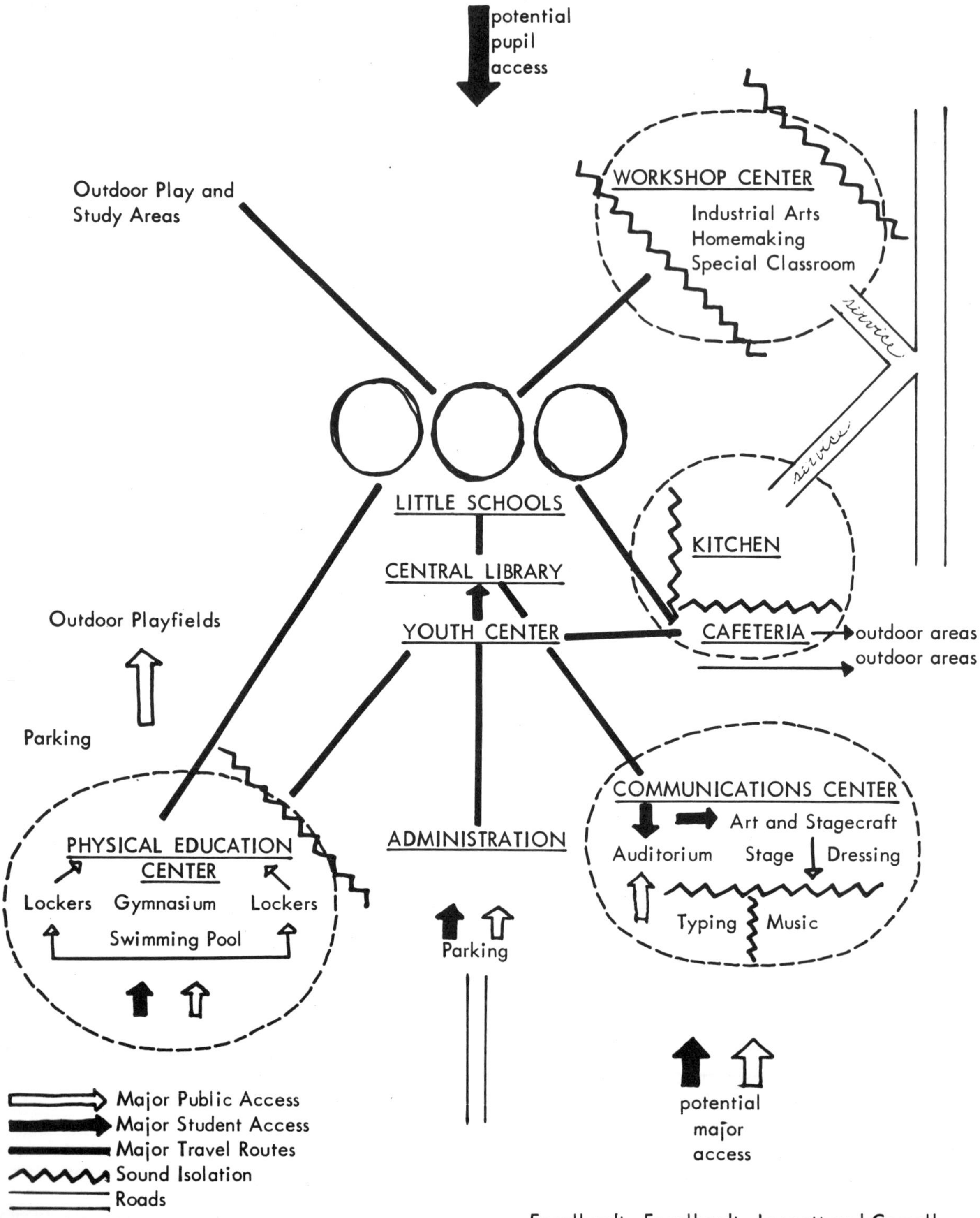

Engelhardt, Engelhardt, Leggett and Cornell
Educational Consultants

SUGGESTIONS FOR SPACE RELATIONSHIPS IN PLANNING A 1,000-PUPIL JUNIOR-SENIOR HIGH SCHOOL

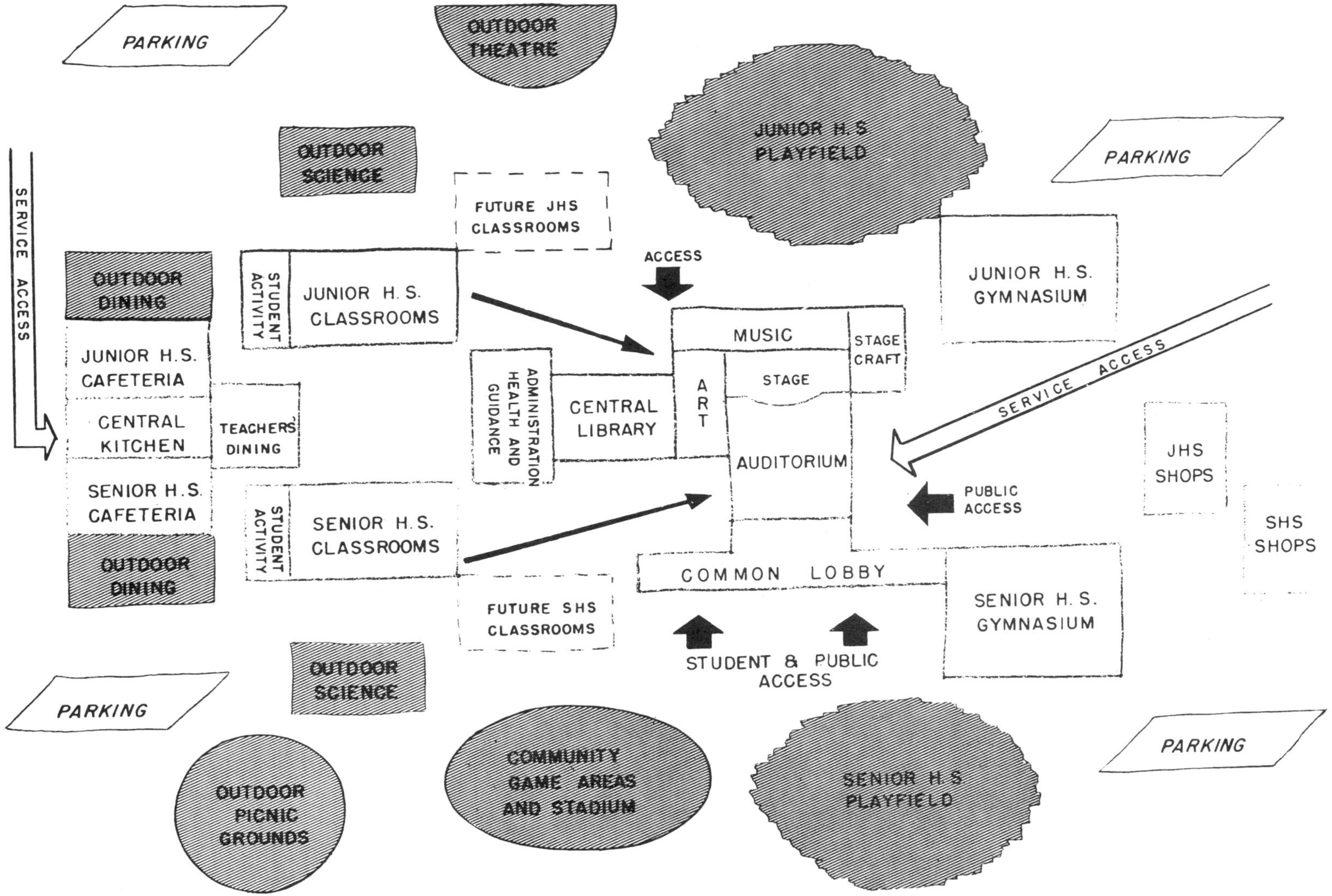

ENGELHARDT, ENGELHARDT AND LEGGETT
Educational Consultants

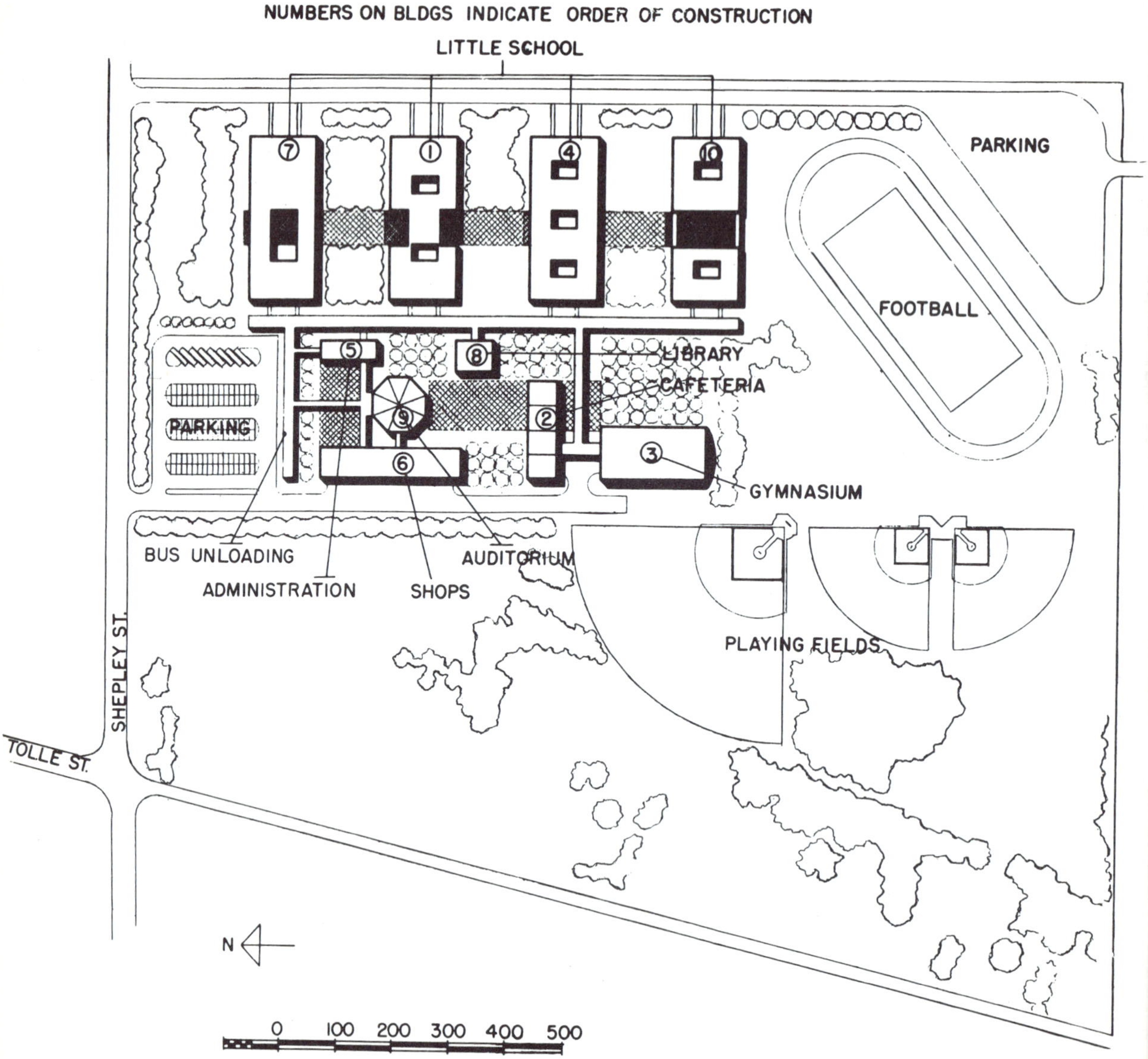

RIVERVIEW GARDENS SENIOR HIGH SCHOOL

HELLMUTH, OBATA & KASSABAUM, ARCHITECTS
W B MANSKE, ASSOCIATE ARCHITECT

ENGELHARDT, ENGELHARDT AND LEGGETT
EDUCATIONAL CONSULTANTS

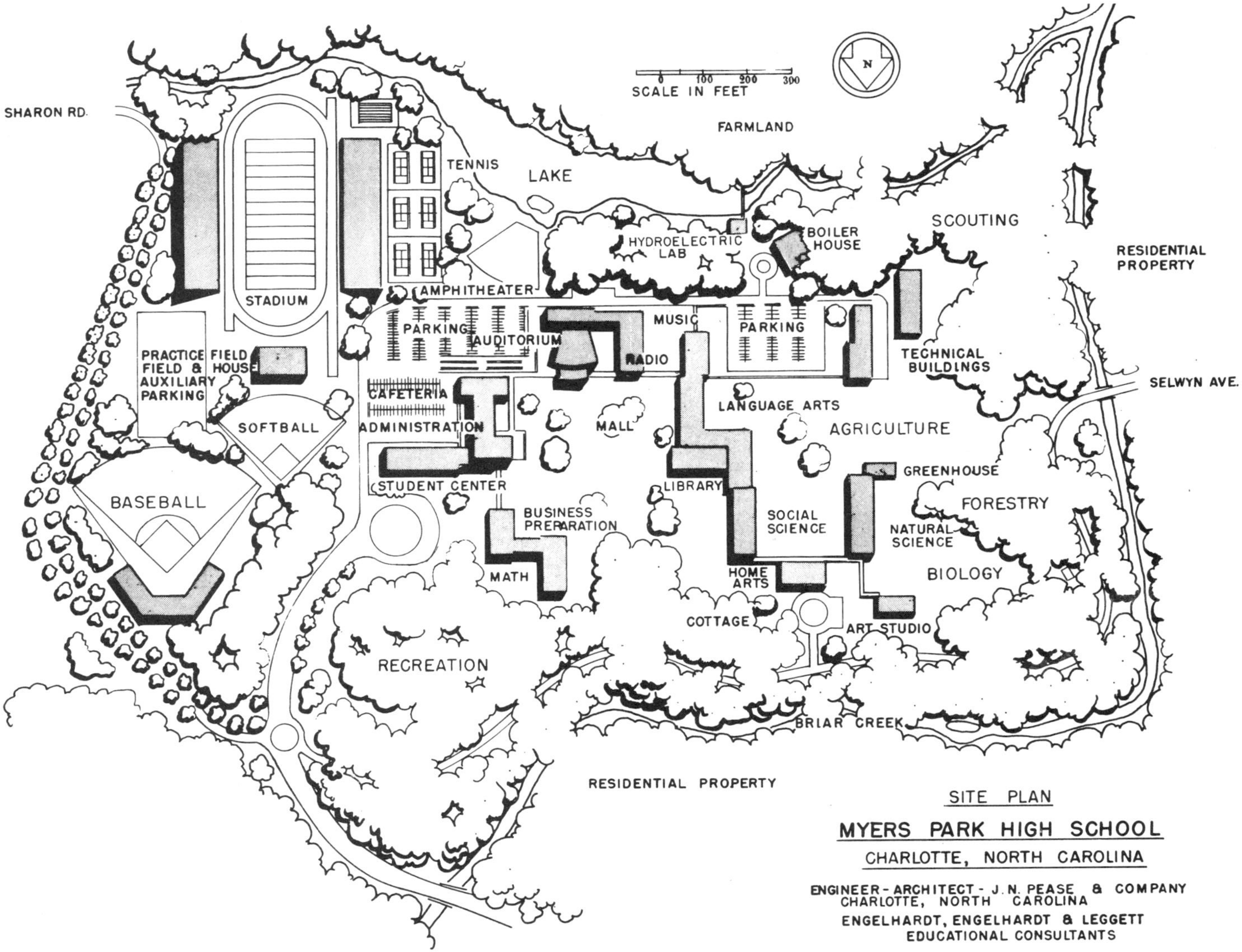

SITE PLAN

MYERS PARK HIGH SCHOOL

CHARLOTTE, NORTH CAROLINA

ENGINEER - ARCHITECT - J. N. PEASE & COMPANY
CHARLOTTE, NORTH CAROLINA

ENGELHARDT, ENGELHARDT & LEGGETT
EDUCATIONAL CONSULTANTS

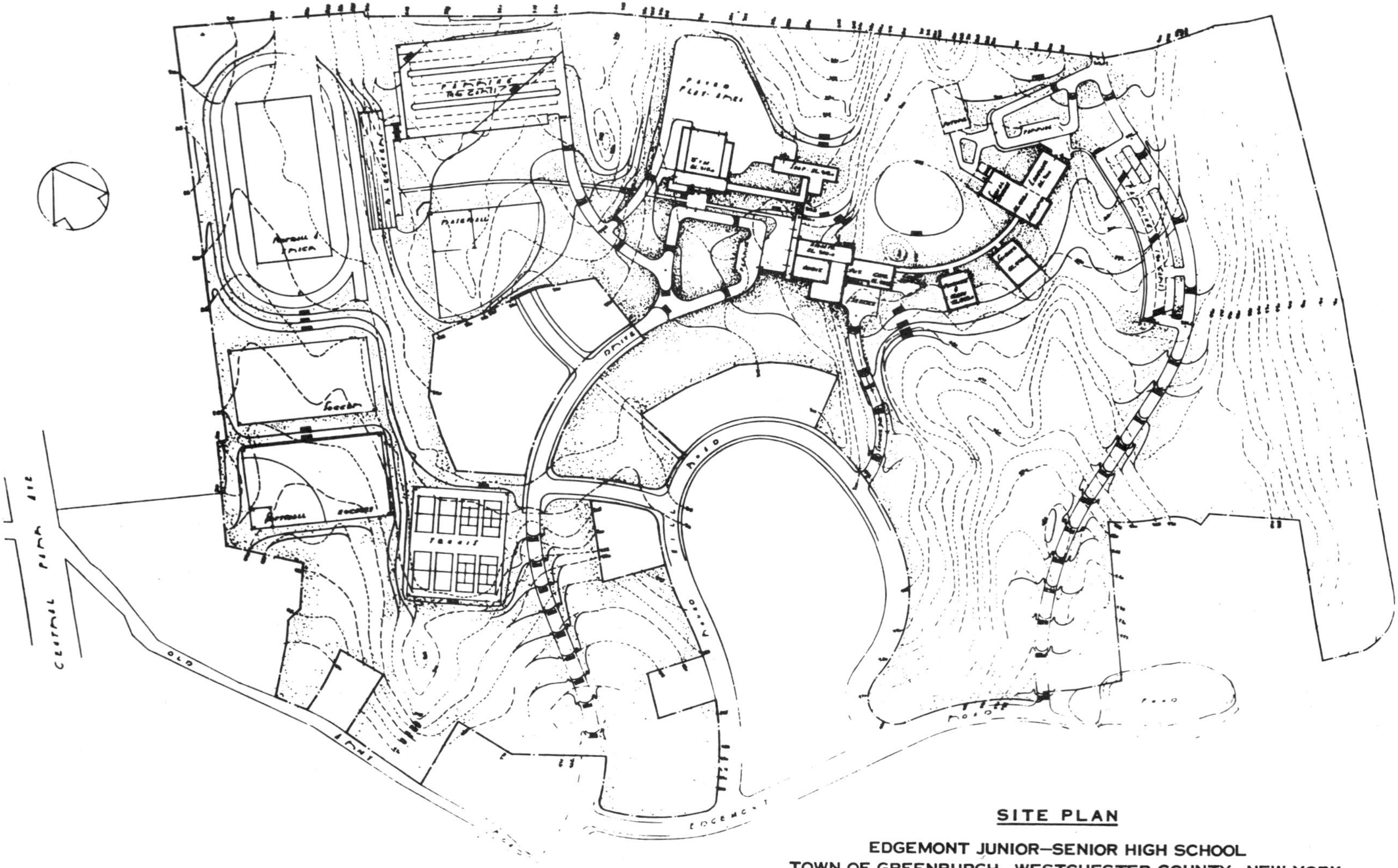

SITE PLAN

EDGEMONT JUNIOR–SENIOR HIGH SCHOOL
TOWN OF GREENBURGH, WESTCHESTER COUNTY, NEW YORK

WARREN H. ASHLEY	WEST HARTFORD, CONNECTICUT	ARCHITECT
CHARLES A. CURRIER AND ASSOCIATES		SITE PLANNERS
MARCHANT AND MINGES		ENGINEERS
ENGELHARDT, ENGELHARDT AND LEGGETT		EDUCATIONAL CONSULTANTS

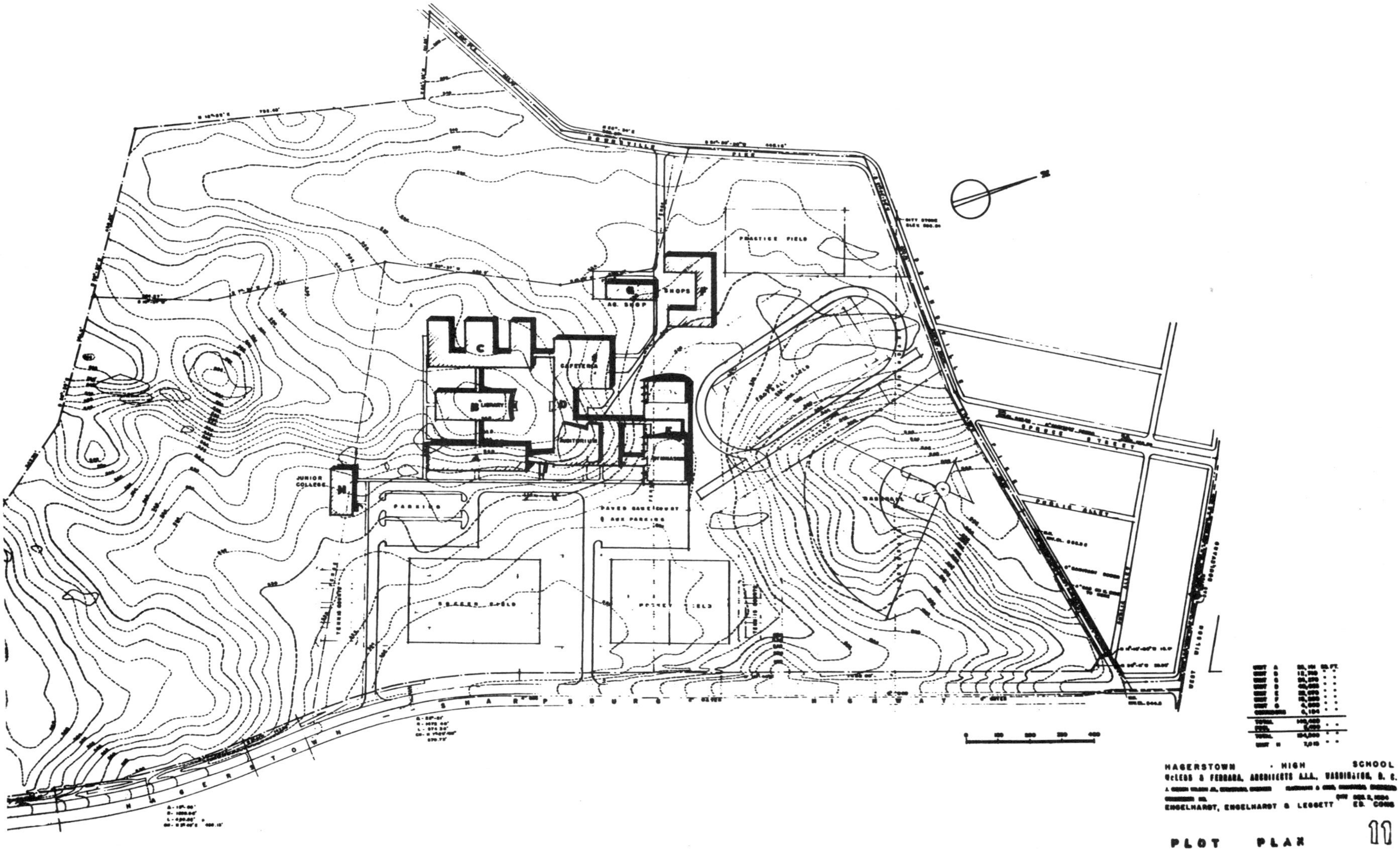

PRACTICE FIELD
SHOPS
AG. SHOP
C
CAFETERIA
LIBRARY
D
AUDITORIUM
GYMNASIUM
JUNIOR COLLEGE
PARKING
PAVED GAME COURT & BUS PARKING
SOCCER FIELD
HOCKEY FIELD
SPRUCE STREET
PUBLIC ALLEY
SHARPSBURG HIGHWAY
HAGERSTOWN
HAGERSTOWN HIGH SCHOOL
McLEOD & FERRARA, ARCHITECTS A.I.A., WASHINGTON, D. C.
ENGELHARDT, ENGELHARDT & LEGGETT ED. CONS
PLOT PLAN
11

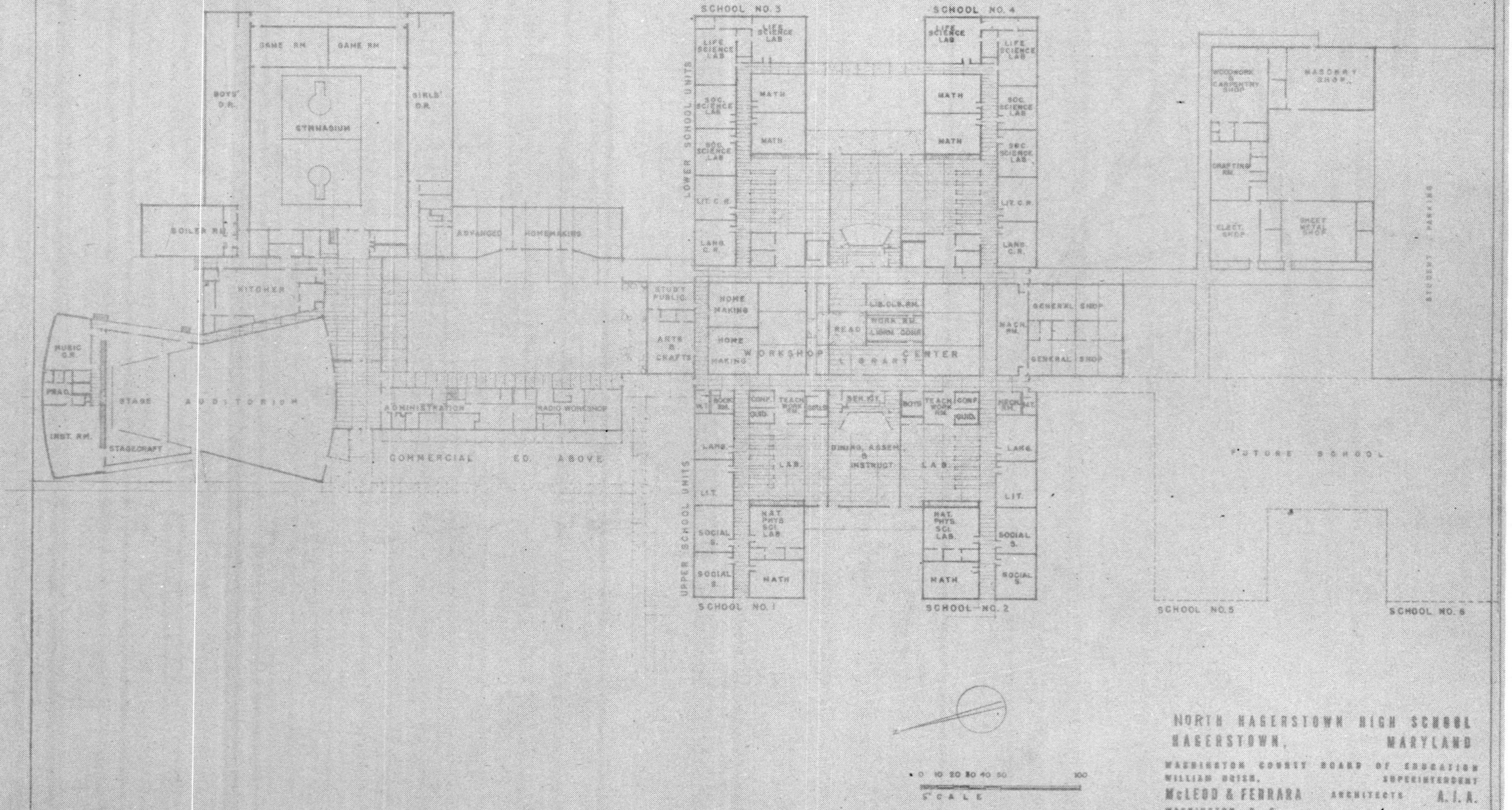

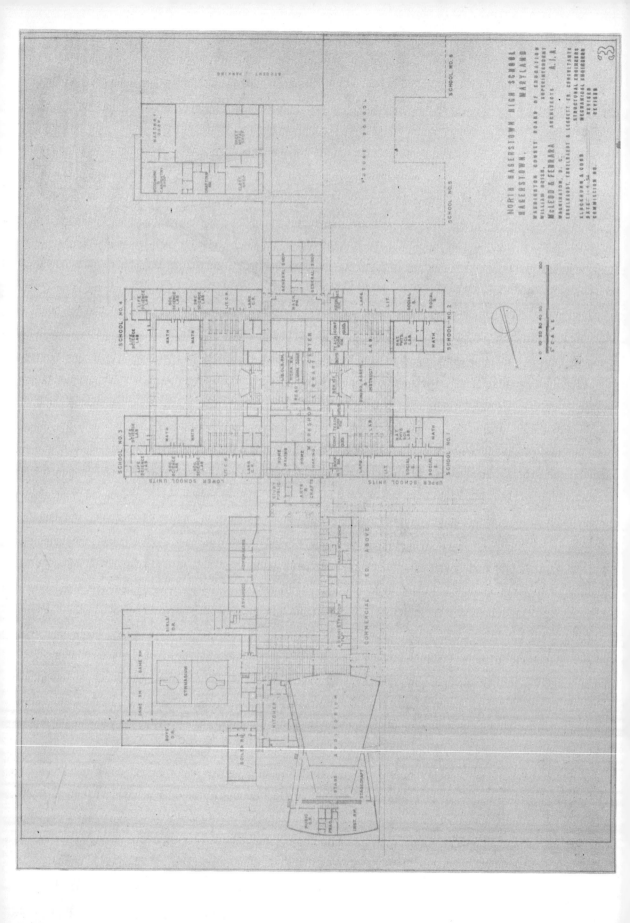

NORTH HAGERSTOWN HIGH SCHOOL
HAGERSTOWN, MARYLAND

WASHINGTON COUNTY BOARD OF EDUCATION
WILLIAM BRISH, SUPERINTENDENT
McLEOD & FERRARA ARCHITECTS A.I.A.
WASHINGTON, D. C.
ENGELHARDT, ENGELHARDT & LEGGETT ED. CONSULTANTS
STRUCTURAL ENGINEERS
KLUCKHUHN & COBB MECHANICAL ENGINEERS
DATE 1-4-56 REVISED
COMMISSION NO. REVISED

3

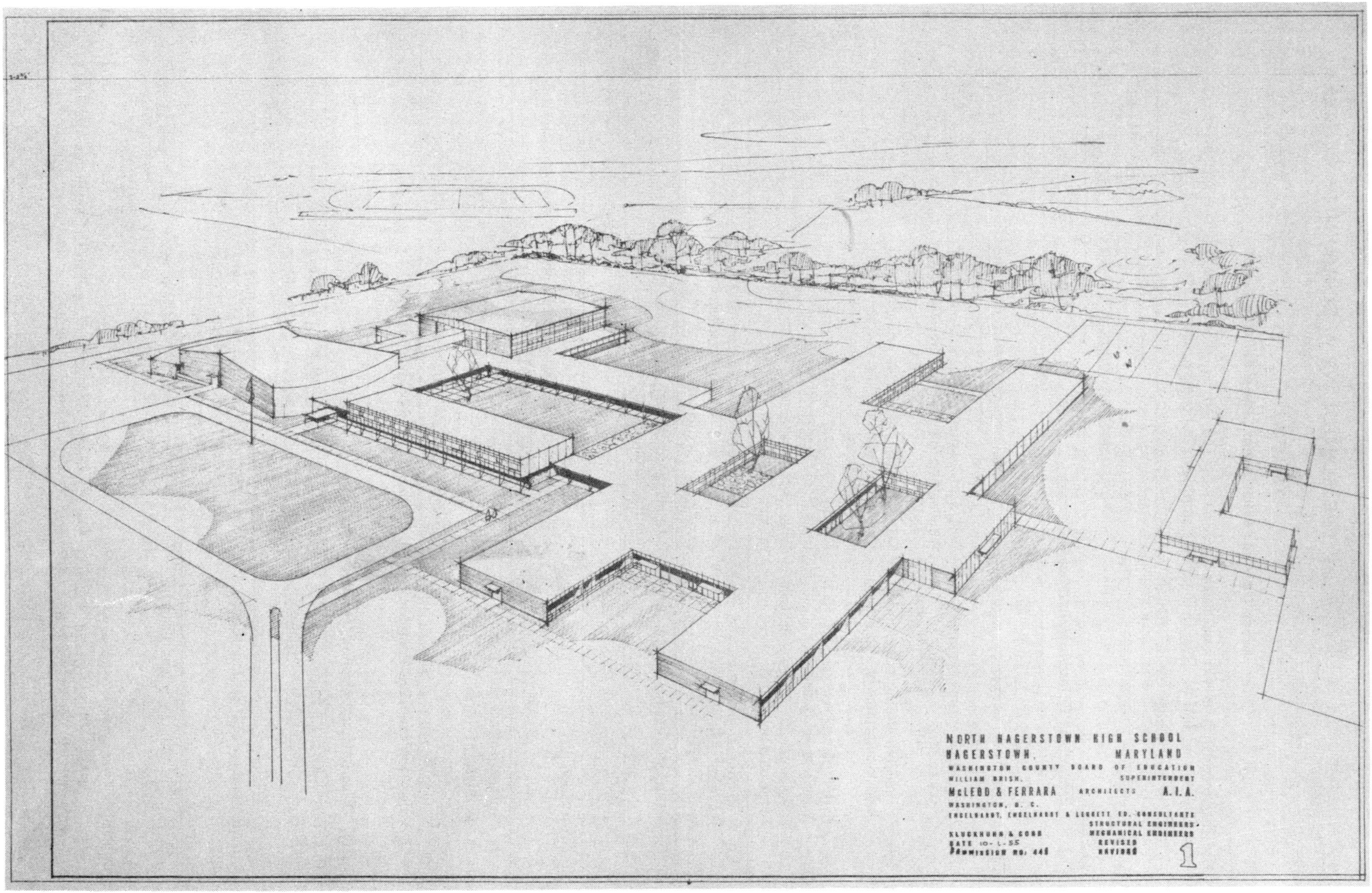
NORTH HAGERSTOWN HIGH SCHOOL
HAGERSTOWN, MARYLAND
WASHINGTON COUNTY BOARD OF EDUCATION
SUPERINTENDENT
McLEOD & FERRARA ARCHITECTS A.I.A.
WASHINGTON, D. C.
CONSULTANTS
STRUCTURAL ENGINEERS
MECHANICAL ENGINEERS
DATE 10-L-55
REVISED
1

TABLE 2-3

Score Card for Selection of School Building Sites*

Use the second half of Column 1 for the scores on the lettered subdivisions when a specific site is being rated. The second half of Column 2 permits summation of these scores.

Location of Site Under Consideration ______________________________

ITEM	*DESCRIPTION*	1	2
I. *Present and Future Environment*			75
A. Nature of present surroundings			
1. Character of nearby residential housing	General locality should offer only the most favorable social influences		
2. Freedom from business distractions	Not near commercial centers or shops which take on undesirable characteristics		
3. Freedom from noise, odors, dust, and traffic of industry	Set distinctly apart from industry and its inconveniences. Prevailing winds fully considered	50	
4. Remoteness from railroads, landing fields, docks	Without impact of disturbing conditions from these traffic centers		
5. Remoteness from heavily-traveled highways	Sufficiently protected from highway noises and hazards		
B. Protection from present and possible future air travel routes	Location approved after careful study of take-off and landing practices and low-flying of airplanes	10	
C. Future prospect for surroundings	Conservation of an attractive community setting seems assured	15	
II. *Integration with Community Planning*			75
A. Acceptability in complete community plan	The site satisfies the requirements of the comprehensive community plan and contributes its share of values	50	
B. Non-interference with other community projects	Sufficiently remote from hospital, church, and other community zones so that they will suffer no disturbance from large groups of children	15	
C. Value for extensive community use	Accessible and readily adjusted to adult use	10	
III. *Role in Comprehensive School Building Plan*			100
A. Scientific determination of location with respect to present and future population	Objective techniques used to measure population in all aspects contributing to best choice	25	
B. Integration with existing schools	Serves a territory without overlapping or duplication with existing schools which have the promise of permanence	25	
C. Place in ultimate school program	Permanent dedication to education as far as foreseeable	25	

* From *School Planning and Building Handbook*, pp. 186 ff. by Engelhardt, Engelhardt and Leggett. New York: F. W. Dodge Corporation, 1956.

ITEM	DESCRIPTION	1	2
D. Official approval of general location	Satisfactory to Board of Education and approved by current faculty	25	
IV. *Size of Site*			300
A. Conformity to present and future educational programs	Makes for satisfactory educational use and for educational expansion	50	
B. Compliance with following suggestions as the minimum in each case 1. Ten acres for an elementary school 2. Thirty acres for a junior high school 3. Forty acres for a senior high school	The minimum should be met. Characteristics of locality and costs affect the final decision Fifteen acres may not be found excessive Present and future junior high school programs make this a defensible minimum Acreage in excess of this minimum usually makes a good purchase	150	
C. Safeguarding of future educational extensions	The vision in selection encompasses all foreseeable extension needs	50	
D. Provision for present and future play areas for all groups	Character of land and orientation ensure play and recreational facilities for all	50	
V. *Accessibility*			100
A. Accessibility for general public	Free from approach and exit hazards. No dangerous gradients	25	
B. Optimum travel distances for children 1. 1½ to 2 miles for senior high school 2. 1 to 2 miles for junior high school 3. ½ mile for elementary school 4. ¼ to ½ mile for home-school units	Based upon national practices and not in conflict with local traditions. Distances measured as the crow flies. Travel routes protected by traffic lights and with police cooperation. These distances usually make possible schools of acceptable enrollments	25	
C. Feasibility of approaches 1. Pedestrian 2. Bicycle 3. Automobile 4. School bus	Pedestrian and vehicular approaches possible without congestion Attractive and readily traversable Possible planning without cross conflicts Without cross currents and excessive grades Easy access to loading center possible	25	
D. Safety of approaches 1. Freedom from hazardous cross roads 2. Provision of sidewalks and good roads 3. Elimination of conflicting travel currents 4. Provision of underpasses, pedestrian bridges	Safety is first consideration Entrance and exit routes unhampered by conflicting traffic Assurance of sidewalks and preferred road approaches Freedom from heavy travel at school opening and closing hours Man-made protection from crossing heavy or through traffic lines	25	

ITEM	*DESCRIPTION*	1	2
VI. *Site Characteristics*			200
A. Shape of site	Square or rectangular is preferred over very irregular or "shoestring" sites	50	
B. Present utilization	Site should be free of structures involving high costs for removal	25	
C. Aesthetic value of site	Maximum capitalization of views at a distance and at close range	25	
D. Influence of site on building design	Stimulation of community-acceptable design through characteristics of site	10	
E. Possibility of preferred orientation for all rooms and all game areas	Dimensions of site offer no restriction to freedom of planning	25	
F. Prevalence of characteristics usable to educational advantage	Abundance of natural resources such as trees, water, and elevations	15	
G. Ease of surface adaptation for buildings, play areas, and parking	Surface and near-surface conditions offer no known handicap to planning	25	
H. Subsoil conditions	No excessive fill, rock, quicksand, or subsurface water conditions known	25	
VII. *Utility Services*			50
A. Proximity of utility connections	Ready access to utilities should be possible		
1. Water connections	Excessive trenching not required		
2. Sewage connections	Reasonably near connections are possible	25	
3. Gas	Distance for gas connections reasonably short		
B. Feasibility of making serviceable utility connections	Freedom from undesirable subsurface conditions	25	
VIII. *Costs*			100
A. Cost of land	Favorable comparison with other nearby land costs per acre	50	
B. Cost of site preparation	No unusual site features necessitate excessive costs		
1. General adjustment of land contours for building and play areas	Site characteristics lend themselves to complete and distinctive planning		
2. Sufficient elevation for safeguarding drainage at reasonable cost	Sufficiently commanding location for buildings and reasonable adjustment for play areas		
3. Freedom from drainage from contiguous land	Proposed site, rather than adjoining land, controls the drainage problem	25	
4. Ease of preparation of parking areas, entrances, and service roads	Parking areas feasible for teachers, visitors, and students. Ready creation of roads possible		
5. Additional charges for piling, rock excavation, tree removal, and the like	Site conditions make for no serious costs for these items		
6. Removal or razing of existing buildings	Salvage value of existing structures establishes low cost		

ITEM	DESCRIPTION	1	2
C. Cost of utility connections	Reasonably low		
1. Length of trenchwork necessary	Not excessive	15	
2. Extent of pumping needs	Not beyond average expectation		
D. Cost of new improvements adjoining and approaching site	Much of this cost not chargeable to the school		
1. New street paving required	Payment follows local practice	10	
2. New sidewalk installations	This requirement will entail costs chargeable to the school building budget		
	MAXIMUM POSSIBLE SCORE	1000	1000

CHAPTER 3

A GUIDE TO PLANNING AND CONSTRUCTING NEW FACILITIES

M. Alexander Gabrielsen

PLANNING NEW FACILITIES INVOLVES CONSIDerably more than the mere birth of an idea. It includes all the processes essential to the successful completion of a facility. Many individuals, departments, community groups, commissions, and school boards have failed to achieve their desire for new facilities because of inadequate or poor planning. Any proposed new facility that is not an outgrowth of a master plan requires careful consideration of its relationship to the total enterprise.

In the construction of educational and recreational facilities American communities have become great "imitators." Community leaders see something they like in another community and often come to the conclusion that it is exactly what they need. They borrow the plans, or hire the same architect and, except for minor changes to avoid being accused of outright plagiarism, they duplicate a facility. Some planners justify this type of planning on the basis that it saves time and argument. Furthermore, they rationalize their actions by saying, "If the facility has proven to be good elsewhere, why don't we capitalize on proven experience!" Every community is different in some respect. Each has its own particular desires, and resources or ability to pay. These differences must be taken into consideration in planning.

A fact that is too often overlooked is that a new facility may be used not only for the present but for many years to come. Since schools or recreation plants should be usable for at least fifty years, buildings that contain the greatest degree of flexibility in design are most apt to meet future educational demands as well as current needs. Planners

Illustration: A planning group in action

must have the courage to project their thinking into the future.

The two aspects of planning that are fundamental if a facility is to be good are "cooperative" and "functional" planning.

The chief administrative official, whether it is the Superintendent of Schools, the Superintendent of Recreation, or the Superintendent of Parks, should be responsible for the planning of new facilities. He may delegate some of the details, but he can never delegate his responsibility. There may be others involved in approving plans, but the over-all responsibility of the planning rests with the top administrative official.

A principle basic to good planning is that those who will eventually use the facility should have a part in its planning. Similarly, those agencies in the community which are engaged in related programs, or which might on occasion use the facility, should be represented in the planning process. Often there are individuals living in the community who possess special talents and abilities that make them valuable to the planning team. Do not overlook retired men and women. These people, as well as others who might have something to contribute, should be a part of the "planning team." This is what is meant by *cooperative planning*. Once the requirements have been determined, further cooperation between the architect and planners is essential in order to bring the ideas of the group to fruition.

Physical education and recreation personnel have been notably weak in the area of planning. Consequently, they are frequently by-passed. There are very few Superintendents of Schools or Recreation who would not welcome help from the physical education director, teacher, or recreation leader in planning physical education and recreational facilities, provided he had assurance that this help represented knowledge of both educational needs and professional standards.

29 Steps in the Planning and Construction of New Facilities

Naturally, the procedures required in the development of any building or outdoor facility will vary according to the type and philosophy of the agency for which the facility is being constructed. States and municipalities with their public works departments and corps of architects and engineers have well established operating procedures. Nevertheless, the steps below give a general outline of the procedures involved, and with slight deviations can be applied to most school and public or private agency situations.

1. The idea of a new facility is born within an individual, or as a result of group discussion.
2. The actual need for the facility is determined. The question of "why do we need this facility?" must be answered.
3. Visits to similar facilities in the community or adjacent communities are made by the individual or group with the idea of becoming familiar with similar types of facilities.
4. Data on cost of construction and operation of such a facility are obtained.
5. The idea originator or group now submits the idea to the appropriate administrator. This is usually the person's immediate superior (supervisor, principal, director, etc.).
6. The supervisor determines whether further preliminary study is desirable and usually involves other members of the staff in the discussion.
7. The idea, accompanied by collected data, is presented to the board, commission, or any other form of managing authority for its consideration.
8. The managing authority (board, commission, or committee) may establish a planning group involving professional and lay personnel to study further the need for the proposed facility.
9. After the necessary study is made of the educational or recreational needs, the planning group makes specific recommendations back to the managing authority on such matters as

   a. Desirability of project
   b. Need for special consultants or services
   c. General scope of the project
   d. Suitable site or sites for the facility.

10. The managing authority interviews several architects, and on the basis of criteria established by them selects the architect for the project.

11. The selected architect receives statement of educational or recreational needs and specifications and draws up preliminary plans and cost estimates.

12. Preliminary plans and cost estimates approved by the managing authority.

13. Discussion of the plan for financing and the possible selection of bond attorneys, if necessary, by the managing authority.

14. Managing authority begins to promote idea with public through the newspapers, radio, television, public meetings, discussion groups, special brochures and special displays of proposed plans in prominent places.

15. Submit issue to the voters for approval if necessary. (In some instances public hearings must be conducted before a referendum is held.)

16. If the plan is approved by voters, draw up educational or recreational specifications for the facility for the architect.

17. Contract with the architectural firm for the preparation of final drawings and specifications. (It is usually the same firm that drew up the preliminary plans.)

18. Approval of working plans and specifications by the managing authority and any other approving body, such as the State Department of Education, and Public Works Department.

19. Advertise for bids on construction and equipment.

20. Opening of bids and awarding of contract for construction. One of the steps involved in this process is the legal approval of the contract and the establishment of the schedule of payment.

21. Supervision of construction. There are usually two kinds, one supplied by the agency for which the facility is being constructed and the other by the architect who drew up the plans. In some instances both are used. Supervision by the architect is usually written into his contract.

22. Progress reports to the managing authority on various stages of construction (such as grading of site, excavation, foundation, first floor, second floor and so forth).

23. Inspection and acceptance of facility by the contracting agency (managing authority).

24. Construction contract completed.

25. Insurance arrangements made.

26. Equipment, supplies, and machines brought in.

27. Staff orientation to facility. Instructions in care and use of facility.

28. Dedication of facility and occupancy of premises.

29. Periodic inspection of facility, checking for operating deficiencies for which contractor is responsible.

Check List for Those Responsible for Planning New Facilities

The chief school officer or the Superintendent of Recreation is usually responsible to a board or commission for the planning of any new facility. He will naturally seek help in his planning and will undoubtedly delegate a considerable portion of the responsibility to members of his staff. In order to assure that nothing is overlooked the person in charge should prepare a check list as a guide. A typical check list of this type is shown below. Once a step has been accomplished it should be checked off.

1. Has the actual need for the facility been fully determined?

2. Have the people who will be operating the facility had a part in the planning?

3. Have the operating and maintenance costs been determined and incorporated in the budget, so that when the facility is completed funds will be available for full operation?

4. Has it been determined that the architect has on his staff, or will secure, specialized technical services, such as site planners, landscape architects, illuminating engineers, structural engineers, acoustical engineers, and others as required for special areas, such as swimming pools?

5. Have all the legal implications been explored and legal advice sought in connection with bond elections?

6. Has a time schedule for planning and construction been worked out?

Planning committees produce the best facilities.

7. Have lay and professional committees been established to assist in the preparation of the recreational and educational specifications and requirements?

8. Have all local building codes, state regulations, and laws been considered in the planning?

9. Is the proposed site for the facility the best possible location, adequate for both present and future needs?

10. Is the facility part of a master plan of school or community recreation development?

11. Has it been determined that the contractors who bid on the plans are qualified to handle the job?

12. Has the administrator in charge made a list of all the things that need to be accomplished in a sequential order?

13. Has resource material been provided for individuals and groups to study in helping to arrive at desirable specifications?

14. Has provision been made for the planning group to visit other similar facilities in the community or adjacent communities?

15. Has the eventual program to be conducted in the facility received consideration in order to help establish size and design of the facility?

16. Has the planning taken into consideration population growth and possible changes in the social structure of the community?

17. Has someone been designated as the

Steps in the planning process.

"clerk of the works" or building inspector who is qualified to do a thorough job of checking the construction with the plans and specifications?

18. Has the expected life of the facility been determined and incorporated into the planning and specifications?

19. Have the equipment needs of the building been included in the cost estimates?

20. Have careful procedures and criteria been established to select the architect?

21. Has a policy been established for effective working relations between such people as the builder, surveyor, educational consultants, advisory groups, "clerk of the works," inspectors, architects and technical engineers?

22. Have the services of professional advisory groups at the local, state, and national level been sought? (State departments, county planning groups, fire departments, safety engineers, and various federal departments.)

23. Has a procedure been established to handle all "change orders" in order to prevent hasty changes to plans which were carefully developed over many months?

24. Has the installation of fixed equipment, such as machinery, basketball backstops in the gym, and apparatus floor fixtures been made a part of the contractor's responsibility in order to prevent tearing down walls by equipment people immediately after the completion of the building?

25. Has community interest been placed above personal and political interest in the selection of sites, awarding of contracts, and in the general planning of the facility?

SELECTION OF THE ARCHITECT

The architect is a key figure in the planning and construction of any new facility. He should be brought into the planning picture as soon as the board or managing authority has approved the project. The architect should be carefully selected. Boards should establish criteria for the selection based on local needs and professional architectural ethics. The American Institute of Architects (AIA) has available a "Standard Form of Questionnaire for the Selection of Architects for School Building Projects."[1]

Some general guides in the selection of the architect are:

1. No architect should be selected merely because of local residence, friendship with anyone connected with the project, or the artistry of his sketches.

2. Once a tentative selection of three or four architects has been made, visits should be made by members of the Board to facilities recently completed by the architects in order to see at first hand the kinds of buildings they have erected. By talking with the local superintendent it is possible to learn about the ethical and businesslike relations of the architect with the board, contractors, and others involved in the planning and construction of the facility. Other questions that might be raised are: Did he complete the work on time? Were there many "change orders"? Was the final cost more or less than the original estimate? Was he willing to take suggestions?

3. Each architect should be interviewed, individually if possible, in order to obtain necessary information and provide him with the opportunity to explain the services of his office and to demonstrate some of his work.

4. Architects who propose to violate the codes of the architectural profession should not be hired.

5. Because an architect has never constructed a building or facility of the type desired, it does not hold that he is not competent. The architects who designed the Swimming Stadium at the 1956 Olympic games at Melbourne, Australia, had never before designed a swimming pool. The architect who has creative imagination, a willingness to learn through research and study, and the ability to cooperate can usually overcome any lack of experience.

6. It is essential to obtain a clear determination of the services which are to be rendered under the architect's fee. This should be included in the architect's contract. Particular items to watch out for are: The extent of engineering services provided

---

[1] Available from the AIA, 1735 New York Avenue, N.W., Washington 6, D.C.

under the fee; the type of supervision provided during the actual construction; and the number of sets of plans and specifications that are to be provided.

7. A time schedule should be agreed upon by the architect and the board in order to establish target dates for completion of various phases of the project.

8. It is best to engage a local attorney to handle the legal problems related to the building program. The cost of legal service should be figured as a part of the cost of the facility.

DETERMINING REQUIREMENTS FOR A FACILITY

It is obvious that the architect must be supplied with certain specific information in order to draw up the plans properly. This information will include such data as:

1. The community's conception of what the facility should be like. This idea is important since it represents the philosophy of the planning group. If it is not adequately set forth the architect will come up with his own conception which might be in conflict with the function the facility is to serve.
2. Location of the facility.
3. Topographical survey of the site including the result of borings to determine foundation requirements.
4. Availability of funds and the approximate amount to be spent.
5. Suggested size of the facility as related to the number of people expected to use it (peak capacity and average daily use).
6. The nature of the program and ages of prospective users.
7. Any special design features, such as the height of ceiling, wall material, location of doors and windows, and special wiring for television.
8. Any special features related to lighting, acoustics, storage, and materials to be used in construction, such as asphalt surface, tan bark surface, ceramic tile walls, electric wall fixtures, drinking fountains, and any other special features.
9. Any special safety features that should be incorporated such as fences, night lights, and so forth.
10. The specific requirements for every area in the building (gym, auditorium, locker rooms, special rooms, classrooms, and administrative suite).

The above requirements and specifications must be carefully planned and all potential users, both professional and lay, should have the opportunity to contribute suggestions rather than "rubber stamp" the ideas of other people. Discussions should be held between the architect and school officials or recreation administrators. In many instances, the architect will be able to give considerable advice and suggestions. There are times when the architect might request certain information which is not included in the original specifications.

The facilities that are represented in the sports, physical education, and recreation programs consist of so many kinds that it is impossible to provide a detailed check list for each facility. However, it may be helpful to potential planners to illustrate a typical check list for a high school indoor physical education plant.

Physical Education Plant Check List

1. *Number of Teaching Stations Required*. The number of stations will also indicate the size of gym needed and whether one or two gyms will be required and the nature of the other teaching stations such as swimming pool, special exercise rooms, and so forth.
2. *Location* in regard to site and balance of the school or recreation plant.
3. *Dimensions* of all areas such as locker rooms, showers, gyms and other rooms.
4. *Height* of gym ceiling and other teaching or service areas.
5. *Material* for floor covering in gym.
6. *Wall* material.
7. *Acoustical* treatment desired.
8. *Lighting* requirements; actual foot candles of illumination desired at eye level.
9. *Heating* and *ventilation* requirements.
10. *Storage space* desired.
11. *Office space*.
12. *Spectator requirements* and type of seats; roll-away or fixed type bleachers including size.

13. *Apparatus*, floor, wall, and ceiling fixtures or mountings to accommodate all types of apparatus.

14. *Lobby* or *foyer* size requirements for gym.

15. *Type of basketball backstop* to be used; swing up, roll-away or fixed.

16. *Bulletin board* location and number.

17. *Type of folding partition* if one is recommended.

18. *Wainscot* and eye *bolt* locations in wall.

19. *Type of floor finish.*

20. *Location and type of court markings* desired on floor.

21. *Any special electrical fixtures*, such as special wiring for public address system or television.

22. *Exit doors*, both within building and those leading to outdoor play fields.

23. *Locker room at peak load* and average daily load.

24. *Storage lockers* or baskets required (size and number).

25. *Dressing lockers* required (size and number).

26. *Floor material* recommended in locker and shower rooms.

27. *Height* of locker room ceiling.

28. *Special dressing facilities* for interscholastic sports (if required).

29. *Is community* use to be made of the facilities and will any special dressing facilities be needed for adult use?

30. *Other features* of the locker room, such as number of drains, color of walls, air temperature desired, number of shower heads, drinking fountains, toilets, width of aisles, bulletin board, mirrors, and size of the toweling room.

31. Requirements for *drying room equipment*.

32. Size of *towel issue room*.

33. *Amount of illumination* required throughout the locker room.

The more detailed the data supplied the architect the better. Inevitably there will have to be compromises; nevertheless, this should not occur at the initial stage of the preparation of the requirements and specifications.

CONSTRUCTION COST FACTORS

It is always perplexing to the layman to learn that one building costs twice as much as another building of comparable size. It should be realized that there are many factors that influence the ultimate cost of a facility. The major variables are: Cost of land and preparation of site for use; cost of labor at time of construction; building material cost at time of construction; building design, cubage space, and total square footage of facility being planned; climatic conditions; extent of landscaping; "frills" or "gingerbread" included in building.

The standard budget items of a building project usually include the following:

1. *Preliminary cost:*

   Acquisition of site
   Site development
   Legal fees
   Cost of bond issue
   Promotion and publicity
   Preliminary architect fees for preparation of preliminary plans
   Consultant fees (educational or specialist)

2. *Architectural fees:*

   Preparation of architectural and engineering plans (working plans)
   Supervision of construction
   Engineering requirements

3. *Construction cost:*

   Building contract and sub-contracts
   Supervision cost ("clerk of the works")
   Building permits

4. *Equipment and furniture:* (up to 15 per cent of the total budget)

   For buildings
   For outdoor play areas

5. *Insurance*

6. *Contingencies:* (usually 10 per cent of total cost)

OPERATING COST FACTORS

Once the facility or building has been completed it must be operated and maintained. The major operational items to be considered are:

Instructional cost
Administrative and supervisory cost
Maintenance cost (staff, supplies and material)
Insurance (property, liability)
Utilities (fuel, electricity)

It is essential that a sound maintenance policy be established. New buildings should be planned to reduce the maintenance cost to a minimum. Often in trying to keep construction cost down the maintenance cost is increased to the point that it offsets the saving in construction cost. Provision must be made in the operating budget to properly maintain new buildings. Usually, the older a building the higher will be the maintenance cost.

GUIDING PRINCIPLES IN PLANNING FACILITIES

In summary the following sixteen principles may serve as a guide in planning any new facility:

Principle 1: The facility should be planned to meet future demands as well as immediate needs.

Principle 2: The facility should implement the kind of program desired.

Principle 3: The concept of the multiple use of a facility should receive due consideration in the planning period.

Principle 4: People who will be affected by the facility should have a part in its planning. This applies particularly to the professional staff.

Principle 5: The location of any facility should be influenced by a master plan of the community or the school system.

Principle 6: The needs of the people to be served must be accurately determined as a part of the planning stage.

Principle 7: There must be cooperation between educational consultants, planning groups, architects and administrative officials in the planning of facilities.

Principle 8: The chief administrative official responsible for construction should have a clear-cut plan of procedure to guide his actions.

Principle 9: Facilities should be located where they will receive maximum use.

Principle 10: Maximum flexibility of design should be sought in order to easily effect change if future needs so dictate.

Principle 11: The facility should be planned to achieve maximum safety of all participants and provide a healthful environment.

Principle 12: The facility should comply with all local and state laws and other regulations, including professional standards.

Principle 13: The operating and maintenance cost of the facility must be considered in the planning stage.

Principle 14: When the cost of rehabilitating a facility exceeds 50 per cent of the cost of replacement it is more prudent to raze the old facility and construct a new one.

Principle 15: The effect any facility may have on adjacent properties and the community and neighborhood as a whole should receive careful consideration.

Principle 16: "A thing of beauty is a joy forever." This concept should not be lost sight of in planning a new facility. It is often overlooked in the haste to acquire new facilities. The Acropolis in Athens and the Coliseum in Rome are examples of facilities whose beauty has survived the span of time.

CHAPTER 4

THE ELEMENTARY SCHOOL—A NEIGHBORHOOD CENTER

Caswell M. Miles

THE MODERN ELEMENTARY SCHOOL PLANT that is also designed to function as a neighborhood center combines the best features of the school, the small park or playground, and the neighborhood recreation building. It is the neighborhood center for the program of public education, recreation, and related activities.

THE NEIGHBORHOOD AND COMMUNITY CONCEPTS

The neighborhood is a unit or area of the urban or suburban community within about a half-mile radius of the school. The size of the neighborhood will vary according to the density of population, physical barriers such as traffic arteries and the master plan of the school district and the community. The size of the neighborhood area will be larger in rural sections but because of good roads, highways, and school bus transportation, it can be an effective unit of the school district or community. The number of such neighborhoods in a community will vary according to the master plans for the county, town, municipality, and the school district, but the number will usually correspond to the number of modern elementary schools in the community.

The community is a major section of a municipality or school district of a size that can be served by a single high school and containing a major business center. It contains two or more neighborhoods and varies in size and population depending upon the master plans for the county, town, municipality, and the school district. The larger municipalities and school districts may contain two or more communities.

The school district is defined as a unit of government with legal powers for the conduct of public education as authorized by qualified voters in the district and ad-

Illustration: Barthelme Elementary School, West Columbia, Texas
Photo by Photo Associates (Ulric Meisel), Dallas, Texas

Many activities of the elementary program have implications for recreation.

Courtesy of *The School Executive*

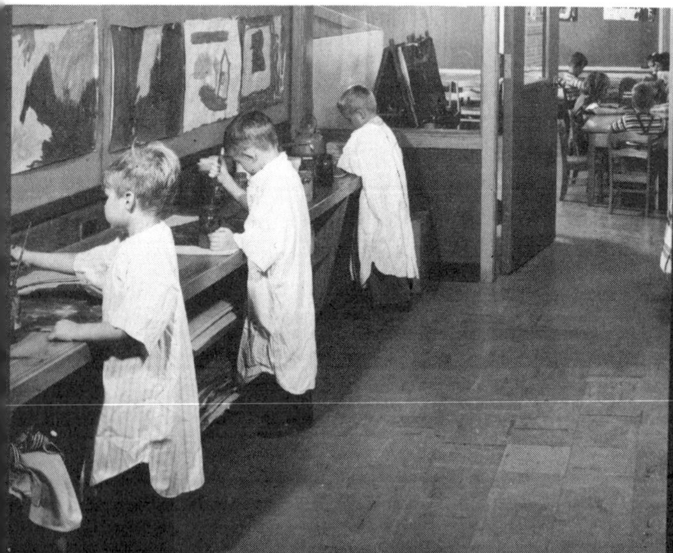

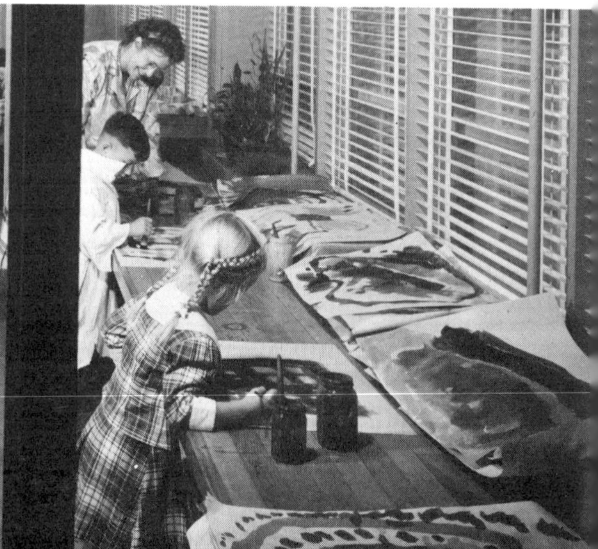

ministered by the chief education officer under the direction of the board of education. Some such districts are fiscally independent of the municipal board or council and some have boundaries that are not contiguous with those of the municipality. The municipality is defined as a unit of local government such as a city, village, or town, which has legal powers for governmental services as authorized by the qualified voters and administered by the chief municipal officer and the board or council.

Cooperative action by municipal, school district, town, and county officials is the basis for effective neighborhood and community organization. Schools, parks, churches, hospitals, voluntary agency centers, residential areas, business sections, industrial centers and traffic arteries are all factors in the master plan for a municipality, a school district or a town.

The rapid shift of population to suburban areas accompanied by a like increase in the number of new school plants provides a golden opportunity for school district and town officials to plan for the kind of neighborhood and community development that will strengthen the foundations of American democracy. In urban centers the planners are limited in planning large new developments but they do much with redevelopment projects to rebuild neighborhoods and community centers. Housing projects in areas without adequate elementary school-neighborhood centers may still be what Frank Lloyd Wright termed "sanitary slums."

THE MODERN SCHOOL IS A CHILDREN'S COMMUNITY

Homes, churches, schools, parks, playgrounds, streets, stores, hospitals, voluntary agency centers, and people are some of the factors in the child's environment that influence his education and development. The total of all experiences, including the impact of the natural and man-made resources of the community and all planned programs of education, recreation, health, and social welfare, is called the *community curriculum*. This concept of the community curriculum refers to all the creative learning experiences of the people in the community. Within this changing pattern of community life, the school, as an organized social institution, undertakes to provide systematic instruction for the child in the heritage, resources, opportunities, and responsibilities of a democratic society and to aid him to become the person he is capable of being.

In the modern elementary school, children and teachers act together. They recreate the life of the community by words, games, projects, and experiences so that the child may become a citizen of the community who not only enjoys the fruits of democracy but contributes to its continued success. The thinkers and the voters have shared in the development of such schools. Here the course of education flows into the life stream of the community. Here the child can develop into a master in the art of living who makes no distinction between his labor and leisure, his education and his recreation. He learns to follow his own vision of excellence in creating and recreating things, friendships, and situations, and gains satisfaction from his achievements.

THE PARK-SCHOOL AND COMMUNITY SCHOOL CONCEPTS

The park-school is a modern school on a park-like site which is designed to function as a center for programs of education and recreation throughout the year. The park-school for the neighborhood serves the children of the elementary grade age level during the day throughout the year and is used during the evening for youth, adult, and family education-recreation programs and related neighborhood activities.

The park-school for the community likewise serves the youth of the secondary grade age level during the day and functions during the evening hours for youth, adult, and family education-recreation programs and related community activities. The rapid growth of state-aided adult education program, which in many sections of the nation has an enrollment greater than the total of high school pupils, has stimulated the design and the use of schools as neighborhood and community centers. The "Lighted School House" program of Milwaukee has been a shining example of such use for many years.

The community school concept holds that the school has an obligation to serve all learning needs of the people in the community except those incompatible with the function of public education. The concept rests on the premise that personality is best developed in a community that understands and solves its social problems. The community school has a professional staff that has special abilities and interest and a flexibility in schedule and assignments that enables it to serve in an informal consultant relationship to indviduals and groups in the community. It operates during the day and evening the year round. The Flint, Michigan community school program is a good example of this concept in action.

INFLUENCES ON THE MODERN ELEMENTARY SCHOOL

There has been much research, study, and discussion of the needs, characteristics, interest, and growth patterns of children during the last 30 years that has had a profound effect on the conduct of the elementary school and the design of the plant. Research reports, professional books, and articles in many newspapers and popular magazines have been widely read and discussed by teachers, parents, and interested citizens. This has resulted in widespread understanding of child growth and development. Discussion at meetings of the school district, citizens committees, the parent-teacher group, the board of education, and professional organizations have all influenced the development of the modern elementary school.

Emphasis on Needs of Individual Students

In 1953 the Mid-Century Committee on Outcomes in Elementary Education, sponsored by the Russell Sage Foundation, the United States Office of Education, the National Education Association, Department of Elementary School Principals and the Educational Testing Service, emphasized nine program areas. They are: (1) physical development, health, body care; (2) social and emotional development of the individual; (3) ethical behavior, standards and values; (4) social relationships; (5) the social world; (6) the physical world; (7) esthetic development; (8) communications; and (9) quantitative relationships. Emphasis is given in each of these areas to: (1) knowledge and understanding; (2) skills and competencies; (3) attitudes and interests; and (4) action patterns appropriate to children at the third, sixth, and ninth grade levels.

These statements of the objectives and important areas of elementary education reflect the thinking of the voters and the teaching profession, that the elementary school program should be as broad as the life of the community. This philosophy encompasses modern programs of recreation as well as education. It envisions an elementary school plant that is designed to serve as a neighborhood center which encourages rather than restricts the full development of such programs.

ACTIVITIES IN MODERN EDUCATION AND RECREATION PROGRAMS

The design of the plant for the neighborhood center should be functional for the activities of modern programs of education and recreation. Fortunately, the two programs have much in common. Both are obligated to fit the characteristics, needs, and interests of individuals and groups. Both are attuned to life situations of the neighborhood, the community, and American democracy. Play and work under the flame of intense interests merge into the fine art of living, the mastery of which is the goal of both programs. Play, which has long been considered the serious business of childhood, is now regarded as essential for the adult too, before and after retirement.

Many of the activities in a modern program of elementary education such as arts, crafts, music, dramatics, games, hobbies, and dances, carry on into adulthood as avocational interests and recreation. Adult use of neighborhood centers has increased in the last decade along with the modernization of the elementary education programs and plants. Such "education for living" programs where the watchword is "learn by doing" contain many activities for which

Upper Photo by Rondal Partridge, Berkeley

Outdoor work and play areas adjacent to classrooms provide many additional class activities.

These areas extend the classroom to the out-of-doors.

Photo by Roger Sturtevant, San Francisco

there is a continuing and unfolding interest from early childhood through later adult life. These activities constitute the core of both the recreation and the education programs. The many learning experiences inherent in the modern elementary school program are illustrated by the following list of activities:

Art—painting, drawing, designing, crafts
Communication—writing, speaking, reading, story-telling, discussion, meetings, forums
Science—projects, collections of plants, animals, and minerals; demonstrating, repairing, using gadgets
Projects—recreating community enterprises
Games—team activities, relays, and individual, dual, informal group and party games
Music—singing and playing instruments, records and parts in shows, musicales
Dances—creative rhythms, folk, square, social; parties, demonstrations, shows
Crafts—building models, using wood, metal, fabrics, leather, paper, clay, yarns, in design and construction
Pets and animals—care, food, shelters, products, collections, shows, exhibits
Puppetry—making puppets, stage scenery, and costumes and having exhibits, shows
Gymnastics—stunts, tumbling, vaulting, demonstration exhibits
Needlecraft—beadwork, sewing, weaving, knitting, upholstering projects and exhibits; making and repairing costumes, clothing
Cooking—playing house, making cookies, cake, jellies, butter, outdoor fireplaces; picnics, camping, foods and meals
Hobbies—recognizing and developing lasting interests in collecting, making, doing things; demonstrations, exhibits, shows
Aquatics—swimming, water safety, boating, fishing, water games, pageants, demonstrations
Outdoor education—field trips, conservation projects, collecting plants, insects, minerals, soils, hiking, swimming, boating, fishing, camping

THE SITE AND OUTDOOR PLAY AREAS

The comprehensive plant for the elementary school-neighborhood center includes the outdoor areas and building facilities. These areas should be as carefully planned as the indoor areas in order to create the facilities that encourage the full development of all program areas and make wise use of every foot of space. The site should provide for the following types of areas:

Building, lawn, walks, and driveway space
Paved surface and play area
Turf area for game fields
Play equipment space
Space adjacent to classroom for outdoor projects
Kindergarten, first grade, totlot space
Digging and growing space
Park and outdoor education area
Automobile parking and bus loading space

Selection of Site

The selection of the site should be preceded by surveys and studies that involve education, park, recreation and planning staff members, and citizen committees. Both education and park officials should coordinate the planning and purchase of school and neighborhood playground areas that are adjacent in order to develop a comprehensive neighborhood plant. Such cooperation is essential in new and redevelopment projects of thickly populated urban centers where large tracts are scarce and expensive and both boards are seeking such space. In suburban and rural areas where there is no park board, the school district has an obligation to select sites for the elementary school that are adequate for both programs.

Factors to consider in selecting the elementary school site are:

Use—Functional for all the outdoor activities of the modern elementary school-neighborhood center programs and related activities.
Topography and drainage—Fairly level, with a sandy loam or porous type of soil, and no extensive stone formations near the surface so that large level turf areas can be developed, drained, and maintained without excessive cost in time and funds.
Size and shape—Are the areas suitable in size and shape to permit the development of large, rectangular fields? Not less than 15 acres are needed in rural and suburban areas where cluster-type, one-story buildings are used, and at least 5 acres in built-up, thickly populated urban centers.
Location—Within a quarter to half mile

radius of the homes of the neighborhood from which children walk to the center; fits in the plans of distant future development and considers zoning and traffic arteries.

Cost—Including purchase, development, and maintenance of site. Better sites are more serviceable and economical; long-range planning and purchase in advance of need gets more adequate sites at a reasonable price that, including development, is usually less than 5 per cent of total cost of a large plant.

Trees and water—Trees are needed for park, borders, and shady areas around fields and courts; a small stream or a pond is a valuable asset for outdoor education and landscaping.

Court Games and Multiple Use Area

The area for court games should be functional for class and extra class physical education activities for elementary school pupils. It should be designed also for the use of neighborhood youth and adults in the recreation program. If the courts are lighted, as described in Chapter 13, four or five hours of evening use is possible. The first and most important kind of multiple use of the court games area is the service for both educational and recreational programs. Such multiple use of the court games area for both programs, in day and evening hours twelve months of the year, for children, youth, and adult groups is a practical way to extend recreational services to the people of the neighborhood. Such extensions of services can be provided at a moderate cost if facilities are wisely planned. Such multiple use of the court games area is a sound investment for the neighborhood.

The second kind of multiple use is possible if courts of similar size and function are grouped according to types. For example Type 11, as shown in Table 4-1, can be used for badminton, paddle tennis, and deck tennis. The space for this type of court provides for eight courts, three sports, and 32 player stations. By providing 32 player stations, they can be scheduled for the three sports, each player in a class of 30 to 40 can get the individual instruction and practice he needs to become proficient in each sport. Such instruction and practice is the foundation for improving the quality of players and programs of class, intramural, extramural, and recreation activities.

The other types of courts shown in Table 4-1 likewise provide enough player stations for class instruction as well as for intramural and recreation groups. There are specific courts for 16 or more different sports and enough space for 184 player stations.

The carry-over from class instruction to recreation and from childhood to adulthood is a worthy goal for the school and the neighborhood. The first step toward this goal is the provision for each type of court as shown, for example in Table 4-1, so that there are enough player stations for each member of the class of 30 to 40 pupils for instruction and practice. The second step is to plan the courts games area to function also for the intramural and the recreation program. The third is to provide adequate personnel for physical education and recreation who are willing and able to achieve the goal. The courts games area will serve its purpose if it is properly planned, constructed, and maintained. It should be ready for use when needed by any phase of the program during day and evening hours and for as many days of the outdoor sports season as possible. A paved surface can be used on many days when an unpaved area would be too wet because of rain or thawing. It costs less to maintain.

Lines of different color for each sport can be painted on the paved surface to mark separate courts within each type of court area. This aid improves the quality of instruction, practice, and play. Also, net posts can be set in sleeves which can be capped when posts are removed. This arrangement makes possible the use of the tennis, volleyball, and badminton type courts for many other activities. Nets that are supported by steel cables and attached to posts so that the height can be adjusted add to the serviceability of the courts.

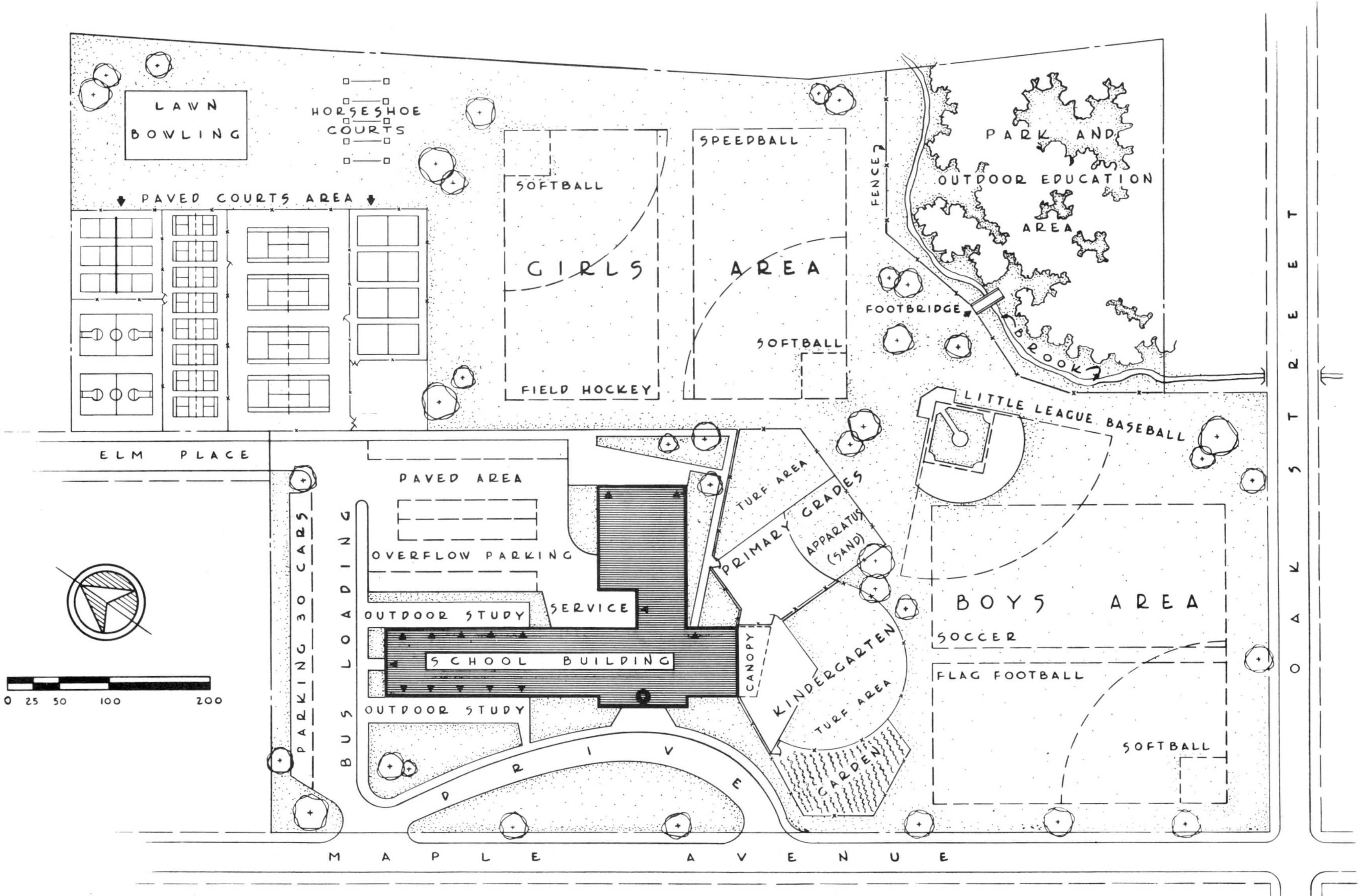

Architects: The A. Carl Stellings Associates, Inc.

Elementary school site showing distribution of outdoor play areas.

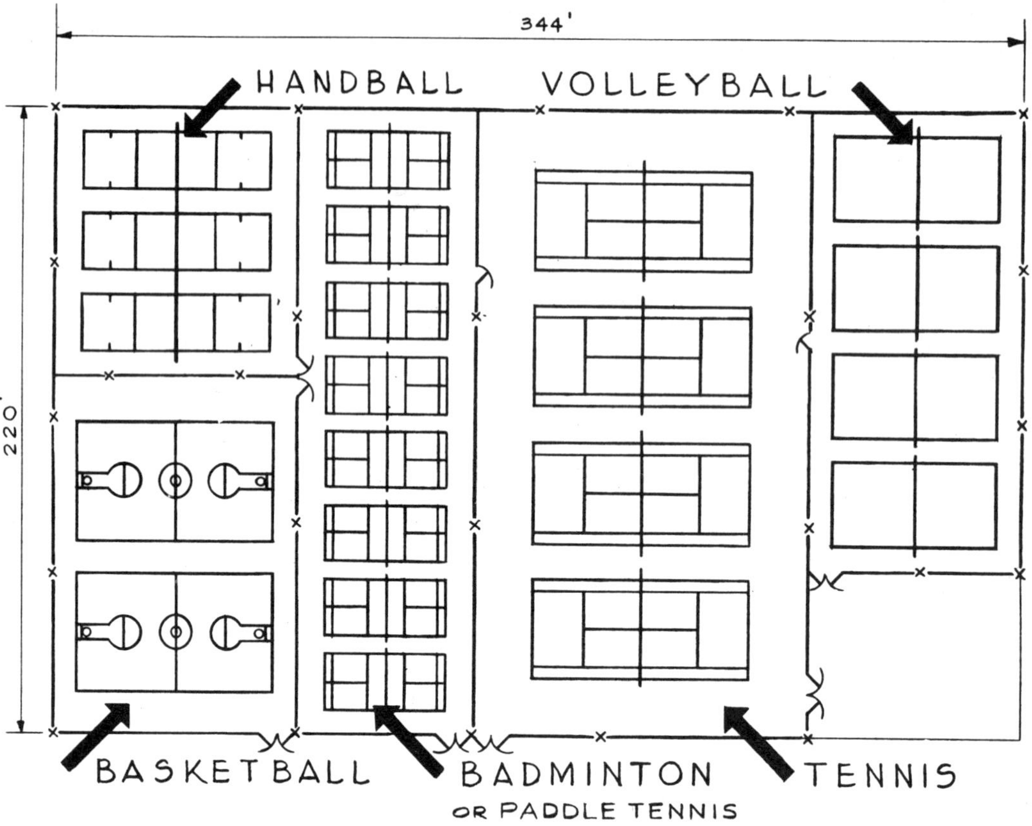

Architects: The A. Carl Stelling Associates, Inc.

Layout of a paved courts area for elementary school.

PLAYGROUND APPARATUS AREA

An area of about 8,000 to 10,000 square feet should be provided for the pre-school, kindergarten and primary grades groups. The choice of the types of equipment will vary with community and school district. Equipment such as climbing towers, horizontal ladders, balance beams and horizontal bars, climbing poles or ropes, sand box, and sections of large concrete drainage tile are more favored by many recreational planners because of safety, challenge, and contribution to physical development. Other educators add slides, swings, and merry-go-rounds, which are considered less safe and developmental than those listed above.

The space under equipment from which children are likely to fall should be covered with soft material such as tanbark, sand, shredded rubber cork mixed with asphalt, or coarse sawdust. Asphalt paving for spaces between equipment makes the area usable for many days when the ground would be too wet or muddy. The apparatus should be located so that lines of travel do not cross the paths of swings, ropes, travelling rings or other such equipment. The area should be enclosed by a low fence and gates that can be locked for the protection of equipment when the playground is closed.

OUTDOOR CLASSROOM SPACE

Each classroom should have an outdoor space for large construction projects, art, dramatics, growing plants, sand modeling, and quiet games. A large percentage of the activities usually conducted in the classroom can be carried on in an outdoor space during moderate weather. Part of the space should be paved and part of it should be a grass surface. There should also be an area for digging, for plants, and for pets. The outdoor space should be accessible to the classroom through a door in the outside wall or from open walkways. The building should be designed and located so that such spaces are protected from extremes of sunlight, shade, and prevailing winds. The space should also contain such equipment as a covered sand box, storage box and work bench.

Kindergarten, Pre-School, and Primary Grade Age Area

An area of about twenty thousand square feet should be provided for kindergarten, pre-school, and primary grade age levels. The area should be enclosed by a low fence or hedge that separates it from the areas used by the intermediate grade or older children's groups. Such separation protects the younger players from being hit by balls and bats, and from collision with older players.

The area should be located close to the building and adjacent to the apparatus area so that the equipment is readily accessible for use by the pre-school and primary grade children. The area should have some turf, some paved surface, and a shady place.

FIELD GAMES AREA

The intermediate grade or middle childhood groups as well as youth and adults in

TABLE 4-1

Basic Outdoor Court Areas for Elementary Schools and their Relationship to Player Station and Size

Area Type	*Activities*	*Players per court*	*Number Courts*	*Player stations*	*Court size**	*Courts area**	*Sq. ft. in area*
I	Volleyball	12	4	48	30 x 60	150 x 76	11,400
	Newcomb	12	4		30 x 60		
	Captainball	12	4		30 x 60		
II	Badminton	4	8	32	20 x 44	214 x 64	13,495
	Paddle Tennis	4	8		20 x 44		
	Deck Tennis	4	8		18 x 40		
III	Tennis	4	4	16	36 x 78	195 x 120	23,400
	Group games when ground is wet						
IV	Handball	4	6	24	20 x 34	80 x 88	7,040
	Squash Tennis	4	6		22 x 36		
	Squash Racquets	4	6		18′6″ x 32		
V	Basketball	10	2	20	42 x 72	102 x 84	8,568
VI	Horseshoes†	4	5	20	10 x 50	100 x 70	7,000
	Quoits	4	5		10 x 50		
VII	Lawn Bowling	6	4	24	14 x 110	69 x 120	8,280

* Size is in feet.

† Set horseshoe pitching stakes 40′ apart for men and imbed pitching board in ground 30′ from stakes for women and players under 16. Set quoits pins or hobs 30′ apart for seniors and locate pitching boards 21′ from hobs for juniors.

SAFETY LANES AND BORDERS IN MULTIPLE COURTS AREAS

Lane Width by Area Type							*Location of Lane or Border*
I	II	III	IV	V	VI	VII	
6	6	12	5	6	5	3	Between sidelines of outer courts and fence
6	6	9	5	6	10	3	Between sidelines of inner courts
8	10	21	10	6	10	5	Between endlines of courts and fence

the neighborhood will be the most frequent users of the field games area. These groups will also make intensive use of the courts area. The area should include fields which can be used for soccer, speedball, flag football, softball, baseball, and field hockey. In the colder sections of the country a space for skating and ice hockey can be provided by packing a good layer of snow and then building up an ice surface by spraying when temperatures are below freezing. Multiple use of this area is possible because of seasonal games and different groups.

There should be a definite allotment of space for girls' and women's games so that their schedule can be maintained independently from that for boys and men. The size of the field games area will vary according to this schedule, the range of activities in the program, and the different groups served.

Many school districts in suburban and less densely populated sections acquire sites that are much larger than the 15 acre minimum. Quite often the site contains 20 acres or more. This is wise because such districts usually do not have municipal parks and have added obligations to provide for organized recreation programs. Also, much more space is required for the popular single-story or cluster type of building which, with lawns and parking space, requires 5 or more acres. Fortunately a larger site often costs little more than a smaller one and will add only a small percentage to the total plant cost.

The size of the field games area under these circumstances should range from 5 to 10 acres. Ten acres of level turf area is a wise investment since this area is the most extensive and most important part of the neighborhood park-school site. Field games involve vigorous and sustained activity and involve team play for large groups, providing rich opportunities for developing physical fitness and desirable social behavior. The

Elementary school strategically located to serve educational and recreational needs of the neighborhood. White Oaks Elementary School.

Courtesy of *The School Executive*

Courtesy of *The School Executive*

Attractive floor covering in a kindergarten classroom. Hinsdale Central School, Hinsdale, New York.

neighborhood park, or school, or a combination of the two, offers the only hope for neighborhoods to acquire the space needed. More details on development of the field games area are shown in the site sketches in Chapter 9.

PARK AND OUTDOOR EDUCATION AREA

The park and outdoor area should include shade trees, flowers, shrubs, tables, benches, fireplaces, a council ring, a small pond or stream, and space that can be used for informal games, dramatics, and picnics. Rock formations, soil types, plants, and wild life add to the value of the area for outdoor education projects and field trips.

The size of the area may vary from one-half to five or more acres. Often a site has a low or rugged section which can be used for outdoor education projects without much development. Such experiences in the living environment add interest and stimulation to many classroom activities.

THE CLASSROOMS

The modern elementary school classroom is designed for a wide range of activities and experiences in programs of public education and recreation. (See pages 48-51 for a list of such activities.) The modern classroom includes large, open work areas and activity centers, part of which are indoors and part outdoors, such as:

Library and individual study space
Crafts and handwork area
General work and construction area
Space for dramatics and party games
Facilities for art and music.

These areas and the tables, bins, shelving, benches, platform units, aquarium, cages, equipment and supplies, make a classroom an activity area for a wide range of age groups. The size of the classroom with activity centers and equipment for 30 children should range from 900 to 1,000 square feet. Many modern schools have classrooms over 900 square feet. Extended use and better quality of programs that such rooms make possible is a good investment in education and in neighborhood life.

THE GYMNASIUM

The gymnasium in a modern elementary school-neighborhood center serves all the pupils in physical education class and extra-class activities. It is also the focal point for a large part of the evening recreation program. It is perhaps the most extensively used space in the building. (For detailed information on the gymnasium see Chapter 6.) Municipal parks have a great deal more outdoor recreation activity space but relatively few buildings with a modern gymnasium. In suburban and rural areas that have no such park systems, the school district has a greater obligation to provide a gymnasium that serves both school and neighborhood center needs.

The gymnasium size is based on:

Number of class or group stations needed for pupils enroled (as determined by the formula shown below)
Size of courts and safety lanes for important sports
Use of the school as a neighborhood center.

Some important types of courts are: (see Table 4-2 for area requirements.)

Volleyball—official size 30 by 60 feet, which can be used also for newcomb and captain-ball
Badminton—official size 20 by 44 feet, which can be used also for paddle tennis and deck tennis
Basketball—official size 42 by 74 feet, for elementary or for junior high and 50 by 84 feet for senior high school; 40 by 60 feet where use is limited to ages below the seventh grade
Dodgeball—circle, diameter 30 feet, which can be used for class formations and a variety of circle games.

Formula for Number of Class or Group Stations Needed

A class station is defined as a space that can be regularly scheduled for a class or a group under the direction of a teacher or leader.

The planning for physical education class or group stations should include provisions for intramural, extramural, and recreation groups. The number of stations needed for an elementary school-neighborhood center depends upon:

Number of physical education classes or groups to be scheduled
Number of minutes for each group during the week, and
Number of minutes one station can be scheduled for the week.

The modern school schedules pupils in grades 3 to 6 for a daily period of about 45 minutes so that they will have about 30 minutes of class activity and about 15 minutes for showering and dressing. Pupils in lower grades who do not change clothes or shower are scheduled for at least one 30 minute period each day. The use of gym suits and shoes enables pupils to get more enjoyment and benefit from class activities and is safer and more hygienic.

The formula that follows has been successfully used to calculate the proper number of stations that are needed by the modern elementary school for physical education classes:

$$\frac{\text{Number of groups to be scheduled} \times \text{Number of minutes each group is scheduled during the week}}{\text{Number of minutes one station can be used during the week}} = \text{Number of stations needed}$$

Application of the formula to an elementary school with about 500 pupils that has 2 rooms for 4 kindergarten groups and 3 rooms for each of the other six grades is shown below. Pupils are scheduled for physical education on the basis of 150 minutes per week for grades K to 2 and 225 minutes for grades 3 to 6.

$$\frac{(\text{8 groups in K-2} \times \text{150 min.}) + (\text{12 groups in 3-6} \times \text{225 min.})}{\text{1500 minutes per week for one station}} =$$

$$\frac{\text{1200 minutes} + \text{2700 minutes}}{\text{1500 minutes}} = \frac{3900}{1500} = \text{2.6 stations}$$

According to the above illustration such a school needs 2.6 stations for the physical education classes. The intramural and neighborhood recreation programs will make heavy demands of these stations. In fact, the peak load for the stations will be during the afternoon and evening intramural and recreation periods. Therefore, the school needs at least three full stations.

It is sound long-range planning to figure the stations on the basis of ultimate pupil enrolment. Adequate planning provides enough stations for the school when it reaches full capacity and avoids the extra cost of adding to the gymnasium. Quite often another wing of classrooms is added after the school has been in operation for some time. These additions overload the gymnasium and result in restricted programs or costly additions.

Priority in Types of Stations

Wise planning establishes some priority for the types of stations. For the above school, which needs three stations, it seems wise to give first priority to a gymnasium with two stations and second to a pool for the third station. Chapter 12, The Indoor Swimming Pool, tells how a good pool can be had for an elementary school-neighborhood center, at a reasonable cost. A pool is a valuable asset to physical education and recreation programs that, because of intensive year round use, will have a low cost in terms of time used and number of groups served. The need for teaching swimming and water safety in the elementary school is as urgent as it is for the high school.

The next priority, if a swimming pool is not possible, is a single station playroom like the one shown in Floor Design I and in Type 1 of Table 4-2. It would be wise to plan this station so that a similar one could be added to form a two-station gymnasium, especially if the school is in a rapidly growing neighborhood. If the enrolment is stable, the 36 by 52 foot station with a ceiling height of 12 to 14 feet will give satisfactory service for classes and small group or club activities.

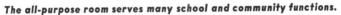

The all-purpose room serves many school and community functions.

The room for remedial or corrective exercises or activities adapted to the needs of pupils with physical defects is next on the priority list. Studies have shown that about 10 per cent of the pupils have physical defects that such exercises and activities will help remedy. The room need not be a full-size station since remedial groups usually total about 15 pupils permitting a standard classroom-size room to be used. However, a 20 by 36 foot room joined to a 36 by 52 foot station by a folding door would make available a 36 by 72 foot room for many special uses involving larger groups.

Size of Stations and Gymnasiums

The dimensions of a gymnasium and class station have been in the past in multiples of 5 and 10. Little or no thought was given to selecting the size that would function most efficiently for the class and extraclass activities of a broad program for all the pupils. Sometimes the choice was made on the basis of an official size basketball court and some extra space for seating spectators. An early standard was expressed in a number of square feet per pupil that was based on the space each pupil in a large class would need for extending arms and legs in calisthenics.

The size of a station and a gymnasium composed of two or more stations in a modern school is determined by the size of courts and surrounding safety lanes for many types of activities included in the program and not by the square feet per pupil a class needs for calisthenics. The increasing popularity of basketball is in some part responsible for the larger size of modern gymnasiums. However there are many other excellent activities that have a high carry-over value into recreation for longer periods of years. One of the best ways to insure such carry-over values is to provide the official-size courts for such activities so that instruction and practice needed to produce skillful players begins at the appropriate age and is carried on through the grades.

The size of the station and gymnasium should be based on usable floor space measured from wall to wall or to the folding seats when closed. The space for seats when closed will vary with the number of rows, and should be added to the usable floor sizes after the number of rows have been determined.

Table 4-2 and Floor Designs Types, I, II, III, and IV show the size and the arrangement of stations and gymnasiums that have been determined on the basis of size

Hard surfaced play area. Fresno school playground, Fresno, California.

Courtesy of American Bitumuls and Asphalt Company

and shapes of certain types of courts and the width of safety lanes. Careful study was made of many sizes to determine the most efficient use of floor space and to select the size and type of gymnasium floor needed for the courts for many important sports. Floor spaces for official courts for these activities also provide stations of sizes needed for improved class, extraclass, and recreation programs. Included are provisions for basketball courts, with seats for spectators when needed. The last two columns in Table 4-2 show the number of players for one court and for two or more courts. The figures given can be doubled if one substitute is allowed for each player, which is the general practice in most games. See Table 4-2 and the Floor Designs for more details.

TABLE 4-2

Stations, Courts, and Gymnasium for Neighborhood Elementary School

	Units		*Safety and Seat Lanes*		*No. Players†*	
*Type of Floor Plan**	*No.*	*Size*	*Side*	*End*	*1 Court*	*2 Courts or more*
DESIGN I						
I. *One-Unit Station–36 x 52*						
Class stations	1	36 x 52			20-30	
Volleyball type court	1	30 x 46	3	3	12	
Badminton type court	1	20 x 44	8	4	4	
Dodgeball type circle	1	30 diam.	3	21	20-30	
See floor design I, p. 62						
DESIGN II						
II. *Two-Station Gym–52 x 72*						
Class stations	2	36 x 52			25-35	50-70
Basketball intram. court	1	42 x 66	5	3	10-20	
Volleyball type court	1	30 x 60	6	6	12-24	
Badminton type court	3	20 x 44	3	4	4-8	12-24
Dodgeball type circle	2	30 diam.	3	11	20-30	40-60
See floor design II, p. 62						
DESIGN III						
III. *Two-Station Gym–68 x 82*						
Class stations	2	41 x 68			30-40	60-80
Basketball intram. court	2	35 x 60	3	4	10-20	20-40
Basketball inters. court	1	42 x 74	13	4	10-15	
Volleyball type court	2	30 x 60	4	4	12-24	24-48
Badminton type court	3	20 x 44	5	12	4-8	12-24
Dodgeball type circle	2	30 diam.	5½	19	20-30	40-60
See floor design III, p. 63						
DESIGN IV						
IV. *Four-Station Gym–72 x 104*						
Class stations	2	52 x 72			35-45	70-90
Class stations	4	36 x 52	3	21	25-35	100-140
Basketball intram. court	2	42 x 66	3	3	10	20
Basketball inters. court	1	50 x 84	11	10	10	
Volleyball type court	3	30 x 60	3½	6	12	36
Badminton type court	6	20 x 44	3	4	4	24
Dodgeball type circle	4	30 diam.	3	11	30	120
See floor design IV, p. 64						

* Floor dimensions are in feet of usable floor space measured from wall to wall or to seats when closed. Space is included for extending seats to accommodate a reasonable number of spectators for interschool basketball and some other sports.

† If one substitute is used for each team position the number of players served in one period would be the higher figure in the player columns.

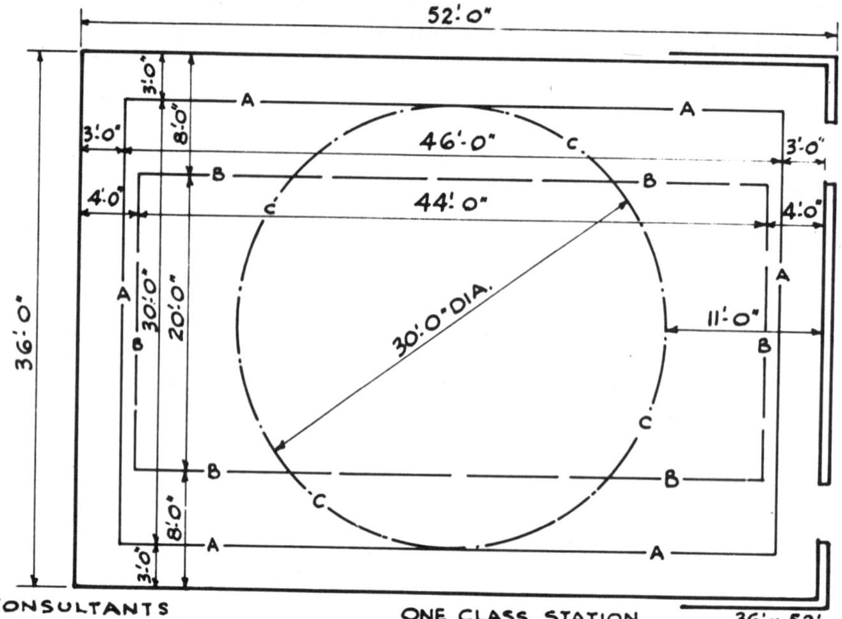

CONSULTANTS
WILLIAM R. SHIRLEY ARCHITECT
GEORGE R. PEDERSEN

ONE CLASS STATION	36' x 52'	
A-ONE VOLLEYBALL TYPE CT.	30' x 46'	——A——
B-ONE BADMINTON TYPE CT.	20' x 44'	— —B—
C-ONE DODGEBALL TYPE CT.	30'-0" DIA.	—·—C·—

DESIGN I - ONE STATION GYM

52' x 36' USABLE FLOOR SPACE

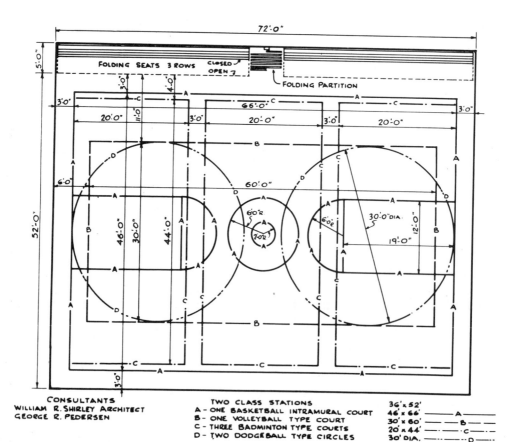

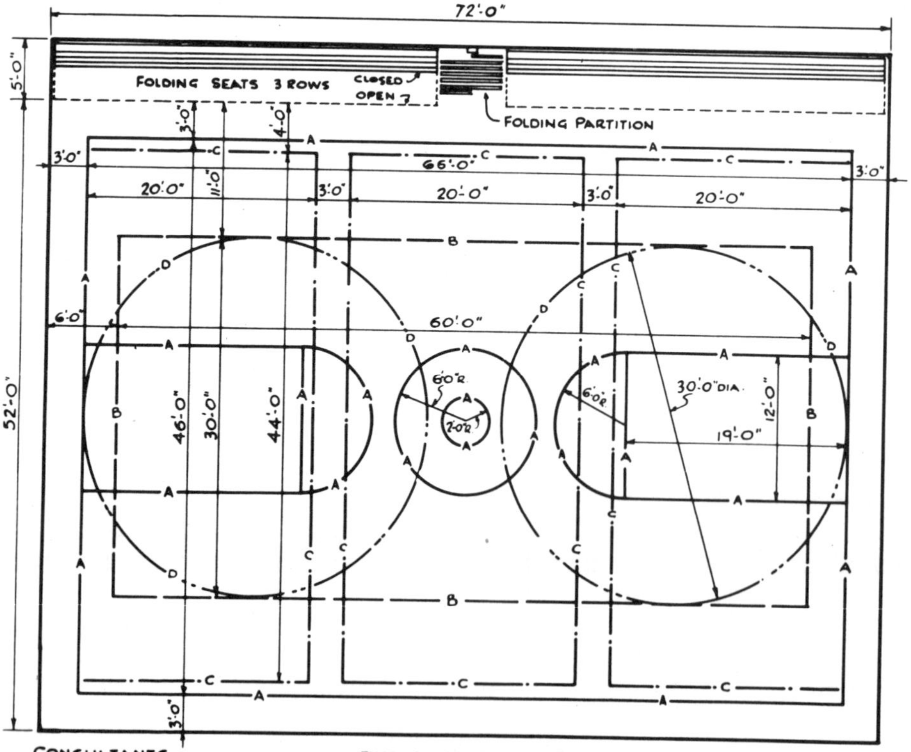

CONSULTANTS
WILLIAM R. SHIRLEY ARCHITECT
GEORGE R. PEDERSEN

TWO CLASS STATIONS	36' x 52'	
A - ONE BASKETBALL INTRAMURAL COURT	46' x 66'	——A——
B - ONE VOLLEYBALL TYPE COURT	30' x 60'	— —B—
C - THREE BADMINTON TYPE COURTS	20' x 44'	—·—C—·—
D - TWO DODGEBALL TYPE CIRCLES	30' DIA.	—··—D—··

DESIGN II TWO-STATION GYM

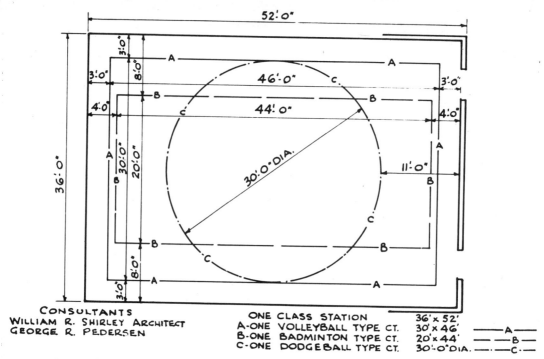

52' x 72' USABLE FLOOR SPACE

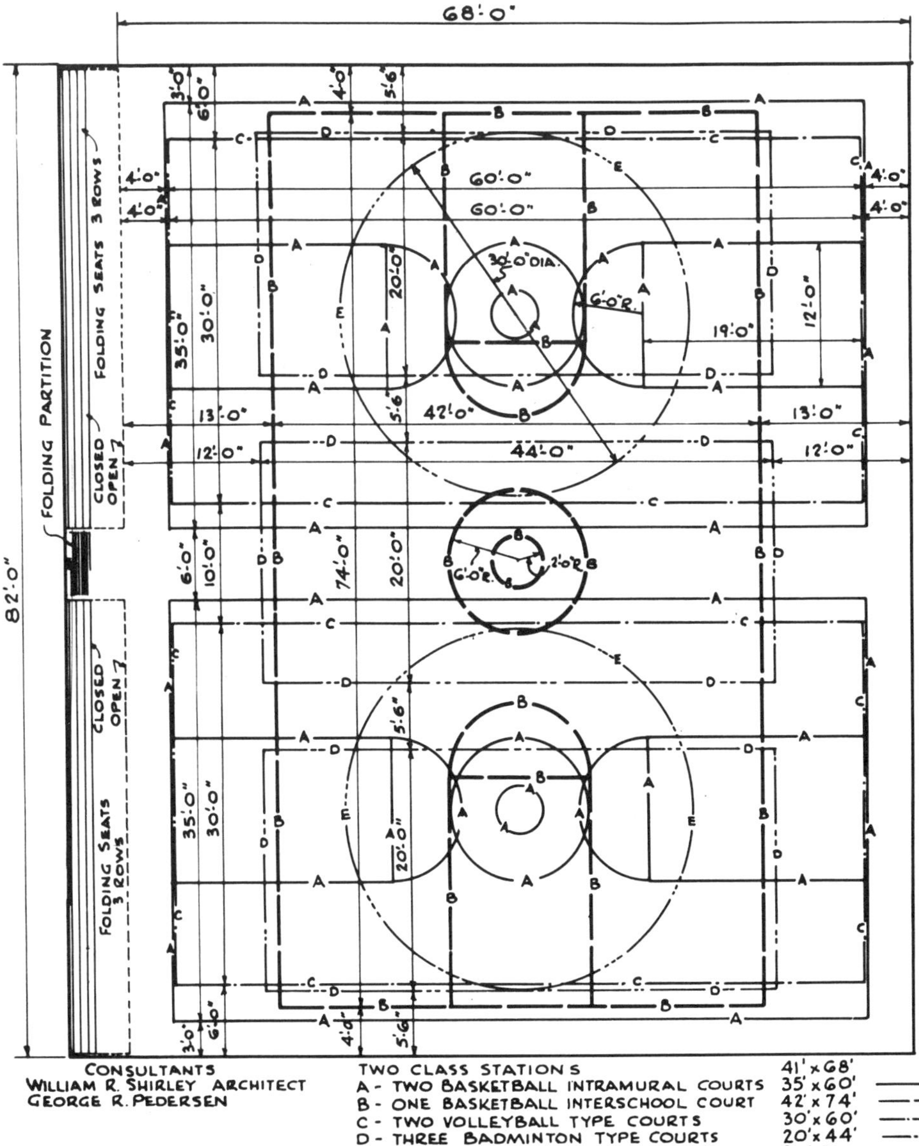

CONSULTANTS
WILLIAM R. SHIRLEY ARCHITECT
GEORGE R. PEDERSEN

TWO CLASS STATIONS	41' x 68'	
A - TWO BASKETBALL INTRAMURAL COURTS	35' x 60'	—— A ——
B - ONE BASKETBALL INTERSCHOOL COURT	42' x 74'	—— B ——
C - TWO VOLLEYBALL TYPE COURTS	30' x 60'	—·—·C—·—
D - THREE BADMINTON TYPE COURTS	20' x 44'	—··—D—··—
E - TWO DODGEBALL TYPE COURTS	30'-DIA	—···—E···—

DESIGN III TWO-STATION GYM

68' x 82' USABLE FLOOR SPACE

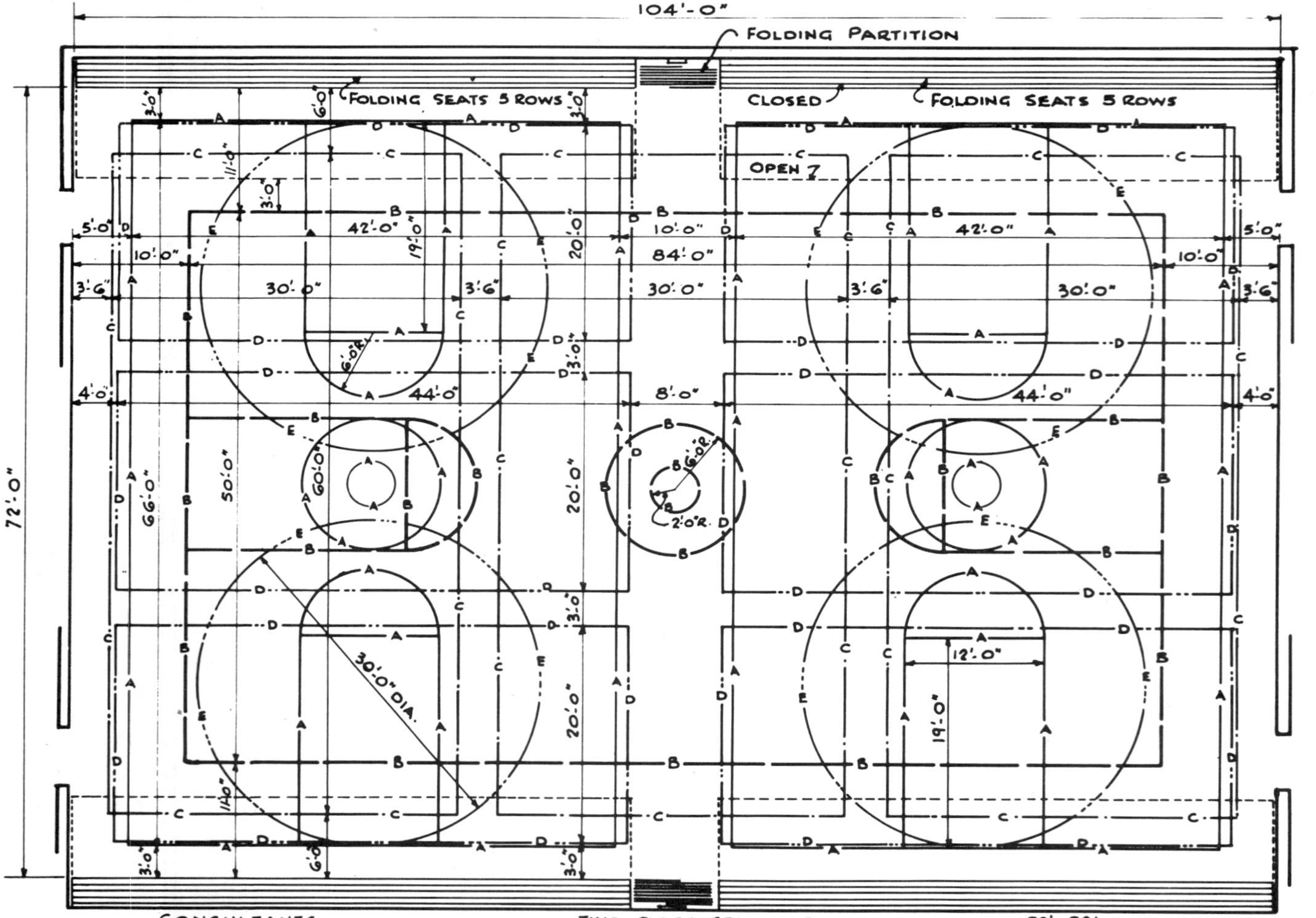

CONSULTANTS
WILLIAM R. SHIRLEY ARCHITECT
GEORGE R. PEDERSEN

TWO CLASS STATIONS	52' x 72'	
A - TWO BASKETBALL INTRAMURAL COURTS	42' x 66'	——A——
B - ONE BASKETBALL INTERSCHOOL COURTS	30' x 84'	——B——
C - THREE VOLLEYBALL TYPE COURTS	30' x 60'	—·—C—·—
D - SIX BADMINTON TYPE COURTS	20' x 44'	—··—D—··—
E - FOUR DODGEBALL TYPE CIRCLES	30' DIA.	——E——
FOUR CLASS STATIONS	36' x 52'	

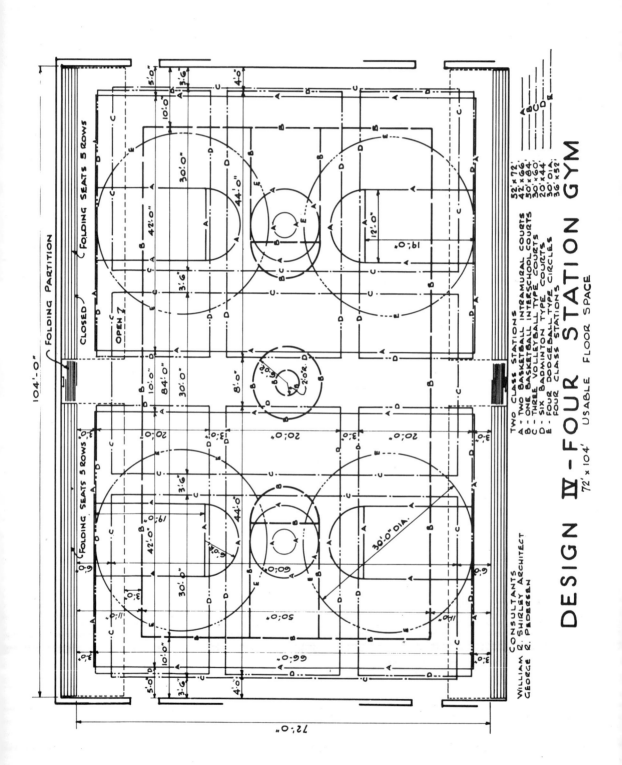

DESIGN IV - FOUR STATION GYM

72' x 104' USABLE FLOOR SPACE

Photo by Roger Sturtevant, San Francisco
Architect: Ernest J. Kump

Outdoor work areas and garden. Dolores Elementary School, Carmel, California.

OTHER SCHOOL FACILITIES FOR RECREATION

The auditorium, cafeteria, lunchroom, the community room, and multiple purpose room for club activities all have a place in the school facilities that are functional for a program of recreation. There are often work benches for assembly and stage prop construction and the auditorium will serve as a Little Theater for a community group and for other dramatic presentations.

The cafeteria and the lunchroom in the modern elementary school-neighborhood center serve both the pupils and community groups. The lunchroom can serve as a snack bar for the neighborhood youth center.

The community room serves as a center for the activities of parent groups and neighborhood committees. It may also serve as a place for school clubs and other meetings.

The program of activities outlined on pages 48-51 forms the foundation for a program that is related to the life of the neighborhood and carries on through the high school years and into adulthood.

CHAPTER 5

THE HIGH SCHOOL—A COMMUNITY CENTER

Caswell M. Miles

THE MODERN HIGH SCHOOL SERVES AS A CENTER for many community activities. By precept and practice education has become more closely related to the life of the community in the following ways:

A broad secondary school program of education attuned to the life of the community

A community for youth which offers for each member opportunities to participate in its government and in a wide range of work and recreation activities

A center for youth, adult, and family-group programs of adult education, recreation, and community activities.

THE COMMUNITY-SCHOOL CONCEPT

The modern secondary school is operated according to the community school concept as outlined in Chapters 2 and 4. It is the capstone of the modern K to 6 grade elementary school and serves also as a community center. The broad range of activities of the modern education and recreation programs outlined in Chapter 4, carry on throughout the six years of secondary school and into adult life. More opportunities are provided for specialization in the senior high school and the adult program, but the junior high school offers a broad exploratory program that sets the pattern for the *community curriculum* described in Chapters 2 and 4.

This pattern of a broad program for the junior high school and more specialization at the senior high school and adult levels guides the course of secondary education into the life stream of the community. It makes the high school a functional community center.

OBJECTIVES AND CHANGING NEEDS

The objectives of secondary education as originally stated by the Commission on the

---

***Illustration:* Conestoga High School, Berwyn, Pennsylvania**
Architects: Howell Lewis Shay and Associates

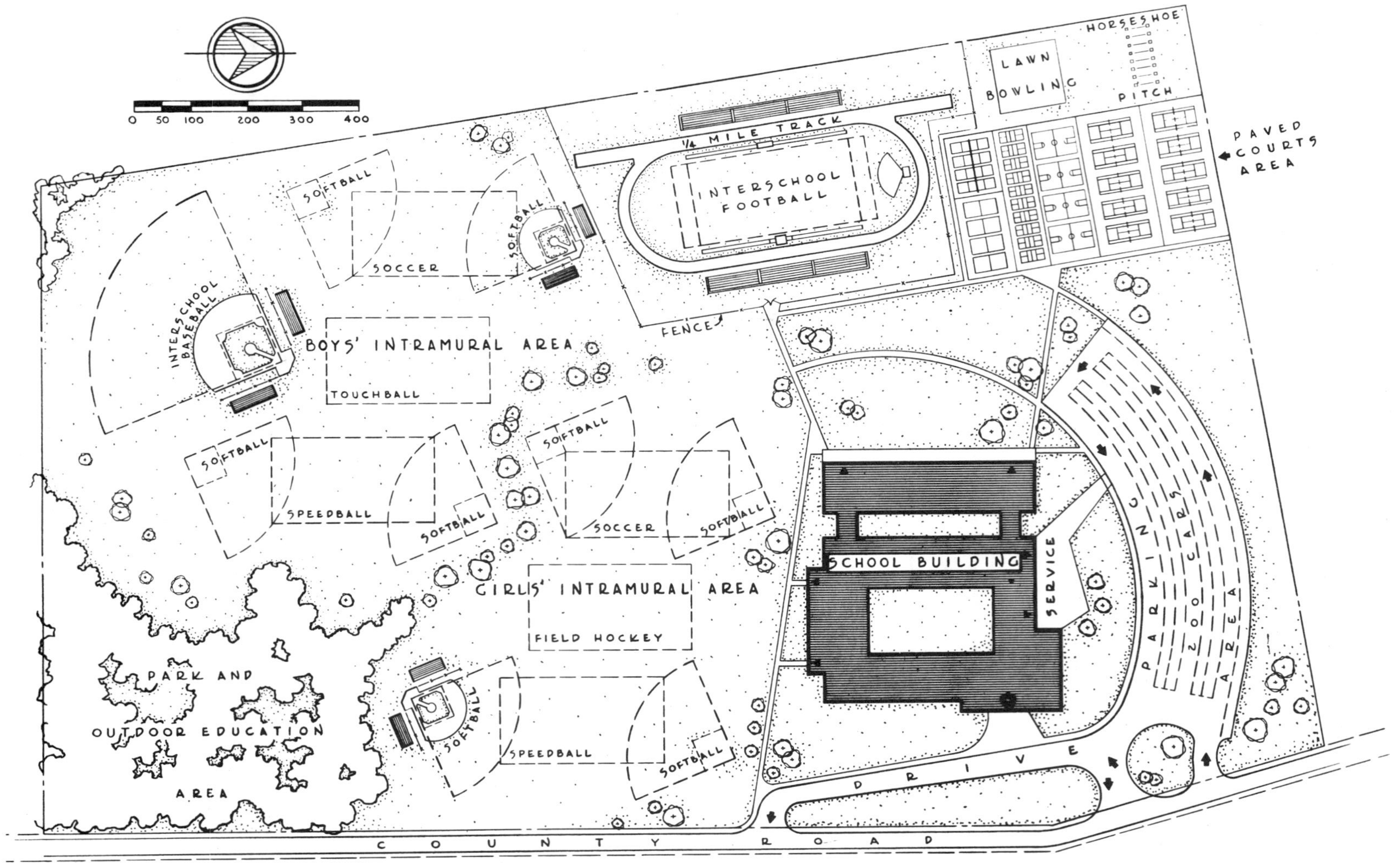

The modern school is a laboratory for human experiences.

Reorganization of Secondary Education in 1918 recognized changes in youth needs. This statement of the objectives has been widely accepted by the education profession, citizen groups, and the voters. They are: (1) health, (2) command of fundamental processes, (3) worthy home membership, (4) vocation, (5) citizenship, (6) worthy use of leisure, and (7) ethical character.[1]

The Educational Policies Commission of the National Education Association in 1944 listed six aspects of living that affect personal development and the education of youth as follows:

Health of body and mind
Family life
Recreational and leisure-time interests and activities
Understanding and appreciation of the cultural heritage
Intellectual achievement
Character, conceived as conduct in relation to other persons, motivated by ethical ideals and principles.[2]

The two statements, which have much in common, reflect the efforts of education to meet the needs of youth during a period in which there were great changes in American community life that have carried on to the present at an increased rate.

Social and technological research and development have brought to this nation the highest standard of living and the greatest amount of time for leisure that has been achieved in the history of man. The greatest change has been in the substitution of machines for physical labor in business, industry, farm, and home. The decrease in physical labor and the increase in leisure and income poses many serious problems for the community. These changes also offer much promise for advancement in the culture, happiness, and health of all citizens.

The community school and other improvements in education and community services have brought education and community life closer together in a concerted effort to meet changing needs. Programs of physical education have been extended and improved to meet the physical fitness and recreation needs of youth and the community. The modern high school-community center that provides an on-going program of education and recreation is a powerful force in meeting fitness and leisure needs. It has facilities for physical education and recreation that are adequate and functional for a year-round program.

THE PATTERN OF GRADE ORGANIZATION

The prevailing pattern of grade-group organization now provides for six secondary school grades with junior and senior high school units. Moving the 7th and 8th grades from the old 8-grade elementary school and the 9th grade from the traditional 4-year high to form the junior high school has broadened and enriched the 7th and 8th grade programs. The 9th grader has become a senior citizen of the junior high school rather than an harassed freshman of the 4-year high school. The boys and girls from 12 to 14 years of age, where the growth and development are greater than in any other corresponding age-grade span, are grouped in a school that is organized to meet their needs.

TABLE 5-1

Pattern of School Grade Organization

Grade Group Organization Plan	Per cent of Districts	No. of Cases
6-3-3	35	478
8-4	23	321
6-6	16	215
6-2-4	12	168
6-3-3-2	4	54
7-5	3	42
5-3-4	2	25
7-2-3	1	14
6-2-4-2	1	13
Other	3	42

The elementary school grade plan now generally includes kindergarten through grade six. The National Education Association study of school organization in city school districts in 1949 showed that 59 per cent of the schools operated kindergartens

[1] U.S. Bureau of Education, Cardinal Principles of Secondary Education, Bulletin No. 38, 1918.

[2] NEA Educational Policies Commission, *Education for All American Youth*. Washington, D.C., 1944 (p. 102).

Architects: Daniel, Mann, Johnson, and Mendenhall

The Spiral School, a new concept in design. New Narbonne High School, Los Angeles, California.

and 2 per cent had pre-kindergartens. The study also included data on grade plan organization.[3]

According to these data, about 70 per cent of the districts in 1948 operated on a grade plan of six elementary grades and six grades of varying junior and senior high school units. In 1910 practically no cities operated this type of six-grade-unit pattern. About 23 per cent of the districts used the 8 to 4 plan and about 3 per cent used the 7 to 5 pattern.

In suburban or rural areas many small or common school districts have been brought together in a large administrative unit such as a central or consolidated school district. Sometimes such a district houses grades K-12 in a single building. Often there are several K-6 schools, two junior high schools and a senior high. Even when grades 7-12 are housed in one building, grades 7-9 are administered as the junior high school unit and the other three as a senior high. Sometimes a large junior high school of 800 to 1200 pupils is organized so that there are two or three units of about 400 pupils.

By organizing the school in this way the advantages of larger administrative districts and schools are gained while provisions are made for smaller classroom units housed in separate wings of the building and operated so that more opportunities are offered for pupil participation in government and in extraclass activities. This arrangement also enables the teachers to work more closely with pupils and parents. Each unit, however, should have its quota of facilities for a full program of class and extraclass activities such as stations for indoor and outdoor physical education classes, intramural, and extramural activities.

THE PROGRAM DETERMINES THE FACILITIES

The design for the high school-community center should include facilities that are functional for the broad range of activities in high school and community center pro-

[3] National Education Association Research Bulletin, Vol. XXVII, No. 1, February, 1949, pp. 10-13.

grams. Many of the activities in a modern secondary education program grow out of the elementary education curriculum and carry on into adult vocational, avocational, and recreational pursuits. Many of the activities are related to the pursuits of the community.

The six high school years offer opportunities for acquiring more advanced knowledge, skills, and social competencies, and for greater specialization in subject areas. Even though secondary education may be more formal and specialized than elementary education, such courses as art, crafts, English, languages, health, homemaking, mathematics, music, physical education, science, and vocational education offer more abundant opportunities for youth and adults to develop a wide range of skills, knowledge, and appreciations. For example, music and

An excellent five-station physical education plant. Linton High School, Schenectady, New York.

Architects: Perkins and Will, Ryder and Link

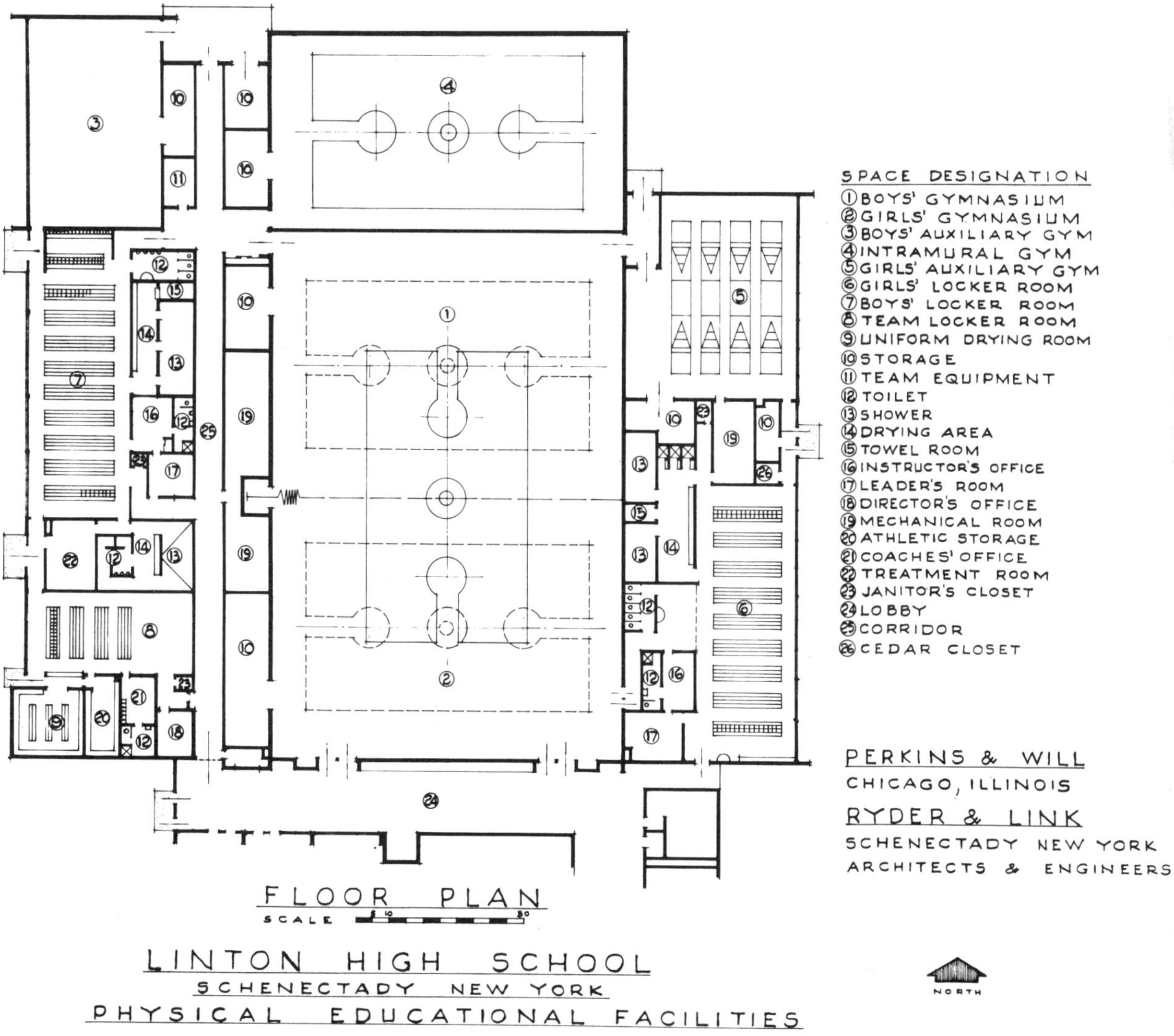

physical education, which have much in common, offer opportunities for developing competencies which range from a simple folk dance to a fine production of a ballet or a musical comedy. Art, science and other courses likewise offer opportunities for developing vocational, cultural, and avocational competencies which lead to a finer life for the individual.

The program of physical education for a high school includes activities in each of the following areas: (1) team games, (2) individual and dual sports, (3) rhythms and dance, (4) aquatics, (5) gymnastics, (6) remedial activities and (7) camping, hiking, scouting, hunting, and fishing. Instruction, practice, and participation in the many activities of each group is provided in class, intramural, extramural and interschool activity schedules. Through this range of instruction, practice, and participation, youth develops the skills, knowledge, and appreciations which carry over into adult life and into the worthy use of leisure.

There are variations in specific goals and activities to suit varying needs of boys and girls. There are also many coeducation activities. The difference in programs and needs calls for separate schedules for girls and boys and an equitable provision of facilities for the girls' program. Too often the girls' program has not had a fair share of facilities because of traditional emphasis on interschool athletics in some communities.

Sound planning for both program and facilities for physical education gives emphasis to all the scheduled activities and in the following order: (1) class, (2) intramural,

A trend in school design is the commons room for study, class group activities, and after school programs. Lakewood High School, New Jersey.

Courtesy of *The School Executive*
Architects: Hays and Ruth

(3) extramural, (4) interschool. It will include activities in the areas of those listed above and facilities for them.

PLANNING OUTDOOR FACILITIES

Planning outdoor facilities for physical education and recreation programs of a high school-community center is closely tied with the selection of the site. The wide acceptance of the park-school and community school concepts in the last decade has helped increase the size of sites for junior and senior high school plants. In 1946 the National Conference on Facilities for Athletics, Recreation, Physical and Health Education in its Guide for Planning Facilities formulated the park-school concept with the elementary school as a neighborhood center and the public high school as a community center.[4]

It recommended a site of at least 25 acres for a junior high school community center and 40 acres or more for a senior high school community center.

In Chapter 2, it is pointed out that many communities from coast to coast have acquired 40 to 100 acres and more for high school sites. The list of acreages for 5 senior high schools in 14 states shows only one school that has less than 40 acres, while 4 have sites of 100 acres or more. The other site sizes are: 40-59 acres, 23; 60-79 acres, 12; and 80-99 acres, 11 schools. Similar increases

[4] *A Guide for Planning Facilities for Athletics, Recreation, Physical and Health Education.* The National Conference on Facilities, The Athletic Institute, Chicago, Ill., 1946 (pp. 5-11).

A & M Consolidated High School, College Station, Texas.

Photo by Roland Chatham, Bryant, Texas
Architects: Caudill, Rowlett, Scott and Associates

have been made in the size of sites selected for junior high schools. One important factor in providing larger sites for senior high schools is the greater emphasis on interschool fields and courts. One good reason for increase in size of sites for both junior and senior high schools is the additional space required for building of the campus and one-story construction. One school in New York State required 13 acres for building, lawn, and parking space.

The items affecting the size of high school sites and a score card for the selection of school buildings are given in Chapter 2.

OUTDOOR COURT GAMES AREA

The outdoor court games area should be planned so that there is a battery of courts for each important sport, sufficient in number to provide enough player stations for a class of about 40 pupils. This enables each class member to have a station for the instruction and practice he needs to become a skilled player. A battery of 10 tennis courts, for example as shown in Table 5-2, provides 40 players' stations for class instruction and practice.

This number of stations makes a good intramural, extramural and tennis center for interschool competition in the afternoon. Furthermore a battery of courts serves as a tennis center for recreation groups during the evening and vacation periods. Class instruction during the days and intramural competition in the afternoons is the best way to develop tennis players who will carry the sport on into their recreation pursuits. This multiple use of the courts for the three programs lowers the cost of the courts per player and time period.

There are six other types of courts shown in Table 4 that in like manner serve for class instruction, for intramural, extramural and interschool competition, and for recreation. These seven types provide official courts for 16 or more sports and for 280 player stations. By such planning the high school-community center can have a broad program of court games and enough player stations to do an effective job in class instruction, team competition, and recreation.

Courts for other sports such as roque and boccie can be added and the list of sports may vary with the sections of the country.

Games courts layout for a high school.

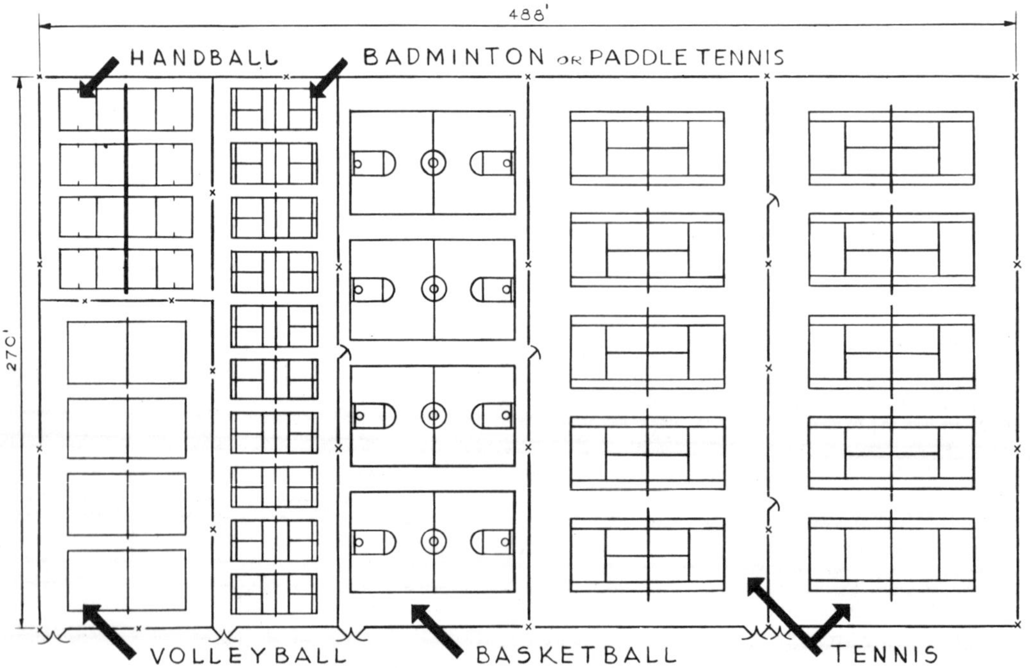

TABLE 5-2

Outdoor Court Areas for High Schools by Type, and their Relationship to Player Stations and Size

Area Type	Activities	Players per court	No. courts	Player stations	Court size*	Multiple courts area*	Sq. ft. in area
I	*Volleyball***	12	4	48	30 x 60	150 x 76	11,400
	Newcomb	12	4		30 x 60		
	Captainball	12			30 x 60		
II	*Badminton*	4	10	40	20 x 44	266 x 64	17,024
	Paddle Tennis	4	10				
	Deck Tennis	4	10				
III	*Tennis*	4	10	40	36 x 78	465 x 120	55,800
	Group games when ground is wet						
IV	*Handball*	4	8	32	20 x 34	105 x 88	9,240
	Squash Tennis	4	8		22 x 36		
	Squash Racquets	4			22 x 36		
V	*Basketball*	10	4	40	50 x 84	230 x 96	22,080
VI	*Horseshoes*	4	8	32	10 x 50†	160 x 70	11,200
	Quoits	4	8		10 x 50†		
VII	*Lawn Bowling*	8	6	48	14 x 110	120 x 120	14,400

* Size is in feet.
** The dominant activity is italicized.
† Set horseshoe pitching stakes 40 feet apart for men and imbed pitching board in ground 30 feet from stakes for women and players under 16. Set quoits pins or hobs 30 feet apart for seniors and locate pitching boards 21 feet from hobs for juniors.

SAFETY LANES AND BORDERS IN MULTIPLE COURTS AREAS

I	II	III	IV	V	VI	VII	Location of Lane or Border
6	6	12	5	6	5	3	Between sidelines of outer courts and fence
6	6	9	5	6	10	3	Between sidelines of inner courts
8	10	21	10	6	10	5	Between endlines of courts and fence

(Columns I–VII: *Lane Width by Area Type*)

The essential factors which the planner must consider are:

Provide courts for many different sports to permit a broad program
Provide for enough player stations in each sport for effective class instruction, team competition, and after school recreation
Provide for efficient multiple use by grouping courts of similar size and function in a common area
Provide for paved surfaces and fences for better games, extended periods of use, and better maintenance
Locate the courts area near the building and the parking area
Provide for lights to extend the use of the courts to evening hours and more people.

The courts games area is needed for the girls' as well as for the boys' program of physical education and recreation. The area is needed for the junior high as well as for the senior high school, both of which serve as recreation centers for adults.

FIELD SPORTS AREAS

The field sports area should provide spaces which are suitable for broad programs of physical education and recreation. In senior high schools the area should include space allocations for: (1) sports fields for girls and

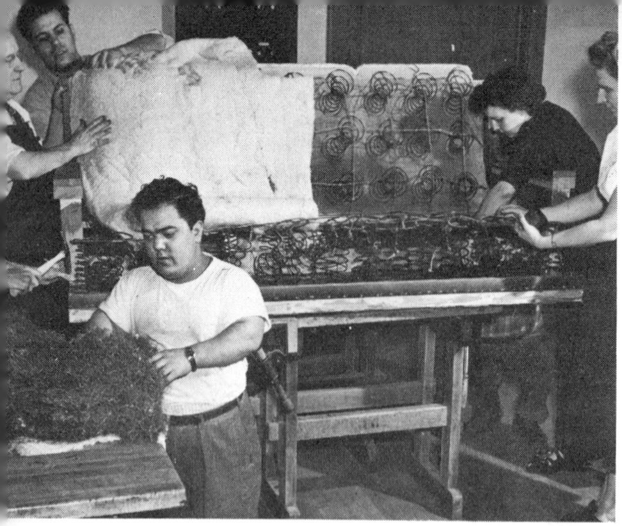

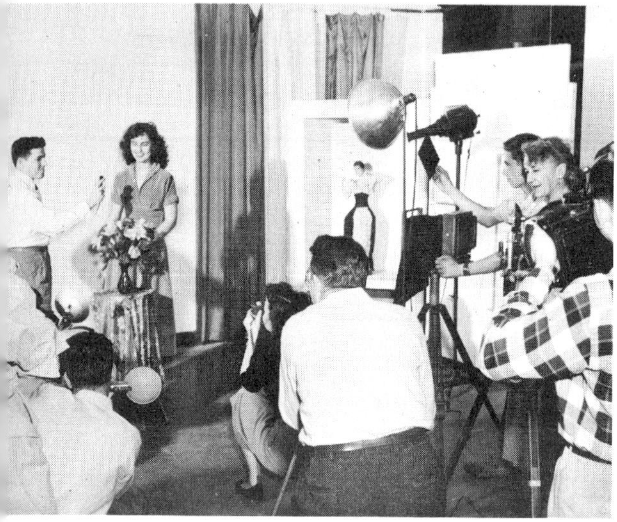

Adult groups use school facilities for many evening activities.
Courtesy of Engelhardt, Engelhardt and Leggett

women, (2) sports fields for boys' intramurals, and (3) sports fields for boys' interschool activities. This allocation is needed in order that these three phases of the physical education program can be scheduled and conducted during the same afternoon periods. All three areas should be planned for and used by recreation groups during evening and vacation periods.

The area for girls and women should be large enough to provide space for scheduling intramural, extramural, and some interschool activities. Separation of intramural and interschool areas is not made as for boys because the girls' program does not usually emphasize interschool competition on a league schedule basis. Instead their program is basically intramural with some extramural games, play days, and sports days which are conducted for the players and not for spectators. Such a program needs space enough for many groups in the afternoon peak-load periods when, for example, several softball fields are needed.

In junior high schools the boys' program is basically intramural with the interschool activities organized on an extramural pattern rather than a fixed league schedule for a limited sports program. The extramural game may be between an outstanding intramural team of the host school and a similar one from a school nearby. There may be sports days for boys from several nearby schools. Such a program requires enough fields for several intramural games at the same time in one afternoon.

Some of the sports and activities in the high school-community center physical education and recreation program needing space in the sports areas are: archery, baseball, cageball, camping, cricket, cross country, fieldball, field hockey, flag football, football, golf,

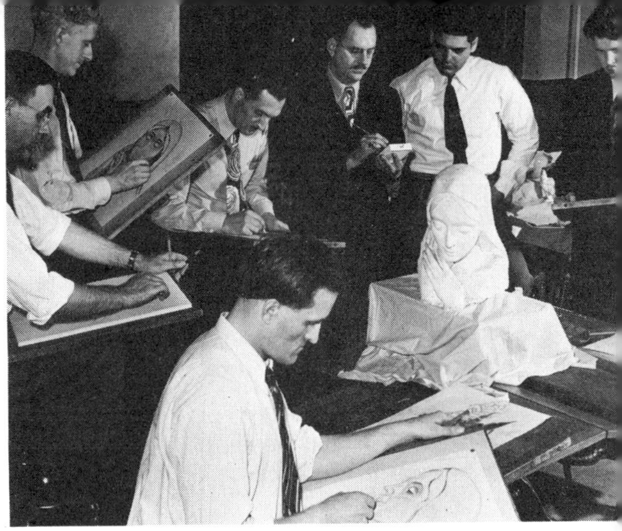

ice hockey, lacrosse, outdoor education, riflery, skating, skiing, speedball, softball, tobogganing, coasting, track and field.

Some of the sports and activities require large level grassy areas. Others such as tobogganing, coasting, riflery, archery, golf, and skiing can make use of a more rugged topography. For activities such as golf, cross country, and skiing, some provision can be made for instruction and practice. Multiple use can be made of field areas because of seasonal schedules.

The size of field areas will vary depending upon scope of program and availability of large sites in the section. Occasionally a large tract of land or a whole farm can be secured for about the same cost as a smaller tract, particularly if the topography of part of the tract is too rugged for house lots or cultivation. Some school districts are purchasing sites of over 100 acres. These large sites are in keeping with the park-school concept. In the rural and suburban areas where large central or consolidated districts are being formed, these schools and sites are useful and practical community school centers. Cooperative action by park commissions and boards of education in joint acquisition of park and school sites can often bring about the purchase of large tracts in more densely populated centers too.

A site of 50 to 60 acres, which is quite common, could have an allocation of about 10 acres for the girls' and women's fields and similar amounts for the intramural and the interschool games area for boys and men. In the interschool area, the track and football field would take four acres and the baseball field three acres, leaving about three for soccer. For the girls' area, 2 to 3 fields for hockey, soccer, and speed ball, and four softball diamonds can be included in the 10 acres. See junior and senior high school site plans for an example of planning for outdoor areas (pages 24-31).

The space for the modern building of the campus or one-story type with lawns, walks, driveways, and parking area will often require 10 to 12 acres. The park or quiet recreation area, to be used for class picnics, outdoor cooking, and has shade, tables, benches, and fireplaces, may include about five acres. The outdoor education projects and activities would make use of the wooded and more rugged section of the site but space may be allocated for certain special projects. Each site requires a plan prepared specifically for that site so that it functions best for school and community activities. The planners have an obligation to present plans for the more desirable site development for the modern high school–community center, because many voters don't know what they want until they see what they can get.

Planning for Indoor Class Stations

An indoor class station is a space in the school building which can be scheduled regularly for a physical education class or group in intramural or recreation activities under the guidance of a teacher or leader. Providing one gymnasium for a school with little or no relation to the number of pupils enrolled or to future plans for added classrooms is not wise planning. Physical education is required by law in most states for all pupils. Such general use of a facility which is also a large one should be planned to serve the pupils of ultimate enrolment and for a broad program of physical education and recreation.

The gymnasium size and number of stations should be planned on the basis of:

The number of class or group stations needed for the pupils of ultimate enrolment as determined by the formula given below
The size of courts and safety lanes for important activities in the program
The need for the extraclass groups during the afternoon peak load periods
The use of the high school as a community center.

Formula for the Number of Class Stations

The number of physical education class stations a high school needs is based on:

The number of pupils of ultimate enrolment
The average number of pupils in a class
The number of periods each week one station can be scheduled for classes.

The formula is for scheduled physical education classes. The peak load for a station or a gymnasium, which can be separated into two or more stations by folding partitions, comes during the after school periods. A modern program for a senior high should provide intramural activities for about 70 per cent of the pupils during the week and interschool activities for about 25 per cent. Some compensation can be made for this peak load by using an extraclass weighting figure such as 1.5. Further compensation can be made by efficient management and flexible school schedules that allow more afternoon time in spring and fall for outdoor activities. The formula follows:

$$\frac{\text{No. pupils of ultimate enrolment}}{\text{Average size of class as desired}} \times \frac{\text{No. periods for each pupils per week}}{\text{No. periods per week one station can be used}} \times \text{Extraclass weighting} = \text{No. Stations Needed}$$

The application of the formula to a school that has an ultimate enrolment of 1000 pupils follows:

$$\frac{1000}{40} \times \frac{5}{30} \times 1.5 = \frac{5000 \text{ pupil periods}}{1200 \text{ station periods}} \times 1.5 = 6.2 \text{ stations, which is rounded off at 6 stations}$$

Skylights provide natural light for this shop. South Central Junior-Senior High School, Seattle, Washington.

Photo by Chas. R. Pearson, Seattle
Architect: Ralph Burkhard

Photo by Tierney and Killingsworth, Miami

New concept of auditorium design provides maximum flexibility. Above: Ring Auditorium, Kinlock Junior High School, Miami, Florida.

Below: Circular Auditorium.

Photo by Roland Chatham, Bryan, Texas
Architects: Caudill, Rowlett, Scott and Associates

***Above:* Music rehearsal room, Cumberland Valley Joint High School, Pennsylvania.**
Photo by Ken Smith, Camp Hill, Pennsylvania
Architect: Edmund Good

***Below:* Folding partitions provide great flexibility in rooms. Clara Bryant High School, Dearborn, Michigan.**
Photo by Elmer L. Astleford
Architect: Eberle M. Smith

Size and Type of Courts Determines Station and Gymnasium Size

The size of the gymnasium and the class or group station is as important as the number of stations. The gym and the stations should be planned so that they function efficiently for a broad program of physical education and recreation. Many sports have official rules which have been evolved over a period of many years and are widely accepted as the way to play the game. Basketball, badminton, and volleyball, among other sports, have official rules which require specific size and shape of courts and safety lanes.

By careful planning, the size of usable floor space of a gymnasium can be determined as the most suitable for a high school-community center. Table 5-3 shows how six types of floor plans can be designed to provide batteries of courts needed to serve programs of class instruction, extraclass competition, and recreation participation. By selecting floor dimensions for the gymnasium that provide for the courts and safety lanes, efficient use is made of floor space and the stations are of a size that serve many other activities.

TABLE 5-3

Size of Stations, Courts and Gymnasium for Community High School

Type of Floor Plan*	UNITS		Safety and Seat Lanes*		No. Players†	
	No.	Size	Side	End	1 Unit	Total Units
Design III						
I. *Two-Station Gym—68 x 82*						
See Type II in Table 4-2 and Floor Design III p. 62						
Design V						
II. *Two-Station Gym—76 x 92*						
Class stations	2	46 x 76			30-40	60-80
Basketball intramural court	2	40 x 70	3	3	10-20	20-40
Basketball interscholastic court	1	50 x 84	13	4	10-15	
Volleyball type court	2	30 x 60	10-6	8	12-24	24-48
Badminton type court	3	20 x 44	8	16	4-8	12-24
Dodgeball type circle	2	30 dia.	23	10-8	20-30	40-60
Design IV						
III. *Two-Four Station Gym—72 x 104*						
See Type IV in Table 4-2 p. 61 and Floor Design IV p. 64						
Design VI						
IV. *Two-Station Gym—80 x 102*						
Class stations	2	51 x 80			30-40	60-80
Basketball intramural court	2	42 x 74	4	3	10-20	20-40
Basketball interscholastic court	1	50 x 84	15	9	10-15	
Volleyball Type court	3	30 x 60	3	10	12-24	36-72
Badminton Type court	6	20 x 44	5	3-6	4-8	24-48
Dodgeball Type circle	4	30 dia.	10-6	6-8	20-30	80-120
Design VII						
V. *Two-Station Gym—80 x 109*						
Class stations	2	54½ x 80			35-45	70-90
Basketball intramural court‡	2	42 x 74	(inn-3) (out 9-4)	3	10-20	20-40
Basketball interscholastic court	1	50 x 84	15	12-6	10-15	
Volleyball Type court‡	3	30 x 60	(inn-3) (out 7-6)	10	12-24	36-72
Badminton Type court‡	6	20 x 44	(inn-3) (out-7)	6-4	4-8	24-48
Design VIII						
VI. *Four-Station Gym—104 x 144*						
Class Station	4	52 x 72			30-40	120-160
Basketball intramural	4	42 x 66	5	3	10-20	40-80
Basketball intramural	2	50 x 84	11	10	10-20	20-40
Basketball interscholastic§	1	50 x 84	(23-6) (30-10)	32	10-15	
Volleyball Type court	6	30 x 60	5	3	12-24	72-144
Badminton Type court	12	20 x 44	3	4	4-8	48-96

* Floor dimensions are in feet and inches of usable floor space measured from wall to wall or to seats when closed. Space is included for extending seats to accommodate a reasonable number of spectators for interschool basketball and some other sports. See floor design for each type.

† If one substitute is used for each team position the number of players served in one period would be the higher figure in the player columns.

‡ Outer lanes are wider to allow use of 1-3 rows of seats.

§ Goals are located nearer to one side because of folding partition.

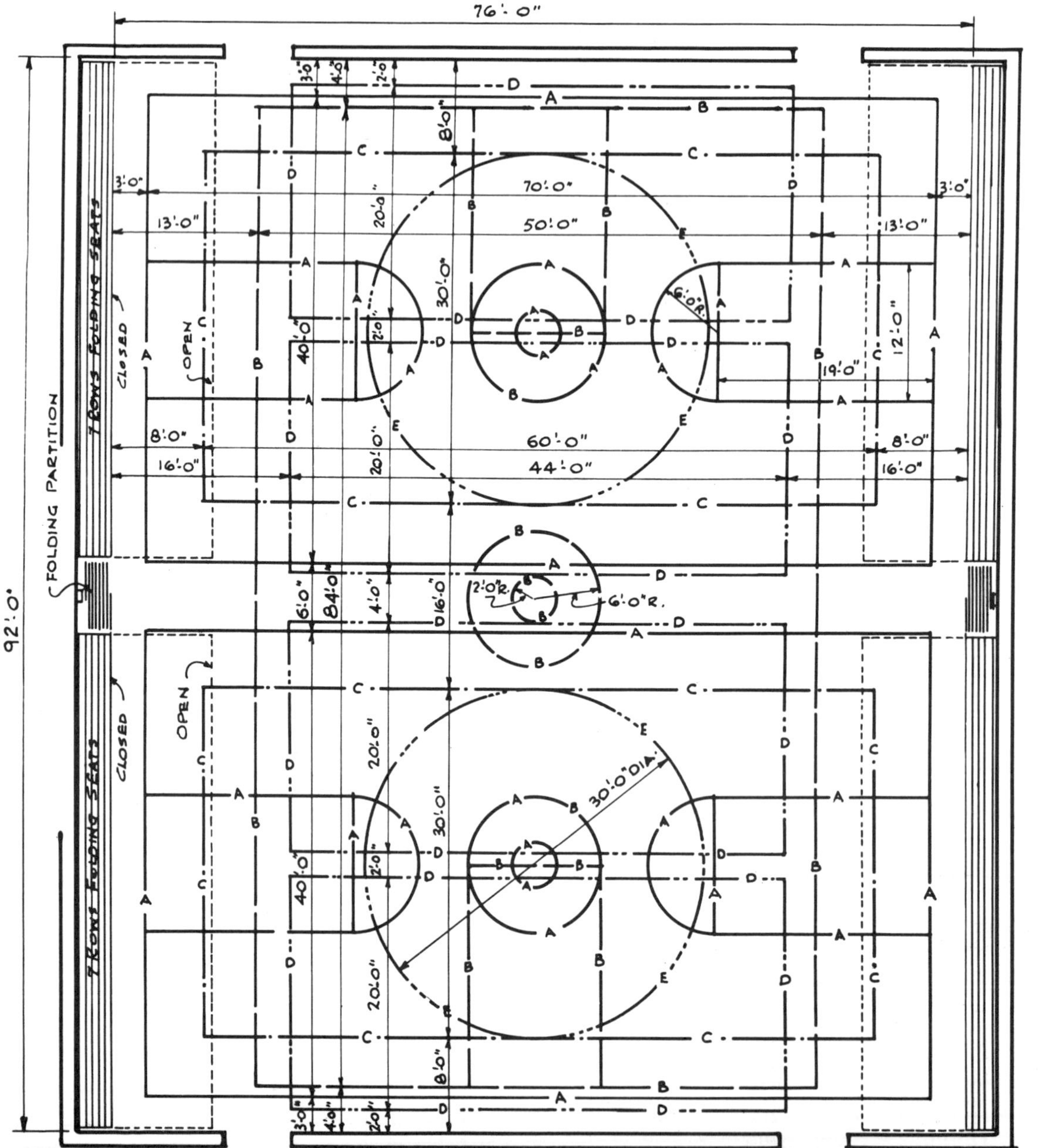

CONSULTANTS
WILLIAM R. SHIRLEY ARCHITECT
GEORGE R. PEDERSEN

	TWO CLASS STATION	46' x 70'
A–	TWO BASKETBALL INTRAMURAL COURTS	40' x 70'
B–	ONE BASKETBALL INTERSCHOOL COURT	50' x 84'
C–	TWO VOLLEYBALL TYPE COURTS	30' x 60'
D–	FOUR BADMINTON TYPE COURTS	20 x 44'
E–	TWO DODGEBALL TYPE CIRCLES	30' DIA.

DESIGN V - TWO STATION GYM

76' x 92' USABLE FLOOR SPACE

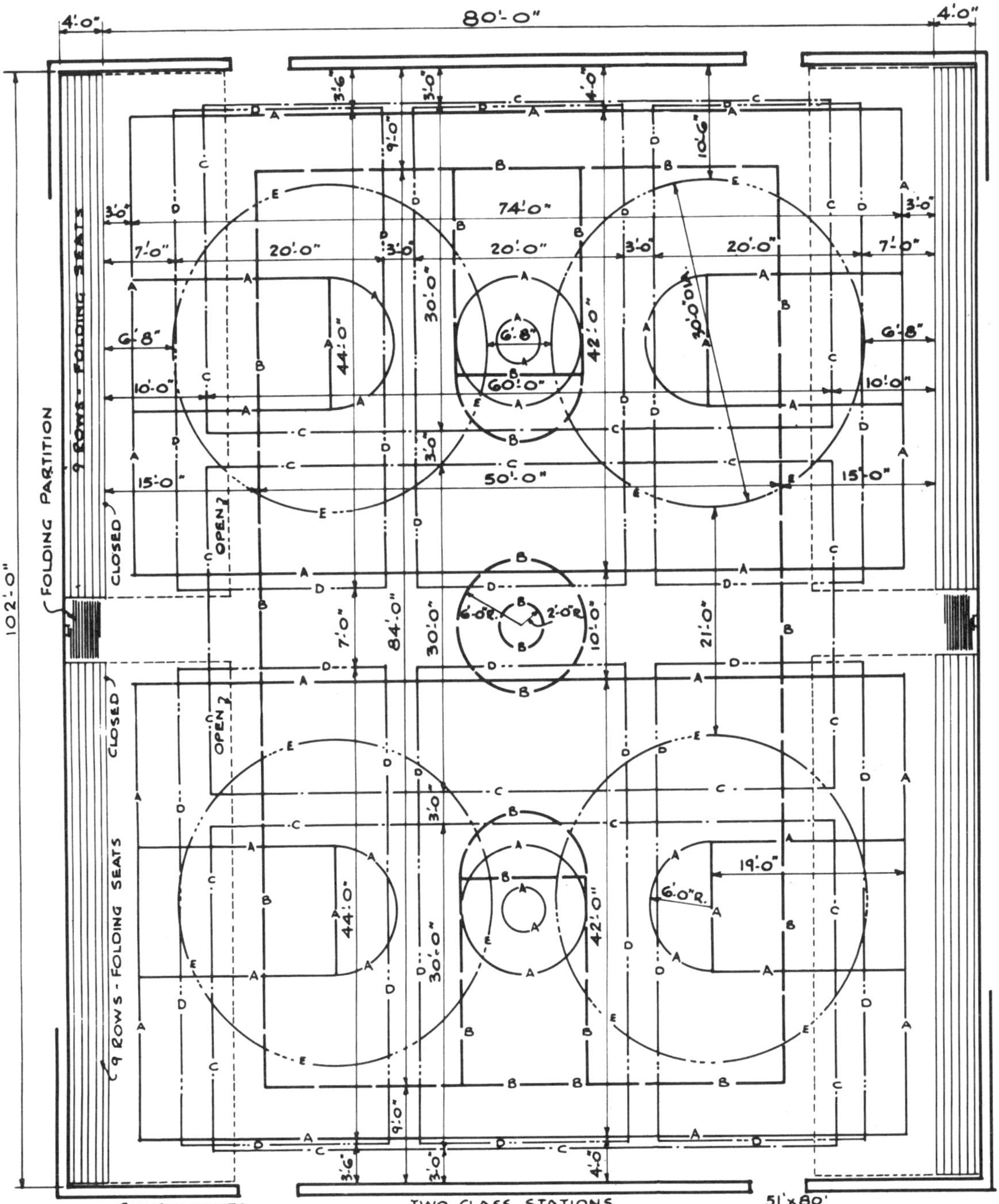

CONSULTANTS
WILLIAM R. SHIRLEY ARCHITECT
GEORGE R. PEDERSEN

TWO CLASS STATIONS		
A-TWO BASKETBALL INTRAMURAL COURTS	51'x80'	——A——
B-ONE BASKETBALL INTERSCHOOL COURTS	42'x74'	——B——
C-THREE VOLLEYBALL TYPE COURTS	50'x84'	——·C·——
D-SIX BADMINTON TYPE COURTS	30'x60'	——··D··——
E-FOUR DODGEBALL TYPE CIRCLES	20'x44' 30' DIA.	——···E···——

DESIGN VI - TWO STATION GYM

80' x 102' USABLE FLOOR SPACE

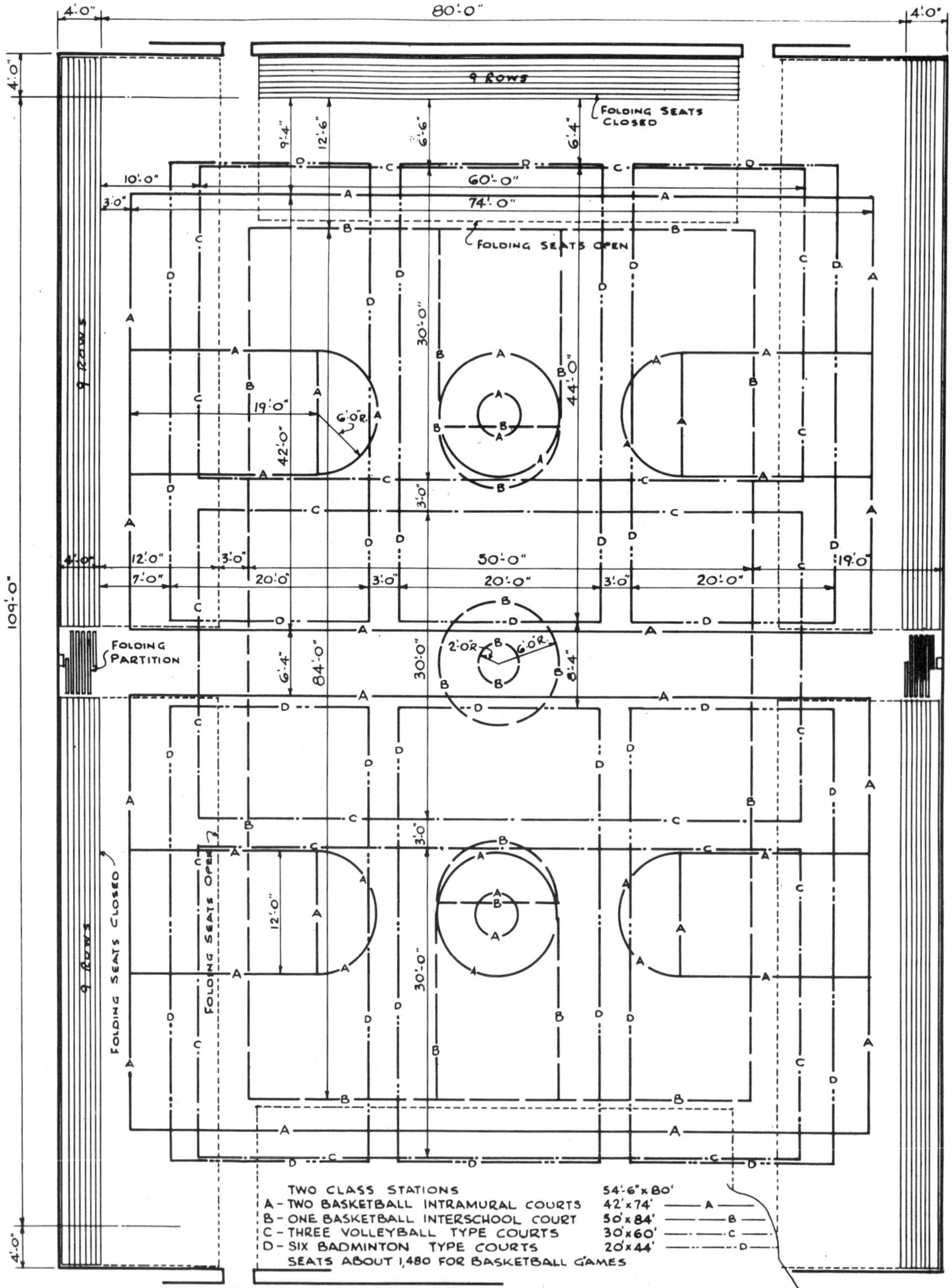

DESIGN VII TWO-STATION GYM

80'x109' USABLE FLOOR SPACE

EXPANSIBLE TO TYPE VI FOUR-STATION GYM

CONSULTANTS
WILLIAM R. SHIRLEY ARCHITECT
GEORGE R. PEDERSEN

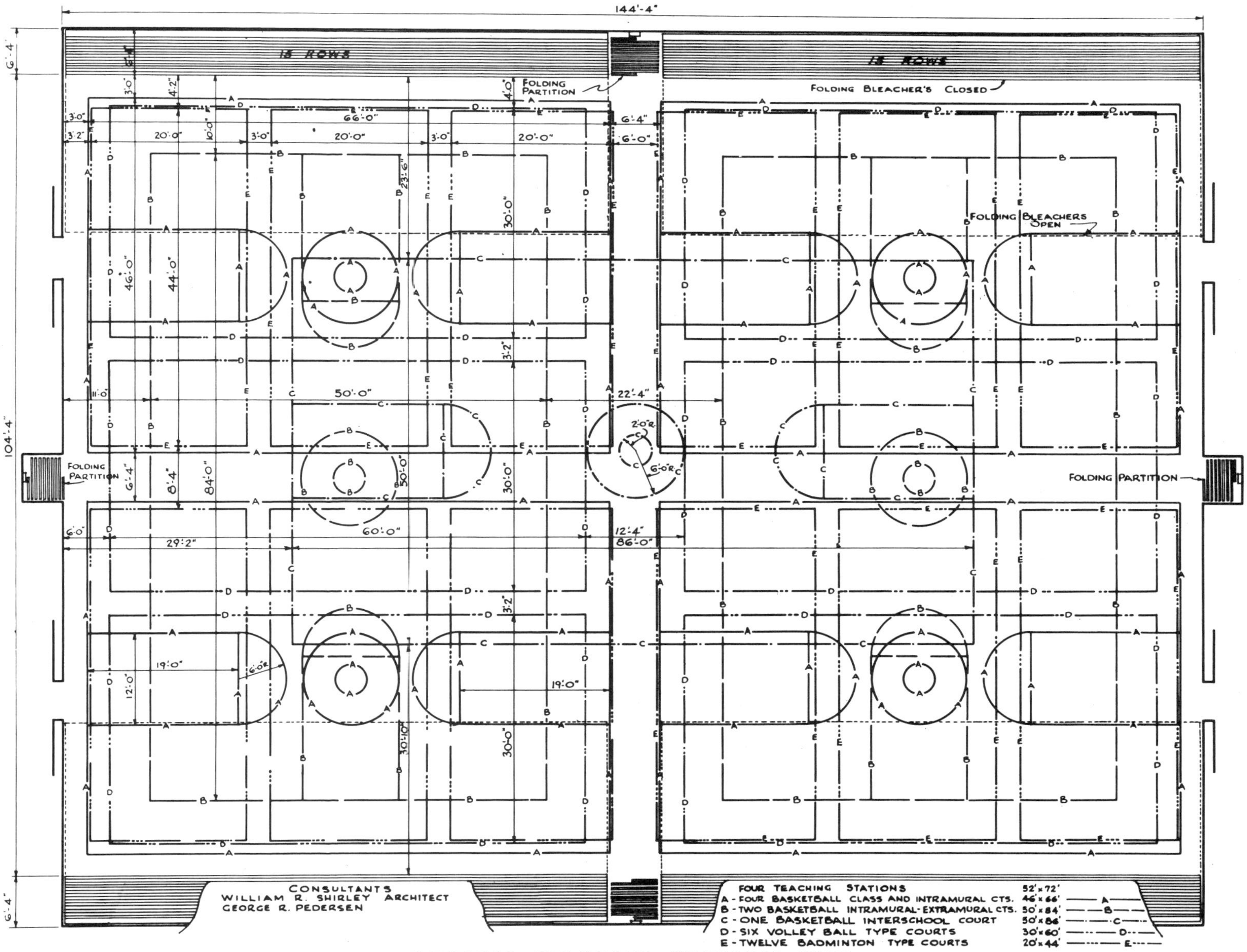

DESIGN VIII FOUR-STATION GYM

104'-4" x 144'-4" USABLE FLOOR SPACE

For example, a community, because of size and resources, may find it necessary to select Type II Plan as shown in Table 5-3. It will get 1 class station each for boys and girls; one regulation basketball court which will seat about 500 people for interschool games; two small intramural basketball courts; and two regulation volleyball and three regulation badminton type courts. Another community with more resources and a long range viewpoint may select Type VI. It will get twice as many stations and basketball courts; three times the number of volleyball type courts; four times the number of badminton type courts; enough player stations to make a real recreation center; and seats for about four times as many basketball spectators.

Type V is a two-station gym that can be expanded to Type VI by adding only 56 feet to the 80-foot dimension. This kind of expansibility is needed in growing communities which often have to add more wings to the building for classrooms. The roof trusses should span the 109-foot dimension rather than the 80-foot width.

OTHER TYPES OF CLASS STATIONS

The swimming pool should be next to the gym on the priority list. (See Chapter 12 for details.) The room for remedial exercises is often included for the estimated 10 per cent of the pupils who need such individualized attention. A suitable size is 36 by 52 feet with a minimum height of 12 feet. Although it is not a full station, it may

Photo by Joseph W. Molitor
Architect: Warren Ashley

Above: Art Room, West Springfield High School, West Springfield, Massachusetts.

Below: Homemaking room, Old Saybrook Junior-Senior High School, Saybrook, Connecticut.

Photo by Joseph W. Molitor
Architect: Warren Ashley

Photo by Joseph W. Molitor

Shop, South Berkshire Regional High School, South Berkshire, Massachusetts.

also be used for such activities as the dance. Some schools provide a room about 40′ x 70′ x 12′ which serves as a class station for activities that do not require a high ceiling.

Other Facilities Functional for Recreation

Facilities such as rooms for music, science, industrial arts, art, homemaking, and vocational education should be planned so that they are functional for use by adult groups and community center recreation programs. The same applies to the auditorium, cafeteria, shops, little theater, and multiple use rooms for meetings, community groups, adult education, and club activities.

The cafeteria should be a place for wholesome food in a relaxed social atmosphere for pupils and teachers. It should also serve for student and community group dinners. There should be provision in smaller rooms for snack bar "teen" center activities. Steam tables should be provided to transport hot food to the smaller rooms. The modern high school is generally open in the evenings for adult education courses that serve avocational as well as vocational interests and needs. The community high extends the program and serves youth, adults, and family groups in a wide range of activities.

The community high school makes the transition from the broad life experiences and activities of the modern elementary school-neighborhood center (outlined in Chapter 3) into the life of the community. Extensive and continuing programs of education from junior high school through adulthood leads youth into participation in many community affairs as responsible citizens. By this kind of education the improvement of community life and better citizenship in American democracy can be attained.

CHAPTER 6

THE GYMNASIUM

William R. Shirley

THE GYMNASIUM IS FIRST ON THE PRIORITY list for indoor physical education and recreation facilities. In a modern school that is also a neighborhood or community center the gymnasium is a multiple-use unit. It is used for physical education classes during the *formal school day*, for extra class group activities *after school*, and for the community center recreation program during the *evening hours*.

The gymnasium is a good investment for education for all the pupils and for community living. The cost is very low when calculated on the basis of the use per unit per participant. The heavy demand on the gymnasium for class, extra class, and recreation schedules indicates the need for a new emphasis in planning the gymnasium. Too often in the past plans have just met minimum standards for minimum physical education class requirements with little attention to after school and evening program needs. Planning for the gymnasium should emphasize the more desirable rather than the minimum. Planners have a responsibility to show people that each gymnasium presents problems in design, construction, and equipment that must be satisfactorily solved so as to be safely, efficiently, and economically operated, and should present their solutions in such a manner that the layman receives a complete and comprehensive picture of the finished gymnasium.

The gymnasium should be planned so that it is adequate and functional for:

The physical education classes for all the pupils.
The intramural program, which includes sports for all pupils.
The interschool contest for a great many high school pupils.
The special school events such as dances, demonstrations, exhibitions, socials, and meetings.
Special community events of similar types.

***Illustration:* Gymnasium, Roosevelt Park High School, Minnesota**
Photo by Oxley and Sons Studio

Chapter 4, The Elementary School-Neighborhood Center, includes information on program activities, the formula for class stations, and the arrangement of courts to be included in the gymnasium. Chapter 5 includes like details for the high school-community center. Each chapter contains tables and designs that show the arrangement of courts and class stations for the more desirable program of physical education and recreation. The duty of the planner is to design the gymnasium in order that all floor space is usable for the program. To cut a few feet from such a floor plan, which would eliminate a whole battery of courts, is not wise planning or good economy.

Gym Location and Exits

The extensive use of the gymnasium indicates that it should be located at grade level and where it is readily accessible to both pupil and community groups. It should be in a wing of the building nearest to the parking area so that spectators for special events do not have to go through other parts of the building. Because of the extensive use of the gymnasium it should be located so that it can be lighted, heated, and closed off from other parts of the building.

The gymnasium wing or section of the building should have a lobby type public entrance and an exit to the outdoor courts and fields. This exit may be from halls that have exits from the boys' and girls' dressing rooms and the gymnasium or from the gymnasium and dressing rooms directly to the outdoor areas. The gymnasium should have an emergency exit with walks and lights for access to street or parking area. The doors into the gymnasium from dressing rooms and halls should be located so that they are not under the main basketball goals or in the way of the seats when unfolded.

Combination of Gymnasium with Other Facilities

Sound economy can be achieved by the type of planning that fits the facility to the program rather than one that curtails the program to fit the facilities. Such planning provides opportunities for program improvement and prevents costly additions. Combination of the gymnasium with other facilities should be judged on the basis of:

- needs of school and community groups
- space requirements of the program, and
- best value for the facility dollar

Many combinations of other facilities with the gymnasium have been tried and special names such as gymatorium, cafetorium, and gymnateria have been used to popularize them. The gymnasium-auditorium has been the most common combination in the past particularly in the small schools. It has also been the biggest concern to the administrator and staff because:

- function and design are quite different
- heavy demands on the gym for class, intramural, interschool, and recreation schedules
- the increased demand for the auditorium for many other school and community programs, and
- the cost of time and labor to remove and replace seats.

Most of the above points apply to the combination of gymnasium and cafeteria. However, small schools have made some good use of the lunchroom for extra class activities and as a playroom by installing folding tables and seats. There are other combinations in the use of the cafeteria and the auditorium more practical than such use of the gymnasium. The demand for the cafeteria comes in the middle of the school day and for the auditorium at certain periods, but the gym schedule is continuous.

The development of larger school units, the enrichment of education, and the use of schools as community centers justifies the inclusion of recreation facilities in the education plant without the use of combinations that restrict programs.

More Usable Floor Space for the Gym Dollar

Getting more usable floor space for the gymnasium dollar is a goal which can be achieved by the administrators, the program staff members, and the planning specialists. Wise planning includes:

A study of school and community needs
A plan for programs to meet these needs
An outline of usable floor space needed as class stations and courts for the physical education and recreation programs
A design for the gym around the floor space selected for the program, and
A real effort to use new ideas, materials, and techniques to hold down cost without cutting the floor space needed.

Technological research and development has provided many new materials and construction techniques that have been used on many types of buildings including some school plants. The elimination of building ornamentation and frills has resulted in more beautiful structures. Modular construction and the use of prefabricated parts are used to build modern gymnasiums more efficiently.

Savings can be made in selecting a lower ceiling height for the gymnasium. It is better to cut the ceiling height than to curtail the usable floor space. Basketball literally raised the roof on the old low-ceiling basement gymnasium to the height in some gyms to 24 or more feet. Now basketball has taller and more skilled players who do not use the long high looping shots, making it possible to lower the ceiling to 20 feet and invest the saving in floor space for courts and class stations.

In such games as volleyball and badminton the more skillful players use lower shots. Therefore, similar savings can be made on gymnasium ceilings where these sports are played. For volleyball and badminton a ceiling height of 18 feet is suitable. The same height will serve also for the Junior High School and the girls' gymnasium. In many cases the arch type of roof construction provides extra height needed over the center of the courts and for equipment such as ropes and rings.

Glen Burne High School, Baltimore, Maryland.

Photo by Williams and Meyer, Chicago
Architects: Perkins and Will

Two full-size class stations. Notice that basketball backstop swings to one side to permit folding partition to be opened. Glenbrook High School, Glenview, Illinois.

GUIDE LINES FOR PLANNING AND CONSTRUCTION OF THE GYMNASIUM

General Consideration

1. It is axiomatic that program needs should serve as the basis for planning the gymnasium plant. Too often programs are adapted to a gymnasium in which the only planning involved was the determination of the size of the plant. To accomplish proper planning there must be extensive involvement of both lay and professional personnel. Future needs as well as current needs should receive consideration.

2. There is no doubt that the "Campus Type" school provides the best plan for the development of the physical education plant. This type permits isolation of the gymnasium from other school activities and affords greater control of the plant when it is used for after school activities or community programs. When the size of the site does not permit the development of the "Campus Type" school the gymnasium should be located in a separate wing of the school building. One of the classic errors in school construction occurred when the gymnasium was placed over the study hall. An order was finally passed on to the physical education staff to cease all running in the gymnasium.

3. Provision should be made for seating spectators for school and community athletic events. Until the introduction of the folding or roll-away type bleachers it was necessary to provide permanent stands or to build the gymnasium as a part of a combination auditorium-gymnasium. The roll-away bleachers are space savers. For example, bleachers that cover approximately 18 feet of floor space when extended fold up into a space of about 5 feet.

4. The practice of planning a gymnasium in combination with other school facilities such as the cafeteria or auditorium is never satisfactory. Invariably, conflict in scheduling results that affect other school programs.

Photo by Williams and Meyer, Chicago
Architects: Perkins and Will

Two-station gym, East Junior High School, Kankakee, Illinois.

Design and Construction of Gymnasiums

1. The most costly part of the gymnasium is the roof. This cost results from the tremendous span that requires that the roof be supported on braced columns as bearing walls are not usually of sufficient strength. The panel walls may be of solid masonry furred, a cavity type wall, stainless steel panels, insulated and serviceable interior, such as masonry, exposed light weight concrete units, terra cotta tile or other unit panel construction to give the required insulation and fire resistance, aluminum panels, enameled steel panels, precast "Tilt Up" concrete panels or one of several other types of construction.

The roof construction on braced columns may be made by the use of steel or wood bowstring trusses or by the following alternate construction:

(a) A rigid frame steel construction with intermediate steel purlins with the shape of the roof determined by required head rooms at center and walls.

(b) A rigid frame laminated wood construction if frames are not over 6 feet apart, 2 inch tongue and groove plank can be used and frames and plank left exposed and painted. Acoustical treatment can be applied directly to the plank. Rigid insulation should be applied over the plank under the roofing. If frames are more than 6 feet apart, intermediate purlins are required and can be left exposed or furred. If furred, bat insulation can be used above the finshed ceiling.

(c) A new type of heavy corrugated steel panel arch construction has been developed that seems to offer a very economical method for long span roof. This system does not require built-up roofing over it. The ceiling can be finished with "sprayed on" insulating and acoustical plaster. Since this system is new, it would require the service of a structural engineer to adapt it to any particular building requirement.

2. A wood finish floor is preferable for the

gymnasium and the best form of construction is as follows:

A 6 inch porous fill on the ground over which is placed a 5 inch depth of concrete (1:2:3½ mix). A one-half inch premoulded joint filler should be provided at exterior walls only separating porous fill and concrete from the wall. In the space above the concrete slab 2 x 3 inch beveled creosoted wood sleepers spaced 16 inches apart and set with Bulldog clips should be placed. Place 1 inch by 4 inch square edge North Carolina pine or equivalent, set 3⁄16 of an inch apart at right angles to sleepers and over this provide 23⁄32 of an inch tongue and groove maple, first grade. The flooring should run lengthwise on the main basketball court.

3. Before the finish can be applied to the gymnasium floor it must be sanded smooth with the final sanding being made with 3/0 or Fine sandpaper. After the final sanding the sawdust should be removed by sweeping, followed by dry mopping with a cloth or towel slightly dampened with turpentine. One or two prime coats should be applied followed by rubbing with fine steel wool. The residue should be removed by sweeping and dry mopping. The first coat of gymnasium finish is then applied. After this coat has dried the court and game lines should be laid down using a high grade glossy enamel. Two final coats of finish should then be applied, steel wooling lightly between coats. The reason for painting lines on the first coat of finish is to prevent paint from penetrating the wood. It also facilitates the removal of lines either by light sanding or by use of varnish remover.

Once the finish is down, proper maintenance is essential. It should not be necessary to resand and refinish the floor for a 10 year period. It is well to clean the floor thoroughly and add a coat of finish each year or two. Instructions for maintenance provided by the suppliers of the floor finish should be followed explicitly.

4. Steam or hot water heating with heating coils, filters and fans should be installed adjacent to the gymnasium preferably in the space above the teacher's office. Duct work should be installed between roof framing with down flow spread over gymnasium area. Supplementary fin radiation should be placed on exposed walls at a distance of 6 feet above the top row of bleachers. This supplementary heating will keep the gymnasium above freezing during week-ends and holidays when the space is not in use. The fresh air system should include fresh air intake and exhaust controls, including automatic dampers.

5. A master switch control should be provided for the electrical circuits of the gymnasium so that circuits not wanted at a particular time can be shut off. Incandescent low or high bay units, with guards, mounted on swivel stems and hung so that they are level with the bottom of the chord of the roof truss should be provided. If the ceiling is furred flush the use of multiple unit is recommended so that the level of lighting intensity can be varied for different functions. Complementary convenience outlets should be spaced around the wall to take care of special lighting effects for special functions. A sound amplifier system should be provided which is under control of the main sound track in the administrative area. A multiplicity of speakers should be set flush in the ceiling so that sound will come down from overhead and operate the speakers at a low level of impact. Microphone outlets should be arranged for the primary functions for which the gymnasium is to be used. Program and fire alarm bells should be mounted in each quadrant of the gym. Clocks should be mounted in each section of the gymnasium. A scoreboard should be mounted in such a manner that a majority of the spectators seated on bleachers can see it, preferably placed in a corner at a forty-five degree angle to the long wall in one of the corners.

6. If spectator seating is provided, one or two of the walls will probably accommodate the bleachers, and consequently do not need more than a smooth concrete or brick finish. The other walls should contain 10 to 12 feet of glazed brick or ceramic tile of sufficient strength to permit a ball to be thrown against it. This preparation will permit handball to be played on the wall.

7. Cupped eyes should be spaced 12 to 16

feet apart on the wall 10 to 12 feet above the floor. Eye bolts should be included to accommodate volleyball and badminton nets.

8. There should be direct access from the gymnasium to the outdoor play fields. If the gymnasium is divided by a folding partition, provision should be made for an exit on both the boys' and girls' sides.

9. There is seldom adequate space provided for storage. There are three types of storage space that must be provided. These are: storage of apparatus and gymnasium equipment such as mats, standard gymnastic equipment, and other supplies; storage of daily use material and supplies such as balls, rackets, fencing equipment, and nets; and dead storage space for uniforms and other athletic supplies. There should be three separate storage areas for the above items just for the boys and at least two such storage spaces for the girls. In addition a separate space should be provided for storage of outdoor athletic equipment such as jumping standards, hurdles, football and baseball gear. The latter space should be attached to the gymnasium or locker room, preferably with a door leading into the building as well as to the exterior. Some schools have incorporated storage space in a field house type of dressing building, which is a separate building usually located adjacent to the football field. See the chapter on Service Facilities for further details on this building.

10. Considerable expensive space is often wasted by constructing ceilings in gymnasiums that are too high. Although a 22 foot ceiling is usually recommended for boys, a 20-foot ceiling is adequate. For girls, a ceiling 20 feet high is sufficient for all types of games and activities.

11. The illumination in the gymnasium should yield a minimum reading of 20 foot candles of illumination. Controls should be included to permit lights to be dimmed during dances and other types of social events. Diffused light provides a better source of non-glare illumination. Light fixtures should be readily accessible for cleaning and repair.

Open steel beam roof construction with closed panel above folding partition. Note that main basketball court is set off from center to permit passage of folding door. High School, Barrington, Illinois.

12. Lines for the different courts should be shown in distinctive colors on the gymnasium floor. Plastic or synthetic tapes can be used or the lines may be painted before the final coat of floor finish is applied.

13. Windows should be avoided at the end of the main basketball court since the incoming light, whether the sun shines directly in or not, makes it difficult to see the basket. In the event that glass is desired in these locations it should be of the tinted variety.

14. The best orientation for the gymnasium with respect to the sun is to have the main basketball court run north and south.

15. The gymnasium is considered a noisy area. Hence, the ceiling should have acoustical treatment and when possible it is well to have some treatment of the walls. There are several materials that give satisfactory results.

16. The heat should be thermostatically controlled. The most desirable temperature for the gymnasium is 60 to 65 degrees. Drafts should be avoided particularly in the spectator section. Competent heating and ventilation engineers should be called in to advise on proper equipment and installation.

17. When gymnasium walls are made of concrete or cinder block, they should be painted up to a height of 10 feet with cement enamel or some other washable paint.

18. Drinking fountains should not be located in the gymnasium. Fountains are best located in locker rooms, foyers, or corridors.

19. At least one fixed tackboard should be located in the gymnasium and also a chalkboard for instructional purposes.

20. The gymnasium need not have a drab appearance. Light pastel colors on the walls and ceiling adds not only to the appearance of the gymnasium but aids the general illumination of the gym area. Red bricks should not be used on the walls when light yellow and beige bricks are available.

21. The installation of floor plates in the gymnasium floor for various types of apparatus should be kept to a minimum. When it becomes necessary to install a horizontal bar in the gymnasium the floor plates should be anchored into the concrete sub-floor in order to provide maximum support.

22. The instructor's office should open directly into the gymnasium.

23. The foyer to the gymnasium is essential when the gym is to be used by spectators at athletic events. A coat room, toilets and ticket booths are desirable facilities to be included in the foyer area. The floor in the foyer should be made of terrazzo.

24. The minimum seating capacity should be two thirds of the student enrolment. Therefore, a school of 1800 pupils should have a minimum of 1200 seats for athletic events.

25. Ten feet should be provided between the end lines in a basketball court and the nearest wall. On the side lines a minimum of 6 feet should be allowed between the first row of bleacher seats and the basketball court.

26. The installation of permanent fixtures, such as basketball backstops, climbing ropes, and floor plates for apparatus should be part of the general contract.

27. Condensation sometimes presents a problem in field house type gymnasiums or in situations where skylights are used. Proper construction including ventilation and insulation of roofs will aid in controlling condensation.

28. The top of floor saddles between gymnasiums and storage rooms should be on a level plane with the top of adjacent finish floors. Raised saddles should be eliminated since they present the problems of transporting heavy apparatus such as parallel bars, horses, and trampolines between the gymnasium and the storage rooms.

29. In general the swing-up type of basketball backstop is the most desirable. In elementary school gymnasiums the side backstop should be of the adjustable type to yield the desired height for young children. See Chapter 24 for details.

30. The use of mat trucks as opposed to mat hangers on the wall has proven to be best.

31. When a folding partition is used to divide the gymnasium into two classroom stations it should be motor driven, suspended from the ceiling. In dome or peaked shaped roofs provision must be made to extend the divider above the horizontal line.

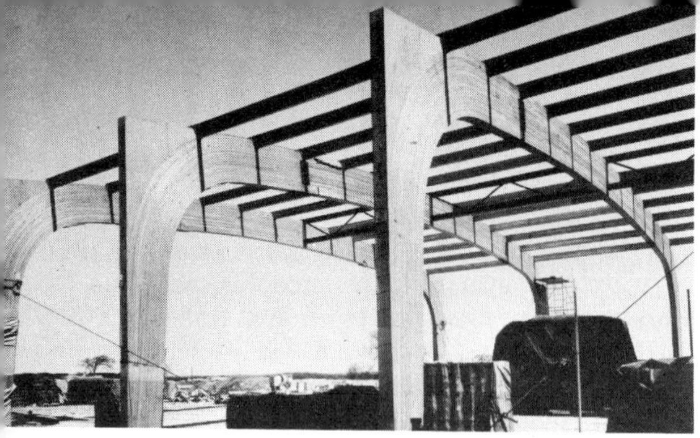

Architect: Ronald S. Senseman

Shenandoah Valley Academy, New Market, Virginia. Span 72 feet.

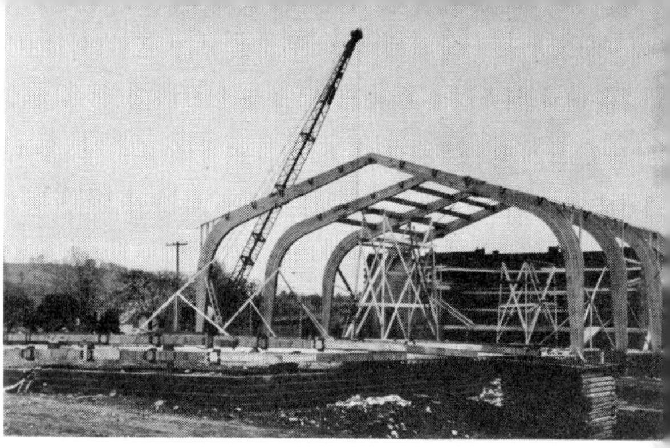

Architects: Grasshold-Johnson & Associat

Brookfield Union Free High School, Wisconsin. Span 100 feet.

Architects: Haarstick Lungten and Associates

High School, Maynard, Minnesota. Span 84 feet.

Architect: Byran Hale Kauf

High School, Bennett, Colorado. Span 74 feet.

Architects: Rowlett, Scott and Associates

Junior High School, Laredo, Texas. Span 72 feet.

Architects: Smith and Voor

High School, Eagle Grove, Iowa. Span 87 feet.

Wood laminated trusses help reduce cost of gymnasium and fieldhouse construction.

American Institute of Steel Construction, Inc.

American Institute of Steel Construction, Inc.

Fieldhouse, Boystown, Nebraska.

High School Gymnasium, Muscatine, Iowa.

Steel truss construction for fieldhouses or gymnasiums.

INFORMATION TO SUPPLY THE ARCHITECT

1. *Number of classroom and group stations required.* This information should also indicate the size gymnasium needed and whether one or two gymnasiums will be required and the nature of the other teaching stations needed, such as swimming pool, special exercise rooms, and so forth.
2. *Location.* The gymnasium should be located with regard to the site and balance of the school or recreation plant.
3. *Size.* Dimensions of all areas such as locker rooms, showers, and gymnasiums.
4. *Height* of gymnasium ceiling and other teaching or service areas in the building.
5. *Material* for floor covering.
6. *Wall* material.
7. *Acoustical* treatment desired.
8. *Lighting requirements.* Actual foot candles of illumination desired at eye level.
9. *Heating* and *ventilation* requirements.
10. *Location* and *size* of *storage space* required.
11. *Office space* and location.
12. *Spectator requirements* and type of seats. Roll-away or fixed type bleachers including number and size.
13. *Apparatus.* Floor, wall, and ceiling fixtures or mountings to accommodate different types of apparatus.

Fieldhouse, Ohio State University.

Photo by Chas. R. Pearson

Above: South Central Junior-Senior High School, Seattle, Washington.

Fieldhouse type of gymnasium is economical and provides greater playing area.

Below: Gymnasium, Palm Springs, California.

Photo by Gayle's Studio

14. *Lobby* or *foyer* size requirements of gym with list of accompanying facilities.

15. *Type and location of basketball* backstops to be used. Swing-up, roll-away or fixed.

16. *Bulletin boards* location and number.

17. Type of *folding partition* if one is recommended.

18. *Wainscot* and *cupped eye* locations in wall.

19. Type of *floor finish*.

20. Location and type of *court markings* desired on floor.

21. Any special *electrical fixtures*, such as special wiring for public address system or television.

22. Location of *exit doors* both within building and those leading to outdoor play fields.

23. *Number of students* to use the gym at peak-load and average daily load.

24. *Whether community* use is to be made of the facilities and any special dressing facilities needed for adult use.

25. *Color* of walls and ceiling.

26. Location of *electrical outlets*.

27. Location and number of *drinking fountains*.

The more detailed the data supplied the architect the better. Inevitably there will have to be compromises; however, they should not occur at the initial stage of the preparation of the requirements and specifications.

FIELD HOUSE TYPE GYMNASIUM

The field house is primarily a development of colleges that require large areas for indoor sports. In recent years high schools have begun to incorporate the field house idea into gymnasium planning. There are numerous advantages to this type of construction that make it desirable for high schools. Among these are simple construction, larger floor area for equivalent money, greater seating capacity for spectators, and a higher ceiling. Where gymnasiums are added to existing school plants it is particularly desirable to consider this type of design.

AUXILIARY GYMNASIUM

The auxiliary gymnasium, sometimes called the special exercise room, multipurpose room, or remedial exercise room, is a desirable addition to the physical education and recreation plant. The ceiling does not need to be more than 16 feet high, and in some instances it may be lower. The auxiliary gymnasium provides one additional teaching station, or two if the room is long enough for a folding partition.

CHAPTER 7

THE SERVICE AREAS

Gerald J. Hase

THE SERVICE AREAS ARE THOSE SPACES OR rooms which are intended primarily for the health, safety, comfort, and convenience of the participants in the school physical education program and the school and community recreation program. These include dressing rooms, showering rooms, team rooms, toweling areas, storage rooms, laundry facilities, equipment drying rooms, toilet facilities, and personnel offices.

The number and size of these areas will depend on the type, grade level, and size of the schools, as well as the school-community recreation needs. A checklist for planning service facilities appears on page 106. This list should be used by local school and community officials in planning functional facilities.

DRESSING ROOMS

The dressing rooms should be provided in all schools that house pupils in grades 3 to 12. These rooms should provide enough storage lockers so that each pupil will have one in which to store his physical education clothing and enough dressing lockers for each pupil to have one during the peak-load period of the extraclass program. These rooms should be directly accessible to the shower rooms, indoor teaching stations, and the outdoor teaching areas. It should be possible for pupils to pass directly to the gymnasium from the dressing room and vice versa without going into the corridors of the school. It is desirable for pupils to be able to pass directly between dressing rooms and outdoor teaching areas without going through the gymnasium or using the corridors. Also, it should be possible to enter the dressing rooms from the corridor without passing through the gymnasium.

Floors should be constructed of an impervious material such as ceramic or quarry tile and should be abrasive and non-slip. They should be properly sloped toward the floor drains which should be adequate in number so that waste water is properly taken away.

Illustration: Corner of a football locker room

Walls should be resistant to moisture and should be smooth so that they can be cleaned easily.

Ceilings should be acoustically treated and resistant to moisture. The arrangement of the lockers should be taken into consideration when planning the proper placement of moisture-proof light fixtures.

Benches should have rounded edges and be secured to the floor. The space relationship between locker and bench, and bench to bench, should be carefully planned so that there is adequate traffic control and dressing comfort.

Mirrors should be installed in the dressing rooms. The location, number, and size will be determined by the arrangement of the lockers and the availability of the wall space.

Sufficient number of hair dryers are recommended for the girls' dressing rooms and all dressing rooms in schools that have swimming pools.

Elementary School Dressing Rooms

Since dressing and showering are recognized as being integral parts of the health and physical education programs, it is necessary that pupils in the elementary schools have an opportunity to dress and shower during the physical education class and extraclass program.

Also, it is necessary for pupils to be properly dressed in order to participate safely in many of the activities in the physical education program.

Eight to twelve-year-old pupils are ready for showering and should not be denied the opportunity of establishing this desirable health practice. With these youngsters, it is not a problem of getting them "into the shower" but it is a problem of getting them "out of the shower."

Because the health and safety of youngsters has been one of the prime concerns of the schools, many programs of physical education are having their pupils dress and shower at grade three or four. In the schools where dressing and showering are initiated in these grades, there are usually fewer problems with this phase of the program at the junior and senior high school grades than in schools where dressing and showering are started in the junior high school.

Lockers are needed for all of the pupils who will use the dressing rooms. Storage lockers are used for the physical education uniform and dressing lockers for the street clothing. The number of storage lockers should be equal to the total number of pupils in a school that use the lockers plus ten per cent to allow for expansion. The number of dressing lockers should be equal to the peak-load at any one period of time plus ten per cent to allow for variation in class size, scheduling, and the extraclass program.

In order to ascertain the area needed for the dressing room, it is necessary to know the following facts: (1) Total number of different pupils that will be using the locker room; (2) number of storage lockers in each unit of battery arrangement; (3) peak-load of pupils using the dressing room at one time. Use the following formula to find the correct area:

First, it is necessary to determine the number of locker units needed.

$$1.\ \text{No. of locker units needed} = \frac{\text{No. of pupils using the locker room} + \text{10\% of No. of pupils using the locker room}}{\text{No. of storage lockers in each unit}^{1}}$$

When this number has been determined, the area needed for the dressing room is figured by using a second formula.

$$2.\ \text{Area needed for dressing room} = \text{Area required}^{1}\text{ for each unit} \times \text{No. of locker units needed} + \text{Peak load of pupils using dressing room at one time} \times 14\text{ sq. ft.}$$

[1] This number will vary, depending on the size and number of storage and dressing lockers.

STORAGE-DRESSING LOCKER ARRANGEMENTS
FOR ELEMENTARY SCHOOLS

Size of Lockers and Battery Arrangement	*Arrangement of Lockers*	*Area Required for Each Unit Including 4″ for Ventilation*
1. 1 dressing (12″ x 12″ x 48″) 6 storage (9″ x 12″ x 24″)		3.79 sq. ft./unit
2. 1 dressing (12″ x 12″ x 48″) 8 storage (9″ x 12″ x 24″)	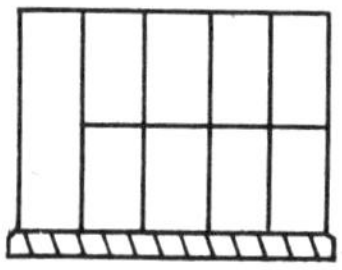	4.67 sq. ft./unit
3. 1 dressing (12″ x 12″ x 48″) 8 storage (12″ x 12″ x 12″)		3.45 sq. ft./unit

STORAGE-DRESSING LOCKER ARRANGEMENTS
FOR SECONDARY SCHOOLS

Size of Lockers and Battery Arrangement	*Arrangement of Lockers*	*Area Required for Each Unit Including 4″ for Ventilation*
1. 1 dressing (12″ x 12″ x 72″) 6 storage (9″ x 12″ x 24″)	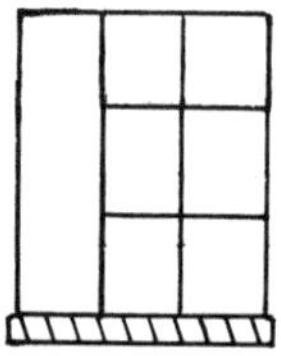	2.88 sq. ft./unit
2. 1 dressing (12″ x 12″ x 60″) 6 storage (9″ x 12″ x 20″)		2.88 sq. ft./unit

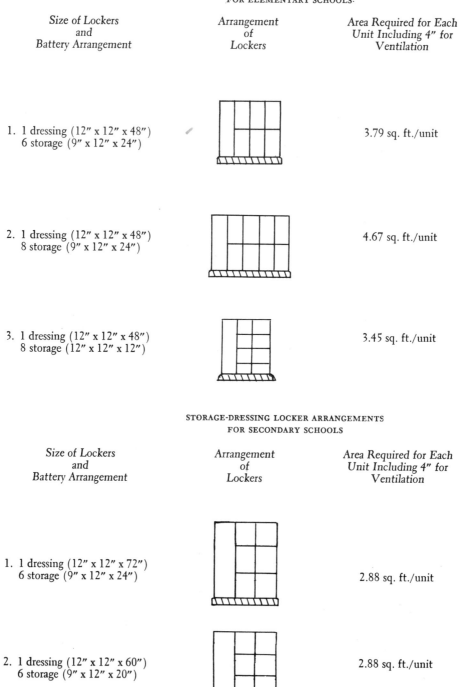

Illustration: An elementary school is being planned for 680 pupils of which approximately 400 pupils will be in grades 3 to 6. Since the pupils in grades 3 to 6 will be the ones dressing and showering during the physical education program and assuming that approximately one-half of these pupils are boys and one-half are girls, the two dressing rooms should be planned for *200* pupils each. The peak-load of pupils using *one* of the dressing rooms at one time will be during the extraclass program when there will be approximately 40 pupils. The number of locker units needed for each dressing room can be determined by using the first formula as follows:

$$\text{Number of locker units needed} = \frac{200 + 20}{8} = \frac{220}{8} = 27 + \text{ or } 28$$

The area needed for the dressing room can be figured by using the second formula as follows:

$$\text{Area needed for dressing room} = 3.45 \times 28 + (40 \times 14) = 656.6 \text{ or } 657 \text{ sq. ft.}$$

If this elementary school has lockers in a battery arrangement of one dressing locker (12 by 12 by 48 inches) and eight storage lockers (12 by 12 by 12 inches), it will need 657 square feet for the dressing room exclusive of shower room area. If the same school selected lockers in a battery arrangement of one dressing locker (12 by 12 by 48 inches) and eight storage lockers (9 by 12 by 24 inches), it would need 691 square feet for the dressing room exclusive of shower room area. It may also be necessary to allow for additional space if the school is used as a neighborhood recreation center for indoor recreational activities.

Secondary School Dressing Rooms

Everything that has been stated concerning dressing rooms for the elementary school should be repeated for these rooms in the secondary school.

In order to ascertain the area needed for the dressing room in the secondary school, the same two formulas should be used that were used for determining this area in the elementary school.

Illustration: A secondary school is being planned for 600 pupils in grades 7 to 12. Assuming that approximately one-half of these pupils are boys and one-half are girls, there should be two dressing rooms planned for 300 pupils each. The peak-load of pupils using *one* of these dressing rooms at one time will be during the intramural and interscholastic activities when there will be approximately 100 pupils. The number of locker units needed for each dressing room

Athletic trainer's room (half of total area shown). Clifton High School Field House.

can be figured by using the first formula as follows:

$$\text{Number of locker units needed} = \frac{300 + 30}{6} = 55$$

The area needed for the dressing room can be figured by using the second formula as follows:

$$\begin{aligned}\text{Area needed for dressing room} &= 2.88 \times 55 + 100 \times 14\\ &= 158.40 + 1400\\ &= 1558.4 \text{ or } 1558 \text{ sq. ft.}\end{aligned}$$

If this secondary school needs to have lockers in a battery arrangement of one dressing (12 x 12 x 72 inches) and six storage lockers (9 x 12 x 24 inches), it will need 1558 square feet of area for the dressing room exclusive of shower room area. It may also be necessary to allow for additional space if this school is used as a secondary school-community center for indoor recreational activities.

Shower Rooms

Since there is usually a limited amount of time for dressing and showering during the physical education class period, it is important that there be enough shower heads so that every youngster has sufficient time to take a shower. These shower heads should be shoulder height so that it will be easier for the pupils to keep their hair dry if they desire.

The showering room should be accessible to both the toweling room and the dressing room. When the showering room is designed to serve a swimming pool, this room should be located so that the pupils must pass through the showers before entering the pool.

The showers for boys should be of the group type, while for girls, they should be mostly of the group type with a few individual shower stalls.

The size of shower rooms is based upon the types of showers and the number of shower heads. There should be a shower head for every four users during the peak-load period and shower heads should be installed at least 4 feet apart.

Floors should be non-slip and constructed of impervious material such as ceramic or quarry tile. There should be sanitary means of drainage with drainage gutters or a slope to the floor leading to a recess covered by a removable nonferrous metal grating.

Walls should be resistant to moisture and smooth so they can be easily cleaned. Such materials as ceramic or glazed tile and marble are excellent.

Ceilings should be moisture resistant. Such materials as tile or portland cement plaster have been used satisfactorily.

Toweling Room

The body-drying area is an essential adjunct to the shower room and should have approximately the same total floor area. It should be designed so that the pupils showering must pass from the shower room into the body-drying area before entering the dressing room proper from the shower. It should be large enough to take care of as many pupils as will be showering at one time. Sufficient hooks for hanging up of towels should be provided on the walls of the body-drying area. A hamper or a receptacle for used towels should be near the opening between the body-drying area and the dressing room.

Many schools are using a dwarf type wall from 4 to 6 feet high between the drying room and the dressing room. The opening between the toweling room and the dressing room should be wide enough to permit pupils to pass each other. The opening between the toweling room and the shower room should be the same width and should have a sill approximately six inches high to prevent water on the floor of the shower room from running into the toweling room. Adequate drains should be located in the toweling room so that water dripping from the body will be carried away.

Team Room

In the senior high school, a separate home-team dressing room should be provided for boys on the interscholastic squads. These rooms should be designed so that the showers of the dressing-shower rooms are directly accessible. Large size full length lockers are usually put in home-team dressing rooms.

Use of the team room by the home teams permits visiting teams to use the regular dressing and showering rooms for boys and keeps the visiting teams from using the facilities for girls.

Drying Room for Equipment

The equipment drying room should be located in close proximity to the team room and should be of sufficient size to take care of the peak-load of equipment to be dried at any one time. Sufficient air at high temperature should be circulated to insure proper drying of the equipment.

Storage Rooms

Towel Storage Room. Towel service is desirable and is found in an increasing number of schools. A towel room or cubicle with a window opening into the toweling room should be provided. A soiled towel storage is needed adjacent to the exit from the toweling room to the dressing room.

Current Supply Room. A supply room of approximately 250 square feet is needed for storage of physical education equipment that is issued daily. It should be adjacent to the dressing room and should have lockable checkout windows to serve both inside and outside facility users.

Off-Season Storage and Repair Room. This room should have sufficient space for the storage of all out-of-season, new, and extra equipment and supplies. There should be an appropriate number of cabinets, shelves, and hangers so that all materials are properly stored. There should be a portion of this room set aside for a repair unit including a workbench. This room should be separated from the current supply room with a solid partition and a door.

Gymnasium-Equipment Storage Room. This room should be on the same level as the gymnasium and directly accessible to it. There should be one storage room of approximately 300 square feet for each teaching station. The door opening should be at least 6 feet wide and with a flush threshold.

Outdoor Equipment Storage. Provision should be made for equipment that is used out-of-doors. Where there is no outside storage, such storage should be located within the building and readily accessible to the outdoor playing areas.

Laundry Room

Sometimes the physical education laundry can be serviced in the general school laundry. However, if special laundry facilities are installed, it is necessary that they meet the local public health regulations. This special unit should be of sufficient size to accommodate the equipment and personnel needed for the service and should be located close to the area it serves.

Toilets

Toilets should be located in the dressing rooms and not in the body-drying areas. Two waterclosets and one lavatory in the girls' dressing room is sufficient equipment for classes of 40 pupils. In the boys' dressing room, there should be one watercloset, one urinal, and one lavatory. These facilities should be directly accessible to the outdoor activity areas. Toilets for public use should be conveniently available to the foyer, auditorium, gymnasium, and outside facilities.

Physical Education and Recreation Offices

There should be separate offices for men and women staff members. Where individual offices are provided, there should be 100 to 130 square feet of space and when group offices are provided, there should be 70 to 90 square feet of space for each staff member. In large schools, it may be desirable to plan group offices for the several staff members with a separate office for the chairman or department head.

Each office or group office should contain a desk, files for records, and limited cabinet space for the storage of some equipment such as basketballs, footballs, baseballs, and volleyballs.

Opening off these offices, there should be a combination dressing, shower, and toilet room. This room should be adequately lighted, heated, and ventilated. It is desirable to locate these offices adjacent to the teaching stations and the dressing rooms and to provide a means of entrance into each of these rooms. Vision panels between the offices and the dressing-shower rooms and, also between the offices and the indoor teaching stations are recommended as desirable means of providing additional safety and supervision of groups using these facilities during a period of time when the person in charge of the group is called to the office.

Storage area in a high school gymnasium.

CHECK LIST FOR PLANNING SERVICE FACILITIES

1. Is the locker room properly located with direct access to the playing floor, pool and outdoor facilities?
2. Does the size of the dressing area provide a minimum of 10 or up to the desirable 15 square feet per person at the peak load?
3. Are the lockers placed on a pedestal with a coved base?
4. Is there a system for providing forced ventilation of lockers for drying purposes?
5. Is the floor covering of non-slip impervious material? If concrete, has the surface been sealed?
6. Are there adequate floor drains in the locker room and is the floor pitched towards the drains?
7. Have mirrors been provided?
8. Is there a storage locker, basket or bag for every person scheduled to use the facilities on a regular basis? Have enough dressing lockers been provided for peak load plus 10 per cent?
9. Is there a separate toweling (drying) area adjacent to the shower room for people to dry themselves in order to keep the locker room floor dry?
10. Has at least one drinking fountain been provided in the locker rooms?
11. Has the ceiling been acoustically treated?
12. Does the illumination provide a minimum of 15 footcandle power?
13. Are all light fixtures moistureproof?
14. Have all wall fixtures been eliminated to avoid possible electric shock as a result of wet feet and a faulty fixture?
15. Has radiant floor heating been considered?
16. Are all windows operable and of translucent glass?
17. Are all doors made of aluminum or some other non-corrosive material?
18. Are the walls finished with smooth, waterproof, washable material such as tile, glazed brick or cement enamel?
19. Are all benches properly secured to the floor?
20. Are there sufficient toilet and washing facilities to accommodate peak loads?
21. Does the locker room provide for efficient traffic control?
22. Have shower heads been lowered on the girls' side to help prevent the hair from getting wet?
23. Is the ceiling a minimum 9 feet?
24. Have all local and state health laws and regulations been adhered to?
25. Is the temperature of the locker room thermostatically controlled?
26. Does the instructor have direct access to the locker room and gymnasium from his office?
27. Has storage space been provided for cleaning supplies and equipment?
28. Can the temperature of the hot water be controlled from a central point?
29. Have soap dispensers been provided?
30. Are there hot water hose connections in the locker room to permit proper cleaning of the floor?
31. Has adequate dressing provision been made for interscholastic athletic teams, both home and visiting teams?

32. If facilities are to be used by the citizens of the community have provisions been made for dressing and storage of special equipment?
33. Are hair dryers recessed in the wall to avoid possible danger as a safety hazard?
34. Are there shelves on the wall below mirrors and above washbasins?
35. Is there a bulletin board in the locker room?
36. Is there a towel issue room?
37. Have laundry facilities been provided if program calls for such equipment?
38. Are pipes so placed as to be easily accessible for repairs?
39. Are towel racks in the toweling area?
40. Has provision been made for drying athletic uniforms?
41. Is there a room for storage of all out-of-season equipment and supplies?
42. Is there a non-shatterable vision panel between the offices and the dressing-shower rooms?
43. Is there a non-shatterable vision panel between the offices and the indoor teaching stations?

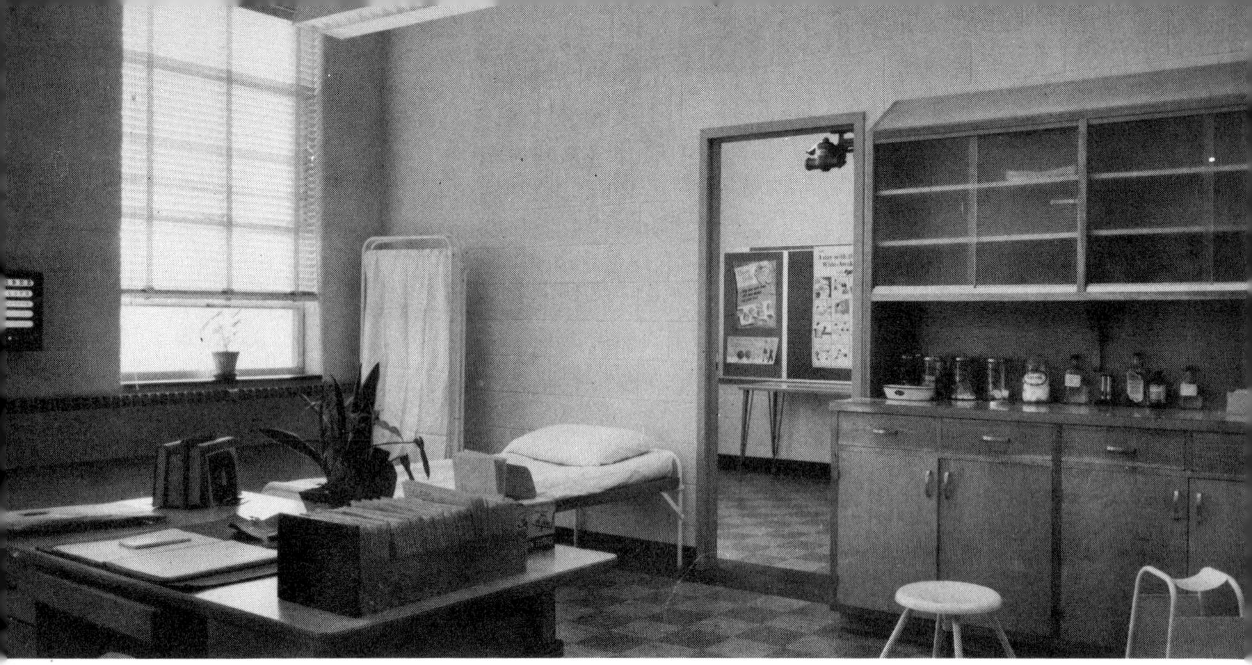

CHAPTER 8

SCHOOL HEALTH FACILITIES

H. Frederick Kilander

THERE IS A GROWING RECOGNITION OF THE IMportance of the school health program by educators, school administrators, parents, and the community in general. The scope of the school health program has been evolving and today is considered by health authorities to comprise three major areas: *The School Health Services*, a *Healthful School Environment*, and *Health Education*. These three areas have been defined[1] as follows:

School health services are procedures established to (1) appraise the health status of pupils and school personnel; (2) counsel pupils, teachers, parents, and other persons involved concerning appraisal findings; (3) encourage the correction of remediable defects; (4) help plan for the health care and education of handicapped children; (5) help prevent and control disease, and (6) provide emergency care for the sick or injured.

Healthful school living means the provision of a safe and healthful environment, the organizaion of a healthful school day, and the establishment of inter-personal relationships favorable to emotional, social, and physical health.

School health education is the process of providing learning experiences for the purpose of influencing knowledge, attitudes, or conduct relating to individual, community, or world health.

Specific evidence of growth in school health service programs is indicated in a national survey, made in 1950, of cities with a population of 2,500 and more.[2] School health services were reported in 91 per cent of these cities with such services comprising

[1] Report of the Committee on Terminology in School Health Education. *Journal of the American Association for Health, Physical Education, and Recreation*. 22: No. 7. September 1951.

Illustration: Health Suite at West Park Elementary School, Newark, Delaware

Courtesy of *American School and University*. Photo by Alfred A. DeLardi, Philadelphia, Pa.

[2] H. F. Kilander, *Health Services in City Schools*. Office of Education Bulletin 1952, No. 20. (Washington, D.C.: U. S. Government Printing Office, 1952.) 68 pp.

at least a medical examination and a dental examination or inspection.

The administrative authority for the school health program, reported by 2,886 city school systems, was as follows: Board of Education, 60 per cent; Board of Health, 11 per cent; jointly by Boards of Education and Health, 23 per cent; by other authorities, 6 per cent. The administration of the school health program is ordinarily performed by the group which finances it.

The study showed that professional school health personnel were available in the following percentages of city school systems: physicians, 63 per cent; nurses, 85 per cent; dentists, 40 per cent; dental hygienists, 16 per cent; other personnel, 12 per cent; nonprofessional, 9 per cent.

Of the various school health personnel involved, it is the nurse who is likely to be present most often. The trend is to supply a full-time nursing service in school buildings that have 1000 or more pupils. In small schools, a nurse will probably spend one-half a day of her time per week for each 125 to 150 children.

An increasing number of secondary schools include health instruction courses in the curriculum. Many of the states require that such instruction be given on both the junior and the senior high school levels as well as on the elementary level. In the secondary schools, the courses in health instruction are increasingly being given the same recognition as other subject areas in the matter of teacher qualifications, textbooks, and teaching facilities. Certain teaching procedures make it desirable that special consideration be given to the planning of the classroom for health teaching in the same way that attention is given to the planning of facilities for the teaching of biology, shop, music, and other subjects.

The remainder of this chapter offers suggestions for the planning of the facilities for the school health service unit and for the classroom for health teaching.

HEALTH SERVICE FACILITIES

The health service unit should be planned with very definite purposes in mind. These purposes may vary for various schools according to needs and resources in the community, as well as according to whether the school is small or large, urban or rural, elementary or secondary. It should also be kept in mind that the health service unit is not a treatment center and should not be so designed.

The criteria that should be used in planning a health service unit include such elements as a healthy and safe environment, utility, economy, flexibility, expansibility, and attractiveness. Because of these, and other factors, the health service room or suite should be planned and equipped with unusual care.

Purposes and Functions of Health Service Unit

1. *As an emergency center for the care of sick or injured children.* The health room first of all serves as an emergency center for the administration of first aid to school children and to school personnel. Included is the proper care of accident victims until they can be placed in the care of their parents or guardian, or returned to their classroom.

An additional emergency purpose is the care of children who have become ill during the school day until they can be returned to their classroom, or until they are moved from school.

The health room also serves as an emergency center where children with suspected communicable diseases can be cared for and can be separated from other pupils until their parents take over the case.

2. *As a place to rest* for pupils who on the advice of their family physician require a rest period at school during the school day.

3. *As a place for supplies.* The health room serves as a center where first aid and other supplies and equipment may be stored and kept in readiness at all times for use in emergency situations and for use in rendering other health services to the school children.

4. *As a place for the health records.* A central place is needed where the health records of the pupils and other information necessary to the administration of the school health service program are filed for ready

use as needed. The records include the accident and illness reports and a complete card index file for each pupil of information necessary for notifying parents or guardians in case of any type of emergency.

5. *As working quarters for the school nurse.* Here the nurse will inspect pupils who have been referred to her by the teachers and carry out many of her numerous responsibilities.

6. *As a place for screening tests.* Included in such screening procedures are vision testing, individual hearing testing, height and weight measuring, and dental inspections or examinations.

7. *As the place where the health examinations are given.* Such examinations of school children include the periodic and special health examinations by physicians, and the dental examination by dentists. Some schools, however, depend entirely or largely on such work being done in clinics outside of the school or by private physicians and dentists in their own offices.

8. *As an immunization clinic.* The health room can serve as an immunization clinic for both pre-school and school-age children.

9. *As a place for health counseling.* Such a room serves as a place for individual conferences on the part of the school nurse, physician, dentist, health educator or guidance person with pupils, parents, and teachers. Such conferences need to be held in a place free from disturbances and should have sufficient privacy. In some schools, certain of the aforementioned personnel have their own offices. It is the nurse who is most in need of the health room for private conferences.

10. *As a center for certain community activities.* In some communities the health suite may be used for well-baby conferences and other pre-school health activities.

When planning facilities for the health unit, the above ten purposes or functions should be checked through to determine how many of these the health unit should serve. If all or most of these are to be met, then it is necessary to consider other factors in planning the type and location of health facilities.

Location of Health Service Unit

In deciding upon the location of the health unit, thought should be given to the various functions that will be carried out there. Its location should be one that facilitates the accomplishment of the greatest number of the functions for which the health suite is designed and which permits such functions to be carried on efficiently and conveniently.

The following principles should guide planners in determining the proper location for the health suite:

The health service unit should be centrally located on the ground floor and convenient to the main building entrance for ready access by staff, pupils, and parents. It needs to be accessible to pupils since they will visit the unit for various reasons including counseling and permission to re-enter following sickness.

Also, since much emphasis is placed on having the parents present at the medical examination (particularly in the elementary school), it would be helpful if the unit were easy for parents to find.

It should be near or adjoining the administrative unit of the school. Such a location facilitates the carrying out of those functions that have both an administrative aspect and a health aspect. Illustrations of some of these functions are: (1) the exchange of information between the health staff and administrative personnel; (2) the use of files and records connected with the health services by those concerned with health guidance and counseling; (3) provision for administrative personnel to supervise when health service personnel are not present; (4) making possible in some schools the joint use of a waiting room.

Certain information contained in the health records is of value to all teachers and, therefore, should be used by them. The principal or his office assistants must carry on many of the health service activities in schools that have only part-time service from nurse and physician. For these reasons, the health unit should be convenient for the principal and all teachers. Strictly confidential medical information should be kept either by the nurse or the principal.

It should be in a quiet area of the building. Examination procedures and especially the individual hearing tests and individual conferences require a quiet room. It is important, therefore, that the health suite not be near a gymnasium, shop, band room, or cafeteria.

The health suite should be reasonably handy to toilet and lavatory facilities, particularly when these are not supplied, or are not adequate, in the health suite itself.

The window arrangement should be such as to provide for natural light from outside windows. Adequate ventilation is also essential.

In a number of schools, outside groups use the health suite for a variety of purposes. Therefore, *a separate entrance and exit is desirable so that the health unit can be used without opening, lighting, and heating the entire building.*

THE HEALTH SUITE

All the purposes or functions previously listed can be carried out in one large health unit or suite which may be subdivided into the following areas: (1) a waiting area, (2) an examining and counseling room, (3) a rest room for girls, (4) a rest room for boys, (5) toilet facilities, and (6) storage space.

It is advisable that a suite of rooms rather than one room comprise the health service unit. In the small elementary schools, the services can be taken care of in one room provided screens are placed between the cots. A space equal to one standard classroom can be divided into the several areas or rooms here needed. In some instances, it is advantageous to have the walls of the areas comprising the health unit built in such a way that they can be taken out and changed as the school grows or changes.

In addition to the rooms already mentioned, it would be desirable—where money and space permit—to have certain adjuncts to the health unit. In large secondary schools where the school physician spends a large amount of his time in the health suite, it is best to have a separate office space for him which can also be used for examination and consultation. Similarly, in schools having an extensive dental program, a separate room for this purpose is desirable. However, ordinarily, the space used by the nurse, the physician, and the dental hygienist may be shared. In the larger schools, it may also be advantageous to have a sound-proof room for hearing testing and separate dressing booths.

Regardless of school size, location or general arrangement, the health service suite or room should be attractively decorated, adequately heated and lighted, and easily ventilated. Ceilings should be acoustically treated, floors should be resilient and of easily cleaned materials, and walls should be washable. Outside windows should be provided for good ventilation and lighting. In some plans, sliding doors are an advantage.

The Waiting Room

The waiting room should have approximately 100 square feet of floor space in the large elementary school and up to 300 square feet for the large secondary schools. It should open into a main corridor.

Some school experts recommend that the waiting room and the two rest rooms open onto a sub-corridor. Such an arrangement makes it easier for the individual to move within the health unit without going into the main corridor. It also serves as a noise buffer between the main corridor and the health rooms.

In small schools, the waiting room of the administrative office suite may serve as a waiting room for the health service room.

The waiting room should be a comfortable and cheerful area informally furnished with curtains and drapes. There should be chairs or benches available. No special lighting is required in the waiting room, but it should be adequate for reading purposes. A bulletin board is recommended as is also a small reading table or a rack for magazines.

In those large health service suites having a record clerk, it is suggested that her desk and files be at one end of the waiting room and that she have a phone provided with an extension to the examination room.

The doors connecting the waiting room to

the rest rooms and the examination room should be shielded by screens, if necessary, in order to maintain privacy of the latter rooms.

The Examination and Counseling Room

The space that is used for the health examination should be ample and should also provide for privacy and quiet. Its size will vary with the extent to which provision is made for certain facilities within this area rather than as separate rooms. It should contain a minimum of 200 square feet of floor space. The various diagrams which follow will show several variations in size, shape, and related facilities. The following points need to be given careful consideration in planning this room.

Since a 20-foot distance is required for the Snellen eye test, a 22-foot clear distance is needed. When this distance is not possible, a minimum of 12 feet is recommended with the Snellen eye test being performed with a mirror. An electrical outlet should be available for illuminating the chart placed on a wall opposite to the window.

Doors should lead into the waiting room and to each rest area.

The examining room needs such lighting as is necessary to facilitate examination.

There is need for several exits from a health examination room so that it can be used for procedures, such as immunization, where children need to file through in groups. If they can go in one door and out the other, confusion is avoided. In this way it is also possible to use the rest rooms for dressing rooms and thereby expedite the giving of health examinations.

Equipment Space

In planning the size, shape, and arrangement of the examination room consideration should be given to the need for the following equipment spaces: (1) basin with hot and cold running water 30 inches from floor; (2) first aid cabinet over the basin or under the work space; (3) work space of about 20 square feet close to basin for first aid materials when being used; (4) toilet; (5) space for scales; (6) eye chart with electric outlet; (7) plate glass mirror on wall opposite eye chart at 10-foot distance; (8) bulletin board; (9) double pedestal desk five by two and one-half feet; (10) examining table 30 by 72 inches; (11) telephone on nurse's desk; (12) small table on casters; and (13) filing cabinets for records.[3]

Additional factors which need to be considered include adequate electrical convenience outlets for appliances and equipment, the examiner's desk and chair, a chair for an attending parent, possibly a screened corner for disrobing, storage and supply space, perhaps an examining table, although the latter will not be used routinely in most health examination programs, and perhaps a sterilizer.

If a separate room for hearing tests is planned, it should be soundproofed. The examining room needs such lighting as is necessary to facilitate examination. The decoration of the examination and counseling room need not be the usual hospital white or gray, but rather any color that is desired. Pastel colors are considered best.

Dental Room

In the smaller school, the dental program is usually taken care of in the regular examination room. In many of the larger schools, a separate room is provided for the dental health program in which the school dentist and the dental hygienist perform their duties.

In some school systems the dental program is conducted with the use of portable equipment and, therefore, the dental room can be used for other school health purposes during parts of the school year.

It is recommended that the dental health room open directly off the waiting room. An area of 100 square feet is adequate for carrying out this program. The necessary plumbing must be provided to accommodate the dental chair and basin, and a lavatory is needed. Provision need also be made for a desk, a dental chair, two chairs, files for the dental records, and a cabinet for dental supplies and instruments. A bulletin board or a table for dental health education displays should also be made available.

---

[3] From a communication from Dr. L. M. Corliss, Director of Health Service, Denver Public Schools.

Rest Areas

Separate rest areas are needed for girls and boys. In high schools, more space should be provided for girls than for boys. In the large secondary schools, the suggested size of the rest area for girls is 16 by 18 feet and for boys it is 9 by 12 feet. For small schools the size recommended is 6 by 8 feet.

Certain other space in the health service unit can be converted into rest area use under special circumstances. For example, a dressing room equipped with a cot can be used for rest and isolation. A cot should also be placed in the physician's office, if this is a separate room, so that it can be used as a rest area when necessary.

The number of cots needed is determined by the size of the school and the likelihood of occupancy. One standard suggested is that of one cot for each 300 children in the building. In the elementary school, one bed should be set up at all times for immediate use, and in the high school two or three beds for each sex should be ready at all times. Additional beds might be folding types that can be stored when not in use, thereby allowing the space to be used for other purposes of the health service program. There should be a minimum space of three feet between beds. If funds are available, the cots should be in separate glass cubicles; on a modest budget, sheets hung from wires between cots will suffice.

Storage space may also be provided in the rest areas for roll-away beds and for linens and blankets to be used in this area. It is also desirable to have a bedside table or a half shelf over the head of each cot for the student's books and other articles. Hooks and other facilities for hanging wraps and clothing are needed. There should be no lights convenient for reading or studying as the student is there for a rest. Rather, the lights should be subdued and below eye level.

Toilet and Washing Facilities

Toilet and washing facilities should be an integral part of the health service unit accessible to the waiting room, the examining room, and the rest areas. For the larger units, a toilet and lavatory is recommended for each rest area. Washing facilities are also recommended, when possible, for the waiting room and the examining room. In small health units, one toilet and lavatory will suffice for the entire unit.

Dressing Room Cubicles

Some of the larger schools include dressing areas in the health suite. In smaller schools the rest areas, the lavatory, or areas in the examining room protected by a screen are used for this purpose. New York State suggests two dressing cubicles each containing 45 square feet and communicating directly with the waiting room and the nurse's or doctor's office. Hooks and clothes hangers should be provided in each cubicle. If equipped with a cot, they can be used for rest and isolation when necessary.

Storage Facilities

For the storage of equipment and supplies, a 20 square foot area should be planned. A separate clothes locker should be provided for each staff member using the health unit.

Telephone

An outside telephone or a telephone extension is needed on the nurse's desk. In some small schools, it may be possible for the health service staff to use the telephone in the school's office.

SUGGESTED LAYOUT AND DESIGN OF HEALTH SUITE

The layouts for school health service units shown here contain the composite elements that should be included in a health service unit. Examples have been taken from several sources and, therefore, the plans will differ in various details. Spaces may need to be varied in size and in arrangement as dictated by the over-all layout of the building and the design program established by the local school. The plans indicate variations for different sized schools.

Small Elementary School

A school of this size does not need an

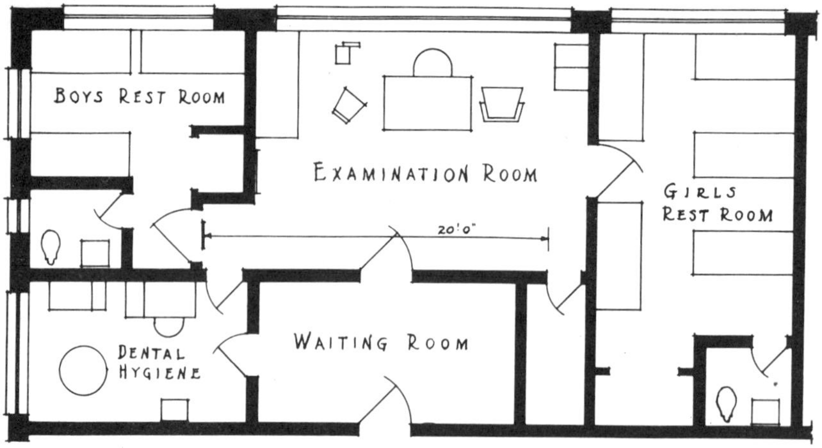

1200 PUPIL SCHOOL

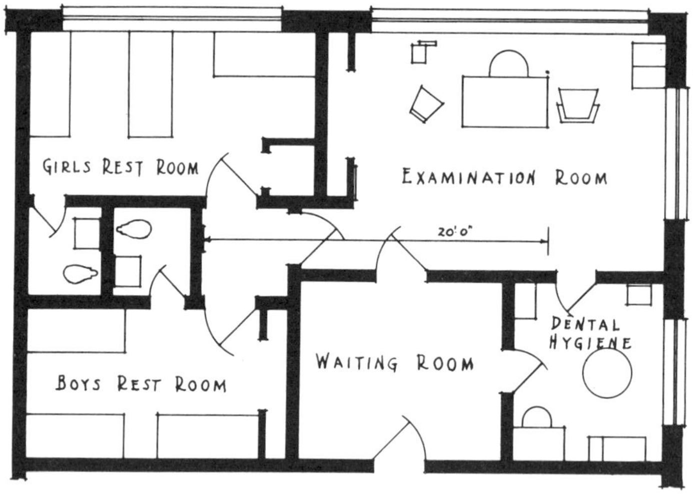

800 PUPIL SCHOOL

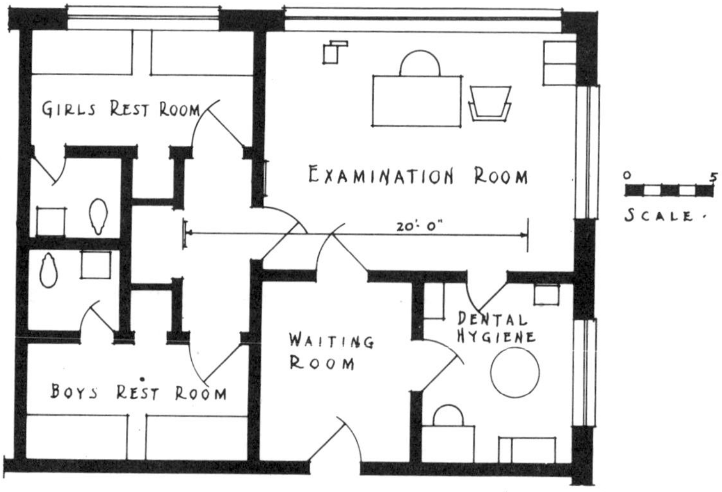

400 PUPIL SCHOOL

WILLIAM R. SHIRLEY ARCH'T.

HEALTH·SERVICE·FACILITIES..

elaborate health unit. Since the health service staff functions only part time, the classroom teacher conducts much of the health work in the school. If there is a possibility that the school will be increased in size, then the health unit should be planned for a school of larger size and the following layout does not apply.

The most important functions carried out in the health unit in a small elementary school include emergency care, health counseling, medical, nursing and dental examinations and inspections, vision and hearing testing, immunization programs, rest facilities and pre-school examinations.

The waiting room of the general administrative office can also serve for the health unit, and a dental room can be used on occasion for other purposes such as a dressing room.

A Large Elementary School

A school with more than 350 pupils will differ in plans from those of the small school in only a few respects. A separate waiting room is needed as is a separate dressing room.

A Secondary School

The health unit in a secondary school will need to differ from the elementary school units in several ways. A larger dressing room with individual cubicles is necessary. More space is needed for cots, with a separate section for boys and another one for girls. Dental health service facilities will vary depending upon the community dental program in that part of the school system. Personal counseling is important and calls for a room that is quiet and private.

Usually the junior and senior high schools have full-time nurses and, therefore, the nurse's office and the examining room should be combined. The school physician who visits the school only once or twice a week need not have a separate office. However, if he is regularly in attendance in the school, he will need an office separate from that of the nurse and the examining room.

The Small Rural School

The school health services for rural school children should be in general just as adequate as those provided in larger communities. But, because of the smallness of the school building and the greater reliance upon the teacher for the school health program, the layout plans are different in many ways from those already described.

Certain services are provided in some communities by mobile units or traveling clinics. For example, dental work, tuberculosis examinations, and preventive inoculations are provided in this way. Other mobile units may provide multiple uses.

Most important in a small school is a room that can be used for individual conferences and examinations and for emergency care. Such a school may also serve the community in other ways in addition to the regular school health functions. It is essential to have telephone service available.

HEALTH EDUCATION FACILITIES

In the elementary schools, instruction in health education is usually done in the regular classroom. In the junior and senior high schools, however, separate classrooms are needed for the various subject fields, including health education, which require special facilities.

In many communities, the local schools are used for a variety of community health purposes. Included are health education meetings of parents and other adult groups. They may wish to use the health teaching room for pre-natal classes, for studying nutrition, first aid, and home care of the sick, and for other health purposes. The room, therefore, needs to be planned so that it can readily and adequately meet such needs as well as those of the regular classes.

The health education room should be near the health service unit. If parents and community groups are to use it on occasion, it should also be near the entrance to the school.

In order to make it possible to teach the various health areas, it is important that the classroom be equipped to provide adequate facilities.

The most important facility for teaching health classes is a classroom adapted to the special needs of the health field.

Provision is needed for audio-visual aids as health teaching can often best be presented through these media. Such aids include films, slides, opaque projectors, film strips, and recordings.

Space and facilities are needed for the storing and displaying of charts, anatomical models, health posters, and health exhibits.

There is need for ready availability of pamphlets, bulletins, magazines, newspapers, and references in the study of health. Therefore, the classroom should either have a health library of its own or have regular library facilities available.

Adequate bulletin board space is essential in this classroom and in various rooms of the health service suite to contribute to health education.

Certain laboratory experiments, especially in the field of nutrition and bacteriology, should be included in the study of health. When facilities for such experiments are not readily available in or from the science laboratory, it is well to provide them in the classroom.

For home-hygiene classes, as well as for other purposes, a wash basin with hot and cold water and a roll-away bed is needed.

The practice of using some other teacher's classroom for health instruction is unsatisfactory, since it limits many desirable teaching methods. Nevertheless, certain teaching materials can be shared with the science department. Other types of material are needed exclusively by the health teacher and should be readily available in the classroom.

CHAPTER 9

OUTDOOR PHYSICAL EDUCATION FACILITIES

A. Carl Stelling Associates

OUTDOOR ACTIVITIES CONSTITUTE A MAJOR part of both physical education and recreation programs. The fields, courts, and other areas that are needed in variety and quantity to serve many groups at one time require an extensive part of the school site or park. However, such areas offer the greatest hope for these programs to meet the needs of all the community at a relatively low cost. The cost of these outdoor facilities is generally less than 5 per cent of the total cost of the school plant.

Physical education and recreation facilities for schools and communities generally include a substantial area devoted to outdoor physical education and recreation activities. Because of climatic conditions and the seasonal aspect of many of these activities, careful planning is essential to insure maximum use of all facilities on a year-round basis. Planning requires a knowledge of the area and facilities required for each activity so that maximum effective use may be made of the space available. The continually increasing cost of school facilities and the land to accommodate them, the steady population growth requiring more new schools, and the corresponding decrease in other open areas suitable for recreation has emphasized the need for greater use of joint school-community planning in the field of recreation. The planning, selection, and design of recreational areas for maximum year-round use is particularly necessary in communities with limited space for recreation programs, limited funds for their development, or both.

This chapter deals with the planning, selection, layout, and construction of outdoor areas devoted to specific athletic, physical education or playground use. The total facility (school athletic field, community playground, and so on) will consist of such combinations of these specific uses as are appropriate to the area available, the age

Illustration: Baseball, a major form of outdoor recreation

level of the intended users, and the recreation or physical education program.

SITE SELECTION AND PLANNING

The selection and development of sites for outdoor recreational areas requires careful study and analysis by all parties concerned in the planning stage, if adequate facilities are to be provided at reasonable cost. Disproportionate cut or fill, extensive rock excavation, subsurface water conditions, and poor drainage are all factors that can create excessive costs as a result of improper site selection or planning. The increasingly high cost of acquisition of available land, as well as the high cost of its development, indicates greater need for thorough studies and a competent analysis of site construction problems to insure that the site finally selected will produce the most economic development of the facilities required.

The study of potential sites can be facilitated through the careful analysis of the required facilities, natural features, development aspects, and costs. It should be noted, however, that in many instances the cost of acquisition is a poor guide since cheap land may be so expensive to develop as to be prohibitive. The initial high cost of site development in many localities can be partially offset through multiple use of areas and facilities. In this respect the outdoor play area of an elementary school, because of its central location in neighborhood or rural community, represents a potentially dual purpose facility providing year-round use to school and community and achieving the most for the tax dollar by eliminating

Anthony Wayne Recreation Area, showing parking field, swimming and diving pools, bathhouse, children's play area, athletic field, and three tree-shaded picnic groves. Palisades Interstate Park, New York.

Photo by Decker

the need for separate neighborhood parks or playgrounds.

The use of a check list similar to the following will facilitate the study and analysis of areas for various uses. Characteristics not included can be added as required.

TYPES OF RECREATION FACILITIES

Nursery and Kindergarten Area

The kindergarten area may vary from one eighth to one quarter of an acre and should include a turf area, a small paved area marked with squares and circles for individual and group activities, a sand box, and possibly an apparatus area surfaced with tanbark, shavings, or sawdust. For control it should be enclosed with a low fence and should be located immediately adjacent to the school building and preferably with direct access from the classroom. The addition of shade trees is particularly desirable in the apparatus section and for a quiet reading or story telling corner.

Primary Area (Ages 6 to 8)

Six- to eight-year-old children often make joint use of the kindergarten area during a staggered outdoor program. However, when this happens the area required should be increased up to one-half acre where additional facilities may be furnished. More emphasis should be given in this area to apparatus that will encourage developmental activities, such as jungle gym, horizontal bars, and other climbing devices. Small wooden backstops 4 to 5 feet high for use in ball throwing and hitting games are desirable as well as a turf area for running and group games.

Intermediate Area

An area of from two to five acres (exclusive of area required for buildings and parking) is required for adequate facilities at the intermediate age level, depending upon the size of the school and the instructional program.

This area should include an apparatus

SITE SELECTION CHECK LIST FOR SCHOOL OR PARK

General:	Distance from center of population to be served________
	Distance from other similar facilities________
	Accessibility________; Maximum distance________
	Relation to future growth________
Traffic:	Existing public roads (name) (width) (condition) (maintained by)________
	Future roads or highways (name) (width) (condition) (maintained by)________
Utilities:	Sanitary sewer (at site) (distance from site) (size)________
	Public water supply (at site) (distance from site) (pressure)________
	Storm sewer (at site) (distance from site) (size)________
	Electricity (at site) (distance from site) (size)________
	Gas (at site) (distance from site)________
Property:	Total available________
	Breakdown (owner) (area) (frontage)________
	Estimated percentage usable________
	Frontage on public roads (roads)________ (frontage)________
	Other access, right-of-way________
	Easements and other factors limiting use of property________
Topography:	Steep grades and slopes____%; Gently rolling____%; level____%
	Heavily wooded____%; lightly wooded____%; open____%
	Rock outcrop (extensive) (occasional) (none)________
	Water (streams) (lakes) (ponds) (springs) (swamps)________
	Sub-surface water condition (good) (poor)________
	Existing buildings and structures________
Soil:	Topsoil (depth)________ (quality)________ (% usable)________
	Subsoil: Clay____% Sand____% Gravel____% Loam____% Other____%
	Estimated bearing________

area, an all-weather multi-purpose paved area, and turf areas for field sports. The following facilities should be provided in the paved area: volleyball, basketball, badminton, deck tennis, tetherball, handball, and shuffleboard.

Field sports areas should be provided for softball, soccer, touch football, speedball, or such other field sports as may be locally popular. The nature of the site itself as well as the climatic conditions of the region might indicate certain additional special types of areas such as water sports or ice skating.

Junior and Senior High School Area

The amount of land needed here may vary from 10 to 20 acres and upward depending upon the school population and the nature of the program. In general, space should be provided for duplicate facilities for boys and girls, with the girls' area located closer to the buildings.

A portion of the area near the building should be paved for all-weather multi-purpose use, such as the following games: volleyball, basketball, badminton, deck tennis, handball, roller skating, dancing, and shuffleboard. If tennis courts are to be provided they should be separate from the multi-use area if possible.

Turf areas for field sports should include softball, baseball, football, soccer, lacrosse, and speedball. Whenever possible, practice fields should be provided to reduce the traffic on fields used for interscholastic games so that the turf can be kept in good condition.

Interscholastic Sports Area

This area is usually planned not only for use by the high school, but also by members of the entire community, and may well be incorporated in a joint community-school recreation facility since the interests of the two groups are greatly overlapping.

The interscholastic area should contain football and field sports areas with a stadium or some form of seating facilities. A baseball diamond is also included but the location of this area within the football-track oval is not recommended. This arrangement causes overuse of the turf areas and results in less satisfactory location of the stands. It also causes some interference with the track and baseball schedules.

An important part of this area, because of its emphasis on competitive sports, is adequate provision for spectator seating, parking, fencing, and sanitary facilities.

The Community Park-School

In many communities the location of

Archery range at Jones Beach State Park, New York.

Photo by Ed Schwalb Studio, Wellsville, New York

Little League baseball diamond.

school recreation facilities, with the addition of certain features, would serve admirably as a neighborhood or community park and recreation area. Because of the excessive costs of duplicate facilities this is often the only way many communities can provide needed recreation areas within the community.

In addition to the facilities provided by the school area, there should be additional parking with access from several public streets; picnic areas; areas for social and group gatherings, and arts and crafts; and in some instances a recreation center building.

The public park. Public park facilities may vary from a small neighborhood play lot of a quarter of an acre to national forests covering hundreds of square miles. The major considerations are the handling of the public traffic flow, parking areas, sanitary facilities, and policing. A brief list of some

Forest Park picnic area.

Outdoor amphitheater, U. S. Naval Training Center, Bainbridge, Maryland.

of the types of public parks and the facilities that should be provided follows:

The play lot. The play lot is found almost exclusively in larger cities where open areas are limited, and consists of one-tenth to one-fourth acre located generally in the center of a city block or apartment project. The play lot usually consists of a turf area with some shade trees, fencing for control, benches for mothers, and if possible, apparatus for children of pre-school age. It is generally not supervised.

The Neighborhood Playground

This park facility may vary from two to six acres in area and serve a population up to 6,000 as a neighborhood recreation center for children from six to 14 years of age. Because of its location, the playground may also serve to provide space for special features such as holiday celebrations, festivals, and other special events. In general the playground should be within walking distance of the population it serves so that parking facilities need not be emphasized except in special situations.

The playground should contain an area for pre-school children, a sitting area for mothers, fields and courts for a variety of games, an apparatus area, open turf areas and shaded areas for quiet activities. A wading pool, which may be used for ice skating during the winter months, and a pavilion or shelter house are features that should be considered in the plans.

The Community Playfield

Ranging in size from 10 to 50 acres this facility serves as a center of athletic and recreational activities for large neighborhoods or even for an entire city, depending upon the local situation. In general, one acre of playfield area is required for every 800 population of the area served, and one playfield will serve about four times the population of the neighborhood playground.

The playfield provides recreational facilities for adults and older children and provides many of the features found on the high school athletic field. For this reason it is often developed in conjunction with the high school area.

Facilities usually provided in the complete playfield are baseball and softball diamonds, football or soccer fields, open turf areas for other field sports, tennis courts, paved areas for multiple-use including handball, basketball, volleyball, and shuffleboard. For larger areas the playfield may include a swimming pool, picnic area, or outdoor theater, as well as municipal or memorial gardens and possibly separate areas for smaller children and older people.

Because of the larger number of people served, the nature of activities and the distance the people must travel, ample provision must be made for traffic control and parking.

The Community Park

Here the emphasis is upon achieving an environment of natural beauty, preserving points of outstanding scenic interest, or providing an area of natural woodland or water for informal outdoor activities. The area required should be not less than 50 acres and may go as high as 100 or 500 acres. In this type of park the emphasis is upon natural features such as lakes, beaches, streams, hills, and woodland. Development should be limited to providing facilities such as gardens, picnic areas, boating areas, bathing beaches, and other activities.

There will often be certain areas in the park set aside for field sports or court games where access is readily available at the perimeter of the area. Ample provision must then be made for parking and comfort facilities. If the park is to be open at night, lighting of roads and walks will be necessary.

The Large Park or Reservation

Large parks and reservations encompassing a thousand acres or more are generally developed and maintained by county, state, and federal agencies, and may contain any or all of the facilities found in smaller areas depending upon the natural features. Large portions of the area may be completely undeveloped with access only by foot path, while other specialized areas such as bathing areas around a lake, picnic centers, camping areas, and ski centers may be intensively developed. An example of this type of facility is the Palisades Interstate Park outside of New York City, which covers 50,000 acres.

DESIGN AND CONSTRUCTION FEATURES OF MAJOR SPORT FACILITIES

Most field sports are played on large turf areas, that if properly planned and constructed, can be adapted to maximum uses permitted by local seasonal and weather conditions. Heavy uses presuppose a good turf cover. The problem of obtaining an adequate stand of grass for turf areas subjected to heavy usage is an extremely difficult one. Careful program planning, utilization of best type of grass and topsoil, and proper maintenance are major factors con-

Offset basketball backstop.
Photo by F. J. Higgins, Highland Park, New Jersey

Improvising facilities. Deck of a U. S. Navy carrier at sea.

Model sailboat race, Conservatory Lake, Central Park, New York City.

Photo by Rountree, Bakersfield

Stadium with 220 yard straightaway track on each side. Note ample parking area. Bakersfield Junior College, Bakersfield, California.

tributing to an adequate turf surface (see Chapter 17). Although the dimensions of playing areas given in this chapter indicate the official or accepted layout, it is often necessary to modify these conditions to meet local conditions, such as limited space or budget. Such modifications may well be the only way to provide play space and should not be discouraged. For college, school, and municipal areas devoted to competitive or tournament play, however, the layout should conform to official rules and regulations.

Running Track (quarter-mile)

Layout: The running track consists of a straightaway for a minimum of 140 yards and a maximum of 240 yards for 100- and 220-yard dashes, and a quarter-mile oval track. A minimum area of four acres is required for the track, and its orientation should show the long axis running north and south. (See Figure 9-2 for dimensions and layout of track.) When combined with a football field for average school use, the football field within the track determines the orientation.

Details of construction data to be heeded are as follows: The *grading* of the area inside of the track (the football field) should be at a pitch of 1 per cent from center line to sides. The track straightaway should be level, with the curves level or slightly banked (3 inch pitch to outside). The *composition* of the base course of the track should be 3 to 10 inches of cinders or crushed stone; the middle course 5 to 12 inches of cinders (medium size); and the top or wearing course 3 to 6 inches of cinders passing a one-quarter to one-half inch screen mixed with a clay binder in a ratio of 4 parts cinders to 1 part clay. The curb may be constructed of concrete, asphalt, treated wood or steel, 2 inches above the track (except for multi-use areas where 1 inch is preferred), with the upper surface rounded.

Drainage. One plan for draining the track and football field is indicated in Figure 9-1. Under the track and about two feet from the inside curb open joint agricultural tile drain lines are installed in a bed of broken stone or screened gravel. Two-thirds of the surface of the joints are covered with a strip of wired on tar paper (see Figure 9-1). The drain lines connect to four leaching type catch basins or dry-wells in areas where ground water is not encountered. Otherwise they are connected to a storm sewer line. The catch basins are located roughly in the four "corners" of the track and about 10 to 15 feet from the track curb. An inexpensive but effective catch basin can be constructed using two sections of 30 inch diameter reinforced concrete pipe set on a 12 inch deep bed of gravel and a drain type top grating. Where impervious material is encountered, a sub-surface tile field is a commonly used method of drainage. The grading of the area inside the track should produce swales between track and football field leading to each of the four catch basins.

Starting and finishing posts. These should be provided for all events. The posts are generally of rigid wood construction (¾ by 3 inches by 4 foot 6 inches high), and are placed with the 3 inch width at right angles to the track. The track curb should be permanently marked for ease in locating the posts.

Warm-up track. If space is available, a warm-up track is a desirable adjunct to the main running track. The warm-up track may be a full quarter mile or smaller circular track, or it may be only a short straightaway for practice starts and sprints, depending on space considerations. It should, in general, be located near and oriented with the main track.

Fencing. Particularly during the football season, the track area is usually the focal point of athletic activity. It is essential, therefore, that adequate fencing for controlling spectator traffic be provided. Chain-link fencing is most commonly used for this purpose. It is strong, comparatively inexpensive, and easy to maintain.

A six-foot-high fence around the perimeter of the track area, including the grandstand or bleachers, is useful in excluding all except authorized personnel during periods when the area is not in public use. Strategically

Figure 9:1. Cross section of a running track.

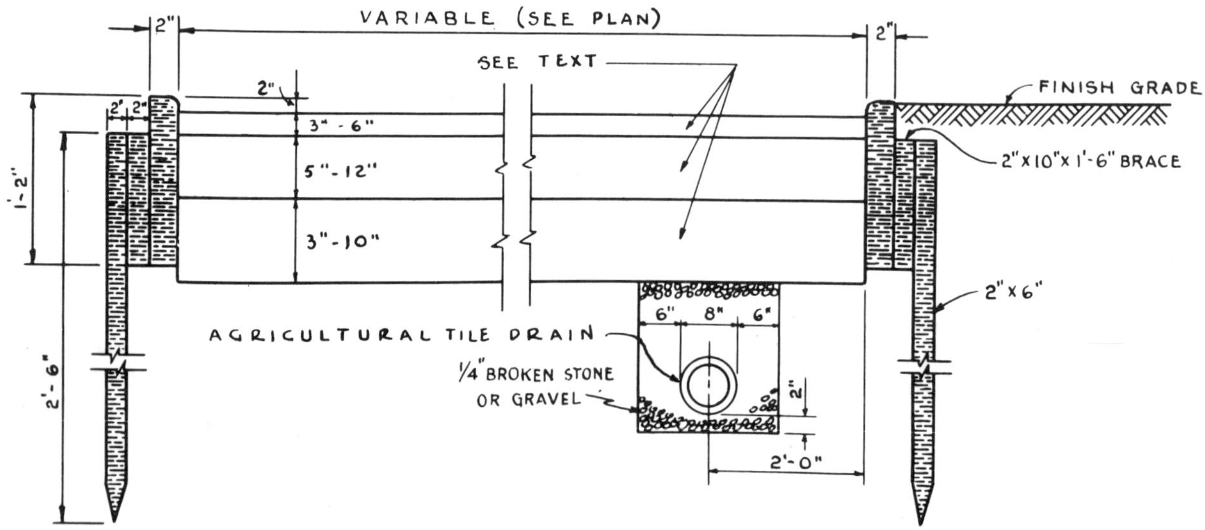

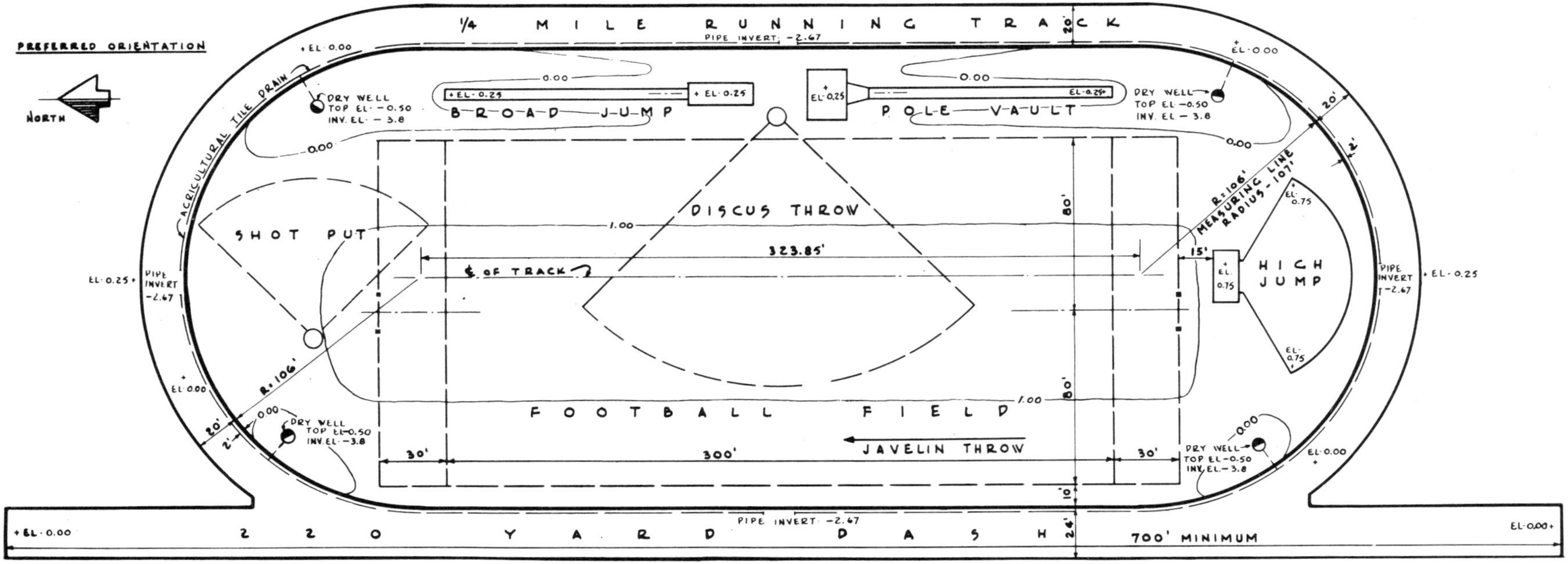

Figure 9:2. Layout of a quarter-mile running track with a 220 yard straightaway.

placed gates should permit orderly access and egress of crowds when the area is in use. The location of the gates should be considered in relation to the parking areas. A 4 foot fence placed between track and stands will prevent spectators from entering the playing areas, and a 4 or 6 foot fence might also be necessary to separate the players' dressing quarters from spectators if the individual situation requires it.

Judges' platform. A portable judges' platform is usually provided at the finish line of track events. There are various designs, but in its simplest form, a judges' platform is similar to a short flight of steps (6 risers maximum about 3 feet wide) mounted on wheels for easy movement from finish line to finish line.

Scoreboard. If football games are to be played on the field inside the track a scoreboard is essential, and a simple hand operated board is adequate in most cases. The board should be large enough, and located for easy viewing from the farthest bleacher seat. For football, the scoreboard should, in general, indicate the location of the ball, the team having possession, the down and yards to go, and the score by quarters. An electric clock showing the timing of the game is a desirable feature where funds permit. The board should be adaptable to other sports such as soccer, lacrosse, track, or any other sport that may be played in the area.

Certain variations are possible in the designing of the quarter mile running track. The radius may vary from a minimum of 95 feet to a maximum of 125 feet, depending on the shape of available land and the facilities to be included inside, if any. A radius of 125 feet will permit the largest space for baseball and football within the track area, and availability of space may dictate whether or not a 220-yard straightaway can be provided.

Hurdles. In races up to 120 yards, the hurdles are 3 feet 6 inches high and placed 10 yards apart with the first hurdle 15 yards from the starting line. In races of up to 220 yards the hurdles are 2 feet 6 inches high and placed 20 yards apart with the first hurdle placed 20 yards from the starting line. In races up to 440 yards the hurdles are 3 feet high and placed 38.277 yards (35 meters) apart and the first hurdle is placed 29.213 yards (45 meters) from the starting line.

The running track is used primarily by athletic teams in highly organized competitive events, for age levels running from junior high school through college and AAU. For this reason this facility usually draws more spectators than participants, increasing the need for parking, bleachers, sanitary facilities, and fencing. The sport demands adherence to regulation dimensions in order to qualify the track for maximum use, competitions, and so forth. The popularity of the track among competitive users will rest upon its standardized layout, sound construction, and good design. If expenses are to be met through admission charges, careful attention must be given the needs of the spectator, particularly in the form of adequate seating and parking facilities (see later sections of this chapter).

Layout of field events. Field events usually include high jump, broad jump, pole vault and shot-put, as well as space for hammer, discus, and javelin throwing. For maximum use of available area, they are usually placed within the running track, but clear of the football field if possible. Runways for pole vaulting and broad jumping are usually located along the straightaway (see Figure 1) parallel to and at least 5 feet from the inside edge of the track curb. These runways are a minimum of 4 feet wide by 125 feet long, level throughout, constructed of a 3 to 6 inch layer of clay and cinders on a base of cinders or sand 6 to 12 inches in depth. The high jump pit is generally located in the semi-circular area at the end of the football field near the finish line for track events. The ground in front of the high jump pit should be level in the form of a semi-circle with a minimum 50 foot radius from the center of the bar so that jumpers may approach from either side. Weight throwing, discus, and other field events can utilize any portion of the remaining turf area. Landing pits are usually constructed of loose sand, sawdust, or shavings 8 to 12 inches deep on a 20 inch base of sand or cinders. For pole vaulting, the pit should be 24 feet wide by 14 feet long; for broad jumping 8 feet wide by 30 feet long; and for high jumping 24 feet wide by 12 feet long.

Uprights and crossbars (pole vault—high jump). Uprights are usually of wood inserted in a metal stand and set a maximum of 13 feet and a minimum of 12 feet apart. Crossbars are made of triangularly shaped wood of uniform thickness, each side measuring 1 and 3/16 inches. Ends must project not more than 6 inches beyond supporting pegs of the uprights, and measurements are made to the upper side of the bar at its lowest point. Take-off board for broad jump is a 4 by 8 inch joist at least 4 feet long, set in the ground level with the runway. See Figure 9-1 for location and Figure 9-3d for details of take-off box for the pole vault.

Weight events. The circle for the discus throw has a maximum inside diameter of 8 feet 2½ inches and must be outlined with a band of iron, steel, or wood, sunk almost flush in the ground. A 90 degree quadrant should be outlined on the ground with a radius of 125 feet from the circle.

The circle for the shot-put, weight throw, and hammer throw has an inside diameter of 7 feet. The use of a protective cage is sometimes recommended in the hammer throw event.

See Figure 9-2 for typical location of field events, and Figure Series 9-3 for construction details of field events.

Football

The area required for the football field is 3 acres minimum. The long axis of the field should run north and south and the dimensions should be 160 by 360 feet (see appendix for diagram of football field). Variations of the football field that can be incorporated in the design include practice fields, and areas for touch football, six-man football, lacrosse, soccer, and field hockey.

Construction. The football field is generally graded from the center line of the long axis to the sides, with a pitch or slope of approximately 1 per cent. Runoff from this slope is collected in catch-basins located along the inside edge of the track.

Drainage. Grading should be so designed that drainage structures can be located clear of all play areas to avoid danger of injury from players tripping over or falling against them. Local soil and climate conditions will determine the most feasible type and layout for the drainage system.

Goal posts. Except for professional football, goal posts are located on the end lines (instead of the goal lines) for reasons of safety. The posts should be at least 20 feet high, 18 feet 6 inches apart, with the crossbar 10 feet from ground level to top edge of the bar. Maximum flexibility can be provided through the use of removable goal posts (see Figure 9-4 for details) so that after the football season the field may be used for other sports and activities. In many cases a

Figure 9:3a. Cross section of a high-jump and pole-vault pit.

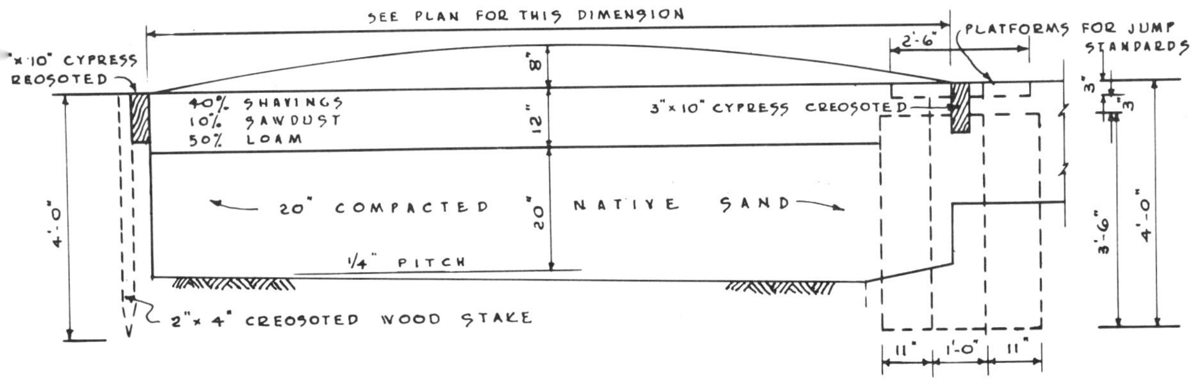

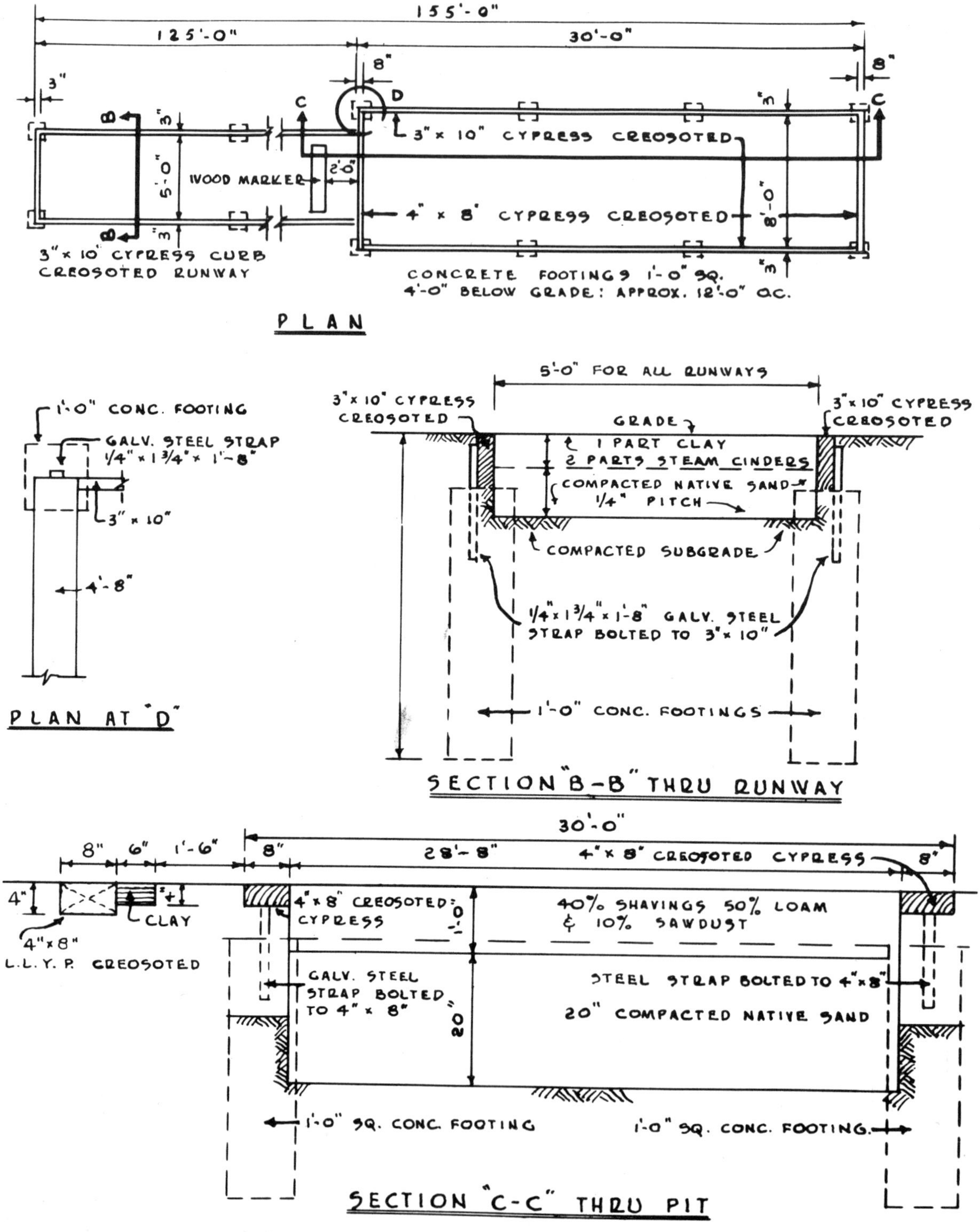
155'-0"
125'-0"
30'-0"
8"
8"
3"
C
D
C
B
B
3"
3"
3"
3"
5'-0"
8'-0"
WOOD MARKER
2'-0"
3" x 10" CYPRESS CREOSOTED
4" x 8" CYPRESS CREOSOTED
3" x 10" CYPRESS CURB
CREOSOTED RUNWAY
CONCRETE FOOTINGS 1'-0" SQ.
4'-0" BELOW GRADE: APPROX. 12'-0" O.C.
PLAN
1'-0" CONC. FOOTING
GALV. STEEL STRAP
1/4" x 1 3/4" x 1'-8"
3" x 10"
4'-8"
PLAN AT "D"
5'-0" FOR ALL RUNWAYS
3" x 10" CYPRESS
CREOSOTED
3" x 10" CYPRESS
CREOSOTED
GRADE
1 PART CLAY
2 PARTS STEAM CINDERS
COMPACTED NATIVE SAND
1/4" PITCH
COMPACTED SUBGRADE
1/4" x 1 3/4" x 1'-8" GALV. STEEL
STRAP BOLTED TO 3" x 10"
1'-0" CONC. FOOTINGS
SECTION "B-B" THRU RUNWAY
30'-0"
8"
6"
1'-6"
8"
28'-8"
8"
4" x 8" CREOSOTED CYPRESS
4"
2"
4" x 8"
L.L.Y.P. CREOSOTED
CLAY
4" x 8" CREOSOTED
CYPRESS
1'-0"
40% SHAVINGS 50% LOAM
& 10% SAWDUST
GALV. STEEL
STRAP BOLTED
TO 4" x 8"
STEEL STRAP BOLTED TO 4" x 8"
20" COMPACTED NATIVE SAND
20"
1'-0" SQ. CONC. FOOTING
1'-0" SQ. CONC. FOOTING
SECTION "C-C" THRU PIT

Figure 9:3b. Running broad jump details.

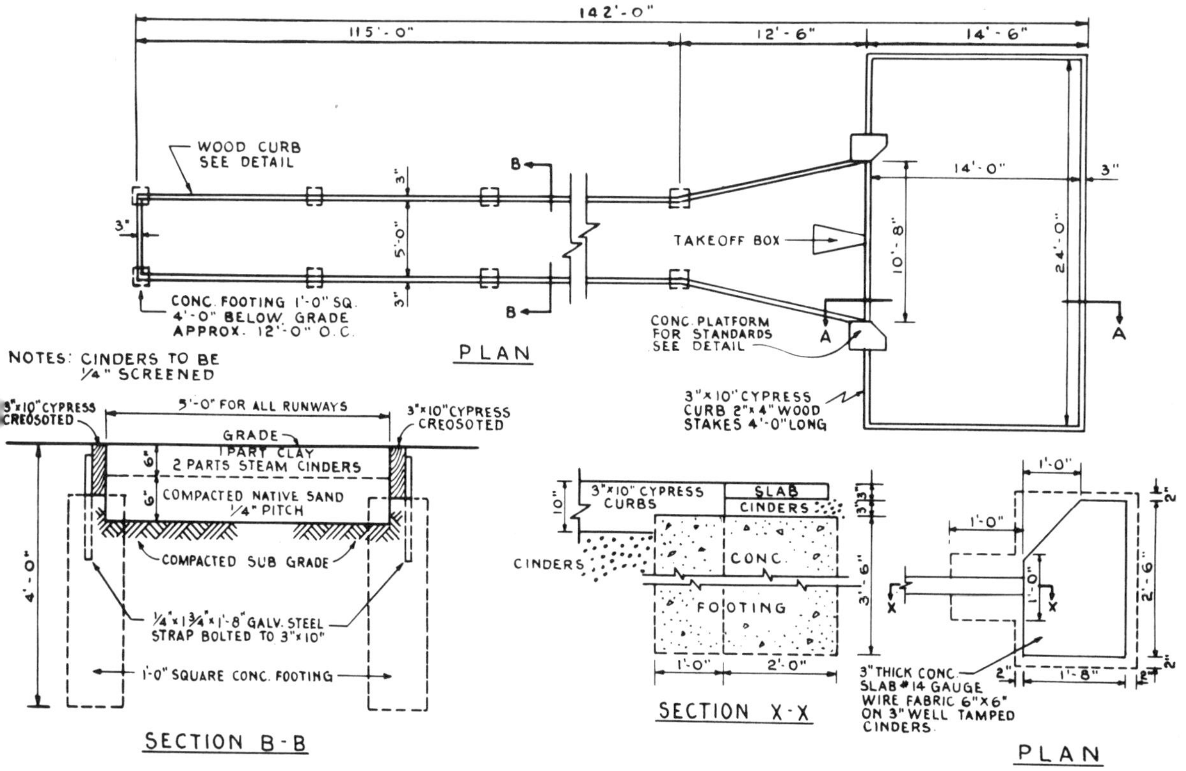

Figure 9:3c. Pole vault details.

Figure 9:3d. High jump details.

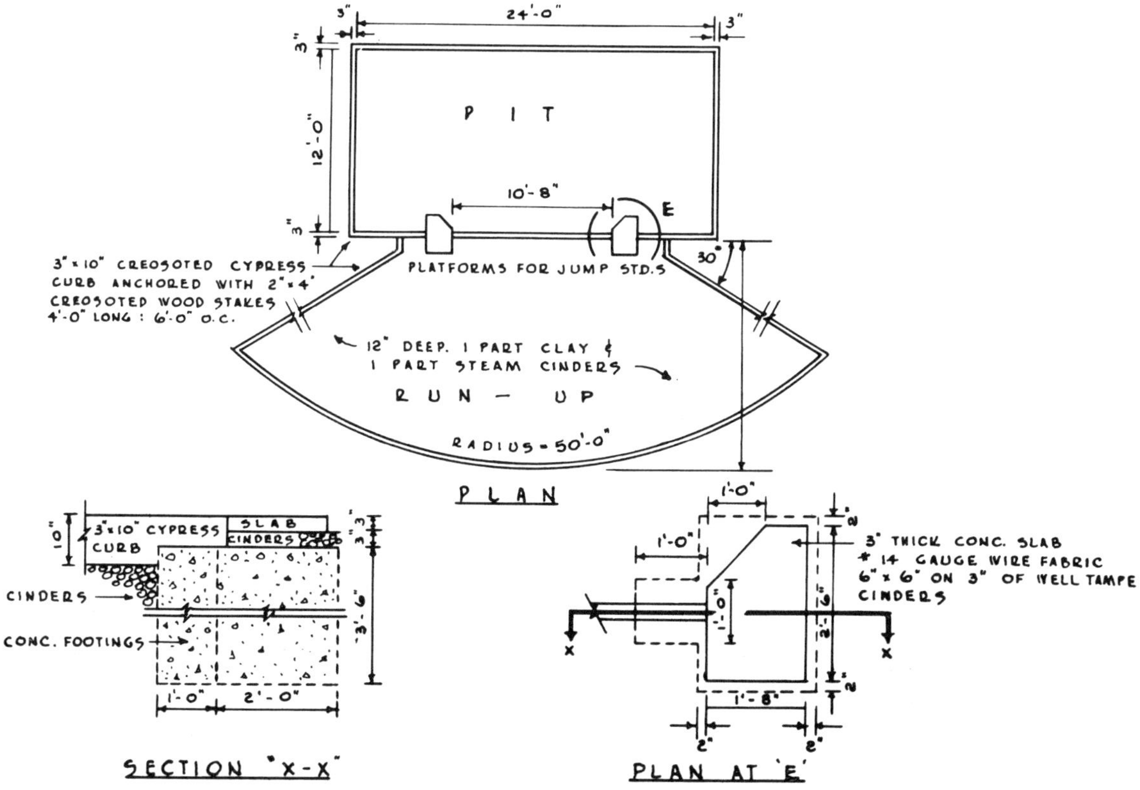

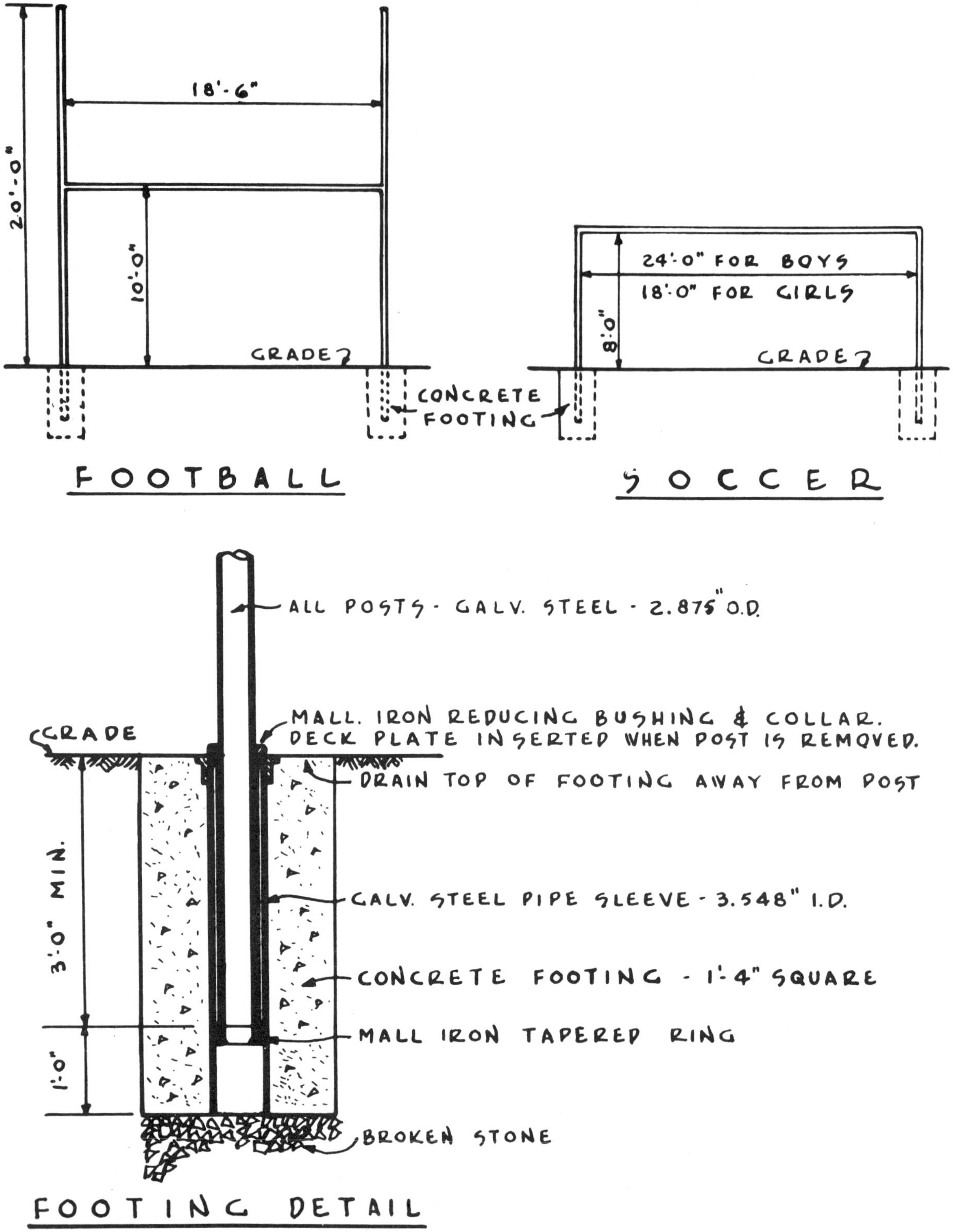

Figure 9:4. Detail of football and soccer goalposts.

combination football and soccer goal is used successfully.

Markings. Boundary lines are known as end lines and side lines, which define the 160 by 360 foot playing area. Inside this area are the end zones (30 feet wide at each end of the field) and the field of play. Goal lines bounding the field of play are drawn across the field at each end between the side lines and 30 feet in from the end lines. The end zones are usually further marked by diagonal lines. The space between the goal lines is marked off by lines drawn across the width of the field at intervals of 15 feet. Each line is intersected at right angles by short lines at a distance of 45 feet in from each side line. In addition, short lines are drawn 2 yards from and parallel to each goal line and directly in front of the goal posts. The length of the short line is not specified. All lines are in white, usually lime thoroughly slaked. The width of lines is not specified, but side lines, end lines, goal lines, 20-yard and 40-yard lines may be wider than the other lines (see Appendix 2).

General use. The playing field is used primarily for team play in intramural and interscholastic athletics. In larger communities there is also the opportunity for semi-professional use when facilities are designed to handle spectators adequately. Because of the appeal of football as a spectator sport, adequate seating and parking facilities should be provided whenever possible. Proper fencing facilities are also necessary. The age level for this facility ranges from junior high school age through adulthood.

Baseball

The area required for the baseball field is at least 350 feet by 350 feet (2.8 acres). Its orientation may vary somewhat due to location and usual time of play (twilight or afternoon), but generally the back point of home plate should be set to point due north-northeast, or the line from the pitcher's box to home plate should be within 20 degrees east or west of north.

Dimensions. The diamond is 90 feet on a side; distance around the bases is 360 feet. The dimensions across the diamond are 127 feet 3-3/8 inches. There should be a minimum of 60 feet from home plate to grandstand or seats unless they are protected by adequate fencing. Batting range is at least 250 feet and where two fields are laid out back to back there should be at least 550 feet between the two home plates. For details of layout and other dimensions see Figure 9-5.

Bases. Home plate is a plate of whitened rubber set into and flush with the surface of the field (see Figure 9-6).

The pitcher's plate is a plate of whitened rubber set into and flush with the ground. The plate should be not more than 15 inches above the level of home plate, and the ground should slope gradually from it to the base lines (see Figure 9-7).

First, second, and third bases are of white canvas bags, 15 inches square and 3 to 5 inches thick, filled with a soft material. Bases are attached to pegs driven into the ground at locations shown in Figure 9-5.

Marking. Foul lines consist of extensions of the line between home and first and home and third to the boundary lines of the ground, and also from home plate back to the backstop lines. All lines shown solid in Figure 9-5 are marked with lime, chalk, whitewash, or other white substance. The width of the lines is 3 inches.

Construction. The infield is graded to conform to the requirements listed above governing the construction of the pitcher's plate. The outfield area may be graded in different ways depending upon the terrain. However, a slope or pitch of 1 to 2 per cent should be obtained; and, if possible, drainage should be away from the infield.

The entire area is turfed except for a specified area along the base lines and the pitcher's plate (see skinned area designated in Figure 9-5).

Drainage. Surface water should normally be handled by good grading and a well developed turf if the subsoil is sufficiently porous. A high concentration of clay or other impermeable material in the subsoil might require tile subdrains or other expensive construction. If drainage structures are necessary they should be located clear of actual play areas to avoid hazard.

Details. There are no official specifications

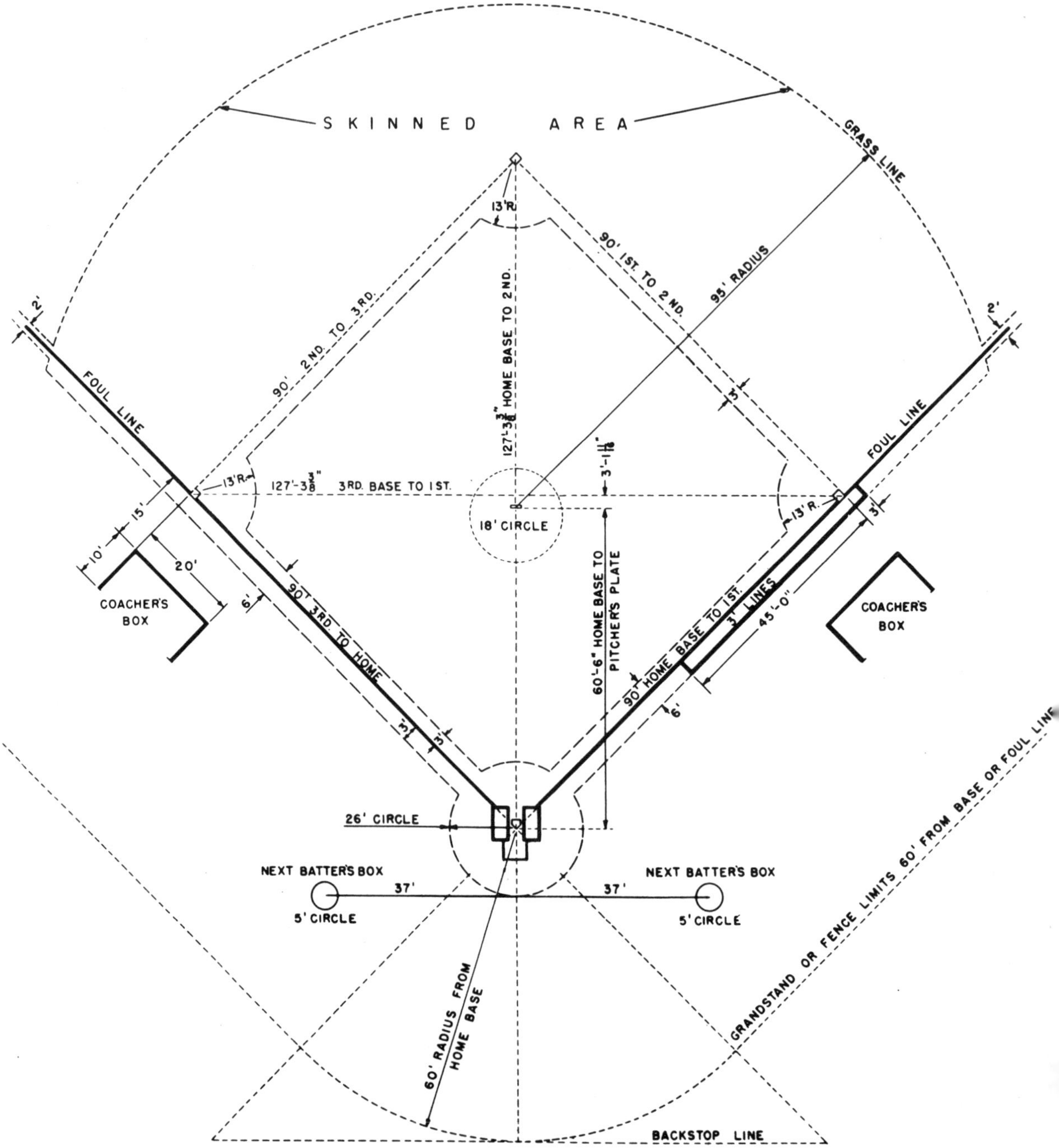

Prepared by L. H. Billing, Sports Engineer for the Falk Corporation, Milwaukee, Wisconsin. (Copyright 1956.)

Figure 9:5. Baseball diamond.

for the backstop, the dimensions and construction depending upon the use, space available, location of seats, and other variables. In general, if there is ample space, the vertical type of backstop is used. This type is constructed in three sections, a center section and two side sections turned in at an angle parallel to the base lines, the width of each section varying from 24 to 40 feet and the height from 15 to 20 feet. The hooded type of backstop is useful where space is limited, and can be located 12 to 16 feet behind home plate with an overhang extending out almost over the plate. A typical hooded type backstop is shown in Figure 9-8a. There is also the multiple backstop for two fields side by side or opposite each other. Most backstops are constructed of woven wire mesh supported by pipe framework and permanently set in concrete footings. The lower section up to 4 or 5 feet above the ground is usually faced with boards to avoid cutting the baseballs on the wire mesh.

Little League field. For a Little League diamond, the area required is 225 by 225 feet

Figure 9:6. Layout of home plate area and detail of base locations.

Prepared by L. H. Billing, Sports Engineer for the Falk Corporation, Milwaukee, Wisconsin. (Copyright 1956.)

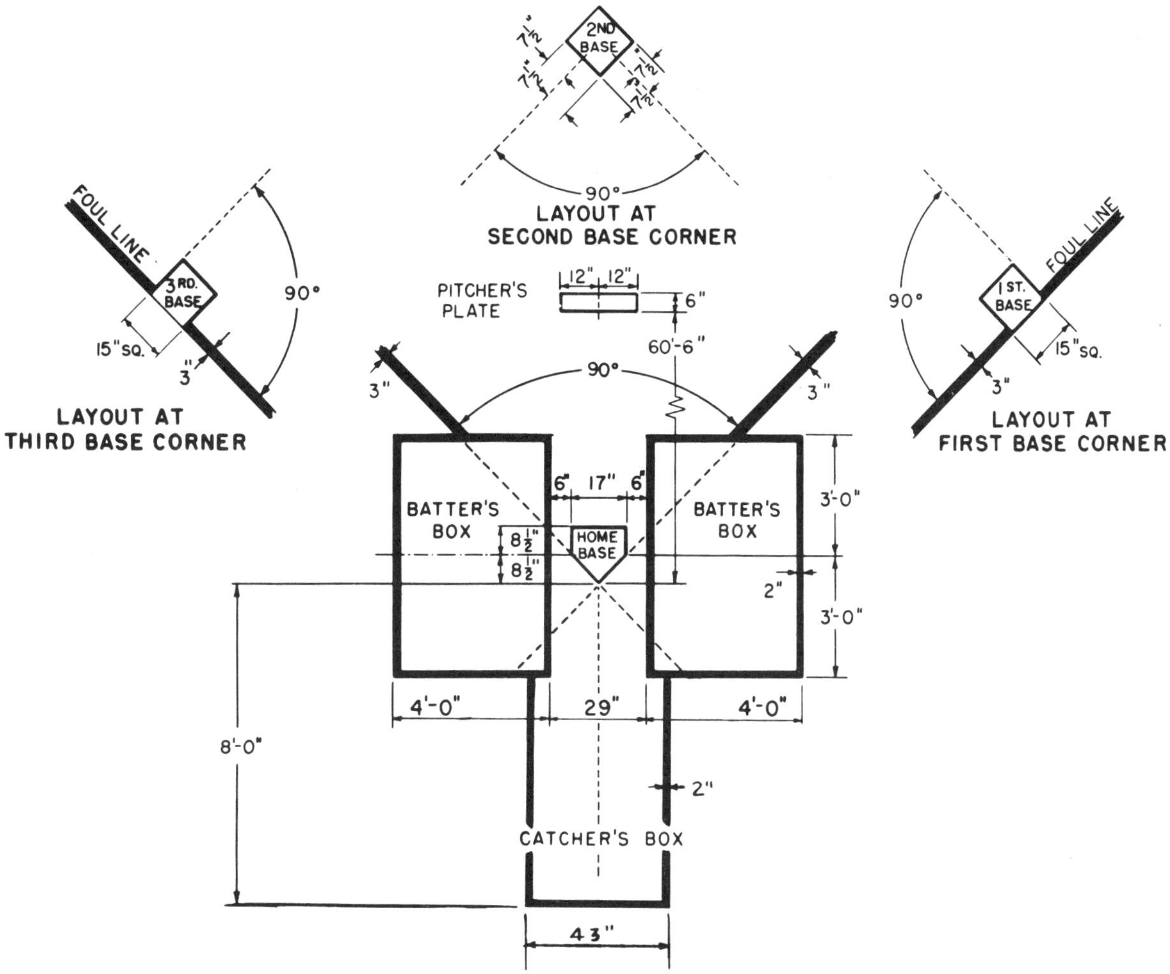

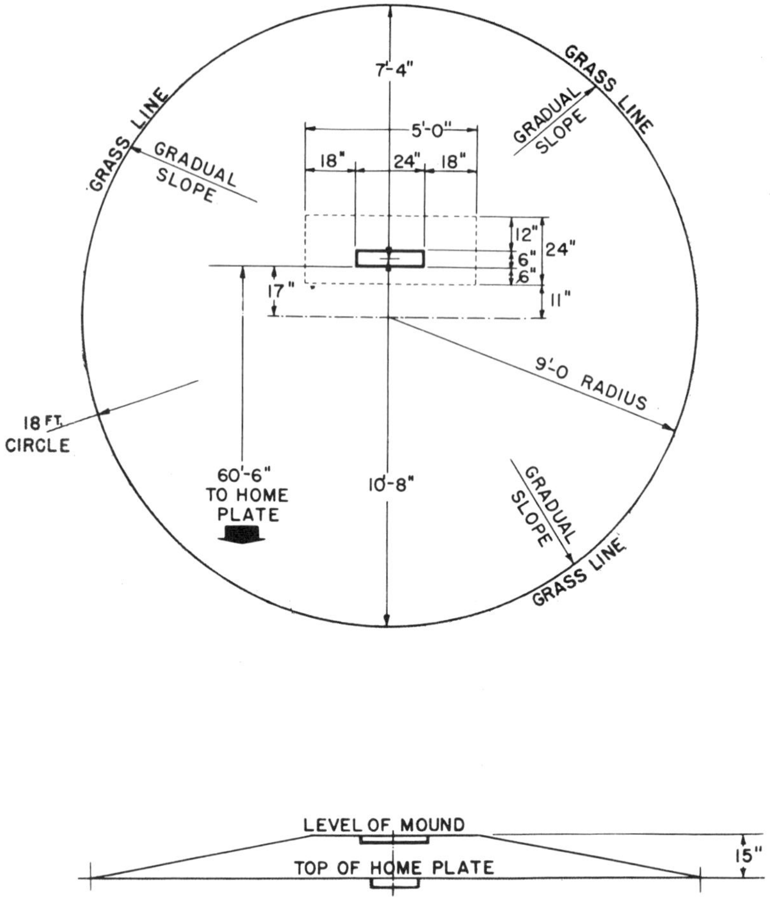

Prepared by L. H. Billing, Sports Engineer for the Falk Corporation, Milwaukee, Wisconsin. (Copyright 1956.)

Figure 9:7. Detail of a pitcher's mound.

(approximately 1 and ¼ acres). The dimensions are similar to 60 foot softball with pitching distance 44 feet and foul lines 175 feet. The bases are the same as for baseball, with the pitcher's mound 6 inches higher than home plate.

Junior baseball. For junior baseball (13 to 16 year age group), the distance between bases is 82 feet, the distance across the diamond 115 feet 11½ inches, the pitching distance 50 feet, and the batting range is 200 to 250 feet.

General use. Baseball can be adapted to a wide range of age levels from elementary school to adult, and the variations listed above may be adapted to meet local needs. Baseball is one of the most popular team sports played in the United States, not only in interscholastic competition, but in Little League, college, semi-professional, and professional circles. There is also a high degree of spectator interest in all phases of baseball. Baseball traditionally begins in the early spring and carries through the summer. In some areas it can be continued almost on a year-round basis, depending on possible conflicts of interest with other sports, such as football.

Alternate uses. Because of the skinned area the baseball infield cannot be satisfactorily used for other sports, but the outfield may well be designed to overlap football, soccer, or other turfed fields devoted to sports popular at different seasons. A typical school athletic field layout usually provides some sort of overlap of this type.

Softball

The area required for softball is 275 by 275 feet (approximately one and three quarters acres), and the orientation of the field is the same as in baseball.

Dimensions. The diamond is 60 feet between bases and the distance across the diamond is 84 feet 10 and ¼ inches. There is generally a minimum of 15 feet of additional space around the diamond with a minimum batting range of 175 feet. The pitching distance for men is 46 feet and for women 35 feet. For typical layout of softball diamond, see Appendix 2.

Marking is generally the same as in baseball.

Construction. Grading, surface, and drainage are similar to the baseball diamond except that the base lines are generally not skinned, but remain as turf areas, and therefore the softball diamond may overlap other turf areas (of seasonal uses) to a greater extent than does the baseball diamond.

Details. The backstop is similar to that used for baseball, but smaller. The center and side sections vary from 15 to 20 feet; the height from 12 to 15 feet.

Bases. The pitcher's plate is the same as for baseball, except that the elevation is not required. Material may be rubber or wood.

Home plate is also the same as in baseball,

Figure 9:8a. Plan of a baseball backstop.

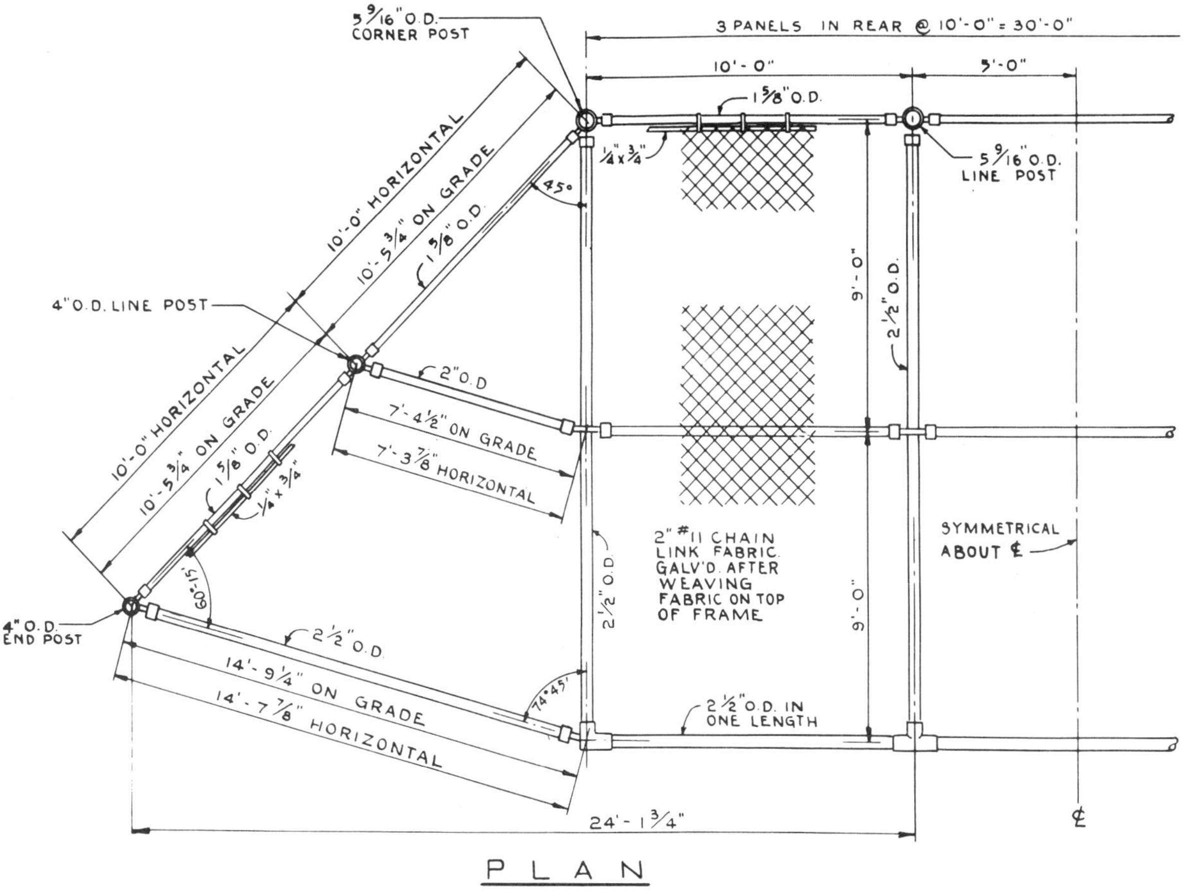

except that the material used is not specified.

First, second, and third bases are the same size as in baseball. They are located inside the base lines (instead of having second base at intersection of lines).

Variations. For the use of women and children, it is possible to vary this facility to a 45 foot diamond, using a 12 inch ball for "slow pitching." The dimensions of the diamond should be 45 by 45 feet, with the distance across the diamond 63 feet 7 inches, and the pitching distance 37 feet 8½ inches.

General use. Probably the most popular form of baseball in light of the number of actual participants, is softball. The equipment is simple, and there is greater flexibility in the size of the diamond, all providing for interesting activity at almost all age levels, from elementary school age to adulthood. The time of use for the softball diamond is similar to that of baseball, only less formal. It is generally dependent only upon suitability of turf playing surface. In addition, its flexibility is increased by the fact that the diamond is essentially just a turfed area, with removable bases and backstop, so that the field may be used for any other field sports.

Field Hockey

The area required for field hockey is 210 by 330 feet (approximately 1.6 acres), with the orientation generally the same as in football.

Dimensions. The official and maximum field is 180 by 300 feet, and the smaller mini-

Figure 9:8b. Elevation of a baseball backstop.

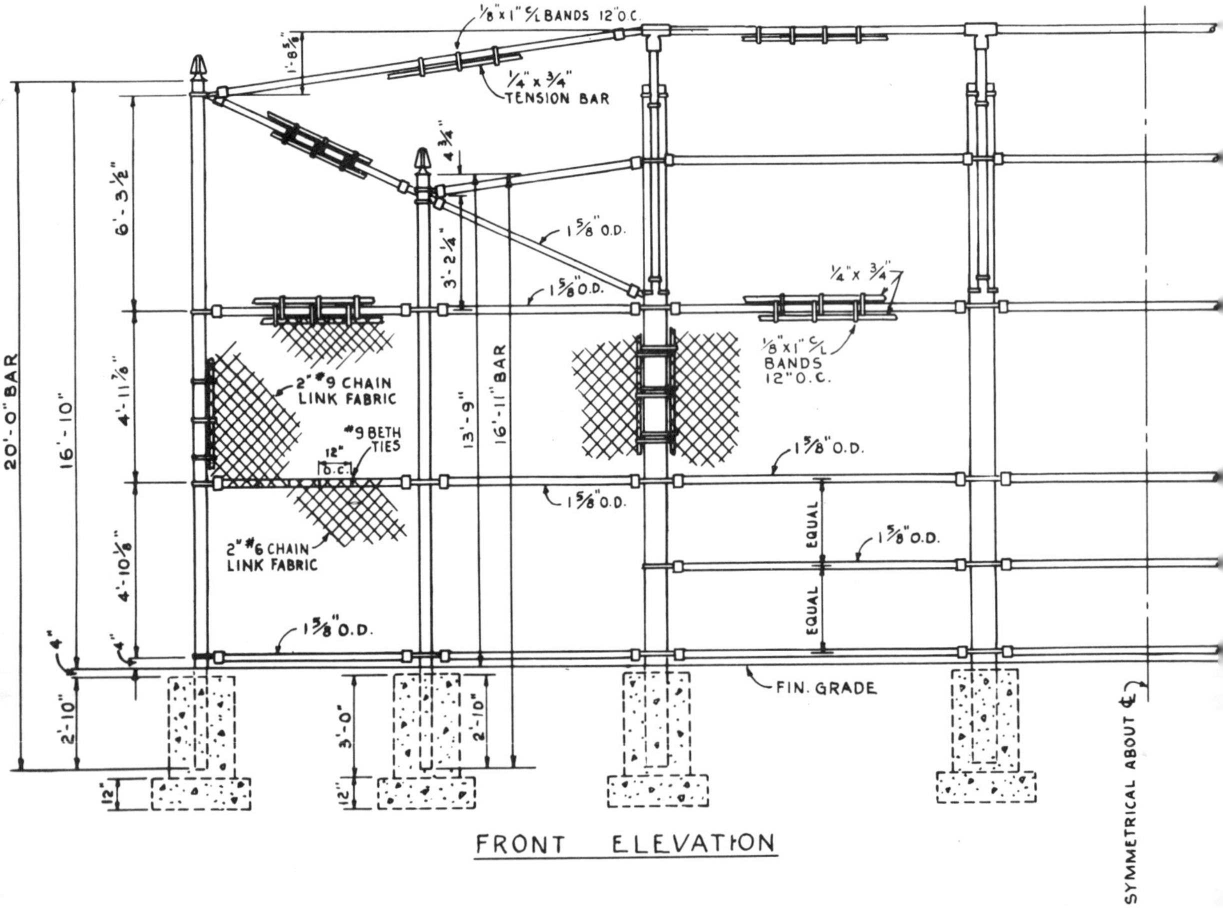

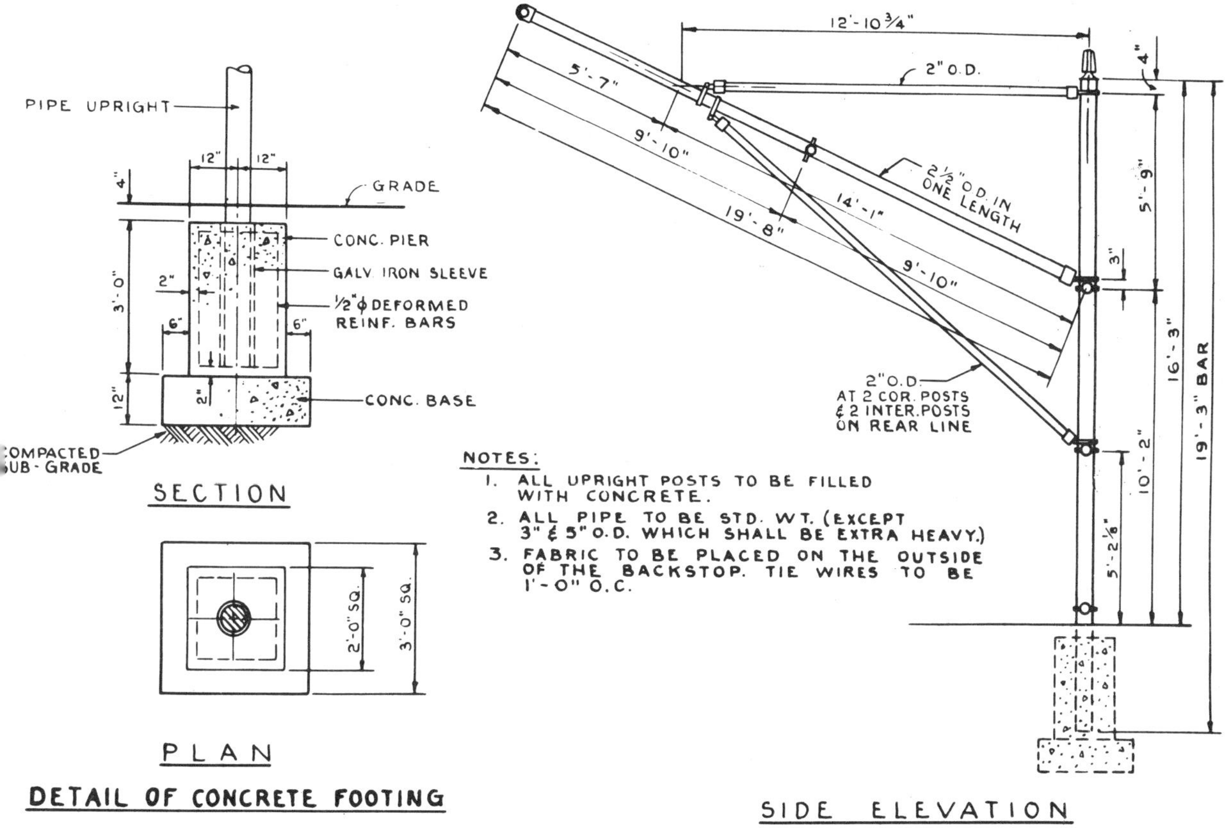

Figure 9:8c. Details of footings for baseball backstop.

mum field for younger children is 150 feet by 270 feet (see Appendix 2 for a detailed layout of the field).

Marking. Lines are drawn across the field between side lines at intervals of 25 yards (in smaller fields the lines consist of two lines across the field 25 yards in from each goal line, and a center line). A broken line called the 5-yard line is located 15 feet inside of and parallel to the side lines for the full length of the field. All lines are 2 inches wide, placed as in football.

Construction. Grading, surface and drainage are the same as for the football field. Goal posts are located on the center of the goal line, 12 feet apart (inside measurement) joined by a cross bar 7 feet from the ground. The posts are 2 inches wide by 3 inches deep. Posts and cross bars are painted white. Uprights do not extend beyond cross bars, and cross bars stop at edge of upright.

General use. The field hockey field is used by senior high school and college students. The popularity of the sport ranges from intramural to intermural.

Soccer (Men)

The area required for this sport is 225 by 360 feet (approximately 1.8 acres), with orientation similar to that of the football field.

Dimensions are a minimum of 100 yards and a maximum of 120 yards for length, with a minimum width of 55 yards and a maximum width of 75 yards.

Marking. The lines at the ends of the field

are called "goal lines," those at the sides are "touch lines." A "halfway line" running between the two touch lines divides the field into two equal areas. At the center of the halfway line is drawn a circle with a 10-yard radius. The "goal area" is marked by two lines extending 6 yards inside of each goal line, 6 yards from each goal post, and connected by a line parallel to the goal line 20 yards in length. Within each penalty area a suitable mark called the "penalty kick mark" is located 12 yards from and directly in front of the midpoint of the goal. From each penalty kick mark an arc of a circle with a 10 yard radius is drawn outside the penalty area only. A quarter circle is usually drawn from each flag post at the corners of the field with a 1 yard radius.

Construction. Grading, surface, and drainage are the same as for the football field. Goal posts are 8 feet high and are set 24 feet apart with a cross bar at the top. Inside width of the uprights is 8 yards. Uprights and cross bar are not more than 5 inches in depth (see Figure 9-4). Flagposts should not be less than 5 feet high with a knob on the top.

Variations. In soccer for women, the dimensions of the field are 60 by 100 yards, center circle radius of 6 yards, and the goal posts are 6 yards apart. A "restraining line" is drawn across the field between the touch lines 6 yards from and parallel to the halfway line. The "penalty area" is formed by a line 4 yards long 15 yards in front of and parallel to each goal. From the ends of this line are drawn quarter circles with a radius of 15 yards and their center 1 yard inside each goal post.

When space does not permit the regulation dimensions, the field can be reduced to a minimum (for men) of 55 by 75 yards, with a greater width if possible.

General use. All age groups from junior high school students to adults play soccer.

Figure 9:10a. Cross section of a handball court wall.

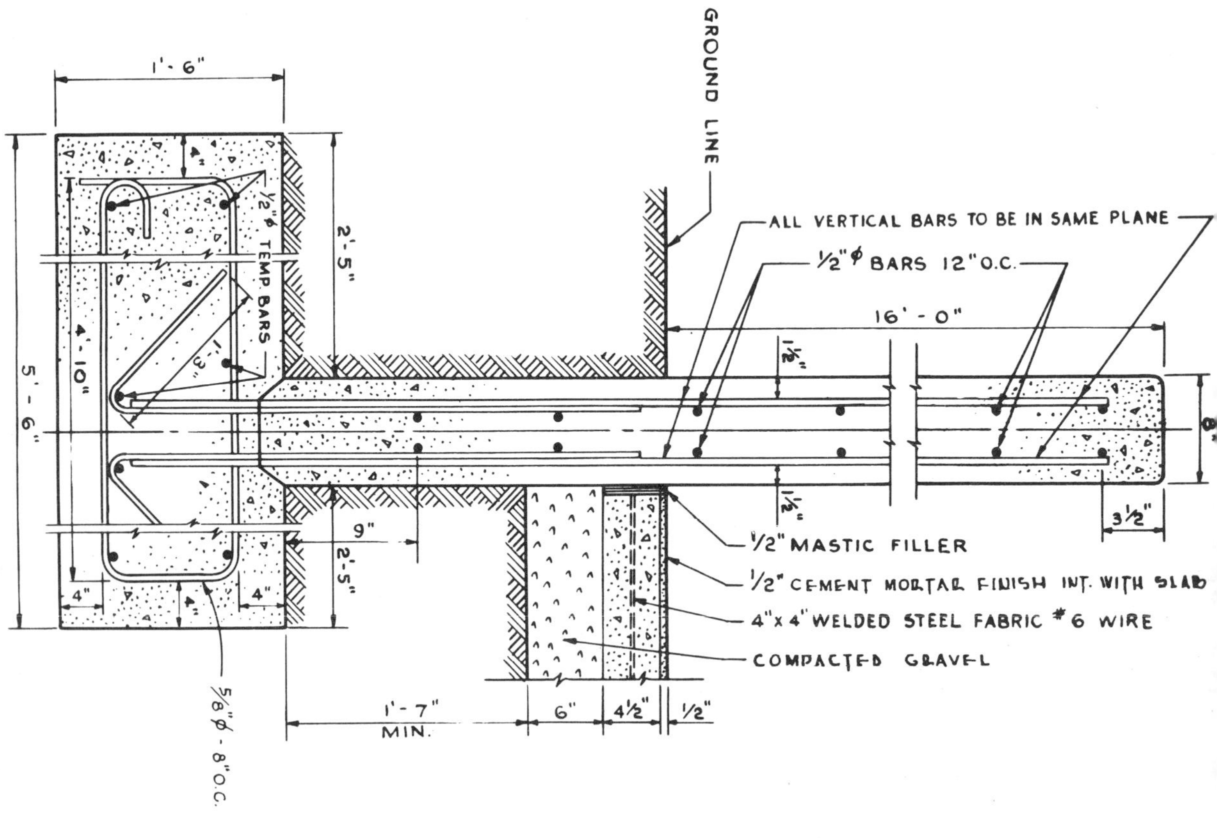

Soccer is played not only in schools, but also among adults in areas with high percentages of population from European countries where soccer (called football) is usually considered a national sport.

Lacrosse

The area required for lacrosse is 225 by 360 feet (approximately 1.8 acres), with orientation similar to that of football.

Dimension. The field is 60 to 70 yards wide and 110 yards long. A barrier fence 5 to 6 feet high is desirable and should be located 10 feet from the boundary lines of the playing field. The goals are located 15 yards in from each end line (see Appendix 2 for men's lacrosse field layout).

Marking. The boundaries of the field are known as "side lines" and "end lines" while a center or "offside line" is drawn across the field between the side lines, in the center of which is marked a circle with a radius of 10 feet. Twenty yards from each side of the center is drawn a line 10 yards long at right angles to the center line designating the "wing areas." The "goal area" is designated by a line 6 feet long drawn parallel to the goal lines 20 yards in front of each goal. A rectangle 12 by 18 feet known as the "goal crease" is marked off around each goal with lines 6 feet from the goal posts in each direction.

Construction. Grading, surface, and drainage are similar to that required for the football field. Goals consist of two poles 6 feet high located 6 feet apart with a rigid cross bar. Attached to these poles is a pyramid-shaped net fastened to a stake in the ground 7 feet back of each goal. The net, usually 1- to 1½-inch mesh cord, is fastened to the ground with tent pegs and staples to catch balls thrown into the goal.

Variations. In lacrosse for women the goals are located on the goal line, from 90 to

Figure 9:10b. Plan of a handball court.

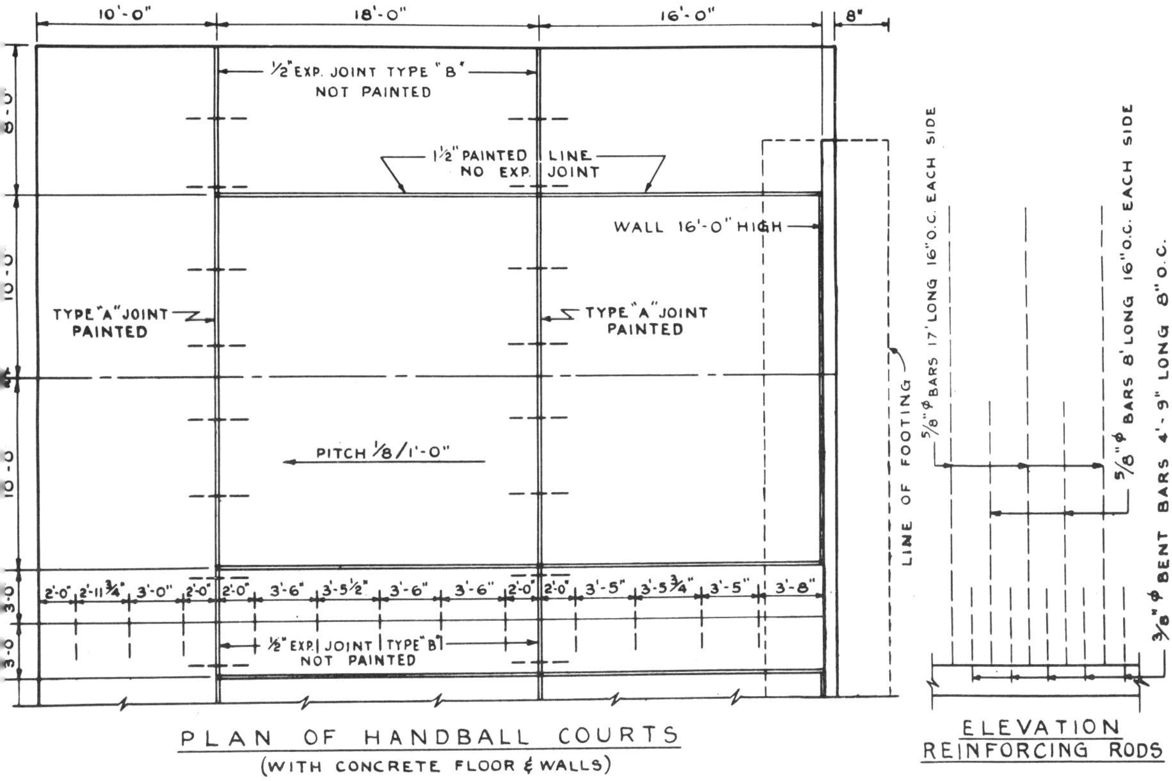

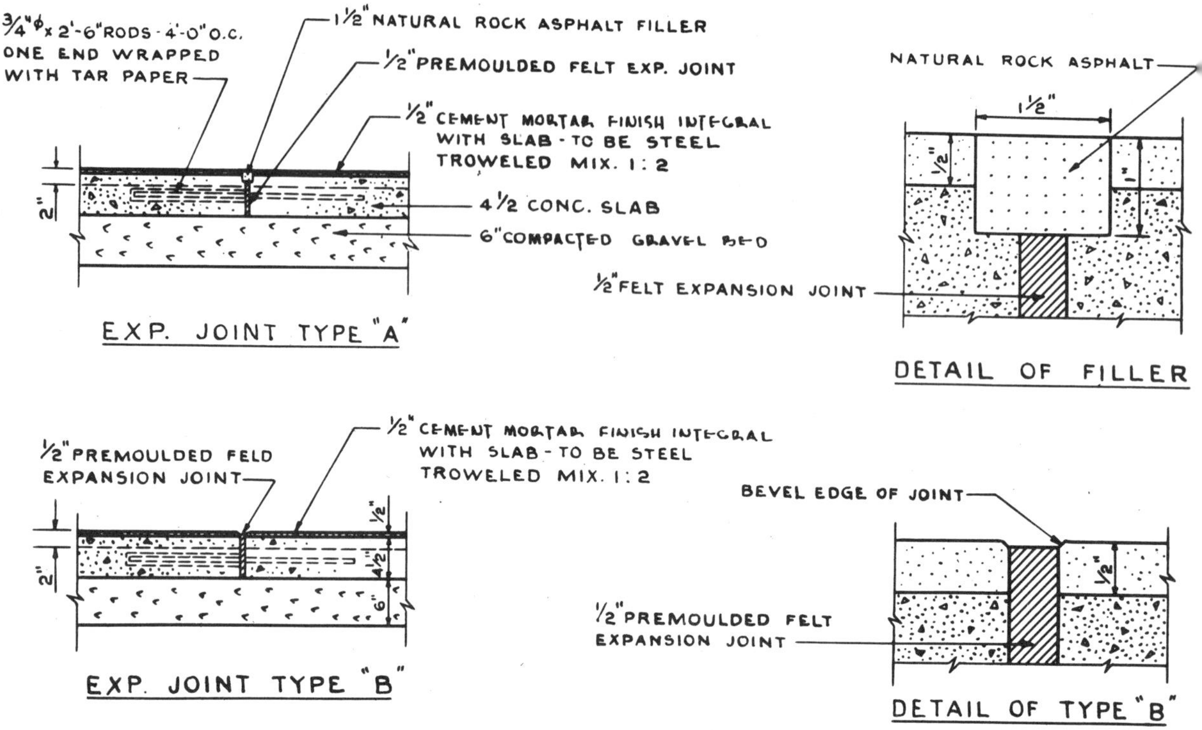

Figure 9:10c. Details of handball court expansion joints.

110 yards apart; the goal crease is square, 12 by 12 feet, and the center line is omitted except for a short line 4 yards long in the center of the circle. The net for the goal is pegged to the ground 6 feet behind the goal instead of 7 feet.

General use. The age level for lacrosse runs from senior high school age to adulthood, and the game is played mostly in colleges and senior high schools.

Archery

The archery area should be level, located in an isolated or protected section of the facility situated so that stray arrows are directed away from other play areas. The area should be sheltered from winds if possible. The range is approximately 150 yards in length, the width of the range depending upon the number of targets, which are usually set up 10 yards apart (except for official meets which require 15 feet spacing). Targets are 4 feet in diameter and made of spirally sewn straw covered with a face having five circles, set up with the center 4 feet above the ground. In the interest of safety the area behind the targets should be protected by an earth bunker, or bales of hay or straw piled up to the height of the top of the target. (See photo on page 120.) The range is usually marked off in lines at 10 yard intervals beginning 20 yards from the target. The common shooting distances are 30, 40, 50, 60, 70, 80 and 100 yards.

Practice Fields

Because of the intensive use of turfed areas for sports such as football, it is wise to provide practice fields that can be used during the week (if space is available) in order to save the turf on the playing field for games. Practice fields may also be used for other sports in off-season periods, thus increasing the over-all facilities available. Dimensions and construction of practice fields should conform to the regulation field size.

Pitch and Putt Golf Course

Golf is a sport that has enjoyed a sharp increase in popularity during the past few years, but a full size golf course requires about 100 acres, thus making it impractical for schools. The pitch and putt course, which requires but 6 to 10 acres of land, could be incorporated in a school site. See Chapter 19 for construction details.

SPECIAL USE AREAS

This section deals with outdoor areas that are surfaced or paved for specific sports, multiple-use all weather areas, and other sports facilities of more specialized interest than those covered in the preceding section.

The ideal paved sports area should be well drained, durable, smooth, and resilient for maximum safety and all weather use, and it should be available at reasonable cost. There are many different types of surfaces available today but most of them fall within one of three categories: cement concrete, asphaltic concrete, and turf. (See Chapters 14, 15, 16, and 17.)

Handball

One-wall handball has become the popular outdoor version of four-wall indoor handball. The area required is 30 by 45 feet (single court). As an economy measure two courts are often constructed back to back in order to share the cost of the wall. It is also often possible to lay out the court areas so as to utilize high retaining walls or blank walls of a building by construction of the playing court against it and improving the surface. The line of the wall should run east and west if possible.

Dimensions. The standard court is 20 feet wide by 34 feet long, and the wall is 16 feet high. The court surface generally extends 10 feet beyond the back line (long line) and at least 4 feet beyond each side line making the total area 28 by 44 feet over-all. It is usually of reinforced concrete construction, but any other smooth, hard, paved surface will suffice. The surface should be constructed on a well-graded base of cinders or gravel with a pitch away from the wall of one-eighth of an inch per foot. The wall is usually constructed of reinforced concrete varying from 8 to 12 inches in thickness, and rests on a concrete footing carried 4 feet below grade. Additional strength may be added by construction of short wing walls at sides at a 45 degree angle to a height of 4 to 6 feet. The wall should extend a minimum of 3 feet outside the side lines on individual courts but is usually continuous in a battery of courts (see Figure 9-10). Although the initial cost is high, the reinforced concrete court and wall requires practically no maintenance. Where a battery of courts is laid out, a minimum of 6 feet between courts is recommended. Courts are generally fenced, and a 10 or 12 foot high chain link type fence is preferred.

Markings. The short line extends across the court 16 feet from and parallel to the wall. The Service line is composed of two lines extending 4 inches into the court from either side line 25 feet from and parallel to the wall. The long line (back line of the court) is 34 feet from and parallel to the wall. All lines are 1½ inches wide and are generally painted white. Side lines are extended 3 feet beyond the long line, and up to the top of the wall. A 2-foot high wire fence may be mounted on top of the wall to stop balls hit high and out of play.

General use. Handball is played by junior high school and other students and by adults. It holds a strong appeal to people of all ages who prefer a very active sport, and is particularly popular in large city playgrounds.

Tennis Courts

The area required for two tennis courts is 105 by 120 feet (each additional court requires 45 by 120 feet). (See Chapter 18 for details in construction and layout.)

Outdoor Basketball Courts

Originally an indoor sport, basketball has become increasingly popular in its outdoor version, usually as part of the paved all-weather play area.

Layout. A minimum area of 60 by 80 feet to 70 by 114 feet is required depending upon the age group to use the courts.

Orientation. The long axis of the court should run generally north-south.

Dimensions. The following dimensions are generally recommended for various age levels: Elementary school level, 40 by 60 feet; junior high school 42 by 74 feet; high school 50 by 84 feet; college 50 by 94 feet. The court is divided in half by the "division line" drawn across the court from side line to side line. Other markings include the center and restraining circles, and free throw circles and lanes at each end of the court. (See Indoor Court Markings in Chapters 4 and 5).

Backboards. The backboards may be rectangular (6 feet wide x 4 feet high) or fan shaped, located at opposite ends of the court midway between side lines with the face of the backboard parallel to and 4 feet in from the end line. Board may be attached directly to upright or for greater safety supported by projecting arms from posts set on the end line.

Baskets. The baskets consist of metal rings 18 inches in diameter mounted in the center of the backstop, 8 feet from the court surface for elementary level and 10 feet for standard use. Nets of cord, leather or chain are usually suspended from these rings. To maintain maximum flexibility of use, the uprights may be set in flush sockets so that they may be removed for roller skating, dancing, or other uses. It has also been found helpful to provide an extra basket at the opposite side at each upright for shooting practice and other games that can be played around a single basketball goal.

Goal-Hi

Goal-hi is an adaptation of basketball played around a single goal. The court is usually circular with a 20 to 30 foot radius from the goal at the center to the outside boundary circle, a free throw line with a radius one-half that of the court, and a restraining circle with a 4 foot radius. The basket is similar to a basketball backstop, placed 8 to 10 feet above the court surface, depending upon the age group.

Several other games have been developed for use around the single goal such as Hi-Lo Goal, Center Ball, and Solo Ball.

Volleyball

Volleyball is an increasingly popular group sport at almost all age levels. It may be played on any hard surface, or even good level turf if it is not wet.

Area required. 45 by 80 feet, more or less.

Orientation. Long axis runs north and south.

Layout. Official dimensions are 30 by 60 feet. For children a court size of 25 by 50 feet is recommended. The net across the center divides the court into two 30 by 30 foot playing areas as in the photo on page 124. The net, 3 feet wide by 32 feet long, is tightly stretched by the four corners to two uprights erected outside the court along the center lines at a height of 8 feet above the court surface (for women the net should be lowered to 7 feet 6 inches and for children the net may be lowered to 6 feet). Posts are usually provided with eye bolts at the various levels to accommodate varying age groups on the same court.

Badminton

Badminton is another popular sport for all age levels. It can be played on any level surface and may be adapted either to the multiple-use area or a level turf surface.

Area required. 25 by 60 feet.

Orientation. Same as for volleyball.

Layout. The doubles court is 20 by 44 feet with a 2½ by 24 foot net stretched across the center at a height of 5 feet to the top of the net. The singles court differs from the doubles court only in its width which is 17 feet. (For layout of combined doubles-singles court, see Appendix 2.)

Paddle Tennis

Paddle tennis is a popular playground game that can be played on a court the same dimensions as badminton.

Area required. 25 by 60 feet.

Orientation. Same as for badminton.

Layout. The official doubles court is 20 by 44 feet with a net across the center 2 feet 10 inches high at midpoint (see Appendix 2).

Deck Tennis

Deck tennis was originated for use on shipboard, but has achieved popularity in many recreation areas. The singles court is 12 by 40 feet, the doubles court 18 by 40 feet. The net is 1½ feet wide and its top is 4 feet 6 inches high at the center, supported by posts set 2 feet outside at the side lines (see Appendix 2 for layout).

Shuffleboard

Shuffleboard is another shipboard game that has become increasingly popular in recreation areas, particularly in resort areas. The court is 6 feet wide by 52 feet long. The game must be played on a smooth, level surface preferably with a waxed finish. With some additional treatment a portion of the paved multiple-use area can be adapted to this use. Courts are generally provided in batteries with drains separating the courts with a low concrete curb or wooden bumper at each end of the courts, behind which are seats for the players. A scoreboard is required with each court, and marking of the court is shown in Appendix 2.

OTHER USES FOR ALL-WEATHER PLAY AREAS

Paved all-weather play areas may be utilized for numerous less formal purposes in addition to the games listed above. Some of the more common are:

1. *Overflow parking.* By proper planning and design this area may be utilized as additional parking space when not in use as a play area. It is especially useful in conjunction with evening use of school facilities. In the event this use is contemplated, a removable gate or chain should be provided so that vehicles cannot use the area during play periods.

2. *Roller skating.* The application of a sealing compound to asphalt play areas will usually provide a surface smooth enough for roller skating and also provide a less abrasive surface reducing the danger of injury resulting from skids and falls.

3. *Dancing.* An outdoor paved play area properly surfaced may provide an excellent location for outdoor dancing during summer months.

4. *Ice skating.* The addition of a low concrete or asphalt curb and modification of drainage structures makes possible the flooding of paved play areas during winter months in northern areas for ice skating without the hazard of falling through thin ice on lakes or ponds. If paved areas are to be utilized for ice skating it is important that the grading be designed to create a minimum difference in grade. Generally, if the area can be pitched from the long axis to both sides proper leveling can be achieved.

DRAINAGE

In designing large surfaced areas for all-weather use the increased run-off due to surfacing must be considered and adequate drainage provided for. Whenever possible the area should be graded to drain from the center to several sides in order to:

avoid location of catch basins within playing areas

reduce concentration of run-off at one point

minimize grade differential from one side to the other.

Surfaced play areas should generally have a maximum pitch of 2 per cent and a minimum pitch of 0.5 per cent, with catch basins or inlets located at a ratio of one for every 15,000 square feet of paved surface.

In areas with low water table and sand or gravel subsoil, it will probably be practicable to utilize a combination catch basin and dry well (see Figure 9-11). In areas where ground water and soil conditions are unsuitable, positive drainage must be provided either by piping or by means of paved ditches to proper discharge points in an existing water course or storm sewer.

In areas subject to frost action it may be necessary to provide additional sub-surface drainage in the form of porous foundation construction, tile underdrains, or both. Such construction, with adequate provision for surface run-off, will greatly increase the useful life of the facility and protect surrounding turf areas from erosion.

SPECIAL FACILITIES

In addition to the various facilities and activities enumerated thus far, it is well to mention other facilities that may be required, particularly where interscholastic, municipal, and competitive play is envisaged. These may include the stadium seating facilities, parking areas, fencing, and other special facilities.

The Stadium

Many books have already been written on the subject of stadiums, and it is not appropriate in this book to go into too much detail on the topic. However, most previous works have reference to the large university and municipal stadiums that are the homes of big-league baseball or football.

The handling of spectators for sporting events requires a separate study in itself where the anticipated capacity is large and provision for adequate seating facilities is of major importance. The large athletic field will usually be provided with a permanent grandstand, which, depending upon the size of anticipated crowds, may range from a single unit along one side of the field to a complete stadium accommodating upwards of 40,000 people.

For the small college or larger high school, a permanent installation is required that will adequately fulfill the several functions of the larger stadium and will also remain within the reach of the school budget.

A concrete or steel grandstand is more permanent and should be considered whenever adequate funds are available, but stands can also be constructed of wood or wood and steel if economy dictates. When the latter type of stands are used it is customary to construct them in prefabricated sections that can be dismantled for storage or for reerection elsewhere on the site. For ease in moving, wheels are mounted under the sections. In many school facilities a small permanent grandstand is supplemented by removable bleachers used only during big games. In either instance, local ordinances and fire laws must be rigidly observed in respect to methods of construction, kinds of materials employed, and in the placing of fire exits, passages, and gangways in the various sections of the stands. The use of removable or portable bleachers permits greater flexibility in the surrounding area, and the units themselves may be utilized at other locations for other spectator sports.

The location of the track and field events has already been discussed in another section, and reasons given for its particular orientation. In locating the grandstands, therefore, it follows that they should be placed at each side of the track so that the spectators command a view of the entire track. The stands are set back a distance of 10 to 15 feet from the track curb to provide for access if necessary, and to allow track and other officials to move about clear of the actual running area.

In the event only one stand is contemplated, it should be placed on the west side of the straightaway so that the spectators, in addition to having a clear view of the track and field event, do not look into the sun. This arrangement has the further advantage of giving some protection against glare to players and contestants when the sun is at a low angle, as it will then be behind the grandstand.

If a baseball diamond is included within the same facility, the bleacher layout will have to be revised by the addition of temporary stands extending parallel to the base lines. If stands are located close to the base lines, as behind home plate for example, they should be protected with wire fencing.

Generally, the stands are of the open type, but where funds permit, they may be designed to afford protection against the weather for the spectators seated therein. Maximum visibility may still be achieved by use of ramped and terraced seating extending upwards and backwards towards the roof, which is usually projected out beyond the front seats to ensure full shade and protection. It is important also for those sitting high up in the back of the stand that their view of the far side of the field is not curtailed in any way by the leading edge of the roof

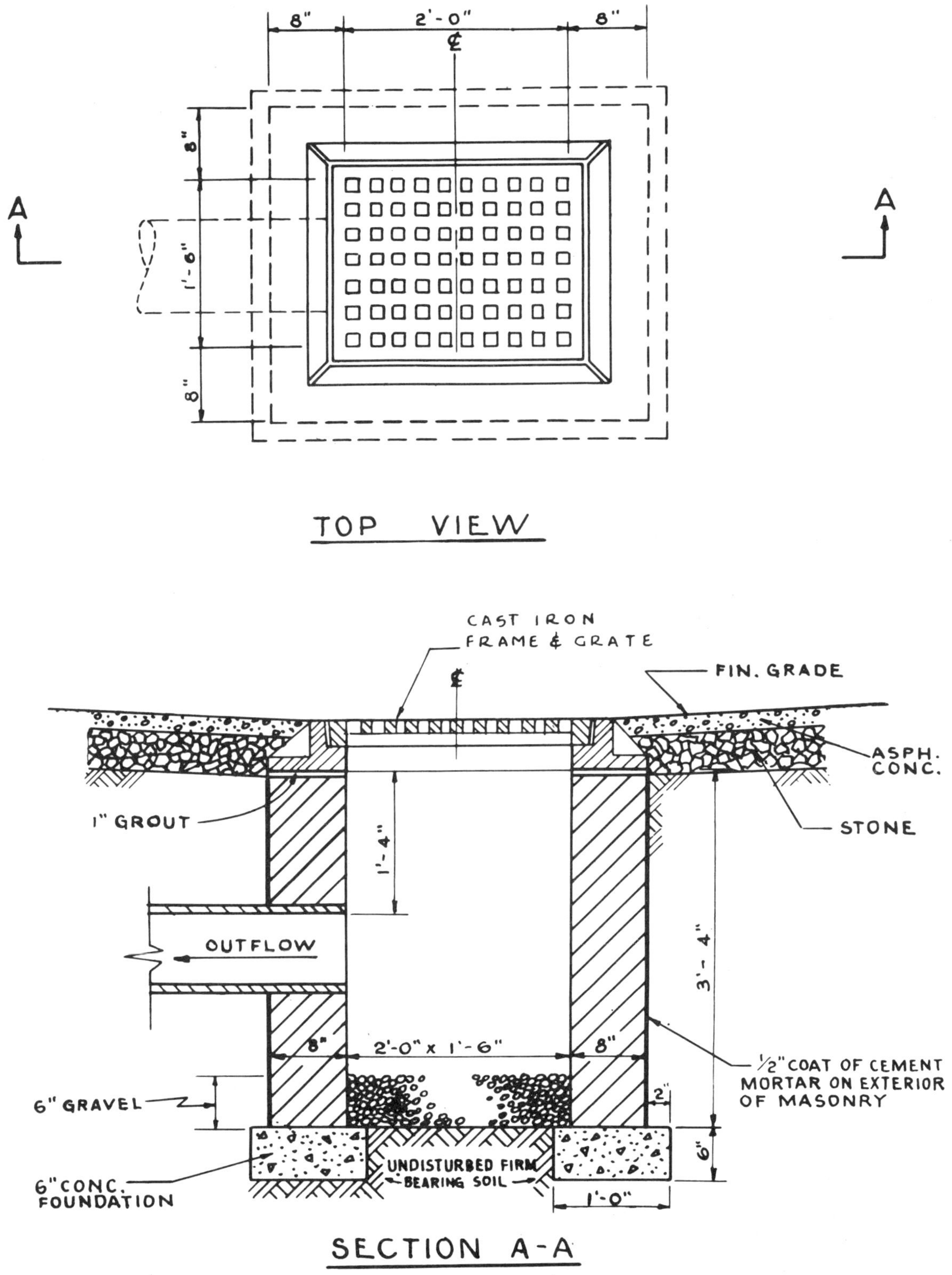

Figure 9:11. Detail of catch basin.

canopy. Similarly, glassed in ends enable the play at both ends of the field to be followed.

Seating. Stands should be designed so that all spectators have an unimpaired view of the playing field. In order to improve the visibility of spectators in the upper seats the height of risers is increased slightly from lower to upper levels. Risers will vary from 9 to 16 inches, with seat width from 18 to 24 inches.

The usual seating for football stadiums consists of strips of wood or planks fixed to pedestals. These may be supported on the treads or fastened to the riser joists. More leg room is afforded by the pedestals than by the riser type bench. Precautions should be taken to avoid sharp points or hooks that will catch or tear clothing and a kind of paint that will not stain clothes should be used. Most seating of this type is not provided with back rests. The minimum allowance per person is 18 inches, and in all cases it is necessary to allow a greater tread width when backs are provided.

Further functions. In addition to providing seating accommodation for spectators, permanent concrete stands can also be made to serve a double duty by providing space for storage of ground equipment, locker rooms, and showers, team and public toilets, and in some cases, refreshment rooms.

Team quarters. Separate quarters are provided for home and visiting teams, or for men and women where co-educational track events are held. Team rooms are furnished with showers, lockers, toilets, and rubbing tables. They should be located within easy reach of the play field and track with exits that are separated from the public section of the stand.

Public toilets. Toilet facilities should be adequate, both as to the number of fixtures and location, and provision made for light and ventilation.

Storage. Storage space is usually provided for athletic paraphernalia, ground equipment, tools, and so forth.

Scoreboards, lighting, and public address systems. In addition to the aforementioned facilities, provision should be made for a scoreboard. Reference has already been made to the hand operated type of scoreboard, but in a stadium layout such as described above an electrically operated board would be the ideal. It should have provision for indicating the score or state of the game for all events for which the stadium is likely to be used. The installation of a public address system and tower lighting for night games would greatly increase the efficiency and scope of the stadium.

Parking

Adequate facilities for parking should be considered in the early stages of site selection, since the parking requirements of a stadium or baseball field may be considerable. For preliminary estimating purposes assume an average of 110 cars can be parked on an acre of level parking space. The space need not be paved unless the use is regular and continuous, although a paved area is usable under all weather conditions, is not dusty, requires a minimum of maintenance, and can be marked with painted lines for best control of parking.

The parking area design should permit easy accommodation of a maximum number of cars within a short distance of the facility served. In the case of stadium parking it is desirable to work out a traffic pattern for before and after games, which may involve one way traffic through the area. For planning purposes an individual parking space is figured at 10 by 20 feet with a minimum of 25 feet for travel lanes between parking rows. (See Figure 9-12 for typical parking layouts.) For smaller facilities it is often possible to provide parking bays along existing or proposed roads bordering the area, but larger facilities and public recreation areas may require one or more parking fields, located as close as possible to the area. Because of various factors such as cost and availability of space it is not always possible to construct regular paved parking areas capable of accommodating all the traffic at an intercollegiate football game. Whenever extra heavy automobile traffic does occur, it is generally the practice to designate certain areas normally given over to play facilities for "overflow" parking. Since these areas are not ordinarily used for parking during regular school hours, their dual role does

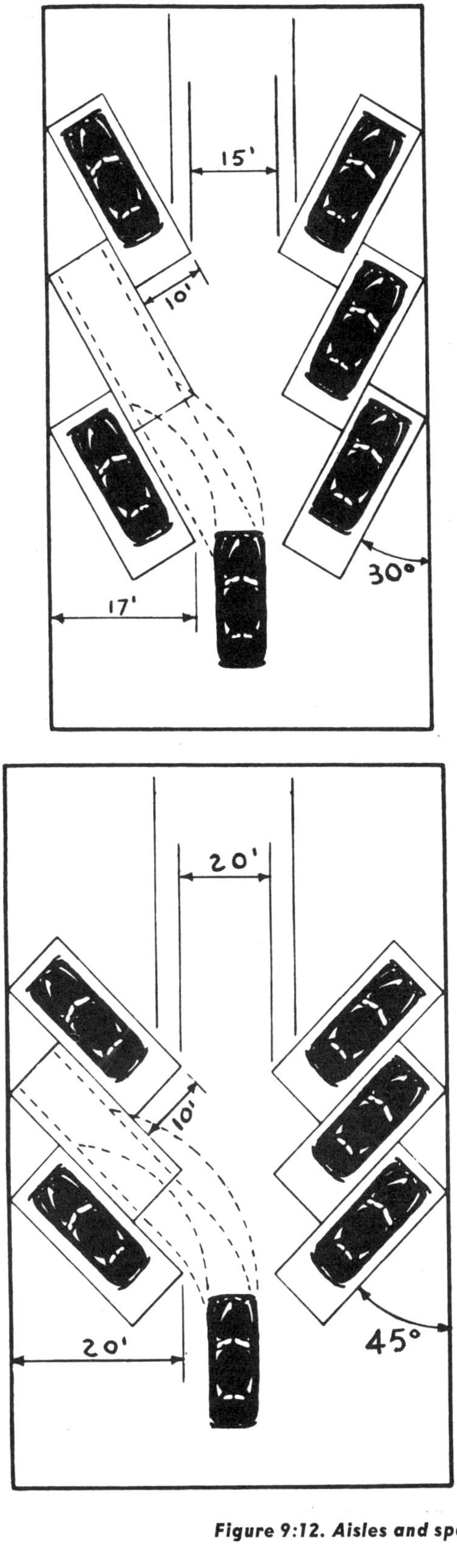

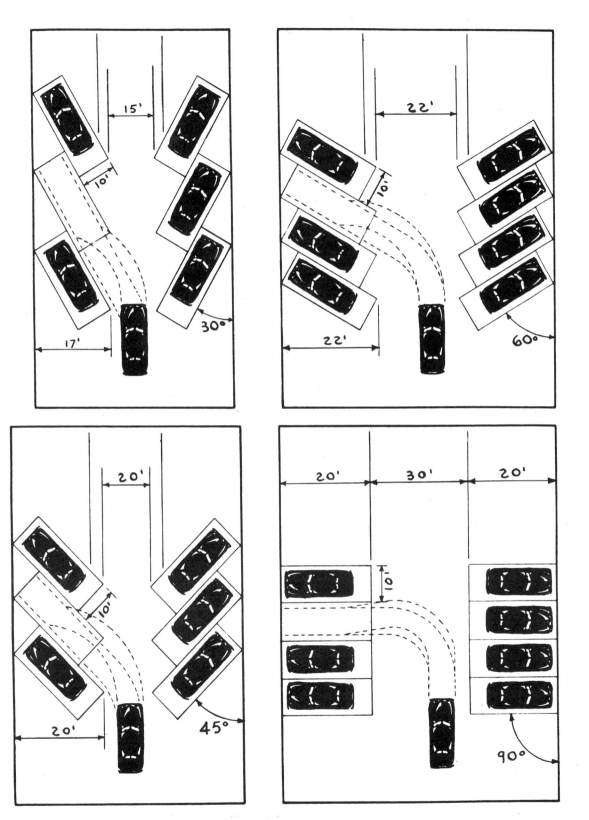

Figure 9:12. ***Aisles and spaces required for various angles of parking.***

not interfere with the school's normal athletic program. The same remarks regarding accessibility to the stands, circulation of traffic, and so forth, apply, since control of traffic on turfed areas is effected by roped enclosures rather than by the use of painted lines.

Fencing

Fencing is required for various purposes throughout the sports area to control crowds, to keep children from wandering off of play areas onto private property, to divide play areas of different types, to protect against hazardous site conditions, to provide a barrier or backstop for various ball games. Most common are several varieties of chain link fence with metal posts set in a concrete footing.

For smaller children's areas and barrier fencing, a height of 4 feet is usually adequate. For older children's areas and property lines, 6 feet is generally used, and for play areas, heights of 8 to 12 feet are recommended, depending upon the sport and age level of participants. All fence posts should be set in concrete footings constructed about 3 inches above the grade and which slope away from the post to prevent the post from rusting due to collection of water around the base. For simplified maintenance, fencing around paved areas should be located within the limits of paving to prevent grass and weeds growing up around the fence. In children's play areas specifications should call for knuckled finish for safety reasons.

Except in scenic parks and recreation areas wooden fencing is not recommended because of the problem of maintenance, and the initial cost will not differ greatly from that of the chain link fence.

Along roads and drives, and for some parking areas, it is well to utilize a guardrail that may be of wire rope or one of several beam types mounted on wooden or metal posts.

Drinking Fountains

In designing recreation areas for schools and communities, there are certain additional features that are often overlooked or omitted to save costs, although without these features no scheme is really complete. For example, provision should always be made for drinking fountains, strategically placed at various points. These should be of the automatic type that shut off when not actually being used, and should be fitted with mouth guards in the interests of hygiene.

Benches

Benches for non-participants and for players resting between game periods are other useful adjuncts, and their location should be given particular attention. Since a great deal of foot traffic around the benches can be expected, it is recommended that they be set on paved areas either adjoining paved walks and play areas in the form of seat recesses, or in a part of the turfed areas where they can command a view of the proceedings without interfering in any way with the play.

Landscaping

Attractive and well landscaped grounds provide a pleasant and relaxing setting for the school grounds or recreational area, and reflect credit upon the community. In addition to the aesthetic advantages, the use of trees and shrubs in accordance with modern planting design concepts can provide many functional advantages. Properly located shade trees are highly desirable for kindergarten play areas, apparatus areas, and sitting areas adjacent to younger children's play areas. An effective, pleasing, and inexpensive screen between different types of play areas can be achieved by use of low-growing dense hedges which also serve to reduce sound transmission. The inclusion of thorny types of shrubs in these screens will discourage traffic through them. Trees are especially valuable in connection with park and picnic areas, and such special uses as the outdoor theater, council ring, and around playground buildings.

The services of a competent site planner or landscape architect are required when planning the planting design, so that consideration is given to all aspects of the landscape plan. Large trees, for example, must be placed so that shadow will not interfere with court games or prevent rapid drying of fields or tennis courts after a rainfall. The

Architects: Kenney and Cullmore

Above: A unique concrete sun shelter. Below: A small recreation center and equipment storage area. Heritage Park, Bakersfield, California.

wide range of climatic and soil conditions from one section of the country to the other makes it impossible to list specific plant materials for use in recreation and sport areas; however, the local landscape architect will be thoroughly familiar with native plant materials most suitable for the various uses required. Major consideration in the choice of plant materials is the stressing of the use of hardy and native plants and a consideration of the degree of maintenance to be required. Consideration should also be given to selection of best lawn seed mixture when seeding to attain the desired turf. (See Chapter 17 on Turf Surfaces.) In some cases the use of flowers and gardens as a decorative addition to the recreation area can be tied in with children's classes in nature study, or with the operation of a municipal greenhouse for providing materials to various municipal parks and playgrounds.

The landscape architect, however, deals not only with plant materials but with the land itself. Hills and valleys, streams and lakes are all a part of the total site and with functional design can play an important part in the educational and recreational picture of the community.

CHAPTER 10

THE COMMUNITY CENTER BUILDING

The Charles M. Graves Organization

A COMMUNITY RECREATION BUILDING IS usually administered by the city recreation department as a public building open to people of all ages for their leisure time use. The program includes a wide variety of scheduled activities, as well as unorganized activities such as an occasional table tennis game, dancing to an automatic record player, or just sitting and relaxing. It is a place to meet one's friends and to participate in an activity of one's choice.

The construction, maintenance, administration, and operation of a recreation building is a community responsibility. Occasionally such centers are financed through a foundation or by contributions, but this method has many disadvantages. It is a municipal responsibility and since everybody benefits from it, everybody should share in its expense through a tax program.

Ordinarily the use of the center is free to the public. Many activities, however, pay their own way financially, and others provide additional revenue which is used for building operation cost. It is not unusual to have revenue-producing programs pay twenty-five per cent or more of the total administration cost. A community recreation building is for all the people all the time.

Undoubtedly, the community center idea came from the neighborhood or settlement house field as well as from the YMCA and YWCA programs. More recently Jewish community centers, often in combination with a synagogue, have been constructed in many communities.

THE COMMUNITY CENTER BUILDING

Other types of facilities related to the

Illustration: Community Center Building, Rockmart, Georgia

Architect: The Charles M. Graves Organization, Park and Recreation Engineers

"community center" concept include student unions found today on many college campuses, as well as boys' clubs and certain church-social centers.

Area Served

Community center buildings are planned primarily to serve specific geographical areas. In communities of up to 25,000 population, a building could be designed to serve the entire community, and would be a building with 15,000 to 25,000 square feet of floor space. The minimum size should be 15,000 square feet. The same size building could serve as a neighborhood recreation building in a city of 50,000 or larger. Many community recreation buildings have served effectively with only 7,000 to 10,000 square feet of floor space, but a well-rounded program is hardly possible in a building of that size.

Within the past 30 or 40 years, the neighborhood playground and neighborhood recreation building have proved to be most effective. This is especially true where people can walk to the building and the distance traveled is not more than one-half to three-quarters of a mile. Then, too, during the past few years people have become more mobile (with the exception of the very low income groups) and children, as well as family groups, ride to the community recreation building, even if it is only three or four blocks away. Where automobiles are not available, paved streets and sidewalks provide a medium for easy bicycle travel. Larger buildings, serving several neighborhoods and including more floor space, more program possibilities, and more leadership, have proved quite effective in many communities.

Site Location

Many community recreation buildings are operated very successfully in a "down town" location, without outdoor play space, although this is certainly not ideal. Even in northern communities where the weather limits outdoor play in the winter, there is need for space for winter activities, such as ice skating. Therefore, for a community recreation building to be successful, there should be 15 to 20 acres of land on which the building will be properly located from the points of view of accessibility and appearance. The outdoor facilities should be related to the activities within the building like spokes in a wheel. Some community center buildings are located in city parks. The building need not be in the center of the park but possibly on one side, and, therefore, adjacent to a main street, with parking adjacent to the street and to the building with an entrance drive of minimum length.

Basic Units to Be Included

In a well designed community recreation building certain basic units should be included, primarily in the following order:

1. *Central Administrative and Lobby Area.* The building must have a focal point and a central spot for administration, and this should be adjacent to the entrance of the building. This central area should be so located that it will be adjacent to the avenue of approach for the majority of the users, and should be near the street or driveway and parking area. The lobby should be centrally located in the building so that persons can readily reach the various activity areas of the building. It is important to have offices for administrative and control purposes adjoining the lobby. Rest rooms should also be located nearby.

2. *Small Activity Areas.* Various types and sizes of clubrooms, meeting rooms, craft and game rooms, and activity rooms for small groups are the next important features. These rooms should be properly arranged for accessibility, ease in administration, heating, and control. The rooms should be located so that it is not necessary to pass through one activity room to get to another.

3. *Social Hall-Gymnasium Auditorium.* A community recreation building should have a large space for social and athletic activities and meetings. Such a room should be well designed in order to accommodate the average activity planned for it. Ordinarily, the room should be large enough to accommodate a junior high school size basketball court and space for 200 to 300 seats, using telescopic folding bleachers of two or three rows. For this purpose, a room approximately 60 by 90 feet would be required. A minimum size of 80 by 100 feet would be preferable and 100 by 110 feet would be even better. The room should be easily accessible to the central lobby and administrative unit.

4. *Dressing and Shower Rooms and Clothes Check Room.* These facilities should be properly planned and located to serve the gymnasium, and should be accessible to the lobby without passing through the gymnasium. If an outdoor and/or indoor swimming pool is a part of the building, the above mentioned rooms should be properly located to serve both the pool and gymnasium. Adequate control must be maintained, and easy access to pool and gymnasium, with minimum walking distances, is necessary.

5. *Maintenance and Custodial Facilities.* Of major importance is adequate and properly located storage space for equipment and maintenance supplies, janitorial closets, equipment rooms, and space for heating and air conditioning equipment. If a pool is included space must be provided for a filter room.

Elements of the Community Recreation Building

1. *Lobby.* The lobby should be placed so that it will be the first room through which visitors to the building will pass. There should be adequate space for the groups who will be using it, but it should be neither too large nor too small. The lobby should be the central element of the building and the activity areas should radiate from it. Offices should be adjoining, especially an office to serve as an information center. The lobby must of necessity have double doors for adequate exit, and, in the case of larger buildings, should have two or more sets of double doors. The lobby must be attractive, as it will be the "front cover" of the building and will convey to the visitor his first impres-

Community Center with accompanying outdoor recreation facilities, Wilson, North Carolina.

Architects: The Charles M. Graves Organization and Charles C. Benton and Sons

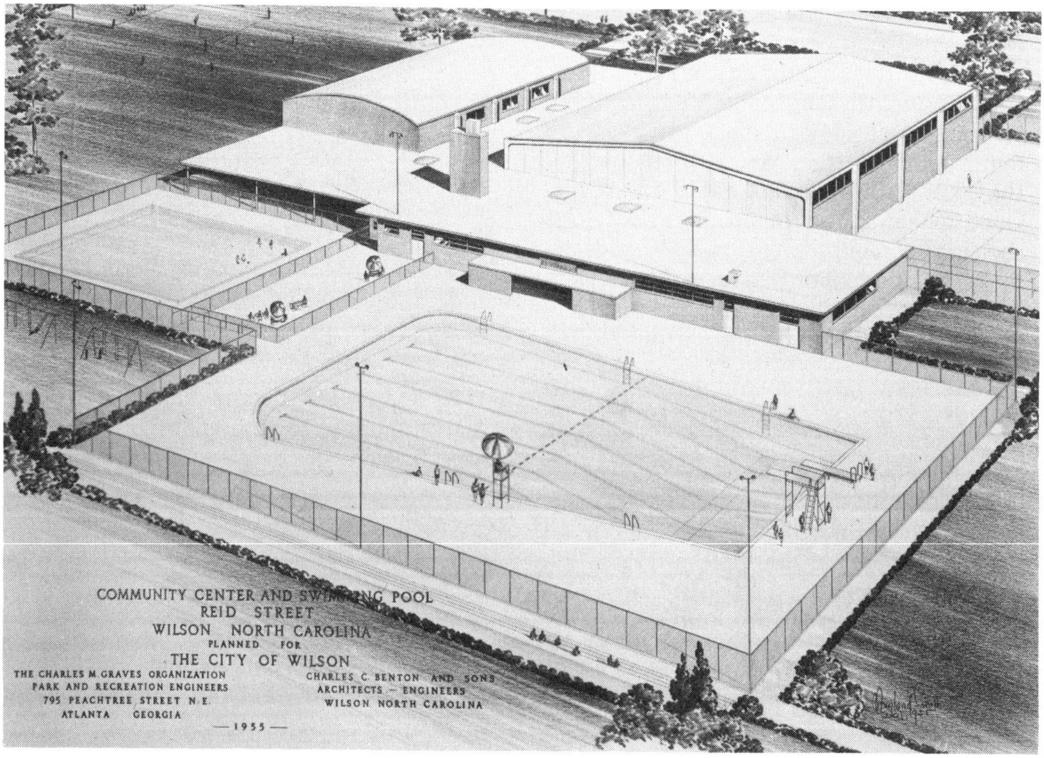

Photo by the Department of Photography, Ohio State University

Student Union Building, Ohio State University, Columbus, Ohio.

sion of the building. The lobby should be well lighted, have comfortable lounge furniture, and include bulletin boards for publicizing activities. Pay telephones and restrooms should be located nearby.

Space and facilities should be available for temporary storage of coats, overshoes, raincoats, hats, overcoats, school books, and the like. Ordinarily this space can be provided by the use of coat and hat racks and shelves for books along one side of the lobby or corridor, or in a special coat room. In some cases, the coat room serves as a check room during large scale activities.

2. *Lounge.* Every recreation building, especially a large one, needs space for comfortable lounge furniture arranged in groupings, to be used by individuals or by groups in social relaxation or conversation. Sometimes the lounge is combined with the lobby, thereby making it multiple-use, with the furniture grouped in the corners away from the main traffic pattern. Often, the lounge is a separate room and doubles as a club room; it can open off the lobby, with one or two sets of double doors, and serve as an overflow area for the lobby.

Attractive and adequate overhead lighting is important in all cases. In some buildings, table lamps are secured to tables for proper maintenance and care. Sometimes small pin point lights are installed in the ceiling, throwing directed light in specific sections of the lounge. Attractive cove or indirect lighting adds a great deal to the appearance of such a room. In some recreation buildings, the lounge is called a "memorial lounge" and is equipped by an individual or an organization in memory of a certain individual, or group of individuals.

3. *Offices.* Even the smallest recreation building needs an office. If the building serves as a central administration building, a series of offices will be required. In a building of 15,000 square feet or more, two offices would be considered a minimum. One office should be adjacent to the lobby and provide space for a clerk, secretary, and information clerk. Counter space should be located on the lobby side, and windows in the other walls where appropriate, making it possible to observe activities in all adjacent activity areas, such as the club rooms, gymnasium, and corridors. This office should have storage space for equipment and supplies. It should also include the control equipment for loud speaker and amplifier for making announcements and for provision of music over the entire building, or for any one room. A control panel should be available for channeling music to specific rooms, and speakers should be located in all the rooms and lobby, as well as at the swimming pool and multiple-use paved area.

The office for the director or administrator of the program should adjoin the clerk's office, and the partition walls should include windows for ease in administration and observation. Book shelves and cabinet space for storage of equipment and supplies should be provided. Arrangements should be such that the room can be closed off for private conferences of small groups. Although the director's office is often planned for a conference room, it is not always considered essential, since staff conferences, board meetings, committee meetings and similar activities could be held in a small club room away from the noise of an office and annoyance of the telephone.

4. *Club rooms.* One club room is a must in any community recreation building, and additional rooms should be provided in proportion to the need and the size of the building. The minimum size of a club room is 12 by 20 feet, and a more desirable minimum size is 20 by 30 feet. Where space is available, it is highly important to have a series of two or three club rooms, located adjacent to each other, and separated by an effective folding wall, thereby making provision for one large or several small rooms. Only the best folding walls, with acoustical treatment, should be used. Each room should be readily accessible from the corridor and each room should have separately controlled lights. Whenever possible, the folding wall should fit into a pocket to protect it from damage and to clear the room.

Photo by the Department of Photography, Ohio State University

A series of meeting rooms that open to one or more rooms by the use of folding partitions. Student Union Building, Ohio State University, Columbus, Ohio.

Each room should be provided with storage space or a series of storage cabinets for the storage of tables, chairs, craft and equipment supplies, projector equipment, and other necessary items.

Often a number of different groups will use the club rooms for meetings. The groups will have various types of flags, books, and other equipment they would like to leave at the meeting room so that it will be readily available at the time of the next weekly or monthly meeting. In these instances it is highly desirable to have a series of cabinets built into the wall, each fitted with a lock, thereby providing each organization with its own storage space.

Adequate window coverings should be provided, so that either one or all rooms can be used for showing movies and slides. If a room is to be used a great deal for showing films, it is desirable to have adequate electrical connections, designed so that the projector can be plugged in at one end of the room and the amplifier at the other, with adequate wiring installed in the floor or in the wall, so that it will not be necessary to have the amplifier cord lying on the floor down the middle of the room.

If the end club room is small, it could be constructed with the floor slightly higher than the rest of the rooms (possibly a foot or 18 inches), thereby allowing it to serve as a stage for lectures or dramatics. However, this procedure is undesirable in some cases as it splits up the room and makes it impossible to use the combined large room for dancing.

5. *Game room.* The game room is an essential part of any recreation building and ordinarily would be designed to include billiards, ping pong, checkers and chess tables, and, in some cases, junior size billiard tables and other games. In some buildings, where the game room serves as a club room, only ping pong and card tables are used, since they can be folded and stored efficiently and quickly. Folding ping pong tables can, of course, be set up in any room of the building, or on the outside terrace or playground. Most recreation buildings have pocket billiards and when this is the case a room must be definitely set aside as a game room, since billiard tables are not portable. Billiard and ping pong tables are approximately 5 by 9 feet. The minimum space to be allowed at the end of each table is 6 feet, although 7 feet is preferable. Space should also be available along one wall for a raised platform with seats. This is most desirable in case of billiards, so that persons waiting their turn to play can watch the game and this is possible only from an elevated position.

With the above requirements in mind, the game room should be designed around the location of the tables. If the room is to be a long narrow room, with tables side by side, the minimum width should be 22 feet, or, if possible, 24 feet. The length of the room must be adjusted to fit the number of tables to be installed. Space should be available at one end of the room for storage of equipment and supplies.

Overhead lights should be carefully located to give proper illumination at each table.

Windows are not essential, particularly around the billiard tables where they might be broken by cue sticks. Forced ventilation would certainly be more desirable than window ventilation. The wall covering for at least four feet above the floor should be a washable type, because persons leaning against the wall in either ping pong or billiard rooms have a habit of placing their shoes against the wall and leaving footprints. In a room where billiards are played the floor must be a permanent type of concrete, terrazzo, or asphalt tile. Wood has been used satisfactorily, but care must be taken to design the floor to take care of the extra weight, and to eliminate any possible vibration.

Space should be available at one end of the room for table games, such as checkers, chess, and dominoes. In some cases, billiards and ping pong are combined in the same general room with bowling alleys, thereby making it possible for one person to control all facilities. This provision is especially desirable where a charge is made for the use of the billiard tables. The experience of most recreation directors is that free billiard play is not always a good thing. Players have a habit of mistreating the table covering and other equipment, but if a charge is made and supervision is nearby, the facilities are better taken care of and are more appreciated. Billiards is a special service, provided at an extra cost, and a charge is therefore justified.

A "senior" type game room, Enlisted Men's Center, U. S. Naval Training Center, Bainbridge, Maryland.

6. *Music room.* In large recreation buildings a music room is usually included and in smaller buildings a club room equipped for music activities usually serves the purpose. Proper design and equipment should provide for instruction and practice for piano, orchestra, and vocal groups. Adequate acoustical treatment of the room, with acoustical plaster or acoustical wall and ceiling tile, is highly desirable.

Portable stage-type platforms for vocal and orchestral groups should be provided for members and be available for performances. Storage space for music, instruments, and uniforms is highly desirable.

7. *Music listening rooms.* A series of small rooms, 5 by 10 feet, with proper equipment for individuals or two or three persons to listen to records is an excellent addition to any recreation building. Such rooms are usually found in the larger buildings, and are also used for individual practice on musical instruments. The rooms should be properly equipped with acoustical tile or plaster, and comfortable furniture should be provided.

8. *Arts and crafts rooms.* Arts and crafts are fast becoming a major activity in any recreation building. The heavy increase in commercial arts and craft supplies stores is indicative of the increase in this very popular activity. In many communities, a special arts and craft center is being constructed, designed specifically for this activity alone. Such activity rooms should be designed for large groups. In many cases, the senior citizens programs, especially for women, are centered around craft rooms.

Recreation buildings with limited space may possibly not have a special room for crafts but would utilize one of the club rooms having storage closets or storage space adjacent thereto. A large closet with sink, running water, and hot-plate facilities should also be available. Under such arrangements, craft equipment supplies and unfinished articles would necessarily have to be stored between craft classes. It is much more desirable, then, to have a special room set aside for this activity alone, where unfinished articles, especially ceramic, metal, and objects requiring painting, can be left in the open on tables and shelves. In some cases, craft equipment is of such large size that it cannot be readily moved—this is especially true in ceramics. Special electrical outlets should be included for kilns and other heavy duty equipment.

9. *Photography room.* The larger buildings should provide space for at least the printing and enlarging of photographs. With the recent increase in emphasis on photography, and the need for reproduction of pictures of activities for the recreation public relation program, a photography room is highly desirable. Adequate space, water, and electrical equipment should be provided for developing and enlarging photographs, and the room should be of sufficient size to enable several people to work in it at the same time. Such a room would not have any windows, and could, therefore, be located in the interior of the building. The room should have double doors for proper protection of those developing films.

10. *Gymnasium.* As mentioned earlier in this chapter, the minimum size gymnasium should have space adequate for a junior high school size basketball court, 42 by 74 feet, with at least 6 feet on one side and 9 feet on the ends for the safety of the players, and space on one side for 200 to 300 spectators. It should be approximately 60 by 90 feet. The ceiling height must be at least 21 feet, and all windows and wall obstructions should be mounted at least 6 feet off the floor for protection of the persons using the room. Windows should be controlled with mechanical or electrical equipment. For further details on the construction of the gymnasium see Chapter 6.

11. *Dressing, shower, and clothes check rooms.* Space for these facilities could be limited to extra large restrooms with showers, or could occupy a space 4,000 to 6,000 feet or even larger. The facilities usually include shower rooms, dressing rooms, drying rooms, toilet and lavatory facilities, and a room for checking clothes. The clothes checking is by lockers, or by plastic bags or baskets locked on portable or permanent shelving. Where lockers are used, they should be set on a permanent base at least 6 inches off the floor for ease in cleaning. Gang showers are desirable for the men, but the women should have individual shower and dressing booths. In some cases, a small gang shower is also included.

For ease in maintenance and cleaning, the shower and dressing rooms should have glazed tile walls to a height of at least 6 feet (preferably the entire height) and unglazed ceramic tile floors. In many cases, a concrete floor with the proper finish has been satisfactory. The difficulty with a concrete floor is that if the floor is finished rough so people will not slip, it may be hard to clean. If the floor texture is smooth for ease in cleaning, it is dangerous to walk on, as it will be slippery when wet. The use of unglazed ceramic tile is, therefore, highly desirable as it provides ease in cleaning and at the same time affords traction for wet feet.

Ventilation can be by windows, but skydomes for natural light and forced ventilation are preferable. Provision should be made for the removal of steam from hot showers.

Toilet facilities should be away from the immediate dressing area and should be accessible when passing to shower room. In cases where dressing rooms will serve swimmers, some of the toilet facilities should be located near the passageway going to the swimming pool. Dressing rooms should be functionally arranged so that one central clothes check room can serve both sexes. Check room counters should be arranged so that a person of either sex can administer the check room without seeing into either dressing room.

12. *Restrooms.* Restrooms should be located as centrally in the building as possible and are one facility that can be placed in the center of the building without outside window space. Proper artificial or natural light can be provided without windows, and in all cases forced ventilation, with exhaust fans in the ceiling, is essential. The restrooms should include glazed tile walls and unglazed ceramic tile floors. It is highly desirable to

Jewish Community Center, Columbus, Ohio.

have the toilet fixtures hung from the walls and toilet partitions hung from the ceiling so the rooms may be readily and easily cleaned. Facilities in the room should be properly designed and arranged so that even with doors open persons in the corridor could not see into the room. Where space is available, double doors should be used, with a short passageway between. Otherwise, partitions should be installed in the room to block vision from the corridor. Toilet partitions of marble or some other non-absorbent material are highly desirable, although a bonderized steel partition is effective. The women's restroom should provide space for large mirrors and powder room facilities. These rooms should be no larger than actual need dictates. It is not necessary to make restrooms as large as clubrooms, or they may serve as such, and thereby be a source of trouble. They should be kept as small as possible from the point of view of maintenance and construction costs, as well as from the point of view of administration and possible problem areas.

13. *Auditorium.* In the majority of recreation buildings, the gymnasium doubles as social hall and auditorium by the use of portable seats and a portable stage. Although it is difficult for one room to serve all three purposes properly, it is being done in the smaller buildings. A special auditorium to seat three to five hundred people, with a stage and a projection booth, is most desirable. An auditorium with an inclined floor and permanent seats will serve its purpose much better than a level floor and removable chairs. However, such an arrangement can be justified only when there is a large demand for this type of room. In most cases, it has been found necessary to use a level floor, with removable chairs, making the room flexible and useable for dinners, banquets, dances, and other activities, rather than for meetings only. The room must be properly finished from the standpoint of acoustics and lighting. Air conditioning is definitely essential, since natural ventilation from windows is objectionable for many reasons.

14. *Kitchen.* The kitchen should be designed to serve the purpose for which it is intended. In most cases, however, very little cooking is actually done in the kitchen of a community recreation building. Food is usually prepared in commercial kitchens and catered, so it is only warmed and served from the recreation building kitchen. In a small or medium size recreation building, a kitchen 14 by 20 feet has been found to be quite adequate. In some cases, the kitchens have been even smaller. It is usually considered advisable to have the kitchen planned so that it will have an outside entrance for bringing in supplies and taking out refuse.

In many buildings it has been found much more desirable to have the kitchen centrally located so that service can be through Dutch doors or over counters in one direction into a large club room, in another direction to a small club room, or in still another direction into the corridor. This arrangement makes for a functional kitchen and has been found very satisfactory in most instances.

When kitchens are to be used for the preparation and storage of food, and especially where food is served each day and often twice a day to various civic clubs and other groups, it is important that the kitchen be larger. Adequate table and counter space, ranges, ovens, and sinks can be included for the preparation of full meals for groups of 50 to 500 or more. Equipment for such a kitchen should be of the commercial type and should be planned by a commercial kitchen designer. Adequate sinks, dish-wash-

Outdoor patio and covered terrace. Student Union Building, Bakersfield Junior College, Bakersfield, California.

ing facilities, and sufficient hot water are items often overlooked. A kitchen of this size should definitely have an outside entrance because of the need for delivery of supplies without passing through the corridor and/or lobby.

The kitchen should be properly ventilated so that gases and heat can be efficiently and effectively removed, thereby maintaining proper temperature for adequate operation of the kitchen.

15. *Snack bar.* A snack bar has long been considered an essential facility in a recreation building. Space and service should be provided for serving ice cream, cold drinks, crackers, cookies, candy, and similar prepared or prepackaged food. This need can usually be met by automatic dispensing machines, eliminating the difficulties encountered in maintenance, operating personnel, and bookkeeping, that accompany the receipts and disbursements of moneys.

The snack bar can be more readily justified where hot dogs, hamburgers, ice cream sodas, and other specially prepared food are required. Such a snack bar is usually included only in large recreation buildings having bowling alleys and game room operations, where the same personnel can handle the money for operation of the bowling alleys, and game rooms, at least during periods of minimum use. When use is heavier, additional personnel may be added. Wherever snack bars are included, it is important that adjoining storage rooms be available, and that counter stools, booths and/or tables and chairs be provided.

16. *Automatic food dispensing machines.* These machines are adaptable to small recreation buildings or to the largest building. Such machines can be secured for dispensing practically any type of food needed in a recreation building. Machines maintain food at the proper temperature—whether hot or cold —and provide clean storage. Food is readily available and money changing facilities are usually included. The principal disadvantages are the space required and the cost of the machines, but these disadvantages are often outweighed by the effectiveness and functional values of the dispensing machines. Definite provision should be made for the required number of machines when the building is designed. Most of the machines will require only proper electrical service outlets, but some will require water and waste facilities. Machines can be rented, leased, or purchased.

17. *Custodial space.* A proper janitorial and cleaning program is essential for the operation of a building. Sufficient storage space for cleaning equipment should be provided on each floor level. Some of the storage rooms should be of sufficient size for a chair, so that the janitor or maid may rest at intervals, especially in larger buildings where the rooms are often termed "custodial offices."

18. *Exercise room.* A comprehensive recreation program will include space and equipment for individual or small group exercise activities. Included would be the use of weights, mats, place for boxing and wrestling, and other individual exercise and equipment activities. Although a small recreation building might not afford separate space for this activity, it could be conducted in one corner of the gymnasium at certain periods. Adequate storage space for the equipment should be located nearby. In larger recreation buildings, a separate room would serve a real purpose. The room should be a minimum of 24 by 35 feet, thereby providing space at one end for full size boxing or wrestling ring. During boxing and wrestling activities the floor in this area would be covered with a heavy mat. Matting would be hung on three walls, with possibly a rope on the fourth side dividing the ring from the rest of the room.

Other equipment in this room would include wall exercise equipment, weights, mats, bicycle, and similar equipment. The floor should be paved with wooden blocks set on edge. Otherwise the weights may be dropped and damage an asphalt tile floor. In case a concrete floor is used, the equipment could be damaged.

Lights for this room would be artificial, and forced ventilation would be required.

19. *Heating and service room.* In small recreation buildings unit blowers of the au-

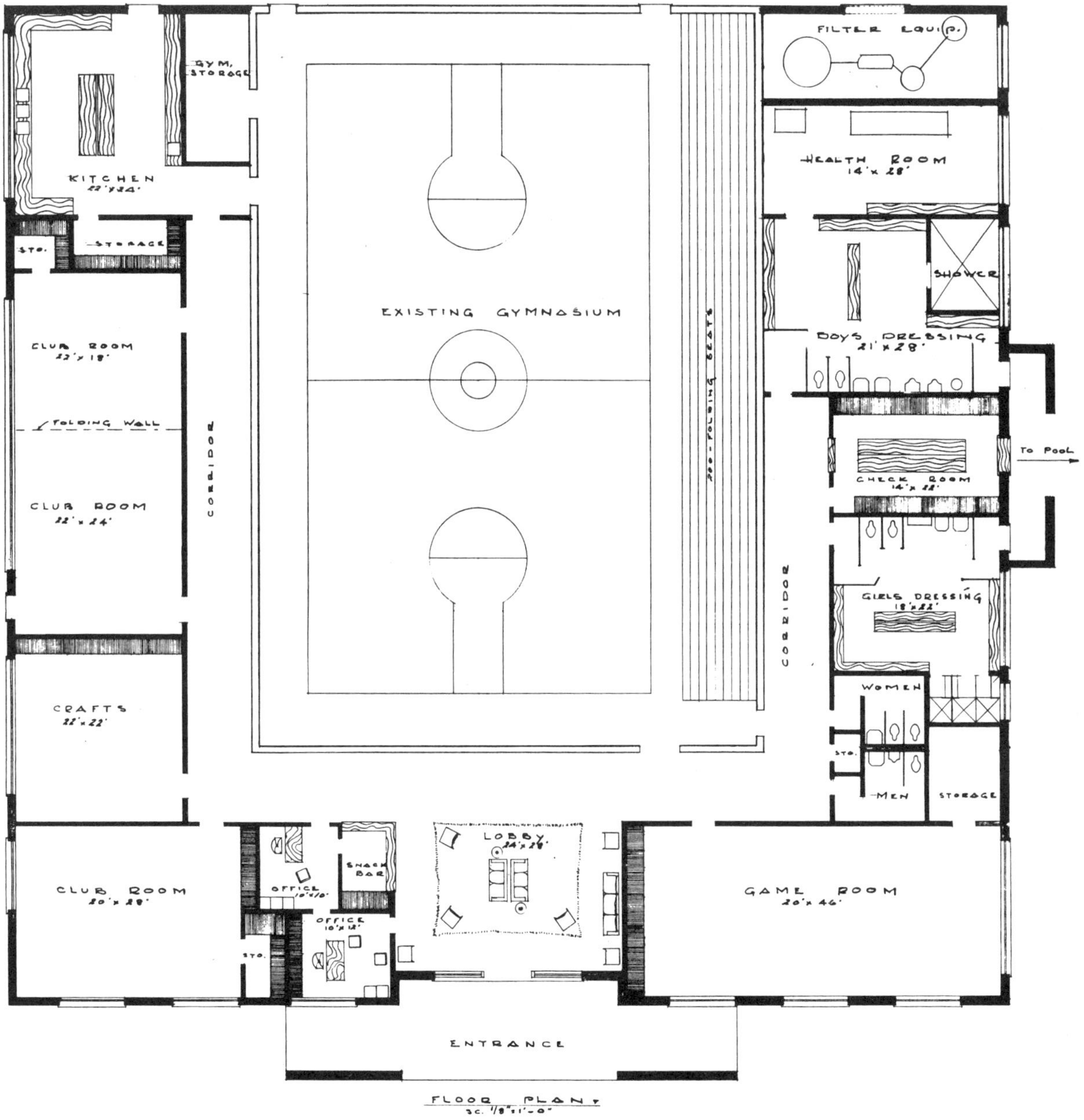

Architects: The Charles M. Graves Organization

Figure 10:1. Floor plan of a medium sized community center. Lowe Park, Reidsville, North Carolina.

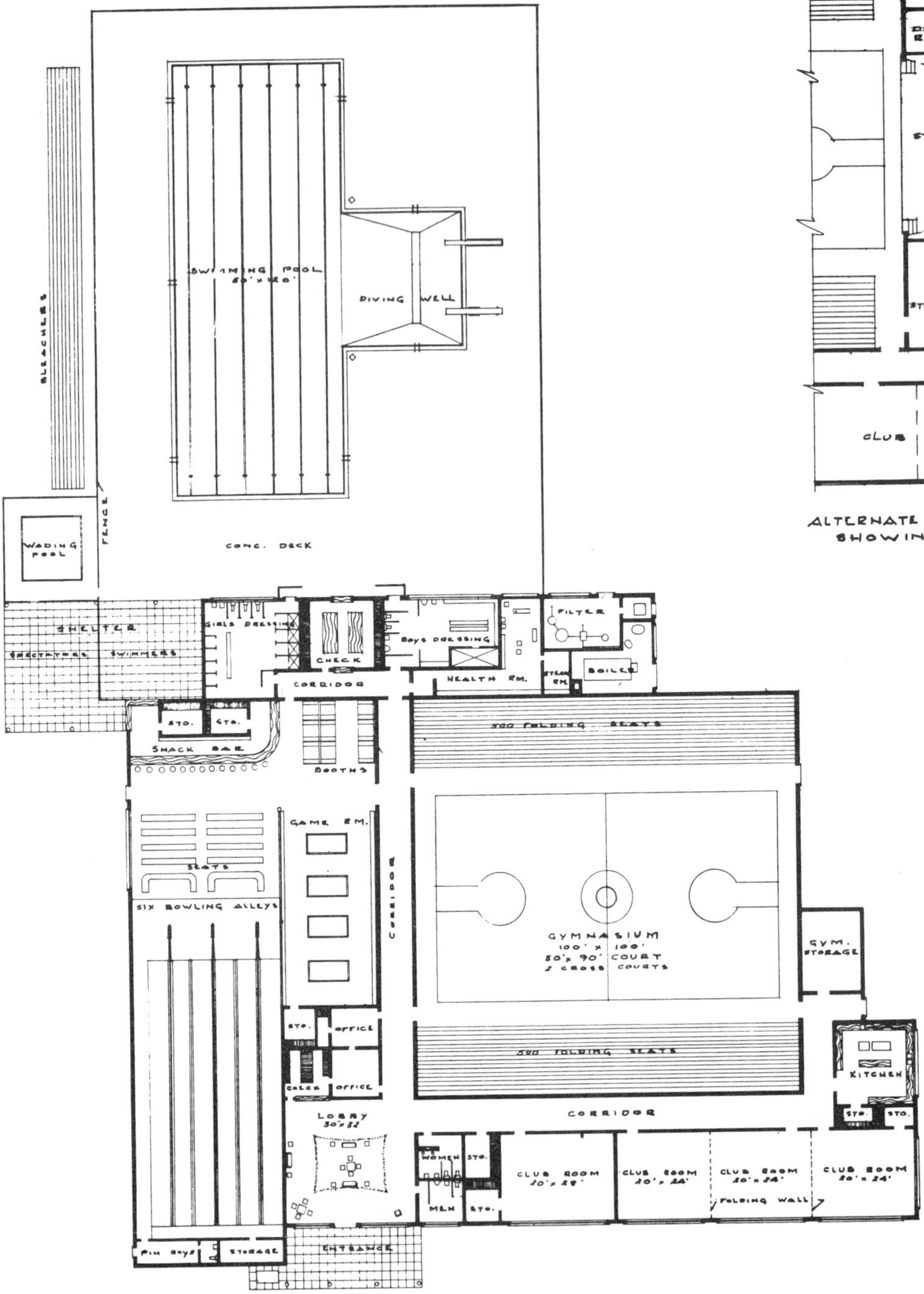

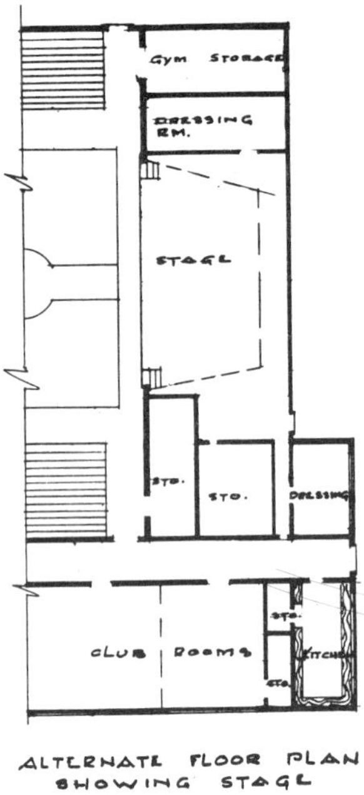

Architects: The Charles M. Graves Organization

Figure 10:2. Floor plan of a large community center. Pettygrew Park, Reidsville, North Carolina.

tomatic type are hung from the ceiling or attached to the wall. These are usually gas fired. Small blowers are used for the smaller rooms and in some cases electric radiant heaters are used in the restrooms and offices. Modern blower equipment is very quiet, but sometimes not quiet enough for rooms where meetings and lectures are to be held. Therefore, it is usually considered preferable to have a central heating plant, with the large rooms served by individual blowers and wall hung radiators serving other rooms. In many communities it has been found highly desirable in recreation buildings—as well as in other types of buildings—to install ceiling mounted outlets for distribution of hot air. The same outlets and air ducts can be used in summer for the distribution of cool air. This arrangement is economical, but each building must be worked out individually by specially trained heating and ventilating engineers.

Whatever heating and air conditioning equipment is installed, it should be properly selected for automatic features, controlled by thermostats, so as to require little if any manual operation.

20. *Corridors.* Adequate corridors of proper width to meet the fire code are essential, and sufficient exits from each room must be provided. Many recreation buildings have been designed so that access to some rooms is through the gymnasium, auditorium, or other rooms. This design is used to economize on corridor space, but it is definitely poor economy. All activity areas should be connected by corridors. Economy can be practiced by proper design of the building to limit the length of corridors and stairwells. Corridors should have permanent floors. Terrazzo and patio tile have proved successful. Walls quickly become soiled with use and should be properly surfaced to a height of at least six feet for ease in cleaning. Glazed tile or similar material is recommended. If drinking fountains are installed in corridors, they should be recessed in order to conserve space in the passageway.

21. *Multi-floor versus one floor.* In large congested communities where land is at a premium, two or more floors in a recreation building may be justified. This is an economy measure on the use of land, but construction costs are generally higher. Economy in construction is not effected, since it is sometimes just as economical to construct the building all on one floor. Certainly the latter rule applies where rooms are to be built over a swimming pool, gymnasium or some other large room where closely spaced supporting columns cannot be used.

Administration of a multi-floor building is more difficult than that of a one-story building. The large number of recently constructed one story school buildings is indicative of the recent trend toward the one story building. Except in rare instances, a one-story recreation building is desirable for many reasons. Rooms can be added on the same level more easily and more economically than they can in a basement, and without the disadvantages of basement rooms.

22. *Activity areas on roof.* In highly congested communities, space is provided on the roof for tennis, basketball, volleyball, handball, social activities such as dances, general lounging, and, in some rare instances, campfire activities. This provision is usually made where adequate acreage is not available. The provision of activity space on a roof presents many problems, such as the difficulty of installing a roof garden type floor so that leakage will not occur in the rooms below, the proper fencing or railings so that persons will not fall or jump off, and the proper administration of the activity area. All in all, there are many disadvantages and certainly these activities can be provided more economically on the ground level.

Master Plan

A master plan for each recreation building should be prepared. The plan should include the total needs of the community or neighborhood to be served, regardless of the cost. The building should be planned for construction by units, the units to be completed at any one time depending upon the funds then available. By following such a plan, the entire recreation building will be completed earlier and will better fill the community needs than if each unit is planned and built separately without relation to the whole.

CHAPTER 11

THE OUTDOOR SWIMMING POOL

The Charles M. Graves Organization

AT THE END OF WORLD WAR II, POOLS OF ALL types in the United States numbered only 8,000; 10,000 were built in the next seven years and by January 1, 1954 another 10,000 had been constructed. During the year of 1954, 15,000 more pools were completed, making a total of approximately 43,000 in the United States in 1955. Although records for 1957 have not been compiled, more pools were built in this period than in any one previous year.

Because of new liberal financing, introduction of new materials, various new methods of construction, and higher family incomes, the construction of residential pools will be greatly increased in the future.

The construction of public and commercial pools will also show a marked increase in the future. This increase will result from the popularity of swimming and the availability of money for construction.

Hotel and motel owners have found that swimming pools are "must" in attracting trade. It is now considered standard practice to include a swimming pool in plans for new motels and resort hotels.

PLANNING THE SWIMMING POOL

When a new home is planned, it is planned with economy. This plan insures comfort, durability, and beauty. The better the plan, the more economical and inclusive are the features in the home. Planning, after all, is figuring accurately the best way to get the best results for the least expenditure of money and effort.

A well-designed swimming pool is planned and designed in much the same manner. The swimming area that makes full use of the sun's rays all during the day, that has the bathhouse between the swimmer and the prevailing winds, that affords seats in the shade for the spectators with their backs to the late afternoon sun, and that gives deck area in the sun to those who wish to sunbathe, is the result of a well thought out plan.

Where would be the best place to build

Illustration: Swimming Pool at Palisades Interstate Park, Bear Mountain, New York

a single outdoor swimming pool in a community of 10,000 to 25,000 population? A home is built on the most logical piece of land available. Likewise, a pool should be built on the most suitable land available. During the day the pool will be used primarily by children. The major concern, therefore, is, "How can the swimming area be made convenient for the most people?" City maps can quickly show the industrial and business areas. With these areas ruled out, the next step to consider is, "Where are the most heavily populated residential areas, at present and for future development?" The area decided upon should offer the convenience of the facilities to the most people, but at the same time be away from busy streets and heavy traffic.

Considering convenience, cleanliness, safety, and healthful swimming conditions, the plan begins to take shape. The swimming pool is being accurately planned to get the best results, through the most economical and best organized plan.

Much thought and research have gone into the proper selection of construction materials and swimming pool finishes. The use of reinforced concrete, if the proper type of reinforcing steel is used and the proper supervision given during construction, guarantees a pool that will not leak.

If a pool is to be used for competitive swimming, all necessary depth and lane markers should be put in the pool during construction. The deck area surrounding the swimming pool, the gutters necessary to take off the overflow, and the drainage systems are all integral parts of the well designed pool. The bathhouse should be located at the shallow end of the pool as an added safety factor for small children. In numerous instances, in poorly planned swimming pools where the bathhouse is at the deep end of the pool, small children upon leaving the bathhouse have fallen and drowned in deep water.

The bathhouse for a well planned pool will have walls of glazed ceramic tile, floors of unglazed tile, and the roof will have a steel frame. The unit will be constructed so as to allow high pressure cleaning by hose. The locker versus the basket or plastic bag checking system has been studied and the basket or plastic bag system is found to be superior in most cases. This system allows more dressing space, a smaller building, and fewer operating personnel.

In order to have a pool that operates smoothly, it is necessary to consider the relationship of each part of the pool to each of the others. One of the most important features of a pool is the proper water treatment equipment, and an extensive study of the various types of filters has been made. Sand filters and Diatomaceous Earth (solidified organic matter) have proved to be the most satisfactory. Scum or overflow gutters, pipe tunnels, pool drains, deck drains, tile work, fresh water inlets, underwater lights, floodlights, swimming pool equipment, and fence arrangement are other very important items in the construction of a first class pool.

A PLANNING CHECK LIST

A committee concerned with the construction of a swimming pool will find the items included in the following check list useful for sound planning:

1. *Plan the pool project for the future*, even exceeding present aspiration. Have the plans and specifications prepared by an experienced engineering or architectural organization that specializes in swimming pool design.
2. *Accept for consideration all recommendations*, as from these you will gather valuable information as to site, water supply, drainage, landscaping, prevailing winds, sun and shade, accessibility to bathhouse, club and parking facilities, and so on.
3. *Consult with local swimming authorities*, recreation, and physical education personnel. These are the people who will use the facility and they represent the "experience" you need.
4. *Include in pool design outline* specifications for style, size, features, location of ladders and boards, lighting—both underwater and overhead, pool capacity, drainage, filtration and chlorination, diving and wading depths, type of earth —sand, clay, hardpan, rock, and so on.
5. *Have a complete set of blueprints prepared* of the pool, as well as complete specifications.

6. *Shop around the market* for builders and contractors who cover all phases of actual installation. Allow all competent contractors a proper audience with the entire committee to study proposals.
7. *Inspect other installations* of the respective builders. Talk with owners, or at least correspond with them.
8. *Obtain bids* based on plans and specifications.
9. *Be sure that all specifications* meet city and state Board of Health requirements.
10. *Study final bids* for all details. Obtain unbiased professional and non-professional opinions.
11. *Have a final consultation period* with parties who have submitted favorable bids—not necessarily with only the lowest bidder. Consider their rating, reliability, and pool building experience.
12. *Arrive at a final decision and contract on a firm price.* Consult your legal advisers on the wording of this phase.
13. *Obtain a written guarantee* that protects your organization for at least one year from possible construction flaws, such as leaking and cracking.

COMMON ERRORS MADE IN THE CONSTRUCTION OF SWIMMING POOLS

1. *Planning one pool by copying another is a common practice in many communities.* The engineer is told to build a pool just like an existing pool in the community, or a neighboring community, so he makes the same errors that were made twenty years ago. The pool costs just as much as a modern pool, but is twenty years behind the times by the day it is finished.

2. *The mistake of locating the pool and bathhouse on property of insufficient size.* This is a very common error and a bad one. Adequate space is needed around a pool, not only to dignify its setting and location, but

A well-planned swimming pool with accompanying facilities. Goldsboro Country Club, Goldsboro, North Carolina.

Architects: The Charles M. Graves Organization

Swimming pool and bath house, Tift Park, Albany, Georgia.

to serve as a buffer from nearby streets and residences. Space must also be provided for parking and for other recreational areas and facilities.

3. *A swimming pool that is not related to other park facilities is never as successful as a pool planned in conjunction with other recreation facilities,* such as ball diamonds, tennis courts, volleyball courts, craft centers, community centers, and other facilities. One activity advertises and publicizes another. A pool thus related to other sports facilities will be much more successful and can be more easily administered.

4. *Many people are of the opinion that digging the hole for a swimming pool is an expensive part of the pool, so they look for a low spot or a ravine in which to build the pool, thereby saving trouble and money for digging the hole.* This is a very common and very expensive error, since the excavating of the hole is actually a small part of the expense, probably not more than 1 per cent of the cost of the entire project. Building a pool in a ravine has many disadvantages. Water from the surrounding area drains into the pool, and, unless precautions are taken for proper drainage around the edge of the pool, considerable water will penetrate the area under the deck and floor and be a source of constant annoyance. Do not place a swimming pool in a low area.

5. *Many people feel there should be trees around a pool to give shade.* In some cases, a pool is built in a park where there is a grove of trees and an effort is made to retain as many trees as possible. Trees are a menace to a swimming pool. Leaves fall into the pool and keep it dirty. They clog up filters and the hair and lint catcher and in many ways keep the pool in an unsatisfactory condition. Trees also keep the sun away from the pool—and to be successful a pool must have sunshine. Most people who visit a pool want to sunbathe.

6. *The pool itself must not be too near a busy or dirty street.* Location in relation to streets is most important. A pool must be

Multiple-type pool with separate diving pool. Anthony Wayne Pool, Palisades Interstate Park, Bear Mountain, New York.

Good distribution of diving boards in a separate diving pool. Anthony Wayne Pool, Palisades Interstate Park, Bear Mountain, New York.

A multiple pool. Astoria, New York.

near the main traffic arteries for good circulation and for accessibility. However, the dirt and filth from the street will blow into the pool and give considerable trouble in the filtration system. The pool should be set back from the street 200 or 300 feet or more.

7. *In many pools the water leaks out as fast as it runs in.* This is the result of poor design and faulty construction, and is very common in inadequately designed pools.

8. *Many engineers make the mistake of putting too many expansion joints in a pool.* The results are that the pool leaks and the expansion joint material comes out of the joints and gets on the bathing suits of the swimmers. The average pool needs few expansion joints if properly designed by a qualified specialist and constructed by a competent contractor.

9. *Too often the floor and walls of a pool are not of the proper texture;* they are either too rough or too smooth. If the floor is too smooth—such as glazed tile—the swimmer will slip down; if too rough, the swimmer's feet will be scratched and hurt, and the pool will be difficult to keep clean.

10. *Many communities make the mistake of building an odd-shaped pool that does not meet any standard requirements.* This kind of pool is merely a concrete pond.

11. *Many pools are too shallow or too deep at the shallow end.* Three feet of depth is adequate and proper to serve all ages and all purposes.

SOME GUIDING PRINCIPLES FOR CONSTRUCTION

1. Sufficient inlets should be installed to make sure that the water is properly circulated in order to keep the entire pool clean. The same size inlets are not required in all sections of the pool, so inlets must be designed for special locations.

2. The walls of a pool should be designed

to withstand the pressure of the earth outside the pool and the pressure of the water inside.

3. The pool outlet should be of sufficient size to drain the pool in four hours or less.

4. The overflow gutter should project 2 or 3 inches in front of the edge of the deck. Many mistakes are made in the construction of overflow gutters. Often they are built level so that they do not drain properly. This method is used to save trouble and expense but is never satisfactory. Many pools are built with a fully exposed gutter, others with a depressed type (one that is wholly depressed into the wall). The gutter that projects from the wall is open to the sunshine, can be kept cleaner and more sanitary, and any water that may run off the coping or walk will drop into the gutter rather than into the pool.

5. A pool should be planned to meet A.A.U., interscholastic or intercollegiate standards. These standards require a size of 25 yards or 25 meters (usually indoor pools), or 50 yards or 50 meters (outdoor pools). Any pool in between these standards should be in multiples of five yards, *i.e.*, 90, 105, 120 feet. To make certain a pool meets competitive standards it should be constructed 1 inch longer than the specified length; thus a 25 yard pool would measure 75 feet, 1 inch.

6. Anchors should be installed in the walls when the pool is constructed. Swimming lanes are painted on the pool floor or, preferably, built into the pool in unglazed tile. Many times no thought is given to swimming events, so anchors for swimming lane markers are not installed in the pool when it is built. This is a definite mistake and requires makeshift arrangements for setting up float lines for swimming meets.

7. Pools should have 75 to 85 per cent of the water area less than 5 feet deep. This is important, because more than 85 per cent of the bathers will swim in shallow water. Only 4 to 6 per cent of swimmers are in the deep water at any one time. Many pools have only 40 to 45 per cent of the water area shallow, or less than 4 to $4\frac{1}{2}$ feet in depth. This is a serious mistake.

8. Proper orientation of the pool and bathhouse in outdoor pools is important, because the bathhouse should always be on the side of the prevailing wind. A swimmer

Rectangular pool with a 10-meter tower. University of British Columbia, Vancouver, B. C.

does not want the wind to dry him off too fast and cause him to become chilled, so he must be protected from the prevailing wind. Sometimes a canvas is hung on the fence, or a glass or masonry wall is installed.

9. The water temperature should be at least 70 degrees, and when the weather is cooler, the temperature should be 75 degrees. In some instances city officials feel they have plenty of water and can save money by just running water into the pool continuously; that by letting it flow through the pool the pool will be clean at all times. In many cases the water for a flow-through pool is from a well or spring and is so cold that the swimmers find it uncomfortable.

10. But even more important, water introduced into a pool must have chlorine residual or it will have no ability to combat the germs and bacteria in the pool or that come from the air, leaves, and swimmers. Therefore, a flow-through pool is never clean and sooner or later it will be necessary to install filters; hence, they should be installed when the pool is constructed—it will cost less that way.

11. Filter equipment should be of proper size and design. Many pools have inadequate filter equipment, and that is just as bad as not having any at all.

12. The location of the recirculation pump should be given careful consideration. When the filter room is below the deck area there is no difficulty. The filter room can be placed on the level with the deck or walk but the pump should be depressed below the water line so that it can be primed by the water in the pool.

13. Chlorine gas is dangerous and the chlorinator should be in a separate room, with an exhaust fan in the roof and a vent extended to the floor to keep the room clear of any escaping chlorine gas.

14. The depth of the water at various parts of the pool should be properly indicated in order to prevent accidents that might occur by diving into too shallow water.

15. The deck of an outdoor pool should entirely surround the pool and should be 18 to 20 feet or more in width. Decks that are too narrow are a common error in the designing of many swimming pools. There are many outdoor pools whose deck or walk is only five to ten feet wide; crowding and congestion around the pool result.

16. Slides and other play equipment should not be placed in a pool because they can be dangerous. The only equipment that belongs in a swimming pool is the diving board, and the board should be properly located in order not to be dangerous, and so that its use will not endanger the lives of the swimmers.

17. Steps and ladders placed in the end walls of a pool interfere with swimmers during swimming meets; therefore, ladders should be placed on the sides of the pool in order not to interfere with swimmers.

18. Sand is acceptable, but not desirable, around a wading pool if it is separated from the swimming pool, but should not surround the swimming pool. Grass has been successful where the best grass is used, good care is given, and the grass is properly cut and collected.

19. The wading pool, varying in depth from 6 to 18 inches, should be enclosed by a fence and separately controlled for the safety of small children. It has been common practice to wall off one section of the swimming pool to serve as a wading or junior pool for small children. This is not considered a good practice. It is dangerous to have them together, because large children will run through the wading pool and knock the small children down. Filtered and treated water can be introduced into the wading pool and as the pool is emptied the water should not be used again because of the high degree of contamination from sediment, debris, and other forms of contamination carried into the pool by the children.

20. Wooden diving boards are accepted as satisfactory but they should be carefully maintained. If they are light enough in weight to have the desirable flexibility they will eventually break—they are dangerous. There are many new diving boards on the market at present, but the most practical appears to be the aluminum board. Champion divers demand this board for competition because of its outstanding permanent uniform lifting action. In the event that wooden

boards are used, there should be extra ones on hand so they can be changed or rotated to increase the life of the boards. Boards covered with fiberglass will outlast other types of wooden boards. The aluminum board has another advantage over the wooden board in that it does not require a cocoa mat, which in itself transmits athlete's foot.

21. A bathhouse should be properly ventilated. There is nothing worse than an inadequately ventilated bathhouse, one that is damp and wet, with water standing on the floor. Such a condition is altogether unnecessary. In outdoor pools the roof may often be left off the dressing area entirely, or vents may be provided in the walls with skydomes in the roof.

22. Lockers should not be used in bathhouses. The basket or plastic bag system is highly preferable. Lockers take up too much space, get dirty, keys often get lost, and lockers are hard to administer and must continually be repaired.

23. Footbaths should not be installed in either outdoor or indoor pools. In many pools footbaths are still used. This is an antiquated custom and the baths are not at all satisfactory. The footbaths are dangerous and actually do very little good, as swimmers will run through them, jump over them, or do anything to keep from going through them.

24. A separate place should be provided for swimmers to sit and eat. It is a mistake to let swimmers eat around the pool; however, swimmers do get hungry and want to eat, so a special area should be provided for this purpose. Food is a definite revenue-producing item but its sale should be properly controlled.

25. Spectators with shoes on should not be allowed inside the pool area. To permit the wearing of shoes is a definite mistake and violates most state health department laws. Spectators should stay on the outside unless they want to put on a bathing suit and take off their shoes.

26. A shelter should be provided for spectators. Bleachers or seats should be arranged so that the spectators will have their backs to the sun, since a glare results from facing the sun across the water.

Determining Cost of Construction

Construction cost is one of the major problems to be taken into consideration. Like other aspects of pool design and construction, cost figures cannot be standardized, for they are influenced by many factors. Cost is affected by such elements as local labor wages, material cost, size of pool, type, location and shape of pool, the type and size of the bathhouse, the water treatment system, and numerous other construction and equipment items. Some indication of the probable cost ranges may be obtained, however, from communities that have recently completed pools. The cost analysis shown in Table 11-1 affords a basis for estimating roughly the comparative cost of outdoor pools of various sizes. This table does not include the cost of the bathhouse.

This cost analysis is based upon the construction of a moderate priced, yet first-class swimming pool, incorporating paved deck area, fencing, underwater and overhead lights, vertical poured reinforced concrete walls, marble plaster finish on walls and floor, filtration equipment, tile swimming lanes, and limestone curb and overflow gutters.

The difference between the cost of a "moderate priced" pool and an "expensive" pool would be governed by the shape, such as "abstract," for example, which would increase the cost because of the complicated forming of the walls, the landscaping, cabanas, and other extra items that might be included.

In the moderate priced pool, galvanized steel ladders and diving stands are indicated in the cost analysis. If chrome ladders and diving board stands are substituted, the price would be increased by approximately 22 cents per square foot of water surface. The cost for equipment for heating the water in a swimming pool is approximately $1.50 per square foot of water surface. The cost of filtration equipment as shown in the cost analysis chart is based on Diatomaceous Earth filters. In some locations the installation of sand filters would increase the price 75 cents per square foot of water surface.

TABLE 11-1

Estimated Cost for Outdoor Swimming Pools

Pools of various types or shapes	*Total area in square feet*	*Depth 3'-4½' area in square feet*	*Depth 4½'-12' area in square feet*	*Total capacity*	*Approximate cost*	*Estimated cost per square foot of water surface*
1. "T" shaped 50 x 165' (40 x 60' diving area)	10,650	8,250	2,400	484	$110,110	$ 9.40
2. "T" shaped 56 x 165' (40 x 40' diving area)	10,840	9,240	1,600	498	101,896	9.40
3. "T" shaped 42 x 165' (35 x 40' diving area)	8,330	6,930	1,400	382	91,630	11.40
4. Oval Pool "A" 56' swim width (8 lanes) No diving	13,600	13,600	—	680	107,440	7.90
5. Oval Pool "B" 42' swim width (6 lanes) Swimming only	12,000	12,000	—	600	96,000	8.00
6. Diving Pool 40 x 45'	1,800	—	1,800	48	24,840	13.80
7. Diving Pool 42 x 60'	2,520	—	2,520	72	32,760	13.00
8. Diving Pool 42 x 75' Also for 25-yard swimming meet	3,150	—	3,150	72	40,950	13.00
9. Rectangular Pool 42 x 165' swimming only	6,930	6,930	—	396	76,923	11.10
10. Rectangular Pool 42 x 120'	5,040	3,360	1,680	204	59,472	11.80
11. Fan shaped 105' (35' deep end, 75' shallow end)	5,775	4,030	1,745	237	66,990	11.60
12. Fan shaped 120' (35' deep end, 75' shallow end)	6,600	4,900	1,700	281	73,920	11.20
13. Fan shaped 105' (30' deep end, 60' shallow end)	4,725	3,305	1,420	201	56,700	12.00
14. Rectangular pool 40' x 120'	4,800	3,200	1,600	196	57,800	12.00

At the present time, most pools are being constructed of *reinforced concrete*, with others being made of *steel, concrete units, brick, plastics* and *gunite concrete*. *Gunite concrete pools* of proper design will be comparable in cost to the vertical poured wall pools. From all indications, swimming pools constructed of *concrete units*, finished with white plaster cement, will reduce the cost of the swimming pool in comparison with reinforced concrete, but with the disadvantage of having entirely too many joints. This type of pool is still in the experimental stage and an accurate cost analysis cannot be made at this time. *Plastic pools* have not been developed to the point where they are satisfactory for commercial or municipal pools. There are companies producing residential pools of reinforced plastic and sold as packaged units. The cost of the plastic pool, because of their limited volume, is comparable in price to the reinforced concrete pool. Before plastic pools will be accepted by the public on a large scale, considerable experimenting and developing must be carried out by the plastic industry and the fabricators.

Constructing a swimming pool of *brick* is a relatively new process and is being promoted by the brick and tile associations throughout the country. Structurally, a brick swimming pool may be satisfactory with proper design. However, due to the limited number of skilled mechanics available for this type of construction, and since the cost is comparable to that of concrete, it will be some time before brick pools will effect sufficient savings to put them in popular demand.

Steel pools are being fabricated by large companies and offered to the public as packaged units, including all necessary equipment such as filtration, inlets, and deck equipment. In some instances erection of the pool is included. The cost of the steel pool is usually greater than the cost of reinforced concrete pools. Steel pools have an advantage in certain localities, especially in the northern states, because they can be installed during the winter months. The steel pool is not affected by freezing weather, which prohibits the pouring of concrete. Where the soil contains chemicals that would affect steel, it is definitely recommended that concrete, rather than steel pools, be installed. At present, the manufacturers of steel pools will not extend the guarantee on the steel hull for more than five years. Research is being made to perfect coatings that will preserve the steel, guaranteeing a life time of service free of maintenance cost insofar as rust is concerned.

Pools constructed of *aluminum* are comparatively new. On projects where alternate bids were taken on concrete and aluminum pools, aluminum exceeded the price of concrete. This material should be used with discretion, since it is evident that aluminum is very active in water that contains the chemicals necessary for sterilization.

TABLE 11-2

Break-down of Construction Costs; Swimming Pool,* Trussville, Alabama

Construction item	Cost	Per cent
1. Grading	$ 490	1.38
2. Concrete Work	14,666	41.35
3. Gutters	2,200	6.20
4. Pool Finish	965	2.72
5. Tile Work	500	1.41
6. Fence	1,420	4.00
7. Pool Equipment	527	1.49
8. Filter Equipment	6,230	17.58
9. Piping	3,216	9.07
10. Electrical Work	1,450	4.09
11. Concrete Walks	2,990	8.43
12. Wading Pool	810	2.28
	$35,464.00	100.00

* This is a fan-shaped pool, 75 feet long, 30 feet wide at the deep end and 50 feet wide at the shallow end. 3,000 square feet water surface.

Tables 11-2 and 11-3 show the percentage cost of the individual components of two swimming pools in relation to the total construction cost. It is interesting to note that these two swimming pools, constructed in different localities, vary considerably in cost, although the square footage of water surface is approximately the same. As the charts clearly show, the cost of grading can vary greatly, depending upon the type of earth at the pool site. It so happened that at the two pools shown on these charts, no rock or other difficult formation existed. Had the conditions been otherwise, the grading cost would have been considerably increased.

Tables 11-3 and 11-4 indicate cost breakdowns of two pools, both constructed in Morganton, North Carolina. Contracts for these two pools were awarded at the same time. The smaller pool contains 3,150 square feet of water surface and cost a total of $44,000, or $13.96 per square foot of water surface. The larger pool, containing 8,085 square feet of water surface, cost a total of $67,509, or $8.35 per square foot of water surface. These two pools are identical in construction features. The only difference is in the size. It is interesting to note that the larger pool cost $5.61 less per square foot than the smaller pool.

TABLE 11-3

Break-down of Construction Costs; Swimming Pool,* Bouchelle Community Center, Morganton, North Carolina

Construction Item	Cost	Per cent
1. Hand excavation	$ 258.00	.60
2. Concrete Footings	910.00	2.20
3. Concrete Pool floors	2,743.00	6.70
4. Reinforced concrete slabs	990.00	2.40
5. Reinforced concrete walls	4,194.00	10.30
6. Concrete pool aprons	1,932.00	4.80
7. Integral waterproofing	429.00	1.00
8. White marble plaster	1,654.00	4.00
9. Ceramic tile markers	864.00	2.20
10. Reinforcing bars & mesh	2,570.00	6.30
11. Metal fencing	1,305.00	3.10
12. Filter equipment	17,603.00	43.00
13. Limestone scum cutter	1,912.00	4.60
14. Pool equipment	1,225.00	3.00
15. Supervision	2,400.00	5.80
	$40,989.00	100.00

* This is a rectangular pool, 42 x 75 feet. 3150 square feet of water surface.

TABLE 11-4

Collett Street Pool, Morganton, North Carolina*

BREAKDOWN OF COST

Item	*Description*	*Cost*	*Per cent*
1.	Grading	$ 196	.3
2.	Concrete Work	14,516	21.5
3.	Gutters	3,601	5.3
4.	Pool Finish	3,320	4.9
5.	Tile Work	1,928	2.9
6.	Fence	1,922	2.9
7.	Pool Equipment	1,950	2.9
8.	Water Proofing	527	.8
9.	Supervision and Overhead	2,600	3.8
10.	Filter Equipment	27,600	40.9
11.	Reinforcing bars and mesh	3,850	5.7
12.	Electrical	5,500	8.1
		$67,509	100.0

* "T" shaped pool
Swimming area 165 x 42 feet. 6,930 square feet of water surface.
Diving area 33 x 35 feet. 1,155 square feet (total of 8,085 square feet).
Depth 3 to 4½ feet. Diving area 8 to 12 feet.
Capacity in Gallons 336,000
Capacity in Persons 299

ADDITIONAL FEATURES OF THE POOL

In designing a pool for a neighborhood or community, the size of the swimming pool should be in direct relation to the number of people to be served. In a study of pool attendance made at the Iowa State College by Elgin-Refinite, Division of Elgin Softener Corporation, Elgin, Illinois, the following facts quoted below were established. This study is helpful in arriving at the number of swimmers that may be anticipated at the peak-load.

"The smaller the community, the greater the percentage of the population using the pool. In cities under 30,000 population, the *maximum* daily attendance will be between five and ten percent of the population; the average daily attendance will be about two to three percent of the population. The maximum daily attendance at any one time during the day is about one-third of the daily attendance."

After determining the maximum number of swimmers, allow 15 square feet of water surface for each bather and 30 square feet of water for each swimmer. A person using water less than 5 feet in depth is considered a bather, one using water over that depth is a swimmer.

The deck area should always equal or exceed the square footage of the water area of a pool, allowing ample area for sun-bathers and non-swimmers. It is evident from many surveys that in recreational pools not more than one-fourth of the swimmers will be in the water at any one time. The minimum width of any deck area as mentioned above should be not less than 20 feet. Adjacent to the deck area should be a refreshment stand and lunching area. This area should be fenced off so that no food can be taken into the pool area.

It is of utmost importance that the *slope of the deck* be not less than one-quarter inch per foot, so that the deck can be hosed and kept clean. The deck should be of a non-slip surface. It can be obtained in concrete decks by giving the concrete a light brushing with a horsehair brush during the finishing operation.

If chrome plated, in lieu of galvanized, ladders are used, they should be procured with utmost precaution. If the ladders are not plated according to strict specifications, the chlorine in the water may change the color of the ladder, and may also cause corrosion.

Recessed ladder in side wall of pool.

Gutter drains can be either angular or rectangular. The spacing of gutter drains depends entirely upon local health regulations. Because of variations in state regulations, the drains will vary from 10 to 15 feet apart.

Main drains for the swimming pool have been improved in the past few years. Today there are a number of manufacturers producing what is known as *Anti-Vortex* drains. The drain differs from the grate type in that the water enters the drain from the side, rather than from the top, thus eliminating the tremendous suction that occurs with a grate drain. A grate drain that would not be dangerous from the standpoint of suction can be installed, but to eliminate the powerful suction, the opening area of the grating must be at least four times the size of the main drain pipe. Therefore, it is easy to see that the grating would not be in proportion to the pool size and it would be more expensive than the Anti-Vortex type.

Swimming lane markers and *depth markers* should be constucted of tile, preferably of black unglazed ceramic tile. Wherever the depth of the water changes in the pool, tile depth markers should be located on the deck, preferably a foot back from the face of the pool wall. The markers should be at least 12 inches square to insure good visibility. The tile swimming lane markers should be 10 inches in width if the pool is to be used for competitive swimming, and should be of black unglazed ceramic tile.

Since diving is one of the most popular pool activities, *diving boards* should be installed at all pools with the exception of shallow neighborhood pools. One-meter boards are most widely used, although it is customary to install a three-meter board if adequate space and depth are available. High diving platforms (10-meters) are usually installed only at Olympic-size pools or pools intended especially for official competition. Installation of boards which comply with A.A.U. or N.C.A.A. specifications (14 or 16 feet long and 20 inches wide) is desirable, and safe, tested equipment is assured. Laminated boards have long been used, but aluminum boards are gaining in popularity because of their durability and performance. Fibreglass boards have also proven very satisfactory.

One-meter boards should never be placed closer than 12 feet to another board or a parallel pool wall. For the three-meter diving board, at least 14 feet of clearance should be allowed.

Benches, constructed preferably of concrete or steel frame with wooden seats and backs, should be installed around the perimeter of the pool.

In order to provide ample circulation of filtered water, it is of the utmost importance that the proper size *inlets* and *inlet pipes* be

Diving board at Americana Hotel, Miami Beach, Florida.

installed. A revolutionary idea in the inlet fitting is the development of the plastic or metal jet type inlet. This inlet extends no more than three-quarters of an inch beyond the wall, thus eliminating a projection that could be dangerous. Also, because of its design, the jet inlet can be drilled by the manufacturer to supply a fixed stipulated amount of water in the proper location. Because of the tapping of the inlet, the water can be disbursed in any desired direction. The inlet, therefore, serves a dual purpose: It supplies the necessary amount of water, and directs the water to the floor and sides of the wall, thereby cleaning the floor and wall by the jet action.

The material for and the type of *coping* and *gutter* will largely be determined by the health regulations of each state. For instance, in the state of Florida, the coping must extend 6 inches above the finished deck. This height is necessary because of the sandy soil and the wind that prevails in the beach areas. The six inch rise in the curb serves as a stop for sand blown by the wind. In some localities, flush deck pools are proving very satisfactory and popular. There are a few states in which the health regulations require an overflow gutter to provide a handhold for swimmers. A gutter constructed of limestone, with the overflow water level nine inches below the top of the deck, is the most widely used type of gutter in outdoor pools at the present time, and this type is accepted by the majority of the state health departments.

HEATING SWIMMING POOL WATER

Heating of water for an indoor pool is a must and for an outdoor pool is desirable. A heated pool will receive much more use and the length of the swimming period will be extended.

Scale and condensation are the problems encountered and these must be given careful attention by a skilled technician in the planning of the system. The condensate of water and waste gases is very corrosive and damages the pipe coils. Scale forming on the pipes is detrimental and most water contains calcium salts and other solids. All these problems must be taken into consideration in planning the system.

There are several methods by which water

Diving board, University of British Columbia, Vancouver, B. C.

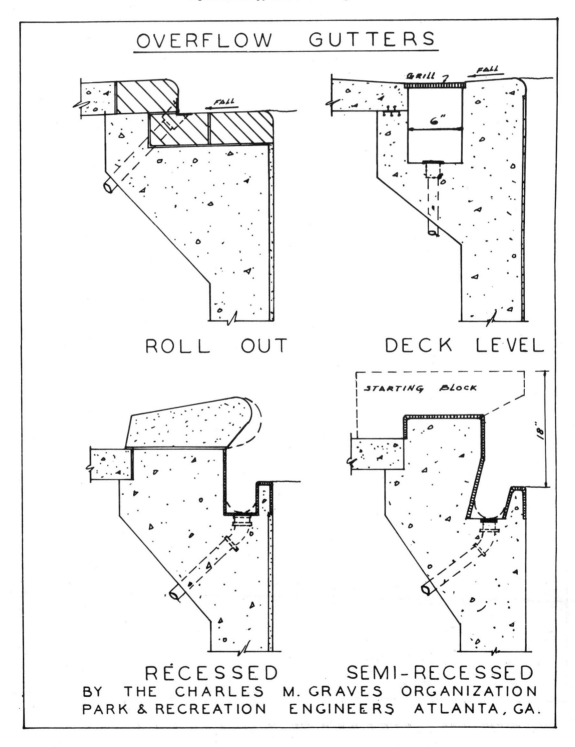

Figure 11:1. Types of overflow gutters.

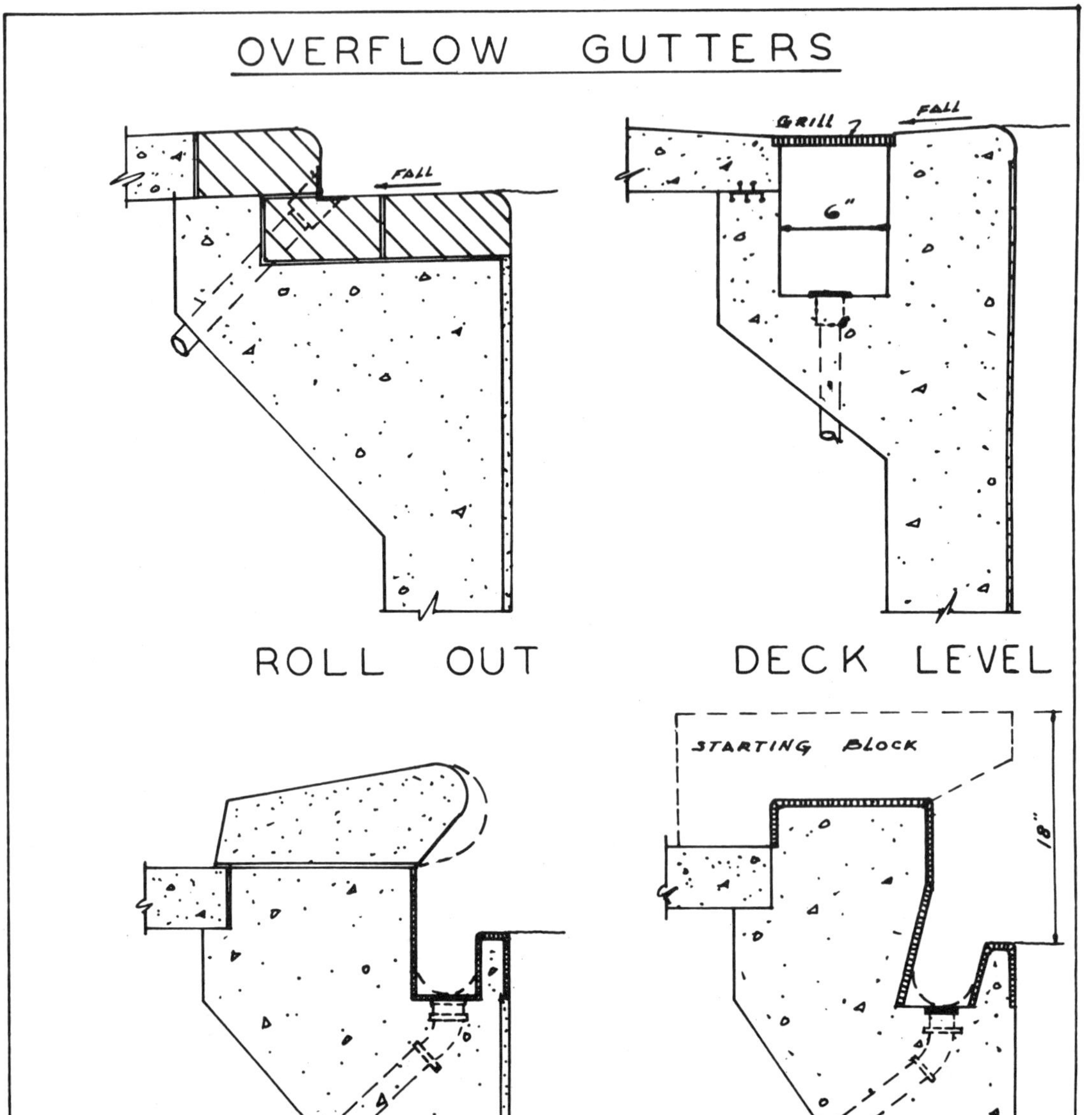

can be heated, and the following are suggested:

1. *Heat exchanger system.* The water is heated and circulated through the exchanger. The pool water is circulated through adjacent chambers of the exchanger to absorb the heat, but the water does not pass through the fire box coils. Therefore, it is not exposed to scale temperature. This is probably the best system but the initial cost is high and the controls require more attention.

2. *The principle of using the jet pump.* The water is circulated through coils by water operated jets. This system is probably the least expensive, since it is relatively simple and less scale is formed.

3. *Direct or flow-through principle.* This is the least expensive system to install but can give the most trouble in operation. Scale will form more quickly in this system and the descaling adds considerably to the over-all cost.

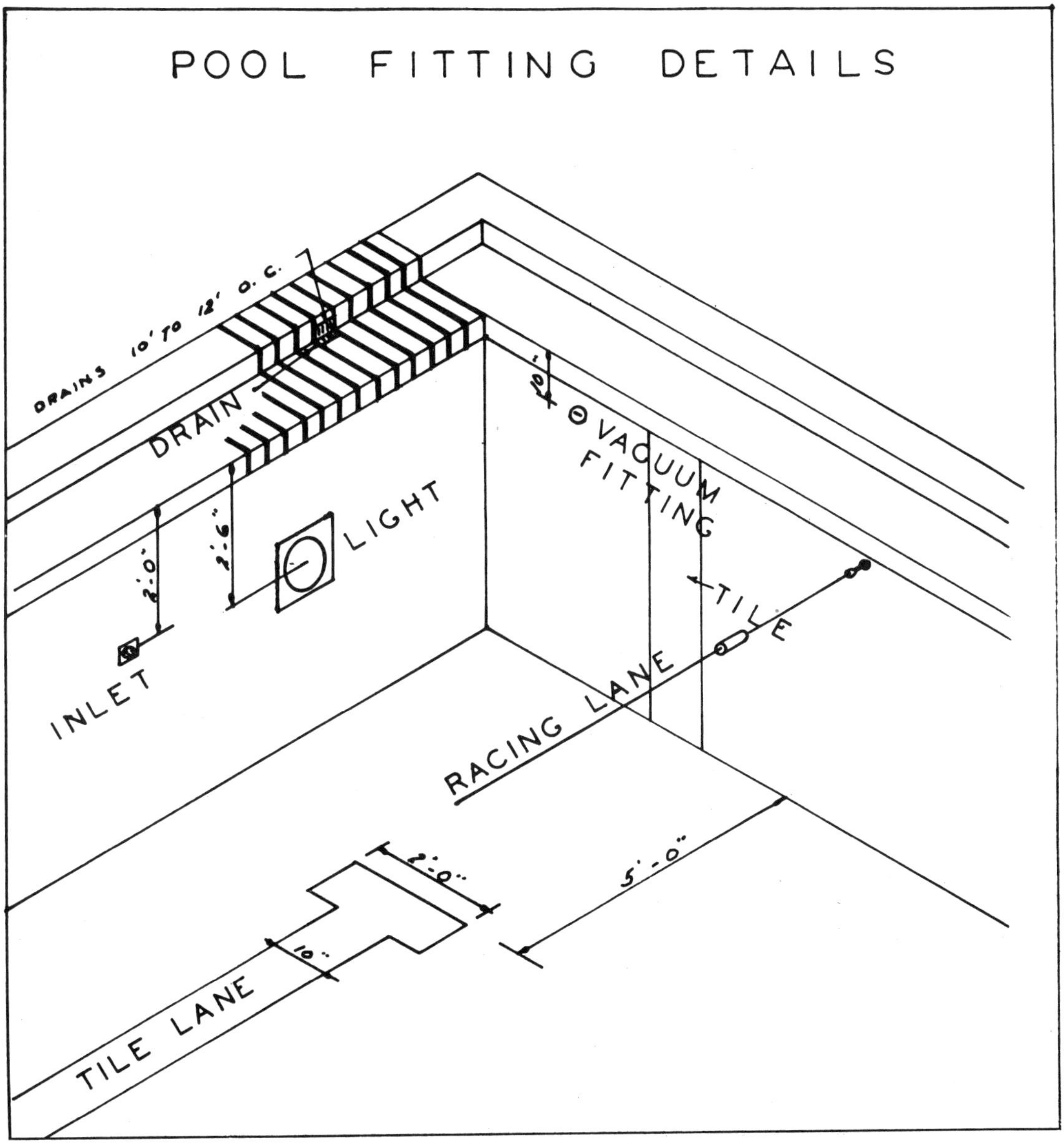

LIGHTING

Three types of lights are used in connection with a swimming pool, *underwater*, *overhead*, and *spot*, each serving a particular purpose. By installing the proper type of lights in the proper locations, the swimming pool can be operated for a longer period each day, thereby serving more people during the swimming season.

The primary purpose of *underwater lights* is to illuminate the water surface during night use, not only for safety reasons but also for the effects achieved for swimming activities, particularly during water shows, ballets, and other special features. The underwater lights afford better vision for the lifeguard and thus add to the safety of the pool, and at the same time enable the spectators to better see and enjoy the swimming activities. The placing and selection of size of the underwater lights should be handled by an electrical engineer who has had experience in the swimming pool field. It is very important to have an adequate number of lights installed, so that the entire area is illuminated and all dark danger spots are eliminated. By staggering the lights on the side walls of the pool, overlapping of the lighted area can be accomplished. The lights should be installed in light niches far enough below the water surface to ensure that a swimmer, when swimming near the surface, will not come into forceful contact with them. Two types of underwater lights are used, *wet niche* and *dry niche*. The wet niche is preferable because of the simplicity of installation and relamping. Where the dry niche light is used, it is mandatory that a tunnel be built around the pool walls under the deck, so that the lights can be relamped. This tunnel also serves as a pipe tunnel for easy access to pool plumbing. It must be noted that this tunnel will add considerably to the over-all cost of the pool and is prohibitive where a pool is being built on a limited budget. It is recommended that the underwater lights be on more than one circuit, since there may be times when only a portion of the lights are required for special events. The switches should be located in a convenient place so that all the lights can be controlled from one point.

If the swimming pool is to be operated after dark, *overhead lighting* is of prime importance. The overhead lights do not always ensure proper illumination of the pool water, but they do afford safety for the bathers using the deck area and the adjoining areas. Flood lights are located around the perimeter of the swimming pool, preferably outside the fence, and are attached to metal poles. The grouping of the lights and the height of the poles are determined by the size of the area to be illuminated. The metal poles should be rigid enough not to be affected by the wind, and the wires leading to the poles should be waterproof, concealed, and underground, rather than overhead.

Spot lights at a pool are considered a luxury and not a necessity, since they are installed not from a standpoint of safety but rather in connection with water pageants and other pool events. Electrical outlets that are waterproof and tamper-proof should be installed at the base of the light poles. These outlets will be used in connection with public address systems, radios, and other electrical equipment.

SPECTATOR FACILITIES

An important point to consider in connection with the operation of a pool is its financial success. Although the major portion of the pool revenue will come from the swimmers themselves, a large part of the success of the pool will depend upon public interest. Adequate provisions for spectators—who are usually the parents and friends of the swimmers, particularly of the younger age group—will go far toward insuring full utilization of the pool facilities.

Suitable seating and restroom facilities should be provided for spectators, but should be so arranged that the spectators and bathers are completely separated. If at all possible, permanent seats should be built, of a type that will require no maintenance other than ordinary cleaning. The seats should be placed so that the spectators will have their backs to the afternoon sun. The ideal arrangement is to have them parallel to the diving boards, since diving exhibitions are probably the most interesting of water sports.

If the bathhouse is constructed with a flat roof, this space may be utilized for lounging and sunbathing, and may be used for a concession area for both spectators and bathers, but arranged so the two groups will not use the same facilities. This space can also be utilized for deck games, such as shuffleboard and table tennis.

The snack bar, which is a very important feature of outdoor pools, should serve spectators as well as swimmers, but through separate serving windows. This arrangement will reduce personnel and operating cost, as well as reduce the problem of sanitation.

TYPES OF POOLS

Although the majority of public pools prior to World War II were rectangular, pools with curved perimeters—circular, oval, ovoid, or irregular in shape—were fairly common. In the more recent years, the rectangular pool has been modified to include "T," "L," and "fan-shaped" pools. Two or three-unit pools, each designed to serve a specific use, have been built in some cities, especially where the pools are expected to serve metropolitan communities. The pool shape and size are of prime importance and these are determined by the relative importance of the activities to be conducted in the pool. It should also be kept in mind that all pools, other than residential or motel, should be of proper size to meet the A.A.U. and N.C.A.A. regulations for competition.

Because of the promotion of swimming in high schools, colleges, and clubs, competitive swimming is receiving greater recognition throughout the United States. Junior championship meets require a pool at least 75 feet long and 42 feet wide. For senior championship meets, the ideal length is 55 yards long and 56 feet wide. The official short-course record requires a pool 75 feet in length and the long-course requires a pool 165 feet long. To fully meet these requirements it is wise to build a pool one inch longer than the specified length, as the official distance cannot be even a fraction of an inch short.

The width of the pool is governed by the number and width of swimming lanes desired. The competitive pool should never have less than six lanes. The width of the lane represents the full spread of the arm in the breast stroke and widths of 6, 7, and 8 feet have been designated as satisfactory. Lanes 5 feet wide are not recommended. The maximum width of lanes recommended by the Federation International de Nation Amateur, is 2½ meters (8 feet 2 inches).

The slope of the pool floor should be as follows: No sudden changes of slope should be permitted in the area where the water is less than 5 feet deep. For depths less than 6 feet, the slope should be 1 foot in each 15 feet, and from the deep area in front of the diving board, the slope must not exceed 1 foot in each 15 feet.

Standards for the depth of swimming pools have been established by the A.A.U. and these must be adhered to in connection with competitive swimming sanctioned by the organization. For the 75 foot pool, the shallow end should be at least 3 feet deep and slope not more than 1 foot each 15 feet and a minimum of 10 feet and preferably 12 feet under the diving boards. When high diving platforms (10 meters) are used, the depth must be increased to 15 feet, maintaining other dimensions given. The N.C.A.A. recommends 3½ feet of water in the shallow end of the pool.

In any public pool the depth in the shallow end should never be more than 3 feet. For all commercial, municipal, and recreational pools, 80 to 85 per cent of the total water area should be 5 feet or less in depth.

EQUIPMENT FOR RECIRCULATION SYSTEMS

Diatomite filters are ideal for all pools because of the outstanding filtration job and the minimum amount of space required. Pressure sand filters require more space but possibly less attention.

Excellent dirt removal is assumed for a well-operated sand filter which removes micro-organisms and some bacteria. The diatomite filter not only removes micro-organisms, but filters minute non-settling sediment, giving the water a crystal polish.

Authorities differ slightly on the proper

TYPICAL SHAPES AND SIZES OF POOLS

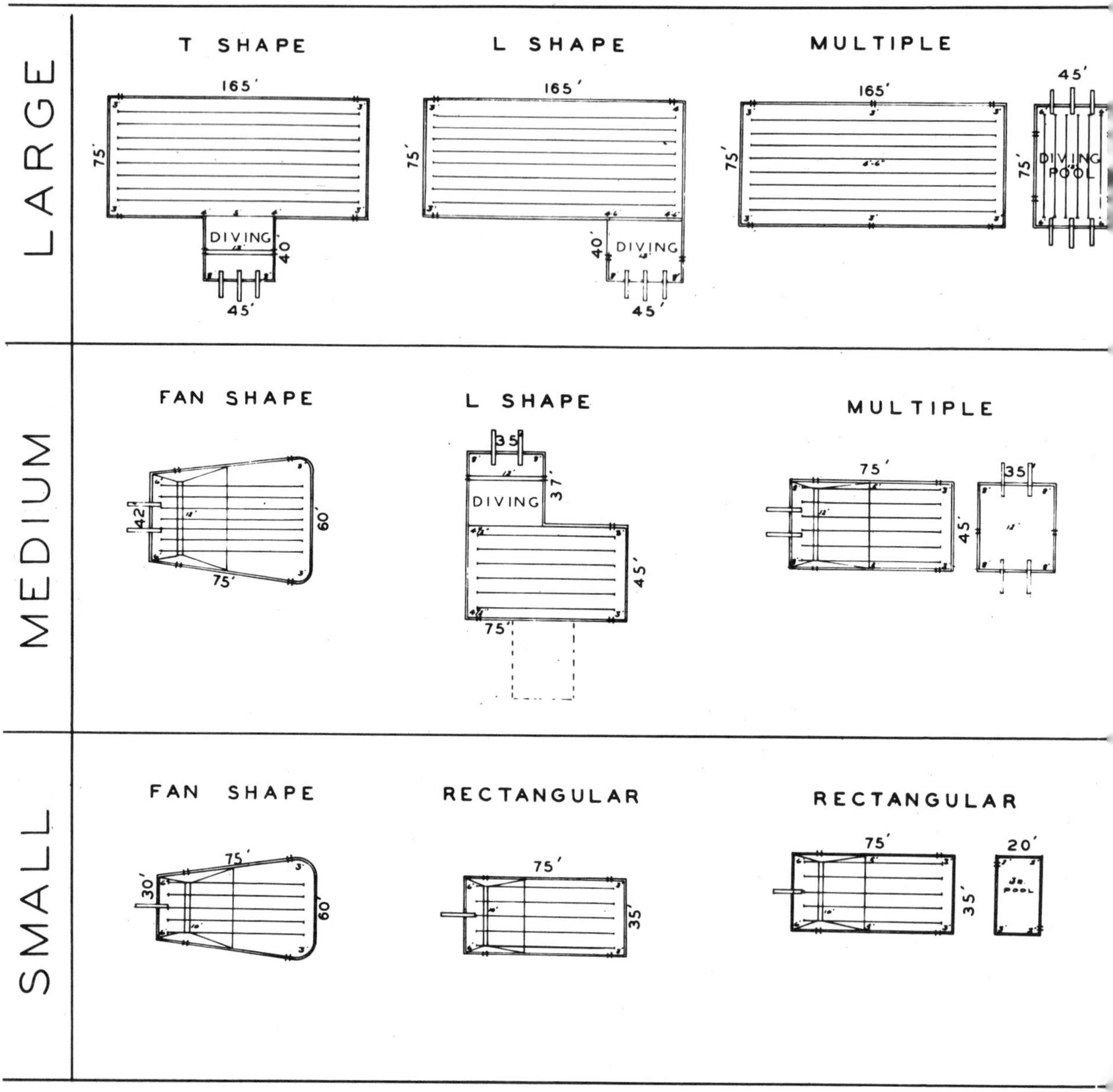

IRREGULAR SHAPED POOLS

HOMES – HOTELS – CLUBS

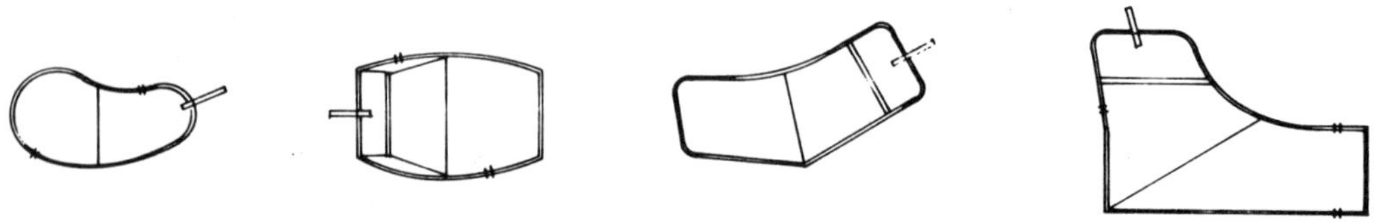

flow rate. Three gallons per minute per square foot of filter area flow rate is recommended by some builders, although most diatomite type filters handle four gallons per minute per square foot of filter area flow rate easily. The backwash flow rate for sand filters is usually 12 to 15 gallons per minute per square foot of filter area. The average backwash time per filter is 15 minutes. The diatomite filter requires only a 3 gallon per minute per square foot of filter area flow rate, and is completely backwashed in three to four minutes.

Rate of flow controllers are desirable on all filters. They can, however, be omitted except on large pools. Pressure gauges are required for both the inlet and outlet pipe for determination of loss of head of back pressure in the filter.

The use of diatomaceous earth as a filter aid in the clarification of liquids is not new. It has been used for years in industry for the removal of finely divided particles of suspended matter from oils and other liquids. The United States Corps of Engineers developed a diatomite filter for military use, which was light in weight, portable, required little space, had high capacity, and removed more finely divided particles from water than did sand filters. (Sand filters failed to remove the cysts of amebic dysentery, when operated at rates necessary for military usage.)

Vertical pressure sand filters range from 36 to 120 inches with flow rates ranging from 21 to 235 gallons per minute. They are designed for a flow rate of 3 gallons per minute per square foot of filter area. The filter containers are usually standard welded steel tanks made to operate at 100 pounds working pressure, with a safety factor of 5. The filter bed itself consists of carefully selected and graded filtering media and four layers of graded gravel.

When pipe lines from the suction vacuum cleaner lead to pump suction, a pump that will develop good vacuum must be used. Pump and piping should be large enough to provide for a turnover of pool water in at least eight hours.

When pressure filters are used, pumps must be designed to pass the required volume under the maximum head that may develop in the filters. When designed to operate with multiple unit filters, it is advisable to have pumps in duplicate with proper cross-connections to permit one filter to be washed with the effluent from another. If pumps are located at an elevation higher than the water line of the pool, a check value must be placed on the pump suction.

CLARIFICATION AND DISINFECTING OF SWIMMING POOL WATER

The type of feeder to be used in a swimming pool depends on several factors: whether or not the feeding is to be continuous, the chemical feed, the size of pool and the convenience desired. The chemical feed pump, due to its efficiency and accuracy, is a great improvement over the other types of feeders and is usually specified for new pools or for replacements in old pools. A chemical pump is used for positive injection of alum, soda ash, and chlorine compounds to the swimming pool at predetermined and adjustable rates.

Chlorine, either as gas or as a hypochlorite solution, should be fed into the pool with the influent water. This method not only gives the chlorine an opportunity to destroy the bacteria before it enters the pool, but also takes advantage of the pool inlet system to get the best possible distribution.

Ideal swimming pool water is crystal clear, free from suspended matter, bacteria, algae, and insects. It is also nonirritating to the bathers. Since in a recirculation type of pool the water is used over and over again, it is easy to see that it must be continuously treated in order to retain its crystal clearness and purity. Various chemicals are required to achieve this result. *Filter alum* (aluminum sulphate) or *ammonium alum* is used for coagulation; for raising *pH* and for *aiding coagulation* the use of *sal soda, soda ash* or *caustic soda* is recommended. For disinfection, *chlorine* in one of its several forms such as liquid chlorine, chlorine gas or chlorine compounds (calcium hypochlorite, sodium hypochlorite, or chlorinated lime), is used. Other disinfectants are ammonia in one of its forms such as ammonium sulfate or ammonium chloride.

For controlling algae and insects, an algaecide and insecticide should be used. These could be copper sulphate (blue vitriol), copper chloride, or some other algaecide.

Pool surfaces can be cleaned with a one per cent solution of calcium hypochlorite or a dilute solution of muriatic acid or a caustic.

Without a coagulant, the rapid sand filter would merely act as a strainer and would not remove finely divided material such as colloidally suspended bits of dirt, scale, dandruff, oil, lint, and coloring matter. It is, therefore, necessary to use a coagulant in the purification of swimming pool water, and alum is the coagulant used. Its point of application is ahead of the filters so that the alum can form flocs. Large flocs are preferable to small flocs as they are more efficient in removing impurities, settle more rapidly, and do not tend to pass through the filter so readily. One factor that is very important to the condition of ideal flocculation is the pH of the water. This characteristic should be within the range of 7.0 to 7.6. Another factor is reaction time. Adding the alum into a reaction chamber or screen chamber is better than adding directly into the piping system. A third factor is mixing. Whenever possible the coagulant should be added to the suction side of the pump so that it will be thoroughly mixed with the water before it reaches the filters. Failure to obtain good flocculation may result in some of the coagulant passing through the filters and into the swimming pool, thus causing turbidity and a residual of free alum that is irritating to the eyes of a bather. Such a condition should be neutralized by feeding soda ash.

Whenever a coagulant is added some of the alkalinity is used up by the coagulating reaction. Unless there are new additions of alkaline material, the swimming pool water will become acid. This condition, of course, must be avoided and consequently alkali in the form of sodium carbonate is added to the recirculated water. The amount to be added should be equal in weight to the filter alum being fed to the system. This is to say, equal amounts of sodium carbonate and aluminum sulfate should be fed. Other materials such as sal soda, ammonium or potassium alum, should be figured back to chemical equivalents.

Various swimming pool water disinfecting agents have been proposed. Chlorine approaches the ideal, although it lacks some desirable characteristics. Bromine appears to have certain desirable qualities, but further research and development are needed to determine, among other items, the effect of pH, temperature, interference with control tests, bactericidal effectiveness and other factors before complete approval can be given the promising agent.

BATHHOUSE

The functional arrangement of the bathhouse is exceedingly important. The entire project should be planned so that the pool and bathhouse can be operated with a minimum of personnel, particularly during low attendance periods.

The clothes check room should be in the center of the building. The wings at either end of the building may house lockers, dressing rooms, toilets, and showers. All facilities should be arranged so that patrons can pass through quickly without confusion. The desirable route from the dressing rooms to the pool should be past the toilets and shower facilities. Each swimmer should take a thorough cleansing shower with soap before putting on a bathing suit. By requiring each bather to pass through a group of showers before entering the pool, at least a superficial bath will be obtained, but this should not be considered as replacing the required shower in the nude. Toilets should be readily accessible and wall-hung fixtures are desirable.

Floors of bathhouses should be sloped to floor drains to provide drainage, allowing ¼ inch slope per foot. Ample hose connections should be readily accessible for cleaning purposes. Floors in dressing rooms and showers should be constructed of unglazed ceramic tile, of a color that is easily maintained.

Individual lockers, baskets, or plastic bags checked in a central room have been used successfully for the storage of clothing, the choice depending mainly upon local conditions. Lockers are more costly and require more space, but keep the clothes in better condition. The basket or plastic bag clothes check system is by far the better from the point of cost, space required, and operation cost.

Individual dressing booths should be provided for women and girls, whereas men and boys will usually dress in the open. Dressing rooms should be arranged to permit a maximum of sunlight and air.

Both individually and group controlled showers are in general use. Control and operation of each group vary and each has advantages and disadvantages. All modern equipment has some type of control so that there is no possibility of bathers being scalded.

Hair dryers are desirable for women bathers.

The bathhouse, as part of the pool and park development, should harmonize architecturally with the pool. It should give the impression of cleanliness and safety.

Exterior walls should be constructed of brick, concrete, concrete units, or stone. Wood construction has a high maintenance cost. Interior walls should be structural glazed tile or glazed ceramic tile for dura-

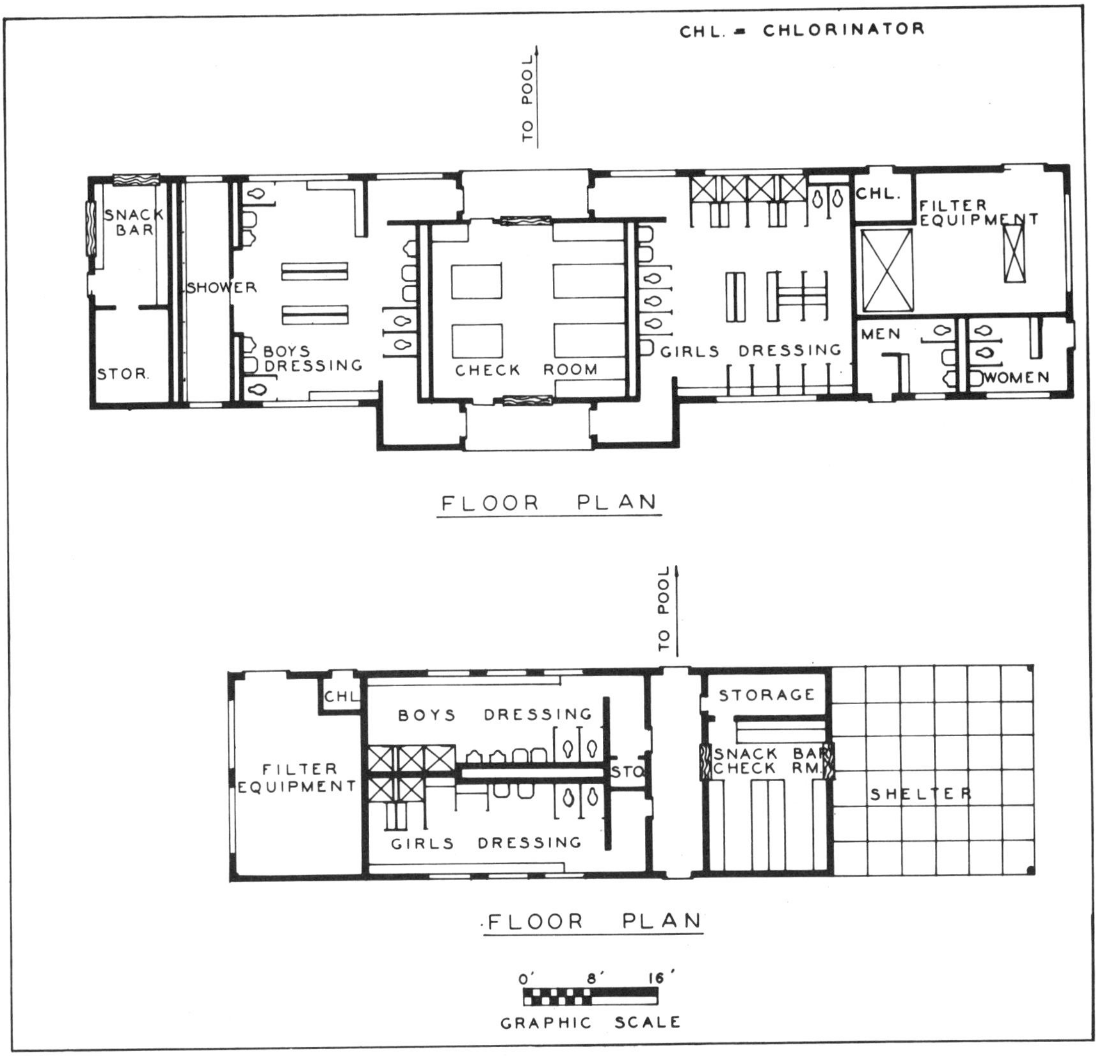

TYPICAL BATH HOUSE PLANS

bility and easy maintenance. Ceilings can be exposed wood, precast concrete panels, steel decking, or finished ceiling of keene cement.

All exterior doors, door frames, and windows should be constructed of bonderized steel. For additional light and ventilation plastic skydomes with built-in fans are very practical.

Mirrors 18 by 24 inches enclosed with metal frames should be installed over each lavatory. Under each mirror there should be a shelf 6 inches wide constructed of tile. Glass shelves should not be used.

Benches should be 11 inches wide, with seats constructed of wood, and legs of strap iron or pipe, bolted to the floor.

Individual shower stalls constructed of marble will prove to be very satisfactory. Gang showers can be built of structural glazed tile or glazed ceramic tile. Exposed masonry unit or plaster walls for gang shower finish should not be used.

After determining the number of swimmers to be served, the bathhouse fixtures will be governed by the following rules which meet most state health department regulations:

1 shower for each 40 bathers
1 lavatory for each 60 bathers
1 toilet for each 40 women
1 toilet for each 60 men
1 urinal for each 60 men

Note: Regulations vary among states and in some instances within states. Architects should consult local health regulations.

In locating a new swimming pool, it is highly desirable to have it properly related to other recreational areas and facilities in the community. It is also important to have it properly related to other recreation developments in the individual park in which it is located.

If a community center building is planned for the same park area, the dressing facilities of the pool should be incorporated in the community center plan. This combination will reduce the over-all cost of the project since one set of dressing and shower rooms will serve the pool as well as the gymnasium. This method will reduce personnel and effect a considerable savings.

CHAPTER 12

INDOOR SWIMMING POOLS

R. Jackson Smith

THE DEVELOPMENT OF INDOOR SWIMMING pools has not kept pace with the growth of outdoor pools. The cost of construction appears to be the major obstacle to a more rapid development of indoor pools. It is the purpose of this chapter to make suggestions in the economies of construction in order to help overcome this problem.[1] Every school building being constructed today should have at least an instructional swimming pool included in its plant, unless there are community swimming facilities adjacent to the school that can be used for instruction by physical education classes.

School swimming pools must be taken out of the class of the so-called "frill facilities." They will be only when state education departments recognize the swimming pool as a required "teaching station" for physical education. In planning a physical education plant the swimming pool should follow directly after the gymnasium in the priority of facilities needed. For example, if the number of teaching stations required to conduct the physical education program is four, the gymnasiums for boys and girls will of necessity be the first and second teaching stations. The swimming pool with its normal capacity of 60 will provide the third and possibly the fourth physical education teaching stations.

The difference in cost between a swimming pool and other facilities that would be needed such as a second gymnasium or two special exercise rooms is insignificant.

The fear that operating costs will make the pool prohibitive is a fallacy, provided the pool is properly designed and equipped. A recent study of twenty school pools re-

---

[1] The subjects of water circulation and sterilization have been adequately covered in the chapter on "Outdoor Swimming Pools." The reader is referred to that chapter for detailed information on these subjects.

Illustration: Uniondale High School, Long Island, New York

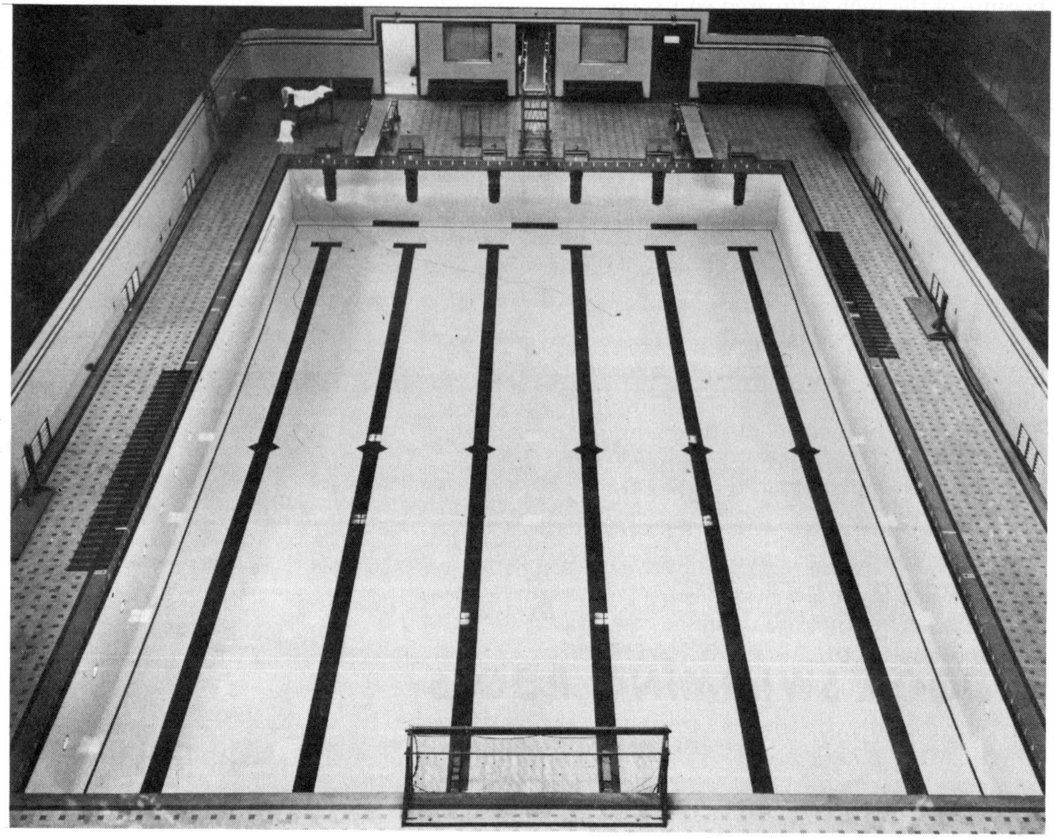

Yale University Exhibition Pool. Size 75 by 42 feet.

vealed a range in the cost of operation and maintenance between $1200 and $2800, exclusive of personnel. Leadership should not be included as an operational factor, since it is part of the over-all instructional staff. Physical education personnel would have to be employed whether there was a swimming pool or not, in order to meet the physical education requirements. In other words, the number of classes of physical education is not affected by the inclusion of a swimming pool.

There are two items that have the greatest bearing on the operational cost of a pool. These are the cost of water and the cost of heating the water. The closed system of circulation was developed to overcome the problem of loss of water. The "balancing tank" is another device that helps to keep the cost of water down. Essentially, the latter method involves the retention of water, which is displaced in the pool by swimmers, in an auxiliary tank. This tank is usually located in the filter room. Water is then drawn out of the tank and pumped back into the pool (through the filters) as required to maintain the proper water level. It is not difficult to understand that if 5000 gallons of water that has a temperature of 72 degrees is spilled down the sewer, it will have to be replaced. The tap water let in will have to be heated, since it may be as low as 40 degrees in the winter time. If replacement must occur very often the operational cost sky rockets. It is not unusual to lose 10,000 gallons of water in the course of a day's operation of an improperly designed pool.

An ironic fact is that numerous communities and school systems have included swimming pools in preliminary plans for a new school or community center, but were eventually forced to cancel plans for the pool because of the high estimated cost submitted by the architect. Some of the estimated costs have actually approached the $500,000 figure. On the other hand completely acceptable pools have been incorporated in school plans at a cost slightly over $100,000. Incidentally, the size of the pools is approximately the same. Why the great range in cost? Here are some of the reasons why high prices are quoted by architects:

1. The school, notably the staff of the physical education department, in setting forth their requirements "shoot for the best." They want a pool with "all the trimmings." A tile basin and deck, as opposed to concrete finish, adds from $4000 to $7000 to the cost of a pool. Underwater windows and lights, special window designs, excessive deep water, deck space, and special acoustical treatment are other factors that are desirable, but may not be essential to a low-cost indoor pool.

2. The inexperience of the architect in planning swimming pools may affect cost estimates. There is a tendency for the inexperienced architect to "protect" himself by adding 20 to 30 per cent to the estimated cost. Another common practice today is to rely on the experience of other communities in the construction of swimming pools. If Community A paid $200,000 for a pool constructed a year ago, the architect adds 10 to 20 per cent to the figure and comes up with an estimated cost for Community *B*.

3. The relatively high cost of certain building materials affects the over-all cost. For example, steel costs more than wood, brick veneer costs more than cement blocks; tile finish costs considerably more than cement finishes, windows invariably cost more than solid walls, and glazed brick or ceramic tile costs more than cinder blocks. Expensive materials do not add to the utility of a facility.

4. The cost of labor in different sections of the country will affect the cost of construction.

New Trier High School Pool. Size 75 by 60 feet.

5. The failure to get an experienced pool architect or planner often proves to be costly. The experienced planner knows where and how to keep the cost down.

6. Certain heating installations can be expensive. The unit heater with attached blower can do an acceptable job in heating the average size indoor pool.

7. Pipe tunnels, although convenient, can be eliminated. Access to underground pipe may be achieved by removable deck sections, or by locating pipes on the side or a shelf of flush-deck gutters.

8. Gutters and drains may be made of precast materials. Tile may be kept to an absolute minimum, *i.e.*, at water-line only; and vitreous glazed wall surfacing may be applied directly on cement, slag, or cinder wall blocks.

9. Attic areas over the pool proper for fans and electric light access may be reduced to a minimum, by locating lights and fans above deck areas and by using glass-block or plexiglass double-dome skylights over the water area. In this regard, the pool planner should remember that reflected window and artificial light may be one of the most disturbing problems in an indoor pool. Overhead illumination, either artificial or natural, is by far the most desirable form of lighting an indoor pool.

Other economies in pool construction may be realized by combining heating and ventilating, *i.e.*, radiant and convected warm-air systems.

LOCATION OF THE SWIMMING POOL

Indoor swimming pools have been located in a variety of places from the basement of the building to the roof. It is quite possible to construct a pool at any level. However, it should be remembered that the higher up in the building the pool goes the greater will be the construction cost. A 100,000 gallon pool represents a lot of weight. This weight requires heavier supports. From many standpoints the ground level is the best location. In addition to more economical construction, the ground level affords direct access from the outside making better control possible.

The following locations are suggested in order of their desirability:

1. As a completely separate self-contained building unit as found in a "campus" type school. This pool would have its own parking facilities adjacent to the pool to facilitate use by the community in the evenings.

2. As a separate wing of a school or recreation center, with a separate locker room.

3. Attached to the physical education plant (gym-locker room) of a school or recreation center with a common dressing room serving both the gym and the pool.

4. On the top floor of a building with separate locker room.

5. Basement location with separate dressing area. In this connection it is not desirable to locate the gymnasium above the pool since moisture from the pool may raise havoc with the gymnasium floor unless proper provision has been made for ventilation and insulation between the pool and the gymnasium.

There are other acceptable locations for swimming pools that will vary from one community to another. However, the locations listed above are preferable, if they are available.

SUGGESTED DESIGN AND CONSTRUCTION OF SCHOOL AND COMMUNITY POOLS

1. The Instructional Pool

The smallest and most simple indoor swimming pool is a shallow water "instruction pool," which may be considered in conjunction with elementary, secondary, or community plant planning. This pool should have a minimum size of 20 by 30 feet with a depth of 3 to 4 feet. A more desirable size would be 24 by 36 feet, but the pool need not be larger than 30 by 42 feet with maximum depth of 4 feet.

The instructional pool should have a roll-out or level deck type gutter for ease of entry and exit to the pool. The water should be slightly warmer than a regular pool, *i.e.*, about 76 to 78 degrees, with the room temperature at 80 to 85 degrees. Since instructional classes should not have more than 24 persons, and preferably fewer, the dressing facilities need not be for the sole use of this pool.

Deck areas around the instructional pool should be ample for seating swimmers, but no space is required for spectators. Minimum size of decks should be 5 to 6 feet, with at least one deck somewhat wider than the minimum. Thus the minimum room for an instructional pool would be 30 by 45 feet, (20 feet plus 5 feet plus 5 feet by 30 feet plus 5 feet and 10 feet). A more desirable room size would be 36 by 60 feet (24 feet plus 6 feet plus 6 feet by 42 feet plus 6 feet plus 12 feet).

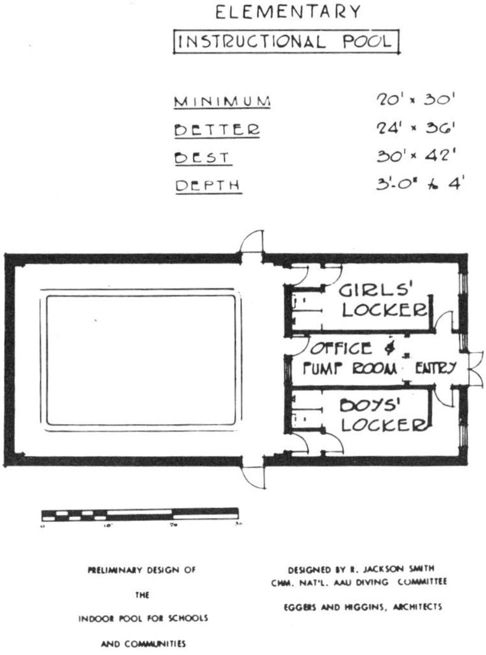

Figure 12:1. Instructional pool for elementary schools.

Ceiling height for an instructional pool should be a minimum of 9 feet and need not exceed 11 or 12 feet. Dressing areas for the instructional pool should be at least 160 square feet, although 200 square feet is a more desirable area. The instructors' control and storage room should have about 100 to 120 square feet of space.

2. The Multi-Use Single Pool

The multi-use single pool indoor swimming facility provides minimum water and deck areas for all of the basic teaching and recreational activities. Such a pool, in its most simple form, would be 30 by 75 feet, with minimum decks and with one or two low boards for diving. A better size pool would be 36 or 44 by 75 feet, with wider decks. Even the minimum size pool should have at least one of the long decks wider than the other.

The minimum ceiling above the low board should be 13 feet, and this height should be maintained in an area 15 feet in front and 10 feet on each side of the end of the board.

In planning the width of the pool, multiples of 7 feet (racing lanes) have been used as the controlling factor, plus an additional small area between the outside lanes and the pool wall. Thus the 30 foot pool provides for four 7 foot lanes plus 1 foot "buffer areas" at each side of the pool. The 36 foot pool provides for five 7 foot lanes, plus two 6 inch "buffer areas," and the 45 foot pool provides for six 7 foot lanes, plus a 1½ foot "buffer area" at each outer lane.

The multi-use single pool is made more attractive and practical if the ceiling height is increased to 24 feet, at least in the diving area to permit high board diving (three-meter springboard).

In each variation of the multi-use single pool, a dual-purpose deck should be provided for special teaching, such as life-saving, body-building, dry-land kicking and arm movement, as well as for folding bleachers for spectators. The number of spectator seats will vary with the community and the school, depending upon general interest in competitive sports, but the deck area for training purposes should not be less than 10 or 12 feet, which will accommodate 200 to 300 spectators or swimmers. Fixed seats are desirable, but in many cases where cost is a controlling factor, it is difficult to justify the sometimes infrequent use of the space.

In addition to the instructional Pool and the Multi-use Single Pool, the pool planner may provide for considerably greater pool capacity by separating the diving and swimming areas either by a deck or a movable bulkhead. By establishing a separate diving pool, the entire 75 foot length of the swimming pool may be used by swimmers, with

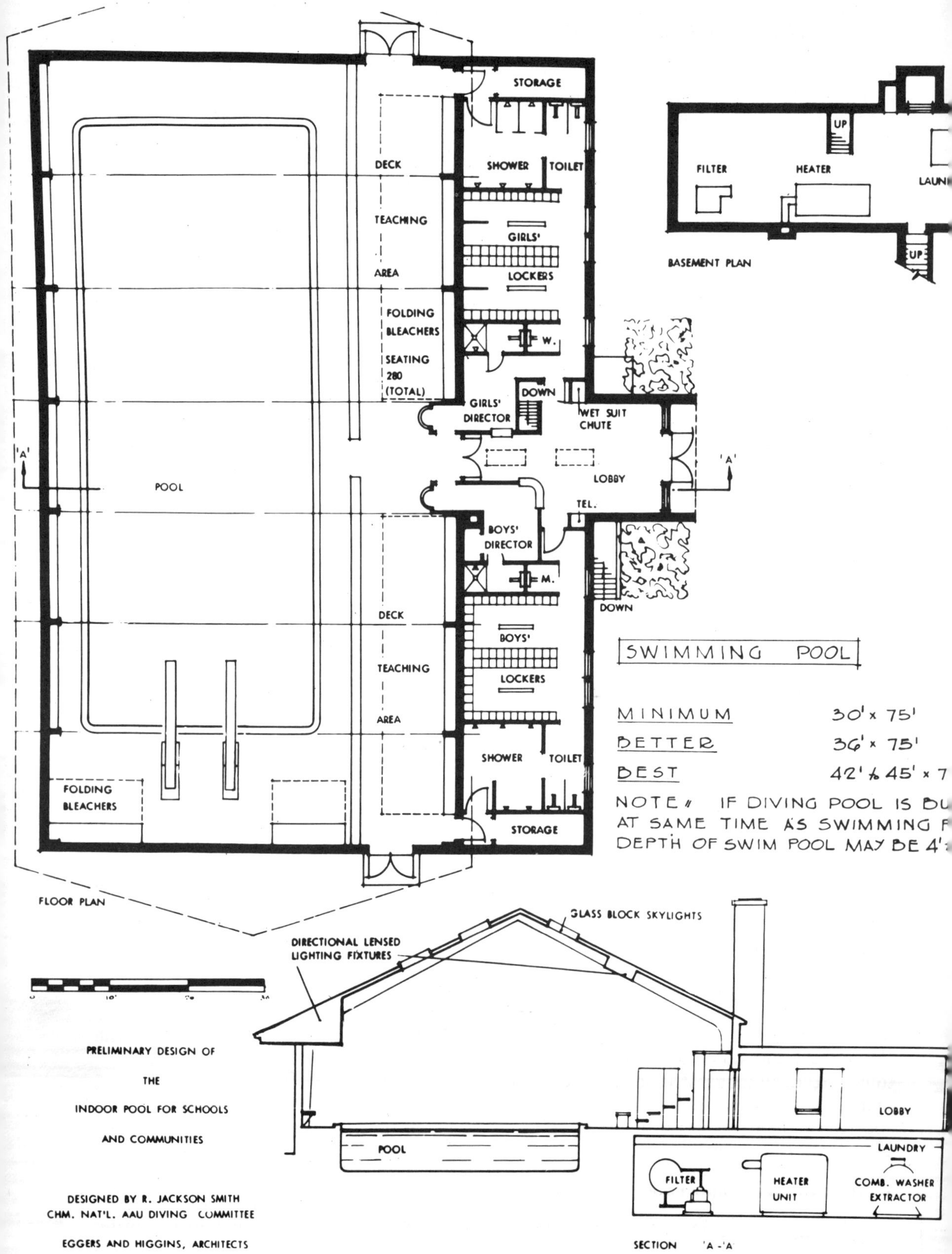
STORAGE
SHOWER
TOILET
DECK
TEACHING
AREA
GIRLS'
LOCKERS
W.
FOLDING
BLEACHERS
SEATING
280
(TOTAL)
GIRLS'
DIRECTOR
DOWN
WET SUIT
CHUTE
LOBBY
'A'
'A'
TEL.
POOL
BOYS'
DIRECTOR
M.
DOWN
DECK
BOYS'
LOCKERS
TEACHING
AREA
SHOWER
TOILET
STORAGE
FOLDING
BLEACHERS
FLOOR PLAN
FILTER
HEATER
UP
UP
BASEMENT PLAN
SWIMMING POOL
MINIMUM 30' x 75'
BETTER 36' x 75'
BEST 42' to 45' x
NOTE" IF DIVING POOL IS
AT SAME TIME AS SWIMMING
DEPTH OF SWIM POOL MAY BE
GLASS BLOCK SKYLIGHTS
DIRECTIONAL LENSED
LIGHTING FIXTURES
10'
PRELIMINARY DESIGN OF
THE
INDOOR POOL FOR SCHOOLS
AND COMMUNITIES
DESIGNED BY R. JACKSON SMITH
CHM. NAT'L. AAU DIVING COMMITTEE
EGGERS AND HIGGINS, ARCHITECTS
POOL
LOBBY
LAUNDRY
FILTER
HEATER
UNIT
COMB. WASHER
EXTRACTOR
SECTION 'A -'A

Figure 12:2. Multi-use single pool.

greater safety and with less depth of water.

The diving pool should be a minimum of 30 feet long as shown on standard international diving dimension tables. The width will be determined by the number and height of diving boards to be provided.

3. The Multiple-Pool Plan

It is apparent that a number of possible combinations can be made using the foregoing pools, either to meet budget demands, or to provide maximum facilities in minimum areas.

The Swimming Center, for instance, with an instructional pool, combined with a multi-use single pool, might be desirable as the first phase of development in a community where teaching and beginning swimming constituted the major aim of the pool supporters.

A more advanced Swimming Center might contain an indoor swimming pool and a diving pool, and a complete indoor aquatic center might well contain three separate pools, *i.e.*, instructional, swimming, and diving.

4. The Indoor-Outdoor Pool

Further developments in planning ideal community facilities should consider combinations of indoor and outdoor pools. This is made possible by either the mechanical removal of the building or roof over the pool, or by sliding wall panels. The Paddock Pool in Detroit and the Wyandotte High School Pool in Michigan are indoor-outdoor pools that have proven to be extremely successful and popular. Both of these pools have sliding glass doors on the west and south sides.

High platform diving, although requiring additional ceiling heights and larger pool dimensions, should be given consideration in schools and communities where swimming and diving interest is keen. There are a limited number of indoor pools in the United States where platform diving is possible. The European countries, however, are well ahead of the U.S.A. in providing indoor pools with high diving platforms. Since the 10-meter platform dive is an Olympic event (along with 3-meter springboard diving), pool planners should use their ingenuity to include it where funds permit.

GUIDE LINES FOR PLANNERS OF INDOOR SWIMMING POOLS

Preliminary Considerations

1. The needs of the program should be fully incorporated into the design of the pool. Program requirements usually involve instruction, competition, recreation swimming, pageants, and exhibitions. Because of the necessity for economy, some program needs might have to be sacrificed.

2. All laws and regulations of state and local Boards of Health should be adhered to in the planning and design of the pool. These laws are related to such matters as the turnover rate of water, use of certain chemicals for water sterilization, type and location of gutters, safety features, bacterial analysis of water, and method of circulation.

3. If the school or agency does not have an experienced swimming pool authority on its staff, it is desirable to engage an experienced pool engineer, planner, or operator. This is not necessary if the architect is an experienced pool builder or if he is willing to employ a swimming pool consultant.

4. The people who will be in charge of the pool, including instructors, should have a hand in the planning of the pool.

5. In the original contract for construction, a written guarantee should be included which provides protection from construction flaws such as leaks or cracks.

6. The future needs of the community and school should be considered. Remember that it is impractical to expand the size of a pool once it has been constructed.

Design and Construction Features

1. Materials used for construction should be evaluated in terms of their serviceability, durability, and cost. There is a wide range in the cost of material that may be used in the construction of the pool basin, decks, walls, ceiling, and roof.

2. The program requirements will have a great deal of influence on the shape and design of the pool. There is no question that a

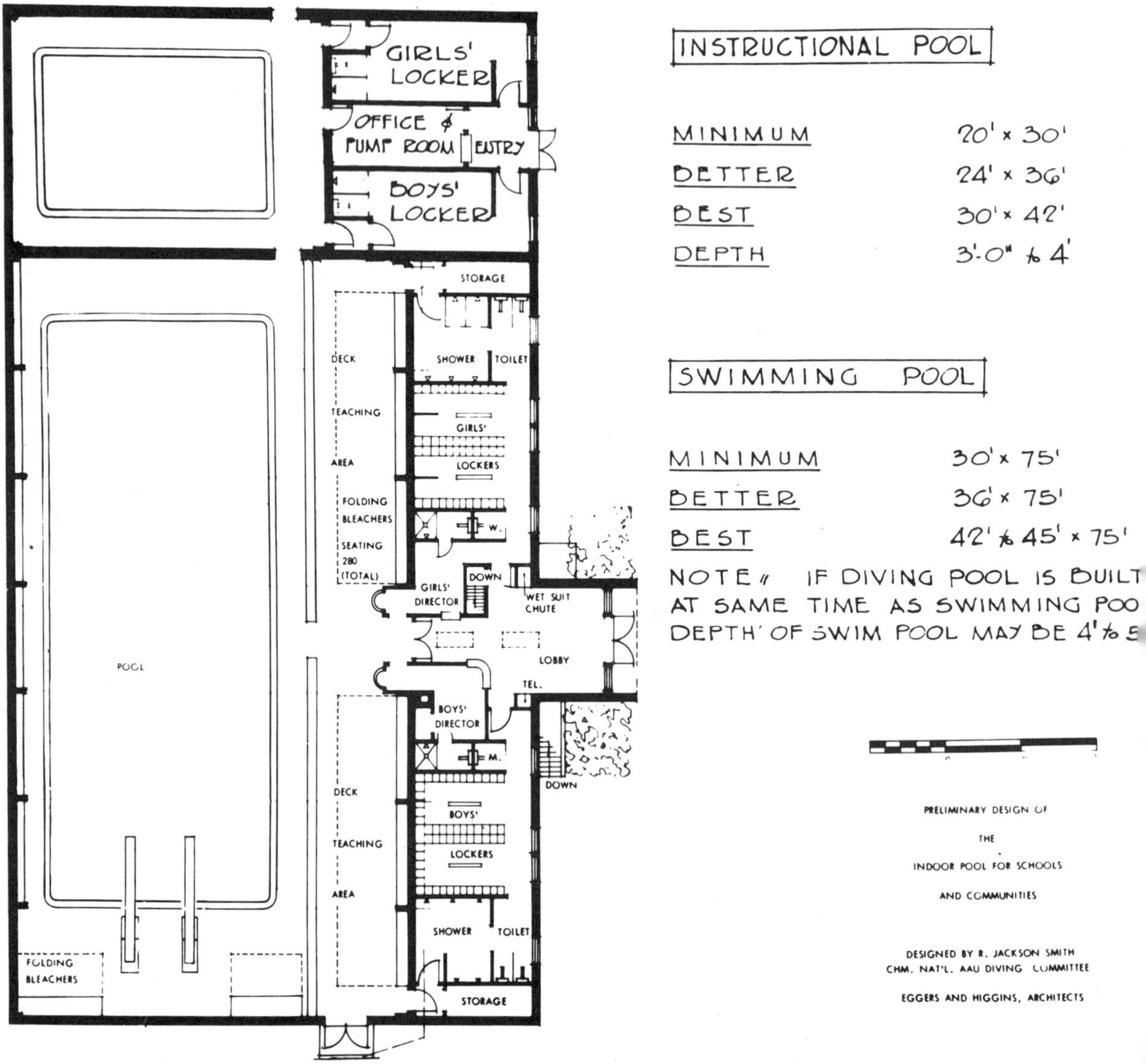

Figure 12:3. Multiple pool plan with separate area for instructional pool.

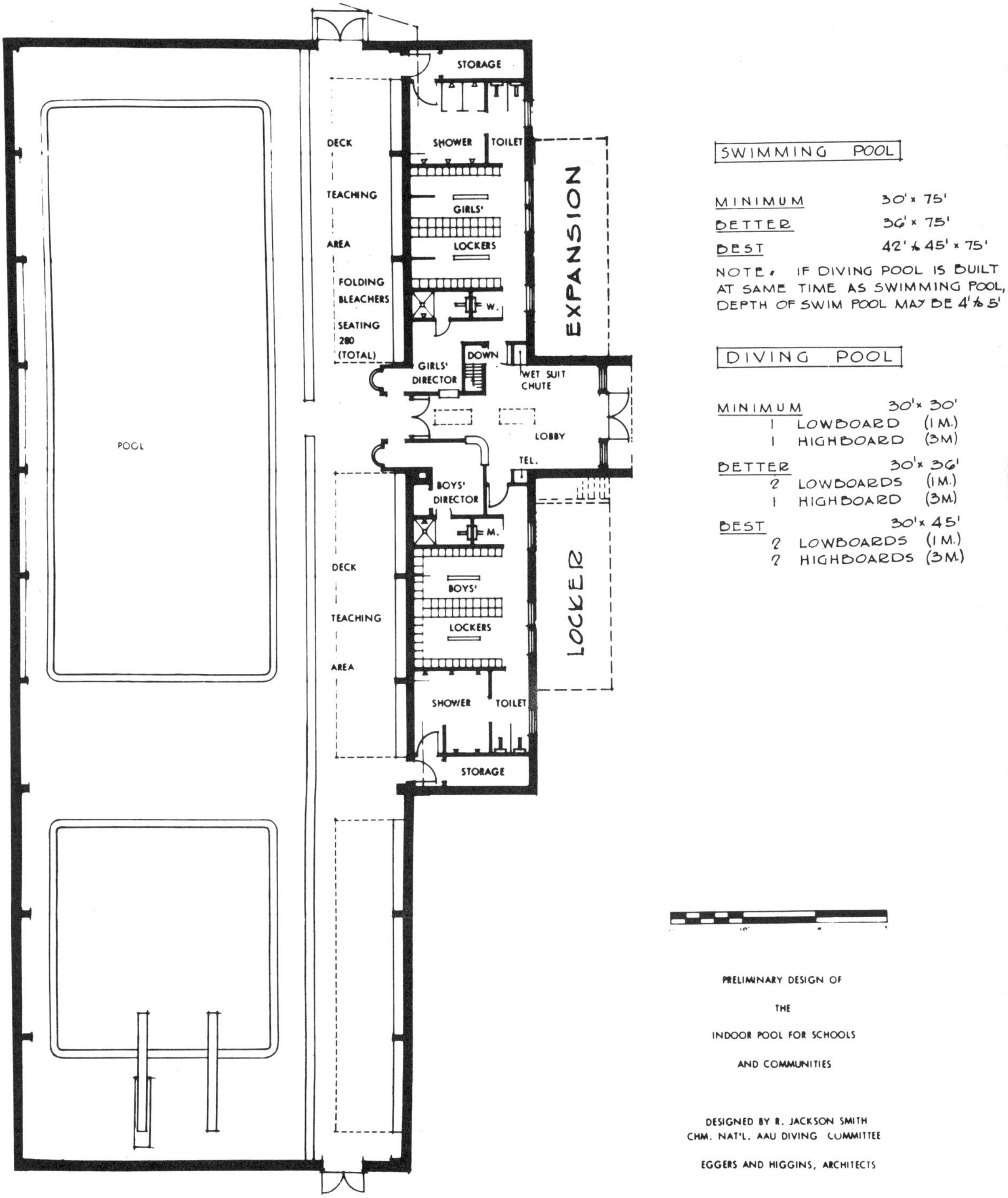
STORAGE
SHOWER
TOILET
DECK
TEACHING
AREA
GIRLS'
LOCKERS
FOLDING
BLEACHERS
SEATING
280
(TOTAL)
W.
DOWN
GIRLS'
DIRECTOR
WET SUIT
CHUTE
LOBBY
TEL.
BOYS'
DIRECTOR
M.
EXPANSION
POOL
DECK
TEACHING
AREA
BOYS'
LOCKERS
LOCKER
SHOWER
TOILET
STORAGE
SWIMMING POOL
MINIMUM 30' x 75'
BETTER 36' x 75'
BEST 42' to 45' x 75'
NOTE: IF DIVING POOL IS BUILT AT SAME TIME AS SWIMMING POOL, DEPTH OF SWIM POOL MAY BE 4' to 5'
DIVING POOL
MINIMUM 30' x 30'
1 LOWBOARD (1 M.)
1 HIGHBOARD (3M)
BETTER 30' x 36'
2 LOWBOARDS (1M.)
1 HIGHBOARD (3M.)
BEST 30' x 45'
2 LOWBOARDS (1 M.)
2 HIGHBOARDS (3M.)
PRELIMINARY DESIGN OF
THE
INDOOR POOL FOR SCHOOLS
AND COMMUNITIES
DESIGNED BY R. JACKSON SMITH
CHM. NAT'L. AAU DIVING COMMITTEE
EGGERS AND HIGGINS, ARCHITECTS

Figure 12:4. Swimming center with separate diving pool.

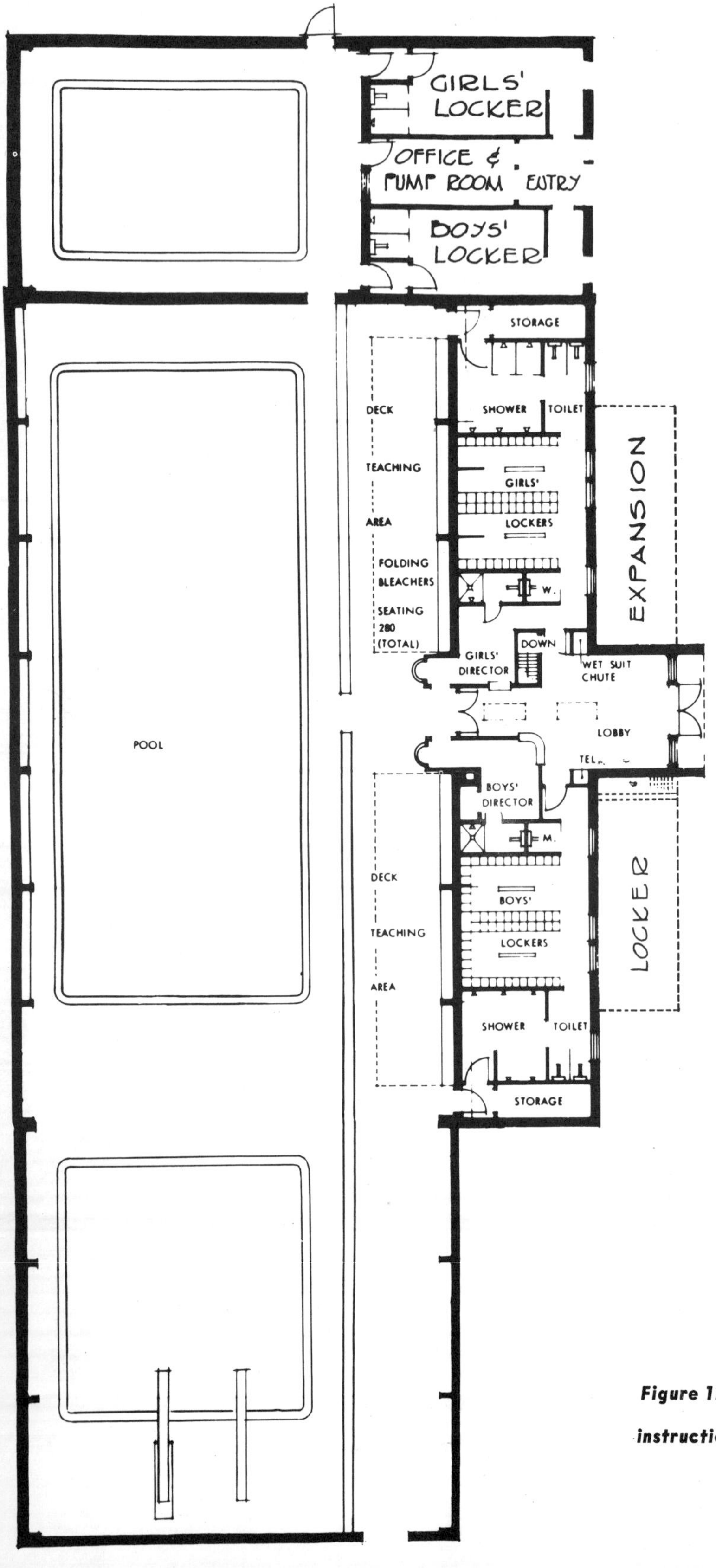

INSTRUCTIONAL POOL

MINIMUM	20' × 30'
BETTER	24' × 36'
BEST	30' × 42'
DEPTH	3'-0" to 4'

SWIMMING POOL

MINIMUM	30' × 75'
BETTER	36' × 75'
BEST	42' to 45' × 75'

NOTE: IF DIVING POOL IS BUILT AT SAME TIME AS SWIMMING POOL, DEPTH OF SWIM POOL MAY BE 4' to 5'

DIVING POOL

MINIMUM 30' × 30'
1 LOWBOARD (1M.)
1 HIGHBOARD (3M.)

BETTER 30' × 36'
2 LOWBOARDS (1M.)
1 HIGHBOARD (3M.)

BEST 30' × 45'
2 LOWBOARDS (1M.)
2 HIGHBOARDS (3M.)

PRELIMINARY DESIGN OF

THE

INDOOR POOL FOR SCHOOLS

AND COMMUNITIES

DESIGNED BY R. JACKSON SMITH
CHM. NAT'L. AAU DIVING COMMITTEE

EGGERS AND HIGGINS, ARCHITECTS

Figure 12:5. Swimming center with separate instructional, swimming, and diving areas.

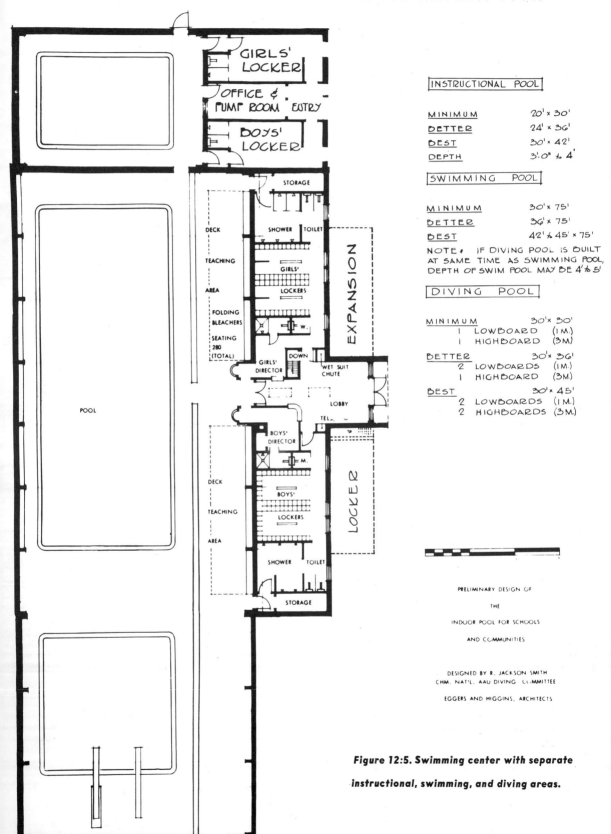

separate diving area provides the most functional layout; however, the cost is often prohibitive.

3. The over-all depth of water is one of the most important design features of a pool. A sound principle to follow is that 65 to 70 per cent of the pool area should contain water that is less than 5 feet deep. When diving boards are included, strict adherence to competitive specification should prevail. A minimum of 9 feet of water under one meter boards, and 11 feet for three meter boards is recommended.

4. It is desirable to have the amount of deck space equal the water surface area. Thus, a 75 by 35 foot pool should have a deck area between 2500 and 3000 square feet.

5. Entrances to the pool from the locker room preferably should lead to the shallow water. The depth of water in a pool is deceptive and the person entering the pool for the first time may inadvertently enter the deep water. To assist swimmers the water depth should be inscribed in tile or painted on the deck at the edge of the pool.

6. Ladders of some sort are essential in a pool. However, ladders or recessed steps should be set back in the wall. They should never be placed on a wall that is to be used for turning in competitive swimming.

7. The circulation of water through the filters is the process that is mainly responsible for producing clear, sparkling water. There are two rules that must be followed if clear water is to be produced. First, adequate size of filters and pumping facilities are necessary to produce the desired rate of flow. Second, proper operation of the pool including the introduction of required chemicals to the water is essential. Most states require that the water in the pool turn over in an eight hour period. In situations where heavy swimming loads occur a more desirable rate is six hours.

8. The use of paint in any part of the pool or pool room should be kept to the minimum, and where it is used for color and decoration, a carefully tested moisture-resistive paint should be used.

9. It is considered essential to provide the instructor's office with a direct view of the pool area. The best location for the office is at the deep end, which offers a full view of the pool. The office window should be large and should be shatterproof glass or clear lucite. The window should be operable, *i.e.*, either horizontal sliding, double-hung or louvered. An opaque blind or curtain should also be provided.

10. When a special area is provided for spectators, it should be separated by some kind of a wall. This prevents them from getting wet and also keeps dirt and debris from being brought onto the pool deck.

11. The best way to keep a pool deck clean and sanitary is by using very hot water. A hot-water outlet must therefore be provided in the pool area. It is best to have two outlets if possible.

12. The distance between diving boards, when more than one board is installed, is important. Low boards (1 meter) should be at least 6 feet and preferably 10 feet apart, and 8 feet from the side of the pool. High boards (3 meters) should be 10 feet away from adjacent boards. When this safe distance is not provided, only one board at a time should be used.

13. The filter room should be readily accessible and should be well lighted. It should not be used for any other purpose such as storage of cleaning gear, suits, or starting blocks.

14. A storage room should be provided off the pool room for storage of instructional supplies, equipment, and cleaning gear. It is best to have a separate room for the cleaning equipment, but the cleaning equipment can be combined with the instructional supplies if necessary.

15. Where the conventional type of gutter is used (not the roll-out or level deck type) a coping should be provided around the edge of the pool to prevent dirt from washing into the pool.

16. The lighting of an indoor pool is important. At eye level there should be a minimum of 20 foot candles of illumination. Underwater lights provide more than an aesthetic appearance. They provide greater safety by illuminating the bottom and serve as an aid to the production of water shows and pageants.

17. Whenever possible the pipes leading

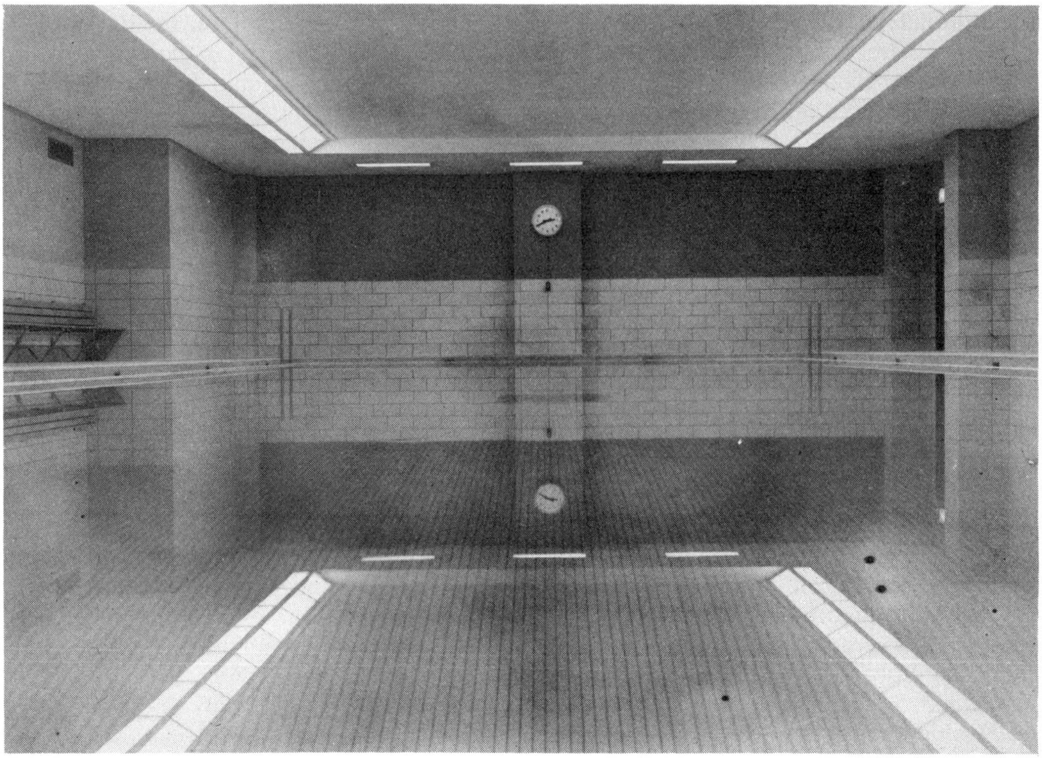

Instructional pool at New York University. Size 60 by 25 feet. Over-all depth is 4 feet.

to and from the pool should be located so that they may be inspected periodically and easily repaired if necessary. The elimination of tunnels will reduce the cost. Troughs may be substituted for tunnels.

18. Eye bolts should be anchored into the gutter or walls to facilitate installation of surface swimming lanes or to divide the pool for instruction or safety purposes. These should be recessed cups if located on the pool walls.

19. It is best to have the circulating pump located below the level of the pool in order to avoid the need for priming the pump.

20. Noise is one of the major obstacles that must be overcome in an indoor swimming pool. This is best accomplished by use of moisture-resistive acoustical material on the ceiling and on at least one or two walls.

21. Reflection of outside light on the water is a condition that must be guarded against. The use of clear glass windows on the south or west side of the pool room should be avoided. Tinted glass such as "solex" helps reduce the sun's glare and reflection, but any glass except in the ceiling area should be provided with sliding opaque drapes of plastic or glass-fiber material.

22. Another problem with which indoor pools are often faced is condensation. The two things that help reduce this condition are good ventilation and proper insulation of walls, ceilings, and windows.

23. It is desirable to have the base of the wall coved to facilitate cleaning. Coved ceramic tile and glazed brick are available for this purpose.

24. It is essential, and in some states a requirement, to include a "safe light" at the entrance of the pool from the locker or shower room. This light should be on whenever the pool is not in use. There have been cases where individuals have stolen into a dark pool and taken a dive into an empty pool basin.

25. All radiators or heating units within

reach of swimmers should be covered and recessed into the wall when possible. Heating by radiation through the floor is a recent trend in indoor pool construction.

26. In order to discourage swimmers from spitting in the pool, cuspidors should be provided, and properly recessed in the wall.

27. At least one drinking fountain should be located in the pool area. It should also be recessed in the wall.

28. It is best to include conduit for wiring for a public address system during the regular electrical installation in order to avoid the necessity of tearing into a wall at a later date.

29. One or two tackboards should be strategically located around the pool. The surface should be made of cork, plastic, or some other similar material.

30. Benches made of concrete, marble, plastic-surfaced hardwood, or ceramic tile provide resting places for swimmers. Recently aluminum folding bleachers have proved to be a boon to class instruction. They also provide seating space for spectators. Radiant heat in the seats, or under them, is desirable if funds permit.

31. Corrosion presents a problem in any indoor pool. Both the humidity and chlorine gas adversely affect non-corrosive metal fittings. Doors, lockers, pipes, grills, diving standards, and other metal fitting should be made from non-ferrous metals.

32. If lane markers are to be installed for competitive swimming they should be permanently installed. This is usually accomplished by the use of block tile embedded flush in the concrete surface or as a part of the tile surface.

33. The deck around the pool and in the shower room should be finished with non-slip material. It is also well to use non-slip material in the pool basin. Falls from slipping on "slick" decks constitute one of the major hazards in most pools.

34. Gutters should not be thought of only as a device for water circulation. There are many types and shapes of gutters. Hence, utility should be combined with such ele-

Roll-out gutter. YMCA, New Britain, Connecticut.

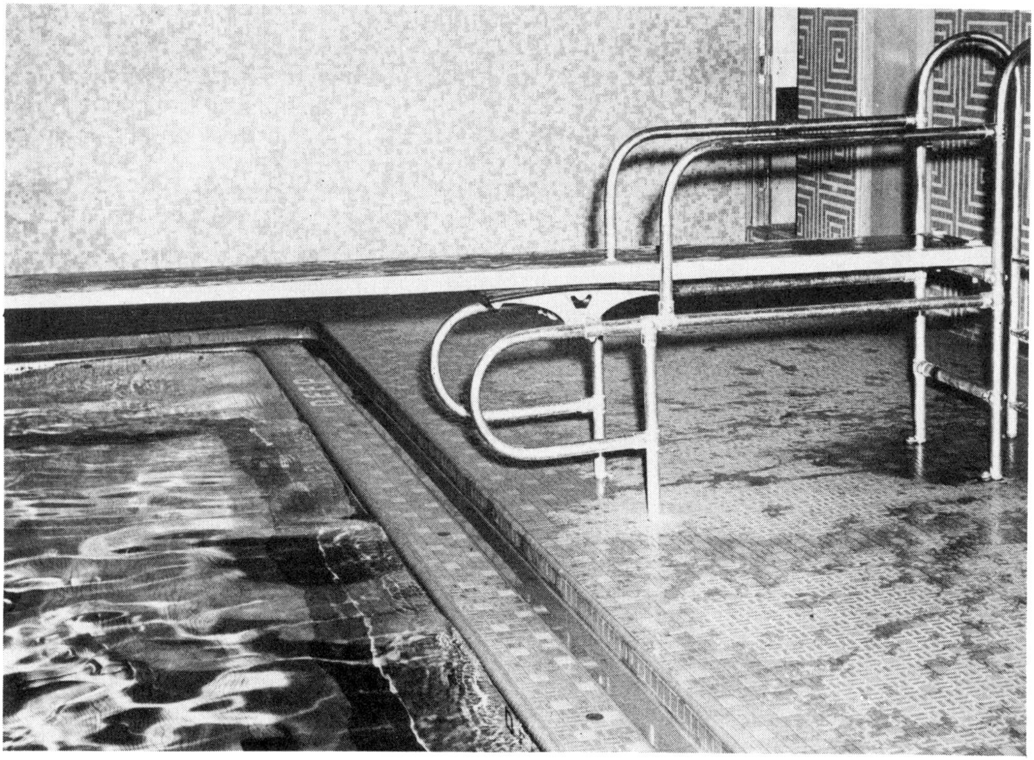

Left: Lint and hair catcher located in the balancing tank type of trench and gutter. New Britain Boy's Club, New Britain, Connecticut.

Right: "Level deck" type of pool with concrete covers placed over trench and gutter. New Britain Boy's Club, New Britain, Connecticut.

ments as appearance, cost, ease of getting in and out of the pool, program needs, and the problem of maintenance. The "roll-out" and "level deck" types of gutters seem to meet most of the criteria established by pool operators.

35. Footbaths located at the entrances to pools are often a nuisance, and in some instances are more harmful than they are good. They should not be included in the design of a new pool.

36. The ceiling height above diving boards is an important factor in designing the pool. A minimum of 12 to 14 feet of overhead clearance is recommended above the board. Thus, a pool with a one meter board would have a ceiling 15 to 17 feet high, and a pool with a three meter board would have a ceiling of 22 to 24 feet high in the area of the springboard.

37. The air temperature in the pool area should be thermostatically controlled. The air should be maintained at approximately 5 degrees above the water temperature. The relative humidity should not exceed 60 per cent.

38. In many outdoor pools which are painted there has been a tendency to paint them a light aqua blue. This practice is not recommended. Pool basins should be white to give the greatest degree of water clarity.

39. The interior of the pool room should be finished in light colored material in order to provide a cheerful, pleasant atmosphere.

CHAPTER 13

LIGHTING FOR SPORTS AND RECREATION FACILITIES[1]

Illuminating Engineering Society

THE PAST DECADE HAS WITNESSED AN UNPARALLELED growth in sports and recreational lighting. Fifteen years ago only two major league baseball parks were lighted; today only one major league park remains unlighted. During the same period the number of lighted football fields has quadrupled, and softball diamonds lighted for night play have multiplied six times. Today, boxing, bowling, badminton, and practically all sports and recreations, may be illuminated so that both player and spectator requirements are satisfied.

The lighting of areas used for various sports activities, especially those located outdoors, involves problems not encountered in other fields of lighting. Some of these problems include the selection of proper floodlight locations, aiming techniques, and provision for multiple uses of the area.

This chapter covers the recommended footcandle levels satisfactory to both players and spectators, and gives typical layouts of lighting systems for certain outdoor recreation and sports facilities.

FACTORS OF GOOD ILLUMINATION

Levels of Illumination

1. It is important that levels of illumination be sufficient for comfortable and accurate seeing and to enable the players to perform their visual task and allow the spectators to follow the course of the play.

2. In facilities in which games are played that attract large numbers of spectators (such as football and baseball stadiums), the illumination level is determined by the

[1] The material in this chapter has been adapted from the Bulletin, "Current Recommended Practice for Sport Lighting," prepared by the Committee on Sports and Recreational Area Lighting of the Illuminating Engineering Society.

Illustration: Bakersfield Junior College at night, Bakersfield, California

amount of light required for the spectators in the row of seats farthest removed from the playing area to follow the course of play. This requirement may require several times the amount of light found satisfactory for the players. The illumination levels suggested by Table 13-1 are those which are currently considered necessary taking into consideration the needs of both players and spectators.

3. The illumination values in Table 13-1 are in most cases stated as "Average Horizontal Footcandles in Service." It is recognized that the vertical component of the illumination on the playing area is important in most sports. Particularly in the "aerial" games, both players and spectators rely to a considerable degree on the vertical illumination on or near the playing area and in some cases well above the playing area. In full recognition of the importance of *vertical* illumination, the recommended footcandle values for most sports and recreational areas are given for *horizontal* illumination for two reasons:

a. Values of horizontal footcandles are much less complicated to compute and to measure in the field, and

b. The vertical components of illumination have been found adequate where the horizontal illumination meets the values prescribed in Table I, and where lighting equipment of the proper type (I.E.S. type of distribution) is positioned at mounting heights and locations conforming to accepted good practice. Unless otherwise noted, the recommended values in this table are in horizontal footcandles on the playing surface. For aerial sports the values are in horizontal footcandles on a plane 36 inches above the ground or floor.

Quality of Illumination

The quality of lighting whether natural or artificial is highly important in providing good seeing conditions. Glare, uniformity, and direction are the most significant factors in determining the quality of illumination.

Uniformity. Reasonable uniformity of illumination over a playing area is required for satisfactory seeing by players and spectators. Expressed in terms of horizontal illumination, acceptable uniformity occurs when the ratio of maximum to minimum illumination does not exceed three to one for those sports in which play is skillful, or the visual task is severe, or where there are likely to be spectators.

Luminaire location.

1. The effects of glare are diminished as the luminaires are removed from the normal line of sight of players and spectators. The angle between the luminaire and the normal line of sight is affected both by the luminaire location in a horizontal plane as well as by the mounting height.

2. The typical layouts show luminaire locations that reflect balanced judgment with regard to providing light from the proper direction and at the same time locating the luminaires out of the normal line of sight. Where physical obstructions require changes from these typical locations, care must be taken to evaluate carefully the possible lines of sight of both players and spectators.

3. Recommended mounting heights are also shown on the typical layouts. Where for physical or economic reasons it is considered necessary to utilize lower mounting heights, the problems of possible glare must be carefully considered. For floodlighting applications the following basis may be used to determine minimum mounting heights from the standpoint of glare:

a. The angle between the horizontal playing surface and a line drawn through the lowest mounted floodlight and a point one-third the distance across the playing area should not be less than 30 degrees, and
b. in addition to meeting the requirement above, the minimum mounting height should not be less than 20 feet for ground sports and 30 feet for aerial sports.

Luminaire brightness. Glare is reduced by reducing the brightness of the luminaire.

Indoor. 1. In applications where fixed equipment is mounted on or near the ceiling this consideration involves two angular regions:

a. The angle from the vertical within which the lamps are not directly

TABLE 13-1

Current Illumination Recommendations for Various Sports and Recreation Facilities

Sport	*Average horizontal footcandles in service**	
	Target	*Shooting Line*
Archery		
Tournament	10†	10
Recreational	5†	5
Badminton		
Tournament	30	
Club or school	20	
Recreational	10	
Baseball	*Infield*	*Outfield*
Major league	150	100
AA and AAA league	75	50
A and B league	50	30
C and D league	30	20
College	30	20
High School	20	15
On seats during game	2	
On seats before and after game	5	
Basketball		
College and Professional	50	
College intramural and high school with spectators	30	
College intramural and high school without spectators	20	
Recreation (outdoor)	10	
Billiards	*On Table*	
Tournament	50	
Recreational	30	
General Area	10	
Bowling	*Lanes*	*Pins*
Tournament	20	50†
Recreational	10	30†
Boxing and Wrestling		
Professional (ring)	200	
Amateur and schools	100	
Seats during bout	2	
Seats before and after bout	5	
Croquet		
Tournament	10	
Recreational	5	
Golf		
General on the tees	10	
At 200 yards	3†	
Putting green	10	

Sport	*Average horizontal footcandles in service**	
Gymnasiums		
Exhibitions, Matches	30	
General Exercising and Recreation	20	
Assemblies	10	
Dances	5	
Lockers and Shower Rooms	10	
Handball		
Tournament	30	
College and school	20	
Recreational	10	
Horseshoes		
Tournament	10	
Recreational	5	
Ice Hockey		
College or Professional	50	
School or club	20	
Recreational	10	
Football		
(Index: Distance from nearest side line to the farthest row of spectators)		
Class		
I Over 100′	100	
II 50′ to 100′	50	
III 30′ to 50′	30	
IV Under 30′	20	
V No fixed seating facilities	10	
(It is generally conceded that the distance between the spectators and the play is the first consideration in determining the class and lighting requirements. However, the potential seating capacity of the stands should also be considered and the following ratio is suggested: Class I for more than 30,000 spectators; Class II for 10,000 to 30,000; Class III for 5,000 to 10,000 and Class IV for less than 5,000 spectators.)		
Rifle Range	*Outdoor*	*Indoor*
On target	30†	50†
Firing Point	10	10
Range	—	5
Shuffle Board		
Tournament	10	
Recreational	5	

* On the playing surface; for aerial sports on a plane 36 inches above the ground.
† Vertical

TABLE 13-1 (continued)

Sport		*Average horizontal footcandles in service**
Skating		
Roller Rink		5
Ice Rink		5
Lagoon, Pond or Flooded Area		1
Skeet Shoot		
Target (surface at 60′)		30†
Firing Point (General)		10
Soccer		
Professional and College		30
High School		20
Recreational		10
Softball	*Infield*	*Outfield*
Professional and Championship	50	30
Semi-Pro	30	20
Schools and clubs	20	10
Recreational	10	5

Sport		*Average horizontal footcandles in service**
Squash		
Tournament		30
Club or school		20
Recreational		10
Swimming Pools		
General (Overhead)		10
Underwater (Outdoors 3 watts per sq. ft. of surface)		
Underwater (Indoors 5 watts per sq. ft. of surface)		
Tennis	*Lawn*	*Table*
Tournament	30	50
Club	20	30
Recreational	10	20
Trap Shoot		
Target (at 150′)		30†
Firing Point (General)		10
Volley Ball		
Tournament and Colleges		20
Schools and clubs		15
Recreational		10

* On the playing surface; for aerial sports on a plane 36 inches above the ground.
† Vertical

visible (called the shielded zone), and

b. the angle within which the lamps are visible (called the unshielded zone).

2. Excessive brightness within the shielded zone may cause glare, particularly in large spaces. Brightness in the unshielded zone may cause direct glare, or glare by reflection, in the specular surfaces of bowling lanes, the surface of water in swimming pools, or polished floors and walls. In addition the brightness of the luminaire in the unshielded zone may cause discomfort or even disability glare if players or spectators look upward. This possibility is minimized by locating the luminaires so that they are removed from the normal lines of sight as far as possible, and/or by using low brightness sources.

Outdoor. The brightness of floodlights, particularly narrow beam types, is lower as they are viewed at increasing angles to the axis of the beam. For this reason, particular emphasis is placed on location and aiming so that, within practical limits, floodlights are not directed along the normal lines of sight of spectators or players.

Surrounding Brightness

1. Increasing the brightness of the surrounding area reduces contrast and improves visibility.

2. One of the most effective ways to reduce the effects of glare is to keep the brightness of the surrounding area to a reasonable level. This can be done very effectively for indoor sports by finishing the walls and ceilings of the rooms in light colors. Control

of the surrounding brightness is much more difficult in outdoor locations; however, a great deal can be done in this regard. Adequate light in the stands and light-colored fences, together with provisions for providing some illumination on the ground immediately around the playing field, will aid considerably in improving the lighting conditions of the surrounding areas.

Direction of Light

1. The eye sees by brightness contrast. The brightness contrasts between an object and its surroundings, as well as the brightness differences between the various surfaces of an object, provide the amount of contrast required to see. Since the visual tasks of the spectators and players involve seeing vertical surfaces as well as horizontal surfaces, it is essential to provide adequate illumination on both the horizontal surfaces and the vertical surfaces of a solid object. Since the objects of view in sports are not flat faced solids it is not essential to provide uniform illumination on all surfaces; in fact, semi-directional illumination produces shading which aids seeing by its modeling effect. Model studies (see illustrations) and stationary ball analyses are useful in determining proper pole locations, mounting heights, and method of aiming floodlights.

2. For unidirectional sports, such as bowling, racing, handball, and archery, it is desirable and possible to provide much higher vertical footcandles from one direction as well as to locate the luminaires so that they are almost completely removed or shielded from the normal field of view.

3. The aiming of the floodlights, even with correct luminaire locations and mounting heights, determines to a large extent whether the uniformity, direction, and candlepower towards the eye are satisfactory.

CLASSIFICATION OF PLAY

Player Requirements

Player requirements vary with the class of play. *Tournament* classification applies to the caliber of play as found in tournaments and exhibitions. *Club* or *school* classification applies to good, fast play. *Recreational* classification applies to play for fun and relaxation. High schools can generally be classed under the *club* classification, and colleges as either *club* or *tournament*.

Spectator Requirements

Spectator requirements for satisfactory seeing vary with the type of sport, distance from and orientation to the playing field. A stadium in which the last row of spectators is several hundred feet away from the playing area must be lighted to a high level of illumination if they are to follow the play. If the spectator section is limited to small bleachers along the sides of the field, the same illumination level that will provide good playing conditions will adequately serve the spectators.

EQUIPMENT CLASSIFICATION

General. 1. The optical characteristics of the luminaire effect to a large extent such important factors as direct and reflected glare, shadows, distribution, and diffusion. Because there are wide variations in these optical characteristics the selection of the correct luminaire for a particular application deserves careful consideration.

2. Luminaires should be designed so as to describe the manner in which the light from the lamp is controlled by the lighting unit, the degree of concentration of zonal lumens, and mechanical details. Since in sports and recreational area lighting there are both outdoor and indoor lighting problems the lighting equipment should be selected to qualify for the service designated. There are therefore separate designations and classifications pertaining to outdoor and indoor lighting equipment.

Outdoor Floodlight Luminaire Designation

Floodlight classes.

1. *Heavy duty* (HD). This class is weathertight, having a substantially constructed housing into which is placed a separate and removable reflector. The assembly is enclosed by a cover glass.

2. *General purpose* (GP). This class is weathertight, and constructed so that the housing forms the reflector surface. The as-

sembly is enclosed by a cover glass. Reflectorized lamps designed for outdoor use fall into this classification.

3. *Open* (O). This class is weatherproof,[2] and constructed so that the housing forms the reflecting surface. There is no cover glass.

4. *Open with reflector insert* (OI). This class is weatherproof,[2] and constructed so that the housing forms only part of the reflecting surface. An auxiliary reflector is used to modify the distribution of light. There is no cover glass.

Beam data. The choice of the light distribution of a luminaire may be selected and designated by type as indicated in the following table.

TABLE 13-2

Light Distribution of Various Types of Luminaire

Luminaire Type	*Beam Spread in Degrees*
1	10° to less than 18°
2	18° to less than 29°
3	29° to less than 46°
4	46° to less than 70°
5	70° to less than 100°
6	100° and over

Method of designation. Floodlights covered by these standards may be designated as Heavy Duty Type 1, 2, 3, etc., General Purpose Type 1, 2, 3, etc. and Open Type 4, 5, 6, etc.

Performance characteristics. The suggested typical layouts for outdoor sports assume the use of floodlights having efficiencies that equal or exceed the NEMA Standards.

Photometric data. For the purpose of classifying floodlights the method of determining and recording the beam spread and beam efficiency should be in accordance with the adopted report of the I.E.S. Committee on Testing Procedure of Illumination Characteristics.[3]

[2] For definitions of *weathertight* and *weatherproof* as used here, refer to: American Institute of Electrical Engineers, *American Standard Definitions of Electrical Terms* (New York: 1942).

[3] Illuminating Engineering, Vol. XXXI, No. 6 (June 6, 1941).

Interior Lighting Luminaire Designation

1. Interior lighting luminaires may be classed into five different types, based on the manner in which light is distributed from the luminaire. These classifications apply to luminaires with either filament or fluorescent sources. These types are convenient in describing the manner in which the light is distributed from the luminaires, and do not in themselves imply quality of lighting. The figures given below indicate the percentages of light emitted by the luminaire upward and downward:

	Approx. Distribution of Light Emitted by Luminaire	
Type (C.I.E. Classification)	*Upward*	*Downward*
Direct	0- 10%	100-90%
Semi-direct	10- 40	90-60
General Diffuse	40- 60	60-40
Semi-indirect	60- 90	40-10
Indirect	90-100	10-0

2. Direct luminaires may be further classified to denote concentration of zonal lumens such as concentrating, medium spread, and wide spread.

Method of designation. 1. Interior direct type lighting luminaires covered by these standards may be designated in accordance with the recommendations of the I.E.S. Committee on Illumination Performance Recommendations.[4]

2. For the purpose of calculation in the design of the typical layouts the photometric performance of the luminaires is assumed to be approximately the value shown in Table 9-2 of the I.E.S. *Lighting Handbook*.[5]

TYPICAL OUTDOOR LAYOUTS

Illumination levels obtained with the typical layouts presented in this chapter may be expected to meet substantially the I.E.S. recommended footcandle values. In any in-

[4] Unpublished report of the Committee on "Recommended Practice for the Illumination Performance of Direct and Semi-Direct Luminaire."

[5] Illuminating Engineering Society, *Lighting Handbook*, 2nd ed. (New York: 1951).

stallation, the illumination obtained is subject to unpredictable variations in installation, aiming, luminaires, lamps, voltage at the lamps, and atmospheric transmission.

TYPICAL LAYOUTS FOR INDOOR SPORTS

Sports played indoors may generally be divided into two classes:

1. Sports played within one general area, i.e., gymnasiums, where the lighting is provided by one lighting system.
2. Sports played in specific areas designed expressly for that sport with a lighting system designed specifically for that one sport, such as in bowling or shooting.

Gymnasiums

The school gymnasium is a multi-sport center that serves the student body during the daytime and in many cases the community at night. It is used for dances where the preferred lighting key is low and colorful, for assemblies where the lighting is primarily for atmosphere, for general exercise and recreation where the lighting assures safe and adequate performance, and for games and exhibitions where substantially higher levels are required both for players and spectators. The higher levels needed for exhibition events may be attained by means of a supplementary system.

The illumination levels recommended for a gymnasium depend on the purposes for which the gymnasium is used (see Table 13-1). Uniformity of illumination well within the maximum-minimum brightness ratio of 3 to 1 is particularly important for multi-sport gymnasium use and is readily attainable by proper design of the lighting system. Glare may be minimized by a choice of luminaires of low brightness at the higher angles and by the use of a ceiling of light color. Luminaires should be suitably protected from mechanical injury.

In most cases these lighting requirements are met with general illumination from a direct lighting system. However, in some cases consideration is given to semi-direct or even indirect lighting systems. Where the gymnasium is to be used for interschool games, the basketball court or similar area should be provided with supplementary lighting by concentrating industrial types of lighting units.

Specialized Areas

This chapter contains typical layouts to illustrate good lighting practice for certain specialized sports usually played indoors. Illumination levels obtained with these typical layouts may be expected to meet substantially the I.E.S. recommended values. In any installation, the illumination obtained is subject to unpredictable variations in installation, reflectors and lamps within manufacturing tolerances, and in voltage at the lamps.

DESIGN FACTORS

The correct choice among the various design factors depends upon a balancing of economic costs against such factors as appearance, relative safety, and reliability.

The over-all cost for lighting should include:

1. An amortization of the first cost
2. The cost of electrical energy consumed
3. Cost of lamp replacement
4. An estimate for maintenance expense exclusive of lamp replacement.

Comparison of lighting systems on this basis, perhaps with different luminaires or different wiring methods, may be made by means of a cost analysis. A true comparison should involve systems providing comparable quality and quantity of illumination.

Lamp Voltage

Many sports lighting installations are utilized for a comparatively small number of hours per year. In such cases good economy dictates the operation of the filament lamps at voltages above those for which they were designed. In general, the operation of general lighting service lamps at 10 per cent over the rated voltage should prove economical when filament lamps are in use 200 hours or less per year, and 5 per cent over voltage operation when the annual use is from 200 to 500 hours. Where annual operation exceeds 500 hours, lamp operation at the rated voltage is recommended. Operation at 10 per cent

Figure 13:1. Layout for Double Tennis Courts—8 Poles.

Courtesy of *Illuminating Engineering*

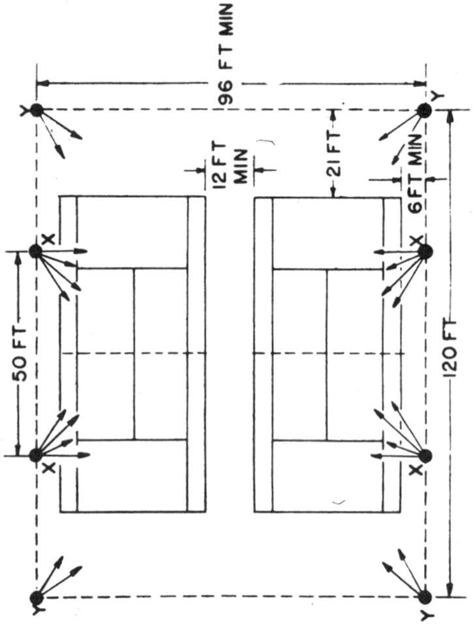

Class	IES Current Recommended Practice—Footcandles Maintained in Service	Floodlights Type	Class	No. per Pole X	Y
Club	20	5 or 6	GP	4	2
			O	5	3
Recreational	10	5 or 6	GP	2	1
			O	3	1

LAMPS: 1500-watt general lighting service operated at rated voltage.
MOUNTING HEIGHT: 30 feet above courts.
POLES: 8.

Figure 13:2. Layout for horseshoe courts.

Courtesy of *Illuminating Engineering*

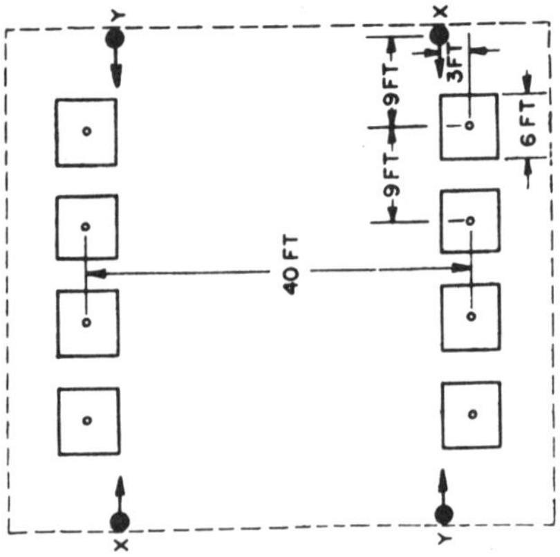

Class	IES Current Recommended Practice—Footcandles Maintained in Service	No. of Courts	Floodlights Type	Class	No. per Pole X	Y	Lamp Size (watts)
Tournament	10	4-6	5 or 6	GP	1	1	1500
				O	2	2	1000
		1-3	5 or 6	GP	1	*	1500
				O	2	*	1000
Recreational	5	4-6	5 or 6	GP	1	1	750
				O	1	1	1000
		1-3	5 or 6	GP	1	*	750
				O	1	*	1000

*For 1-3 courts no "Y" poles are required.
LAMPS: General lighting service operated at rated voltage.
MOUNTING HEIGHT: At least 20 feet above courts.
POLES: Four for 4-6 court layout, two for 1-3 court layout.

Figure 13:3. Layout for football.
Courtesy of *Illuminating Engineering*

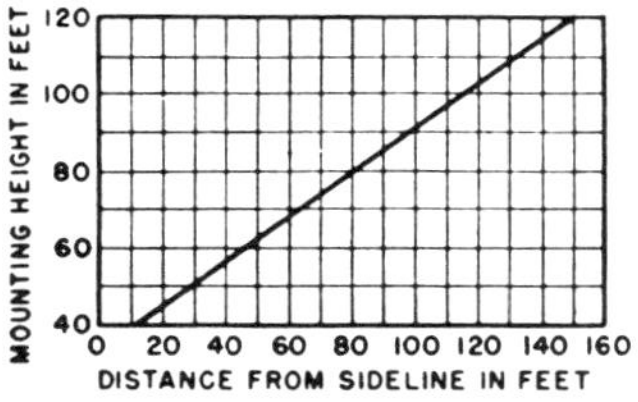

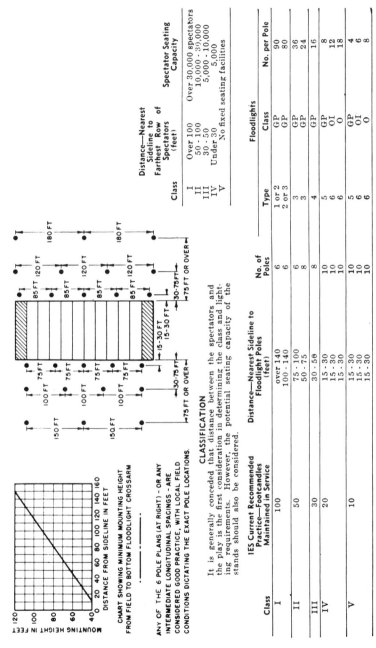

CHART SHOWING MINIMUM MOUNTING HEIGHT FROM FIELD TO BOTTOM FLOODLIGHT CROSSARM

ANY OF THE 6 POLE PLANS (AT RIGHT) - OR ANY INTERMEDIATE LONGITUDINAL SPACINGS - ARE CONSIDERED GOOD PRACTICE, WITH LOCAL FIELD CONDITIONS DICTATING THE EXACT POLE LOCATIONS.

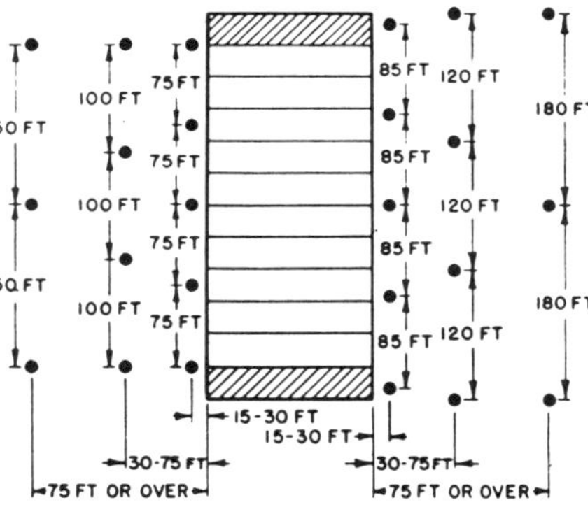

Class	Distance—Nearest Sideline to Farthest Row of Spectators (feet)	Spectator Seating Capacity
I	Over 100	Over 30,000 spectators
II	50 - 100	10,000 - 30,000
III	30 - 50	5,000 - 10,000
IV	Under 30	5,000
V	No fixed seating facilities	

CLASSIFICATION

It is generally conceded that distance between the spectators and the play is the first consideration in determining the class and lighting requirements. However, the potential seating capacity of the stands should also be considered.

Class	IES Current Recommended Practice—Footcandles Maintained in Service	Distance—Nearest Sideline to Floodlight Poles (feet)	No. of Poles	Floodlights: Type	Floodlights: Class	Floodlights: No. per Pole
I	100	over 140	6	1 or 2	GP	90
		100 - 140	6	2 or 3	GP	80
II	50	75 - 100	6	3	GP	36
		50 - 75	8	3	GP	24
III	30	30 - 50	8	4	GP	16
IV	20	15 - 30	10	5	GP	8
		15 - 30	10	6	OI	12
		15 - 30	10	6	O	18
V	10	15 - 30	10	5	GP	4
		15 - 30	10	6	OI	6
		15 - 30	10	6	O	8

LAMPS: 1500-watt clear general lighting service operated at 10% over rated voltage.

Class of Baseball	IES Current Recommended Practice—Footcandles Maintained in Service		Floodlights		Approx. No. per Pole			Minimum Mounting Height to Bottom Floodlight Crossarm (feet)
	Infield	Outfield	Class	Type	A	B	C	
Major League	150	100	GP	3, 4 or 5	100	200	100	120
AAA and AA	75	50	GP	3, 4 or 5	50	100	50	110
A and B	50	30	GP O or OI	3, 4 or 5 4, 5 or 6	32 44	64 88	32 44	90
C and D	30	20	GP O or OI	3, 4 or 5 4, 5 or 6	24 32	48 64	24 32	70
Semi-professional and Municipal	20	15	GP O or OI	3, 4 or 5 4, 5 or 6	16 22	32 44	16 22	70

LAMPS: 1500-watt clear general lighting service operated at 10% over rated voltage.

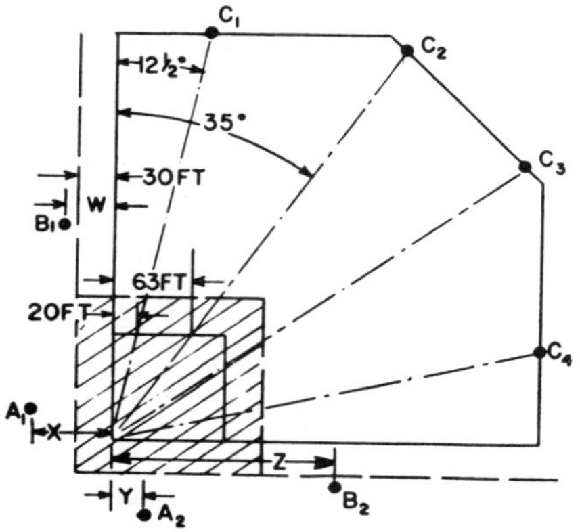

DIMENSIONS

W = 30-60FT
X = 40-80FT
Y = 20-30FT
Z = 130-180FT

THESE LAYOUTS ARE BASED ON THE FOLLOWING:

TOTAL PLAYING AREA, INCLUDING A STRIP 30 FT OUTSIDE OF EACH FOUL LINE —— 132,500 SQ FT

INFIELD AREA (SHADED) 22,500 SQ FT

OUTFIELD AREA 110,000 SQ FT

Figure 13:4. Layout for baseball.

Courtesy of *Illuminating Engineering*

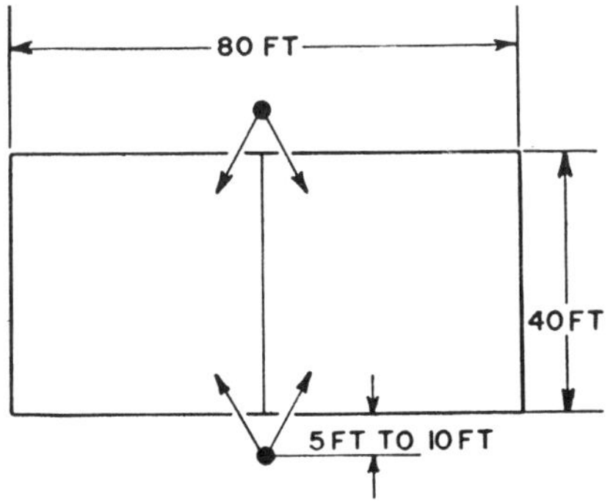

Class	Footcandles Maintained in Service	Floodlights Type	Floodlights Class	Floodlights No. per Pole
Tournament	20	5 or 6	GP / O	3 / 5
Recreational	10	5 or 6	GP / O	2 / 3

Lamps: 1500-watt general lighting service operated at rated voltage.
Mounting Height: 30 feet above court.
Poles: 4.

Courtesy of *Illuminating Engineering*

Figure 13:5. Layout for outdoor volleyball courts.

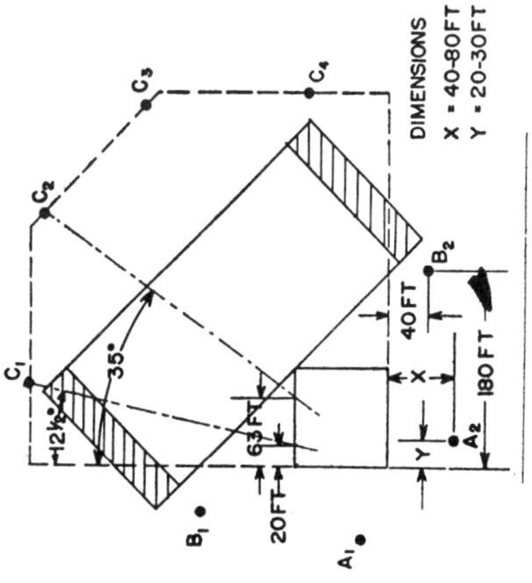

Class	IES Current Recommended Practice—Footcandles Maintained in Service: Infield	Outfield	Floodlights: Class	Type	Approx. No. per Pole: A	B	C
Baseball (Semi-Pro)	20	15	GP or O or OI	3, 4 or 5	16	32	16
Football		15		4, 5 or 6	22	44	22

Lamps: 1500-watt clear general lighting service operated at 10% over rated voltage.
Mounting Height: 70 feet minimum.

Figure 13:6. Layout for combination baseball and football areas.

Courtesy of *Illuminating Engineering*

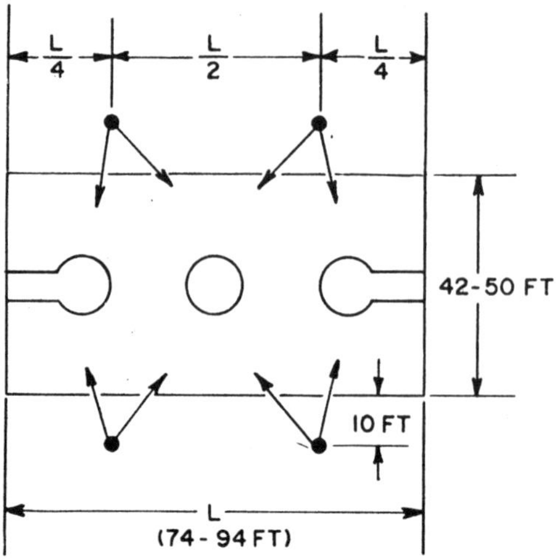

Figure 13:7. Layout for outdoor basketball courts.
Courtesy of *Illuminating Engineering*

Class	IES Current Recommended Practice—Footcandles Maintained in Service	Floodlights Type	Floodlights Class	Floodlights No. per Pole
Recreational	10	5 or 6	GP / O	2 / 3

LAMPS: 1500-watt general lighting service operated at rated voltage.
MOUNTING HEIGHT: 30 feet above court.
POLES: 4.

Figure 13:8. Layout for bathing beaches.
Courtesy of *Illuminating Engineering*

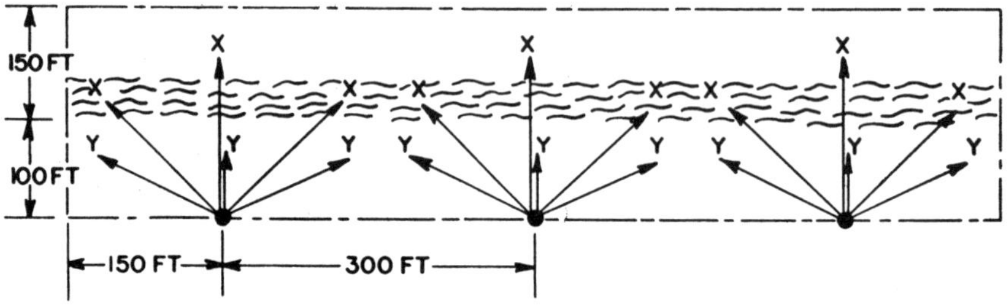

IES Current Recommended Practice—Footcandles Maintained in Service	Floodlights Aiming Point	Floodlights Type	Floodlights Class	Floodlights No. per Pole
3 (vertical) in surf at 150 feet	X	3	GP	3
1 on beach	Y	5	GP	3

LAMPS: 1500-watt general lighting service operated at rated voltage.
MOUNTING HEIGHT: 60 feet above beach.
POLES: One pole every 300 feet.

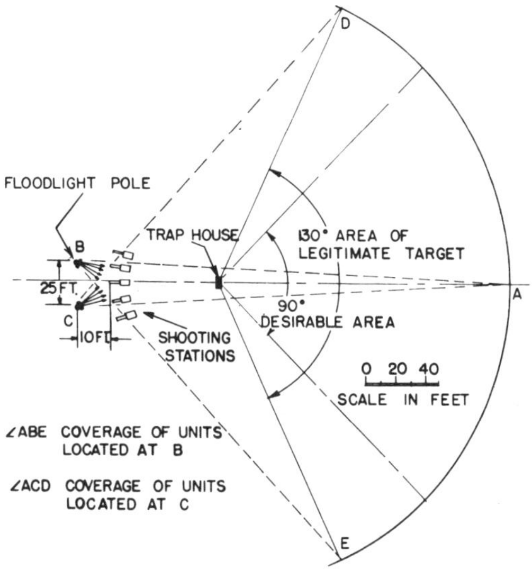

	IES Current Recommended Practice—Footcandles Maintained in Service	*Floodlights*		
		Type	*Class*	*No. per Pole*
Target (vertical surface at 105 feet)	30	2	GP	4
Firing Point (general)	10			

LAMPS: 150-watt clear general lighting service operated at 10 per cent over rated voltage.
MOUNTING HEIGHT: 20 feet above ground.
POLES: 2.

Courtesy of *Illuminating Engineering*

Figure 13:9. Layout for trap shooting.

Figure 13:10. Layout for outdoor swimming pools (overhead lighting).

Courtesy of *Illuminating Engineering*

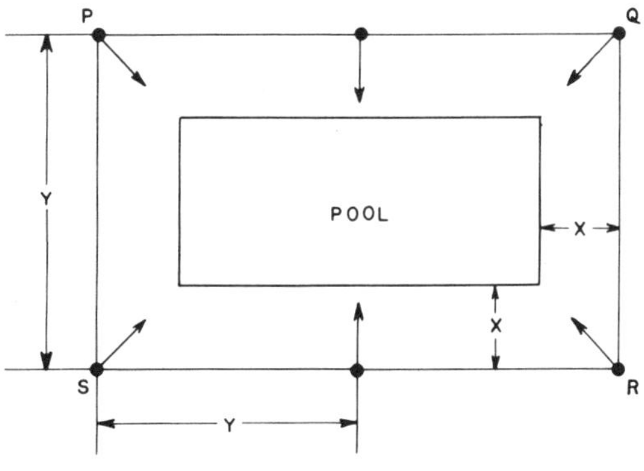

IES Current Recommended Practice—Footcandles Maintained in Service	Floodlights		Watts per Square Foot Area P-Q-R-S*
	Type	Class	
10	5	GP	1.7
	6	O	2.5

*The rectangle P-Q-R-S outlines the area to be lighted.
The number of floodlights and lamp size are computed from table above.
LAMPS: 500, 750, 1000 or 1500-watt general lighting service operated at rated voltage.
MOUNTING HEIGHT: At least 20 feet above water.
POLE SPACING: Not to exceed 4 times mounting height.

over voltage increases light output 35 per cent, power consumed, 16 per cent, and reduces lamp life to approximately one quarter of rated life. Operation at 5 per cent over voltage increases light output 18 per cent, energy consumption 8 per cent, and reduces lamp life to approximately one half of rated life.

The typical layouts in this recommended practice take advantage of over voltage operation where justified to reduce the amount of equipment required. Although over voltage lamps are referred to in many layouts there is no expressed or implied restriction on the use of any other suitable lamp of equivalent output and life at rated volts.

Choice of Equipment

Floodlights, because of their larger size, more elaborate mounting requirements, and in some cases cover glasses, are more expensive than normal indoor type luminaires. The use of floodlights is economically justified on any outdoor area where the light must be projected a considerable distance.

Floodlights are available with beam spreads of various degrees and can be used economically to concentrate light on and near the playing area even when they must be mounted several hundred feet from the playing area. On the other hand, some of the playground sports such as horseshoe pitching and shuffleboard, may in some cases be lighted by indoor type luminaires suitably adapted for outdoor use.

Choice of Beam Spreads

Most open floodlights provide inherently wide beam spread. Enclosed floodlights are available in a range of beam spreads from wide to narrow. The choice of beam spread depends largely on the distance from the floodlights to the area to be lighted—the greater the distance, the narrower the beam spread for high utilization efficiency. Although the cost of specularly-reflecting equipment is higher than that of wide beam types the over-all installation cost with specular reflectors is less when the floodlights are located at a considerable distance because fewer units are needed. Conversely, when floodlights are located relatively close to the playing area wide beam spreads can be used with good economy.

Open and Enclosed Floodlights

The choice between open and enclosed floodlights depends chiefly on differences in cost and in rate of depreciation. Open floodlights cost less, but depreciate more rapidly due to collection of dirt, soot, and insects on reflecting surfaces and light sources. It is generally accepted practice to allow a maintenance factor of 75 per cent for enclosed floodlights and 65 per cent for open floodlights when calculating the maintained footcandle level. The typical layouts are based upon these maintenance factors. Although these factors are empirical, they are based on considerable experience. The cleanliness of the surroundings, the frequency of cleaning of the units, and the replacement of lamps will affect the maintenance factor to a considerable extent.

Reflectorized Lamps

Reflectorized lamps may be used. Their principle application is in small scale sports lighting installations. Reflectorized lamps for outdoor use are made of heat resisting glass that will not crack when subjected to rain while in operation. The relative economy of using these lamps and associated equipment when compared with other lighting systems may be calculated for any installation.

Wiring

Outdoor floodlighting installations are sometimes made with overhead wiring, and in other cases with either direct burial underground cable or wire in a duct system that runs to the base of each pole or tower and extends up the tower in rigid conduit. The type of wiring to use depends on local practices and on economic factors including the value placed upon such items as appearance, safety, and reliability. In addition to the choice in method of wiring an economic study should be made of the method of distribution. Some installations justify a separate transformer on each pole or tower with primary wiring to each location. In other cases it is more economical to reduce the number of transformers and run secondary wiring to some of the floodlight locations. The question of whether or not to fuse each floodlight individually is determined partially by local practice and partly by economic considerations.

In the final analysis architects and planners would do well to consult local illuminating engineers and electrical distributors in order to obtain information on the latest standards and equipment development since every year brings out new changes in lighting and design and practice.

It should be kept in mind that all electrical installations must meet the standards of the National Electric Code of the National Board of Fire Underwriters[6] as well as any local or state building codes and fire regulations that apply to their locality.

---

[6] National Board of Fire Underwriters, 85 John Street, New York, New York.

CHAPTER 14

SELECTING THE PROPER PLAY SURFACE

M. Alexander Gabrielsen

ONE OF THE MOST DIFFICULT DECISIONS PLANners of outdoor play areas have to make is the selection of the type of surface to be used for various play and sports areas. When play fields were first developed, earth surfaces were the only ones used. Subsequently, sand, clay, and turf were added to earth in various combinations to provide a more suitable surface for certain types of activities. The problem of proper maintenance of earth surfaces, and the desire for greater efficiency of play were the major factors that have lead to the introduction of hard surfaces, primarily of the bituminous and concrete varieties.

Ever since the initiation of hard surfaces controversy has existed over the advisability of its use for certain play areas. A few fatalities and some serious injuries have been attributed to hard surfaces used under play apparatus. Consequently some municipalities and school districts have actually ruled out the use of hard-surfaced material under children's play apparatus. However, the evidence to date is inconclusive, as well as insufficient, to accurately judge the reliability of the claims against hard surfaces. Actually there is considerable evidence to support the use of hard surface material for courts and general play areas. Their smooth, even surface minimizes one of the major causes of playground accidents—falls.

During the last decade new surface materials have been introduced in an attempt to reduce the likelihood of serious injuries resulting from falls from play apparatus. None of them have proved to be completely satisfactory; however, they do hold some promise for the future.

At present there is no universal surface on the market that meets the needs for all types of play surfaces. However, satisfactory surface materials have been developed for most sports and recreation areas. The only

Illustration: Asphaltic concrete surface tennis courts

exception at this time appears to be the surface material used under play apparatus.

When faced with the problem of selecting a surface material for any play area, there are certain factors that one must study carefully before a decision can be made. These are:

Level of performance (general play, tournament play, professional play)
Seasonal use (summer only, year-around use)
Multiple use or *single purpose* (surface to be used for more than one activity)
Durability (for quantity of use)
Resilience (the spring or bounce)
Traction (footage)
Appearance (esthetic value, or harmony with surroundings)
Cost (money available for initial construction and maintenance)
Maintenance (availability of funds and personnel for maintenance)
Local climatic conditions (amount of precipitation and range of temperature)

Schools are seldom able to provide adequate maintenance staffs for the proper upkeep of turf areas, and other pervious type surfaces. Consequently, schools have installed all weather surfaces for most of their outdoor play areas. It is the belief of some authorities that they might have gone too far. It seems desirable to include some turf area as well as hard surfaced all weather area.

Recent studies have indicated that the accident rate is lower on playgrounds with "blacktop" surfaces than on playgrounds using other types of surface materials.

Considerable experimentation and research have been carried on in recent years in an effort to provide a more suitable surface for playgrounds, particularly that area accommodating the climbing apparatus. Recent materials that have received a great deal of attention are mats, cork, rubber, plastics, foam rubber, and other types of air cell material. These materials have been used in a variety of ways. Some have been introduced into asphalt along with a fine sand aggregate, thus, providing a more resilient surface. In other situations covers of vinyl, rubber, plastic, canvas, and coatings of asphaltic binder have been used. Sand and tanbark have been used extensively by some communities under children's play apparatus. There is no question that some of these surfaces have possibilities; however, it is too early to go all out for any one surface. More qualitative and quantitative evaluation is necessary. One fact is emerging from all this controversy, and that is that there is no surface material that can substitute for good supervision and safety procedures.

The general types of media in use and their recommended application to various recreation and sports activities are shown in Table 14-1.

TABLE 14-1

Various Surface Media and Their General Application

Medium		
Aggregates	Cinders, slag, gravel, shells, crushed stone	Running tracks, walkways, roads, parking areas.
Asphalt—Tar (Bituminous)	Asphaltic concrete (hot or cold) Sheet asphalt, cork asphalt, rubber asphalt, natural asphalt, and various patented asphalt mixtures	Tennis, basketball, school yards, multiple-use areas, shuffleboard, walks, roads, badminton, volleyball, roller skating, artificial ice skating, paddle tennis
Concrete	Cement with aggregate introduced for binding monolithic-terrazzo, an extremely hard surface with lasting qualities	Same application as asphalt
Earth	Clay, sand, loam, and mixtures of the above	Play yards, baseball and softball infields, tennis courts, under play apparatus, horseshoe courts, badminton, volleyball
Turf	Grasses: Fescues, bent blues and southern grasses	Golf-park areas, tennis, lawn bowling, baseball, football, and other playfields
Miscellaneous	Sandstone, brick, flagstone, tanbark, wood, sawdust, cotton meal, rubber	Special uses, in some instances, of a decorative nature

In the final analysis surface material must be carefully selected. The decision should not be left entirely to the architect. The users of the facility and the general educational requirements should exert the greatest influences on the selection of any surface material.

The succeeding chapters go into considerable detail on the three major types of surfaces, turf, asphalt and concrete. Here specifications may be found to meet almost any type of surface requirement. What is best for a local community will depend on the uses to which the surface is to be put and the funds available.

CHAPTER 15

ASPHALT SURFACES FOR RECREATION AND SPORTS AREAS

The Asphalt Institute

RESILIENT, SMOOTH ASPHALT PAVEMENTS make excellent play surfaces—a fact long recognized by school and recreation authorities throughout the United States and Canada. A survey of current literature dealing with the construction of play area pavements shows that those made of asphalt are highly favored over all other types.

Asphalt engineers and contractors are endeavoring to keep pace with the increasing need for paved recreation facilities in areas of growing population and to develop new uses for this versatile product in a variety of recreational structures. In addition, research and field engineers of The Asphalt Institute and of the asphalt departments of major asphalt-producing companies are constantly investigating new and better uses for their product. Recent experiments have been made with asphalt-paved dance floors, roller and ice skating rinks, sidewalks, multiple-use areas and other surfaces.

Illustration:* *Asphaltic concrete multiple-use area, Encino Park, California
Photo by Spence Air Photos, Los Angeles

ADVANTAGE FEATURES

School and recreation authorities agree that many accidents on play areas result from stumbling. Asphalt surfacing helps reduce injuries caused by stumbling by providing a smooth, yet non-skid surface. An asphalt surface is jointless; that is to say, it is placed as one continuous pavement, not in slabs. In addition, asphalt pavements do not wear slick.

The economical cost of asphalt paving is, of course, of interest to every school and recreation leader regardless of the size of his budget. When bids for paving of comparable design are called for, asphalt paving contractors invariably submit the lower bids. Asphalt is probably the only construction material that has not increased materially in cost since World War II.

In addition to the economical first cost of asphalt construction, this remarkable petroleum product offers these advantages:

The dark surface of asphalt pavement is free from the glare of reflected light.

The natural resiliency of asphalt pavement lessens foot and leg fatigue.

Asphalt pavements reduce the noise of wearing objects such as roller skates.

Asphalt pavements, when properly constructed, resist alternate freezing and thawing so common through the Temperate Zone.

Asphalt pavements can be constructed in a short period of time. There is no long "curing period" or objectionable use of large quantities of water.

Asphalt pavements are waterproof; no prolonged "drying period" is necessary following rain or cleaning.

Asphalt pavements need little or no maintenance. Repair is simple and inexpensive.

Asphalt pavements provide excellent background contrast for white markings necessary in many school playground and recreational areas.

Asphalt pavements are easy to clean with water and heavy-bristle brush brooms.

Asphalt pavement surfaces will not promote the growth of moss or any other vegetation.

DESIGN SPECIFICATIONS

Following are three tables for suggested thickness designs according to load, soil condition, and climatic conditions:

Loading classifications

I. Game courts such as badminton, basketball, tennis, volleyball, multi-use areas, dance floors, light foot traffic, and roller skating rinks

II. Playgrounds, sidewalks, heavy foot traffic and occasional light vehicles

III. Parking areas and driveways for passenger cars

Soil classifications

A. Gravel, sand soils (which drain well)

B. Non-plastic clays and silts (average soil mixture)

C. Plastic clays (unstable when wet)

TABLE 15-1

Specifications for Type I Loading (Game courts, dance floors, light foot traffic, and roller skating rinks)

	Frost Free and Light Rainfall		*Frost Over Four Inches Heavy Rainfall*		
Soil Condition	*Thickness in Inches*		*Thickness in Inches*		
	Asphaltic Concrete	*Base*	*Asphaltic Concrete*	*Base*	*Subbase*
A—Gravel, sand soils	1-2	0-3*	1½-2	3-4	0-3
B—Non-plastic clays and silts	1½-2	2-3	2	3-4	0-3
C—Plastic clays	1½-2	3-5	2-2½	4-6	4-6

* Cohesionless subgrade material should be covered with a two-inch minimum base course of coarse sand.

CONSTRUCTION SPECIFICATIONS

A. Earthwork

Grades for earthwork are established so that the pavement will be free draining, but slopes should not be greater than absolutely necessary. Pavements intended for use as dance floors and for roller and ice skating must be absolutely level.

The first construction requirement is the compaction of the area to be paved. A power roller weighing not less than 5 tons and providing a minimum compression of 175 pounds per inch width of the driving roll, firms up the surface. Hand tamps are used in areas inaccessible to power rollers. All unsuitable material is removed and replaced with acceptable fill. Surplus excavation is removed and, when not needed in the construction, is disposed of.

TABLE 15-2

Specifications for Type II Loading (Playgrounds, sidewalks, heavy foot traffic, and occasional light vehicles)

Soil Condition	*Frost Free and Light to Moderate Rainfall* — *Thickness in Inches*		*Annual Frost Depth Exceeding 4 Inches and Moderate to Heavy Rainfall* — *Thickness in Inches*		
	Asphaltic Concrete	*Base*	*Asphaltic Concrete*	*Base*	*Subbase*
A—Gravel, sand soils	1-2	0-3*	1½-3	3-5	0-3
B—Non-plastic clays and silts	1½-2	3-4	2-3	4-5	3-4
C—Plastic clays	2-2½	4-5**	2½-3	4-6	5-7**

* Cohesionless subgrade materials should be covered with a two-inch base course.

TABLE 15-3

Specifications for Type III Loading (Parking areas and driveways for passenger cars)

Soil Condition	*Frost Free Regions and Light Rainfall* — *Thickness in Inches*		*Frost Over Four Inches and Heavy Rainfall* — *Thickness in Inches*		
	Asphaltic Concrete	*Base*	*Asphaltic Concrete*	*Base*	*Subbase*
A—Gravel, sand soils	1-3	3	2-3	3-5	0-3
B—Non-plastic clays and silts	1½-2½	3-4	2-3	4-5	3-4
C—Plastic clays	2-3	4-5**	3	4-6	6-8**

*Cohesionless subgrade materials should be covered with a two-inch minimum base course.
** When coarse aggregate base or subbase courses are placed on plastic clay foundation soil a 1½-2 inch layer of clean sand, stone or slag screening should be placed first to prevent infiltration of the clay into the coarse aggregate course.

The side forms should be firmly staked. Granular material should be placed to support the edges of the completed pavement, in the form of a shoulder at least 1 and ½ feet wide. All shoulder material is finished flush with the finished pavement, sloped away from the pavement and compacted with regular roller equipment. Vertical pavement faces should never be left unsupported.

B. Drainage

Sub-surface drains should be ordinary farm drain tile laid with open joints or perforated corrugated metal pipe. Storm sewers should be sewer pipe or asphalt coated corrugated metal pipe. Drain slope should be not less than 6 inches per 100 feet, and should connect to outlet drains or open ditches. Surface drainage is directed away from adjoining buildings or property. Where the geological formation is a sloping plain, a cut-off drain at least 3 feet in depth should be constructed across the high side.

Porous aggregate consisting of clean coarse sand, or crushed stone, slag or gravel graded from ⅛ inch to ¹⁄₁₆ inch and free from dust should be used as backfill over and around drains.

C. Weed Control

Any pavement structure (asphalt mixture and base) 6 inches or less in thickness and located in warm regions should be protected against damaging weed growth by sterilization of subgrade soil. Several good soil sterilants are available. The best of these are the borox compounds which are non-poisonous and least likely to kill nearby trees and plants. However, soil sterilants should never be used close to valuable plantings.

with not more than 8 per cent passing the 200 mesh sieve.

Aggregates for the base course are deposited on the subgrade in such a manner as to be completely uniform throughout. Concentrations of coarse or fine materials are not permitted. If segregation occurs in handling, it shall be reblended by blading or other satis-

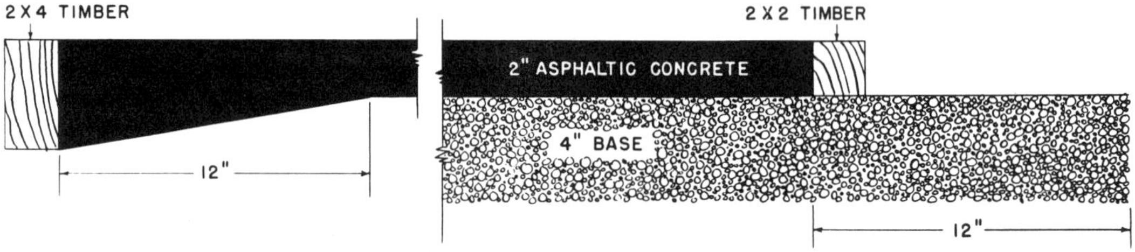

Figure 15:1. Construction for dance floors, roller skating rinks, and game courts such as badminton, basketball, volleyball, and multi-purpose areas. Game courts cross fall for drainage not over 1 inch in 20 feet. Outdoor dance floors and roller skating rinks must be absolutely level. Thicken edge to 4 inches in 12 inches when base is not required and use 2 x 4 timber side forms of redwood, cedar, or treated timber. Extend base 12 inches beyond edge of asphaltic concrete surface when edge is not supported by curb or other structure and use 2 x 2 timber side forms of redwood, cedar, or treated timber.

D. Subbase Course

When specified, this course of granular material consists of good quality crushed stone, slag, gravel, granulated slag or clean sand, or it may consist of bank-run sand provided it is free from clay, organic matter, or other foreign materials.

Subbase material consisting of coarse granular particles is well compacted by means of a power-roller weighing not less than 5 tons. When the subbase is constructed of sand it is compacted by watering.

E. Base Course

Materials to be used in the construction of this course are crushed stone, slag, or gravel, spread evenly and compacted with a power roller weighing not less than 5 tons. The maximum size base course aggregate should not be larger than 1½ inches and should be reasonably well graded from coarse to fine factory mixing methods. The course should be sprinkled during the final rolling.

F. Prime Coat

For the prime coat, 0.25 to 0.35 gallon per square yard of cut-back asphalt MC-0 or MC-1 grade is applied to the base course.

For dense surfaces MC-0 is used; for open surfaces MC-1 is used. When resurfacing asphalt or cement concrete pavements, a tack coat of 0.15 gallon per square yard of SS-1 or SS-1h emulsified asphalt is used and applied evenly. All debris is first removed from the old base or pavement. Surfaces of adjacent structures are protected against marring during application of the prime or tack coat by covering them with paper.

The SS1 or SS-1h emulsified asphalt used as a tack coat should be diluted with about 50 per cent water (½ gallon of water added to each gallon of emulsion).

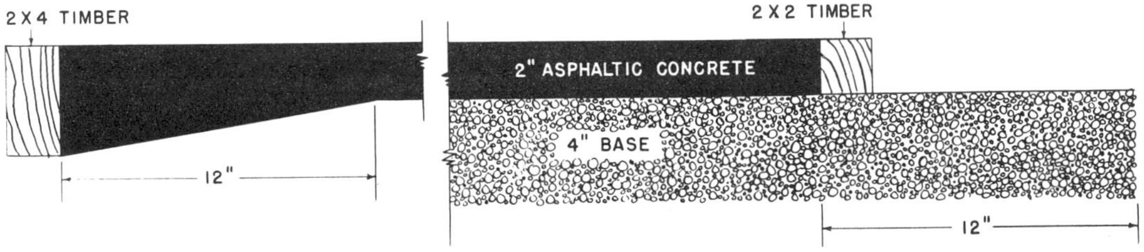

Figure 15:2. Construction for playgrounds, sidewalks, heavy foot traffic, and occasional light vehicles. Thicken edge from 3 to 5 inches in 12 inches when base is not required, and support edge with 2 x 4 timber side forms using redwood, cedar, or treated timber. Extend base 12 inches beyond edge of asphaltic concrete surface when edge is not supported by curb or other solid structure and use 2 x 3 timber side forms of cedar, redwood, or treated timber.

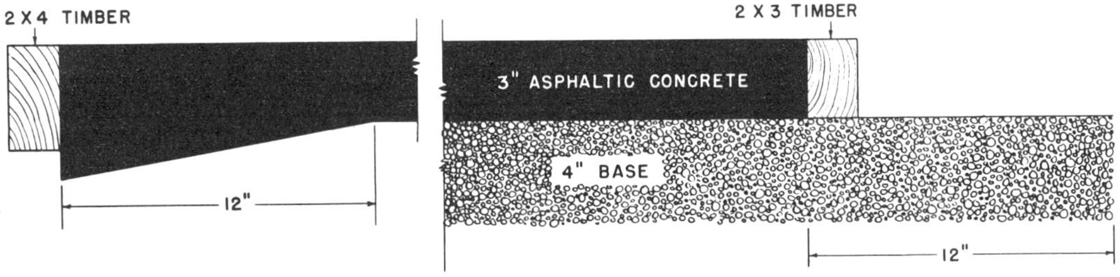

Figure 15:3. Construction for parking areas and driveways. Thicken edge from 2 to 4 inches when base is not required. Use 2 x 4 side forms for unsupported edge of pavement. Side forms should be of redwood, cedar or treated timber. Extend base 12 inches from edge of pavement when not supported by curb or other structure. Sidewalks may be constructed 3 inches thick without thickened edge and without permanent side forms for medium-light foot traffic.

The prime or tack coat should be allowed to cure at least 24 hours before further construction.

G. Surface Course

Asphaltic concrete used for the surface course consists of a mixture of coarse and fine aggregate, mineral filler, and asphalt cement. The hot mix should conform with local Highway Department specifications, insofar as they apply, and the composition tables below can be used as a guide.

The asphalt cement should have a penetration at 77 degrees Fahrenheit of 85-100 for cool and moderately cool regions or 60-70 penetration asphalt for regions with long hot and/or dry seasons. The composition by weight of the finished mixes should be within the following range limits:

TABLE 15-4

Sample Composition of Mixes* for Driveways and Parking Areas

	Mix IV-a	*Mix III-b*
Total Passing Sieve	*Per Cent*	*Per Cent*
¾ in.	—	100
⅜ in.	80-100	60-85
#4	55-75	35-55
#8	35-50	20-35
#30	18-29	10-22
#100	8-16	4-12
#200	4-10	2-8
Normal Asphalt Cement	4-7	4.5-6

The temperatures of the hot-mix asphaltic concrete should be adjusted to within reasonable and workable limits below 325 degrees Fahrenheit.

H. Placing Asphaltic Concrete

Asphaltic concrete mixtures should not be laid when the base course is wet or when weather conditions prevent proper spreading, finishing, or compacting. The base course should be cleaned and a prime and tack coat as described be applied prior to the placing of surface mixtures.

TABLE 15-5

Composition of Mixes* for Playgrounds, Game Courts, Sidewalks, Dance Floors, and Roller Skating Rinks

	Mix V-a	*Mix VI-a*
Total Passing Sieve	*Per Cent*	*Per Cent*
¾ in.	100	100
⅜ in.	85-100	85-100
#4	65-80	
#8	50-65	65-80
#30	25-40	35-60
#100	10-20	15-30
#200	3-10	6-12
Normal Asphalt Cement	5-7½	6-8½

Adjacent, abutting vertical constructions are painted with hot asphalt cement or asphalt emulsion to a slightly greater depth than the thickness of the surface course.

When the pavement design indicates more than 2½ inches of asphaltic concrete surfacing, the concrete is spread and finished in two courses, except as provided hereafter.

If spreading and finishing are done by hand rather than by mechanical means, then the hot mixture shall be placed by methods that will require a minimum of handling and a minimum of time.

Shoveling from trucks or dump boards or the use of other slow methods that permit chilling of the mix should not be permitted.

To construct well-bonded and sealed joints, it may be necessary to paint the joints with hot asphalt cement or to heat them before placing adjacent asphaltic concrete.

It is important to secure a true and uniform alignment and grade along the outside edges. To this end, wood or steel forms may be found useful.

The wearing course should be finished a quarter of an inch above the top of flush structures to maintain proper compaction.

---

* See Asphalt Institute Specification Series No. 1 for complete specifications for materials used in asphaltic concrete and for other mix compositions that might be used.

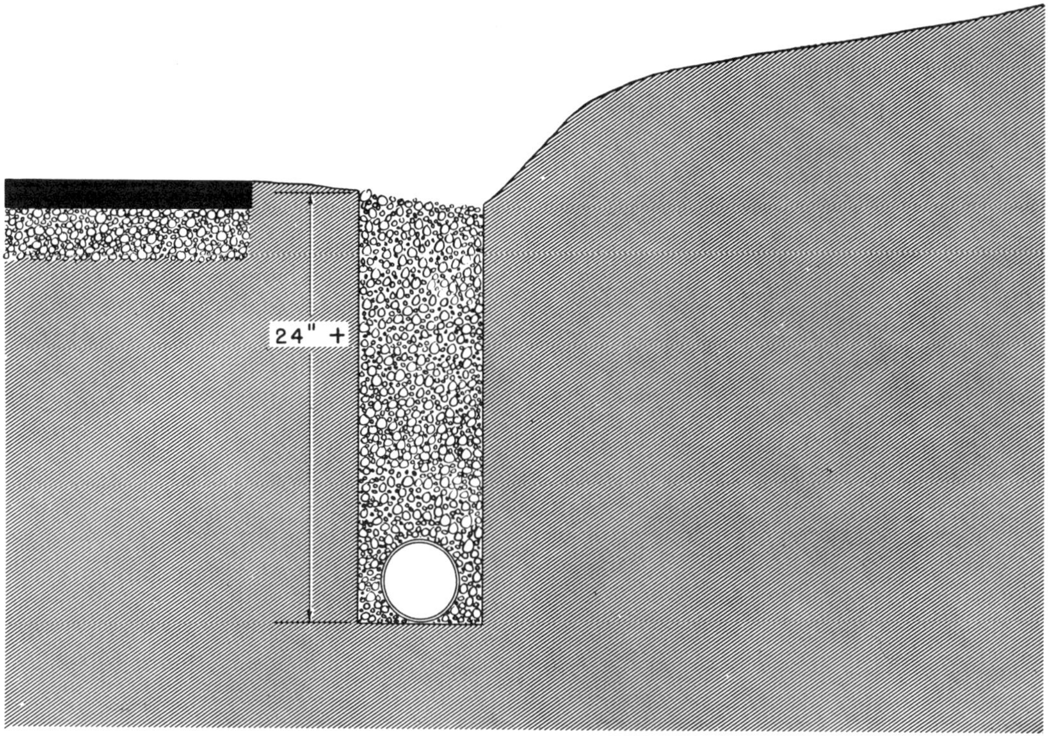

Figure 15:4. Interceptor drain required where location is on a sloping plain.

I. Compaction

Rolling should begin as soon after the mix is placed as possible. The rollers are moistened with water to prevent adhesion. Compaction is accomplished with tandem rollers weighing from 5 to 7 tons. Compaction in areas inaccessible to the power roller is performed with the use of hot smoothing irons, hand or vibrating compactors.

J. Protection of the Wearing Course

No vehicular traffic should be permitted on any portion of a completed hot-mixed asphaltic concrete pavement until it cools sufficiently, which takes at least four hours.

K. Asphalt Curbs

When compaction is completed, asphalt curbs are constructed around the periphery and other areas indicated on the plans. For complete specifications and methods of constructing asphalt curbs and gutters, see Asphalt Institute Information Series No. 92, February, 1958, available from any of the Asphalt Institute offices.

L. Surface Finishes and Seal Coats

Upon completion of each paving course operation the surface is checked for uniformity by the contractor in the presence of the owner or his representative.

The check is accomplished with a 10 foot straightedge at intervals of 5 feet in both directions and at additional intervals as required by the owner.

The surface of the completed work should be of such smoothness that there will not be more than one depression or two points of contact within the length of the straight edge at any place checked. No deviation should exceed the tolerances allowable for the class of finish specified.

In the event of deviations exceeding the maximum allowable, the high points are removed with a floor sander, terrazzo grinder, or other suitable machines. Low places are corrected by patching with the surface dressing mixture described below. All patches are trimmed and smoothed with a floor sander or other grinding tool.

Class A. This surface is suited for playgrounds and sidewalks or for other surface uses not requiring a high degree of smoothness. Deviation from a 10 foot straightedge may not exceed a quarter of an inch. When this requirement is met, the following seal coat is applied:

Diluted emulsified asphalt SS-1 or SS-1h is applied at the rate of 0.05 to 0.10 gallons per square yard. Dilution consists of approximately 30 per cent (by volume) added water (to 100 gallons of emulsified asphalt, add 30 gals. of water). The diluted emulsion may be added by hand spray or broom. The quantity specified includes the dilution water.

Class B. This surface is suited for badminton, basketball, and similar game areas. It will provide a fair surface for tennis courts and when painted makes an excellent dance floor.

The deviation from a 10 foot straightedge may not exceed one-eighth of an inch. A surface dressing mixture like that described below is applied to the surface with a squeegee at the rate of ¾ to 1 cubic foot (7½ gallons of the wet mixture per 100 square feet of surface area).

Class C. This is equal in degree of smoothness to any floor of any type of construction. It is excellent for tennis courts, and when coated with a plastic paint, specifically manufactured for this purpose, it provides an excellent surface for roller skating rinks and outdoor dancing.

The deviation from a 10 foot straightedge should not exceed one-sixteenth of an inch. The surface is treated with a surface dressing mixture, and for roller skating rinks should be free from surface pits or voids more than one-eighth of an inch in diameter.

Upon the completion of the checking described above, a surface finish may be applied

Asphalt roller skating rink, 100 by 150 feet, with 3-inch surface.

American Bitumuls and Asphalt Company

School playground laid with bituminous concrete, Glendale, California.

in the following manner, according to the degree of smoothness required:

Composition of Surface Dressing Mixtures (if desired)

1 part portland cement	94 lb. (1 cu. ft)
2 parts silica sand, 60 mesh	170 lb. (2 cu. ft)
1⅓ in. emulsified asphalt, SS2, (10 gal.)	83 lb. (1.33 cu. ft)
1 part water, 7½ gal.	62 lb. (1 cu. ft)
Total wet weight	409 lb.
Total dry weight (compacted)	314 lb. (2.50 cu. ft)

Note: Must be mixed and stored as directed.

Any commercial grade of cement is satisfactory, but special grades such as "early strength," plastic types, special fine grind, and similar types should not be used. A commercial silica sand product (obtainable from building supply dealers) should be used. Use emulsified asphalt Grade SS2. Use any domestic water supply.

The surface dressing mixture is prepared in a small drum mixer and may be stored for several days in tightly covered cans.

When the surface dressing is applied the pavement surface should be damp (not wet). The dressing is then poured in a small stream immediately ahead of a squeegee. The squeegee rubber blade should measure 36 to 48 inches, and should be worked across the surface from one side to another. The blade should be held at an angle so that the leading end laps over the last strip 3 to 4 inches, making an invisible joint. In this manner the surplus mixture remains at the trailing edge.

The work should go forward rapidly so that the time elapsed between laying each strip is no more than one or two minutes. The entire surface should be covered in this manner. The final result should be uniform in color and texture. If this application is not uniform, a second coat, thinned slightly with additional water, should be applied.

Within 24 hours after application of the surface finish, the surface should be lightly rolled with the lightest self-propelled roller obtainable, either of the pneumatic or the steel-wheeled type. A second rolling should be accomplished within 24 hours after the first. Small ridges and other imperfections are removed by a hot asphalt hand iron.

SPECIAL RECREATIONAL USES AND COLOR APPLICATION

Asphalt mixes are used to construct outdoor (and in many instances, indoor) dance floors and roller skating rinks. For dance floors and roller rinks the floor is finished with a plastic paint, manufactured specifically for this purpose. Colors are available in several bright shades and white. Asphalt surface dressings are manufactured for cold application and are available in black, terra cotta, dull green, and bright green shades. Proprietary color coat materials used to add color to asphalt floors and tennis courts are manufactured by general roofing and specialty firms.

SUMMARY

The foregoing design and construction specifications can be used to excellent advantage by architects, engineers, and recreation and school authorities. The person unfamiliar with engineering terms and construction methods should consult a reputable local engineer for specific construction information and cost estimates. Also available are the technical services of Division, District, and Area Engineers employed by the Asphalt Institute and located in principal cities throughout the United States. Their addresses are:

Division I. Atlantic, Gulf

New York 20, New York, 1270 Avenue of the Americas.
(Long Island, New Jersey, and New York City).

Boston 16, Massachusetts, 419 Boylston Street.
(Connecticut, Maine, Massachusetts, New Hampshire, Rhode Island, and Vermont).

Albany, New York, 11 North Pearl Street.
(New York State, except New York City and L.I.).

Harrisburg, Pennsylvania, 800 North Second Street.
(Delaware, Pennsylvania).

Richmond 19, Virginia, Travelers Building
(District of Columbia, Maryland, North Carolina, Virginia).

Atlanta 3, Georgia, 881 Peachtree Street N.E.
(Alabama, Florida, Georgia, South Carolina, Tennessee).

New Orleans, Louisiana, Maison Blanche Building
(Louisiana, Mississippi).

Division II. Ohio Valley and Great Lakes

Columbus 15, Ohio, Neil House
(Indiana, Kentucky, Michigan, Ohio, West Virginia)

Applying walk-top over cold mixed asphalt macadam.

American Bitumuls and Asphalt Company

Lansing 16, Michigan, 109 West Michigan Avenue
(Michigan, Northern Indiana)

Louisville 7, Kentucky, 4050 Westport Road
(Kentucky, Southern Indiana)

Division III. Midwest

St. Paul 4W, Minnesota, 1951 University Avenue
(Iowa, Minnesota, North Dakota, South Dakota)

Chicago 39, Illinois, 6261 West Grande Avenue
(Illinois, Wisconsin)

Kansas City 3, Kansas, 2500 Johnson Drive
(Arkansas, Kansas, Missouri, Eastern Nebraska)

Denver 4, Colorado, 1250 Stout Street
(Colorado, Idaho, Montana, Western Nebraska, Utah, Wyoming)

Division IV. Southwest

Dallas 6, Texas, Meadows Building
(New Mexico, Oklahoma, Texas)

Austin 1, Texas, Perry-Brooks Building
(Texas)

Oklahoma City 2, Oklahoma, Republic Building
(Oklahoma)

Santa Fe, New Mexico, 10 Radio Plaza
(New Mexico, West Texas)

Division V. Pacific Coast

San Francisco 4, California, Russ Building
(Arizona, California, Nevada, Oregon, Washington)

Los Angeles 17, California, 1709 West Eighth Street
(Arizona, Southern California)

Seattle 1, Washington, White-Henry-Stuart Building
(Washington)

Sacramento 14, California, Forum Building
(Central California, Northern California, Nevada)

Portland 1, Oregon, 2035 S.W. 58th Avenue
(Oregon)

Requests for technical information addressed to the executive offices and laboratories of The Asphalt Institute are welcomed and answered promptly. The address is: Asphalt Institute Building, Campus—University of Maryland, College Park, Maryland.

CHAPTER 16

CONCRETE SURFACES FOR RECREATION AND SPORTS AREAS

Portland Cement Association
Richard G. Knox

CONCRETE SURFACES ARE WIDELY USED OVER the nation for parking areas and many types of athletic and recreational play areas.

Concrete surfaces are especially well-adapted for tennis, handball, badminton and other court games that demand a fast, uniform surface. It also is used for outdoor roller skating and ice hockey rinks, bowling alleys, and shuffleboard courts. Playgrounds paved with concrete may be found throughout the nation, where they serve as multiple-use, year-round play areas. Another very popular use of concrete is discussed in the chapter on swimming pool construction.

Advantages of concrete surfaces. Concrete provides a durable, uniform, easily cleaned surface for play activity. Bumpy ridges and high and low spots that hinder participating activities are not a problem when good construction procedures are used. Particularly is the surface quality important in games such as tennis and handball, where a true, even surface is needed to insure the consistently accurate bounce of the ball.

Concrete play areas are versatile. With proper construction, concrete paved areas may be utilized for winter sports, such as ice skating and ice hockey, while serving other purposes during the warmer months.

Concrete surfaces require little or no maintenance to be kept in playing condition, an essential factor in choosing a surface which does not or cannot receive periodic maintenance. Maintenance costs are usually low and areas need not be closed for long periods of time for repairs and rehabilitation.

For parking areas, concrete pavement meets all the requirements for the ideal paving material: it is durable and economical; it provides an all-weather dustless surface easily cleaned and not injured by standing cars, or oil and fuel drippings; it has low depreciation

***Illustration:* Concrete skating rink, Palisades Interstate Park, Bear Mountain, New York**

and low maintenance costs. Of vital importance, concrete parking areas can be designed to handle any given load capacity, the same as any other engineered structure.

For recreational areas subject to seasonal use, concrete pavements are particularly desirable. Concrete pavement does not require the kneading action of traffic to keep it in good condition, a fact of importance in areas where the pavement may be unused for long periods. Concrete does not become rutted under standing loads. It remains even and uniform throughout the year and does not become soft during hot weather or after heavy rains.

Geographic factors. Geographic location poses no real problem for well-built concrete surfaces. Problems presented by climatic changes and different types of soil may be eliminated by the use of two relatively new developments in the field of concrete paving. The first is *granular sub-base*, consisting of a layer of sand, gravel, or crushed stone, which has been found to be the best protection against frost-heaving in areas subject to severe ground freezing. The thickness of the sub-base will depend upon the severity of the climate and the type of soil encountered. Experienced contractors or soils engineers should be consulted to predetermine the amount and type of granular sub-base required to carry a specified load on a given type of soil.

Air-entrained concrete. This concrete, a second development in concrete paving, eliminates the problem of pavement scaling and damage from repeated cycles of freezing and thawing. Though this type of concrete is of greatest benefit in northern climates where the weather is more severe, it is recommended for concrete pavements and outdoor play areas of all types in all sections of the country. Air-entrained concrete is made by using "air-entraining" portland cement or admixtures that introduce small amounts of air (from 3 to 6 per cent of the total concrete volume) into ordinary concrete in the form of billions of microscopic air bubbles per cubic foot. Air-entrained concrete is available in all parts of the nation at little or no extra cost.

Neither the thickness of the concrete slab nor the amount of steel reinforcement required will be affected by the geographic location of a concrete paved area or playground. Only the use planned for the paved area, which includes the amount and type of activity, will have direct bearing on these factors.

Cost of concrete play areas. The cost of constructing concrete paved areas varies from place to place due to the availability of suitable materials and to varying labor factors. The discussion of construction of concrete play areas that follows is purposely broad and details of a highly technical nature are omitted. However, the material in this chapter will be helpful in formulating plans. The advice or counsel of a competent concrete contractor should be sought in carrying out these plans.

CONSTRUCTION DETAILS AND SPECIFICATIONS

Preparing the Sub-Grade

In constructing any concrete paved recreational or parking area, the first consideration is the sub-grade—the soil on which the concrete will be placed. On some less heavily used play areas, such as shuffleboard courts or outdoor bowling alleys, no sub-base material need be used if the soil is well drained. However, on most projects, a few inches of sub-base material is recommended to prevent frost-heaving of the soil underneath the pavement and to provide a smooth, level surface for the play area.

It is important that the sub-grade be well and uniformly compacted to prevent any unequal settlement of the concrete slab. All organic matter such as sod and roots, should be removed and the ground made level. Any holes and irregularities in the sub-grade and any trenches for utilities should be filled in layers not exceeding 6 inches deep and thoroughly tamped. Fill material should be of uniform character and should not contain large lumps, stones, frozen chunks, or material which will rot.

The entire sub-grade should be rough-graded to an elevation slightly above the finished grade and then thoroughly compacted by tamping or rolling. The finished sub-grade should be carefully checked for elevation and profile. For best compaction, there is an optimum moisture content for each type of soil. A rough idea of the moisture content of ordinary soils, except very sandy ones, may be obtained by squeezing a sample in the hand. With proper moisture content the soil will cling together but will not be plastic. If the soil is too dry, it should be sprinkled with water and mixed to the desired condition before compacting. If the soil is too wet, it must be allowed to dry before compaction. If there is any question as to the moisture content of sandy soil, more water may be added since an excess of water will not be harmful with this type of material.

When a concrete play area is built on a heavy clay soil such as adobe, or any soil having appreciable expansive characteristics, it is recommended that the sub-grade be thoroughly soaked down several days in advance of concreting, and that a minimum of two inches of sand or rock dust fill be used between the base soil and granular fill. The sub-grade should then be maintained in a moist condition until the concrete is placed.

A coarse granular fill should be placed over the finished sub-grade. Generally consisting of coarse slag, sand, gravel, or crushed stone ranging from one-half to one inch in size, granular sub-bases act as an insulating material and as protection against ground moisture. Materials should be of uniform size to insure air-space in the fill. The fill should be brought to the desired grade and then thoroughly compacted before the concrete is placed on it.

Constructing Pavement Slab for Play Areas

After preparation of the sub-grade, including placing of granular sub-base where needed, construction of the playing surface is ready to begin. Placing the concrete slab for all types of play areas, with the exception of shuffleboard courts and outdoor bowling alleys, is basically the same procedure, with minor variations due to dimensions. Shuffleboard courts and bowling alleys require two-course or two-layer construction, and for this reason will be considered in a separate section.

A 4 inch reinforced slab is recommended for concrete play areas of single-course construction. These areas include tennis, bad-

Reinforcing steel and side forms assembled prior to the placing of concrete pavement slab.

minton, and handball courts, ice hockey and roller skating rinks, and concrete playgrounds. The slab should be reinforced with steel bars or wire mesh placed at the center of the slab depth (see photo on opposite page).

The proportion of ingredients in the concrete should be 1:2½:3½ for cement, sand and aggregate, with not more than six gallons of mixing water for each bag of cement, including moisture in the aggregate. *The water used should be suitable for drinking.* Aggregate should be clean, durable, and well-graded, with a maximum size of 1 inch for coarse aggregate.

When concreting is started, it should be a continuous operation until at least one full section, such as one half of a tennis court, is completed. After the sub-grade is prepared and before the placing of the concrete is begun, side forms should be accurately set at the finished elevation of the concrete area. The screed, a strike-off templet used to level the concrete after it is deposited, rides on these forms.

In constructing a slab, the following operations should be followed:

1. As the concrete is placed on the subgrade, the reinforcement should be adjusted to the proper elevation in the middle of the slab thickness from top to bottom (see page 236).
2. Using the screed or strike-off templet, the concrete should be leveled to the elevation established by the previously set screed boards (see page 236).
3. After the concrete has been struck off to the proper elevation, a grid tamp may be used to force the large aggregate particles below the surface (see page 236). The tamp should be used sparingly as over-use will bring an undesirable amount of fine sand, cement, and water to the surface.
4. The surface is smoothed with a long-handled metal float to work out high and low spots and other irregularities (see page 237).
5. After the concrete has hardened sufficiently, a mechanical rotary finisher is used to compact and level out the concrete to a true, even surface (see page 237). This finishing can also be accomplished by hand.
6. For the final finish, a steel trowel is worked in small circular movements to produce a "swirl" pattern (see page 237), providing a uniform, non-glassy surface texture necessary for superior play courts.

As soon as the concrete has hardened sufficiently, it is cured by keeping it continuously wet for at least three days, and preferably for a week. Generally accepted curing methods are the fog spray; "ponding" —building an earth dike around the concrete area and keeping it covered with water; or covering it with wet burlap and moistening the burlap continuously. Any method of curing that might stain, mar, or blemish the surface should be avoided.

This procedure is generally applicable to play areas of single-course construction. However, the different dimensions and requirements of the individual play areas will necessitate variances in the techniques of construction.

Tennis courts. Particularly in tennis, it is desirable to have a court with a *continuous, uninterrupted surface with no joints* to mar the even bounce of the ball. Therefore, each half of the court must be placed in one continuous operation. A 1 inch expansion joint across the court under the net separates the two halves of the court. A 1 inch expansion joint should also be placed between courts when they are constructed in batteries.

A concrete beam 6 inches thick and 18 inches wide should be cast in a trench across the center of the court under the expansion joint at the net line. Bottom photo on page 237 shows construction details of this support beam, how it is thickened at the posts and reinforced.

In selecting the area for a tennis court, the long axis should run in a north and south direction. There should be no cross slope in the court, but a continuous slope of 1 inch in 20 feet may be permitted from one end of the court to the other to provide for drainage of water.

Either portland cement or traffic line paint should be used to paint 2 inch playing lines on the court following curing.

Handball courts. The 37½ by 25 foot

LAYING A CONCRETE SLAB

Above left: *Reinforcing steel is adjusted to the proper elevation as concrete is placed.*

Above right: *Wooden screed is used to strike off concrete to desired elevation.*

Below: *Grid tamp is used sparingly to force large aggregate particles below the surface and provide smooth top layer.*

Opposite page, top left: *After tamping, the surface is leveled with a long-handled metal float.*

Top right: *When the concrete has nearly hardened, it is compacted and finished with a mechanical rotary finisher.*

Center: *Small circular movements with steel trowels produce a non-skid "swirl" pattern for final uniform finish of tennis courts and other play areas.*

Below: *The trench at the middle of this tennis court will be used to construct a reinforced concrete beam under the expansion joint to support the edges of the two abutting slabs.*

concrete floor slab of the single handball court illustrated in Figure 16-2 should be constructed in one continuous operation, with a 4 inch thick slab over 4 to 6 inches of granular sub-base as needed. The concrete wall, 7 inches thick as specified in the diagram, may be placed in 4 foot lifts by removing form boards at approximately this interval. If a double court is desired, a similar floor slab should be built on the other side of the wall, with provision made for an expansion joint under the wall between the two floor slabs.

The slab should contain mesh reinforcement weighing at least 40 pounds per 100 linear feet. The wall slabs should be reinforced with half inch steel bars, the bar spacing varying from 5 to 12 inch centers be-

Figure 16:1. Cross section drawings showing construction of concrete tennis court.

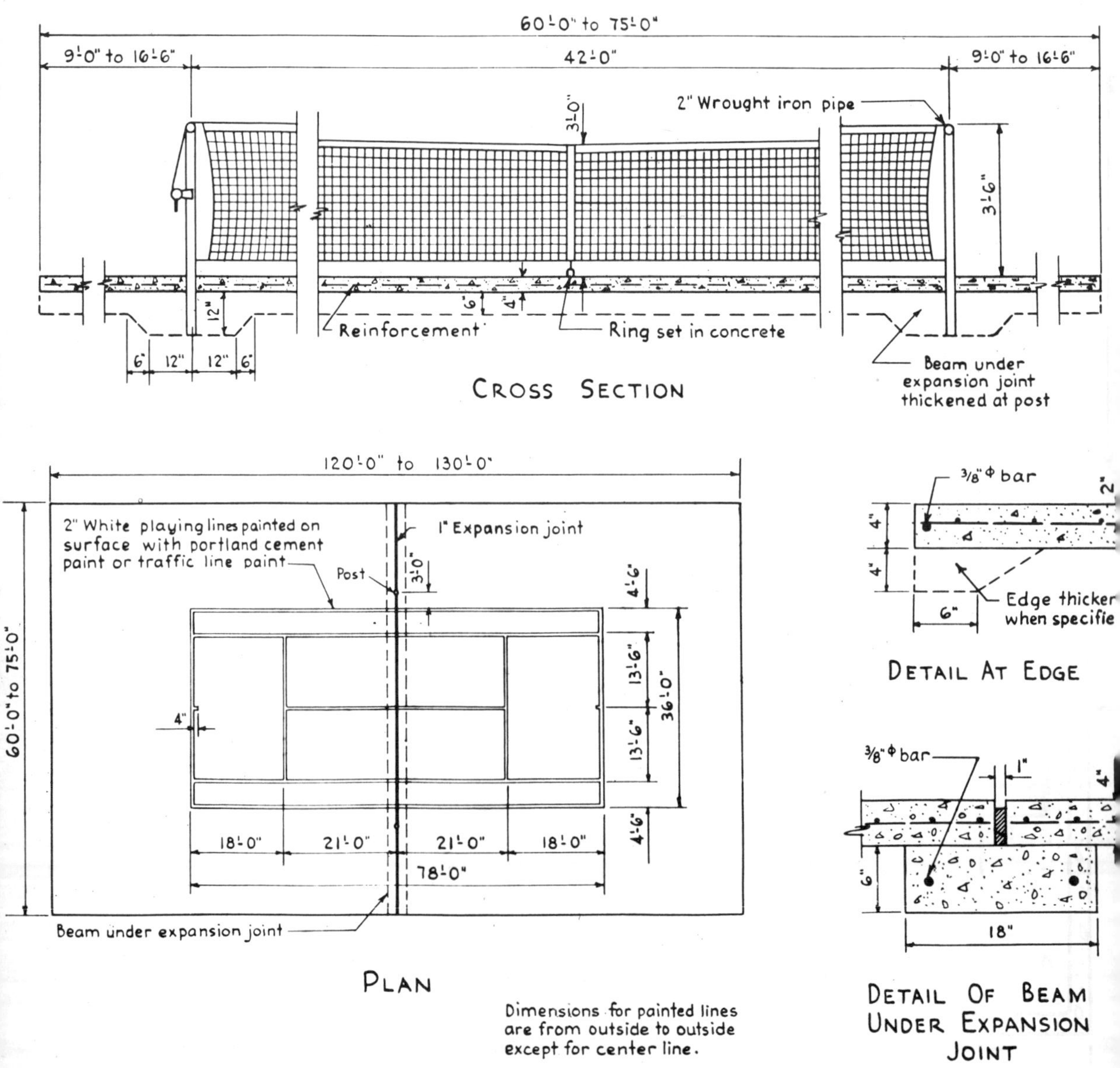

ginning with the heavy concentration near the bottom-center of the wall. As shown in Figure 16-2, an L-shaped foundation block measuring 3 by 3 by 1½ feet should be built under the wall. In constructing a double court, a similar support foundation should be built on the opposite side of the wall.

For a concrete handball court, the forms should be constructed and the concrete placed so as to produce a smooth face on the wall. No plastering should be done. The proportion of ingredients should be 1:2½:3½, the same as for other single-course constructed play areas. The forms should be kept in place at least 5 days and kept wet to allow curing. Form marks may be removed by rubbing with carborundum blocks.

For badminton, deck tennis, or home

Figure 16:2. Single wall handball court showing over-all dimensions and cross section of foundation.

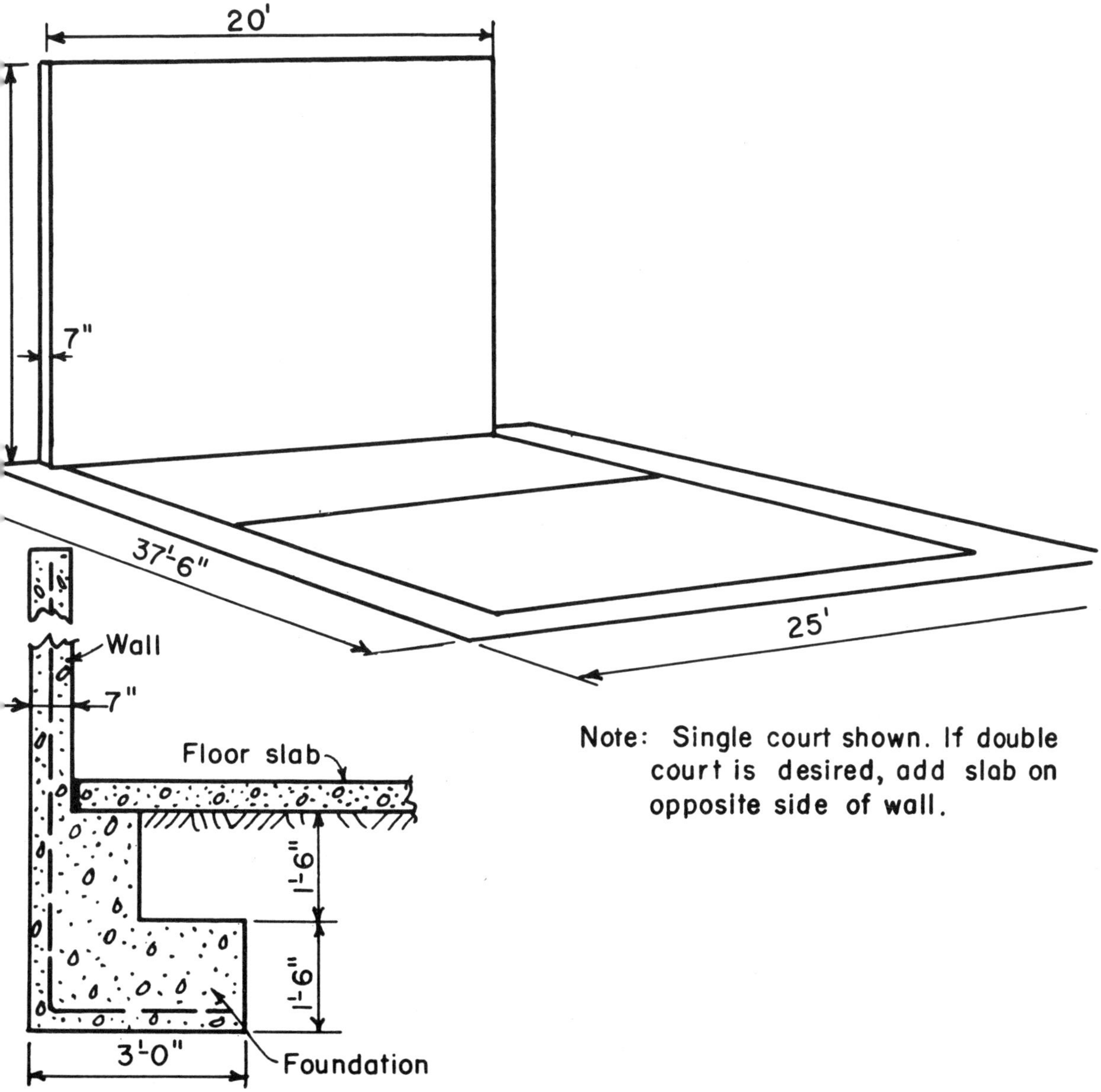

paddle tennis courts, the construction procedure is similar, save for dimensions.

Concrete playgrounds. The size of the paved yard of a concrete playground will depend, of course, upon the number of persons who will use the area. A 40 by 40 foot slab is a convenient size to construct in one section. One-half inch expansion joints should be provided every 40 feet in both directions, and contraction joints every 20 feet in both directions.

Roller skating and ice hockey rinks. Concrete paved areas designed specifically as roller skating or ice hockey rinks will differ only slightly in construction from concrete playground areas. Primary differences will be the possible use of curbs around the skating or hockey areas and the placement of brass dividing strips in contraction joints. Brass strips are specified for the joints rather than flexible joint-filling material in order to insure a continuous hard surface for skaters.

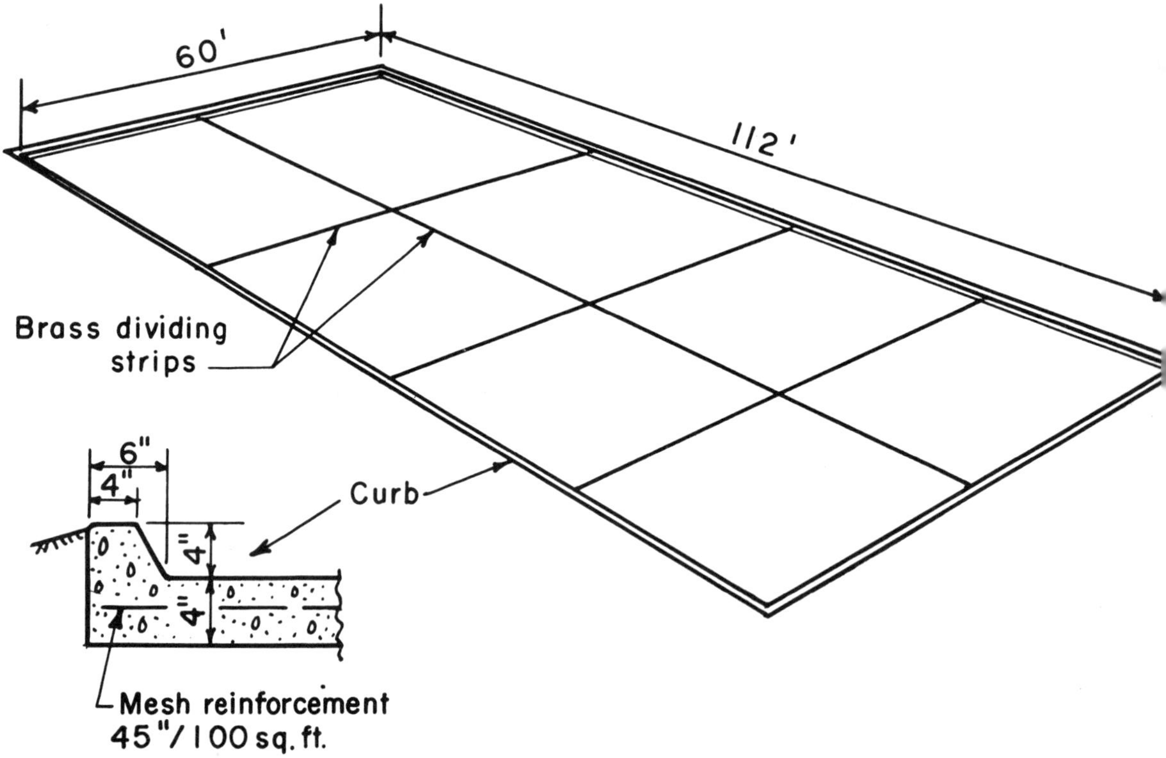

Figure 16:3. Roller skating or ice hockey rink, with cross section showing rounded curb.

Paving procedure should follow that of any other single-course paved area. Special care should be given to an adequate subgrade, properly compacted with granular sub-base, to provide a level area for heavy play use. A concrete mix of 1:2½:3½ parts for cement, sand, and aggregate is generally specified for the 4 inch slab. If a curb is desired around the area, see Figure 16-3 for recommended construction details for a 4 inch rounded curb.

The brass strips also help prevent chipping of the concrete.

The figure above shows a rectangular area measuring 60 to 112 feet, with a 4 inch curb around the entire area. It can be used, as shown, as a roller skating area and flooded with water to make an ice hockey court. Adequate drainage provisions are a must if flooding is planned, and air-entrained concrete should be used.

Figure 16-3 illustrates an oval-shaped roller skating rink with rounded curbs at each end.

Concrete roller skating track with center for figure skating and beginners. Jones Beach State Park, New York.

Shuffleboard courts and bowling alleys. The purpose of constructing concrete shuffleboard courts and bowling alleys in two courses or layers is to insure a smooth wearing surface, necessary for both games, and a durable concrete slab base. Longitudinal cross sections of such facilities are provided in Figures 16-4 and 16-5.

For shuffleboard courts and bowling alleys, the base course should be 3 inches thick and composed of the same type and size of ingredients specified earlier for single-course concrete slab construction. Reinforcing steel, consisting of expanded metal or wire mesh should be put down between the base layer and the wearing or top surface. The 2 inch top layer should have a cement, sand, aggregate ratio of 1:1:1¾, with smaller coarse aggregate (maximum size three-eighths of an inch) and less water (from 4½ to 5 gallons of water per bag of cement). The top layer should be placed within 45 minutes after the base layer has been struck off.

After the top or wearing layer has been

Figure 16:4. Cross section of concrete shuffleboard court.

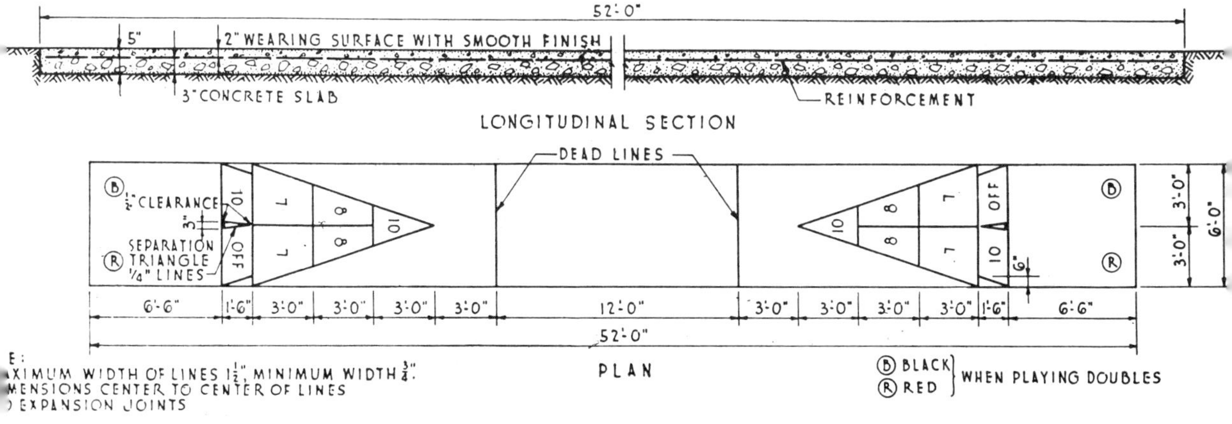

brought to grade, it should be compacted with a wood float and tested for any surface irregularities. Shuffleboard surfaces should be trowelled with a steel trowel as soon as the concrete has stiffened sufficiently. The final smooth finish is attained by careful hand trowelling. The top layer for bowling alleys, on the other hand, should be screeded and floated to finish grade without trowelling. After the concrete has been thoroughly cured for seven days, the surface of the alleys should be given the final finish with carborundum bricks or by grinding. The floor should be kept wet during the grinding process.

Curing is also of prime importance in the construction of a shuffleboard court. The finished surface should be kept continually wet for a period of seven days. After drying for four or five days, playing lines may be painted on the surface.

Coloring Concrete Surfaces

One of the reasons for concrete's popularity as a paving material is its high light-reflectance. However, there are times, particularly for tennis courts, when it may be desirable to color the concrete surface some shade other than its normal gray-white color. Darker surfaces may be desired for tennis courts or other play courts for two reasons: (1) they cut down on the sun's glare by absorbing light and reducing reflection, and (2) they provide better contrast between the

Figure 16:5. Cross section and plan for outdoor concrete bowling alley.

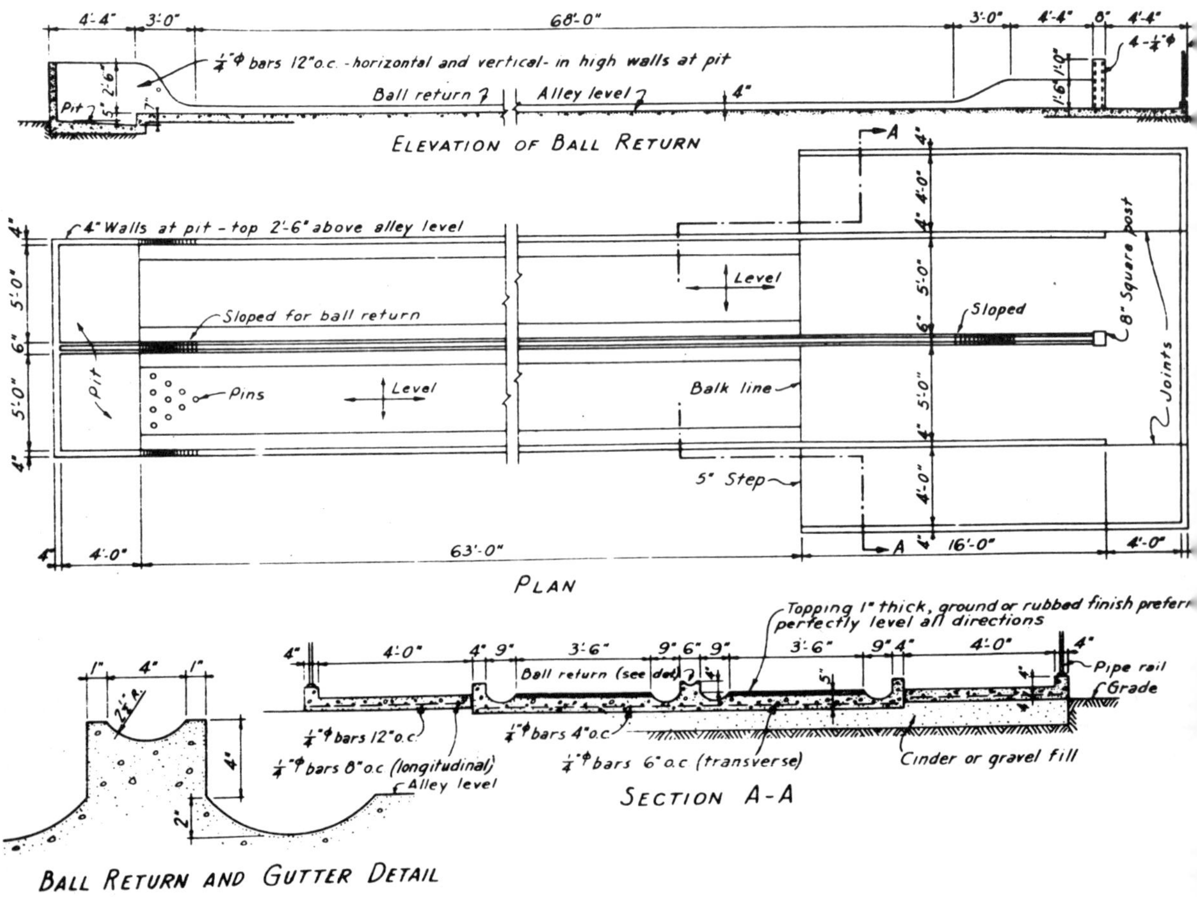

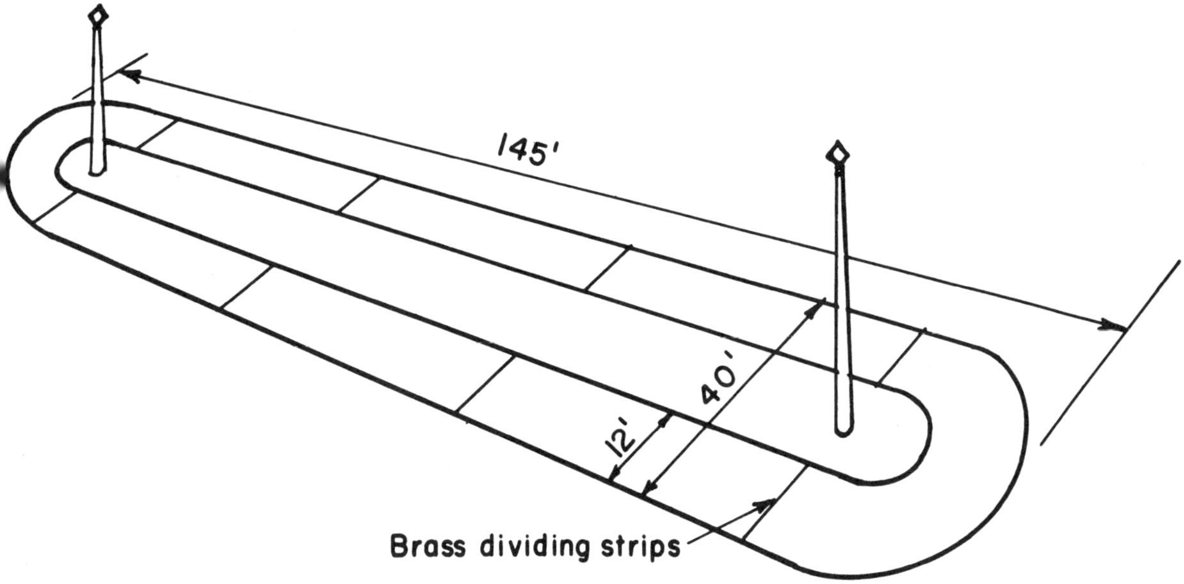

Figure 16:6. Oval-shaped roller skating rink.

playing surface and the light colored tennis balls.

There are several ways to produce colored concrete surfaces. The most widely used methods are: (1) chemical stains applied after the concrete has hardened, and (2) mineral pigments mixed integrally with the concrete ingredients.

Chemical stains are used extensively, particularly in southern California where tennis is a major sport. The stains used are inorganic reaction-type, and are applied to the hardened concrete slab in accordance with manufacturers' recommendations. Usually two applications are specified to develop the desired color.

A number of accepted stains are on the market. Shades of brown, tan, green, and black are the most popular for staining concrete play areas. Black is the predominant choice for concrete tennis courts in the California area, but other colors are used generally over the nation.

Concrete surfaces colored by chemical stains have proved satisfactory in retaining their color for considerable periods of time. The center championship court of the Southern California Tennis Association has been in use for 29 years and has required only two restainings during that period.

In the integral color method, mineral pigments are used as coloring agents and are mixed with the other concrete ingredients before water is added. A color guide will include the following: for blues, cobalt oxide; browns, brown oxide of iron; buffs, synthetic yellow oxide of iron; greens, chromium oxide; reds, red oxide of iron, grays or slate effects, black iron oxide or carbon black, preferably black iron oxide.

Only commercially pure mineral pigments should be used, as others are likely to fade or reduce the strength of the concrete to a marked degree. The amount of coloring materials added should not exceed 10 per cent of the weight of the cement. Deep shades can generally be produced with less than this amount of color by judicious choice of pigments. Different shades can be secured by varying the amount of coloring material used or by mixing together two or more pigments. *The full coloring value of pigments can be obtained only with white portland cement, which must be used to obtain the more delicate shades of lighter colors.*

There are two accepted methods of mixing

pigments with other materials. The first is to weigh out carefully the aggregate and cement. To this is added the predetermined amount of pigment. The new mixture should be mixed dry until the entire batch is of uniform color. Water is added to bring the mixture to the proper consistency.

Another method that has been used successfully for large projects is to grind the cement and pigment in desired proportions in a small ball mill. This mixture is added to the aggregate and the batch thoroughly mixed dry to a uniform color before adding water.

Other methods of producing colored concrete surfaces include: *two-course construction,* in which a base or first course of normal color concrete is topped with a three-quarters to 1 inch layer of concrete containing color; *dust-on process,* where a mixture of color pigment and cement is dusted onto the fresh concrete before final trowelling and worked into the mixture to become part of the finished surface; or by *painting* the hardened slab. Painting is not desirable for a tennis or badminton court, since constant service makes frequent repainting necessary to retain the original color.

Painting of walls and other concrete surfaces is discussed in the following section.

Painting Concrete Surfaces

Factors of importance in considering the selection of a paint for a particular concrete surface include: the condition of the concrete, the service to which it will be subjected, and the effect desired.

Before painting any concrete surface, it is vitally important that the surface be properly prepared. This preparation will differ with the type of paint used.

Portland cement paints. Portland cement base paint consists largely of portland cement ground with coloring materials. It comes in dry powder form and should be mixed and applied in accordance with the manufacturer's directions.

All surfaces must be uniformly damp when the paint is applied. A slightly roughened surface is desired. Portland cement paint can be applied to concrete immediately after the forms have been removed, or to portland cement plaster or stucco as soon as they have hardened, although there are advantages in permitting the surface first to season or "cure." Dirt, oil, grease, efflorescence, or paints of an organic type must be completely removed from the surface before painting. A garden hose providing a fine spray is suitable for dampening. The surface should be sprayed several times, with a few minutes' interval between each spraying to allow the moisture to soak into the concrete.

After the first coat of paint has hardened sufficiently to prevent injury, it should be cured by keeping the surface continuously damp for at least 24 hours. This can be done by spraying. The surface should be wetted down again just before applying the second coat, which should be applied at least 24 hours later than the first coat. The second coat should be kept damp as long as practicable, but not less than two days.

It is good practice in mixing portland cement paints to first add only about half the total amount of water suggested and to thoroughly mix the ingredients to a stiff paste. Water is then added gradually until the desired consistency is obtained. Workability improves by allowing the mixed paint to stand 30 to 45 minutes before using. Frequent stirrings after this will keep the mixture in usable condition for three to four hours.

Organic paints. When painting concrete surfaces with organic paints, the concrete must be perfectly dry and well-seasoned. Oil, grease, and efflorescence should be removed. Old concrete should be wire-brushed or sand-blasted slightly to remove dirt and loose particles. New concrete work should be given at least eight to ten weeks to dry after the moist-curing period. After the concrete is thoroughly dry, it should be given a neutralizing wash to prevent saponification of the paint oils. The neutralization wash may be a solution of water and zinc sulphate or magnesium fluosilicate, or a zinc chloride-phosphoric acid solution with water. After drying 24 to 48 hours, any dust on the surface should be brushed off but the concrete should not be rewetted before paint application. The surface should then be given a binding and suction-killing treatment, consisting of one or more coats of oil or varnish carrying some pigment. The prime coats should be allowed to dry thoroughly, after which any of the organic paints can be applied in accordance with manufacturer's directions. Neutralization treatments are not necessary on old concrete or old portland cement stucco.

General comments. In applying paint to coarse-textured concrete, a brush with relatively short stiff fiber bristles gives best results. For concrete with smooth or sandy finish, whitewash or Dutch-type calcimine brushes are suitable. Spray gun application of portland cement paint is satisfactory for *decorative* purposes, but tests of the rain resistance of painted concrete masonry walls indicate that paint applied by spraying provides less protection than paint that is scrubbed on.

A satisfactory paint job on a floor of any type presents a difficult problem, and in this respect concrete is no exception. It should be appreciated that repainting will be necessary at intervals, depending upon the service requirements.

Most manufacturers of lead and oil paints make special floor paints in which they embody abrasion-resisting pigments. These are suitable for concrete floors when carefully applied. Most manufacturers recommend two coats on concrete floors. Experience indicates that three coats give results which more than compensate for the extra cost.

A number of so-called cement or cold water paints on the market today contain little or no portland cement, and hence offer little resistance to weather, serving only as temporary color coatings when exposed to adverse conditions. On the other hand, portland cement base paint is especially recommended for any exterior concrete surface exposed to damp or adverse outside conditions. A wide range of colors can be obtained. *Portland cement paint is not recommended for application on wood or metal, enameled brick, vitrified or glazed brick or tile.* Nor is it recommended for concrete floors except for swimming pools, wading pools, ponds, and similar facilities not subject to mechanical abrasion.

A good rule is: *For outdoor use and locations subject to moisture, use only paints which the manufacturer can definitely show to have satisfactory service records under similar conditions.*

MAINTENANCE OF CONCRETE AREAS

One of the most generally admired qualities of concrete paved play areas is that they require little maintenance. But it is plain good business to see that the little that is required is done promptly. Such maintenance is not difficult, nor does it require special qualifications. Untrained workmen, properly supervised, can carry out most routine maintenance of concrete areas with dispatch.

Other than periodic cleaning, the only type of maintenance ordinarily required for properly-constructed concrete pavements is the sealing of joints and cracks. And in play areas such as tennis, badminton, or handball courts, these joints are at a minimum.

Maintenance of contraction joints usually involves replenishing or replacing the sealing material (a rubber-asphalt, asphalt, or tar substance). This is placed in joints and cracks to prevent seepage of surface water through the openings and to exclude foreign matter from entering.

The hand-formed groove with a poured seal is easy to maintain. If the original sealing material is of good quality, and if it was not burned or damaged when placed, it should be necessary only to remove any loose or foreign material. The joint should then be thoroughly cleaned and additional seal added where needed. Caution should be taken not to overfill the joint. When the original seal requires replacement, it may be "plowed out" using a power-driven rotary cutter or by use of chisel-pointed hand tools.

Contraction joints formed of pre-molded bituminous strips or ribbons normally require little or no maintenance for many years after construction. Generally, the same procedure of removing foreign particles and thoroughly cleaning and resealing should be followed. Contraction joints formed by the newest method, concrete power saws, are sealed in the same way, but special equipment such as power-driven rotary brooms and air compressors may be necessary in cleaning because of the smaller joint-openings.

No attempt should be made to seal a pavement crack unless it is open wide enough to permit the ready entry of sealing material. Sealing material applied to the surface over narrow cracks is not effective. Much effort and material can be wasted by attempting to seal "hair cracks." Wide cracks should be well cleaned out before sealing. Where compressed air is available, it may be used effectively. Power-driven rotary brushes provide a rapid means of removing dirt and other inert material, although hand-brooming with stiff-fiber or steel-bristle push brooms may be adequate for the job.

In some unusual cases, where cracks are open and seals are difficult to maintain, a groove about 1 inch deep and less than one-half inch wide may have to be made along the crack with a power saw to provide a recess for sealing material.

Periodic cleaning adds to the durability of concrete. The dirt and grit on play areas is subjected to considerable foot traffic in games and sports, and will be ground into the surface.

Most minor stains can usually be removed by a thorough scrubbing with warm, soapy water and stiff brushes. Concrete with oil stains can be cleaned by first scraping off the oil crust, then scrubbing with gasoline. Although it may not fully remove the discoloration, this treatment will remove the objectionable coating of oil and grease. Special solvents are also available for removal of oil and grease.

The best protective material for concrete play areas is boiled linseed oil mixed with turpentine. This mixture gives the slab a good protective coating and brings out the color of the surface.

CHAPTER 17

TURF SURFACES FOR PLAY AREAS

John H. Melady

FIELDS AND PLAY AREAS SPECIALLY SEEDED OR planted and maintained for sports and recreation are mostly a development of the last one hundred years. The practice in previous centuries was to use facilities that already existed, such as grazing fields or lawns. Golf, which was taken to their own by the Scots in the fifteenth century, was played on a suitable sheep pasture. Park-like turf for rest and recreation was largely in the hands of the wealthy; its general use by the common people dates from the "Common grazing ground" of colonial New England, and the grassing over of the plague-pits throughout London where the dead were mass-buried in 1665.

The large class of ball games calling for a group of players endeavoring to hit, kick, carry, shove, bat, or throw a ball into the opposing team's territory while keeping it out of their own, includes football, soccer, shinty or hurley, and lacrosse; these were usually enjoyed in an available paddock or hayfield. Except, perhaps, the two-thousand-year-old polo, the forerunner of this type, which was as often played on the dry and dusty plains of Persia and India as on grass turf.

Cricket was played on the public pasture or Common. The grass around the tavern or the home was always available for the games needing but little space, such as croquet, or pall-mall, horseshoes, and lawn-tennis. Up to the turn of the present century, the abundance of horse manure, much of it old and rotted, enabled a lush, self-repairing turf to be maintained with little effort.

Bowling greens of old, like the one on Plymouth Hoe, where Sir Francis Drake is alleged to have finished his game before tackling the Spanish Armada, or the famous bowling green at the foot of Broadway, New York, were in all probability specially made and kept up. The difficulties encountered can be imagined when one remembers that mowing machines were not available in those days, and that hand scything is a highly skilled operation.

Illustration: Seven gang mower cuts a 10 foot swath

Photo by Worthington Mower Company, Stroudsburg, Pennsylvania

ADVANTAGES OF TURF FOR PLAY AREAS

It is safer. In the absence of a carpet of living grass there are the alternative surfaces such as concrete, asphalt, cinders, gravel, rolled sand, packed clay, or wooden flooring. School yards in many cities are commonly laid with concrete or asphalt, and games played on them usually have to be modified by using rubber balls or improvising the rules. These hard surfaces would be dangerous for such games as lawn hockey, football, soccer, lacrosse, softball, field hockey, or baseball. Grass possesses a quality that enables it to yield considerably under impact and many a sprain or fracture is prevented because of this characteristic. Some asphalt mixtures recently have been compounded with an elastic matrix; however, a deep-rooted fibrous sod comes closer to the ideal playing surface.

It is more fitting. Certain games are entirely out of character if not played upon turf. The quiet conservative game of lawn-bowling played without the lawn becomes the fast raucous effort of the bowling-alley. Hard-court tennis is far from lawn tennis. Croquet away from the lawn becomes a combination of roque and billiards. Polo ponies ran on gravel centuries ago, but it is doubtful if they could work so intelligently as they do today on grass. In many iron shots the golfer is instructed to "take turf." To do this he must be provided with turf to take.

It gives a truer rebound. In many games, such as tennis, football, soccer, and cricket, the bounce of the ball is highly important. Grass possesses qualities that permit a better bounce of balls in these games.

It is more pleasing. The emerald green turf framing the baseball diamond is a time-honored feature. Sun reflection is eliminated and a more practical surface is provided by grass.

THE USE OF TURF FOR PLAY AREAS

For recreation. For park surfaces an important attribute of turf is its restful color; another is its relative softness, making it perfect for sitting or lounging upon, and for picnicking.

For the small fry. Turf is ideal for play areas for younger children to romp upon with their pets, and to play their games. If space permits in a park, an area of grass should be left unmown. Every spring and fall it should be topdressed sparingly with a mixture of twenty parts by measure of screened soil and one part of mixed flower seeds. Some of the larger dealers offer these seeds in two grades: expensive seeds are true wild flowers native to the locality, and cheaper seeds are mixed "seedsman's" flower seeds, a bulk combination of the kinds normally sown in gardens in spring and autumn. Children should be encouraged to gather a reasonable size bunch of flowers when they are in bloom.

For athletics. Turf for sports must be hard-wearing, and quick to recover from injury. This calls for soil that drains well, and requires that plant foods and moisture are always present.

For golf. Three types of turf are aimed for on golf courses: (a) for unwatered fairways, grass that will tolerate drought in midsummer, thick enough to support a ball well above it and thus give a good lie. (b) For irrigated fairways, one that is kept slightly on the acid side, and tooth-harrowed with the harrow-teeth sloped to drag without ever much tearing. This is to discourage the growth of clover. Golf tees would come under one or the other of these turf classifications. (c) For the greens, usually planted with the kinds of bent grass that the green committee may prefer such as colonial, Rhode Island, seaside, Astoria, or highland bent, either alone, in combination one with another, or in combination with redtop as a nurse-grass. Sodding is accomplished by moving and planting turf bodily on limited areas, or "vegetating," by planting portions of the runners developed by creeping bent and covering them with a quarter inch layer of screened soil. See Chapter 19.

For tennis. Tennis courts must withstand the hard wear occurring around the baselines, and must tolerate the continuous rolling that the majority of players insist upon. The wear is taken care of by maintaining a reserve of tennis turf for patching; also by designing the tennis area large enough to permit moving the nets when necessary. The usual distance courts are moved is ten feet, thus taking the worn sections of the court out of play.

For bowls. Probably the best treated turf is that on a lawn bowling green. A woman's high heels are frowned upon on a golf green, but leather shoes for either sex, low or high heels, are banned on most bowling greens, rubber sneakers being the rule. Often the player delivering his bowl stands on a rubber mat. The grass varieties used are mostly bents, or bents mixed with redtop.

South of Washington, D.C., the grasses would be those listed for the southern states in Table 17-9.

CLIMATE AND GEOGRAPHIC LOCATION

No one grass variety will thrive permanently in every part of the United States. South of Richmond, Knoxville, Memphis, Little Rock, Dallas, and Roswell, turf is usually of Bermuda grass on high land, and carpet grass on wet land. Bermuda has a period of winter dormancy ranging from a few weeks in the extreme south to several months. Sports are usually maintained on the browned turf.

However, where extensive winter play is required, the Bermuda turf is scalped with hoes to an even surface of roots and soil. It is then topdressed with a mixture of one part by measure of ryegrass and ten parts of screened soil. This forms a temporary turf which dies out as spring turns into early summer, giving way to Bermuda, which gives a satisfactory summer turf provided the autumn scalping was not too drastic.

North of Philadelphia, Harrisburg, Parkersburg, Cincinnati, Evansville, St. Louis, Wichita, Amarillo, and Santa Fe the varieties listed in Table 17-1 as the "permanent varieties" grow well. The farther one travels northward the better they grow.

Between these two lines of cities is the territory where neither northern nor southern grasses do their best. One solution here is to sow a mixture of northern sorts with Bermuda. Every spring and fall thereafter more of the same seeds mixed with screened soil must be sown.

TABLE 17-1

Grass Varieties

Note: R = Propagated by runners; S = Propagated by seed.

A. THE PERMANENT GRASSES

Used in the Northern two-thirds of the U.S.[1]

AGROSTIS OR BENT VARIETIES

One pound of seed contains 5,000,000 or more living grains. The bents are most valuable in golf and bowling greens, and for other sport areas in a proper mixture with other grasses. They provide an excellent cushion for the ball next to the soil. Alone bent grass has little wear-resistance. Bent grasses are propagated by either runners or seed depending upon the variety.

Agrostis stolonifera R. *Creeping bent.* Many strains of this grass have been segregated, some having fine turf-making qualities. Many thrive in certain localities, but do not do so well in others. Some of the best known and most liked of these strains include the following, any one of which may be used for golf putting greens and lawn-bowling greens: 1, Arlington; C 7, Cohansey; C 19, Congressional; C 52, Pennlu.

Agrostis palustris R.S. *Seaside, Coos county, Cocoos bent.* Makes a wonderful turf, does especially well in the far west and both eastern and western seaboards. Elsewhere somewhat susceptible to fungus diseases.

Agrostis tenuis S. Astoria, Brown-top, Colonial, Highland, Prince Edward Island, and Rhode Island Bent. These are the same botanically, but are collected in various parts of the world, and they show minor differences.

Agrostis canina R.S. Velvet Bent. The dwarfest, narrowest-leaved lawn grass, silk-like and beautiful. Tolerant of shade. Superior strains of Agrostis canina include Bell, Kernwood, and Raritan.

POAS OR BLUEGRASSES

One pound of seed contains about 2,500,000 grains. These grow best in early spring, frequently fade out in hot weather and reappear in autumn.

Poa pratensis. S. Kentucky Bluegrass, June grass.
Poa pratensis B 27. S. Merion Bluegrass. Stands heat better than other bluegrasses.
Poa compressa. S. Canada Bluegrass.

[1] North of Philadelphia, Harrisburg, Parkersburg, Cincinnati, Evansville, St. Louis, Wichita, Amarillo, and Santa Fe.

Poa trivialis. S. Shade grass, bird grass, rough-stalked meadow grass.
Poa annua. S. Annual or biennial bluegrass; a weed that invites crabgrass, disappearing in warm weather, leaving voids which crabgrass fills; an effective turf grass in spring and fall.

FESTUCAS OR FESCUES

The leaf-edges of this group are rolled on themselves, giving a bristly wire-like or mat-like effect. They are resistant to drought and heat. They root deeply and will stand wear. Watering in spring and fall harms them. They also fare better with frequent mowing. All are shade tolerant. One pound of seed averages 600,000 grains.

Festuca rubra fallax. S. Chewing's fescue.
Festuca rubra repens. S. Creeping fescue.
Festuca rubra Illahee. S. Illahee fescue.
Festuca rubra, Penn state. S. Penn. State fescue.
Festuca rubra F 74. S. F 74 fescue.
Festuca tenuifolia. S. Fine-leaved fescue. A narrow leaved grass, but the color is against it for turf; it is a bluish green.
Festuca ovina. S. Sheep's or hard fescue. This is a coarse grass growing in clumps, bluish gray and of value only in such places as the rough of a golf course.

B. THE TEMPORARY OR NURSE GRASSES

These are often mixed with permanent grasses since they are quick growing and their effect is to provide a turf while the slower kinds of grasses are maturing. They keep the soil covered with grass, thus discouraging weeds. Their cost is low, which is one reason for using them in a seed mixture which is low priced. Some of the more common varieties are:

Lolium multiflorum. S. Italian Ryegrass.
Lolium perenne. S. English Ryegrass.
Lolium hybrids. S. Domestic Ryegrass.

Any of the above three may be sown in the southern states as a winter turf over Bermuda grass. For this purpose a fresh seeding with ryegrass is necessary every fall.

Agrostis alba. S. Redtop. The most useful temporary nurse grass.
Festuca elatior. S. Alta fescue. A large plant with flat leaves.

C. SPECIAL DROUGHT-TOLERANT GRASSES

The grasses that are especially tolerant to drought are:

Bromus inermis. S. Smooth bromegrass.
Agropyron cristatum, Fairway strain. S. Crested wheatgrass. Particularly suitable for the northwestern part of the U.S.
Agropyron Smithii. S. Western wheatgrass.
Agropyron repens. R. Couch, twitch, or quack. Because it is a noxious weed, sale of the seed of this variety is restricted, but on a steep hillside or a ski-jump, half a mile or more from a cultivated farm it has value because it resists erosion. Runners may be collected from a field (the farmer will gladly point them out to you and will probably tell you to help yourself). Set each runner half-in half-out in holes dibbled in the hillside nine inches apart.
Buchloe dactyloides. S. Buffalo grass. A coarse, drought resisting, sun requiring grass for the western plains from southern Texas to Canada. Thrives on heavy land only, and prefers alkaline soil.

Bouteloua gracilis. S. Blue grama.
Bouteloua hirsuta. S. Hairy grama.
Bouteloua eriopoda. S. Black grama.

The gramas stand partial shade. They, too, are for the western plains. All four of the above kinds are of value in preventing soil erosion and soil loss by wind surrounding sports areas in this locality. For the playing fields themselves use agrostis, poas, and fescues as in the western, middle Atlantic and New England states, but irrigate generously.

D. SUB-TROPICAL GRASSES

Cynodon dactylon. R.S. Bermuda grass. It gives especially good results on limestone soils. Some of the newer improved strains include Tifton 57 (Tiflawn) and Tiffine.

Axonopus compressus. R.S. Carpet grass. A coarse variety for low, moist land. Prefers acid soil.

Eremochloa ophiuroides. S. Centipede grass. Stands some shade.
Zoysia matrella. R.S. Manila grass. Likes neutral soil.
Zoysia japonica. R.S. Japan or Korea lawn grass.
Zoysia japonica Z 52. R. Meyer zoysia.

SEED MIXTURES

The question is often raised "why sow grass mixtures?" The answer is that different grasses grow better at different times of the year, and not so vigorously at other times; because wet weather favors one kind, whereas dry weather helps another; because a low temperature helps some while a high temperature suits others. So it is customary and desirable to sow, or plant mixtures when building a new turf area.

PREPARING THE GROUND FOR PLANTING GRASS

The surface should be composed of at least four inches of topsoil. If the ground is recently cultivated farmland, prospects for the topsoil layer are good. Topsoil which is light and porous is the best since drying after rain is more rapid. The grass will root more deeply and show maximum resistance to wear in such a surface. Any area to be seeded must be cleared of weeds, young bushes, and trees. Men equipped with handforks, spades, and mattocks will help a lot. Larger trees will need loosening with dynamite to allow a bulldozer to drag them out. The surface should then be plowed to a depth of six inches, disced and tooth-harrowed. A roto-tiller may also be used to prepare the soil.

The following table contains some of the more popular and proven mixtures:

TABLE 17-2

***The Kingston Mixture*[2]**

A fine, hard-wearing turf in the northern half of the United States, which is suitable for football fields and baseball diamonds, may be obtained from the following mixture:

50 parts by weight Chewing's fescue or creeping fescue
35 parts Kentucky bluegrass
15 parts Astoria or Rhode Island bent

Grading

For grading a qualified engineer will be needed. Where plans call for areas for polo, football, cricket, baseball, hockey fields, and even bowling, the greens should be "crowned," or graded to a slight invisible "hog's back" or convex surface .25, .375, or as much as .5 per cent slope (3, 4½ or 6 inches to 100 feet).

When working with sloping or hilly terrain, the engineer should indicate neutral points to which the topsoil should be bulldozed. The stripped surface should then be disced and graded and the topsoil returned in an even thickness over all.

Golf putting greens are graded to the architect's plans. He is careful that all surface water runs off the green and not into surface pockets. Fairways are graded in spots to take care of land-locked rain. Very severe hillocks in the fairways may be lowered, taking care to replace or bring in topsoil. Wet spots may have to be drained. However, the architect can often go around hillocks and avoid wet spots. (See Chapter 19 on golf course construction for details.)

Tile Drainage

Some playing sites are often low-lying and need artificial drainage. Grass grows stronger as a result. The process gets rid of excess water in the soil which is unfavorable to the growth of grass; it does not interfere with the upward course of moisture by capillarity.

When a field has been graded and a minimum thickness of four inches of topsoil is in position over the area, the local agricultural agent, or a nearby agricultural college, or experimental station should be consulted to determine if tile-drainage is necessary. If it is necessary he should be requested to work up a program for you.

It will probably be a system of narrow ditches starting at about 30 inches beneath the surface, perhaps 30 feet apart, with a grade or fall of four and a half or six inches per 100 feet, running into other ditches until unwanted water is conducted off the area into a ditch, pond, brook, or blind-well. Unglazed baked clay drain tiles are placed along the bottom of the ditches, butted end to end, gravel is placed around and over them; the subsoil and then the soil are returned, filling ten per cent over grade to allow for sinkage.

Tile drainage is troublesome and costly, but well worth the expense where it is needed. Football fields usually require tile-drainage.

Testing the Soil

Take several representative pint samples of the soil to the nearest agricultural college. They will do the testing for you. Easily operated soil testing kits are available at horticultural supply houses if self examination of the soil is desired. All soil should be tested twice a year, even after the turf has matured.

The first step is to find out the degree of alkalinity or acidity in the soil, due to the presence or absence of calcium. This is expressed by the symbol "pH" followed by a figure, which if it is more than 7 represents degrees of alkalinity; if it is less than 7 it indicates more or less acidity. A pH of 7 is considered neutral. For example, if a report reveals a pH of 5, it indicates that an application of pulverized limestone should be included in the soil preparation. If the pH is 8.5 it can be concluded that the soil is alkaline and no limestone is advisable.

---

[2] This is recommended by Dr. J. A. DeFrance of the Rhode Island Agricultural Experiment Station, and has been designated the Kingston mixture.

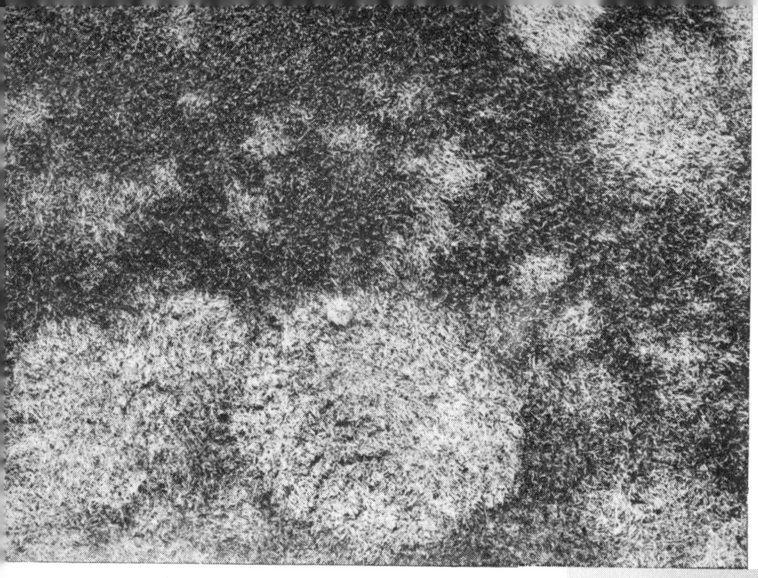

Brown-patch, a turf disease.
Photo from E. I. du Pont de Nemours Company, Wilmington, Delaware

Mower hook-up. Two units are hitched under the tractor and a third is hooked to the rear close to the driver.
Photo from Roseman Mower Corporation

Power mower cutting grass surrounding a tennis court.
Photo from Jacobsen Manufacturing Company

Photo from Skinner Irrigation Company

Battery of revolving sprinklers on the football field of the University of Illinois.

Photo by Don Berg, courtesy of Soilaire Industries

Water-ballast self-powered roller weighing from one-half to one ton. Used on turf, running tracks, tennis courts, baseball diamonds, and blacktop surfaces.

Photo from West Point Products Corporation

When the Aerifier is drawn over a field, thousands of holes are made in the turf, down which air, water, and plant food are carried.

Photo from International Harvester Company

This grader is useful for removing roots and large stones.

Photo from Old Orchard Turf Nurseries, Madison, Wisconsin

Rows of C52 creeping bent in a nursery. Stems and leaves that appear wide and coarse at this stage become narrower and finer in a bowling or putting green.

There are three other elements that must be present in order for soil to be fertile. These are nitrogen, phosphorus, and potassium. If the soil test indicates that one or more of the chemicals is low, materials containing the deficient chemicals are added when preparing the land. Furthermore, the turf would be topdressed with these chemicals for as long thereafter as semi-annual tests indicate that they are in short supply.

These essential elements are termed the "Big Four." In addition, grass needs minute quantities of so-called trace elements. These are present in most fertile soils and are certain to be present when manures, and other materials recommended to be spread at the same time as fertilizers, are used.

To find out the suitability of any material offered or suggested, make up a mixture of one measure of the material and two measures of soil from the field, with a teaspoon of ground limestone to each quart. Bore one fourth inch holes one and one half inches apart in the bottom of a wooden cigar box and fill it three-quarters full with the mixture. Sow domestic ryegrass seeds roughly one fourth inch apart, and with a flour-dredge sift on additional soil mixture to hide the seeds.

Place outdoors during growing weather on the shady side of a building, or stand against a window indoors during the winter and water daily. If the young grass appears and grows to the point where it can no longer support itself upright, and retains its green color without turning yellow, it may be used. If nothing grows, repeat the trial using one half and one-quarter the material. If the results are no good do not use the material.

SOWING SEED

When. Seed may be sown any time in the northern half of the United States except in the midsummer months. However, certain times of the year are better than others. In the order of preference they are (1) end of summer (September), (2) end of autumn (November), (3) during winter, either on frozen soil honeycombed by frost or on a snow covered surface leveled and prepared ahead of time, or (4) earliest spring (April or May). Seed sown in late spring or in summer will probably grow, but more than the average crop of weeds will appear alongside the grass seedlings.

How. The soil must be plowed, disced, tooth-harrowed or raked, or rototilled. The top layer should have organic manure or material containing the essential plantfood elements added to it. The desired type and quantity of grass mixture suited to the locality and to the purpose for which the turf is required should be obtained. The seed should be scattered very evenly over the surface.

When seeding a limited area such as a tennis lawn, a bowling green, or a golf green, it can probably be done by hand. On a day when the soil is dry and there is little wind, the exact amount of seed is divided in half. One of the halves is broadcast over the entire area by casting it in a number of wide circular sweeps. Then the remaining seed is scattered in the same way over the same area.

For a football field one or more wheelbarrow broadcasting drills should be used. With this equipment the principle of double seeding can be taken care of by watching the wheel marks, and assuring that one-half the hopper overlaps the previous path of the drill.

To cover the seeds. Most seeds grow best when placed one quarter inch below the surface. This is taken care of by brushing small areas once lightly with a birch broom, or raking them once lightly with a flat-tined, spring rake. For large areas a brush-harrow may be drawn over once (this is a ten foot long two-by-four to which twenty thin tree branches are spiked). A chain is attached to the brush-harrow of such a length as to hold the wood off the ground. It is drawn over once. Some turfmakers connect a pair of chains from a tractor, one to each end of an eight foot cedar tree, and this serves quite well as a brush.

Planting Stolons

Selected strains of creeping bent, and much Bermuda turf are obtained with runners or stolons. Bent is grown in rows in a nursery, then the plants are lifted and the soil shaken from them. One method of planting is to pass the dirt freed plants through a feed-cutter and scatter the cut grass on a well prepared surface. The clippings are then covered with one-half inch of screened soil. Creeping bent does not produce seed.

The above method also represents the best way to plant Bermuda; however, in most situations, stems are torn apart and planted in holes 6 inches apart made with a sharpened stick. If the holes are made at a 45 degree angle, pressure with the sole of the shoe closes them. Bermuda can be grown from seed readily enough, but to maintain better strains they are best grown from stolons, that is by planting portions of the grass plants themselves.

Spring and fall are the seasons for planting creeping bent. For Bermuda only the spring is suitable.

TURF MAINTENANCE

Rolling

After seeding, the area should be rolled. A tractor drawn or self powered roller is desirable for large fields. A hand drawn one is satisfactory for smaller areas. A water-ballast roller half filled is about right for most soils. Use it nearly empty if the soil is largely clay. Should it rain as seeding is completed omit the rolling.

Rolling is part of the regular upkeep routine, necessary every late spring, and helpful at other times. Always roll only when the soil and grass are dry.

Mowing

The young grass should be mown as soon as it reaches the cutting edge of a mower set for the particular sport. From then on it needs cutting every few days, except that it should not be mowed during rain or when the land is muddy. If bad weather disrupts the schedule for three days or more, raise the adjustment of the machine to where it merely clips the top of the grass leaves, and lower it a trifle at each subsequent mowing as the routine returns to normal. Watering is likely to do more harm than good to newly sown seed, unless very carefully done, by dislodging it or causing bare spots and clumps of crowding plants. It is better to wait patiently for rain on new seed. Established turf, however, may need irrgation in dry weather from June 15th to September 1st, when it should be given plenty. If possible sprinkling is best done in the early morning, late afternoon in cloudy weather, or in the evening. It is best to water when the humidity is high.

Regular Periodic Feeding

As long as the soil shows a pH rating below 7 spread limestone late every autumn or winter. When spring growth commences dress with the organic manure or chemical fertilizer that a soil test indicates may be beneficial. Repeat in late autumn.

TABLE 17-3

Some Sources of Plant Foods: Calcium, Nitrogen, Phosphorus, Potassium, and Trace Elements

Material	Element predominating	Quantity to harrow or rake into bare land before sowing seed		Quantity to topdress or spread on turf in early spring, again in late summer		Remarks
		Per acre.	Per 1000 sq. ft.	Per. acre.	Per 1000 sq. ft.	
LIME						
Pulverized limestone (ground limestone rock)	Calcium	2-4 tons	100-200 lbs.	1-2 tons	50-100 lbs.	Do not mix with other materials, or spread them at the same time.
Gypsum	Calcium	2 tons	100 lbs.	1 ton	50 lbs.	
Superphosphate of lime	Calcium, phosphorus	2 tons	100 lbs.	1 ton	50 lbs.	
CHEMICAL FERTILIZERS OR ORGANIC AND CHEMICAL FERTILIZERS MIXED						
Country Club 10-6-4	Nitrogen, phosphorus potassium	½ ton	25 lbs.	400 lbs.	10 lbs.	
8-6-4		1250 lbs.	27½ lbs.	500 lbs.	12½ lbs.	
5-10-5		1500 lbs.	35 lbs.	750 lbs.	20 lbs.	
duPont Soluble Plant Food 19-22-16					4 ozs.	Dissolved in water, add to fungicide sprays; 4 ozs. in 5 gals. per 1000 sq. ft.
Sulphate of Ammonia	Nitrogen			200 lbs.	5 lbs.	
ORGANIC MANURES						
Agrinite	Nitrogen, trace elements	1 ton	50 lbs.	500 lbs.	12½ lbs.	Use one, two, or more at one time, but reduce the quantities in proportion. If two are employed use one-half of each; if three use one-third of each.
Bonemeal	Calcium, phosphorus, trace elements	2 tons	100 lbs.	1 ton	50 lbs.	
Milorganite	Nitrogen, trace elements	1 ton	50 lbs.	1500 lbs.	35 lbs.	
Tankage	Nitrogen, trace elements	1 ton	50 lbs.	½ ton	25 lbs.	
Tobacco scrap	Potassium, trace elements	2 tons	100 lbs.	1 ton	50 lbs.	

Organic Materials and Soil Ingredients					
Hyper-Humus*	All, trace elements	6-15 tons	275-700 lbs.	3-6 tons	150-275 lbs.
Manure,* rotted horse, rotted or fresh cow		12 tons	550 lbs.		
Poultry manure		2 tons	100 lbs.		
Mushroom soil*		6 tons	275 lbs.	3 tons	150 lbs.
Peatmoss*	Effect mostly mechanical	20-50 bales	½-1½ bales	10-25 bales	¼-¾ bale
Sand		30-60 cu. yds.	1-2 cu. yds.	15-30 cu. yds.	½-1 cu. yd.
Composted leaves and weeds*	All, trace elements	A layer 2 inches thick, forked in			
Seaweed*	Phosphorus, trace elements				
Pond dredgings*	Nitrogen, trace elements				
Dirt from drained marsh*					

*These are invaluable when topsoil is to be made from subsoil.

Correct Hide-bound Conditions

If the soil is unduly hard under the turf in dry weather when contrasted with neighborhood areas, a condition often brought about by heavy rolling when wet, it can sometimes be corrected by spike-rolling or perforating the soil with an aerofier or other punching device. Humus, rotted manure, mushroom soil or peatmoss may be spread along with an equal bulk of coarse, sharp sand. Then with the backs of rakes, or with a cedar tree pulled by a tractor, the materials should be drawn to and fro until they disappear down the holes. The quantities vary with the capacity of the soil to absorb them. As the materials are used up, add more.

Repair Turf Injuries

Worn areas around such places as tennis base-lines or baseball infields should be carefully cut out to a depth of one and one-fourth inches. The exposed surface should be whitened with 8-6-4 fertilizer at one half pound per 10 square feet, and roughened with a rake. From a reserve of turf, mown and rolled as regularly as the courts, cut the necessary number of 12 by 12 inch squares of turf one and one-half inches thick. Place each in a foot square tray with one and one-fourth inch sides, grass side down, and shave the soil side with a scythe blade to give a uniform one and one-fourth inches. Lay the sods in position and tamp them to moderate firmness. Corners and less than foot square holes are filled by cutting sod to shape with a mason's trowel.

A week before repair work is started a bushel or so of topsoil mixed with grass seed should be prepared. The approximate quantity of grass seed is one teaspoon to the quart. Keep the mixture in a shed for a week before using. Then, when the sods have been tamped, scatter the pre-sown seed and soil, and brush it into the cracks.

Patching in this way will heal fertilizer burns, recognized by swatches of dead grass, or spots where the fertilizer spreader overlaps. Fertilizers will usually burn if they are put on when the grass is wet or if too much is used. Oil or gasoline dropped from a tractor or power mower will also burn grass. The shape of the damaged spot often suggests the source of the injury, or by smelling the burnt-out spot it is often possible to detect the source. Make the same kind of patch-repair when turf is damaged by vehicles running over wet turf; however first try prying the turf up with a handfork. If possible then fill in with topsoil underneath and roll.

On large damaged areas turfing is not practical, so mix up a batch of mixed seed and top soil and store it in the shed for a week. Then fill the damaged areas, such as hoof marks on a polo field, the divots on a golf fairway or tee, the lug-skids on lacrosse, soccer, football or hockey fields, with this plain top soil. On top of the plain soil scatter a skin of the presown mixture, and press with the shoe, or roll. The sore will become green in a day or so because some of the "divot" mixture will consist of ryegrass, which is very quick to germinate.

A clever trick is to prepare a mixture of seed and soil six days before an important game, so that the day after the game you can begin work on repairs.

THE COST OF INSTALLING TURF

Soil preparation is so varied that there is no general formula by which cost may be determined. Get a contractor's figures for plowing, bulldozing the topsoil into heaps, grading the subsoil, and returning the topsoil.

If tile-drainage is necessary a contractor or a farmer could give a close estimate of the cost. A local person could give a price for discing and harrowing or rototilling the finished surface, sowing, brushing, and rolling.

The cost of seed varies from year to year, and there is a great difference in the varieties. Bent seed for putting and bowling greens may cost up to $1.75 per pound. Mix-

TABLE 17-4

Tools Needed to Maintain Grass-Surfaced Areas*

Not included are bulldozer, plows, discs, tooth-harrows, and similar implements required only in the construction, and which ordinarily would be supplied by the contractor.

Tractor, medium, light; with rubber tires and sickle-bar
Pick-up truck
Wheelbarrows, pneumatic tires

Rollers, hand, water-ballast
Roller, large, self-powered or tractor drawn
Roller, spike-disc, small, hand
Aerofier or Aerator

Soil-screen or shredder
Fertilizer spreader, small, hand
Fertilizer spreader, medium, hand
Fertilizer spreader, large, tractor-drawn
Seeder, Cyclone, small, hand
Seeder, wheelbarrow, hand
Seeder, large, tractor-drawn, broadcast

Mowers, hand
Mowers, medium, power
Mower, large, self-powered or tractor-drawn
Scythes
Scythe sharpening stones
Sickles or grass hooks
Grass shears
Lawn Sweeper for gathering trash and leaves

Chain harrow
Flexible steel mats
(Both above for distributing materials.)

Champion sod cutter, tractor drawn
Sod lifters, hand
Turf-repairing disc cutters, 2 to 12 inch diameter
Tampers

Sprayers, hand, knapsack and power
Dusters, for applying insecticides and fungicides

Sprinklers
Hose
Hose accessories: washers, menders, couplers, nozzles
Soil-soaker for deep watering
Flame-shooter gun

Soil testing kit
Mole traps
Barometer, wet and dry bulb thermometer

Forks, hoes, shovels, spades
Rakes, steel, flat spring, wood
Trowels

Birch brooms
Bamboo poles, 15 ft., for distributing dew and worm-casts

Reserve supply of seed, screened soil, plant-foods
Reserve supply of insecticides, weedicides and fungicides

* The tools listed are based on the requirements needed to maintain the grounds and play area surrounding a high school of approximately 15 to 25 acres, or a neighborhood park of approximately the same size.

tures for polo, football, soccer, and baseball fields may be worth from $1.00 per pound (where a small proportion of temporary nurse grasses are used in the mixture), to $1.40 per pound for a mixture consisting only of permanent kinds.

WEEDS

The worst weed for turf that is to be used for sports is *clover*. The principal objection to clover is that under wear it becomes dangerously slippery. A second charge against it is that it stains tennis balls, shoes, and clothing. A third disadvantage is that it deflects many a golf ball on a putting green.

If soil tests indicate a pH reading of 7 or higher, reduce the alkalinity by two dressings per year of the following:

	Per Acre	*Per 1000 sq. ft.*
Sulphate of ammonia	200 lbs.	5 lbs.
Sulphate of alumina	200 lbs.	5 lbs.
Shredded cattle manure	1 ton	50 lbs.

Should the soil test indicate a pH reading under 7, use gypsum instead of the annual winter application of limestone.

Rake the turf with rake-teeth filed to sharp points once a month during the mowing season, the object being to comb up the clover runners and present them to the mower. Then spray the turf with a mixture of 2-4-D and 2-4-5-T amine, using two quarts per acre in 200 gallons of water, but reducing the dosage for low cut bent turf in a bowling or putting green to one-half the chemical.

Another pesty weed is *crabgrass*. In bent turf handpick it as early as it can be recognized. You need not dig out the root, but should merely cut it with a sharp knife beneath the surface. For mixed turf that is mown longer, spray with a dilution of one and one-fourth fluid ounces of PMAS 10 per cent in two and one-half gallons of water over 500 square feet. Reduce the chemical to one ounce per 500 square feet for turf less than six months old. Reduce it to three-fourths of an ounce for putting and bowling turf. Three sprayings should be given at ten day intervals in spring.

PMAS 10 per cent is also a proven preventive and control of various fungus conditions that attack turf.

Goosegrass or silver crab is similar to crabgrass, but is shiny. Cut the slender tough single root just under the surface with a sharp knife. Old plants turn white as they mature. Treat chemically the same as for crabgrass.

TABLE 17-5

Mowing Schedule

Surface	*Height of Cut*	*Interval between Mowings*
	Inches	*Days*
Putting green, clock golf	¼	1 to 2
Bowling	½	2
Croquet, golf fairway and tee, roque, tennis	1	2 to 3
Badminton, baseball, basketball, cricket, horseshoes, volleyball	1¼	3 to 4
Archery, football, hockey, lacrosse, pushball, soccer	1½	3 to 5
Polo, rough on the golf course	2	4 to 6

Note: Make and sand a number of hardwood cubes, the sides of each measuring ¼, ½, 1, 1¼, 1½ and 2 inches, insert or attach 12-inch dowel stick handles, and mark the size clearly. Stand the mower on a bench and measure the distance between the cutting point and the bench top.

Spurge appears in summer in new lawns. It is one of the rubber plants, exuding a white sticky milk or latex when the stem or a leaf is torn or cut. Raking to present the plants to the mower is helpful.

A few yellow *dandelions*, or similar-looking blue-flowered *chicory*, may be killed by a stab with a wooden or hard rubber skewer wet with sulphuric acid. Wear rubber gloves, galoshes, and a rubber coat. The same treatment will take care of *dock* and *plantain*.

For large infestations spray with 2-4-D. Be sure to follow the manufacturer's directions exactly as given on the container, or the turf may be injured.

Marsh pennywort and *sheep's sorrel* are signs of an acid soil. The leaf of the former is about the size and shape of a penny. The latter is a small native sourgrass with a halberd shaped leaf.

Snakebit or *hawkbit* is an indication of hungry land. The leaves are hairy, and the flower is like an orange colored dandelion. Fertilizer applications should eliminate it.

TABLE 17-6

Some Fungus Turf Pests

Snow Mold. Caused by Typula itoana. When snow disappears in February or March, many perfect circles 2 inches to a foot in diameter of whitened grass are disclosed. The dead leaves are glued together with a fungus.

Remedies include Acti-dione, Calo-Clor, Calo-Cure, PMAS 10%. They may be used as a preventive last thing before winter sets in or as a cure at winter's end if the trouble is found. The white circles may be raked to break open the stuck leaves.

Damping Off. Caused by species of Pythium. When seedlings are overcrowded and kept too moist they will often die off in groups. When normal conditions return, re-sow the area at one-half the original rate, first shaking up the seed in a container with Arasan seed disinfectant.

Dollar Spot. Caused by Sclerotinia homoeocarpa. From April through October many spots of white dead grass the size of a silver dollar may show up, and may increase in number daily, but seldom in size. Remedies include Acti-dione, Cadminate, Craig 531, Calo-Chlor, Calo-Cure, duPont 531, PMAS 10%, Puraturf, Puraturf 177, Semesan, Special Semesan.

Brown Patch, Summer Blight. Caused by Rhizoctonia solani. From mid-June through September circles of diseased grass may appear, with a dusky margin where the fungus is active. If not treated the circles will grow to 5 feet in diameter or more. Drop everything and apply one or other of the following controls: Acti-dione, Calo-Clor, Calo-Cure, PMAS 10%, Puraturf, Semesan, Special Semesan, Tersan 75.

Copper Spot. Caused by Gloeocercospora sorghi. The numerous small patches are similar to those of dollar spot, but they are copper-red. They are likely to appear from June through September. Try one or other of the following: Acti-dione, Cadminate, Craig 531, PMAS 10%, Puraturf, Puraturf 177.

Pink Patch. Red thread. Caused by Corticium fuciforme. Turf is killed in patches up to a foot across in mid-May. Reddish threads of fungus protruding from the felted leaves give a pink tint. Controls: Cadminate, Craig, Puraturf 177.

Blights, including Melting Out, Going Out, Fading Out, Black Mold. Caused by Helminthosporium and Curvularia varieties. In this group the fading leaves are seen under a magnifier to be blotched with netted, brown, yellow, or red spots. Recommended controls are Acti-dione, Semesan, Special Semesan.

Fairy Rings. Circles of mushrooms or toadstools appearing in warm, damp weather in spring or fall. Ring may be years old and enclose acres. Topdressing with fertilizer will help, but the condition is relatively unimportant. You may plot the position of the mycelium, which may be called the fungus' roots, occupying a strip of ground 3 feet wide around the mushrooms, and close to them; spike-roll over the mycelium, and treat with PMAS 10% or other control.

How to Apply Fungus Controls

Acti-dione. Package contains two vials, Acti-dione and ferrous sulphate. Dissolve in from 7½ to 37½ gallons of water and spray onto 7500 square feet.

Cadminate. Half-ounce in water of any convenient amount on 1000 square feet as a preventive. One ounce per 1000 square feet as a cure.

Calo-Clor. Mix 2 ounces with any convenient quantity of dry sand, say one-half bushel, spread on 1000 square feet as preventive; use double this rate should the trouble get through. Use water instead of sand if preferred, but keep stirred.

Calo-Cure. Two ounces per 1000 square feet mixed with any convenient amount of sand or water.

Craig 531 and *duPont 531.* Mix three ounces per 1000 square feet in ten gallons of water or half bushel of screened soil or dry sand, as preferred.

PMAS 10%. For athletic fields and lawns 2½ ounces in 5 gallons of water sprayed on 1000 square feet. Half this amount in 5 gallons for closely mown bowling and putting greens. Repeat three times at ten day intervals. Sometimes the 10 per cent solution is not obtainable locally and a weaker strength has to be used; then proportionally more of the chemical is mixed with the water. PMAS 10% is the wonder chemical: it is a reliable fungicide, and a weedicide also. It is much used for the elimination of crabgrass.

Puraturf. Mercuric. Half-pint in 50 gallons of water on 600 square feet.

Puraturf 177. A cadmium fungicide. Pound makes 100 gallons of spray, covers 10,000 to 12,000 square feet.

Semesan. Four to eight ounces per 1000 square feet.

Special Semesan. Three to four ounces per 1000 square feet. Either of the above two may be mixed with 10 gallons of water or half a bushel of screen soil or dry sand.

Tersan 75. Three to five ounces per 1000 square feet, mixed with 5 or 10 gallons of water.

Special Note

It must be remembered that no one remedy is 100 per cent effective; it is therefore wise to repeat spraying or dusting at seven or ten day intervals. It is also desirable to change the control from time to time.

Knotweed or *knotgrass* tells of compacted land. It may be seen where people walk or where mowing tracks converge. Run a spike-roller over the patches or prick them with a garden fork, then rub in coarse, sharp sand. In the winter the patches are brown. If they are not hidden by snow, burn them with a flame-gun or blow-torch.

Chickweed and *mouseear* are matting weeds. If few, scarify each mat with an old time curry comb obtained at a harness store and then scatter grass seed. Follow with monthly dressings of arsenate of lead, five pounds per 1000 square feet. For large areas, spray with one pound sodium arsenite dissolved in 100 gallons of water for one acre. Repeat in seven to ten days.

SOME TURF PESTS

Ants may be killed by spreading one-half pound of five per cent chlordane dust per 1000 square feet, first mixing it with a bushel of sifted soil or dry sand.

Army-worms, cutworms, sod-webworms and *grasshoppers* may be controlled with a poison bait. Take two and one-half pounds of bran, one-fourth pint Paris green, one-half pint of molasses, and one pint of water. Mix up as many batches as are necessary to place small gobs of the mixture six inches apart. Keep dogs and cats away and sweep up after three days.

Chlordane may also be used. Spread one pound of the five per cent dust on every 1000

TABLE 17-7

Recommended Seed Mixtures for Washington, D. C., North to the Arctic

(Sow spring or autumn.)

	Sunny turf within 100 miles of coast	*Sunny turf inland*	*Shaded or partly shaded turf*	*Bent greens*	*Polo fields and airports*
PERMANENT VARIETIES *Bent grasses*	*Lbs.* or ozs.	*Lbs.* or ozs.	*Lbs.* or ozs.	*Lbs.* or ozs.	*Lbs.* or ozs.
Seaside	5	5	..	25	..
Rhode Island (Colonial)	5	5	..	25	..
Highland	..	..	..	..	5
Astoria	5	5	..	25	..
Velvet	..	..	5	..	..
Bluegrasses					
Kentucky	..	10	..	..	..
Merion B 27	10	10	..	..	..
Shade bluegrass (Bird grass)	..	..	20	..	..
Fescues					
Chewing's, F74, or Illahee	55	45	55	..	50
Smooth brome grass	..	..	..	..	5
Crested wheat grass	..	..	..	..	10
TEMPORARY VARIETIES (Nurse grasses for quick coverage; they disappear in time.)					
Redtop	10	10	10	25	..
Meadow fescue	..	..	..	..	10
Alta fescue	..	..	..	..	10
Perennial rye grass	10	10	10	..	..
Domestic rye grass	..	..	..	..	10
Total	100%	100%	100%	100%	100%
Amount to sow per 1000 sq. ft.	3½ lbs.	3½ lbs.	3½ lbs.	2½ lbs.	3 lbs.
per acre	150 lbs.	150 lbs.	150 lbs.	100 lbs.	125 lbs.

square feet mixed with a bushel of dry screened soil. Water it in after spreading.

Chinchbugs are gray, quick moving creatures the size of the head of a pin. With their thousands of companions they kill grass in large irregular shaped patches that often turn brick red during hot summer weather. To destroy chinchbugs, scatter one-half pound per 1000 square feet of five per cent chlordane dust, mixed with one-half bushel of screened dry soil. Repeat with another one-half pound mixed with soil two hours later.

White grubs of the May beetle or of the Japanese beetle may feed on grass roots close under the soil surface, giving the effect of walking on a rug. Five pounds of a ten per cent DDT compound spread on 1000 square feet, mixing first with a bushel of dry soil can be used to destroy them. Wear a respirator. Turf may be grubproofed by spreading and washing in ten pounds arsenate of lead per 1000 square feet.

Moles are attracted by earthworms and grubs. Bury a pair of gloves for a day to remove human scent. Then while wearing them open a package of poisoned pellets that can be purchased at a supply store, make holes at six foot intervals in the mole-runs and drop a pellet in each. *Moles will avoid anything carrying the smell of your hands.*

Turf pests of the South and mid-South area include the fat two inch white grubs of the *June beetle* or figeater, making what look like very large wormcasts, and *mole crickets* that act like small moles. They live on grass

TABLE 17-8

Recommended Seed Mixtures for the Mid-South 35th to 39th Parallel

(Sow every spring and autumn.)

	Sunny turf		*Shaded or partly shaded turf*		*Bent greens*		*Polo fields, airports*	
	Spring	*Fall*	*Spring*	*Fall*	*Spring*	*Fall*	*Spring*	*Fall*
PERMANENT VARIETIES *Bent grasses*	*Lbs.* or ozs.	*Lbs.* or ozs.	*Lbs.* or ozs.	*Lbs.* or ozs.	*Lbs.* or ozs.	*Lbs.* or ozs.	*Lbs.* or ozs.	*Lbs.* or ozs.
Highland	5	5	..	..	15	30	..	..
Astoria	..	..	..	..	15	30	..	..
Velvet	..	..	5	5	..	..	..	..
Bluegrasses								
Shade bluegrass (Bird grass)	..	..	15	15	..	..	..	..
Fescues								
Chewing's, F74, or Illahee	45	45	45	40	..	..	20	30
Smooth brome	..	..	..	..	..	..	10	10
Crested wheat	..	..	..	..	..	..	10	10
Bermuda grass	50	..	35	..	50	..	30	..
TEMPORARY VARIETIES (Nurse grasses; they disappear in time.)								
Redtop	..	10	..	10	20	40	..	..
Meadow fescue	..	..	..	..	..	..	10	10
Alta fescue	..	..	..	..	..	..	10	15
Perennial rye grass	..	40	..	30	..	..	..	..
Domestic rye grass	..	..	..	..	..	..	10	25
Total	100%	100%	100%	100%	100%	100%	100%	100%
Amount to sow, per 1000 sq. ft.	2½ lbs.	2½ lbs.	2½ lbs.	2½ lbs.	2 lbs.	2 lbs.	2½ lbs.	2½ lbs.
per acre	100 lbs.	100 lbs.	100 lbs.	100 lbs.	75 lbs.	75 lbs.	100 lbs.	100 lbs.

roots. Both may be controlled with five pounds of ten per cent DDT or with ten pounds lead arsenate per 1000 square feet.

Earthworms in reasonable numbers are helpful, but if excessive they become pests. Ten pounds arsenate of lead per 1000 square feet, watered in, will hold them in check. So will a refined wormkilling grade of mowrah meal at a half-pound per square yard, well washed in. The effect is immediate and spectacular if conditions are right (warm, damp, cloudy weather). They may also be killed with chlordane, preferably in the emulsion form. Observe the strength of your emulsion, then use enough to furnish twenty pounds of actual chlordane per acre. Add the amount of water recommended on the package.

In recent years a new earthworm called the *oriental earthworm* or *stink worm* has made its appearance in the northeastern states. It is 6 to 8 inches long, with a diameter of one-fifth of an inch, and often light green on the upper surface. It is hard to kill, and usually needs a second treatment of chlordane in the fall, if the first was given in the spring; or in spring if the first was given in the autumn (twenty pounds at each occasion, forty pounds of chlordane to the acre in all).

TABLE 17-9

Recommended for Sowing below 35th Parallel (level land)

	Spring	*Fall*
PERMANENT VARIETY	*Lbs.* or ozs.	*Lbs.* or ozs.
Bermuda grass, for dry land / Carpet grass, for moist acid land	100*	..
TEMPORARY VARIETIES		
(They generally disappear in spring.)		
Redtop	..	25
Domestic rye grass	..	75
Total	100	100
Amounts to sow, per 1000 sq. ft.	2½ lbs.	4 lbs.
per acre	100 lbs.	160 lbs.

* Bermuda grass or Carpet grass, depending upon whether the area is normal and reasonably dry, or is marshy.

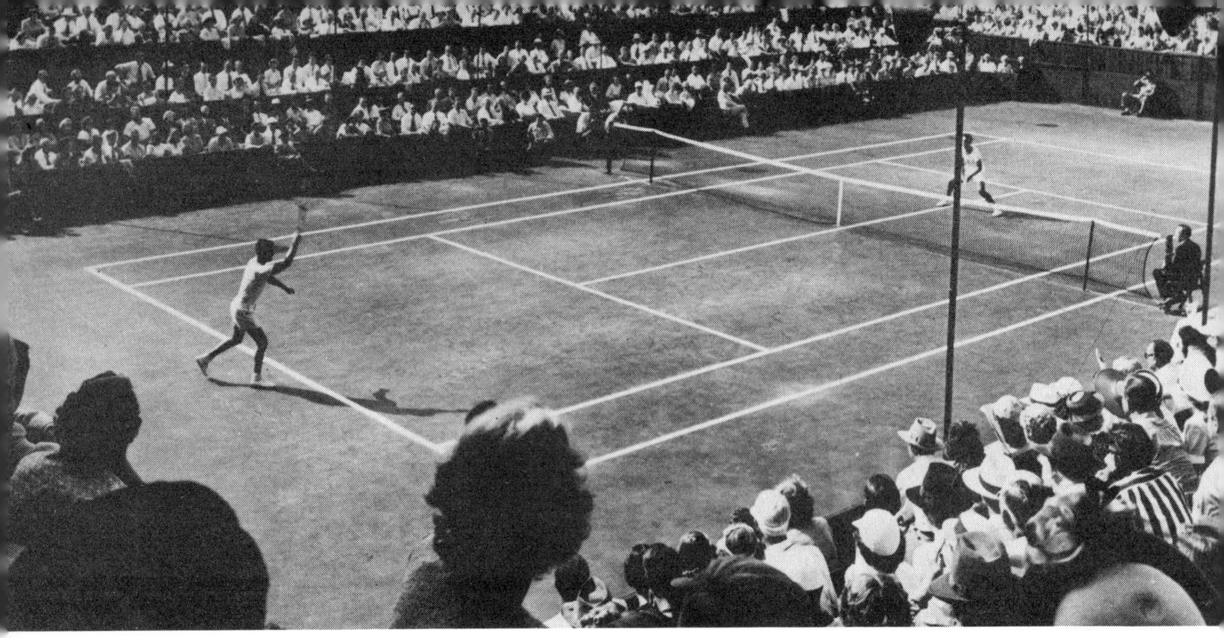

CHAPTER 18

TENNIS COURTS

Walter L. Pate

THERE IS SOME DOUBT AS TO THE LOCATION OF the first lawn tennis court in this country. It was either at the Staten Island Cricket and Baseball Club located at Camp Washington (now St. George), Staten Island or at Nahant, a small town on the coast a few miles from Boston. The preponderance of evidence, however, gives the Staten Island site the call, and the credit to Miss Mary E. Outerbridge who brought from Bermuda in February 1874 a net and some racquets which she obtained from British military officers then stationed there. Miss Outerbridge's brother, Eugenius H. Outerbridge, a director of the Club, arranged to mark out a court and to set up the net on the club grounds. That first court would have a bizarre appearance to the present day tennis player. The regulations (English) specified an hour-glass shaped court, 24 feet wide at the net, base lines 30 feet wide, distant 39 feet from the net and service lines parallel to the net at a distance of 26 feet therefrom.

Illustration: Tennis match

The surface was, of course, turf. The game was known as "Lawn Tennis" and at the beginning it was played only on grass. The growth of the game was so rapid that other surfaces had to be employed because of the scarcity of available lawn and the high cost of construction and upkeep. And so, inevitably, surfaces more serviceable and durable soon came to be more and more prevalent. It is estimated that today less than three per cent of the courts in this country are grass. The remainder consist of a score or more different types such as cement, asphalt, board, clay (of many different kinds), and numerous other surfaces constructed by many different business enterprises and given many different trade names.

The purpose of the chapter is to assist those who must decide on the type of court they are about to install.

Unless cost of upkeep is of no consideration, unless the court may occasionally be closed to play, and unless there is sufficient space behind the base lines so that those lines may be moved back and forth from time to time, grass should not be considered.

Unless a grass court is kept in excellent condition, almost any other surface would be better, and yet there is no finer playing surface than properly maintained grass.

And so grass courts are out for most schools, colleges, and playgrounds. There undoubtedly would be many more good tennis players if there were more grass courts. When great tennis players meet to decide championships they are expected to play their best; therefore, the important championships are played on grass. A few of the "big" tournaments are the Challenge Round Davis Cup Matches and the United States, British, and Australian Championships. In spite of considerable experimentation and research, no surface has been developed on which the game can be played as well as on grass. Most players who learned to play on other surfaces have found, on becoming accustomed to turf, that their shots are more effective and their skills greater on grass courts. The reasons are not hard to find, for the grass surface rewards finesse, subtlety, and strategy more than any other. The effect of spin is greater on grass than on smoother and harder surfaces, just as new felt on a billiard table imparts more "English" to the ivory ball than does an old covering worn smooth. The delicate drop shot and the stop volley may be employed to advantage on grass, whereas it is dangerous to attempt either on hard courts. And, strangely enough, speed, power, and aggressiveness are also more effective on grass. The reason? The bounce is lower, leaving less time for the player to reach the ball while it is still playable. And furthermore, a good grass court has no rival for sheer enjoyment of the game. The glare, dust, and dirt from most other surfaces are lacking on grass. Grass is cooler, cleaner, and much easier on the feet and eyes.

The problems to be faced in the building and maintenance of grass courts are so many and so varied that it is not feasible to discuss them in this chapter. Climate, character of the soil, types of grass and numerous other factors have an important bearing on the subject. For those interested in the subject it is suggested that a perusal of the pamphlet "Tennis Court Turf Management Practices at Leading Eastern Clubs and Notes on Maintaining Grass Courts" by H. Alfrede Langben, issued by the United States Lawn Tennis Association, be made.

PLANNING A COURT

How To Lay Out a Tennis Court[1]

Most accurate results are obtained if a tennis court is laid out by a civil engineer or competent surveyor using proper surveying instruments. However, if such services are not readily available, adequate accuracy can be obtained with the proper use of two good 50 foot tapes as indicated below.

All courts should be laid out for singles and doubles play. However, since the same lines—except for the side line extensions for doubles play—are required for each, it is best to first lay out the singles court, establishing the lines shown in the diagram [on page 269. This diagram shows only one half of a singles court; the other half is exactly the same]. Courts should be laid out with the long way north and south. First establish the net or center line. This is done by driving a peg at Point A, then a second peg—27 feet from A—at Point B. Then take the two fifty foot tapes and attach their respective ends to the pegs A and B. On the first, which will determine the side line A—E, measure off 39 feet and on the second, which will determine the diagonal B—E, measure off 47 feet 5¼ inches; pull taut in such directions that at these distances they meet at Point E. Drive a peg at E. Then establish point D in a similar manner. The distance from E to D should be 27 feet, the same as from A to B.

Check this for accuracy before driving peg at D. Point F, 21 feet from A, and point C, 21 feet from B, should then be established and pegs driven at these points. This provides the lower (or south) one half of the court. The upper (or north) one half is determined in a similar manner. This completes the boundaries for the singles court. The doubles court boundaries are established by prolonging the base lines from points E & D on lower half and similarly for the upper half 4 feet 6 inches in each direction and joining the four new points to establish the side lines for the doubles court. The doubles court is actually 9 feet wider than the singles court, with side lines parallel to those of the singles court.

---

1 From "Care and Construction of Tennis Courts" quoted by permission of the United States Lawn Tennis Association.

Factors in Selecting Court Surface

Many factors must be considered in selecting the type of court best suited to those who will use and maintain it. Among them are climate, cost of construction and upkeep, preference of the players, amount and standard of play. There are a score or more of court surfaces to select from. The advantages and disadvantages of the better known types are discussed in the following pages.

Most of them fall into one of two groups:

1. Porous surfaces that allow water to seep through to a porous base, where it is partly disposed of by drainage, and to some extent draw moisture to the surface in dry weather.
2. Non-porous surfaces through which water does not seep to the base but drains from the surface.

Although the size of a doubles court is 78 by 36 feet a surface of at least 120 by 60 feet is required to provide adequate space between the base lines and the backstops and beyond the side lines. If courts are built in batteries net posts between courts should be separated by a minimum of 6 feet. Avoid locating the court on low ground or where it would be subject to drainage from higher terrain. Select ground that is well drained and that requires a minimum of grading and, if out doors, lay the court in all cases with the long axis north and south so that players will not have to face the sun. In the north the best orientation will be 10 degrees West of North by 10 degrees East of South.

Types of Surfaces

As already indicated, in general all courts fall into one of two general categories, *porous* (pervious) and *non-porous* (impervious). The first group includes grass, clay, En-Tout-Cas and types known as "Fast Drying," surfaces through which water drains to a greater or lesser extent to the base. The second includes, cement, concrete, asphalt, and mixtures of all three, from which water drains from the surface and none seeps through to the base.

Porous Courts

Clay courts. It is estimated that approximately 75 per cent of all courts in the United States are made of some kind of clay. This is due chiefly to the low cost of construction, and that while raw clay varies in quality, and to some extent in color, good clay suitable for courts is available in most sections of the country.

Advantages. The surface can be kept smooth by drag brushing and rolling and when in good condition the rebound of the ball is seldom deflected. Clay surfaces are reasonably easy on the eyes and feet, balls discolor only slightly and wear fairly well. They will stand up well under continuous hard play.

Disadvantages. Clay dries slowly and is unplayable when even slightly wet. Many playing hours and days are lost because of rain. When very dry and hard, balls bounce too high for proper stroking and the effect of spin is considerably reduced. They require rolling and lining with white liquid (lime) at least every day and reconditioning every spring. They tend to become dusty and to soil clothes. Fabric tape should not be used for lining. Metal tape may be used but is not recommended because it deflects the bounce of the ball and when loose presents danger of tripping players.

Maintenance. Clay courts should be rolled and marked once or twice daily. The playing surface should be brushed free of loose sand and dirt, wet down each day after play, and rolled before play the following morning. Before sprinkling, all uneven spots should be smoothed and leveled and depressions filled with clay. An application twice a year of 300 to 400 pounds per court of flaked calcium chloride is recommended for clay, Har-Tru, and other composition porous courts. It is best applied after sundown. It should be spread evenly over the entire area. If fabric tape is used for lining it should be brushed to remove all calcium because the chemical tends to disintegrate the tape. Under most conditions the calcium will dissolve over night by absorbing moisture from the atmosphere. The next morning the court should be lightly watered and then brushed and rolled. If any calcium remains on the court in the morning the court should be well watered before brushing and rolling.

Tennis court layout for singles and doubles.

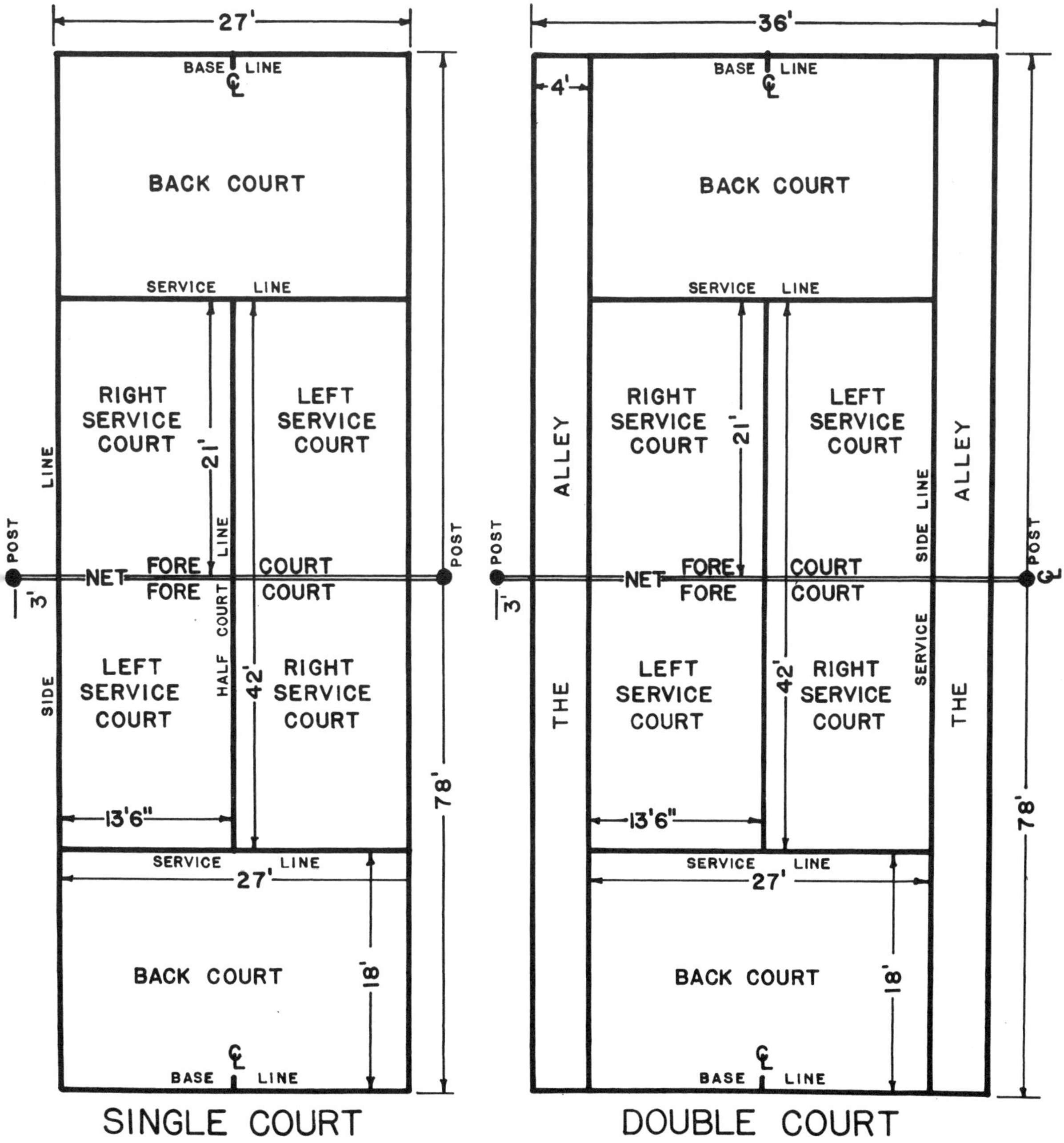

The first application should be made in early spring and the second during July or August.

Clay and grass courts are sometimes unplayable for an entire day or two after a heavy rain. However, "Fast Drying" surfaces have been developed that are playable within an hour or less after a hard rain, which gives them a considerable advantage over clay and grass in that respect.

Grass Courts

The advantages and disadvantages of grass courts have been covered at the beginning of this chapter. In summary, they make the best playing surface and the most difficult to maintain.

En-tout-cas Courts

These courts represent a composition material of crushed mineral laid on a clay base.

Advantages. Very fast drying, non-glare, easy on feet and leg muscles, bounce and action of ball probably nearer that of grass than any other surface. Balls wear well, lose little weight, and discolor very little.

Disadvantages. High installation cost and maintenance. They require heavy daily watering and much rolling. If played on morning and afternoon, they should be watered and rolled before each session of play.

Fast-Drying Courts

Courts may be built nearly level since the drainage is largely through the porous top surface to a cinder, ash, or crushed rock base. A dozen or more concerns build this type of court and each has its own brand or trade name, but in general all have many similar characteristics. All have a porous top surface made of pulverized materials mostly mineral of various kinds and all have most of the advantages of clay courts and few of the disadvantages.

Non-porous Courts

These include concrete, cement, asphalt, and mixtures of those materials. For construction detail and specification see Chapters 15 and 16 on Asphalt and Concrete Surfaces.

Advantages. Little or no maintenance is required, and no rolling. Can be played on the year round. Lines are painted and last indefinitely. Always accurate rebound. Cleanest of all courts. Playable one hour or less after heavy rain. May be finished in any color. Black, red, and green are the most popular. Because of absolutely true bounce players acquire great confidence in ground strokes and half volleys. Many of our greatest players learned to play on concrete courts. Among them are Budge, Kramer, Vines, McLoughlin, Johnston, Schroeder, Mako, and Doeg.

Disadvantages. Balls bounce too high. Surface has little resilience. Under a hot sun the surfaces absorb a great deal of heat and become hot underfoot. In freezing climates cracking and heaving (buckling) of asphalt and cement may occur if improperly laid. Grips feet too tightly—prevents sliding so that running and stopping are jarring and tiring. Severe on feet and leg muscles because of its stonelike hardness and rigidity. However, some companies build such courts with some resilience and "give" by introducing certain ingredients, such as cork and rubber, into the surface material.

Drainage of Non-porous Courts

There are three types of drainage for pervious courts:

From side line to side line
From end to end
From each end toward the net with a narrow gutter (4 inches, covered with a heavy metal grille) running across the court directly under the net and dropping in depth gradually from one side to the other to carry off the water.

The *first is recommended* particularly for porous courts. It gives neither player an advantage and does not impose a handicap on either. The rainfall flows a shorter distance than from end to end, and in case of porous courts, washes away less top dressing and reduces the possibility of gullies.

The *second is objectionable* because the water from the higher side flows onto the lower causing puddles to form near the base line. It delays drying, makes the lower court play slower for a longer period, and creates an inequality of playing conditions.

The *third* presents the same playing conditions for each contestant and makes for quicker drainage, but is objectionable from the playing standpoint because it reduces the height of the net by the fall from the base line to the net, making two surfaces in different planes whereas the entire playing surface should be in one plane.

The side to side method should generally be used also for non-porous surfaces but the problem of drainage is much less important for such courts.

CONSTRUCTION SUGGESTIONS

It is not possible to deal adequately with the many methods followed in court construction in a limited chapter. In planning to build a court the first step is to decide which of many types best suits your requirements and preferences and then consult some reliable concern which builds that type.

To be sure of building a satisfactory and durable court there must be proper *sub-grading*, adequate *sub-drainage* and a *cinder* or *crushed rock base*. Some builders prefer cinders, others crushed rock. Although it is somewhat more expensive, crushed limestone is preferred by some builders because cinders may disintegrate and compact, which will cause the surface to drop and clog subsurface drainage.

In leveling or excavating, care should be taken not to bury any turf, weeds, or vegetation of any sort. All vegetation should be removed before leveling and the roots of trees should be taken out as far as possible, and roots near the court should be cut back as much as possible to prevent their growing out under the court.

Proper leveling, particularly where filling is necessary, is very important for any type of court to guard against settling of parts of the surface. The most economical way of leveling is to fill in the lower section with soil taken from the higher section. Frequently it is possible to excavate just enough to fill in the lower area. To avoid settling, filling should be spread in layers a very few inches in thickness and each layer should be

Layout of one side of a tennis court.

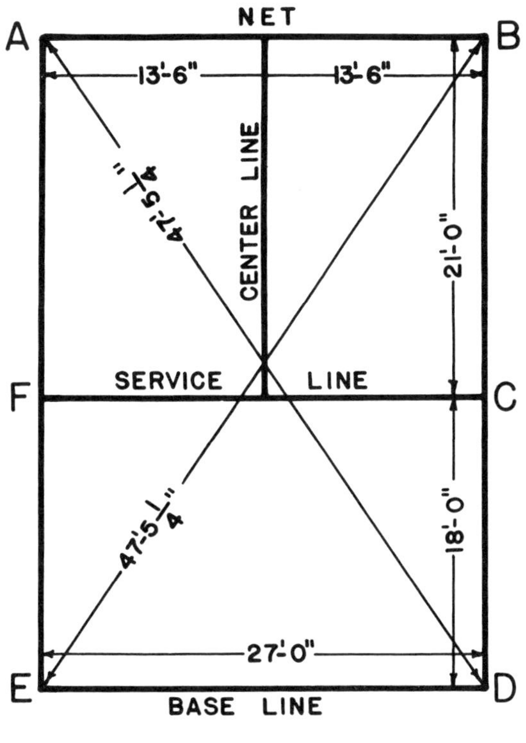

heavily rammed, preferably with a caterpillar tractor or very heavy roller. Watering the fill will help pack it hard and firm.

Great care should be taken in constructing the sub-base because the court will not be satisfactory unless it is properly constructed. If cinders are used for the base they should be clean mixed boiler cinders from any industrial plant. For one court, 120 feet in length by 60 feet in width, approximately 180 cubic yards are necessary for an adequate foundation. Before being laid, cinders should be screened to pass through a one-inch screen to get about 20 per cent of the bulk. These fine cinders should be set aside for use as the top layer. The bottom layer should be laid evenly and leveled to about 4 inches in thickness after rolling. To level and to keep a uniform thickness leveling pegs should be used, but should be withdrawn after they have served their purpose. For leveling, a heavy roller (three to four tons) should be used, and in dry weather the cinders should be well watered before rolling. The fine cinders should then be laid down one inch thick by the use of screed strips and a straight-edge. The fine layer of cinders should be rolled not more than twice as it is not advisable to get this layer too firm and solid because it may affect the affinity between the surface material and the fine cinders. It will help a good union between the surface and the layer of fine cinders if, immediately before laying, the surface cinders are raked lightly so that they will be loosened slightly. The base should be confined by adequate curbing of treated timber, brick, or concrete.

Steel net posts should be installed and set 3 feet outside the side lines in concrete bases and made removable by using "sleeves." Wooden posts are not recommended but if used should be locust or oak, treated with a preservative and deeply and firmly embedded.

It will pay to install substantial fencing of heavy guage galvanized wire (chain link is preferred) of not more than 2 inch diamond mesh, at least 12 feet high and a minimum of 20 feet behind the baselines. The rear fences should extend about 10 feet beyond the side lines. One side of a singles court should be entirely closed. An opening on the other side may be left for spectators. When built in batteries there should be no fencing between courts. Fencing should be attached on the inside of the posts. If placed on the outside of the posts, the balls will bounce in all directions on hitting a post.

Location. The court should have shelter, particularly from prevailing winds, and have the same background at each end—preferably green in color. *Background of open sky-line should be avoided.* There should be no paths or roads at either end or any other condition that permits movement. Shadows should be avoided as much as possible. Choose a nearly flat well drained area with room for placing additional courts. Avoid large trees because roots will work under the surface and leaves are a nuisance in the fall and shadows an ever present annoyance.

COST

The cost of courts listed below does not include grading and fencing, and, naturally, will vary according to local labor costs. The cost will also vary, to some extent, in different parts of the country. Nevertheless, the following table gives the approximate cost of various types of courts. In referring to the table it should be kept in mind that a single court comprises about 800 square yards, while in a battery of two or more the average is about 600 to 750 square yards per court.

Type of Surface	*Cost per Square Yard*
Clay	\$1.25 to \$2.00
Quick drying composition—such as Har-Tru	\$3.25 to \$4.50
All weather—such as Laykold	\$3.00 to \$4.75
All weather—such as Grasstex or Cork-Turf	\$3.75 to \$5.50
Concrete	\$3.00 to \$5.00
Grass	\$6.00 and up

For much of the technical information appearing in this chapter the authors are indebted to the following master court builders, all nationally known and bearing a high reputation in the field. The types of court each specializes in and approximate costs are given.

American Bitumuls & Asphalt Co., 200 Bush Street, San Francisco 4, California

"Laykold" and "Grasstex" in black, red, and green, non-porous. \$3.00 to \$4.00 per square yard

W. A. Burnham Company, 1608 Elman Street, Houston 19, Texas

- Laykold, non-porous, $3.50 to $4.00 per square yard
- Grasstex, non-porous, $4.40 to $5.00 per square yard
- Limestone, non-porous, about $2000
  In black, red, or green colors

David Sedgwick Durant, Inc., Oblong Road, Williamstown, Massachusetts

- Asphaltic (Red or green), non-porous, cost about $2500
- Tuff-Turf (Red or green), non-porous, cost about $2700
- Clay, porous, cost about $1400
- Clay with composition surface, porous, cost about $1600

F. C. Feise Co., Narberth, Pennsylvania

- Corkturf, green composition, non-porous, cost $4000 to $5500
- Teniflex, green composition, non-porous, cost $3250 to $4250
- Teniko Royal, green composition, porous, cost $3000 to $4000
- Teniko Commander, clay mixture, porous, cost $1200 to $2500

Har-Tru Corporation, 100 East 42nd Street, New York 17, N.Y.

- Har-Tru, fast drying composition courts, porous, cost $3000 to $7000

Gene Mako Tennis Court Construction, 2601 Waverly Drive, Los Angeles 39, California

- Concrete courts, non-porous (Cost about same as high grade composition courts)
  Black, brown, red-brown, green

The Markath Trading Co., P.O. Box 102, Ryder Station, Brooklyn 34, N.Y.

- En-Tout-Cas, porous, cost about $4000

Perma-Green Tennis Court Co., 9 Crescent Beach Drive, Huntington 12, N.Y.

- Grasstex, non-porous, cost about $4000 including fencing
- Perma-Green, fast drying composition courts, porous, cost about $2900

C. R. Peterson Construction Co., 5659 No. Newark Avenue, Chicago 31, Illinois

- Peteco Allweather. Non-porous Emulsion Court, green and red, cost about $3400
- Peteco Lay-True Green. Porous, fast drying, cost about $3000

Tennis Courts, Inc., 101 Park Avenue, New York 17, N.Y.

- Fast Drying composition courts, porous, all weather with permanent lining tapes. Cost about $4000
- Asphaltic construction non-porous courts (red or green), lines painted, cost about $5000

Other Tennis Court Builders of Good Reputation

Dixico, Box 11, College Park, Georgia

Green-Lawn Tennis Court Co., Golf Lane, Huntington 5, N.Y.

M. R. Lane & Sons, Ardmore, Pennsylvania

Rubien Construction Co., Westfield, New Jersey

Sim Cote Products Co., Granville, N.Y.

Shrainka Construction Company, 7173 Delmar Boulevard, St. Louis 5, Missouri.

CHAPTER 19

GOLF FACILITIES[1]

National Golf Foundation, Inc., Rex McMorris

IDEALLY, THE GOLF COURSE SHOULD BE DE-signed and constructed so that no major alterations will ever be required. However, even the greatest of golf courses have been revised and the organizers of a new golfing enterprise need not expect that their course will be the one in the world that will not eventually need some changes.

It is always advisable to engage the services of a competent golf course architect. Even if funds do not permit initial construction of the course so that it will be completed with all the trapping of a finished course, the qualified architect's plan will provide for later installation of traps as money is available and the course will develop according to a wise plan instead of being a rather expensive and unsatisfactory exhibit of inexpert experiments.

However, there are hundreds of instances where the initial investment must be kept at the absolute minimum and architect's services, regardless of moderate cost, cannot be used. Hence, the material in this chapter is primarily for the guidance of those who have to go at the course job with their own brains and muscle.

Golf architectural authorities recognize that Nature is the best golf architect. The famed courses of Scotland that are fundamentally the same today as they were almost a century ago are proof that small town club organizers can do a great job if they are fortunate in selecting, or having available, sites that fit golf. Natural hazards make the most interesting and the most easily and cheaply maintained hazards. The genius of the golf architect often shines brightest in his use of natural features of terrain in providing shot problems.

But in many instances the ground is flat and without trees. The problem then is to provide a layout that will call for every sort of shot that the best courses demand. The variety is provided, as far as possible, by judicious variation in the length of holes.

Such tremendous advances have been made in mechanical moving of earth in the past 10 years that at even the flattest of sites not

[1] This chapter on Golf Facilities has been adapted from the booklets "*Planning and Building the Golf Course*" and "*Golf Operators Handbook*" with the permission of the National Golf Foundation, Inc., 407 S. Dearborn St., Chicago 5, Illinois.

Illustration: Teeing off
Photo by Gates Priest

much money is required to move enough soil to elevate a green, taking the earth from locations where grassy hollows or areas for sand traps are needed.

Selection of Course Site

The golf architect usually considers a number of prospective sites for a course and selects the one that can be converted into a good course at minimum construction cost and maintained properly at minimum expense. By considering several sites the club organizers place themselves in a good trading position.

Size of property is important. Fifty acres for a nine-hole course and 110 acres for 18 holes is generally considered the minimum. Even areas this large involve risk of injury of players playing parallel holes. Eighty acres for a nine-hole course and 160 for 18 holes is about right for the better courses. Irregularly-shaped plots often afford opportunities for the most interesting course design.

Land should not be too rugged. A gently rolling area with some trees is preferable. Land that is too hilly is tiring on players, usually necessitates too many blind shots, and is more costly to keep well turfed.

The course should have a practice fairway area close to the clubhouse. Some public and daily fee courses have installed practice ranges, lighted for night use, and adjoining their courses on highways. From these ranges they get considerable income and develop golfers for day play on the courses.

The usual experience of the golf club in leasing land with an option to buy is to find that the installation of a golf course has increased the value of the land enough to make the option an excellent investment when it is exercised.

When finances permit and the community's prospects warrant, it is also well to tie up enough land so property bordering the course may be sold for residential sites, and the proceeds used to pay off the club's loans. Frequently reference to this increase in value of surrounding property, because of the establishment of a golf club, is so attractive to the landowner that enough property exclusively for course use becomes available at a bargain price. The owner correctly figures that the net value of his entire holding is not only increased by the location of the golf course, but that his property surrounding the course is made more readily saleable.

Accessibility

Unless absolutely unavoidable, a golf course should not be off the beaten track. Location is especially important in the case of a small town course that plans to apply the green fees from transients to meet maintenance costs. Locate your course along the main highway into town. All other things being equal, design the course so that one or two holes parallel the highway; it is good advertising.

Another reason for not locating the course in an out-of-the-way spot is that the club should have good transportation for the members. It should be as near to town as possible, cost of land taken into consideration, and the main highway from town to the club should be one that is kept in good condition and is not merely a country lane, unpaved, and liable to become impassable with every heavy rain.

Soil Factors

Condition of the soil is extremely important because in the final analysis the better the stand of turf raised on fairways and greens, the more satisfactory and more popular will be the course. The ideal golf course soil is a sandy loam. It is not impossible but is expensive to grow a good stand of grass on a heavy clay. Be sure to take the character of the soil into consideration when choosing the site.

Soil analysis of areas of the golf course site will be made at low cost by state agricultural departments or county agents. Considerable helpful information can be supplied by state agricultural experiment stations and county agents to help determine the most desirable site from the viewpoint of the possibility of good golf turf development and in recommending the grass seeding, growing, and maintenance program.

Past Use

Closely tied in with the above is the use to which the land has been put in the past. Is

the plot a run-down farm where a large part of the plant-food has been removed from the soil, or is it rich in the elements that will be necessary for successful cultivation of turf? Has the land lain idle for many years, or has it been intensively cultivated by its farmer owner without his returning plant-food to the soil?

The selection of property that has been well kept up as pasture land is highly advisable. Much money is saved in putting the course into excellent condition. For instance, one southern Ohio club built its course on property that had been in blue grass for about 30 years and for that reason its fairways cost practically nothing. Frequently the scenic attractions of a site are such that to the susceptible and uninformed organizers of a golf club, they totally outweigh soil conditions. A happy balance should be maintained between both factors. Pick a site that will offer no serious handicaps to the attempts of the club to grow a stand of grass and maintain it thereafter.

Power and Water Availability

In some instances electric power and water supply are clear out of the picture and the club has to get along without water for its

Above: Golfing green.

Below: Well-laid out fairway.

Photo by *Golfdom*, the Business Journal of Golf

Photo from National Golf Foundation

Above: An open green.

A well-protected green.

Photo from National Golf Foundation

Water is essential for good fairways.

Photo from Buckner Manufacturing Company

greens, tees, or fairways. Quite a few clubs in the arid sections of the country have done that and have had very enjoyable golf.

But if you can possibly get water and electric power without prohibitive expense, by all means select a site where these items are available.

How Much Clearing

Consider next the amount of clearing that will have to be done in building the course. Will it be necessary to move many trees or grub out many stumps? Will it be an expensive proposition removing stones from the soil? Are there large swamp areas that will have to be filled in or drained? Do not misunderstand the statement above relative to clearing out trees. A golf course should, if possible, have patches of woodlands, as trees offer one of the best natural hazards if properly placed with reference to the course. However, it is an expensive matter to remove large growing trees and the site selected should not have too many of these in those portions of the plot that will be fairways in the final picture.

Natural Golf Features

The last consideration in selecting the site is whether or not it possesses natural golf features.

This may seem to the uninitiated to be the first and most important thing to look for, but, as a matter of fact, natural golf features, while extremely desirable, are not nearly as important as the character of the soil and site location.

Rolling terrain, creek valleys, woodlands, ravines, ponds, and the like, of course, make the job of designing an interesting course just so much easier, but all of these features or substitutes for them can be secured with artificial hazards. For this reason the presence or absence of natural golf features is perhaps less important than any of the factors that have been mentioned above.

How to Design a Golf Course

Once the promoters of the golf course have perfected their organization plans, secured sufficient members to assure proper financing of the cost of construction, and definitely decided on the tract of land on which the course is to be built, they should secure an accurate map of the property. An aerial survey of the property can be arranged with the county agent. A topographical map, also, is very helpful as it will help determine what surface features may have to be removed and which ones may serve as interesting and judicious hazards.

On the maps architects usually make a number of preliminary layouts before they decide on the final plan for a course. It is also a good procedure to be followed by the club organizers who are trying to get along without an architect.

Location of the clubhouse, entrance drive, parking spaces, tennis courts, swimming pools, golf practice and lesson tees, fairways and traps, and practice greens, is another job that requires a great deal of thought. Few of the smaller clubs have such an array of facilities around the clubhouse and in such cases an architect's services are required. By locating its practice green and parking space properly, the small club can add to its attractiveness and convenience.

The best location for the clubhouse generally is one that is convenient to, but removed from, the highway. Road construction and maintenance costs must be kept in mind when locating the clubhouse.

Often the clubhouse site is a prominent hilltop, although elderly golfers may bemoan this choice because it means that the finishing hole of the course must of necessity be uphill; they do not like a heavy climb at the end of a strenuous day of golf. Generally, a convenient and practical site can be found at a less elevated spot.

Mapping the Course

Authorities are well agreed on what makes the "ideal" nine-hole course in the matter of distance. All agree that such a course should measure over 3,000 yards, preferably around 3,200 yards. These authorities likewise agree that the par of the course should be 35, 36, or 37, with 35 the most usual. Just how should these 3,200 yards be apportioned among the nine holes? Most experts suggest two par-3 holes, two par-5 holes, the remaining five holes to be par-4's. Par-6 holes should be avoided.

The two par-3 holes, should, of course, vary, for obvious reasons, in length; the shorter one should measure 130 to 160 yards, thus requiring an exacting four or five-iron shot from the tee; the other short hole should have the green a full long iron or wood shot away, say 180 yards or more.

The par-5 holes should also vary in length, one being on the short side for a par-5 (about 480 yards) and the other 520 to 550 yards. Both types of par-5 holes call for two full wood shots and well hit iron approach shots.

Architect Robert Bruce Harris points out that it is advisable to provide a mixture of pars. He suggests a par order of 4—5—4—3—4—5—4—3—4 (36) as one that will be found highly satisfactory.

Under United States Golf Association regulations, the minimum length of a par-4 hole is 251 yards and throughout the country many courses have holes of this length. Yet, only in rare instances where some physical feature redeems the lack of distance do these holes rate as even of average interest. They are too short; after the drive nothing remains but an easy chip-shot or run-up; there is no "kick" to playing so short a hole. The same objection attaches itself to par-4 holes even as long as 350 yards, where physical peculiarities are lacking. This distance, from 251 to 350 yards, is known among golf architects as "No Man's Land," a zone to be avoided if the course is to be genuinely popular with golfers.

Tips on Course Planning

Certain standard practices should be observed in making a course layout, among which the important ones are:

1. The distance between the green of one hole and the tee of the next should never be more than 75 yards, and a distance of 20 to 30 yards is recommended. Trees should not be closer than 20 yards to a green to avoid screening an approaching golf ball.

2. The first tee and the ninth green of the course should be located immediately adjacent to the clubhouse. If it is practical without sacrificing other factors, bring the green of the sixth hole also near to the clubhouse. This is a feature appreciated by the golfer with only an hour to devote to his game, as six holes can be comfortably played in that time and at the finish of his available time he is once more back at the clubhouse.

3. As far as is practical, no holes should be laid out in an east to west direction. The reason for this is that the maximum volume of play on any golf course is in the afternoon and a player finds it disagreeable to follow the ball's flight into the setting sun. If an east-west hole is unavoidable, locate it among the first two or three holes of the layout so that a player will strike it as early in his round as possible. Northwest direction of holes is particularly bad.

4. The first hole of the course should be a relatively easy par-4 hole of approximately 380 to 400 yards in length. It should be comparatively free of hazards or heavy rough where a ball might be lost, and should have no features that will delay the player. The obvious reason is to get the golfers started off on their game as expeditiously as possible.

5. Generally speaking, the holes should grow increasingly difficult to play as the round proceeds. It takes a golfer about three holes to get well warmed up, and asking him to execute difficult shots while he is still "cold" is not a demand that he will appreciate.

6. Whenever practical, greens should be plainly visible, and the location of sand traps and other hazards obviously apparent from the approach area, which is that portion of the fairway extending tee-ward for approximately 125 yards from the green.

7. Generally speaking, fairways sloping directly up or down a hillside are bad for several reasons: (a) steep sloping fairways make the playing of the shot by the majority of players a matter of luck rather than skill; (b) the up-and-down climb is fatiguing to the golfer; (c) turf is difficult to maintain on such an area.

8. If there are ravines or abrupt creek valleys on the property, a splendid short golf hole consists of a tee located on one edge of the ravine with the green on the other,

a suitable number of yards down or up the ravine. This calls for perfect control in carrying the ravine, permits the golfer to "bite off" as much of the ravine as he thinks he can carry, and does not unduly penalize the beginner, who can play straight across the ravine and then progress green-ward on the other side.

9. The par-3 holes should be arranged so that the first of the two is not earlier in the round than the third hole and the other one is not later than the eighth hole. Par-3 holes should not be consecutive.

The old days of golf courses that punished the shortcomings of the dub so severely that the fun was taken from the round have passed, and into extinction along with this penal design are going unnatural looking knobby bunkers, geometrically designed traps and tiny, miserably conditioned tees. Trees, slopes, creeks, lakes, and other natural details provide hazards enough for the average well designed small town course. If sand traps around the greens can be well maintained, their use provides the course with a feature that is of metropolitan course character. But if the construction or maintenance cost rules out such traps, turfed hollows in which the grass is allowed to grow several inches high and of a design that fits in the natural surroundings will do well.

Robert Trent Jones, golf architect, sets forth points that are generally agreed on by members of the American Society of Golf Course Architects. We quote him extensively here:

The backbone holes of the modern golf course are the two-shotters, of 400 yards or over. The length of the two-shot hole offers plenty of opportunity to develop good strategy. Unfortunately, these holes are a little long for the average golfer to be able to reach in two, but this can be remedied by having sets of alternate tees.

The short holes should be kept under 200 yards in length so that every golfer has an opportunity to reach the green with a good shot and thereby obtain his par or birdie. These holes should be attractive and tantalizing in appearance with the greens designed so that they will become extremely formidable or relatively easy depending upon the position of the pin and the angle of the tee in use.

There should be as little walking as possible between greens and tees, but under certain circumstances it is more expedient to break this rule than to adhere to it. For often, where the property is rugged in type, a longer walk between the green and the tee makes it possible to obtain a good golf hole rather than a poor one.

The holes should be so different in length, character, and architectural type, that there is no feeling of duplication.

The three types of golf architecture—penal, strategic, and heroic—should be used in good proportion.

In penal type construction, the traps guard the greens in bottleneck or island fashion. Here the average golfer must either hit the shot accurately, or choose a club to play short in order to avoid the trouble which he would ordinarily find at his normal range. One or two holes of this type are usually sufficient in the composition of an 18-hole golf course, and should be the "short" or "drive-and-pitch" holes.

The strategic type utilizes fewer traps, adroitly placed, so that any golfer can hit with his full power but must place his shots to obtain the most favorable results. The modern golf courses are designed with about 50 per cent of the holes strategic in type. This architecture adapts itself best to holes of 400 yards or over, the par-4 holes.

The heroic is a blend of strategic and penal design. The traps or natural hazards, such as creeks, rivers, and lakes, are placed on the diagonal so that the player can bite off as much as he feels he can chew. The more he is able to carry, the more advantageous will he find his position for the next shot. This type of architecture is adaptable to all length holes, and should be utilized on 30 to 50 per cent of the holes of the course.

There should be no blind shots for approaches, and blind shots from the tee should be kept to a minimum.

There should be a sufficient number of heroic carries from the tee, but the routing should be so arranged that the player, with the loss of a stroke, should always have an alternate route to the green.

The character of the course should be so designed that during one round every club in the bag should be used.

No stereotype design can be used, but the principles of the design have to be applied in accordance with the natural terrain and the location of the proposed green.

On level or flat land a nine-hole course of 3100-3400 yards can be laid out in approximately 50 acres but it will be cramped. An 18 hole course of 6200-6500 yards or more would require at least 110 acres. This is a minimum, making the routing of the course extremely tight. Gently rolling land requires approximately 60 acres for 9 holes and 120 acres for 18. Hilly or rugged land will require considerably more because of the waste land where the contours are severe; at least 70 acres will be needed for 9 holes and 140-180 acres for 18 holes.

Before starting the routing of the course all the natural green and tee sites on the property should be examined, and as many of these as possible incorporated in the routing of the course. Natural sites should not be passed over in routing the course in order to obtain a hole of predetermined length, unless the hole would fall within the undesirable length of 250 to 350 yards.

The minimum length for a standard 18-hole golf course is 6200 yards. A good average is 6500 yards, and championship length is 6700-6900 yards. The short holes should range from 130-200 yards (par-3) and there are generally four of these holes, but there may be five. Par-4 holes should range from 350 to 450 yards, and there are generally ten of these. Par-5 holes should range from 450 to 550 yards and there are generally four of these.

The length of the hole will be determined by the slope of the terrain and the direction of play, the natural features from tee to green and at the green site, and the desire to obtain a variety of lengths throughout the 18 holes.

Fairway width generally is about 60 yards, but will vary depending upon the type of players expected to play the course, and the strategy of the play of the hole. A yardstick of fairway widths is as follows: 75-120 yards from the tee the fairway will be 40 yards wide; 120-180 yards from the tee the width will be 50 yards; 180-220 yards from the tee the width will be 60-70 yards.

The fairways can then narrow again if desired to the next landing area if the hole is long; that is in the area from 330-440 yards.

The green sizes will vary from 5,000 to 8,000 square feet depending upon the length of the hole and the length of the shot called for. The shape of the green will depend upon the strategy of the design, the location and size of the traps, and the length of the shot playing to it.

Where the slope of a green is from front to back, the slope should not be more than five per cent, unless there is a break in the slope by

Golf course lighted for night play.

Photo by Fred Kuehn Studios, Chicago

a depression. If the depression is not too deep, the slopes of the depression can go from 10 to 15 per cent.

The slopes on the approach of a plateaued green can run as high as 20 per cent.

Mounds and slopes running from the surface of the green to the sides or back can run up to 20 per cent.

The slopes of the traps in front or on the sides playing toward the green will run from 30 to 40 per cent.

At the entrance of the traps the slopes should not be over 25 per cent so that the golfer's backswing can be taken with a full, clean stroke.

Golf Course Costs

The cost of golf courses vary so much that to give a flat figure for a 9 to 18 hole golf course that could be applied to any given piece of property would be misleading. On the flat plain country of the midwest with very few trees or drainage problems it would actually be possible for a few public spirited farmers with tractors and other men and boys willing to contribute their time, to develop a golf course for the actual cost of the land and materials such as seed, fertilizer, water pipe and pump, sprinklers, etc. However, such a case is the exception instead of the rule.

There are four factors which determine more than anything else the wide range which one gets when trying to gather from all sources how much a golf course should cost. These are (1) the cost of land; (2) the natural assets and liabilities of the land chosen; (3) the labor and equipment costs in the area; and (4) the type of design.

If a course has to be completely carved out of woods, the costs are naturally higher. If the course is only partly wooded the relationship of the open and wooded areas in the design would have a bearing on the costs. Extensive drainage due to heavy soils would increase normal costs. In general, woods and drainage are to some extent part of every golf course. Land heavily imbedded with or having tremendous outcropping of rock that would require blasting and covering with topsoil is the one factor that makes golf course costs almost prohibitive. It is to be expected that any committee looking for land upon which to develop a golf course would shun such property unless it was the one and only available area in a generally rocky territory.

So important is the choice of land in the development of a good golf course and the cost of such a course that no given piece of property should finally be determined upon until a golf architect has been consulted and given a choice of sites if such a situation is possible.

Labor costs vary so much, and are such a large part of any construction, that even in a normally good situation the cost of construction of a golf course can be twice as much in one area as in another under similar topographical conditions. For instance, in one area and at the same time labor might require paying the men only when they work, in another area the labor might be higher per hour with time and a half for overtime over 40 hours, plus an allowance of from two to four hours on rainy days. The same relative variations apply to rental of equipment in different parts of the country.

One would expect under ideal conditions that the type of design would not be a prime factor in determining costs. Such, however, is not the case. Five different people would produce five different designs for any given piece of property. Therefore, the effective use of the hills and valleys and natural green and tee sites of one designer over another would not only have a bearing on the character of the course but would, also, have a bearing on the cost of the course. Building up artificial features where natural features exist is something that is normally done by the inexperienced designer and not by the competent architect. It is more than likely that the difference in the relative costs of the inexperienced from the experienced designer would be more than compensated for by the savings in the experienced designer's ability to utilize all the natural features to the fullest extent.

Construction and Construction Equipment

Hard and fast rules on how to construct a golf course cannot be given for an unknown site. The best and most efficient method at the site will have to be used, the proportion of mechanical equipment and hand labor to be used at each job will depend upon the cost and supply of each in that particualr area at that particular time. One cardinal rule, however, is that where construction is done on topsoil that is good, always remove the topsoil outside of the area of construction before shaping the particular feature that is to be designed. After the shaping has been done the topsoil is then replaced and mixed with sand or humus to improve the physical condition. Fertilizer is applied and the area is then seeded and rolled.

As to the type of seed that is to be used, in temperate climates the most popular type of seed for putting greens is bent grass, of which there are many acceptable types. In the south a grass of the Bermuda type should be used. Rye grass can be used as a winter cover on top of the Bermuda (topsoiling the area before seeding) making a very good winter putting surface. The rye dies out when the sun gets hot again, at which time the Bermuda replaces it by starting its season's growth.

Staking Out the Course

After the design of the course is determined and accurately mapped, the work of construction begins. If changes in design are to be made, they should be made in the plans and not as construction work progresses or the job will be unduly delayed.

Tees and greens should be staked out according to their locations on the map. After these areas are outlined with stakes, other stakes should be driven to indicate the fairway zone between the tee and the green. Within this zone the grass will be kept close-cropped and in as good playing condition as possible. Outside it is the rough where the grass is permitted to grow longer and act as a temporary obstruction to the ball that has wandered off the straight line of flight. As a general rule, fairways should average from 120 to 210 feet in width.

Do not get the impression from the above that a fairway necessarily extends in a beeline from tee to green. The most popular holes on a golf course are the "dog-leg" holes with a distinct elbow bend to the fairway about 200 yards out from the tee. Even on a short hole it is a good idea to place the fairway to one side of a direct line to the green, thus leaving rough and possibly a sand trap or similar hazard over which the expert player, attempting to drive the green from the tee, must carry. The less expert golfer, who does not feel equal to this, can play down the fairway and then on to the green with a second shot. The nervy player, who tries but fails, pays the price in strokes lost recovering from the hazard; should he succeed, he reaps a rich reward of satisfaction and has gained a stroke.

The best way to stake out a fairway is to plan it on a large sheet of paper. Draw a base line to run up the center of the fairway; point off every 50 feet on this base line and measure from these points at right angles to the edge of the fairway. Having planned the hole definitely on paper, do the same thing on the ground, setting a stake at each of the 50-foot points and measuring from these to find the limits of the fairway.

Much helpful information on preparing the soil for seeding, selection of grass seed for greens, fairways, tees and rough, seeding, and fertilizing can be secured from state agricultural experimental stations; greenkeepers and professionals at courses in the general area in which the new course is to be constructed; from the United States Golf Association, Green Section, Beltsville, Maryland; suppliers of golf course materials; the golf course maintenance magazines and greenkeeper regional organization meetings; and from short courses at state colleges.

The practical advice and recommendations of a successful greenkeeper at a well maintained course not far away will be very valuable and worth far more than the moderate fee and expenses the greenkeeper will ask for his services.

CONSTRUCTION OF GREENS

Construction and care of the greens will determine, next to the design, the quality of any golf course.

On the following pages we quote extensively from Dr. O. J. Noer, a noted authority on green construction and maintenance.

"The turf on a well kept putting green is as near perfect as man can produce. Skill is needed to obtain and keep it that way. Success depends upon selecting a grass adapted to the local climate and proper maintenance practices.

Soil for Greens

"Soil is not just so much dirt, but consists of solid, liquid and gaseous matter. It is half solid by volume with about 70 to 80 per cent minerals which is a mixture of sand, silt and clay particles. The other 20 to 30 per cent is organic matter or humus. The non-solid half, or the voids between the particles, is half water and half air. Stated another way, a cubic foot of soil should contain one half cubic foot of solid matter, one quarter cubic foot of water and one quarter cubic foot of air. Such a soil is well ventilated, and an ideal medium for the growth of grass, or any other crop.

"The subsoil need not have organic matter,

but it should be well ventilated to facilitate drainage, and speed the removal of surplus gravitational water. A system of tile drains should be installed in all greens having a subsoil which does not meet these specifications.

"A putting green is more than a place to grow grass. The surface must have enough resilience to hold the ball of a pitched shot, and, yet be firm enough to have billiard table trueness. Over-watering is one way to make a grass hold a pitched ball. The better way is to have a good soil structure. The surface will have sufficient resilience to hold the ball, irrespective of its moisture content. Then it will not be necessary to resort to the bad practice of over-watering.

"The surface soil on a putting green should not be less than 4 to 8 inches deep. A medium sandy loam containing 20 to 30 per cent organic matter, but no more, is best. This soil has enough sand, with particles varying in size from coarse to fine, and has the right amount of silt and clay to impart the desirable qualities these colloidal substances possess. They give the soil body, enable it to retain and release available plant nutrients, and enhance the water-holding capacity. Too much silt or clay makes for excessive compaction due to heavy traffic, the puddling effect of frequent watering, and the compressing effect caused by constant mowing. Compaction deprives the soil of air, and then the root system becomes shallow because feeder roots breathe. They must have oxygen to live, otherwise they perish.

"The presence of some organic matter in the surface soil is essential to make it slightly resilient and perform other functions connected with growth. It is the energy food for beneficial soil micro-organisms. As the organic matter undergoes decay by them carbonic acid is generated. It is the principal solvent in the soil solution and is responsible for the liberation of the mineral soil nutrients. Organic matter increases water-holding capacity and imparts other benefits of its colloidal nature.

"Too much organic matter is bad from the standpoint of play and maintenance. When overdone, greens become so soft that they foot mark badly. Humus or peat has a high water-holding capacity and may retain 200 to over 300 per cent moisture. Both tend to resist wetting when dry. Greens with more than 30 per cent by volume of organic matter become too wet during rainy weather, and dry out too slowly afterwards. Should they ever become a little too dry it is hard to get water back into them.

Mixing Soil for New Greens

"The topsoil for a new green can be mixed on the green with a roto-tiller, or an agricultural disc. The best procedure is to mix the soil and sand first and then incorporate the peat or other organic material. In practice the soil is spread over the finished subgrade and covered with the proper amount of sand. After they are well mixed the peat is spread and worked in. A good grade of reed or sedge peat should be used. Thorough mixing of thick layers is impossible. The best way is to spread and mix half the amount and then the other half. There is a trick to obtaining a satisfactory mixture with a farm disc. It must pass straight across the green and all turns must be made off the green. Sand or peat pockets develop when the disc turns on the green, or is operated in a circular path.

"The other method is to mix soil, sand and peat in the proper proportions and spread the mixture on the green to the desired thickness. Mixing is done with a Royer or a Wichita grinder.

Tight Subsoil Needs Fine Gravel

"The soil at hand is used to make the sub-grade or elevated greens. It may be heavy in character and rather impervious to water. Working a 3 to 4 inch layer of pebbly fine gravel into the sub-grade before adding top soil will make the subsoil more open and permeable to air and water.

Drainage Within the Soil

"A film of capillary water surrounding the soil particles is the reservoir from which grass satisfies its water requirements. Any other water fills the void between the particles and occupies space which should contain air. This is gravitational water which should not stay in the soil for any length of time. It should pass down rapidly, and will do so provided the subsoil has the many fine passage ways which are present in a well drained soil.

Tile Drains

"A system of tile drains is required when natural drainage is inadequate. The herring-bone system of design is the only satisfactory one where tile is badly needed. It resembles a tree in outline. The main tile line represents the trunk of the tree; the laterals correspond to the branches. The main should follow the direction of the general slope, and should bisect

Left: ***A rubber practice tee.*** **Right:** ***A brush practice tee.***

the green. The lateral lines should make a 45 degree angle with the main line and should be spaced not more than 10 to 20 feet apart. The trenches should be 18 to 30 inches deep and should be back-filled with pea gravel, or similar coarse material, to within 6 to 8 inches of the surface. A three or four inch tile is large enough for the lateral lines, and the four or six inch size is satisfactory for the main. A good quality of burnt clay tile is generally used. Cement tile is satisfactory in some sections.

Drainage of Greens on Hillsides

"The soil underneath greens situated alongside, or at the base, of a hill is often saturated with seepage water. The water comes from the higher ground and flows under pressure. Saturation occurs mostly in spring when the ground everywhere is full of water. It may occur at other times in soggy spots fed by underground springs. The turf becomes thin or it may be killed completely in late winter or early spring. A deep trench located between the hillside and the green is needed to intercept the seepage water which flows under pressure. A line of tile is placed on the bottom of the trench, and then it is back-filled with gravel right up to the top. This is the secret of success. Without this trap the water flows over the top of the tile and into the green. The gravel conducts the water down to the tile.

Surface Drainage

"The important role of surface drainage is overlooked by many. They fail to realize that surface run-off is the quickest way to remove water. A well contoured green with good under drainage never stays wet very long.

"A green raised slightly at the center and sloping away on all sides would have the best surface drainage. A course with every green like that would lack character. Yet, many greens slope from back to front. The back part dries first and surface run-off from it keeps the front of the green wet long afterwards. Traffic concentrates on the front so it should dry first.

"Every green should be shaped so the surface slopes in two or more directions. Sloping in three directions is preferable to two. It will insure more rapid and, hence, better surface drainage. Localized low spots which hold casual water should be removed whenever they develop as a result of settling.

Air Drainage

"The movement of air across the surface of the green is very beneficial in hot weather. It tends to hold temperatures in check and to prevent dew formation. The grass stays healthier and disease is less formidable.

"A dense growth of trees and underbrush around the sides and back of a green stops air circulation even though the green faces the direction of the prevailing wind. The trees and undergrowth act as a barrier. Summer breezes pass over the top of them and leave a dead spot on the green. This happens to greens located on hills as well as those in valleys.

"The underbrush should be removed, and some trees, also, if necessary, to provide air passage through the barrier. When prevailing winds come from the side an open lane can be cut through the trees to make an air passage-

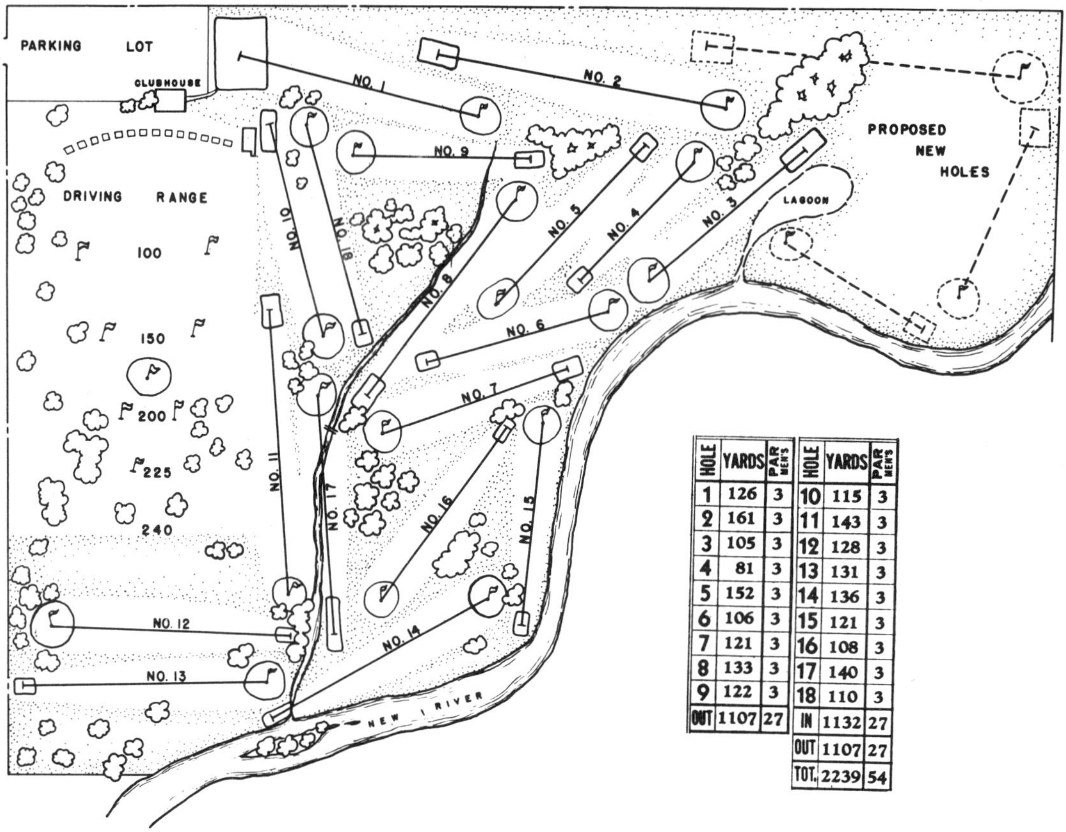

HOLE	YARDS	PAR MEN'S	HOLE	YARDS	PAR MEN'S
1	126	3	10	115	3
2	161	3	11	143	3
3	105	3	12	128	3
4	81	3	13	131	3
5	152	3	14	136	3
6	106	3	15	121	3
7	121	3	16	108	3
8	133	3	17	140	3
9	122	3	18	110	3
OUT	1107	27	IN	1132	27
			OUT	1107	27
			TOT.	2239	54

Typical layout of a par-3 course.

way without detracting from the beauty of the green and its surroundings."

Sand Green Construction Methods

Where lack of water or other factors prohibit the maintenance of grass greens on the right sort of a basis, the course builders might as well reconcile themselves to installing sand greens made along the right lines. In a number of instances in the south and southwest, especially in the southwest, sand greens are about the only possible greens for small town clubs. An interesting combination sand-and-grass green has been installed at some southern courses, the sand part of the green being a circle of about 20 feet in diameter and the sand surface even with that of the surrounding Bermuda grass.

Very satisfactory sand greens are those having at least 4 inches of clay base and having a top of sand (baked in oil) of about 2 inches. Oil drained from crankcases can be bought at a low price and makes a good oil but washes from the sand unless burned beforehand in a furnace or on a large sheet-iron pan.

A medium coarse sand is advised. A dusty, powdery sand makes a slow putting surface, leaving a track of the ball. Coarser sand will handle pitch-shots and putted ball better.

Other greens have an asphalt base and a coating of about one inch of fairly coarse sand, treated with crude mineral oil. The sand is sifted to remove any small pebbles, treated with oil, worked thoroughly and then applied. The green is swept with a coarse fiber broom, using a circular motion.

Construction of Tees

Whenever possible tees should be turfed,

as a golfer derives a great deal more pleasure driving from a grass tee than he does from a skinned clay one or, as are sometimes necessarily used, rubber mats made of used tires, where wear is too heavy for grass. In case it is decided to use turf, care should be taken to build the tee large enough to permit shifting the tee plates, which mark the spot from which the golfer drives, to various locations on its surface. The tee should be large enough to allow plenty of time for a given spot to heal before it must once again be put in service.

It should be obvious that a tee has to be essentially level in order to give a player fair stance for his drive. It should also have good drainage, either natural or physical, so that the player need not play from a wet spot.

Although most tees are rectangular it is not necessary to have such design. Often an irregular design of an elevated tee when properly coordinated with the required direction of the tee shot makes a very interesting feature of design.

Slopes of an elevated tee should be such that the tee can be mowed by the fairway mower.

Ball washers, benches, umbrellas or other shelters (if trees do not provide shade), waste receptacles, and tee markers that are neat and brightly painted add greatly to the "class" look of the smaller course without costing much money.

Trap Design and Construction

One of the most delicate features of golf course architecture is trap location and design. They can "make" a hole or simply make trouble and add to expense. In the absence of competent architectural advice the builders of a new course should go at the trap problem with caution and restraint.

In heavy soil especially, experienced judgment is required for trap location and construction. In such soil it is wise to build the entire trap above the existing grade, borrowing the earth from some location where drainage will not be retarded.

Where there are no natural hazards, such as a gulley, a patch of woodland, or a pond, to increase the difficulty and, therefore, the interest of a given golf hole, it may be necessary to build artificial hazards. These take the form of raised mounds, sand-filled depressions and occasionally grassy hollows. The mounds, or bunkers as they are generally called, should blend with the landscape and vary in height from 3 feet to as much as 8 feet in certain instances, although as a general rule a properly constructed 3 foot high bunker is adequate. The front face (the side toward the tee) of a bunker should be steep as practical and still permit grass to grow, but the backs and sides of these mounds are graded out as gently as possible, not only because it improves their appearance and makes them more natural looking but, also, because such grading simplifies and facilitates the labor of keeping them mowed with fairway mowers. At least 6 inches of good topsoil should cover the mounds in order to establish a good stand of turf.

Like greens, sand traps should be somewhat higher at the back than they are at the front so that a player approaching them is conscious of their presence, can estimate their distance away and can decide whether to attempt to drive the ball over them or play safe and go around with the resulting loss in strokes.

On flat, well drained ground, this raising of the back of the trap can be accomplished by building it up from the material excavated to make the trap. They may be of any size, and should have an irregular outline. The rear edge of the depression should be rather abrupt for a matter of 9 inches or so, in order to make the ball come back into the trap if it does not clear the top edge.

Traps are customarily surfaced with about a 6 inch layer of sand, and this surface on a well-maintained course is kept free of weeds and is raked at frequent intervals to keep the surface soft and in place. Particularly after a heavy rain it may be necessary to rake the sand back into the upper parts of the trap from which it has been washed by the surface water. This expense should be prevented by design. It is permissible to let the grass grow fairly long around the edges of a trap as this adds to the difficulty of playing a ball out of it, but this grass should never be permitted to grow so rank as to make a sand trap unsightly.

Sand traps are frequently placed in the

face of a hill to force a golfer to play over the hill on the fly. Any traps located in such a spot should have a slight rise at the back so that water running down hill will be deflected around either side of the depression and not flow into the trap and wash out the sand.

The location of traps at the base and sides of putting greens often makes them a sort of catchbasin for seepage from the green and nearby parts of the fairway. Should there be a clay sub-soil, water will frequently stand in the traps above the sand layer, thus, causing an unsatisfactory playing condition. Providing the depth will permit a proper fall, a tile line should be laid in this subsoil and connected with the fairway and green drain lines. It is well to use 4 inch tiles. A layer of tar paper over the joints and gravel over tile helps drainage.

Equipment for Maintenance

Maintenance equipment for a nine-hole course can vary just as much as costs of construction and standards of maintenance that are desired.

For the course that wants complete and up-to-date equipment for mechanized maintenance, a leading golf course equipment and supply house suggests:

> 1 five gang fairway mower; 1 tractor; 1 power greens mower; 1 all purpose power mower; 2 hand lawn mowers; 1 wheelbarrow; 1 sod cutter; 1 hole cutter; 9 hole cups; 9 pairs tee markers; 9 flag poles; 9 flags; 1 flexible steel mat; 6 ball washers; 1 compost mixer; 1 fertilizer spreader; 9 greens sprinklers; 1 trailer or dump box; a 1000-foot hose; 1 power sprayer; 1 fairway fertilizer spreader; 1 spiker; 1 leaf sweeper; 1 roller; necessary rakes and shovels.

An equipment storage shed and workshop should be at every course that aspires to first-class operation.

Construction Pointers

1. It is wise to have the man who will be responsible for the maintenance of the course on the job when the course is built so that he will know all details of construction.
2. Even if it costs a bit more it is better to have local plumbers, electricians, drainage contractors, and other workmen on the job so that they will know exactly what conditions are in case emergency repairs are needed.
3. A planting plan for the trees and shrubbery the course may need is highly advisable. This has to be coordinated with the architecture of the course and clubhouse and can be well advanced by the time the course is opened if planting proceeds along with construction.
4. Watering of the new trees and shrubs is an important part of the construction program.
5. See that your creek banks and bridges are put into condition while course construction work is proceeding instead of having to attend to the details later and delay giving the course a finished appearance.
6. Make sure that all construction material is ordered well in advance. There may be a lot of time required for supplying some materials without which costly delays might result.

Other Suggestions

Leave room for practice field. In laying out the golf course it is well to have an area some 250 to 300 yards long, conveniently adjacent to the clubhouse where golfers can practice their golf shots. This area should be kept mowed and in as good condition as the fairways of the course itself, and if the club finances will permit, it is well to construct and maintain a practice green at the near end onto which the members can direct approach shots. If such a green, with a sand trap for practice, is available, members should be specifically forbidden to use any of the regular greens of the course for practice. A well groomed plot, of easy access from the clubhouse will encourage practice and build better golf.

Practice putting greens. If at all possible, there should be a practice putting green of considerable area near the clubhouse. This green should be surfaced with the same turf as the greens on the course, should be gently undulating, and is best arranged with nine or eighteen putting cups spotted about the green and numbered so that a player can putt from cup to cup in regular order. Obviously there will be considerable wear on the turf immediately surrounding these cups and it is necessary, therefore, to have plenty of room in the practice green to shift the cups from spot to spot at intervals.

WATERING THE COURSE

The availability of an adequate water supply is one of the important items to bear in mind when selecting the site for a golf course. The water supply may be obtained from a river, stream, pond, lake, city water main, or by drilling a well on the property.

Water Rights

Anyone expecting to develop an adequate supply for irrigation purposes from a natural lake or stream on the property, no matter how small, should consult the proper state or local official and secure the necessary permission. The construction of a dam on any stream or overflow from a spring-fed lake might limit the flow of water to other users in the downstream area. Two fundamentally different theories or systems of water rights are recognized in different states. These are the doctrines of appropriation and of riparian rights.

Ponds and Water Holes

If a pond or water hole should be excavated on the property for water storage purposes, it has been found that the size of the storage basin be such that at no time must the water be lowered more than 12 inches, for any greater draw-down permits the showing of the non-vegetated area below the high water line, and detracts from the surrounding landscape. Further, the water in any pond or water hole helps to keep the banks from falling in and if the water is lowered too much the banks will, in time, keep slipping and in a number of years it will be necessary to again excavate part of the lake bottom.

Evaporation losses from any body of water, such as a pond or water hole, vary with the surface area and with the prevailing rate of evaporation, and seepage losses vary with the size of the storage basin and the nature of the soil. However, these losses are often compensated for by drainage gains from higher points on the course.

Probably one of the most troublesome items encountered on any pond or water hole is the growth of plankton, which produces an odor and which may cause the clogging of the intake line to the pump. The most widely used method of destruction of plankton is by the use of copper sulphate distributed evenly over the surface. This is only applied when the algae growth causes trouble. If fish are to be raised in the pond or water hole the safe dose of copper sulphate ranges from 0.14 ppm (parts per million) for trout to 2.10 ppm for black bass.

Wells

If the water supply has to come from a well, or wells, on the property a thorough investigation should be made before the expense of drilling them is undertaken to make sure that a sufficient amount of water can be obtained. This investigation is usually done by consulting local well drillers who are familiar with the underground water supply in their respective localities. Where there might be a doubt as to getting the correct volume of water it is always best to drill a test hole, which consists of a 4 or 6 inch casing. The log of the drillings and the various formations are carefully recorded and when this data is submitted to any of the state colleges a report will be furnished on the amount of water that can be expected, along with suggested depths, casing size, screen size, and screen openings. The drilling of a test hole is never very costly for once the data is obtained the driller pulls back, and salvages the casing.

The cost of drilling a well is usually based on a predetermined amount per foot, unless the driller makes a contract on a lump sum basis to produce the necessary amount of water.

Some well waters are not suitable for irrigation purposes because of their mineral or chemical content and this should be investigated by sending a sample to the state college.

The temperature of the well water has little or no bearing on the suitability of the well water for irrigation purposes. Low temperature water quickly gains heat from the air when properly broken-up into droplets by the sprinkler. Consequently, so called "tempering-basins" are not required. The centrifugal and turbine type of pump is most commonly used for taking water from a storage basin; however, it will be found that the centrifugal pump should not be set more than 15 feet above the level of the water in the pond for this type of pump loses much of its efficiency when the lift is greater than 15 feet (at no time should the lift exceed 20 feet). The turbine type of pump is designed so that the pump can be set into the water with a driving unit mounted on top and above the water level. This type of pump is often used where conditions do not permit the use of a centrifugal pump.

Pumps

Well pumps are usually of the turbine or plunger type. The former type is the more commonly used on golf courses as it requires the least maintenance. The nearest representative of any of the numerous pump manufacturing firms will gladly furnish the necessary data on the correct size and type of pump to use once the demand and local conditions are known.

Water Requirements

The depth of water required to produce the desired turf varies with soil texture, climatic conditions, rainfall, and the kind of turf. With all other things being equal, the amount of water to be applied by irrigation depends on the deficiency of the rainfall during the growing season, and, as there are times when no rain will fall for a prolonged period, it is reasonable to assume that any irrigation system should be designed to produce the amount of water required to supply the turf water requirements.

Many agronomists agree that if the top 4 inches of soil is kept moist the turf will get ample water. It is, of course, difficult for the irrigation engineer to determine the exact amount of water required to produce the above mentioned amount of soil moisture.

In the middle-west and some eastern states it has been found that any irrigation system capable of producing one inch of water per week over the turfed area is able to supply the maximum water requirements during any prolonged period of drought. When cool weather, rains, or heavy dews are experienced the amount of irrigation water is reduced accordingly.

Water Application

The amount of water that the average soil can absorb without run-off is one-quarter of an inch per hour; consequently, any sprinkler used should be of such a size that this amount will not be exceeded over the area of coverage.

The formula commonly used to determine precipitation in inches per hour from any sprinkler is as follows:

$$\frac{122 \times G}{D^2}$$

G equals the discharge of the sprinkler in gallons per minute.

D equals the diameter of coverage of the sprinkler.

When the watering of tees and greens is being considered it should be borne in mind that it is not only necessary to water the actual playing areas but, also, the banks or outer edges of the tees and greens, for if they do not receive water they will take, by capillary attraction, a considerable amount of moisture from the watered playing areas.

Green Sprinklers

Although the system of distribution piping, pumping, plant pressure, and topography of the land determine the amount of pressure and volume of water discharged through any hose, or hoseless, type of green sprinkler it would be using good judgment when designing the system to provide for a pressure of at least 50 pounds per square inch at the sprinkler when it is in operation.

This pressure with a modern sprinkler will give a discharge of approximately 17 gallons per minute and will cover an area of 10,568 square feet, or 116 feet in diameter. This quantity will be ample, in most instances, to cover the green and the surrounding banks with one setting. Referring to the precipitation formula given above, the amount of precipitation per hour will be 0.154 inches. This would indicate that 6½ hours would be required to produce one inch of precipitation. This further indicates that if the sprinkler is allowed to operate 65 minutes per day, or per night, for a period of six days, or nights, the precipitation would total in one week the above mentioned one inch of precipitation.

Tee Sprinklers

Although tees vary in size we will consider at this time a tee 40 by 40 feet, or 1600 square feet. This playing area plus 10 feet on either side of banks or aprons might well be construed as being 60 by 60 feet, or 3600 square feet. An area of this size would necessitate a sprinkler capable of covering 68 feet in diameter. Sprinkler manufacturers' catalogs indicate that this coverage can be obtained from a sprinkler operating at 25 pounds pressure per square inch and discharging three gallons per minute. If the precipitation per hour was 0.08 inches, it would require 12 and one half hours to apply one inch of water.

Capacity of Pumping Plant

From the above it will be noted that if all the tees and greens on a 9 hole course are to be watered at one time a total discharge of 180 gallons per minute will be required (153 g.p.m. for greens and 27 g.p.m. for tees).

If electrical energy is used to drive the water pump it might be well to bear in mind that many power supply companies only permit up to 5 horsepower on a single phase circuit. The cost of installing a three phase circuit for greater horsepower is often costly and a schedule of watering tees and greens that does not require an excess of 5 horsepower might be found to be the most economical system. It is always well to check with the local power company before designing the irrigation system.

Pipe

Cast-iron, steel, and cement-asbestos pipe have been used with much success in various localities for course irrigation.

The selection of the correct size of pipe for a known flow is governed to a considerable extent by the cost of the pipe, its in-

Aerial view of the Par-3 Golf Course, Fort Lauderdale, Florida.

Photo by Fred Kuehn Studios, Chicago

The driving range.

stallation cost, depreciation, interest on the initial investment, friction loss, hours of use per year, and power costs. A good rule to follow in selecting the most economical size of pipe is allow a velocity of between 3 and 6 feet per second. These factors would indicate that the following pipe sizes might be used to advantage for the various flows given.

Rate of Flow in G.P.M.	*Size of Pipe in Inches*	*Rate of Flow in G.P.M.*	*Size of Pipe in Inches*
5	¾	75	2½
10	1	90	3
15	1¼	100	3
20	1¼	125	4
25	1½	150	4
30	1½	175	4
40	2	200	4
50	2	250	5
60	2½	300	5

Laying Pipe

Pipe trenches for cast iron and cement-asbestos pipe should be deep enough to provide a soil cover of 24 inches over the top of the pipe as a protection from loaded trucks and tractors that might pass over. Steel pipe should have a coverage of at least 18 inches over the top of the pipe.

Where cast iron, or cement-asbestos pipe, is fabricated with hot poured lead joints a space of 2 inches in the bell of the cast iron fitting should be allowed for the lead. When the lead in the joint is compacted with the caulking iron much care should be exercised not to split the cast iron bell of the fitting by over-caulking. It will be found that half-inch braided jute is much easier to handle and use when yarning the joints than oakum. When an angle of 7 degrees, or more, is required in laying the pipe, a suitable bend should be used in the line.

In laying steel pipe the standard threading is usually construed as eight threads, and when the threaded end of the pipe is made up into a fitting no more than three threads should remain exposed. All male threads should receive a coating of suitable joint compound before being made up. The applying of joint compound to the interior of female threads in fittings or couplings should be avoided for the surplus compound gets pushed ahead into the pipe line where it hardens, breaks off, and is carried into sprinkler nozzles.

Leaded joints act as expansion joints where there are considerable differences in temperature between winter and summer, but some form of expansion joint should be provided in a screwed steel pipe line. These expansion joints should be installed at 150 or 200 foot intervals.

The openings for risers to valves on the pipe line should be set on the side of the pipe and a double swing elbow used in order to prevent the risers from being broken off by pipe movement or by a tractor spud striking the water outlet valve.

All pipe 2 inches in width or smaller should have a pitch of 6 inches per 100 lineal feet towards the drainage outlets. Larger pipes may have a lesser pitch but in any case not less than 2 inches per lineal feet. All water should drain by gravity from the pipe lines. The draining of the pipe system by using air pressure is not recommended.

After the piping system with laterals, water outlets, and valves, is completed, it should be thoroughly tested by filling the entire system with water (care must be exercised to get *all* of the air removed). The water pressure should then be raised to 150 pounds per square inch. After a period of one hour a measured amount of water from a container such as a barrel or drum is pumped back into the line with a hand pump until the pressure again reaches 150 pounds. The measured amount of water pumped into the line represents the amount of leakage in one hour, which should not exceed 2 gallons per 1000 lineal feet.

Backfilling

The backfilling of the pipe trenches is very important. The back-fill should be placed back in 6 inch layers, and each layer tamped to original ground solidity. In lieu of this the back-fill may be flushed back by using a 4 foot long three-quarter inch pipe attached to a hose. The three-quarter inch pipe is pushed down to the bottom of the trench and the water allowed to flow until it appears on the surface. This may have to be done at 6 to 10 feet intervals along the trench line. Once the back-fill has settled, the excess is then removed and the area seeded or the turf laid down. The crowning of the back-fill on the trench line is not recommended, for it rarely settles to ground level and for years the mowers scalp this area and a permanent scar is left.

All boulders, and other solid materials, if used in the back-fill, should be placed at least 6 inches away from the wall of the pipe, for frost movement of these solid materials may damage the pipe in time.

Drinking Fountains

If the water supply is approved by the State Board of Health and is to be partly used for drinking fountains on the course it will be necessary to chlorinate and disinfect the pipe line by a suitable dose of chlorine. The amounts necessary can best be determined by consulting the local water department or the State Board of Health.

Clubhouse Water Supply

Where the clubhouse supply is obtained from a well also used for the irrigation supply it will be, in most instances, necessary to bury the clubhouse supply line below the frost line. If the pressure required for the irrigation system is too high, a pressure reducing valve can be inserted to lower the clubhouse pressure.

Fire Hydrants

It is often possible to secure a reduction in the clubhouse fire insurance policy if one or two fire hydrants can be located near the clubhouse and fed from the high pressure irrigation supply.

Guarantee of Piping System

Where the piping system on the course is installed by a contractor it is often the case that the owner requests a performance bond from the contractor, this bond to equal the full cost of the installation and to remain in full force for one year after the job is completed. It also becomes the contractor's responsibility to drain the entire system free of water during the winter following completion of the job and to turn on the water into the system in the following spring. Should any breaks or leaks show up the contractor, or his bonding agent, is then liable to repair them free.

THE DRIVING RANGE

The golf driving range has enjoyed phenomenal development in this country, largely as a commercial venture, since its inception in 1925. Today driving ranges are found from coast to coast along America's highways.

The modern trend in school planning, which calls for larger school sites, has motivated planners to include a driving range as a desirable addition to the outdoor physical education and recreation facilities.

A separate driving range with 30 to 35 tees will require from 6 to 12 acres of land depending upon whether fencing is used and the general ability of the students. Modified driving ranges of a temporary nature have been set up on athletic areas such as football fields. Usually the limited area reduces the use to clubs not exceeding a number 5 iron.

Planners interested in the development of commercial or municipal recreation golf driving ranges should refer to the guide "Golf Operators Handbook" published by the National Golf Foundation. This contains many excellent suggestions for the construction, operation, and management of golf driving ranges.

Some guiding principles for those planning school driving ranges are:

1. The range should be so oriented that golfers will be hitting towards the north.
2. The natural beauty of a school site should be used in locating the driving range. The land does not have to be flat; in fact, it should simulate a golf course as much as possible.
3. In order to maintain an attractive fairway provision should be made for watering the turf.
4. All necessary safety precautions should be taken. It must be remembered that most students using the range will be non-golfers and, hence, not apt to realize the harm that might be caused by careless swinging of the golf clubs.
5. Rubber tees or brush tees should be provided since they will save the turf area and provide a more uniform hitting surface.
6. For maximum control, tees should be arranged in an arch aimed at a central point 160 yards from the center tee.
7. A minimum of 10 feet should separate each tee (center to center).
8. A restraining line should be provided approximately 10 feet behind each tee to keep anyone from walking into a player.

Tom Thumb or miniature golf course.

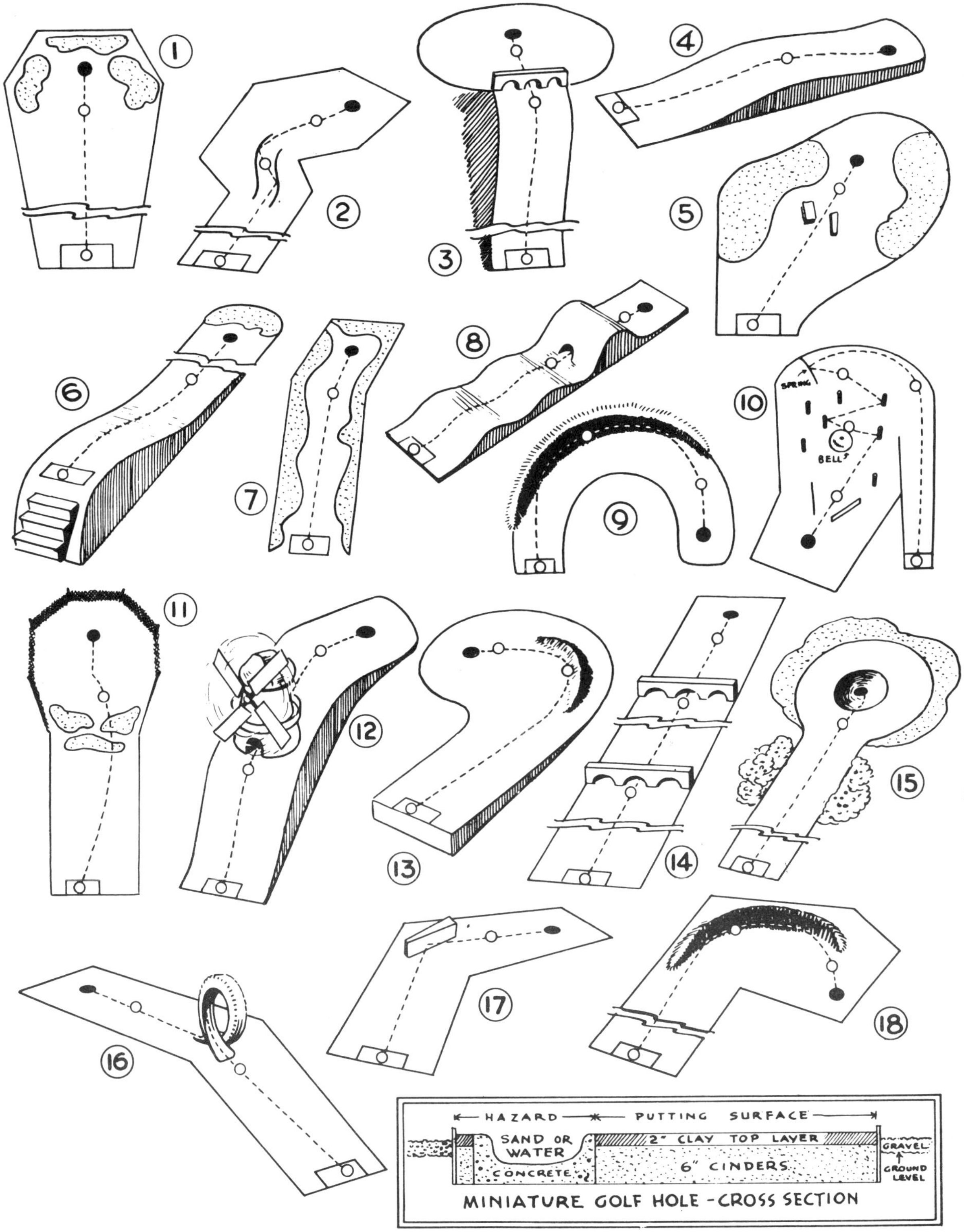

Designs for miniature golf course holes.

9. One or more target greens can be both an attractive and instructional aid. If one green is installed it should be located between 140 and 175 yards from the tees. If three greens are installed they should range between 100 and 250 yards from the tees.

10. Distance signs showing yardage should be located at 100 yards to 250 yards at 50 yard intervals.

11. By installation of lights on the driving range its use may be greatly expanded. Thus, school ranges may become community facilities in the evening (see Chapter 13 on lighting for detail specifications).

The Pitch and Putt Course

The pitch and putt courses, or "pony," par-3, or short course, as they are sometimes called, offer tremendous possibilities for recreation and school use. The holes are all par three ranging anywhere from 40 yards to 250 yards. These courses can usually be constructed on as little as 5 acres of land for a nine-hole course and 9 to 10 acres for an 18 hole course. It is not a substitute for a regulation course, but it does provide an excellent instructional facility, as well as a recreation facility for the person who has a limited amount of time.

A nine-hole pitch and putt course can be constructed for as little as $1000 per hole, as compared with $5000 to $10,000 a hole for a regulation golf course. These figures do not include the cost of the land.

Some of the features of the pitch and putt course are:

1. The maintenance cost is low.

2. Supervision is easier since the whole course is visible from the starting point.

3. It provides all the elements necessary to teach the game of golf including rules of play and etiquette. This means that when students are sent out to a regulation public or private course they will know how to conduct themselves.

4. Nine holes can be played in 30 to 40 minutes which fits into the physical education period very nicely.

5. The pitch and putt course stresses the most basic phases of the golf game, the "short" game, pitching and putting. This phase of the game represents three-quarters of the total par score for an eighteen hole course.

6. By placing a small fee on the use of the course after school and in the evenings the cost of maintenance and operation, as well as amortization may be met. Thus, it may serve the community as well as the school.

7. The pitch and putt course is excellent for older people and those who are handicapped. It is an excellent facility for hospitals, particularly those who have long term patients.

8. The pitch and putt course can be easily lighted for night play. (See Chapter 13 on lighting for details of equipment necessary for lighting the course.)

In addition to school use the pitch and putt course lends itself to the following recreational situations:

1. small cities
2. as a part of a small city park
3. on military bases, both in the United States and overseas.
4. hospitals, particularly veterans' hospitals and old age homes
5. around hotels and resorts
6. at industrial plants for employees' recreation
7. for children's camps
8. as a commercial recreation facility.

The details of construction are basically the same as for the regulation course described earlier in this chapter.[2] The major difference usually lies in the size of the greens and the type of tees. It is almost impossible to maintain turf tees, consequently, the rubber mat or brush tees are used extensively on pitch and putt courses.

Unquestionably as land becomes more expensive the short pitch and putt course will become increasingly popular. At Jones Beach and Jacob Riis Park in New York the pitch and putt courses have been extremely successful.

---

[2] For further information on the "Pitch and Putt" course refer to National Golf Foundation's "*Golf Operators Handbook.*"

CHAPTER 20

NATURAL ICE SKATING RINKS

Lloyd Hollingsworth

ICE SKATING IS AN EXCELLENT WINTER SPORTS activity that provides for mass participation at a low cost. In St. Paul, Minnesota, ice skating and hockey represent the greatest participation count of all the activities in the program of the recreation department. This valuable recreational activity is available to communities of the northern and eastern third of the United States at a low cost by the construction and maintenance of outdoor-natural-ice skating rinks. These rinks are serviceable two to four months of the year, depending upon location and climatic conditions.

The initiative for constructing and maintaining outdoor skating rinks may be assumed by such agencies as the following: park boards or commissions, recreation departments, city councils, public schools, private schools, voluntary agencies, or private groups and individuals. Regardless of the sponsor or the size of the rink, certain basic requirements must be met and certain procedures and directions followed if successful operation is to be attained.

Illustration: Preparing a natural ice skating rink

FLOODED RINKS

Surface Preparation

The area selected for flooding should be as near level as possible. Deviation in the elevation should not exceed 3 inches. Since the human eye is not a suitable gauge, the area should be surveyed long before the freeze-up. When it is found that the deviations are greater than 3 inches, grade stakes should be set and the surface graded to conform to these stakes. If a drain is available in the area, the ground should be sloped to the drain. A slope of 3 inches is sufficient for even a large area. Before flooding the drain should be covered with waterproof paper and packed with dirt. In the spring this can be chopped out to provide for quick drainage of the water, which is important if the area is to be used for spring activities. Grass, weeds, and other vegetation should be cut close to the ground during the fall season.

The area selected to be flooded should be depressed below the surrounding ground if possible, particularly if the area will be used season after season. When such depressed areas are not available or feasible to construct, the area to be used may be enclosed by an eight to twelve-inch dirt bank of clay or loam. Sand will not suffice. A satisfactory method of dirt banking on turf areas is to use a good grade of black dirt and spread this out as top dressing in the spring. Experience has proved that snow and ice banks are unsatisfactory as the flood water will melt through them and permit seepage. An added precaution for non-depressed areas is to be sure that seepage cannot reach adjacent buildings and basements since this may entail damage suits.

The type of surface, soil, and subsoil must be considered carefully in the selection of a rink site. A battery of three to five hard-surfaced tennis courts makes an excellent area, as well as surface, for flooding, providing the surface has been properly constructed. The provisions which must be made in order to accommodate ice skating on tennis courts are:

1. Grade should not exceed three inches over-all
2. A curb six to eight inches should surround the courts on the outside of the fence in order to retain the water during the flooding process. If this curb is not a part of the permanent construction, dirt banks may be used.
3. Tennis posts must be set in sleeves so that they may be easily removed for skating.
4. The surface should be properly reinforced to take the freezing and thawing.

Multi-use hard surfaced areas also are suitable surfaces for ice skating providing they meet the above standards. On pervious surfaces the texture of the soil must be such that it will not permit moisture readily to pass through it. A combination of clay and loam is acceptable. Sand, cinders, and ashes are too porous, and thus unsatisfactory. A turf surface is usually adequate to hold the moisture, but sod will usually be damaged by

Flooding an ice rink.

the "winter kill" caused by the flooding, freezing, and thawing. The subsoil is also important in preventing seepage. Clay, loam, and hardpan are quite satisfactory. Experience has proved that flooding over recently filled areas, old dump areas, and gravel pits is a waste of time, energy, and water.

Flooding and Sprinkling the Area

The ground and dirt banks should be thoroughly soaked by sprinkling and allowed to freeze fully before flooding. If the fall season is dry, it is advisable to do some of this sprinkling before the freeze-up. In situations where the temperature is not well below the freezing mark, best results can be obtained by evening and night sprinkling. Where hard surfaces, cement or asphalt, are to be flooded over, it is also advisable to soak and freeze these areas before flooding to prevent seepage through expansion boards, cracks, and dirt banks.

If any quantity of snow has fallen before the flooding operation is started, most of the snow should be removed; however, about one-half inch of snow sprinkled down into a slush and allowed to freeze provides a very desirable base on which to flood. Weather reports should be checked before flooding to be sure that the flood coat will freeze sufficiently before snow falls on it. Snow falling onto the flood water may result in a rough surface that will be difficult to level out.

The ground should be frozen to a depth of four to six inches before the flooding operation is started. The temperature should not be above 20 degrees for good flooding conditions. In order to attain this condition it may be necessary to flood at night. Normally, this first coat should be about two to three inches in depth. A lighter flood should be used when the ground has frozen to a depth of less than four inches.

Flooding of relatively large areas is best accomplished by means of a fire hose, but it may be done with a one-inch hose or even a garden hose. The hose should not be held or left in one place for any length of time since the water may melt through the frozen surface and/or the hydraulic action of the water pressure may bore through the frozen surface. When a small hose is used on a large surface, or when the temperature is quite low it may be impossible to supply the area fast enough to permit the water to spread out before it freezes, causing a pile-up. Under these conditions the flood water should be applied progressively, from one end of the rink to the other. It may be necessary to work over the rink several times in this manner. When the temperature is above 15 degrees the first flood coat should not be too heavy since the flood water (usually about 50 degrees) may remove the frost from the ground and cause seepage.

After the first flooding has frozen, all the air pockets should be punctured and the shell ice broken up. Holes, cracks, and areas where seepage has occurred should be filled with slush and allowed to freeze before another flood coat is applied. Under good conditions two floodings are sufficient, but, uneven ground or unfavorable weather conditions may necessitate additional floodings.

The *flood coat* often does not provide as smooth a surface as desired. The *finish coat* is best applied as a light spray from a one-inch hose nozzle. It may also be applied by walking back and forth across the rink, holding the open end of the hose so as to apply a light flood to the surface. Under any conditions the finish coat should be a light one as it congeals better with the base ice and provides for less chipping. If warm water is available, it will provide an even better finish coat as it congeals better with the old ice and melts into the cracks.

Cleaning and Resurfacing

The snow-ice (skate shavings) should be removed from the surface frequently. The exact number of times per day will depend on the daily load. It should be removed at least once a day. If it is not removed a light thaw followed by a freeze-up will cause excessively roughened ice. This cleaning is best done by sweeping with a small-wheel tractor with a revolving broom in front and a blade on the side (see page 298). If such a broom is not available, the rink may be scraped by a truck plow, tractor plow, or by handscrapers. It is especially important to clean the rink thoroughly before applying a new surface coat of ice.

Surface sweeper.

Ice surfacer or shaver.

Ice racing track.

Removable ice hockey boards.

A new surface coat should be applied whenever the surface is rough, especially after heavy use or after a thaw. It may be necessary to do this daily for hockey rinks. This resurfacing is best done by applying a light spray coat following the same procedures as previously indicated. After a severe thaw it sometimes becomes necessary to apply a new flood coat.

RINKS ON PONDS, LAKES, AND STREAMS

Ponds, lakes, and streams may be advantageously used for skating rinks where the hazard of thin ice is not a factor. When weather conditions during freezing cause rough ice, the area may be given a spray coat in the same manner as described for flooded rinks. Water for this operation may be obtained from a hydrant or by opening a hole in the ice and using a portable pump.

Smooth ice may also be provided by means of shaving or planing. The ice should be planed until a "blue-ice" surface is obtained. Shaving machines have been developed that are quite effective in providing a smooth ice surface. The cost of the machine is offset by the increased use of the surface for skating.

HOCKEY RINKS

Hockey rinks may be constructed on, or as a part of any recreation skating area, or they may be built as a separate facility. If the hockey rink is a part of the recreation skating area, it should be well fenced to prevent flying pucks from becoming a hazard to skaters. On large round or rectangular areas the hockey rink may be located in the center of the area which provides a natural flow of skaters around the rink. On smaller or odd shaped areas, it is better to locate the hockey rink at one end or in the corner of the skating area. Whenever possible it is best to build the hocky rink in a separate area to eliminate the necessity for fencing. It is less hazardous and permits better accommodation of spectators. Hockey rinks may also be located on lakes, ponds, or streams.

The size of the hockey rink should conform to the standards established by the National Collegiate Athletic Association or the Amateur Athletic Union which provide a minimum of 65 by 165 feet, and a maximum of 85 by 200 feet. The height of the boards should also conform to the hockey rules wherever it is possible; however, slight deviations have been found acceptable, especially for schools or junior hockey. To provide for multiple use of areas, for aesthetic appearance, and for lake, pond, and stream use, it is recommended that the hockey boards be constructed in such a manner that they are demountable and removable. This is best accomplished by building the boards in sections and using triangular frames for support. These frames can be staked into the ground or frozen into the ground or ice. The sections may be made of planks placed horizontally or they may be made of tongued and grooved 6 inch flooring placed vertically and nailed to a horizontal frame. The corners of the rink should be curved.

The hockey board sections and frames should be stored out of the weather between skating seasons. On flooded rinks they may be reassembled before the freeze-up. If a hockey rink is so located that it is not advisable to demount the boards, then permanent posts may be set and a wall attached. Such posts should be treated to prevent rotting and the boards should be painted on both sides. The boards should be painted with a flat paint to prevent sun reflection from melting the adjacent ice. Light poles may be used to serve the dual purpose of supporting the hockey boards. The hockey boards should have at least two three-foot doors along the longside of the rink for purposes of access and for use as a penalty box. These doors should swing out from the rink for safety. A large sectional door should be provided somewhere in the rink to provide access for snow removal and shaving equipment.

SPEEDSKATING TRACKS

In winter sports areas a speedskating track is an added facility. It is an expensive addition on flooded areas, but the costs are modest on lakes, ponds, and streams. The track should measure six laps to the mile and should be the equivalent of ten skaters wide, with the inner side well defined. An inner track for the use of officials and judges is advisable. Provision for spectators should be made available around the outer side of the track. The ice shaver is a necessity for maintaining good ice on the skating track.

LIGHTING

The use of skating rinks is more than doubled by providing illumination for night use. The amount of illumination necessary is small, three to ten foot-candle power for all except hockey rinks. Here the illumination should be at least fifteen foot-candle power. Street lights may be suspended over the area or regular flood lights may be mounted on poles. On multiple-use areas and over lakes, ponds, and streams, this equipment must be removed after each season. On flooded areas the poles should be set before the freeze-up. See Chapter 13 on lighting for details.

WARMING HOUSES

A building should be provided for changing to skates and for warming purposes. It should be as close to the skating area as possible and a wood plank walkway with double hand rails should connect it with the rink. The floor should be of rough wood or planking. The building should be heated and should contain adequate benches or seats. When it is feasible to make this a permanent building, restroom facilities should be provided. If the building is to serve other functions in the summer season, such as a shelter or bath-house, the permanent floor may be covered with rough wood planking for the skating season. For playgrounds and schoolgrounds it usually is not necessary to build permanent buildings, since part of the school building might be used for this purpose. However, in the event that a building must be provided, a removable or demountable type building may suffice. A concession stand is an added convenience and attraction.

CHAPTER 21

ARTIFICIAL ICE SKATING RINKS

C. A. Meadows and Associates Limited

THE PROVISION OF RINKS FOR HOCKEY AND skating is recognized as essential by recreation authorities, but the increasingly mild winters in the northern hemisphere have made the maintenance of natural ice rinks almost impossible. Most cities spend large amounts of money in the attempt to give their boys and girls and grown-ups ice surface for skating, but for the most part those efforts come to naught because the weather is not consistently favorable. For the few days of skating their efforts are hardly worthwhile, and many cities have given up altogether.

Fortunately science has come up with a solution—artificial ice—that may be successfully maintained outdoors throughout the whole winter. The method that is used employs mechanical refrigeration to remove the heat from the water that would otherwise cause the ice to melt.

The main components of an artificial ice rink are the system of closely spaced floor pipes that cover the entire area it is desired to freeze; a machine room or separate building that houses the ice-making machinery; and two large pipes that connect the rink floor piping with the machinery.

The "miracle" of making and maintaining an ice sheet for a skating rink, especially out-of-doors, during those periods when natural ice disappears altogether is illustrated in the diagram shown below. The rink floor piping and the ice surface (below) are shown bearing the heat "load" from the sky, the occasional rain (in the case of an outdoor rink), the warm wind, and the radiant energy of the earth. There is also present the heat radiating from the people on the ice and, in the case of a heated arena, from the heating plant. The refrigeration machinery keeps removing the heat that is impressed on the ice sheet by those several contributing sources and disposes of it to the air, the earth, and to the water, depending upon the system of cooling being used.

Illustration: Artificial Ice Skating Rink, Palisades Interstate Park, Bear Mountain, New York

In order to provide heat removal equipment of sufficient capacity to get rid of this heat, the designing engineer must first calculate the total amount of heat gain from the various sources and then add to it that amount of heat that must be extracted to change the initial rink water to ice. This latter, the latent heat, amounts to 144 B.T.U.'s per pound of water.

Broadly speaking, the type of floor to be used for a proposed rink is, or should be, the first consideration. Up until 1951, when the take-up rink floor was introduced for the first time, there were two main types used, the *sand-fill* and the *concrete slab*, both using steel or wrought iron pipe to circulate the cooling media.

The Sand-Fill Floor

This type of floor (see Figure 21-2) is simply a system of steel or wrought iron pipe, usually 1 inch or an inch and a quarter in diameter laid down on a level, compacted surface with sand deposited and brought flush with the top of the pipe. Since the pipe has no protection against air and moisture, this type of floor should only be used for an indoor rink. If and when corrosion does occur, allowing the freezing solution to leak out, it is possible to make repairs by replacing the leaking pipes.

This type of floor should be confined to an indoor arena, because the exposed pipe must be protected from the elements.

If this type of floor is installed in an arena, the current estimated cost for the ice sheet alone, including refrigeration equipment, is $3.50 per square foot of ice surface. To this must be added the cost of electric power wiring, water supply, provision for housing machinery, accessory installations such as hockey boards, rink lighting, and public address systems.

The Concrete Slab Floor

This type of rink floor (see Figure 21-3) costs the most, takes longest to install and involves the most risk. However, properly designed and installed, it requires little or no maintenance and leaves the area open to a wide variety of uses.

It can be installed indoors and outdoors, either on the ground or above the ground, over a basement for example. The concrete must be a continuous, monolithic slab, poured without any joints whatsoever. Since concrete is not flexible, the slab must be so designed that it does not heave, or so designed that when it does heave it will not crack. A crack in the slab would permit moisture to reach the metal pipe that is encased in the slab and leaks would soon follow. Repairing leaks in the concrete slab rink floor is a much more serious undertaking than it is with the sand-fill floor. In a concrete slab there is a certain amount of horizontal movement because of the temperature extremes it is exposed to, and this must be provided for by the designer.

The drainage of the subsoil underneath the concrete floor and the surface water drainage in the case of an outdoor rink are vitally important to the life and success of the slab-type rink floor. A preliminary study of the nature of the soil and of the surrounding topography can eliminate the possibility of insufficient drainage being provided on the one hand and too much money spent on it on the other hand.

Today the reinforced concrete floor slab, with the one-inch steel floor pipes embedded in it at four-inch centers to provide an ice sheet 85 by 200 feet can cost by itself $35,000 or more. It is to protect this investment that much attention is, or should be, given to the foundation for the slab. With even the most favorable ordinary soil conditions, the cost of such a foundation at today's rates would be $5,000, and this could grow to $15,000 if ground conditions are poor. The rough estimated cost of the concrete slab rink is from $5.25 to $6.25 per square foot of ice surface, including all refrigeration equipment.

Once the type of floor to be used has been established, there is a choice of two different methods of freezing the ice sheet, *direct expansion*, and the "*brine*" as it is sometimes called. The direct method involves the circulation of a refrigerant, such as ammonia or one of the freons, directly in the rink floor piping, whereas in the "brine" method, brine is circulated. In the latter, the brine, usually calcium chloride or sodium chloride, gives up the heat it has absorbed in its travel across the rink floor to the refrigerant in the brine chiller and returns as chilled brine. This low pressure, low velocity cycle is continued as long as the brine circulating pump is in operation. The heat is given up in the chiller to the refrigerant system which is a separate circuit wherein the ammonia or freon is successively compressed, condensed into a liquid and expanded into a gas. The heat that was originally picked up on the rink floor is finally deposited into the air or earth by means of water coming in close contact with the coils carrying the refrigerant in the condenser.

The direct expansion system eliminates the brine cycle entirely, and is often cheaper to install and takes less power to operate for a given size of rink. However, it has the disadvantage of being a much more delicate system requiring considerably more skill and attention to operate, and is therefore seldom recommended for skating rinks.

PLASTIC FLOOR PIPING

In view of the high cost of materials and installation of steel or wrought iron floor pipe systems outlined above, the use of plastic pipe is becoming increasingly widespread.

Plastic pipe, manufactured from virgin Polyethylene, costs approximately 30 per cent of the cost of steel pipe and only about 15 per cent of the cost of wrought iron pipe of similar size.

Over the range of brine flow used in the floor pipe circulation, the resistance to flow in plastic pipe is only about 50 per cent of that encountered when steel pipe of equal size is used, thus further reducing the initial installation cost by using pumping equipment of smaller capacity and reducing running costs on power consumption.

From an initial installation point of view,

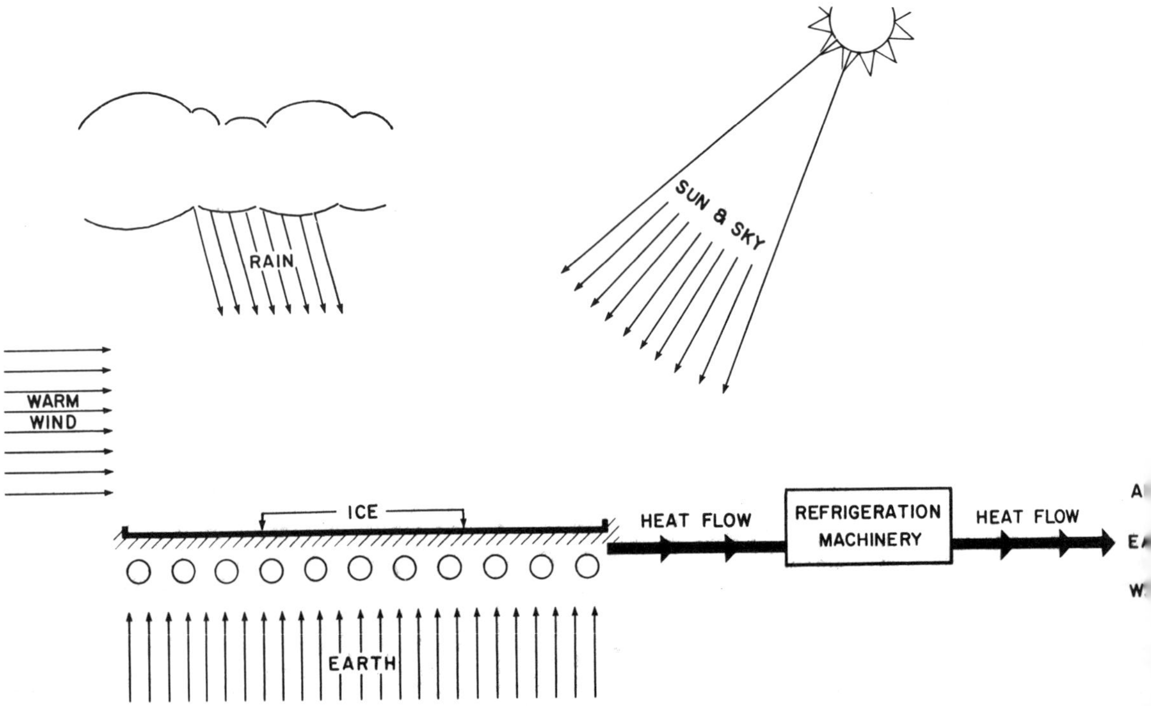

Meadows and Associates Limited

Figure 21:1. Application and dissipation of heat load on ice sheet.

plastic pipe leaves little to be desired. It is manufactured in any length required, the labor involved in its installation is negligible compared with a similar installation using steel pipe, and only two joints are required per length of pipe, giving less possibility of leaks. Plastic pipe does not corrode.

Plastic pipe has the disadvantage of a thermal conductivity equal to only about 30 per cent of that of steel and has a much higher coefficient of contraction.

These faults, however, have no appreciable significance provided the installation is designed to counteract their effects.

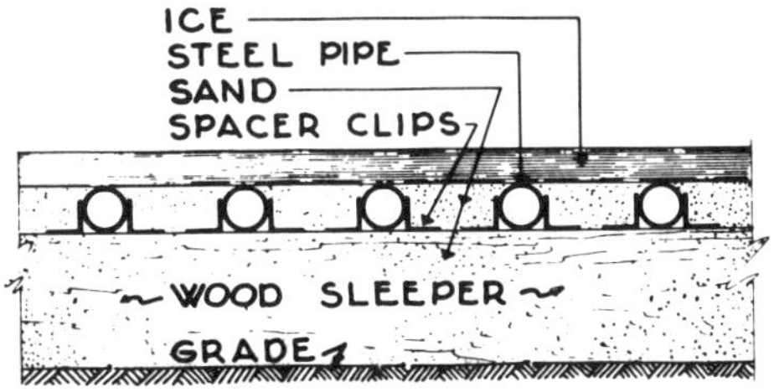

Meadows and Associates Limited
Figure 21:2. Cross-section of steel pipe sand-fill floor.

When it was first realized that public demand required ice rinks that could be installed at a reasonable cost, engineers undertook to design an installation that would be easy to maintain, portable to the greatest extent, and that would have the lowest possible operating cost. The "take-up" rink appears to be the answer.

The "take-up" rink consists of a system of plastic pipes, light in weight and practically indestructible, laid down on any level surface and through which the freezing solution is constantly circulated. Ice forms around the pipes for about an inch above them and is kept frozen by the mechanical refrigeration.

The system of floor pipes is fed by header pipes located at one end or along one side of the rink and enclosed in a tunnel. Where, for purposes of economy, the header pipes are laid along the short dimension of a rectangular rink, a tunnel is also constructed along one side in which the plastic pipes are stored in straight lengths during the summer. If it is considered advisable, depending mainly on the geometric shape of the ice sheet, the header tunnel may be built along the longest side of the rink and used for storage of the plastic pipe also. The tunnel for the headers, and for storage space if it is required, is constructed to form a seat for the skaters, eliminating the need for the usual movable benches.

THE TAKE-UP "SWIM-RINK"

The latest development in the artificial ice rink field is a completely new concept of the swimming pool-cum-skating rink combination.

Hitherto it has been the practice in cases where it was desirable to skate on an ice sheet formed over a swimming pool to install a false floor over the pool and form the ice sheet on that floor.

With a newly designed "Swim-Rink," the very high cost and storage problem of the false floor are eliminated because the ice sheet is formed on the water surface. This design is primarily intended for use with a specially constructed swimming pool but is readily adaptable to suit the particular requirements of an existing pool.

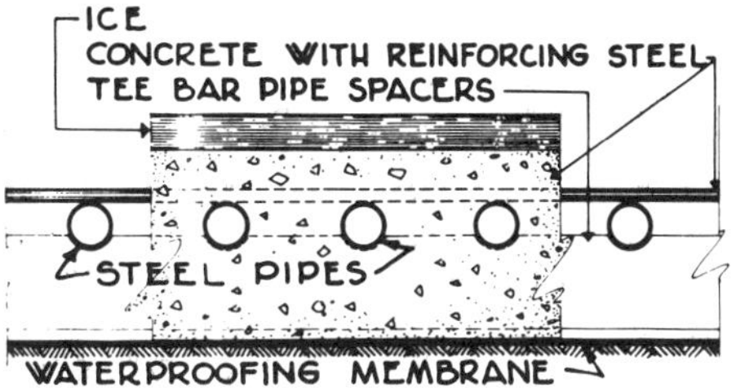

Meadows and Associates Limited
Figure 21:3. Cross-section of steel pipe concrete slab floor.

Static or Portable?

Although as its name implies, the Take-Up type artificial ice rink is designed with a view to attaining 100 per cent portability,

Pouring concrete slab over steel floor piping. Veterans Memorial Park, Hamtramck, Michigan.

it is by no means a "must" to dismantle and store the various units during non-skating periods.

CHAIN RINKS

It is a well-known fact that a much larger refrigeration capacity is required to make an ice sheet in the first instance than to maintain a sheet once it is formed.

For this reason it has been proved to be much more economical to install only sufficient refrigeration capacity at any one site to maintain the ice sheet after it has been made and to obtain the extra capacity required for the initial making of the ice sheet from a travelling *booster unit,* mounted on a truck and serving a number of rinks in one locality.

By using this method of boosting the "resident" units, the cost of the booster unit is spread over a number of installations thus reducing the cost of each installation, yet providing the extra boost required.

SITE REQUIREMENTS

Rink Floor

An expensive type of floor surface on which to install the Take-up type of artificial ice rink is not required.

This type of rink has been successfully installed on a level turf surface. Being portable, it is an easy matter to remove the floor pipes in the spring and repair any irregularities in the turf surface caused by frost heaving.

This type of floor can be equally successfully laid on a stone chip and asphalt surface, or on a concrete slab surface.

Obviously, the more permanent the surface on which the floor piping is to be laid, the better the drainage of the site must be to eliminate as much frost action damage as possible.

Water Availability

Cooling water requirements for the refrigeration equipment is in the region of three gallons per minute per 125 square feet of ice sheet.

The cheapest method of obtaining the necessary water supply on initial installation is to use water supplied by the local authority. Unfortunately, the cost of water, its frequent scarcity, or the lack of drainage facilities for its disposal, very often make this form of supply prohibitive, in which case it is necessary to provide some means of dissipating the heat picked up by the incoming water and recirculating it after cooling.

The latter is by far the most economical over a period of time. Although initial installation costs are higher, the consumption cost is reduced to the electrical power required to operate the recirculating pump.

Various means of removing the heat absorbed are available, the most commonly used being the evaporative condenser. These items are costly and are limited to the function for which they are designed, namely, heat dissipation.

The spray cooling ponds have the added advantage that they provide another form of recreation for the kiddies during the summer months.

Electrical Service

From experience it has been found that electrical service to an existing building or site is usually inadequate and needs to be increased.

Sometimes it is found to be more economical to house the refrigeration equipment in a separate building rather than an existing one and install a completely new

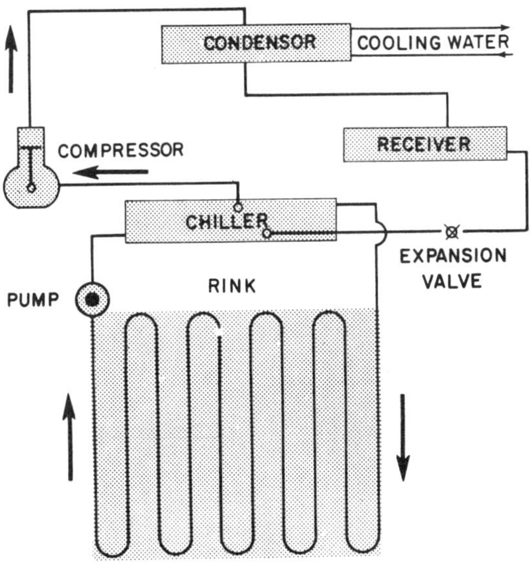

Figure 21:4. Schematic layout of "brine" method of freezing.

Meadows and Associates Limited

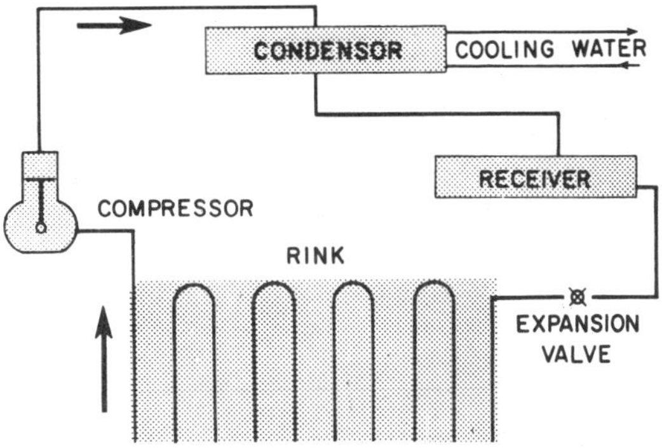

Meadows and Associates Limited

Figure 21:5. Schematic layout of "direct expansion" method of freezing.

electrical service rather than increase the capacity of an existing service.

The power required is in the region of 1.5 kilowatts per 125 square feet of ice sheet plus that required for floodlighting if it is to be installed.

Size of Ice Sheet

Usually, the size of the ice sheet is predetermined by the site available. A full size ice hockey rink is 185 feet long by 85 feet wide.

Where a choice is available, it is usual to estimate that about 25 square feet of ice surface are needed per person actually skating.

For the purposes of estimating revenue where an admission fee is to be charged, a fair approximation may be obtained by allowing one person per 25 square feet of ice surface plus an additional 25 per cent to allow for people sitting out or standing around after paying an admission fee.

ESTIMATES OF COST OF "TAKE-UP" RINKS

Due to the wide variations in labor costs, taxes, and other factors, between Canada and the United States, and even between different localities in each country, it is not possible to give a definite cost on the various types of installation available. Furthermore, cost figures change from year to year. The figures outlined below should be used primarily for making comparisons between initial cost of installation, operating cost, and revenue.

Meadows and Associates Limited

Figure 21:6. Installation complete and ready for freezing.

TABLE 21-1

Outdoor Rink Installation Costs

Ice sheet 85 x 185 feet = 15,725 square feet

Floor surface turf, leveled and compacted

Floor pipes 1 inch diameter plastic pipe, steel spacers galvanized shields

Header pipes 3 pipe balanced flow system housed in steel angle frame tunnel, corrugated iron siding, hinged wood covers, also used for pipe storage

Refrigeration equipment 50 ton brine chilling unit, 30 ton condensing unit in conjunction with a cold storage tank

Electrical Power supply adequate service on site

Estimated cost of installation, including engineering $60,000

In addition to the above, provision should be made for:

Fencing
Lighting
Housing for refrigeration equipment
Electrical power supply if existing service is inadequate
Cooling water supply and discharge

This type of installation would provide good ice at wet bulb temperatures up to 45 degrees. If an evaporative condenser is to be used add $5,600. If a spray cooling pond is to be used add $2,500. Note that it is often possible to utilize an existing wading pool for cooling water recirculating purposes.

Booster Unit

The cost of a "Booster" unit comprising a packaged brine chilling unit of 50-ton capacity mounted on a truck, complete with all necessary flexible quick release pipe connections and pumping equipment, is approximately $25,000.

Amortized Costs

Rates of interest charged will vary with each municipality and will also vary with the length of the term of the mortgage.

For an approximate cost, consider the example in Table 21-1 amortized on a 20 year term at 5 per cent interest.

Wollman Memorial Rink, Central Park, New York City.

Ice surfacing machine.

TABLE 21-2

Amortizing Costs of Outdoor Rink

First capital cost $60,000	
Yearly cost	$4,742.80
Electrical power (assume ½¢ per KW hr.)	1,165.00
Water (assume 15¢/1000 gals.)	1,825.00
	$7,732.80

SALARIES AND WAGES

Refrigerating Operator:
Approx. $400 per month

Cashier:
Approx. $150 per month

Skating Supervisor:
Approx. $250 per month

Snow Removal:
Approx. $250 per month

Assuming above personnel are employed on this work for 4 month period: total labor cost per 4 month season = $4,200.

Total cost of operation less lighting for 4 month season = $11,932.80.

REVENUE

The amount of revenue realized at any particular ice rink will depend on the rate of charges and length of operation. For a rink of the size described above the expected revenue could be as shown in Table 21-3.

TABLE 21-3

Revenue of Outdoor Rink

PLEASURE SKATING	
250 children per day, 2 days per week for 17 weeks @ 25¢	$2,125
500 children on Saturday for 17 weeks @ 20¢	1,700
300 adults per week for 17 weeks @ 50¢	2,550
HOCKEY	
10 practice periods of 1 hour per week for 17 weeks @ $25	4,250
10 practice periods of 1 hour per week for 17 weeks @ $10	1,700
1 big hockey match per week of 2 hrs. for 17 weeks @ $40/hr.	1,360
MISCELLANEOUS	
Figure skating club, 300 members @ $15 per season	4,500
	$18,185

Net profit $6,252 for 17 weeks or $367.70 per week. This figure could be increased by at least $1,500 per season if a method of recirculating the cooling water were employed.

It is important to recognize that the figures cited above are presented for comparative purposes only. The amount of revenue will depend on local policy and the nature of the program. The primary purpose of this discussion is to demonstrate that ice rinks can be made to be completely self supporting.

CHAPTER 22

PUBLIC BEACHES

Lee L. Starr

SELECTION OF BEACH SITES

THE PUBLIC BEACH USUALLY REPRESENTS THE most popular summertime recreation facility in a community fortunate enough to have one nearby. On a hot Sunday afternoon the five major beaches in the metropolitan New York area accommodate over 2,000,000 people. The modern beach with its numerous supplemental recreation facilities ranging from "par three" golf courses to table tennis is a far cry from the old beach facility that provided only swimming. Today when families go to the beach they go for the day. Consequently, they demand many types of recreation facilities in addition to swimming. This factor has greatly influenced the planning of public beaches in recent years.

Unfortunately, all states and cities do not have ocean beach sites, and must seek out lake sites for development of beach facilities. Counties and states that possess properties suitable for beaches have begun to construct such public areas to serve tourists and people from the cities. These beaches are frequently located in state or county park systems.

For the most part beach facilities of the larger variety may very easily be adapted to small waterfront areas and suggested layouts reduced or deleted accordingly.

The selection of a desirable location for beaches and the subsequent development of the area is an important step in securing adequate bathing facilities.

The Ocean Beach

An ocean bathing beach site should have certain characteristics to make it more desirable than any other stretch of ocean front area. The following criteria are recommended as a suitable basis for selection of ocean beach sites:

1. An unobstructed, smoothly contoured, shallow water area at low tide.
2. An unobstructed expanse of clean, sandy beach.
3. Water that is chemically and biologically suitable for bathing.

Illustration: Jones Beach State Park, New York

4. An area readily adaptable to the construction of dressing, parking, and recreational facilities.

5. Popularity and general usage of the area in its present condition. In many instances a stretch of ocean front, though undeveloped and sometimes restricted, seems to be a popular bathing spot. This expressed evidence should serve as a criterion. The community or municipality involved, should wherever possible make a virtue out of what appears to be a necessity.

6. A necessity for new facilities based on a study of overcrowded existing areas.

7. Accessibility by private and public transportation.

The Lake Front Beach

In general the criteria listed for the selection of ocean beach fronts apply to lake front beaches. It should be understood that tide conditions on certain types of lakes are relatively unimportant in making the selection.

Usually, a lake front beach development is of a more localized variety. It will serve a smaller community. The facilities will not be extensive. Control problems will not be serious. In spite of these favorable factors, the success of any beach project will inevitably depend on the type of facilities provided, the cleanliness of the water, the smoothness of the beach and accessibility to it. When a lake front site appears to have the features mentioned but the bottom of the wading depth leaves something to be desired, the problem can be easily resolved. With modern land movers and grading equipment practically any lake site can be developed into a first-rate bathing beach.

GENERAL REQUIREMENTS AND LAYOUT OF FACILITIES

Servicing the public is and always should be the prime objective when determining the final physical arrangement of the essential facilities for a public beach. It is necessary to know what facilities are required and what should be done with them to afford maximum and unobstructed use. Experience over the past twenty years indicates that the facilities listed below are desirable and in most instances essential.

Bathhouse Design

In areas where only one bathhouse is contemplated it should be constructed to include:

1. Admission ticket sales and locker rental booth. Valuables checking section.
2. Suit and towel rental section.
3. An adequate shower and toilet facility for both men and women.
4. Sufficient locker and dressing cubicles (men and women).
5. Centrally located egress from dressing spaces to beach.
6. Food concession.
7. First Aid Station.
8. Employees locker room and sanitary facilities (Lifeguards, Attendants, etc.) In this regard it has been found that a more efficient operation will result if lifeguards have their own quarters.
9. Administration Office.
10. Lobby space of sufficient size to accommodate the patrons of the bathhouse during rain storms.
11. Locker key machine.
12. Storerooms.
13. Maintenance area for repair of equipment, boats, ropes, reels, lifeguard towers, inhalators or resuscitators, beach chairs and umbrellas, etc.
14. Clothing issue room if employees are supplied with uniforms by the facility.
15. Rooms with adequate storage and counter space for rental of chairs and umbrellas.

Bathhouse Construction

Simplicity should be the watchword in bathhouse construction. The trend points to one-story, long, low, ranch-type buildings, one end used for a female dressing and locker section with dressing cubicles and sanitary facilities, and the other, a male section of similar design, without individual dressing cubicles. Cubicles are considered an unnecessary expense in men's facilities. A very satisfactory innovation in modern construction is the locker and dressing area that requires no roof. This open forum arrangement furnishes

One million bathers at Coney Island on a hot Sunday afternoon.

the person who does not desire to check his clothes, a facility in which to get into his bathing suit. The person who wishes to check his clothes can do so by dropping a nickel, dime or quarter in the coin lockers provided. These, of course, are under cover. This idea is similar to the checking lockers in train and bus terminals. Alternate plans are:

1. A flat locker rental fee where a wristband locker tag is issued on purchase and lockers are serviced by an attendant with a master key.
2. Instead of a tag, a wristband key is issued for which a deposit is usually demanded.

Although it is not the intent here to discuss the merits of operational features, the three systems are mentioned to aid the prospective builder or architect. The advantages of the coin locker system are obvious.

Construction Materials

Minimum maintenance and permanency, being of the essence, construction should be limited to the use of concrete and cinder block. The use of brick or fieldstone veneer should be utilized for greater aesthetic appeal.

The "open to the sky" type of construction incorporates the use of corrugated transite for the roof of sheltered sections, such as the locker areas, and smooth transite for all facia treatments. These materials have been time-tested and require little or no maintenance.

Shower Facilities

Holding to the original intent, minimum maintenance and permanency, it is suggested that shower facilities be constructed with the following features:

1. Open to the sky
2. Concrete block enclosure walls
3. Multiple shower installation on three sides
4. Rough non-skid finish decking with quick run-off drainage.

Some shower enclosures are constructed so that drainage is pitched toward a perimeter trough at the base of the enclosure walls.

This general type of construction has been found to be very functional and has also withstood the test of time.

Toilet Facilities

The general and satisfactory practice in bathhouse construction is the installation of toilet facilities close to the exit to the beach. To reduce the cost of laying water and sewer lines for any great distance, the facilities for both bathhouse and general beach patrons are located so that a common separation wall contains the water closet, urinal, utility sink and hand basin lines.

State and city building codes throughout the country vary but it is doubtful whether a set formula for toilet installations exists for public beaches. This statement is not to be construed to mean that codes do not exist for toilet installations at other places of public assembly. In the suggested comfort station layout, a utility closet containing a sink large enough to hold a wringer-type bucket should be included. This compartment should be equipped with shelves for storing essential materials (soap, cleanser, tissue, mops, polish, garden hose rack) and a faucet threaded to receive at least a three-quarter inch hose for swabbing down the decks and walls.

Decks and walls in comfort station facilities, to enable easy maintenance, should be lined with a tile that will withstand hosing down. The decks in particular must be adequately graded to a drain or drains depending on the size of the facility.

Jacob Riis Park, New York.

Drinking Fountains

It is believed that vandalproof drinking fountains for public beaches or public facilities of any kind are yet to be invented. However, a reasonable degree of success has been attained with a trough type installation containing a series of three, four, or five fountain bubblers with individual push button or wheel bubbler controls. These troughs are equipped with filler spigots at both ends for those who wish to fill containers.

The entire trough is constructed of concrete with sufficient access plates or doors for maintenance and repair. The plates or doors (steel) should be equipped with a square or hex nut locking device, opened and closed with a key to fit.

Individual fountains precast of concrete in one piece (pedestal and basin) with the type of maintenance and repair doors mentioned above have also proved to be fairly substantial. In most instances these are equipped with push button bubbler control.

Depending on the size of the beach and the location of the bathhouse, it is believed that drinking fountains should not be located more than 500 feet apart along the line of the boardwalk. Obviously, persons farthest from the fountain would not have to walk more than 250 feet in either direction, plus whatever the width of the beach is at the point they have selected to occupy.

Concessions

The concession generally associated with beachfront operation includes a facility for the sale of food, soft drinks, beer, cigars and cigarettes, bathing and beach accessories, souvenirs, novelties and, where picnic areas are available, charcoal. The larger and more elaborate installations feature complete restaurant facilities where persons strolling the boardwalk or having concluded a swimming

A catamaran used in water safety patrol.

date may finish the day with a seven-course dinner.

The remarks here are confined to listing the equipment necessary for the average beach food concession and its general design. The minimum essential equipment is considered to be:

1. 2 Soda Dispensers
2. 2 or 3 Bottle Coolers
3. 1 30 Cubic Foot Refrigerator
4. 1 Walk-in Ice Box and Freezer
5. 1 Automatic Coffee Maker
6. 1 French Frier
7. I Large Grill (preferably gas)
8. 1 Work Table with 2 inch top
9. 1 Back Bar
10. Display Cases
11. Ice Cream Bar
12. Ample Storage Space

In arranging the floor plan for the installation of this equipment, it should be borne in mind that accessibility to servers is very important. It is, therefore, suggested that the concession area be rectangular in shape, with service counter space on three sides. These counters should be constructed so that roll down shutters or sliding battens may be used to shut off parts or to completely open the entire area.

All equipment, located in the center of the rectangle, would be easily reached by the service personnel and out of reach of the patrons. This arrangement is possible whether it be part of the central bathhouse type installation or a separate unit remote from the main building. There is no set rule for floor plans of concessions. However, research involving concession operations of varying sizes reveals that the aforementioned plan is preferred.

First Aid Station

Whether a First Aid Station is constructed as part of a central bathhouse or is an additional separate entity by reason of a long expanse of beach, certain characteristics and equipment are necessary.

The First Aid facility must be designed to accommodate persons with minor injuries and at the same time provide for the more serious submersion cases. The minor injury section should include:

1. A porcelain footbath equipped with sit-down ledge and hot and cold water taps.
2. A steel porcelainized examining table.
3. Medicine cabinet highboy, porcelainized steel.
4. Steel porcelainized stool.
5. Steel examining chair with leg rest.

This section should be screened from the submersion or serious case section in which the following equipment is considered essential:

1. Rubbing Table
2. Steam Sterilizer
3. Inhalator or Resuscitator
4. Steel porcelainized flat top, 4 drawer medical cabinet
5. Medical desk and chair for Nurse or First Aid Attendant
6. Porcelain sink with single knee-operated water control

The rooms, for maintaining the highest standard of cleanliness, should be constructed with tile or concrete decks and a 4 foot dado of tile around the walls. It is customary to separate the actual working space in a First Aid Station from the entrance by a railing equipped with swinging gate. On the entrance side of the railing an informal waiting area is designated by a row of chairs such as one might encounter in any medical office. The outside of the building should be conspicuously matked so that it can be identified by persons approaching from any direction.

It is also important that this building or designated section of a bathhouse be located so that an ambulance may have free access to it.

Lifeguard Stations

In beach installations where the length of beach available is not more than a half to three-quarters of a mile and the bathhouse is centrally located, the main lifeguard station may be included as part of it.

This station primarily would serve as a point from which lifeguards are assigned to their respective posts and as an operating office for the chief and lieutenant lifeguards. When such an arrangement is possible, this station could very well serve as a separate dressing facility for all lifeguards. As mentioned previously, for better functioning of the lifeguard service, it has been found that lifeguards separately quartered and independent of the rest of the beach personnel maintain better "esprit de corps." This point cannot be emphasized too much.

Lifeguard posts as distinguished from lifeguard stations are two- to three-man chairs, located at intervals of approximately 500 feet along the waterfront. These should extend 6 or 7 feet above the grade of the beach and constructed with a wide base for steady footing. They should also be constructed so that one or two men may easily move them to or from the water as tide conditions change. It is suggested that these seats be constructed of aluminum pipe framing with seat and back rests curved to conform to natural contours of a sitting man. This feature alone is worth its weight in gold in helping the lifeguard to stay alert.

The lifeguard chair should also include a foot rest and platform on which an inhalator or resuscitator may be stored. A footlocker type compartment might also be included for safe storage of extra clothing and lifeguard gear.

Safety Factors

At this point it may be well to mention that each lifeguard chair should be located at a point where the line of umbrellas does not interfere with vision of the lifeguards seaward. In any case where their view might be obscured, flags on 6 or 7 foot staffs should be placed on the beach indicating the closest point to the water's edge that umbrellas are permitted.

To insure that rescue operations do not become confused by interference from the public, it is suggested that each tower or chair be roped off and boats and other rescue gear kept immediately available.

Where jetties have been built to preserve the contour of the beach, it has been found that lifelines with 18 to 24 inch brightly colored floats installed on both sides parallel to the jetties are necessary. These lifelines are secured to the beach by a buried "deadman" or good-sized log. The outboard end is secured to a Danforth, mushroom, or hairpin anchor depending on the type of bottom.

Beaches not having jetties from which the public must be warned or protected are reducing gradually the number of lifelines in use. This reduction has come about because people in general get the impression that the lines were installed so that they might have something to hang on to. Originally, lifelines were supposed to aid the lifeguard in establishing a swimming area that he could easily observe. Unfortunately, these lines tend to give poor swimmers too much confidence and frequently result in submersions that could otherwise have been prevented. Lifeguard stands properly spaced and manned serve to much better advantage than lifelines.

Boardwalk-Beach Area

After the first postwar (World War II) summer season was over a tremendous increase in usage of Metropolitan Area beaches was reported. Overcrowding created an urgent need for further expansion. But statistics are necessary for intelligent planning and design of any facility. The formulas on p. 317 were devised, based on patronage at the five leading beaches around New York and Long Island.

Assuming 1,000,000 people use the beaches on the existing 480 acres, there will be 2,100 bathers per acre. To get an actual picture of what each of the five formulas represented in congestion or comfort, 150 lifeguards at Rockaway Beach were arranged to simulate each condition.

Knowing the size of the area and approximate number of people to be served, planners can get a fairly good idea of how much beach should be seaward of a proposed boardwalk. Where a beach area is long enough to warrant the construction of a promenade or boardwalk, myriad problems present themselves.

To determine the type of boardwalk construction best suited to a particular area, grades are an important factor.

Boardwalks most easily maintained are the concrete or asphalt block surface variety. As a general rule concrete promenades are constructed where flush grade permits. In instances where there is an appreciable change in grade or where inshore installations make it necessary, elevated boardwalks 12 to 14 feet high must be installed. Supporting structures can either be of treated wood piling or concrete. Both have proved satisfactory. The decking of boardwalks as a rule has been constructed of Douglas Fir (Wollmanized). Experiments over the past 10 or 15 years have been made with decking of Greenheart, a South American lumber, which has served remarkably well and may well become the number one choice for wooden boardwalk construction.

Mention should be made of other features of a boardwalk even though actual construction details are not discussed.

1. *Railings* on both the outboard and inboard sides of the boardwalk are usually constructed of pipe and for aesthetic appeal, the top is of wooden ship rail design. Stanchions are on 6 foot centers and fit into flush deck sleeves. Over-all height from promenade to top of ship rail is 3 feet 6 inches.

2. *Benches*. In most instances benches are installed along both rails facing the water. Whenever possible they should be of the wood and concrete type which feature a contour seat of bench slats and back rest of the same material.

3. *Shelters*. A desirable but expensive innovation in boardwalk design includes shelters or pavilions at intermediate distances. They serve the public by affording protection from the sun and sudden storms.

4. *Lighting*. Promenade or boardwalk lighting may be the street post type. Specifications in most recent design call for luminaire with 340 Watt lamp with asymmetric globe on a tapered elliptical arm. Height of the pole including a 20 inch base is 25 feet 9 inches and is manufactured of aluminum alloy.

1. Rockaway Beach: 3 ft. x 3 ft. = 9 sq. ft. per person
4,800 bathers per acre

2. Coney Island: 4 ft. x 4 ft. = 16 sq. ft. per person
2,700 bathers per acre

3. Jones Beach: 5 ft. x 5 ft. = 25 sq. ft. per person
1,700 bathers per acre

4. Orchard Beach: 6 ft. x 6 ft. = 36 sq. ft. per person
1,100 bathers per acre

5. Jacob Riis Beach: 7 ft. x 7 ft. = 49 sq. ft. per person
900 bathers per acre

Space available to bathers at five New York beaches.

Streets and Access Roads

A definite policy regarding streets and access roads must be established to keep a beachfront area on a dignified, desirable level. Various municipalities in long range planning have done an excellent job in this regard. The following steps should be taken:

1. Street systems near the waterfront should be completely mapped to prevent summer bungalows and other seasonal shanties from mushrooming in the area.
2. The waterfront end of the principal streets serving the entrances to the beach and boardwalk should be zoned to permit hotels, restaurants, and bathhouses, but prohibit open front stores, parking lots or commercial garages. Those permitted are only to provide supplemental services by private business not included in the simple beachfront development.
3. The remaining areas in the vicinity of the beach should be zoned "Residential" which would further stop the growth of undesirable beach shanties.
4. Parking should be prohibited if possible on all streets within two or three blocks of the beach.

Landscaping

Plans for landscaping must include a parkway or boulevard tree planting, and a tree and

Recreation area in conjunction with ocean beach front, Jones Beach State Park, New York.

Supporting recreation facilities at Jones Beach, New York.
Above: _Shuffleboard courts._
Below: _Paddle-tennis courts._

Marine Theater, Jones Beach, New York.

shrub screen planting between the main vehicular artery and the parking fields, games areas, and any other facilities between it and the boardwalk.

The selection of trees in the picnic area should receive special consideration. They should be planted to provide shade for the picnic tables and fireplaces. This area in turn should be screen planted to separate it from the adjacent playgrounds or parking fields.

All landscape plans should contain the following:

1. Symbols used to indicate number, types, and species of trees
2. Description of abbreviations used to indicate shrubs
3. Details of tree guying
4. Details of staking (minor and major trees)
5. Details of grades
6. Areas to receive topsoil and seed
7. Detail of skinned area for softball diamonds
8. Detail of edging for shrub beds
9. All notes pertaining to elevations, grades, and planting that may be of special concern.

Some of the more desirable planting materials suggested for the beach area are:

Shrubs

Ligustrum valifolium	Prunus maritima
Myrica Pensylvanica	Rosa rugosa
Rosa floribunda	Ilex crenata

Trees

Platinus acerifolia	Populus alba
Eleagnus angustifolia	Pinus thunbergi
Albizziajulibrissinrosea	Crataegus crusgalli

Selection of material should, however, be based on physical properties and the zone or section of the country where the construction is to take place.

SUPPORTING RECREATION AREAS AND FACILITIES

Satisfactory results have been accomplished in reversing the trend of deterioration in waterfront areas by following the conventional pattern of beachfront improvement. Beach development must, however, provide more than swimming opportunities. Therefore, a list of facilities is included that should receive serious consideration in any beach plan.

1. Behind the boardwalk, long strip park-

ing areas which in modern design are equipped with toll booths, automatic coin stations and parking lot gates. The vehicle operator is only required to insert a coin and a mechanical detector lifts the gate for entry. Several companies manufacture this mechanism.

2. Games areas between parking fields, including handball, basketball, paddle tennis courts and softball diamonds.

3. At every ten or twelve street intervals between softball fields and games areas a picnic area might be included with trees, tables, and fireplaces.

4. Children's playgrounds with swings, slides, and see-saws at appropriate intervals, depending on the length of the beachfront.

5. Comfort Station facilities at not more than six to eight city streets apart.

6. All of the above should in turn be backed up by a pleasant, wide, and possibly malled roadway, boulevard, or parkway. Typical of this type of design is the new South Beach Improvement in Staten Island and such facilities as Jones Beach, Long Island, and Rockaway in Queens.

7. Where sufficient space is available and usually where the beachfront area is well within park limits, pitch and putt golf courses have been included. Although an installation of this kind is initially expensive and requires constant maintenance, the popularity of the game makes it a worthwhile and often profitable enterprise. However, a word of caution is warranted. Construction of a pitch and putt course should not be undertaken unless it can be reasonably established that large numbers of people will patronize the beach. It is doubtful that a pitch and putt beach installation dependent only upon golfers would carry its own weight financially.

Access to the course should be directly from the boardwalk or close to it and control exercised from a starting booth where fees are paid, personal property is checked, and clubs and balls are obtained. In some installations where the terrain and location are not hazardous, it is unnecessary to enclose the area with protective fencing. For details on the layout and construction of the course see the chapter on Golf Facilities.

8. In the larger state parks, facilities for boating, dancing, roller skating and night water shows are also available. A rather successful arrangement is a combination dance floor and roller skating arena. This type of facility attracts people from the promenade or boardwalk and should be accessible on the inshore side. Operationally, this is a night activity with dancing "under the stars," for no fee. Depending on the budget allowances of the agency involved, a minimum fee should probably be charged for skating and rental of skates.

9. With the increase in popularity of boating, efforts are being made to accommodate small boat owners at some beach facilities. Marinas, with docking piers for boat storage, landing floats for transients, gas facilities, launching ramps and fully equipped boat houses are now available. Separate parking facilities for marina patrons are a requirement in any contemplated operation of this kind. In the presentation of the final plan for a marina, care should be exercised in confining all boating activities to an area that is not part of the bathing beach.

CHAPTER 23

CAMP SITES AND BUILDINGS

Charles Pound

PUBLIC INTEREST IN CAMPING AND OUTDOOR living is at an all-time high. Public camp sites in state and national parks are being developed at a rapid rate to meet the demands of family groups and citizens generally for a vacation in camp. The short work week and vacation with pay brings camping within the reach of a large majority of the people. Studies by the American Camping Association and individuals show that less than ten per cent of the youth of camp age attend an organized camp during the summer. The great difference between the millions who desire to go camping and the number of those who go indicates the necessity for more careful planning to get more adequate land areas and facilities for organized camping.

More camps are needed to teach skills, knowledge, and attitudes about outdoor vacations so that the millions who are going camping will profit most from the experience and make wise use of natural resources. The need for more camps calls for careful planning by public agencies such as park and recreation departments and school districts.

School camping has taken firm roots in many states. The essential difference between school camping and the traditional summer camp is that programs are conducted primarily during the school year as a regular part of the school curriculum. This development requires all-weather camp facilities that can be used the year round and is in keeping with the contemporary practice of spreading vacation choices over many months rather than limiting them to the summer. This new trend calls for camp facilities that are useable for several months of the year rather than only two as in the past. Extended use of camp facilities is economical in terms of resources and makes possible the accommodation of more campers by any one camp.

Resident camps should be built for year-round use to meet the needs of organized school and community camps. Cooperative planning is necessary to get the best value

Illustration: Tent frame with bunks hinged to side walls, Camp Bliss. Herald Tribune Fresh Air Fund, Sharpe Reservation, Fishkill, New York

for the community dollar and to make the best use of available land and sites that are available. Although the capital outlay for year-round use will be more at the beginning, the extended use will make the all-weather camp more economical.

The selection, development, and operation of a site for a camp program requires cooperative planning by experienced camp personnel and professional technicians including architects, engineers and contractors. The initial proper selection of a site will greatly influence the future success of the camp program. Although criteria vary with the specific requirements of the camp and the locality in which it is to be situated, certain basic considerations apply to all good camp sites.

SITE SELECTION

The *geographical location* of the site should be determined by the type of program, frequency and duration of the camper visit, and the origin and density of the population served. Extended use of the camp facilities for short term camping, school camp programs, and community services, is increasing and will continue to increase in importance. Therefore, it is generally advisable to select a site that is the most proximate to the density of population that will satisfy the established criteria.

The *tract* should be located on roads traversable during the period of camp operation by autos, busses, and trucks and require approximately three to four hours average driving time from nearby cities.

The *size* of the site to be selected should be governed by the ultimate number of campers to be accommodated, and ideally should contain one acre per person to permit a decentralized plan of development, and sufficient peripheral buffer area to preclude encroachment by, or on, surrounding property activities.

The *topography* of the site should provide good drainage, and preferably be sufficiently irregular and varied to provide privacy and separation for the various portions of the camp development. The *elevation* of the area should be above any possible flood levels of adjacent rivers, streams, or lakes; and should not be in a natural depression with poor air circulation and high humidity.

The *character* of the site should possess sufficient natural beauty and interest to engender in the campers a desire to participate in the activities, and to derive a feeling of exhilaration and satisfaction from their camping experience. It should have open and wooded areas, and be capable of supporting a diversity of program features. Natural hazards such as mine shafts, turbulent waters, precipitous cliffs, extensive swamps, or poisonous snakes, plants, or insects, should be avoided wherever possible; and if encountered, adequately guarded and posted.

A potable *water supply* economically available is mandatory. *Natural water* features for swimming and other aquatic activities are desirable, but if not available, a pool will suffice for a minimum aquatic program.

Sewage disposal must be economically feasible either by subsurface absorption, or treatment and discharge of effluent into a watercourse.

Public utility electric and telephone services are desirable. The site should be located in an area where *codes, ordinances,* and *zoning* permit harmonious integration of the camp and its program into the activities of the surrounding community.

Title to the property should be clear and free from easements or provisions concerning riparian, oil, or mineral rights, or other restrictive stipulations.

MASTER PLANNING

After a site has been carefully selected, a graphic over-all plan of the ultimate camp development should be prepared by competent technicians working in conjunction with experienced camp personnel. Accurately and thoroughly prepared, this plan will serve as a guide for all construction over a period of years into a final integrated design.

Topographic Map

The basic tool for the preparation of a master plan is an accurate topographic map with horizontal scale of 1 inch to 100 feet, and a vertical contour interval of 5 feet. The method selected for preparation of this map will depend on the extent of the tract; photogrammetric projections are generally more economical for tracts in excess of 500 acres, and ground surveys for smaller areas.

Site Analysis

With the map as a guide, a detailed inspection of every portion of the tract should be made, and notations entered on the map indicating areas especially adaptable for specific functions or construction, and also areas to be avoided in the development. Utilizing this information a complete integrated plan of the ultimate proposed development should be prepared indicating the locations of all structures and facilities. Individuality of planning and the specific nature of the site will determine exact placement of facilities. However, some basic criteria apply to any master plan.

Criteria for Location of Facilities

1. Living units should be located within a 500 yard radius of the administrative and program centers of the camp.
2. Distances between units should vary from 150 to 300 yards.
3. Toilet facilities, if centrally constructed for a unit, should not be more than 75 to 100 yards distant from living units.
4. Administrative facilities including office, parking, infirmary, and dining hall should be accessible by vehicles.
5. Structures should be located with reference to elevation to permit gravity flow of water to the buildings, and also gravity flow of wastes from them.

Schedule of Development

To supplement the master plan, a schedule of development should be prepared listing all items of construction, priority sequence and years in which they are to be undertaken, and estimated costs. There are three general categories of improvement: utilities, structures, and program facilities. (See Table 23-1.)

Preliminary Sketches and Tentative Costs

Following the preparation of the master plan and the development schedule, preliminary sketches of floor plans and architectural styles of all proposed structures should be made, and tentative costs determined from square foot construction costs currently applicable in the camp site locality. Actual unit costs will vary greatly with the type of construction and the location; however, an average rule of thumb for current construction costs of an entire camp facility exclusive of land acquisition and swimming pool construction, and based on the size of the camper load is as follows:

*Camp Capacity**	*Cost per Bed*
75-100	$1300-$1500
101-200	1100- 1300
201-400	900- 1100
401-600	700- 900

TABLE 23-1

Priorities for Developing Facilities

Item of Development	Priority and Year	
Utilities		
Water supply, storage	(1)	(1)
Sewage disposal	(3)	(1)
Service road	(2)	(1)
Electricity	(8)	(2)
Telephone	(9)	(2)
Structures		
Living units	(5)	(1)
Latrines	(4)	(1)
Dining hall	(10)	(2)
Infirmary	(7)	(2)
Administration	(11)	(2)
Staff quarters	(12)	(2)
Program and recreation bldgs.	(13)	(3)
Warehouse-garage-workshop	(14)	(3)
Program Facilities		
Waterfront or pool	(6)	(1)
Activities fields	(15)	(3)
Amphitheater	(17)	(3)
Rifle-archery ranges	(16)	(3)

CONSTRUCTION

Buildings and physical facilities at a camp should be of the minimal number and simplest design that will satisfy the specific function for which the structure is intended. An architectural style applicable to all buildings should be selected that is harmonious with the environment and compatible with the climatic conditions prevailing in the location and at the time of the year the camp will be in operation. Construction materials should be available locally, should preferably be indigenous to the area, and selected for their permanence and workability with local la-

* Staff and Campers.

Photo by James Kavallines, Staff Photographer, *New York Herald Tribune*

Modern design can be both beautiful and functional. Recreation Building, Camp Bliss, Herald Tribune Fresh Air Fund.

bor. All structures should be carefully designed and well constructed since initially cheap materials and assembly will often require high future maintenance and rehabilitation costs.

Basic Standards

Although the variety of structures is infinite, certain basic standards apply.

Living quarters.

1. Living quarters in the form of tents, lean-tos, shelters, or cabins, should not house more than eight persons in a single enclosure.
2. Forty square feet of floor area should be provided per person, with beds arranged with a minimum of 2 feet between heads.
3. Provisions should be made for the protection from rain, exclusion of pestiferous insects, and storage of personal articles.

Dining hall.

1. Dining hall area requires 10 to 12 square feet per person and kitchen needs from 3 to 5.
2. Storage area varies with the frequency of delivery, but generally requires 3 cubic feet per person for dry storage and 2 cubic feet per person for refrigerated storage.
3. The design of the dining hall should take cognizance of the factors of traffic flow, sanitation, temperature control, illumination level, and acoustics.
4. The roof system should be suspended between exterior walls to eliminate posts within the dining hall floor area.

Waterfront.

1. Waterfronts should provide an average of 25 to 30 square feet of water per swimmer divided into areas for non-swimmers, beginners, and advanced swimmers with water depths of 1 and ½ to 3 feet, 4 to 6 feet, and 7 to 9 feet respectively.
2. The designated waterfront area should be enclosed with a fence or other physical demarcation, and ingress and egress checked at a control point.
3. Separate areas should be provided for boats and canoes.

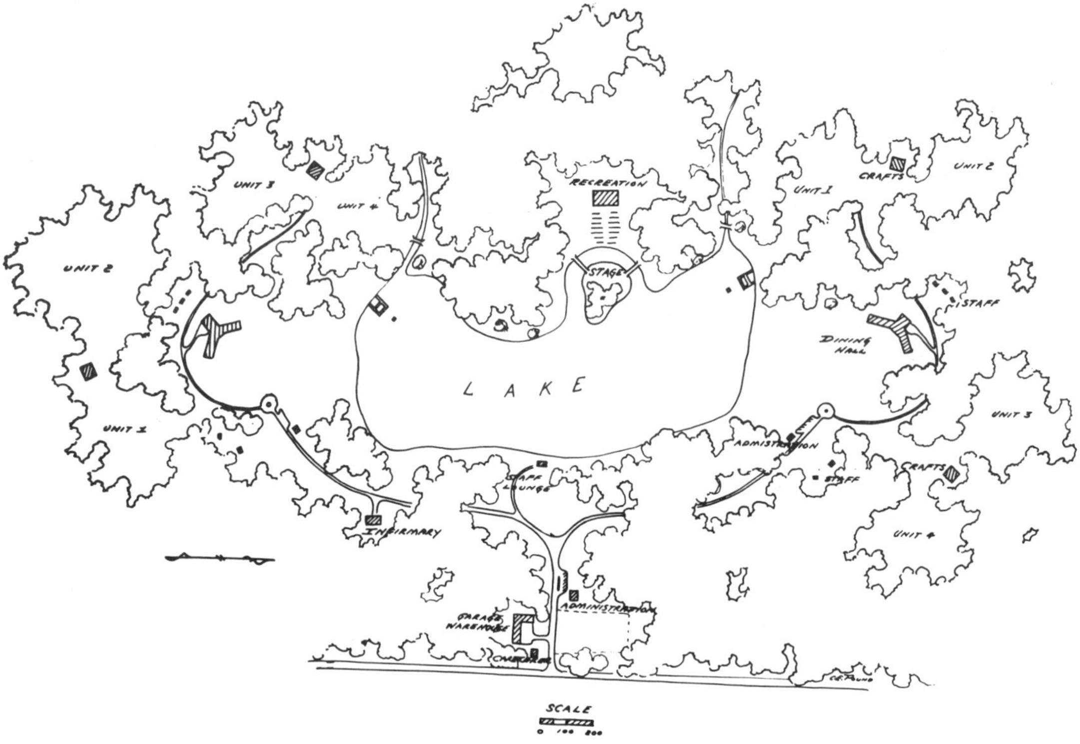

Development plan for co-ed camp with capacity of 400.

Large dormitory type sleeping cabin.

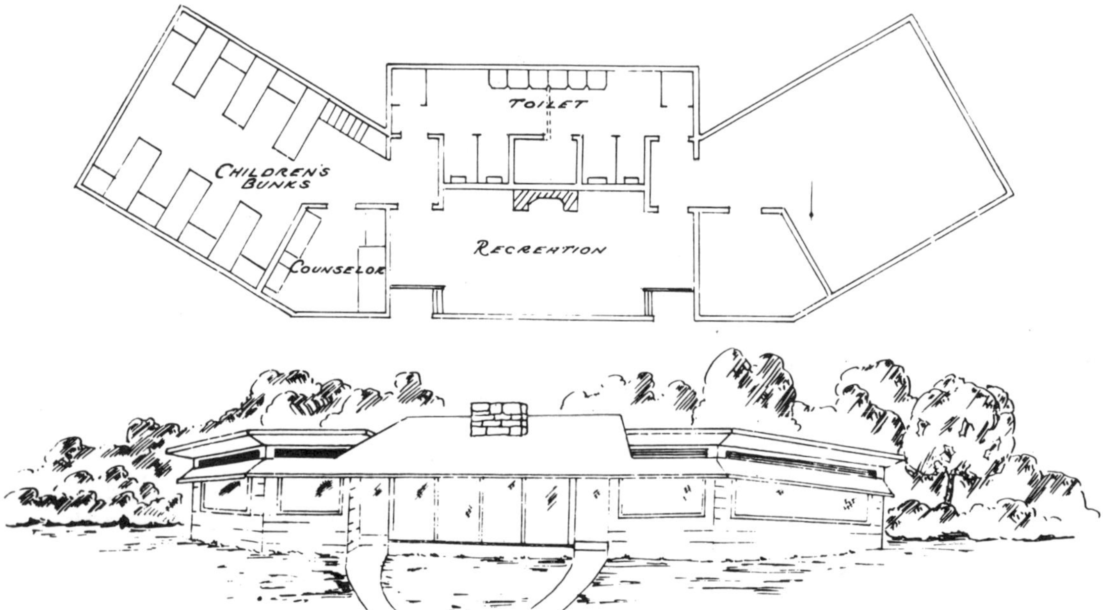

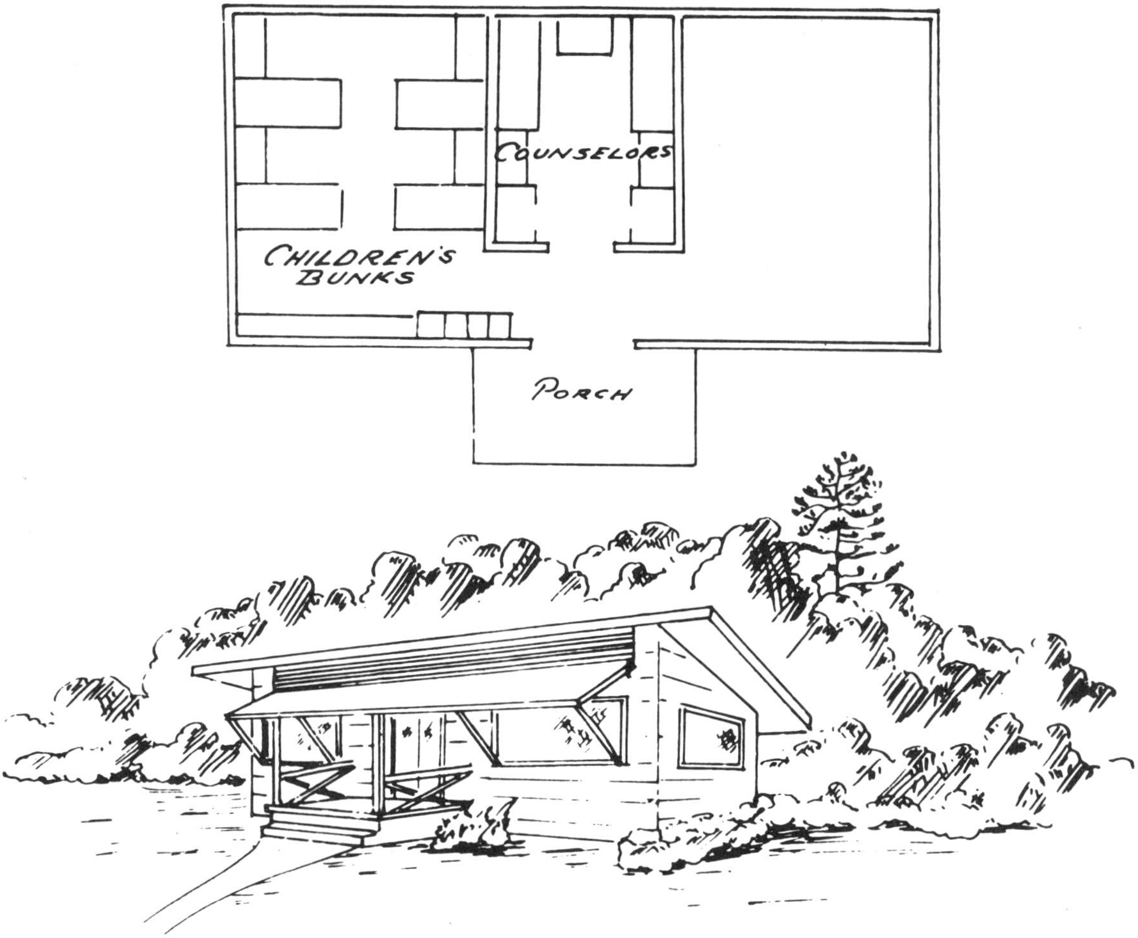

Bunk house for eight children and two counselors.

Lean-to type bunk house.

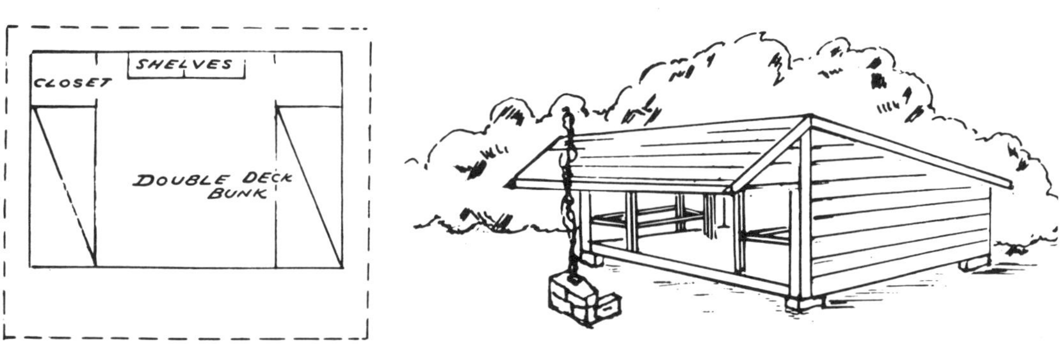

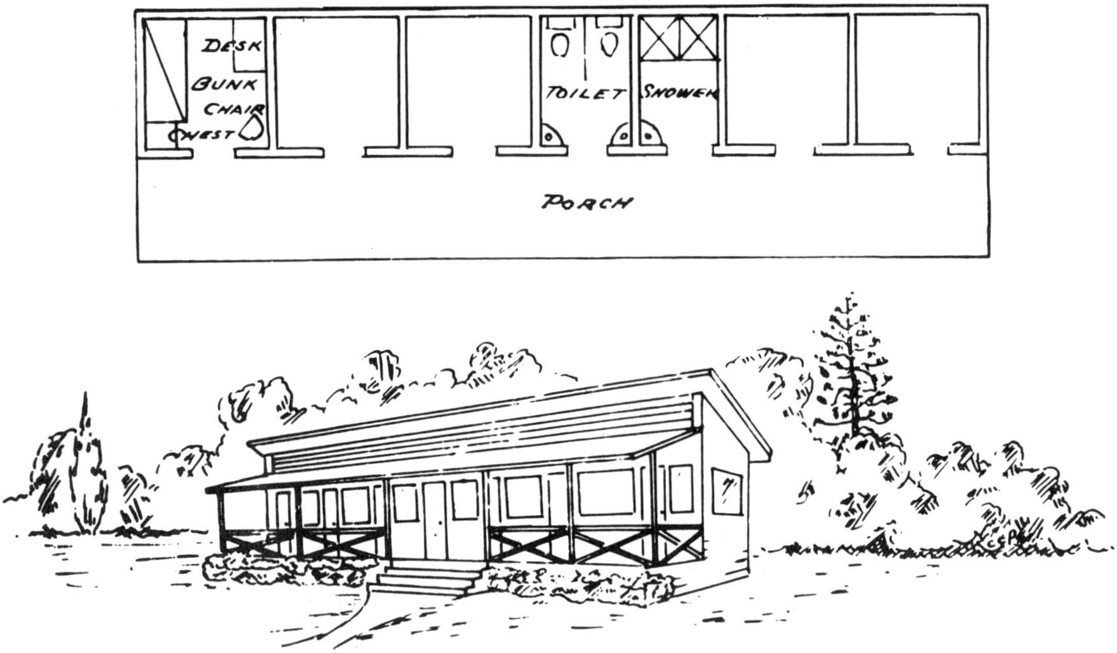

Staff cabin.

Dining hall.

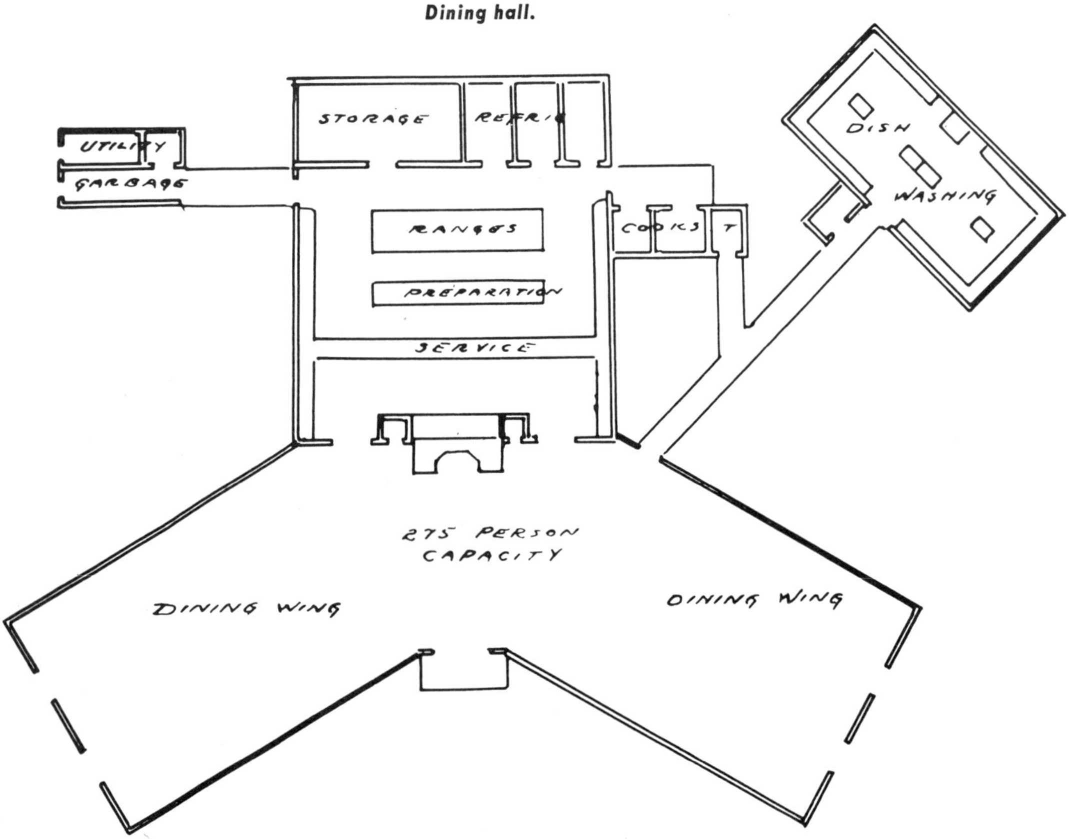

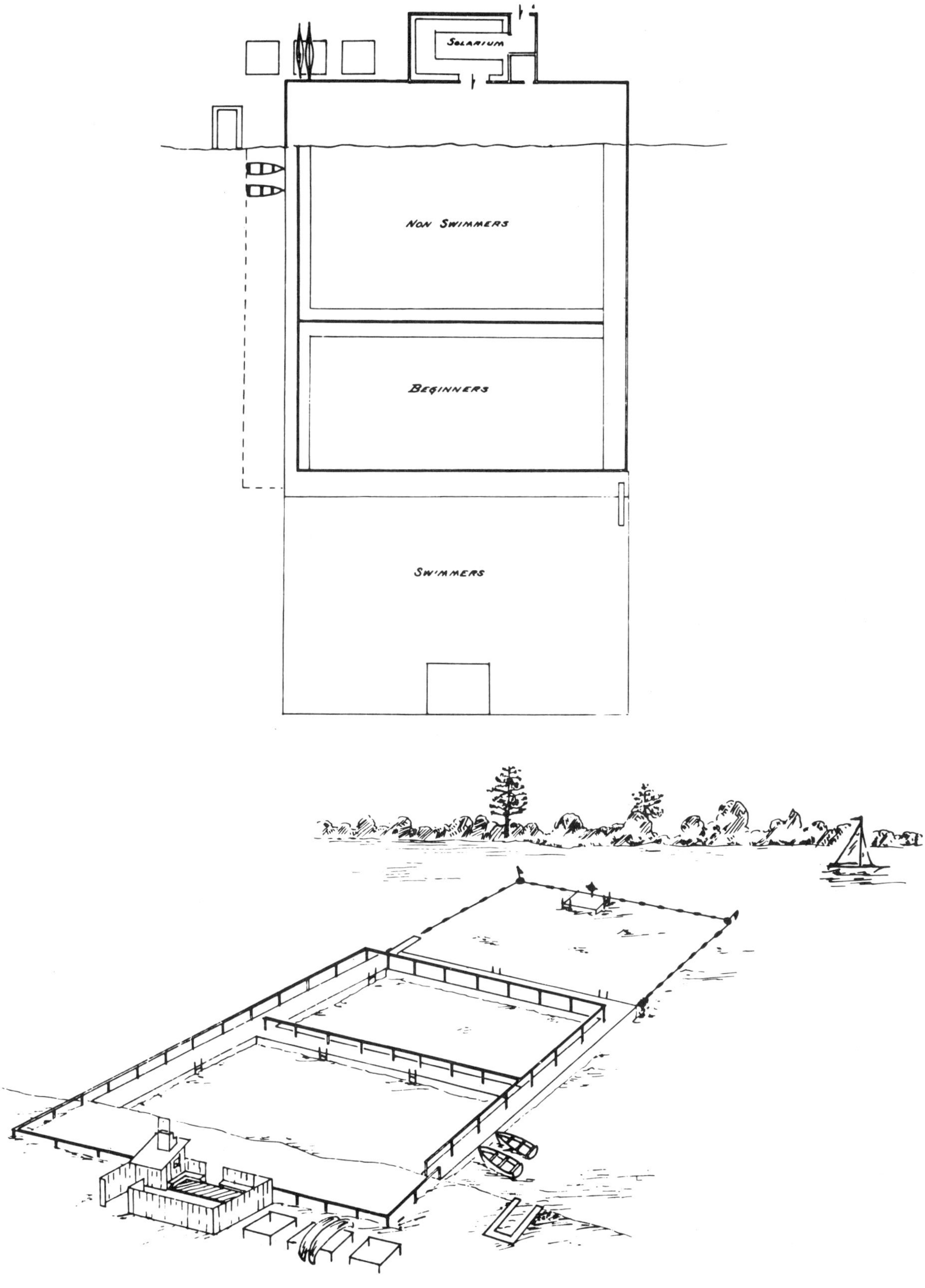

Three station waterfront area.

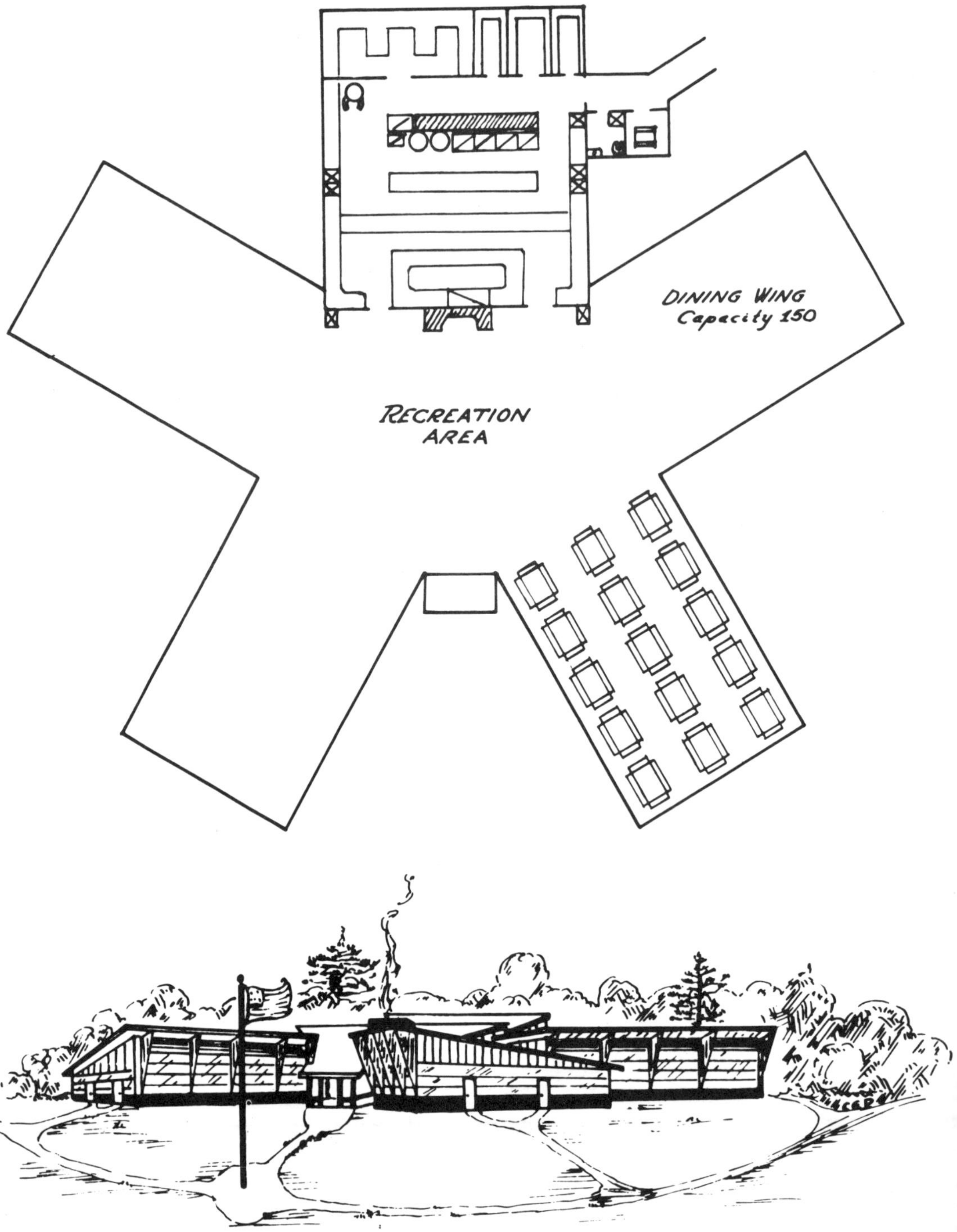

Central dining room with separate dining units.

Infirmary.

1. Infirmary capacity should average 1 bed for each 20 campers.

2. The building should provide facilities for ward, isolation, clinic, and nurse or doctor quarters.

WATER SUPPLY

An adequate potable water supply is the most essential requisite for the establishment of a camp. Its availability should be ascertained before a site is purchased, and the actual delivery of water effected, before any other construction is started. Daily requirements vary with the type of program and extent of facilities from 5 to 100 gallons per person per day. In most camp operations 60 to 75 gallons is average. This amount should be available from its source during eight hours. For example, a camp of 200 persons using 60 gallons per person per day would require 12,000 gallons, or 1,500 gallons per hour, or 25 gallons per minute. Sources of water in order of preference are: (1) municipal supply, (2) drilled wells, (3) dug wells, (4) springs, (5) streams, (6) lakes. The variation in the prevalence of ground water requires that advice of experienced well drillers, engineers, and geologists be obtained before the source of water is decided or the location of a well is established. If a well is drilled accurate data should be maintained by the driller regarding depth of well, diameter and length of casing, residual water level, pumping level and draw down. A 24-hour continuous test is essential to ascertain that the flow is from a continuous supply. As soon as the water is obtained a chemical and bacteriological analysis should be made to determine its suitability for consumption.

Storage can be either in pressure or elevated storage tanks. Pressure tanks are subject to mechanical interruptions of power or pumps and will deliver only one-third of their capacity at usable pressures. An elevated tank, on either high land or on a tower, with a minimum of 24 hours water supply is recommended.

A source of water requiring chlorination should be used only as a last resort because of the possibility of the failure of either the mechanical equipment or the human element in operating the machinery.

Pumping equipment should be selected on the basis of the data determined during the drilling and pump test. Pumps are classified according to lift from the source of water to the pump; shallow pumps for lifts up to 22 feet, and deep pumps for lifts greater than 22 feet. Many types are available, each offering certain specific advantages in specialized circumstances. Principally, a pump should be selected on the basis of an engineer's or well driller's recommendation for the specific source, should be manufactured by a reputable company, and should be repairable or replaceable by distributors in the immediate vicinity.

Distribution piping should be of sufficient size to deliver the required flow at each point of usage with a minimum of 20 pounds pressure. If the camp is located within the limits of an organized fire district the reduction in insurance rates will sometimes justify the installation of 6 foot mains and hydrants. Time proven cast iron, galvanized wrought iron and steel, have been supplemented extensively with asbestos cement and plastic piping. These materials are not subject to corrosion, and the plastic does not burst when water freezes in the lines.

WASTE DISPOSAL

Camp wastes are of several types: sewage, kitchen, shower, garbage, and pool backwash.

Sewage waste can be disposed of in dry pit latrines, concrete vaults, or septic tanks with either subsurface tile fields or sand filters. Pit latrines should be screened structures above a board lined pit at least 4 feet deep. The structure should be located slightly above the ground level to permit surface drainage away from the pit. Earth and lime should be added to the pit daily to cover the excrement, and insecticides should be used to eliminate flies.

Concrete vaults are only used where proximity to water supply or lake is mandatory, or where the subsoil conditions prohibit percolation. The vaults will require periodic cleaning.

Flush systems are the most satisfactory method of disposal; however, their initial high cost, and the amount of water required for their operation sometimes prohibits their use in a camp used only for summer operation. The standard water closet with either flushtank or flushometer is subject to mechanical failure and clogging when installed for general use in children's camps. A modified flush system utilizing a subsurface concrete vault and a dump hopper charged with waste water from lavatories and showers, both reduces the amount of water required for the operation of the system and permits use during periods of freezing weather.

Septic tanks used in conjunction with flush systems can be either prefabricated of steel or concrete, or formed in place and poured of concrete. The capacity of the tank is proportionate to the daily load. Tanks should be placed in proximity to the structure served, and be accessible for cleaning. Final disposal of septic tank effluent can be in either subsurface tile fields or through sand filters.

Kitchen waste containing a high percentage of grease, vegetable parings, and detergents should not be introduced into the same subsurface disposal system as sewage because the suspended greases will completely clog the soil porosity in a very short period of time. While it is true that greases will decompose in the presence of anaerobic septic tank action, the volume of liquid flow in the tanks combined with the emulsifying action of the detergents, does not permit the complete breakdown or removal of the greases, and a heavy carry through into the tile lines occurs. A retention trap should be installed on the kitchen waste line which will partially serve as a grease trap, but mainly as a settling basin for solid wastes. The effluent from this trap should be disposed of either in a separate tile field, or through the sand filter if such final disposal method is used. The retention trap should have a capacity of approximately 6 gallons per person served.

Tile fields for the disposal of septic tank effluent are designed on the basis of sewage flow and the porosity of the soil. The absorption rate is based upon a percolation test which determines the number of gallons per square foot per day that the soil will absorb. Tile fields should be divided into lines not greater than 60 feet in length, and dosed with an alternating syphon. Their location and alignment should be designed by a qualified sanitary engineer.

In areas where subsurface conditions will not permit absorption, sand filtration with post chlorination and discharge of effluent into a watercourse is the recommended procedure. The open type offers the advantage of permitting easy removal of the grease accumulation on the surface of the filter. A properly designed and constructed sand filter will operate indefinitely with minimum maintenance, and in comparison with the relatively short 10 to 12 year life of a tile field, justifies the greater initial expense.

The best garbage disposal service is that offered by professional scavengers. If this is not practical, incineration or sanitary fill operation are satisfactory methods. Garbage waste averages approximately 2 cubic feet per person per day. Commercially designed incinerators are more efficient than camp constructed ones, and should be selected on the basis of the load. Large volume disposal units are available that masticate waste food, paper, and glass into a semi-dry sterile waste.

CHAPTER 24

EQUIPMENT—PROCUREMENT, STORAGE, MAINTENANCE

E. Parker Yutzler

GOOD EQUIPMENT FOR USE IN PHYSICAL EDUcation and recreation programs is necessary for the maximum utilization of the recreation facilities and effective leadership. Just as a competent dentist with his modern office needs good tools and equipment for the successful performance of his skills, the best qualified recreation director with the most elaborate facilities needs safe, top-quality tools with which to conduct his program.

Equipment and supplies are usually divided into three main classes: permanent, semi-permanent, and expendable.

Permanent equipment is that type which usually does not need replacement, except after many years of use. Permanent equipment such as indoor and outdoor basketball backstops, climbing ropes, rings, stall bars, tennis posts, goal posts, and diving boards are best installed at the time the building or play area is constructed. Other types of permanent equipment include side horses, bucks, springboards, trampolines, bleachers, electric scoreboards, parallel bars, goal posts, jumping standards, baseball backstops, table tennis tables, swings and slides. Another method of identifying permanent equipment is through the use of the labels "fixed" or "portable."

Semi-permanent equipment is that which after several years of normal use must be replaced for safety and sanitary reasons. This classification includes protective padding, gymnasium mats, wrestling mats, nets for tennis, volleyball, and badminton, see-saw boards, swing seats and so on.

Expendable equipment is that which must

Illustration: Portable bleachers

be replaced regularly because of wear. This includes all uniforms and shoes, tennis racquets, balls, bats, vaulting poles, cross bars and so on.

HOW EQUIPMENT IS MADE AND DISTRIBUTED

What steps are involved in the manufacture and distribution of athletic equipment? This is a question frequently asked by the user. Almost all manufacturers have athletic or recreation experts on their advisory staffs. An idea for a piece of new equipment or modification of design in some traditional piece soon becomes a working model that undergoes rigorous tests for strength, safety, practicability, and public acceptance. Even a new improvement or change of design on an existing model must pass these tests. The next step is the fabrication of sample models that are tried out at selected recreation areas. After improvements have been made as a result of these trials the production run is started. Simultaneous promotional materials are sent to dealers, trade magazines, schools, and colleges announcing the item.

The manufacturer establishes a "list" or market price according to his cost of production and the expenses of selling. He sells to *dealers* at approximately 50 per cent off this list price, or he may sell to *jobbers*, who buy and stock large quantities, at approximately 50 per cent and an additional 10 per cent off the list price. A jobber, in turn, sells to dealers at about 40 per cent off list price. The dealer sells to the general public at list price or slightly below. In selling to schools or institutions, however, he establishes a "school" price, also referred to as "trade" price, of approximately 25 per cent above his cost. For instance, a manufacturer may set a market value or list price of $10 on #XYZ ball. A jobber pays $4.50 for it and sells it to a dealer for $5 to $6 depending upon what volume of business has been involved. The dealer sells this ball to the general public at $10 or slightly less. His price to schools will vary from a minimum of $6.25 to a maximum of $7.50.

Often purchasers will contact a manufacturer directly in an effort to obtain a lower price than that charged by a dealer. This practice is not recommended inasmuch as reliable manufacturers prefer to sell through their dealers or representatives who are needed to promote products and provide a steady volume of business for them. The purchaser needs the good will of the dealer and the services he is in a position to provide. When manufacturers are contacted directly by the purchaser they usually will follow one of two procedures: Refer the purchaser to their local dealers or representatives, or fill the order at the same school price he would have had paid to a dealer. Invariably, if the dealer is an exclusive representative, his normal commission will be paid to him by the manufacturer, or the order may be sent to the dealer for processing by the manufacturer.

A manufacturer's representative is a salesman who may or may not carry a stock of merchandise, but who nevertheless promotes products and sales. He may work on a commission basis, send all orders to the factory for processing and receive a commission. Or, he may process the order, finance it, issue his own invoice to the school or institution and receive payment from the purchaser. This procedure is common practice when heavy duty equipment, which is difficult to carry in stock, is involved.

QUALITY VS. QUANTITY BUYING

The importance of top quality merchandise cannot be overemphasized. The very nature of athletic and recreation activities suggests roughness and toughness. In no other field of activity is there greater need for sturdy, safe, and durable equipment. The old adage, "Penny wise and pound foolish" has direct implications for the purchaser of sports equipment. A supply of inferior footballs may last for only one season, whereas, fewer top quality footballs will give longer and better service and additions may be made from year to year. It is more prudent to initially purchase one or two pieces of the best available playground equipment and purchase more at a later date, than to have a gym or playground filled with unsafe, inferior equipment. Facilities and play areas must be carefully planned and equipped in order to derive maximum use and efficiency from them.

RECOMMENDED PROCEDURES FOR PURCHASING EQUIPMENT

The best time to purchase equipment for school or community athletic programs is immediately following the completion of a season. It is then that the needs and wants are fresh in the minds of the coaches. Furthermore, at this time manufacturers and dealers are likely to have close-outs for purposes of turning their stock into cash. Even when school purchases cannot be made until the following year for budgetary reasons, detailed lists of requirements and specifications should be made at the close of the season.

In most states, there are laws that govern the expenditure of public funds. All purchasing agents must be thoroughly acquainted with the law and proper procedures that should be followed in the procurement of equipment.

For example: the following is quoted from Section 103 of the General Municipal Law of New York State:

§103. ADVERTISING FOR BIDS; LETTING OF CONTRACTS

1. Except as otherwise expressly provided by an act of the legislature or by a local law adopted prior to September first, nineteen hundred fifty-three, or except in an emergency, all contracts for public work involving an expenditure of more than twenty-five hundred dollars and purchase contracts involving an expenditure of more than one thousand dollars, shall be awarded by the appropriate officer, board or agency of a political subdivision or of any district therein, to the lowest responsible bidder furnishing the required security after advertisement for sealed bids in the manner provided by this section. In cases where two or more responsible bidders furnishing the required security submit identical bids as to price, such officer, board or agency may, in his or its discretion, reject all bids and readvertise for new bids in the same manner provided by this section.

2. Advertisement for bids shall be published in the official newspaper or newspapers, if any, or otherwise in a newspaper or newspapers designated for such purpose. Such advertisement shall contain a statement of the time and place where all bids received pursuant to such notice will be publicly opened and read. All bids received shall be publicly opened and read at the time and place so specified. At least five days shall elapse between the first publication of such advertisement and the date so specified for the opening and reading of bids.

3. Notwithstanding the provisions of subdivision one of this section, any officer, board or agency of a political subdivision or of any district therein located in whole or in part in a county, authorized to make purchases of materials, equipment or supplies, may make such purchases, when available, through the county subject to the rules established pursuant to subdivision two of section four hundred eight-a of the county law; provided that the political subdivision or district for which such officer, board or agency acts shall accept sole responsibility for any payment due the vendor. All purchases shall be subject to audit and inspection by the political subdivision or district for which made. No officer, board or agency of a political subdivision or of any district therein shall make any purchase through the county when bids have been received for such purchase by such officer, board or agency, unless such purchases may be made upon the same terms, conditions and specifications at a lower price through the county.

When it is expected that the purchases will not exceed $1000 informal quotations can be requested from several dealers or manufacturers' agents in the form of a letter as follows:

Gentlemen:

Kindly quote your lowest prices for the following items and return to us on or before (Date), total cost to include delivery charges to destination.

Approximate delivery date should also be included as a dealer cannot be expected to hold merchandise for an indefinite period of time pending a decision.

HOW TO WRITE SPECIFICATIONS

One of the most important steps in the purchasing process is the preparation of specifications. Suggestions for the preparation of specifications are:

1. Determine what is actually needed or wanted according to existing inventory.

2. Become acquainted with the different trade brands usually available of each particular item to be purchased.

3. Select reliable, well-known manufacturers and their merchandise; however, thoroughly investigate new products. Sample them or obtain recommendations from other users.

4. A full description of each item or a reference number should be given. As an illustration, there may be 40 different kinds of basketballs. The choice should either be described in detail or be referenced, "Basketball, J. Doe Co. #166 or equal." This will completely identify the ball. It is not legal to specify a particular brand of equipment and refuse to accept an equal. *The burden of proof that an article is or is not equal rests with the buyer.* A recent ruling defines "an equal" as being an item that will do the job or serve the purpose for which it is intended.

5. Detailed specifications are most essential in permanent equipment. The example below represents the complete specifications for the purchase of "outdoor portable bleachers."

TABLE 24-1

Example of Detailed Specifications

1. Scope of Work

Furnish complete and ready for erection the following sections of Type "AN" or Type "BM" Mobile Bleachers as manufactured by Standard Steel and Supply Co., Three Rivers, Michigan or equal.

__________ Sections __________ Ft. Long x __________ Rows High—Non-Elevated

__________ Sections __________ Ft. Long x __________ Rows High—Non-Elevated

__________ Sections __________ Ft. Long x __________ Rows High—Elevated

__________ Sections __________ Ft. Long x __________ Rows High—Elevated

__________ Pairs of Wheel Attachments

Dimensions and Extras:

Rise per row __________ (Specify 8″ or 10″)
Depth per row __________ (Specify 22″ or 24″)
Single 10″ Footboards __________ Double 8″ Footboards
Elevation __________ (Specify 30″, 36″ or 42″ ground to walkway or 1st row Footboard)
Walkway width __________ (Specify 36″ or 48″)
1st Row Footboard __________ (Specify 18″ or 24″—on elevated bleachers where walkway is not required)
Ramps __________ Steps __________ (Specify number)
Rear Guard Rails __________
End Guard Rails __________ (Specify number of pairs)
Divided front to back for multi-use __________ (Specify Division)

2. Design

Mobile steel frame bleachers shall be designed to support in addition to their own weight, a live load of 120 pounds per linear foot of seatboard plus 120 pounds per linear foot of footboard. Bleachers shall withstand a side sway load of 24 pounds per linear foot of seatboard and a front to back sway load of 10 pounds per linear foot of seatboard.

3. Unit Specifications

A. *Support Structure.* The main support members are to assemble at right angles to the boards and are to be welded, non-bolted, units. Each vertical seatboard support is to be one continuous member from seat to base. Footboard supports, and bracing where used, shall be welded to vertical seat supports to form rigid non-bolted structure. Adequate cross bracing, tie bars and pick-up members to be field bolted to main support members to permit bleacher sections to mount on wheel attachments so there will be no undue stress on seat and footboards during a moving operation.

B. *Seat and Footboards.* Each seat and footboard shall be of Structural Grade Douglas Fir 2″ thick before surfacing, s4s, edges eased and attached to steel support frame with ⅜ inch truss head bolts. Seatboards are to be 10 inches wide before surfacing and shall be jig drilled so as to be interchangeable and reversible. Footboards are to be 10 inches wide before surfacing (unless specified as 8 inch boards under "Scope of Work"), and are to be interchangeable with seatboards. Footboards are to be mounted above their supports to provide obstruction-free passage full length of bleacher. All joints on seatboards and footboards to be flush and lapless.

C. *Guard Rails.* Where required—1⅝ inch O.D. Galvanized Steel pipe guard rails with steel mounting brackets shall be provided. (See "Scope of Work" for location and quantity.)

D. *Walkway or Front Footboard.* See "Scope of Work" for detail. Walkway or front footboard support shall be an integral welded part of the bleacher support structure.

E. *Wheel Attachments.* Each wheel attachment shall be a self-contained unit complete with pneumatic tires. Each wheel shall be self-locking requiring no bolts, fasteners or loose pieces to hold it in place during a moving operation. Wheels shall be of adequate size to accommodate weight of bleacher sections over prevailing terrain.

F. *Painting.* All steel shall be properly cleaned and shall receive one shop coat of rust inhibiting paint and one finish coat of best quality outside aluminum paint. All lumber shall receive one coat of combination color primer sealer and one coat of best quality outside bleacher enamel—both coats to be applied to lumber by a dipping operation.

G. *Hardware.* All bolts, nuts, washers, etc. required are to be heavy cadmium plated for rust prevention.

H. *Sleepers.* Penta treated Douglas Fir sleepers or mudsills shall be furnished.

6. Permanent or semi-permanent equipment should have a guarantee of at least a year. One should insist on a statement to this effect, "All units shall be guaranteed against defective workmanship, operation and materials for a period of one year from the date of final installation."

7. Advertise for bids in local papers using a form similar to the following:

BOARD OF EDUCATION
NAME OF SCHOOL
ADDRESS

ADVERTISEMENT

The Board of Education, U.F.S.D. No. ___ of the Town of __________, County of __________, hereby invites the submission of separate bids for physical education equipment for use in the schools of the District. Bids will be received until 2:00 P.M. __________ (Date) at the Central School, Main Ave., __________, at which time and place all bids will be publicly opened and read aloud.

Information for Bidders, Form of Proposal, Form of Acceptance of Proposal, and the Specifications, may be examined at said office and copies thereof obtained upon request.

The Board of Education reserves the right to waive any informalities or to reject any or all bids.

Dated __________

JOHN DOE
District Clerk

In addition to advertising for bids, requests may also be sent to qualified bidders. A minimum of five days must be allowed for their return; however, to obtain a more desirable competitive bid it is suggested that 15 to 20 days be allowed in order to give dealers ample time in which to obtain the best possible price on which to bid.

Special instructions to bidders set forth the conditions under which the bids are made and received.

Sample Instructions to Bidders

1. PROPOSALS: Sealed proposals for the furnishing, delivery, and installing, where called for, of the services, materials, equipment and/or supplies, as required by the Board of Education of Union Free School District No. X, Town of __________, County of __________, popularly known as "__________ Public Schools" and set forth in the following specifications prepared under the direction of said Board of Education, will be opened on the day and hour stated in the request for bids.

   The person, firm or corporation making such proposal shall submit it in a sealed envelope to the District Clerk or his duly designated representative at the place mentioned on or before the hour and day stated in the request, and the envelope shall be indorsed on the face thereof with the name of the person, firm or corporation making such proposal, the date of its presentation and title of the services, materials, equipment and/or supplies for which such proposal is made. Proposals must be made in duplicate upon the forms provided therefor which will be furnished to the bidders by the Owner. Amounts must be stated both in words and in figures. The signature shall be in longhand. The bidder shall retain one executed original and return to the Owner the other.

2. CONDITIONS OF THE CONTRACT: All bidders should carefully read the General Conditions and the specifications and addenda, if any, for they will constitute a part of the contract, together with the Proposal and the Acceptance of the Proposal.

   The bidder may bid on any or all items on the bid form. The bidder shall insert the price per stated unit and the extension against each item in the schedule hereto annexed, which he proposes to furnish and deliver. In the event of a discrepancy between the unit price and the extension, the unit price will govern. The price inserted must be net and must include delivery charges to destination inside delivery. Computation must be made of the total amount of the bid for all items bid upon and the total shall be stated in the space provided.

3. TAXES: No charge will be allowed for federal, state or municipal sales and excise taxes, in that the Board of Education is exempt therefrom. The price bid shall be net and shall not include the amount of any such tax. Exemption certificates, if required, will be furnished on forms provided by the bidder.

4. ADDITIONAL CHARGES: No charge will be allowed for cases, boxes, cartons, bottles, etc., nor for freight expenses, expressage or cartage. No empty packages, cases, boxes, cartons, bottles, etc., will be returned to the bidder or contractor and none will be paid for by the Board of Education. Such empty cases, boxes, etc., may be removed by the bidder or contractor at his own expense.

5. EQUIVALENTS: When a catalogue reference follows the description of an item, such catalogue reference is intended as a means of more fully describing the item in the shortest possible space and is to be regarded as part of the description of the item. All catalogues to which reference is made shall be available at the office of the District Clerk. The use of such catalogues is not intended to limit competition. Whenever a particular brand or make of material, de-

vice, equipment or other merchandise is shown or specified, such make or brand is to be regarded merely as a standard. If two or more such brands are shown or specified, each is to be regarded as the equal of the other. Any other brand or make which is the recognized equal of that specified and is suitable for the purpose intended will be accepted. The merchandise shall be in every respect in accordance with what in the opinion of the Owner or the Architect/Engineer is the best modern practice and whenever there is doubt as to what is permissible, that interpretation which requires the best quality or materials and workmanship in conformity with the best modern practice must be followed.

6. PROHIBITED INTEREST: Each bidder must state that no member of the Board of Education, Union Free District No. X, Town of ______________, nor any officer or employee thereof, nor any member of or delegate to Congress or resident commissioner, is directly or indirectly interested in the proposal.

7. DELIVERY: Delivery will be made to individual schools or proximate warehouse as directed. Mixed loads of more than one item, color, size, etc. must be sorted when directed by receiving clerk. No help for unloading will be provided by the Board of Education. Suppliers should notify their truckers accordingly. Deliveries shall be made between the hours of 9:00 A.M. and 4:00 P.M. on weekdays other than Saturdays and holidays. All materials and supplies must be securely packed in uniform containers adequately marked as to contents, our order number, and delivered without damage or breakage in such units as are specified in the schedule. Count to be determined at a later date. Inasmuch as the merchandise described in this contract is urgently needed for the operation of a public school, time is of the essence. When a particular order is designated to the attention of a specific person it shall be so indicated on all packages concerned.

8. LIQUIDATED DAMAGES: The successful bidder, upon his failure or refusal to execute and deliver the contract bonds if required within five (5) days after he has received notice of the acceptance of his bid, shall forfeit to the Owner as liquidated damages for such failure or refusal, the security deposited with his bid. It is understood, however, that this forfeiture shall not preclude the Owner from claiming any and all other damages sustained as a result thereof.

9. TERMINATION FOR BREACH: If the person or firm to whom an award is made shall fail to furnish and deliver within the time specified and allowed, the Board of Education may cancel the remainder of the order and may deduct and retain out of the monies due, or which may become due to such person or firm from the Board of Education, such sum as shall be sufficient to pay the difference between the prices on which the award is made and the prices which the Board of Education may or shall be obliged to pay to procure such supplies from other parties.

10. SAMPLES.

General Conditions

1. CUTS AND SPECIFICATIONS: If certain items are not bid on, state the item number and the wording, NO BID. All bids must be accompanied by cuts and specifications of items bid. When stated in the specification "or approved equal," it shall mean approval only by the Board of Education of Union Free School District No. X, Town of ____________, County of ____________, N.Y.

2. ADDENDA: Any addenda sent to bidders shall be as binding and take precedence over the original part of the specification to which they refer. Interpretation and clarification of all parts of the specifications may be had at the Office of the Business Administrator, ____________ High School on or before date of bid receipt if request for same is submitted in writing.

3. DAMAGE TO WORK OF OTHERS: No floors, walls, structural members or existing finished work shall be drilled, cut, or in any way defaced for the installation of furniture, furnishing or equipment herein specified until the Owner has been consulted and its approval obtained in writing. The contractor shall be held strictly responsible for and shall make good at his own expense any and all damage to the work of others resulting from the delivery and/or installation of his work.

4. ACCESSORIES: The contractor shall furnish, deliver and install where called for, furniture, furnishings and equipment described in the specifications, with all appurtenances, parts and accessories not specifically mentioned in the Articles of the Specifications but which are normally a part of the items called for or necessary to render it complete. These shall be included in the bid prices and shall conform to the best practices.

5. LAW COMPLIANCE: The contractor awarded a contract for any portion of the following bid under these specifications must comply with all Federal and State labor, education and other laws governing school work.

6. BID PRICE: The bid price on all items shall be firm until delivery has been made. The Board of Education reserves the right to increase or decrease the quantities of items required without any change in unit pricing.

7. ACCEPTANCE OF BID: The Board of Education reserves the right to accept this bid by items or as a whole, waive any informality in or to reject any or all bids, or to accept that bid or those bids, which in its judgment, is or are best for the school district.

8. Bid Security: No bid will be accepted unless accompanied by a certified check or bid bond of the bidder with a surety or sureties acceptable to the Board of Education in an amount not less than 5% of the total bid. Bid securities will be returned to all successful bidders five (5) days after the Owner and the accepted bidder shall have executed the contract, or if no contract has been executed within thirty (30) days after the date of the opening of the bid, upon demand of the bidder, or at any time thereafter so long as he has not been notified of the acceptance of his bid. The successful bidders will be required to furnish a Performance and Completion Bond in an amount equal to 100% of the bid price, in form and with a surety or sureties acceptable to the Board of Education.

9. Samples: At the request of the Board of Education, samples of the items bid may be called for inspection and held by the Board until same has served its purpose. Said samples shall clearly indicate Item Number bid on and manufacturer's name and model number. The Board reserves the right to retain such samples submitted by successful bidder until completion of contract covering such items. Where sample is requested same must be delivered within five (5) days of request. Samples will be returned, if desired, as soon as award is made, but must be removed by bidder at his own expense.

10. All Bids must be submitted on forms furnished by the Board of Education.

11. Definitions: The word "Owner" is used herein to designate the Board of Education. The word "Contractor" is used herein to designate the person, firm or corporation whose proposal is accepted. The word "Bid" is the equivalent of the word "Proposal."

12. Guarantees: Unless otherwise specified in the specifications, all merchandise shall be guaranteed for a period of one year subsequent to the date of delivery, during which period any defective merchandise shall be replaced by the Contractor without additional cost to the Owner. Failure to reject any merchandise or payment for the same by the Owner shall not relieve the Contractor from this obligation.

13. The Contract: The contract shall consist of the Proposal, the Acceptance of the Proposal, the General Conditions, the Specifications, and the Addenda, if any. The Addenda, if any, shall consist of written interpretations or supplemental instructions mailed to prospective bidders not later than three days prior to the date fixed for the opening of the bids.

14. Title: Title to all merchandise shall remain in the Contractor until final acceptance by the Owner.

15. Assignments: Neither the contract nor any part thereof shall be assigned or sublet without the written consent of the Owner.

16. All items under Instructions to Bidders shall become a part of the General Conditions, and, where applicable, shall become an integral part of all proposals.

BOARD OF EDUCATION
UNION FREE SCHOOL DISTRICT NO. __
Town of __________, New York

When bids are opened, check all unit prices and extensions; the unit price governs. Extreme care must be made in determining if bidder is offering equipment that meets the standards set forth in specifications, and notations should be made to indicate such nonconformance. It is not legal to advertise for a quality item specified in detail and then to accept a low bid on merchandise that does not meet these specifications. The specifications should be rewritten and the bids re-advertised. When one bid is far below the others, it is very possible the bidder has either made an error or he is not meeting specifications. Late bids or those otherwise not in accordance with other conditions set forth should be rejected immediately. A breakdown chart should be prepared similar to Table 24-2 on page 340.

Requesting samples from suppliers, when feasible, to be held until all the corresponding merchandise is delivered, will serve as a protection against the furnishing of "down graded" equipment. An example of "down grading" is as follows: Gymnasium mats have been specified to be 5 feet by 10 feet by 2 inch mats, 100 per cent long goats hair filler, covered four (4) sides with supported vinyl plastic fully tufted on 8 inch centers. The cost of a mat depends largely on the quality of filler such as ozite, long goats hair, plastic foam, standard hair, felt, sisal, rubberized curled hair and so on. Bidder "A" is low bidder and an order is issued for him to furnish mats with 100 per cent long black goats hair. What he furnishes may seem to be exactly as specified from all outward appearances but the filler may be standard felt and not goats hair. Deal with reliable dealers for one who may be unscrupulous may assume that the laymen cannot distinguish standard felt from goats hair.

In order to prevent "down grading" when it is not feasible to request a sample, request the bidder to submit a letter from the manufacturer which definitely states the specifications of the item to be furnished or send an "Informative Copy" of the order to the manufacturer.

RECEIPT AND MARKING OF EQUIPMENT

When equipment is received it should be checked immediately upon receipt from the carrier. Delivery receipts should not be signed without first checking the number of cartons indicated on the receipt; the cartons should be in good condition, undamaged and unopened. There is seldom any recourse once an acceptance signature is given, therefore, any irregularities should be noted on the receipt. All cartons should be opened immediately to determine if the contents meet the specifications. If they do not conform to the specifications the dealer should be notified at once of any shortages, variations or other discrepancies. A dealer cannot be expected to rectify errors months later.

All new equipment should be marked, coded, and listed on inventory records immediately. A ball marked "SHS-A" will identify it as belonging to "Smithville High School." The code letter "A" will refer to information on the inventory record.

Team and equipment managers can be of great assistance in keeping inventories, issuing equipment for use, maintaining, repairing, and so on. A high school program might have eight Freshmen Managers, four Sophomores, three Juniors and one Senior. When equipment is issued for use, a record should be made in an "Issue Pad."

Team and equipment managers may further assist in the following:

1. Storage of equipment
2. Keeping balls inflated properly
3. Replacing lacings, cleats, chin straps, etc.
4. Drying of shoes
5. Oiling leather products
6. Maintenance of First Aid Kits
7. Preparation of uniforms for cleaning
8. Issuance of expendable equipment —sweat socks, T-shirts, etc.
9. Being responsible for team equipment on trips or on athletic fields.
10. Other duties connected with individual athletic or recreation programs.

TABLE 24-2

Breakdown Chart for Recording Bids

		Name of Company		*Name of Company*		*Name of Company*		*Name of Company*	
Item No.	*Item*	*Unit Cost*	*Total*	*Unit Cost*	*Total*	*Unit Cost*	*Total*	*Unit Cost*	*Total*
1	Basketballs								
2	Bats								
3	Bases								
4	Standards								
5	Mats								
	Etc.								

TABLE 24-3

Sample Basketball Inventory

Item	*Manufacturer (Dealer)*	*Catalog Number*	*Code*	*Date Purchased*	*Total on Hand*	*Additional Purchased*	*Cost*	*Comments*
Balls: Topgrade	Wilson (Doe Co.)	B-1000	A	1/56	6		$23.50	Excellent (Re-order)
Medium Grade	Long (Doe Co.)	XYZ	R	10/55	4		$15.40	Unsatisfactory (Do not order any more)
Goals								
Nets								
Shoes								
Warming Suit								
Etc.								

TABLE 24-4

Issue Pad (in duplicate)

SMITHVILLE HIGH SCHOOL

DATE ________________

I acknowledge receipt of equipment as listed below and agree to be responsible for its safe-keeping and return when requested.

____

SIGNATURE

Baseballs ________________

Bats ________________

Catcher's Mitts ________________

First Baseman's Mitts ________________

Fielders' Gloves ________________

Uniforms:
- Shirts ________________
- Caps ________________
- Pants ________________
- Belt ________________
- Shoes ________________
- Etc. ________________

Footballs ________________

Uniforms:
- Shirts ________________
- Pants ________________
- Helmet ________________
- Stockings ________________
- Shoulder Pads ________________
- Shoes ________________

PROPER CARE OF ATHLETIC EQUIPMENT

Athletic and recreation equipment represents a substantial investment and consequently, deserves the best of care. Each item should be treated according to the raw materials of which it is made.

Leather

1. Avoid high temperature drying after exposure to excessive moisture.

2. Dry promptly at normal room temperatures away from heat.

3. Shoes and football helmets should be

placed in forms or shoe trees while wet. If none are available, use newspaper to round out the form and absorb the moisture.

4. Work all gloves and mitts into normal shape while still wet, then allow to dry.

5. Balls should be inflated to normal playing pressure before drying.

6. Repeated wetting and drying have a tendency to harden leather. Neatsfoot oil applied to the surface in thin coats will help to restore leather to its original condition. Apply in thin coats and allow to dry between applications.

7. Clean soiled leather with saddle soap but never use a dry cleaning fluid or other naphtha product.

8. Store in a dry, airy place to avoid mildew.

Rubber Goods

1. Heat, grease, oil, and direct sunlight are the main enemies of rubber.

2. Clean with soap and water; dry cleaning fluids tend to destroy rubber.

3. Store in a dry place; avoid dampness.

Uniforms

1. Mildew is the cause of the greatest damage as it breaks down the fibre and lowers the tensile strength of the fabric.

2. Since mildew spreads rapidly in damp textiles left in a dark place, prompt drying in a well ventilated, dry room is advised. This also applies to body pads, helmets, and shoes, as well as to softballs, basketballs, and other equipment.

3. Perspiration weakens fibres and attracts moths; therefore, wool uniforms should never be stored from season to season without first being thoroughly cleaned and moth proofed.

Wood

1. All wood items such as bleacher seats, footboards, bats, handles, and so on should have a protective coating of paint, lacquer or enamel which must be renewed from time to time.

2. Exposed wood absorbs and loses moisture rapidly. As the moisture content changes, dimensions also change. This leads to the formation of cracks and checks which expose still more wood to the atmosphere. More cracking and checking develops and this leads to the ultimate destruction of the wood.

3. All wood must be kept weather-proofed.

Steel

1. Moisture, causing erosion and rust, is the greatest source of deterioration.

2. Goal posts, backstops, bleachers, and other equipment that is liable to rust should be treated with a rust inhibitant such as a good quality aluminum paint, steel black enamel, or zinc chromate.

3. Proper care and maintenance of steel will prolong the life of the equipment for many years.

RECOMMENDED EQUIPMENT FOR NEW HIGH SCHOOL

In the initial construction of a new high school certain basic physical education equipment should be included in the construction contract; other equipment for physical education may be included in the over-all equipment and supplies for instruction. The equipment listed below is considered minimum. The nature of the program and the size and type of facilities will determine the exact quantity required.

The asterisk indicates that the item should be a part of the contractor's responsibility; however, specifications should be drawn up by the physical education instructor.

Archery (minimum number of units 4)
Indoor: heavy back drops, wooden target stands; 48″ marsh grass (vermin proof) targets; flat storage dollies.
Outdoor: welded iron target stands (if permanent site is available), or wooden stands; 48″ vermin-proof marsh grass targets; truck or dollie for moving equipment.

Badminton, Paddle Tennis, Volleyball (minimum number of courts 2)
Indoor: these games all utilize nets and stand-

ards. Use all-purpose lightweight aluminum standards* that may be adapted for any one of the above games, or wall fasteners for holding cable.

Outdoor: best practice is for permanent installation of standards.* Where these games are played on multi-purpose hard-surfaced areas, permanently mounted sleeves* should be installed in order that net posts may be removed as required for other games.

Baseball

Permanent, heavy duty backstop,* 6-gauge chain link, galvanized after fabrication with overhand; Portable batting cage* on wheels; Players benches* (dugout preferred); Bleachers,* permanent in back of home plate, portable at first and third base lines; scoreboard; pitching rubber, home plate, set of bases.

Softball

One permanent, heavy duty, galvanized backstop (6-gauge chain link).

One or more portable backstops.

Pitching rubber, home plate and set of bases.

Basketball

Outdoor: basketball backstops,* heavy duty galvanized, metal perforated backboards; rectangular, two leg supports, set 6 feet apart to permit player to run through on shot; extended, chain goal nets.

Indoor: basketball backstop* and official "No Tie" goals* equipped with nylon nets for long wear; electric scoreboard and timer;* sound system;* players' benches, bleachers* (rolling telescopic type with flat surface when folded).

Football

Official goals,* heavy duty pipe, combination football and soccer goals. Scoreboard;* tackling dummy installation with fittings for rope climbing;* blocking dummies; charging sleds; steel players benches; rubber line markers; yard marker, and downsmarker.

Gymnasium Equipment

Springboard, parallel bars; climbing ropes;* horse; buck; vaulting box; travelling rings;* flying rings;* horizontal bars (wall adjustable);* horizontal bar* (exhibition); ladder* (adjustable); mats (regular and light weight); mat trucks (flat or vertical with neoprene non-marking wheels).

Most of the equipment suggested for use in high schools is also recommended for junior high schools. Such items as outdoor football score boards would not, however, be essential. See the chapter on the Secondary School.

Kindergarten through grade six schools should have completely equipped playground areas. See Elementary School chapter. Archery, badminton, football, and gymnasium equipment as suggested for high schools and junior high schools should be eliminated completely. The only exceptions to this might be: climbing ropes, vaulting box, traveling rings, adjustable ladders, lightweight plastic mats and mat trucks for gymnasium use. Elementary schools should have multi-play area basketball courts indoors. A practical installation is one in which the height of the backstops can be raised or lowered to the height required for pupils in any one group. The main court might have permanently installed 10 foot backstops; one cross court with 8 foot high backstops, the other cross court with 9 foot high backstops.

Creative Playthings, Inc.

Sculptured play apparatus.

APPENDIX 1

NEW EQUIPMENT IDEAS

The illustrations on the following pages show some of the latest concepts in contemporary recreation equipment design. The pictures represent only a part of the new designs in equipment that is available for use in modern school and recreation areas.

Creative Playthings, Inc.

Sculptured creative play forms.

Creative Playthings, Inc.

A new climbing device.

Swing ring set.

Jamison Manufacturing Company

Standard Steel and Supply Company

Mobile benches made possible by adjustable wheel assembly.

Portable backstop.

Austin Fence Company, Inc.

Bingham Cage Court Company
Photo by Robert L. Perry

Self-contained sports area.

Adjustable basketball backstop.

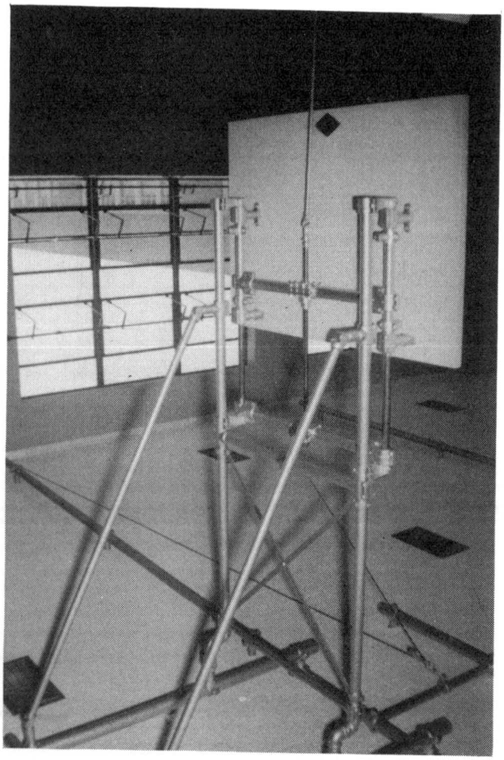

Durable and efficient welded archery stand.

Photo by H. K. Cedar

Wagner and Adler Bowling Company

Port-O-Bowl, portable bowling unit for use on hallways, gymnasium, and cafeteria floors.

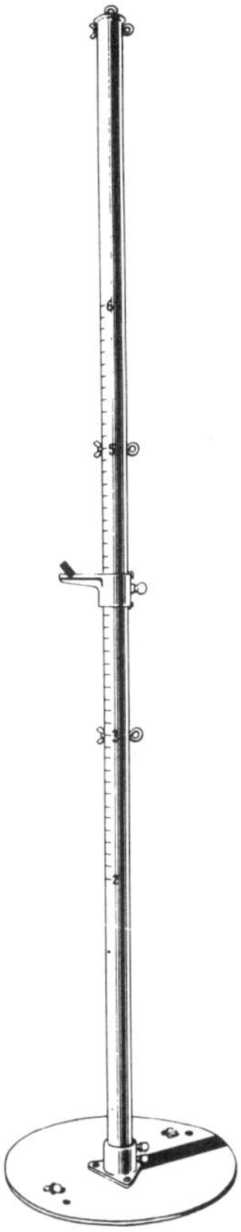

Left: Multi-purpose aluminum standard.

Jay Fro Athletic Supply Company

Space saver and safe takeoff platform.

J. E. Burke Company

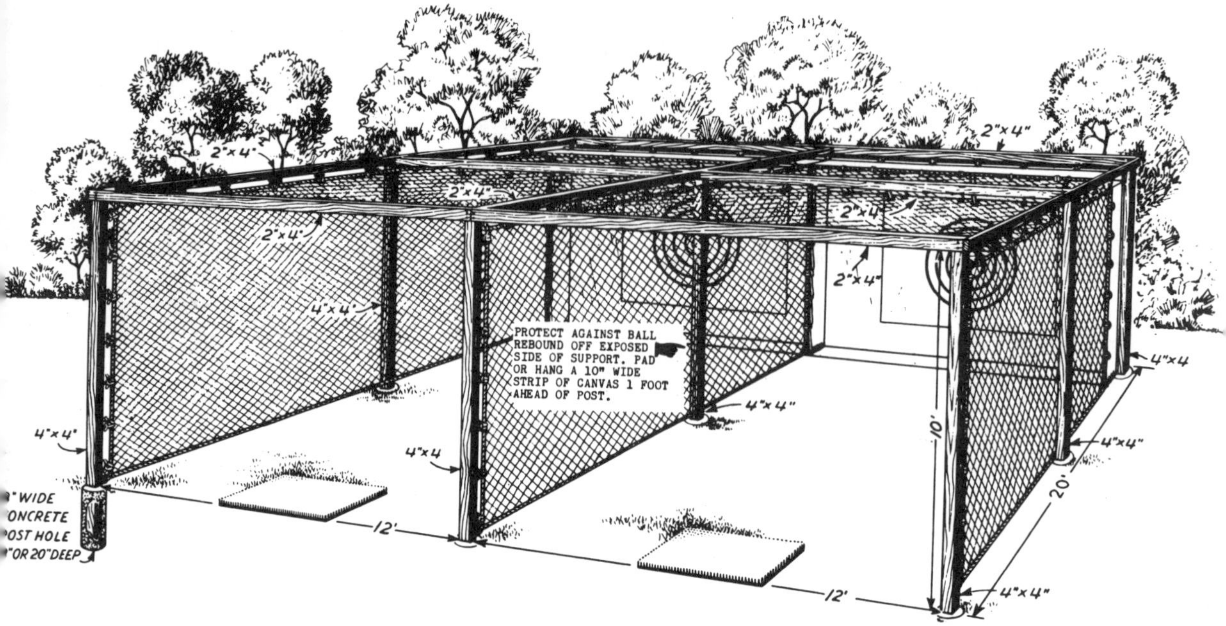

Multiple unit golf driving cage.

A chain link baseball and softball batting cage.

Austin Fence Company, Inc.

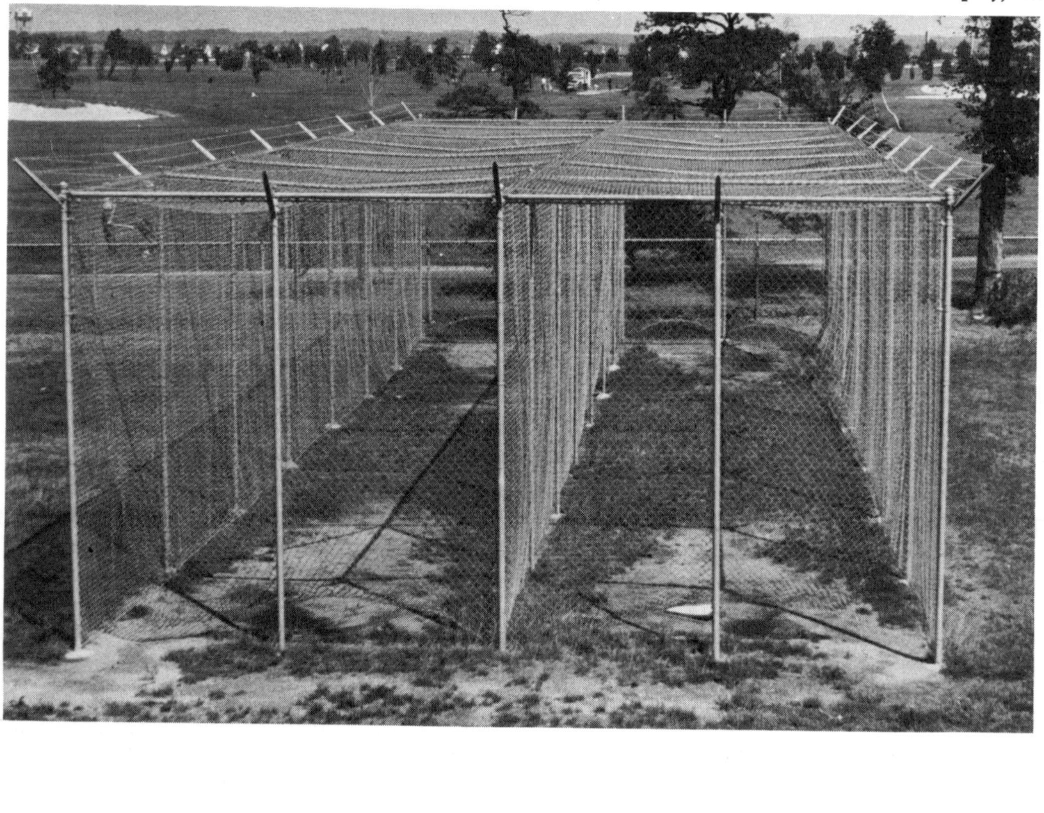

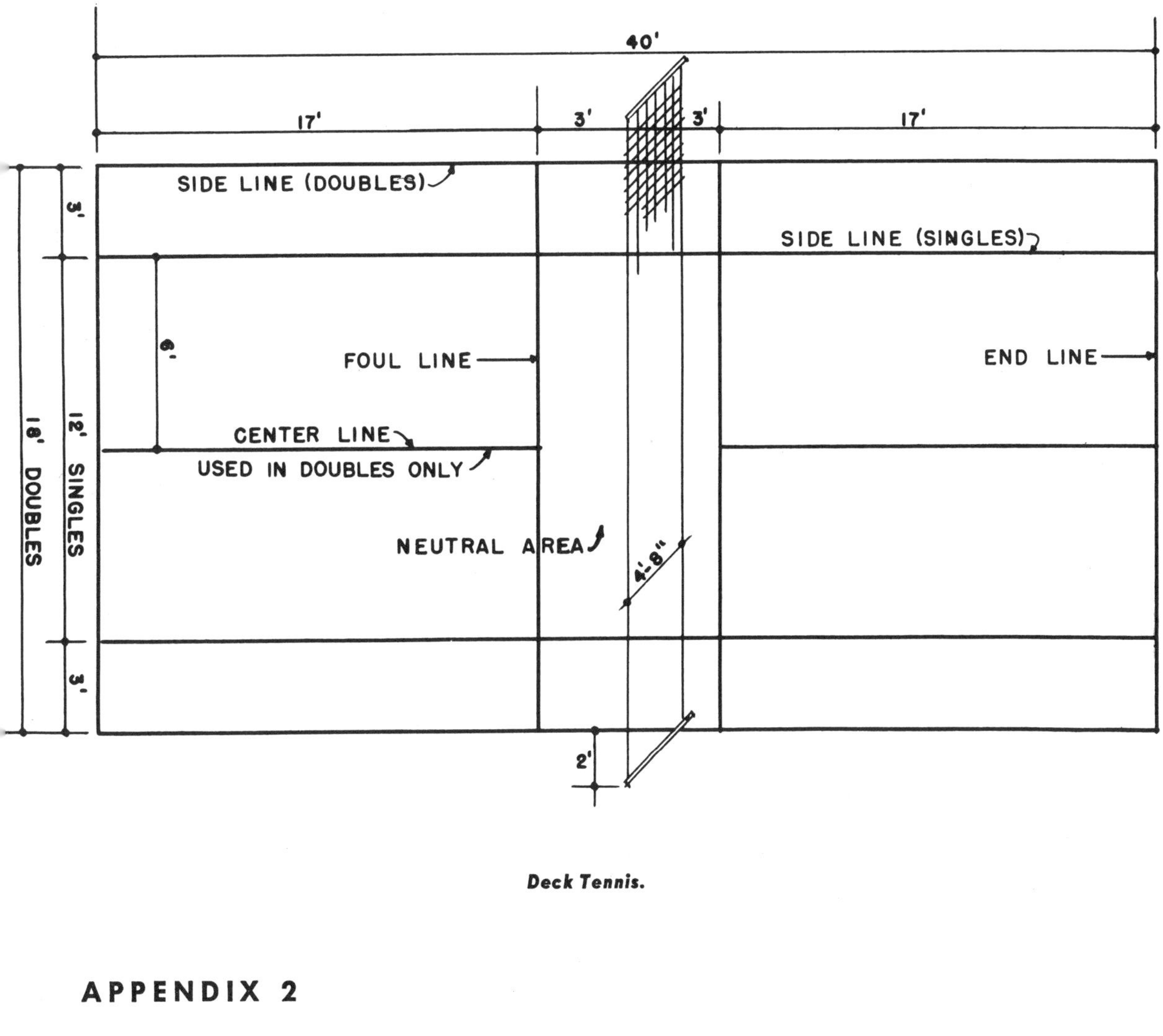

Deck Tennis.

APPENDIX 2

LAYOUTS OF GAME AREAS

The following diagrams specify the correct dimensions for the playing areas of some of the most popular sports. The diagrams were prepared by Carl W. and R. T. Clark, A.I.A., Architects-Engineers, of Syracuse, New York. The orientation studies on page 364 for the layouts of football fields and tennis courts were made by Thomas H. Jones, Division Design and Construction.

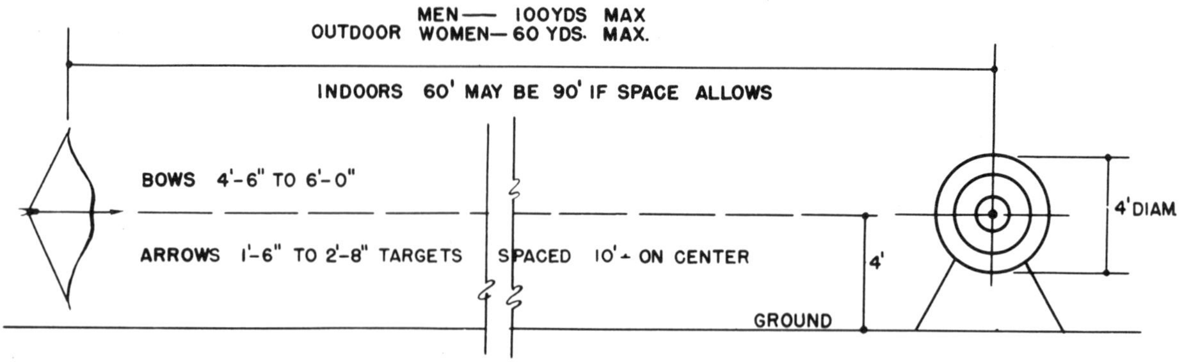

Archery.

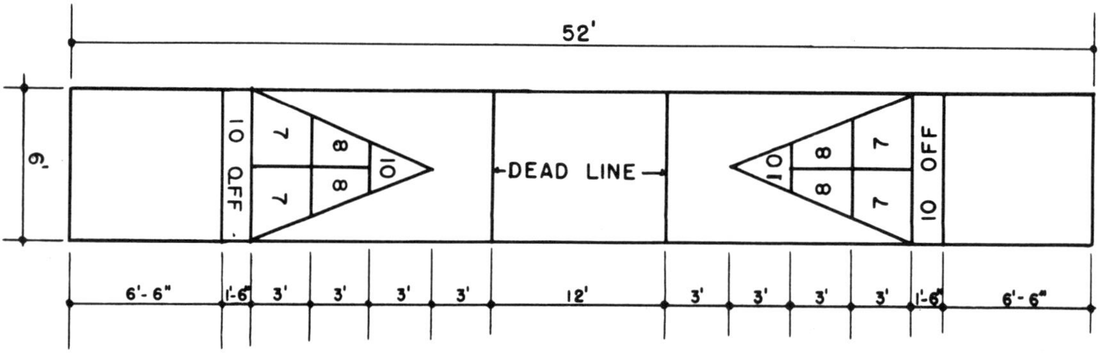

Shuffle Board.

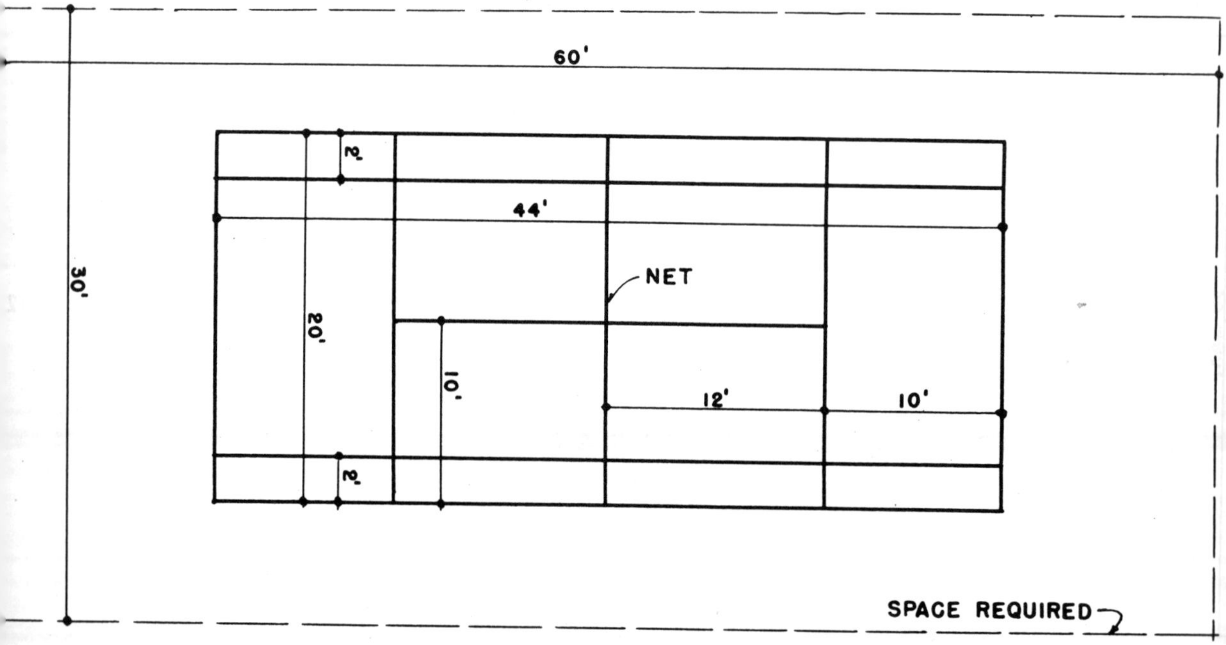

Paddle Tennis.

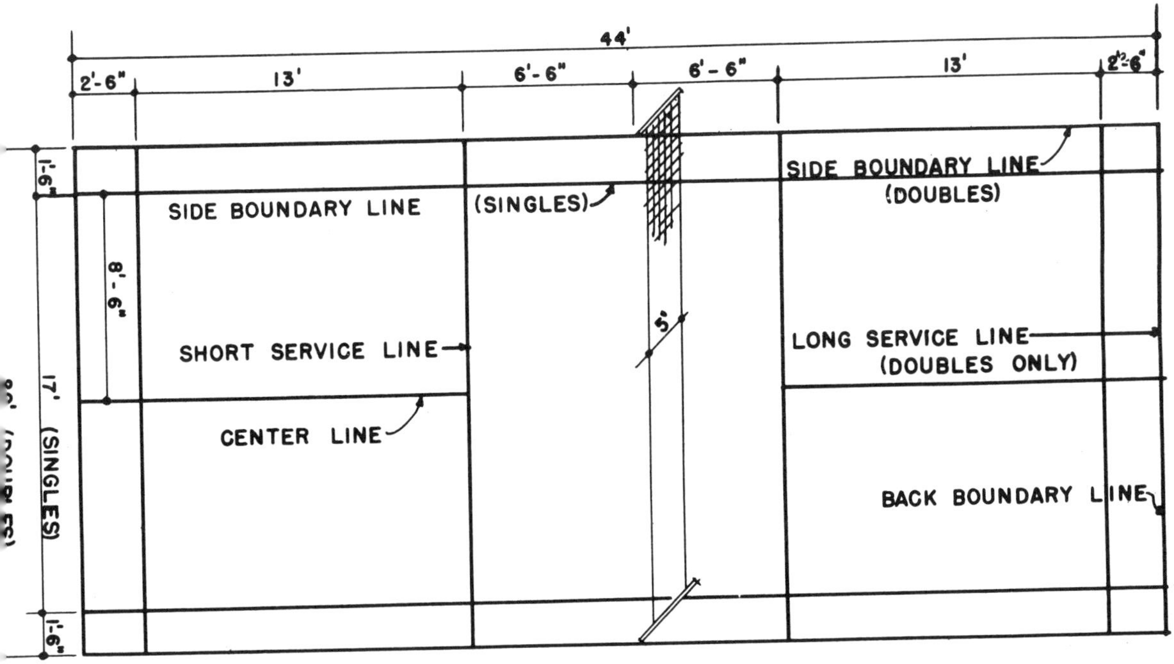

Badminton.

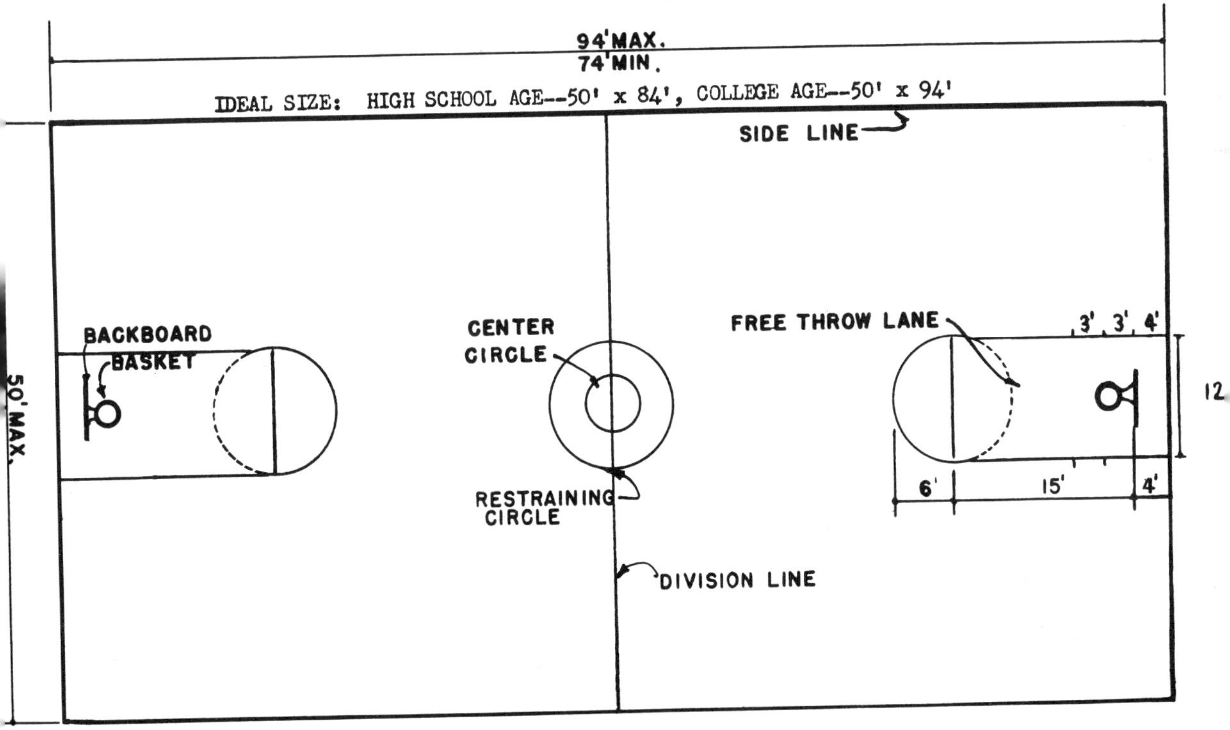

Basketball.

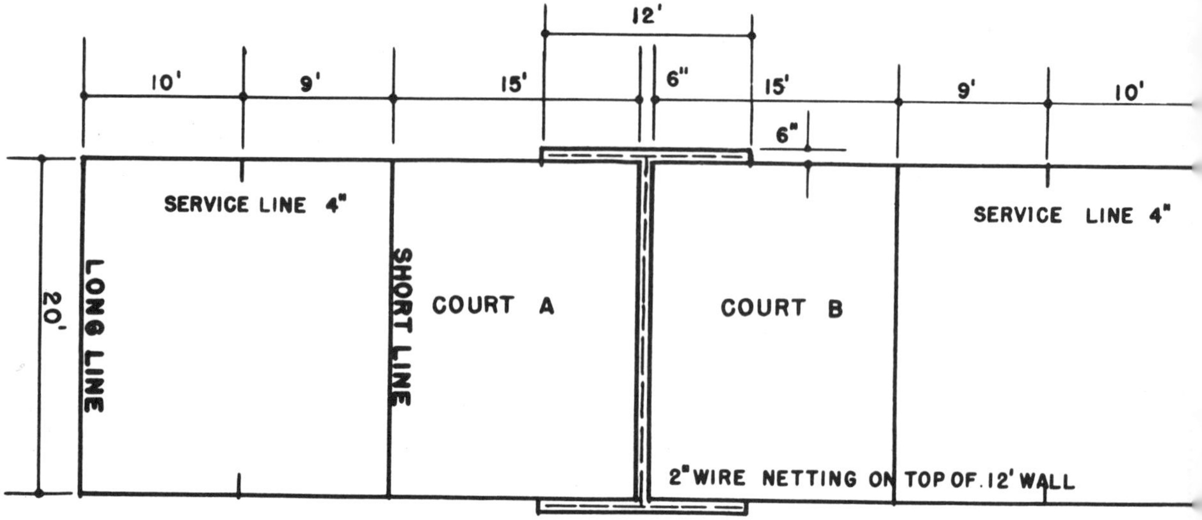

Handball.

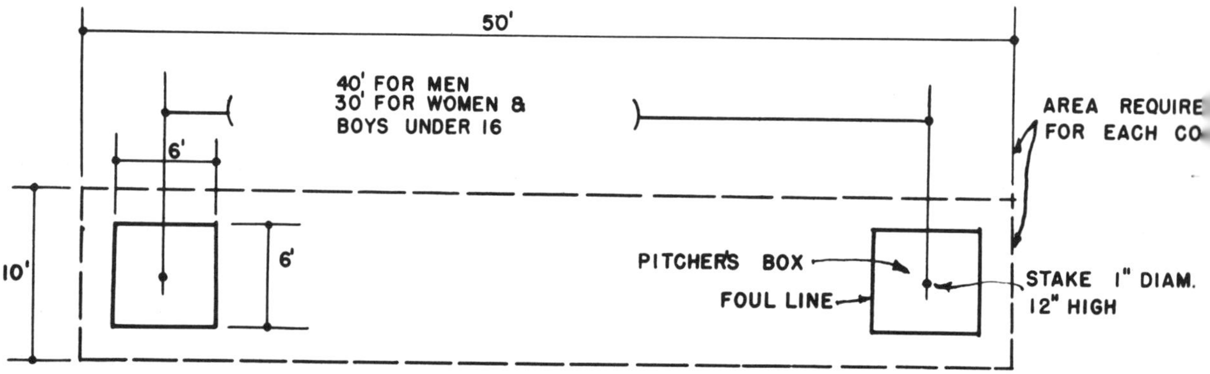

Horseshoes.

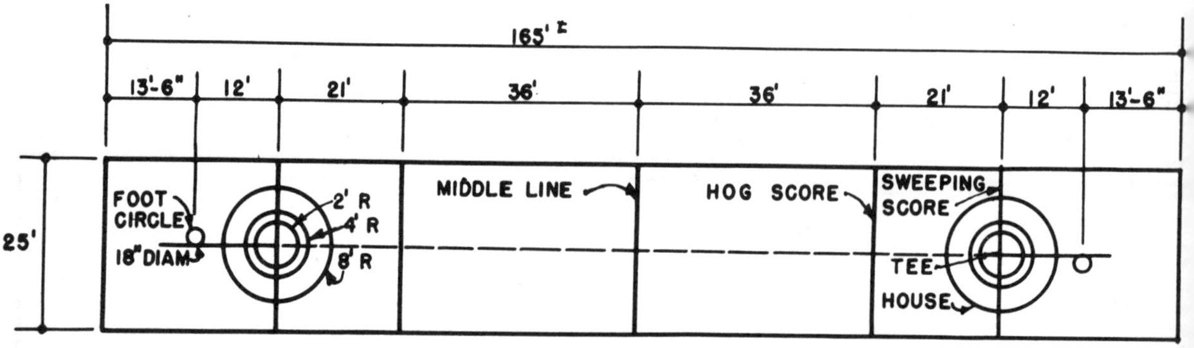

Curling.

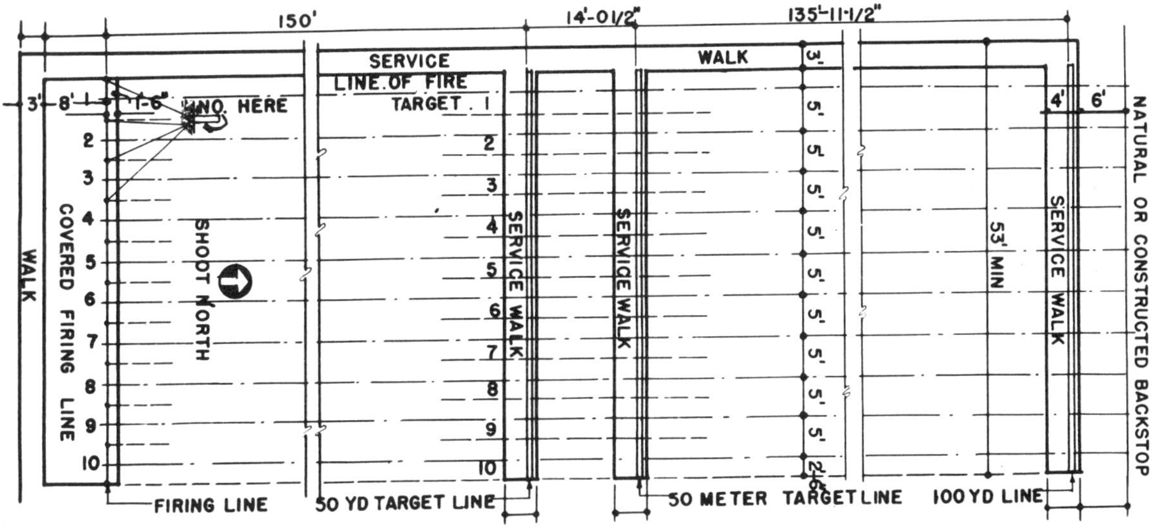

Outdoor Shooting Range.

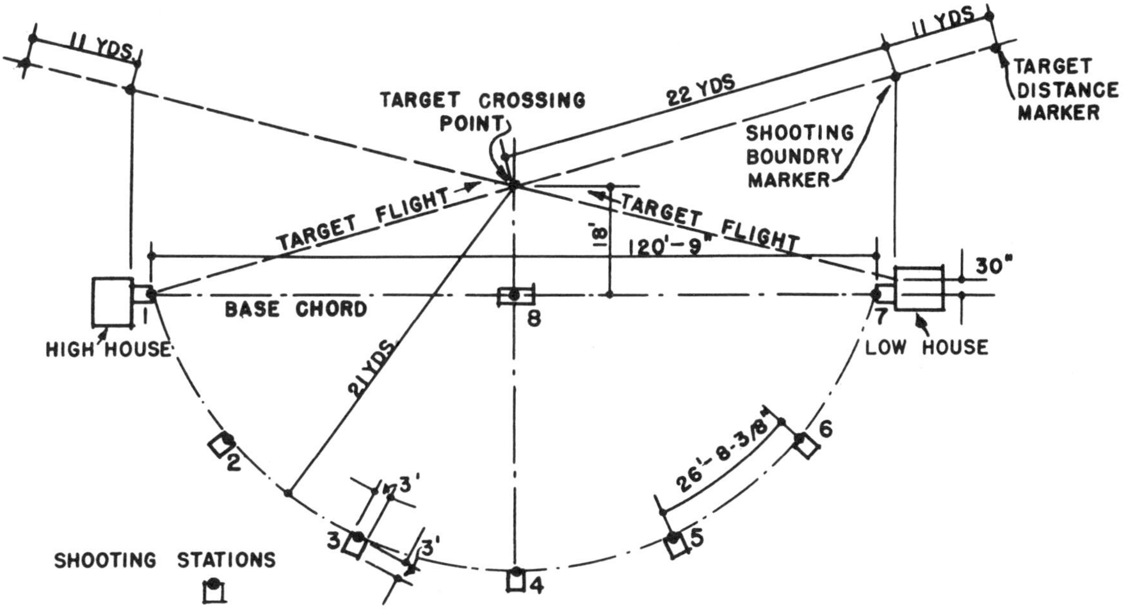

Skeet Shooting.

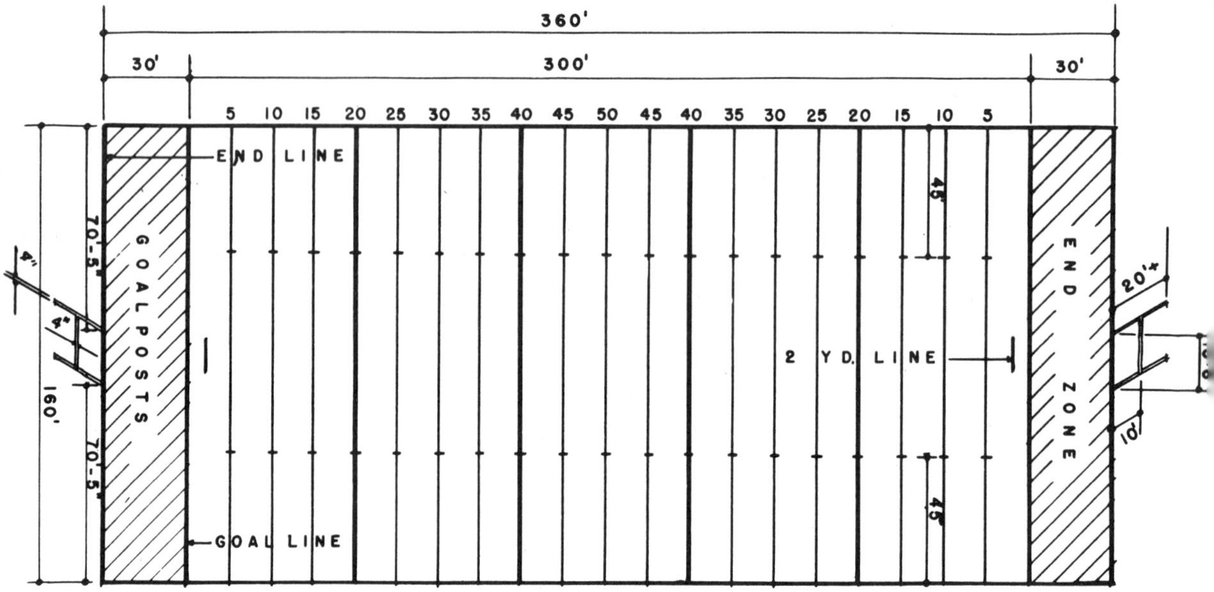

Football Field.

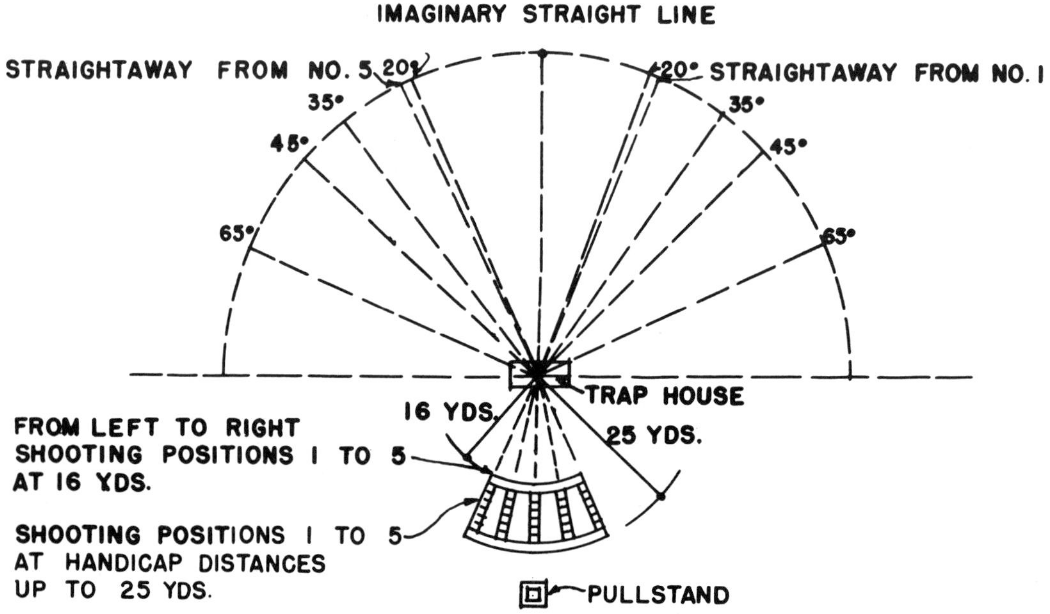

Trap Shooting.

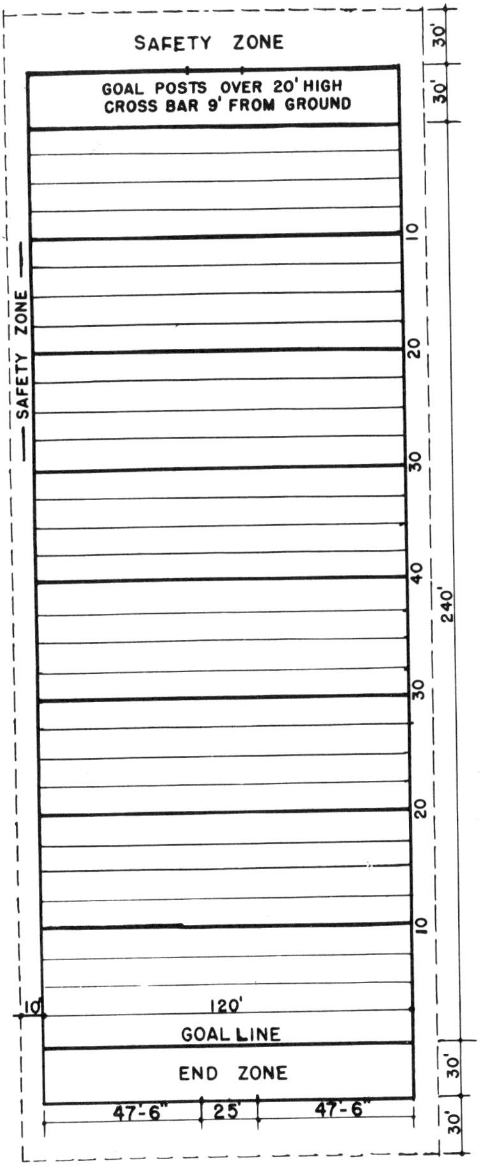

Six Man Football.

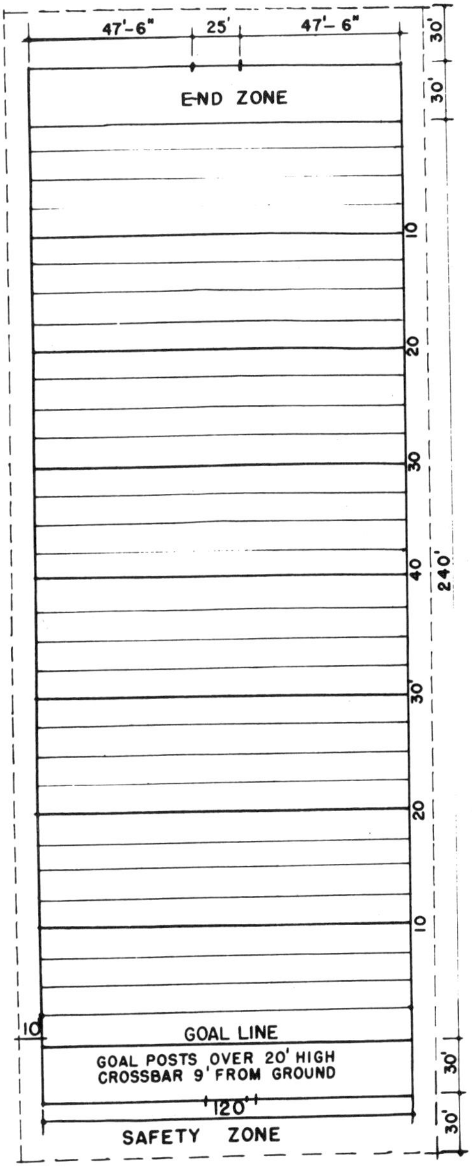

Eight Man Football.

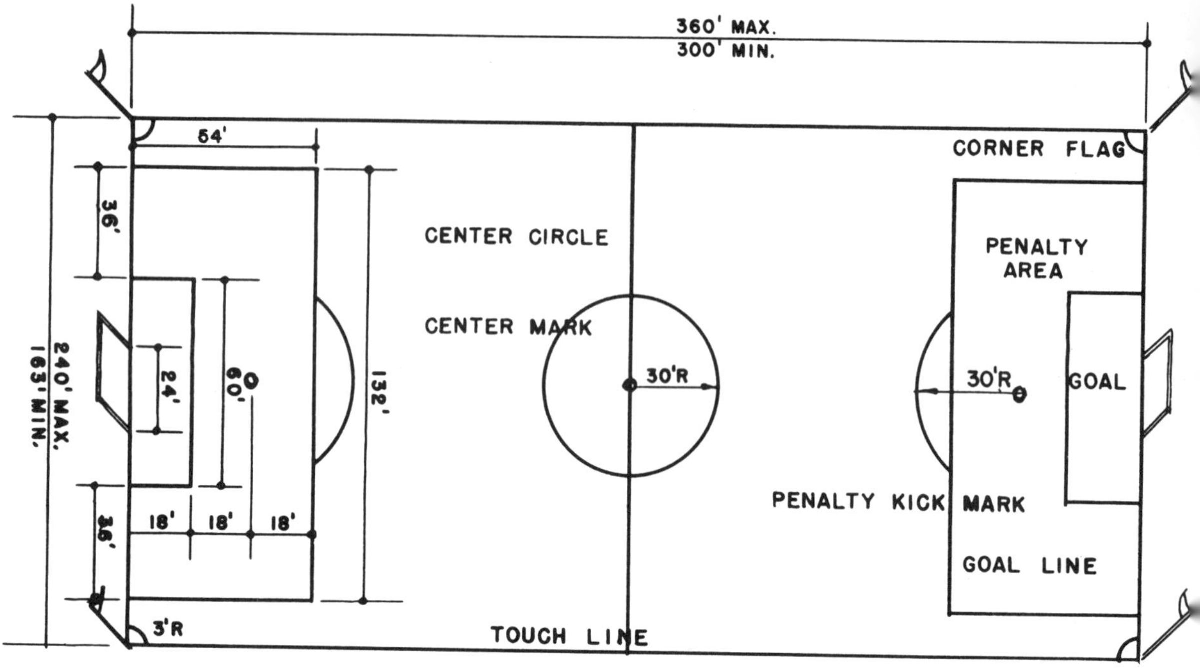

Soccer.

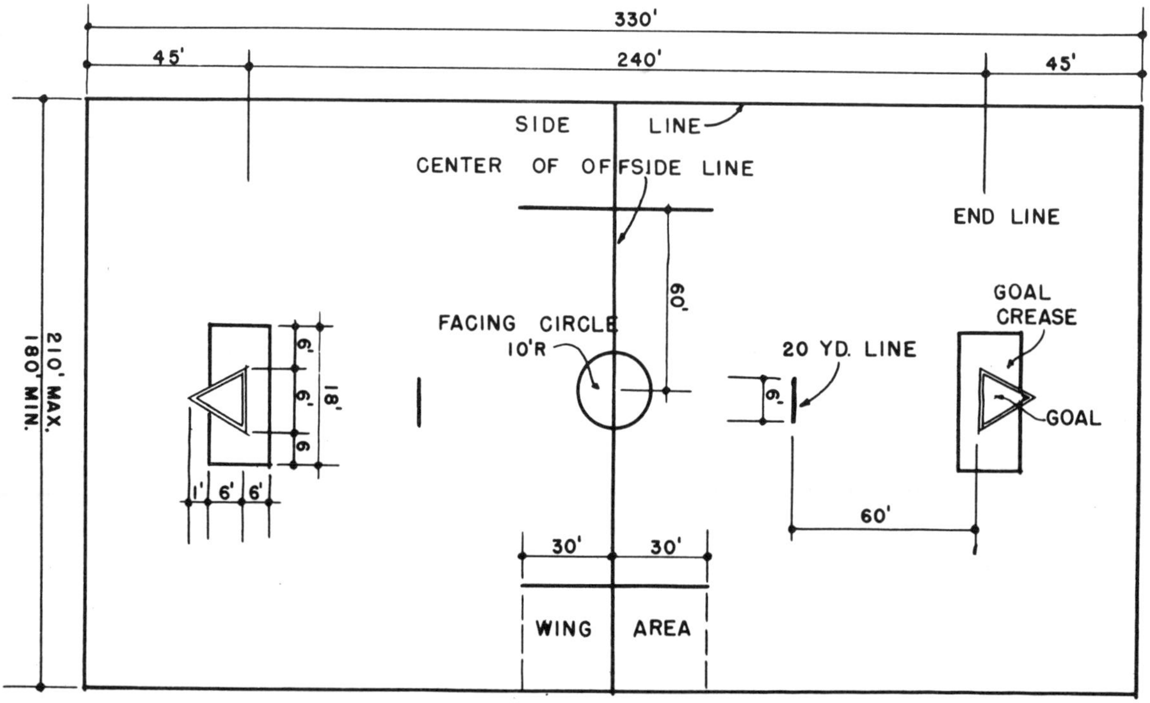

Lacrosse.

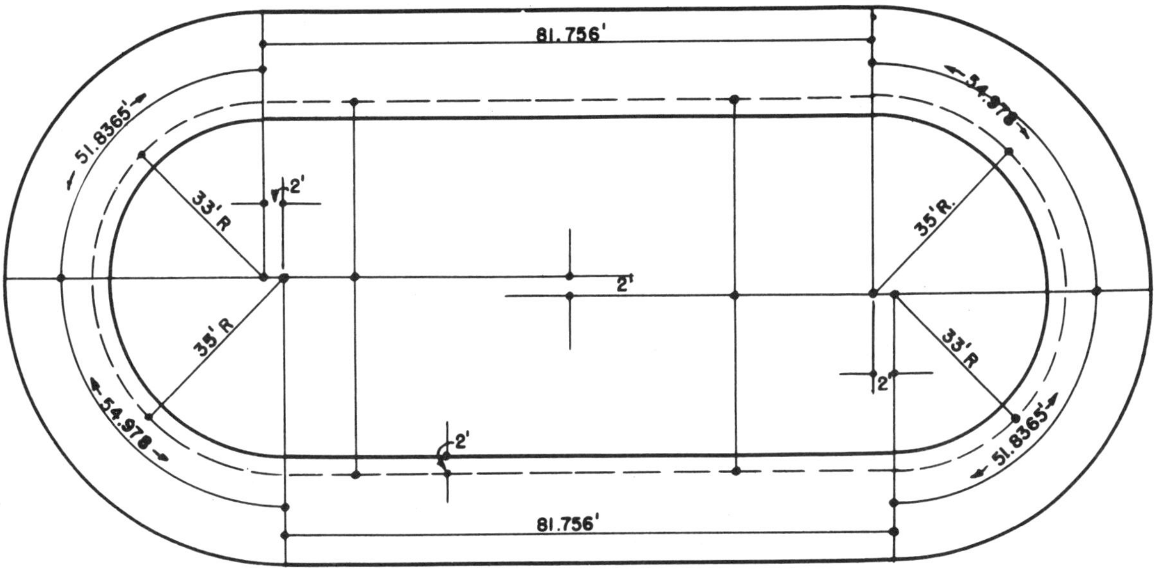

Roller Skating.

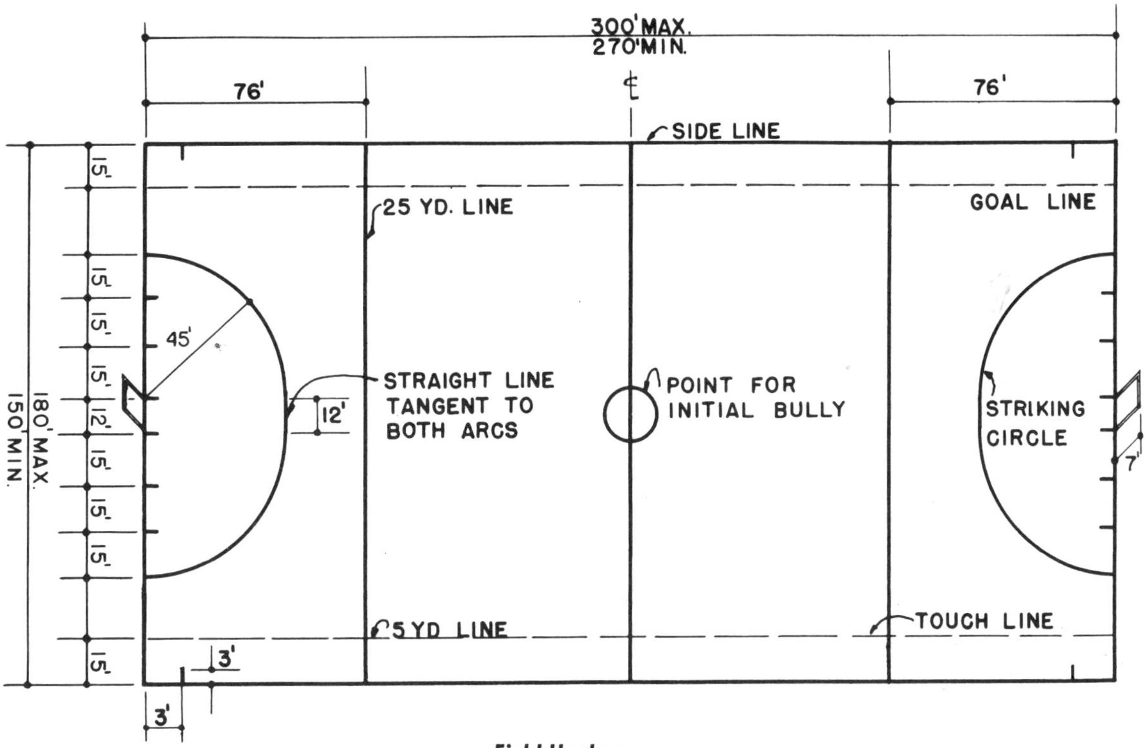

Field Hockey.

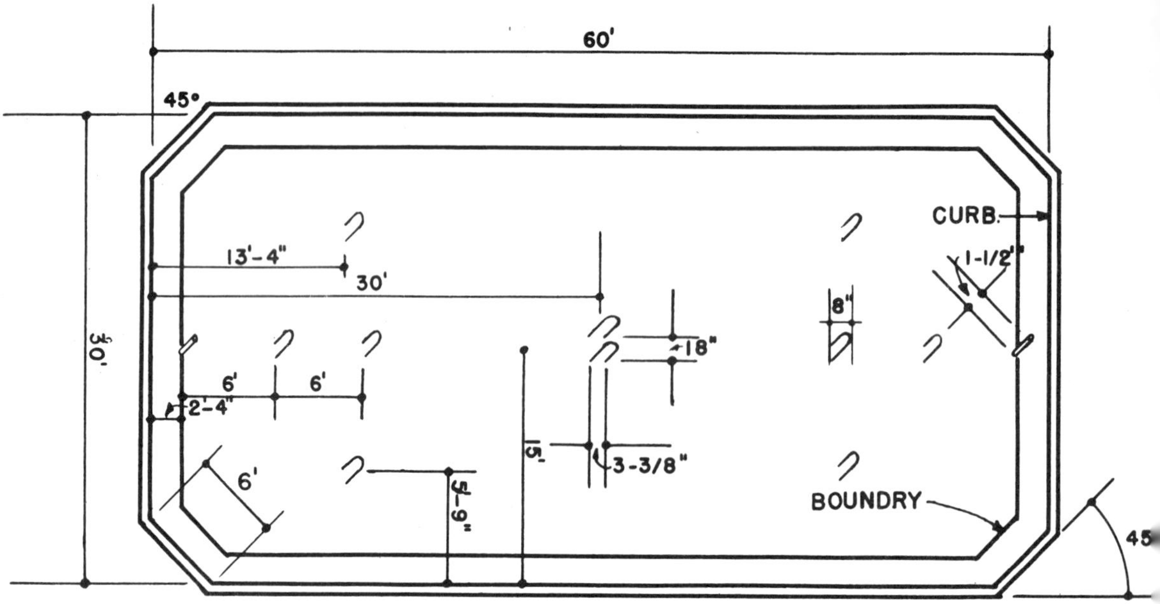

Roque.

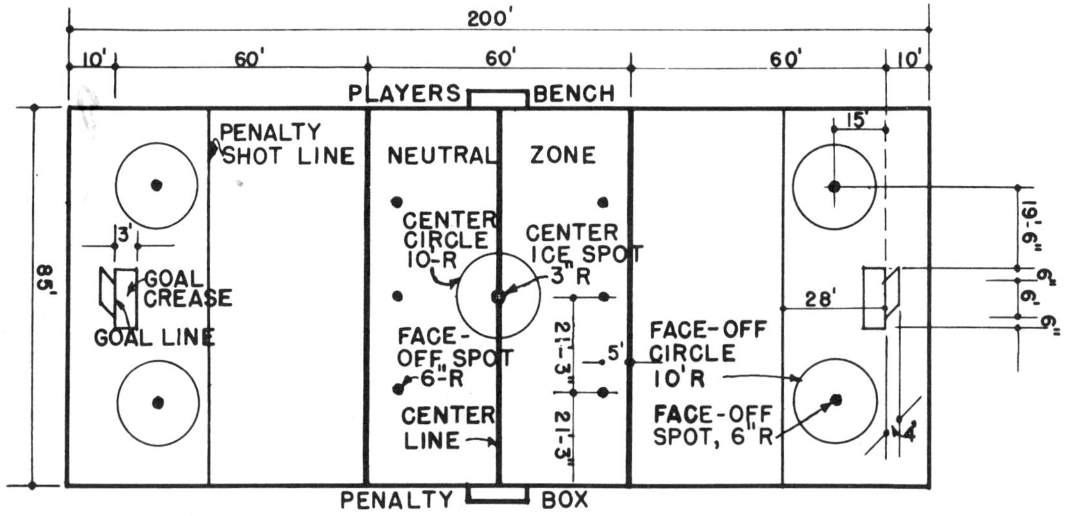

Ice Hockey.

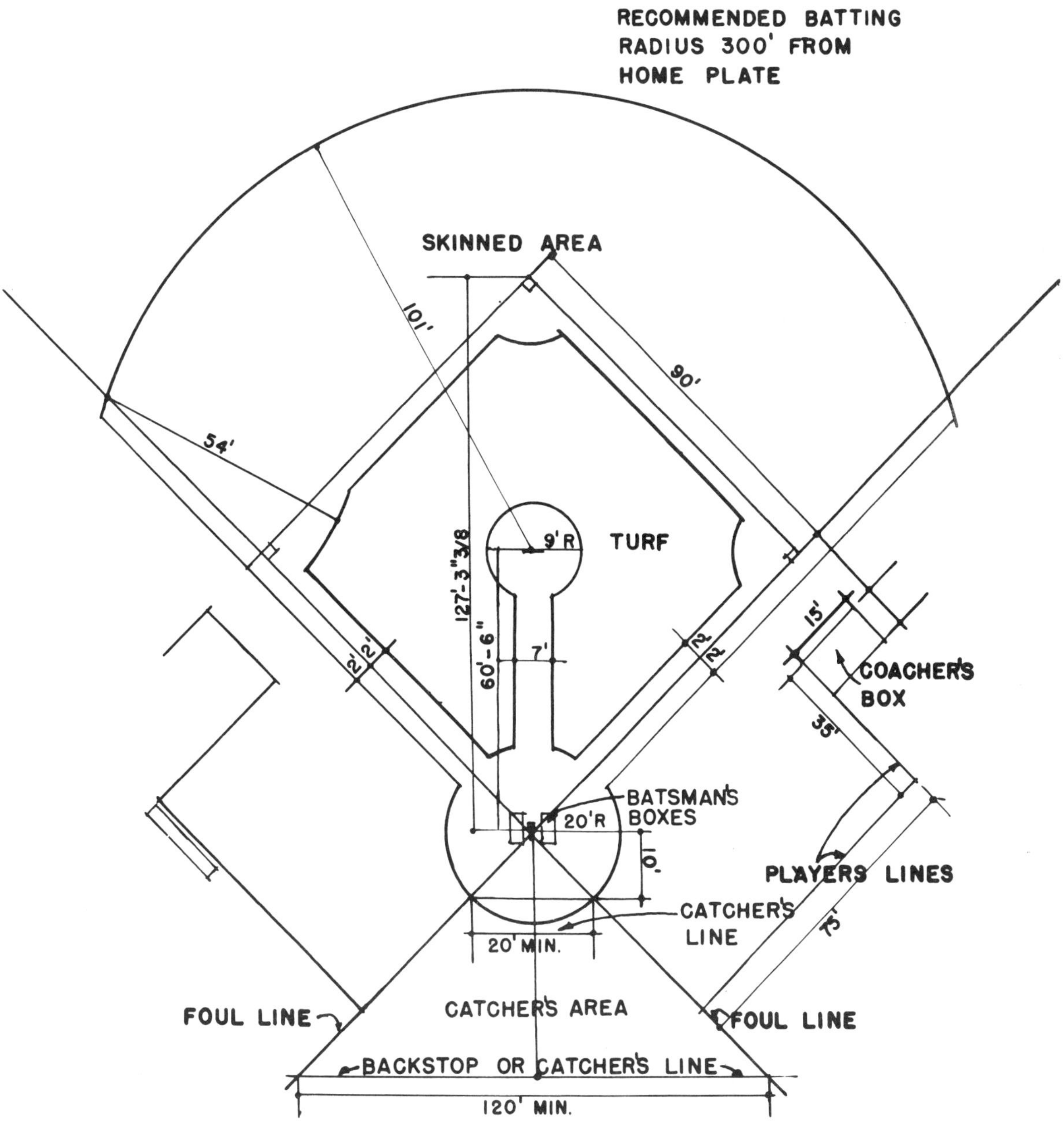

Baseball Diamond.

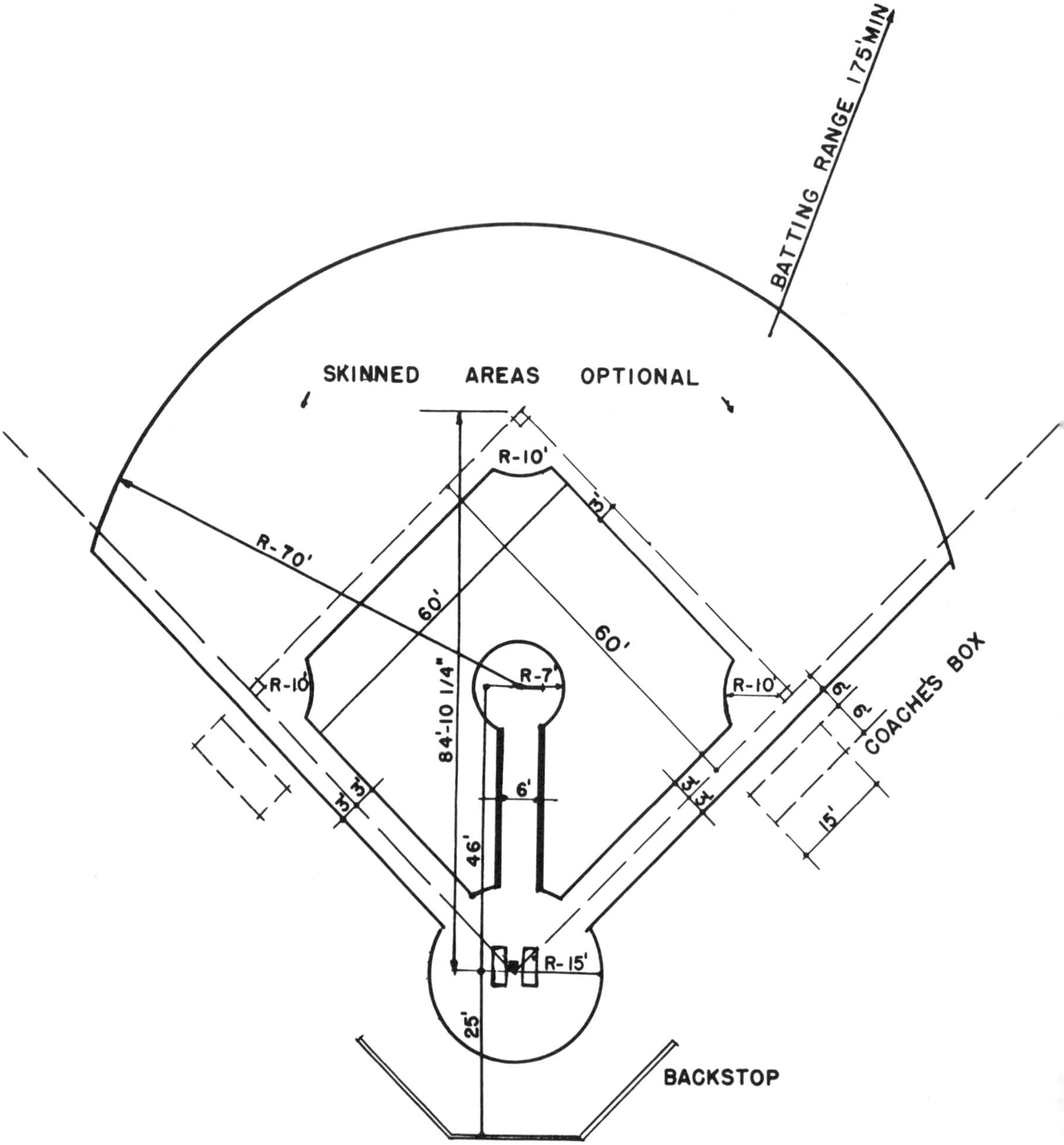

Softball Diamond.

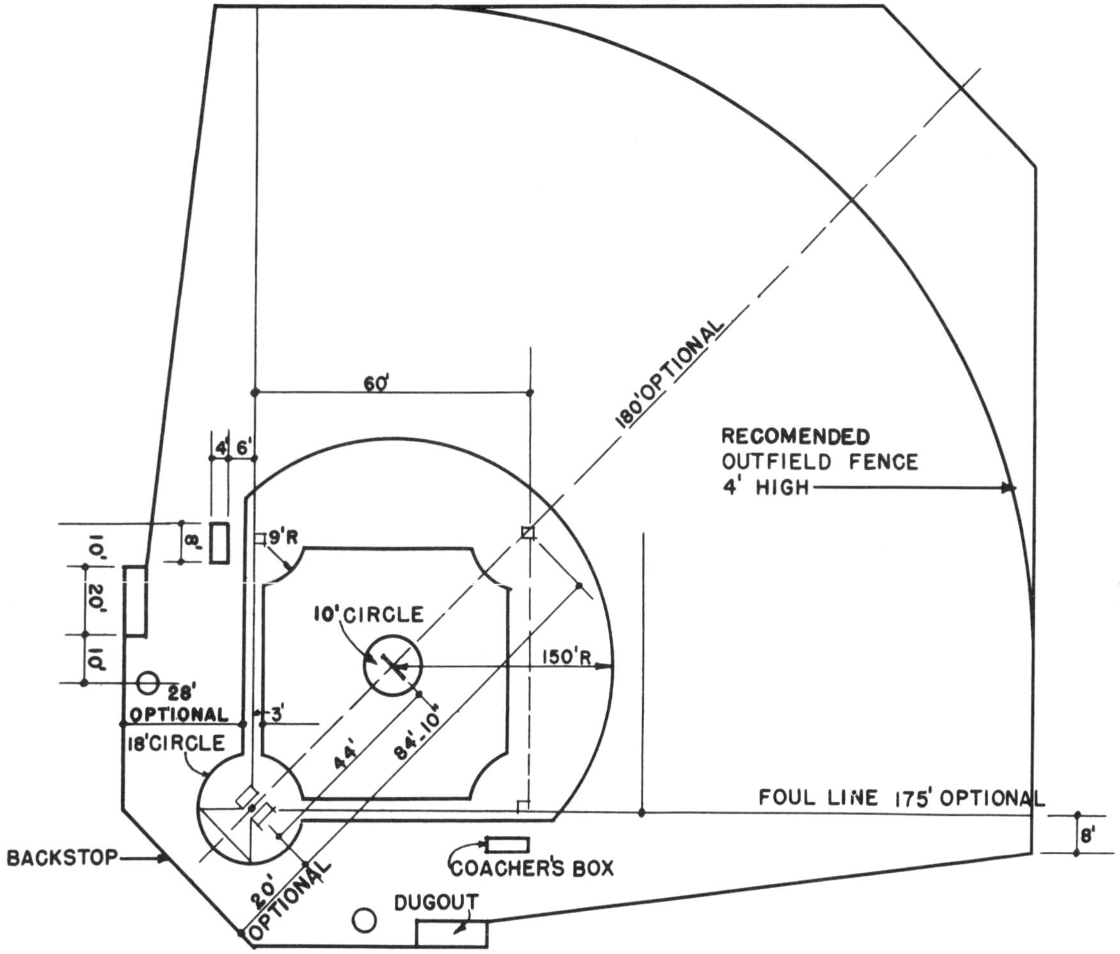

Little League Baseball Diamond.

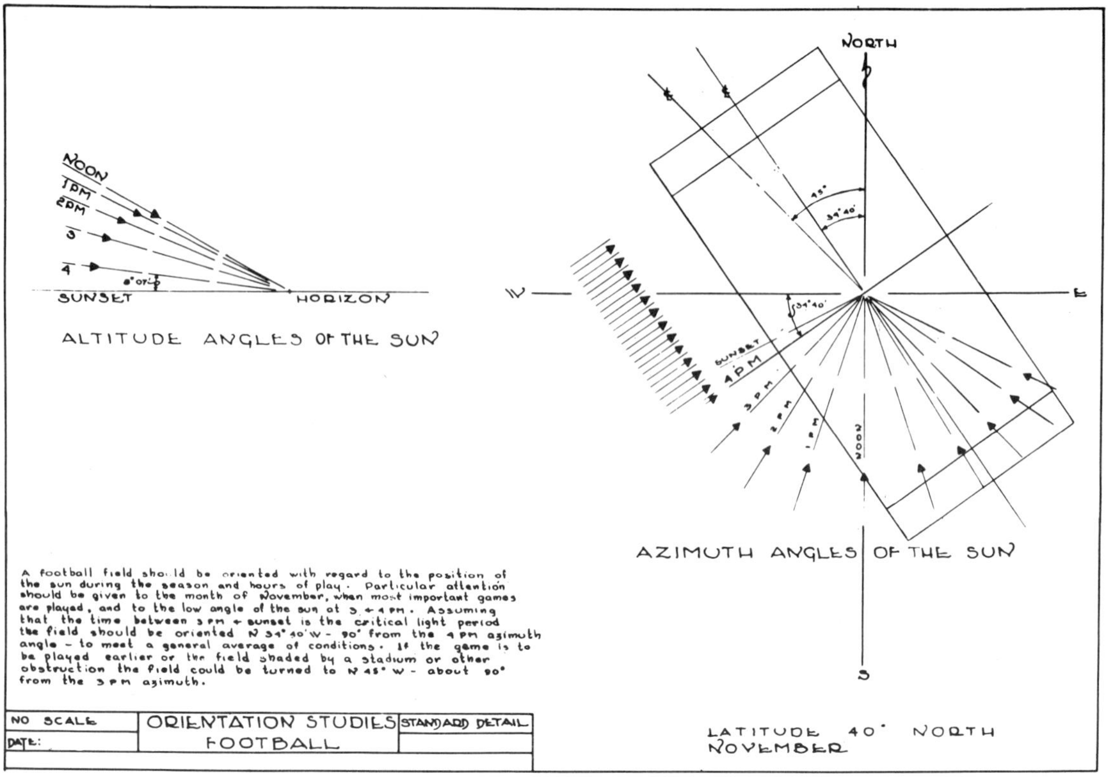
NORTH
NOON
1PM
2PM
3
4
SUNSET
HORIZON
The orientation of Tennis courts in areas where play may begin at sunrise and continued thru the day to sunset is primarily a problem of adjusting the court for the best average condition. This is accomplished by placing the long axis due North + South. If, for any reason, play is confined to either the morning or the afternoon then the axis of the court should be turned at right angles to the direction of the sun at its low altitude say 6 AM or 6 PM. This would place the axis N 15° or 18° W for morning or N15° or 18° E for evening.
ALTITUDE ANGLES OF THE SUN
W
E
45°
34°40'
SUNSET
4PM
3PM
2PM
1PM
NOON
AZIMUTH ANGLES OF THE SUN
S
A football field should be oriented with regard to the position of the sun during the season and hours of play. Particular attention should be given to the month of November, when most important games are played, and to the low angle of the sun at 3 + 4 PM. Assuming that the time between 3 PM + sunset is the critical light period the field should be oriented N 34° 40' W - 90° from the 4 PM azimuth angle - to meet a general average of conditions. If the game is to be played earlier or the field shaded by a stadium or other obstruction the field could be turned to N 45° W - about 90° from the 3 PM azimuth.
NO SCALE
DATE:
ORIENTATION STUDIES
FOOTBALL
STANDARD DETAIL
LATITUDE 40° NORTH
NOVEMBER

Football.

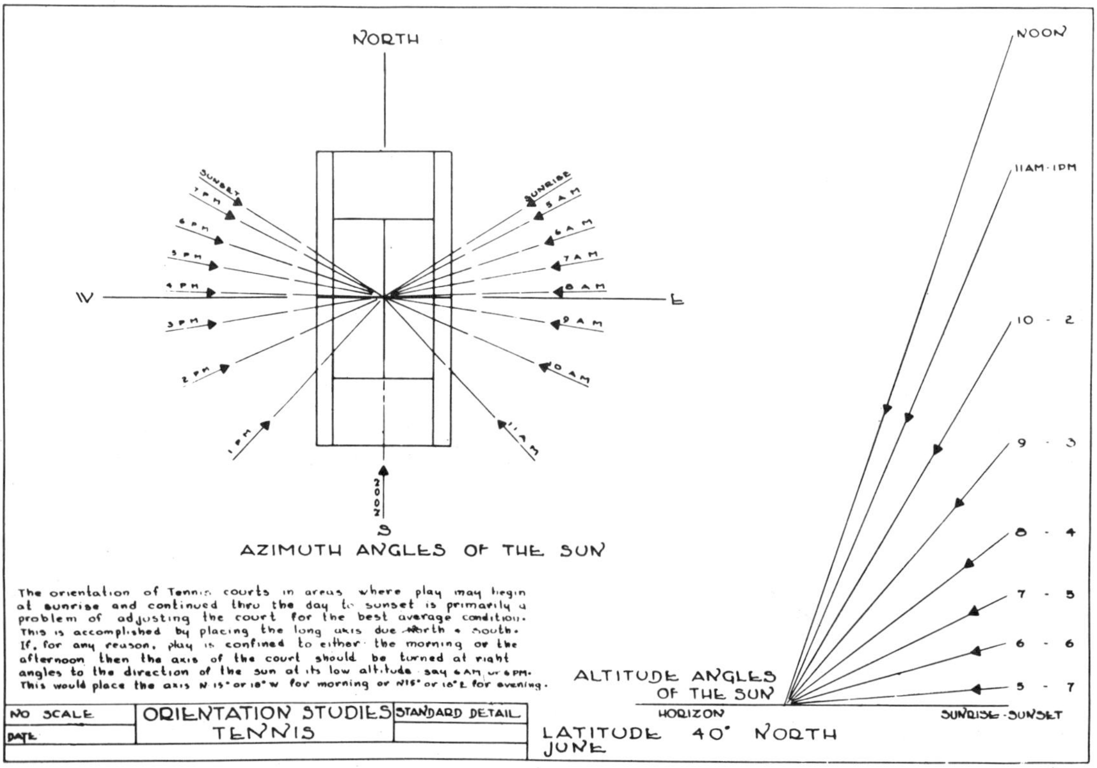

Tennis.

INDEX